Not for Sale

Not for Sale

In Defense of Public Goods

Anatole Anton
San Francisco State University

Milton Fisk
Indiana University

Nancy Holmstrom
Rutgers University

Westview Press
A Member of the Perseus Books Group

Copyright © 2000 by Westview Press, A Member of the Perseus Books Group

Published in 2000 in the United States of America by Westview Press, 5500 Central Avenue, Boulder,-
Colorado 80301-2877, and in the United Kingdom by Westview Press, 12 Hid's Copse Road,
Cumnor Hill, Oxford OX2 9JJ

Find us on the World Wide Web at www.westviewpress.com

Library of Congress Cataloging-in-Publication Data
  Not for sale: in defense of public goods / edited by Anatole Anton,
Milton Fisk, Nancy Holmstrom.
     p. cm.
  Includes bibliographical references and index.
  ISBN 0-8133-6618-6
  1. Public goods. I. Anton, Anatole. II. Fisk, Milton. III. Holmstrom, Nancy.
HB846.5 .N68 2000
363—dc21   00-042864

The paper used in this publication meets the requirements of the American National Standard for
Permanence of Paper for Printed Library Materials Z39.48-1984.

10   9   8   7   6   5   4   3   2   1

Contents

PART ONE
WHY PUBLIC GOODS?

   Economists since Adam Smith have proposed conceptions of public goods that are essentially bound up with a market society and
   the institutional underpinnings of such a society in private property. I argue for an alternative conception of public goods—one
   that does not presuppose either a market society or private property (understood as the right to exclude others). It proposes instead the notion of public goods as commonstock and suggests
   that the concept of the commonstock provides a basis for the critical evaluation of the ongoing privatization, commodification,
   and exclusive control of nature, communicative space, and the social, political, and economic order

   Those who support a global economy of the current neoliberal
   sort claim it promotes justice by promoting full employment and
   harmony among nations. This claim is rejected in favor of the
   view that justice is promoted when public goods are being built
   that realize widely held social values. Doubts about the feasibility of a program of public goods rest on the unfounded assumption that political will cannot put restraints on capital.

A fundamental assumption of neoliberalism is that rational behavior aims always to maximize individual utility—from which
it is inferred that collective action to achieve public goods is irrational. This is an excessively narrow notion of rationality, one
that underestimates the social character of individuals and their
actions, and also obscures the nature of many of our most important goods. I offer grounds for giving priority to the collective point of view in determining what it is rational to do.

A Genuine Critical Internationalism, 89

PART TWO
EQUALITY AND JUSTICE

This interchange between two feminist theorists—one a philosopher and the other an economist—explores the implications of
thinking about care for children and other dependents as a public
good. Much depends on how we define public goods and how we
think they are best provided. The dialogue ends with a list of
questions concerning conceptual issues that need to be resolved in
order to strengthen public policies supporting the provision of
care.

I argue against those proponents of deliberative democracy who
claim that deliberation requires appeal to a common good to get
people to take a distance from their parochial interests. As opposed to this, I argue that social difference can function as a positive resource in a deliberative democratic process, providing the
multiplicity of perspectives necessary for collective wisdom.

Disability Rights, 127

Using Derrick Bell's story, "The Space Traders," to stage a discussion of racism and punishment, I explore historical and contemporary contradictions between civil rights and prisoners'
rights. The emphasis in civil rights discourse on abstract equality

and color-blindness has rendered it difficult to develop an understanding of the way imprisonment practices recapitulate and deepen practices of social regression. Moreover, the historical origins of the prison reveal it to be a peculiarly undemocratic institution inextricably linked to the democratic process in which the rights-bearing subject is implicitly measured against the subject deprived of democratic rights. I argue that this history can help us to understand the pivotal role racism plays in the consolidation of the U.S. prison industrial complex and the importance of incorporating radical critiques of global capitalism into our analyses of the punishment industry.

PART THREE
ENVIRONMENT AND WELFARE

tions. Regulatory and administrative functions, poverty alleviation, and then welfare and civilizing functions were also forced
upon the state in order to build markets, to increase security, and
to reduce conflicts. Currently the "overactive" state is under attack. Yet the claims for the reduction of state spending are selective. They affect first of all the civilizing and welfare functions.
The disturbances that follow may legitimate the strengthening of
the policing and the administrative functions. These processes
may trigger a trend toward decivilization.

Social (In-)Security, 205

Environmental quality ought to be preserved as an inviolate publicly provided good. After analyzing the relationship between publicly provided goods (such as fire or police protection) and "pure
public goods," I argue that the requirements for the delivery of
publicly provided goods are parasitic on the definition of pure
public goods, creating a normative burden on those who would
advocate the privatization of their delivery or maintenance.
Identification of the argumentative burden on privatization efforts
is strengthened by a claim that publicly provided goods represent
a community's understanding that such goods fulfill commonly
held needs and meet obligations to future generations.

The social democratic French system of family assistance represents an alternative to the theory and practice of "pre-reform"
American welfare policy. U.S. welfare policy generated popular
political opposition to redistributive programs and adherence to
individualist ideas of civic virtue. The French system has fostered
popular understanding of the role of public goods in improving
the quality of life for working-class citizens. To provide a cogent
and appealing rationale for the more successful social democratic
family assistance model, we must abandon key tenets of contemporary liberal social philosophy.

Profits or People, 251

The old American Dream, the suburban home, has lost its allure:
popular preference is for a "new urbanism" that stresses human

connection and environmental sustainability. But new urbanist reconstruction requires extensive public action—expanded public regulation of economic development and land use, and increased taxation to create public goods including open space, transit, parks, town centers, historic and environmental restoration, and more—which arouses fierce overpowering corporate opposition. So suburbanization continues, and for the foreseeable future, struggles to save the cities and their regions will generate local activism and starkly and vividly raise progressive alternatives requiring public goods to the rule of wealth and market.

PART FOUR
EDUCATION AND PUBLIC EXPRESSION

Acknowledgments

The editors and publisher gratefully acknowledge the following for permission to reproduce copyright material:

Seven Stories Press: for Subcomandante Marcos, "First Declaration of *La Realidad* for Humanity and Against Neoliberalism" in *Zapatista Encuentro: Documents from the 1996 Encounter for Humanity and Against Neoliberalism* (New York: Seven Stories Press, 1998), published as one of Open Media Pamphlet Series, editors Greg Ruggiero and Stuart Sahulka. ©1998 by The Zapatistas.

MIT Press: for Iris Young, "Difference as a Resource for Democratic Communication" in *Deliberative Democracy* edited by James Bohmen and William Relif (Cambridge: MIT Press, 1997).

For their cartoons: Wiley Miller, Joel Pett, Ted Rall, Tom Tomorrow.

The IEEE Computer Society: for "A Proposed Declaration of the Rights of Netizens"© excerpted from *Netizens: On the History and Impact of Usenet and the Internet*, by Michael Hauben and Ronda Hauben, IEEE Computer Society Press, 1997.

The Nation: for Nation editors "Social (In-)Security," *The Nation* (June 1, 1998).

ColorLines Magazine and Applied Research Center: for Bob Peterson and Barbara Miner, "The Color of 'Choice,'" *ColorLines* (Spring 1999).

Dollars and Sense: for Edward S. Herman, "Privatization: Downsizing Government for Principle and Profit, Part 1," *Dollars and Sense* (March/April 1997).

Copyright's Commons, http://cyber.law.harvard.edu/cc/

Resist, Inc.: for Kim Diehl, Laura Stivers, and Keith Ernst, "Profits or People? Challenging the Privatization of Public Welfare Services," *Resist Newsletter* (January 1999).

The New Yorker for "… And We Should Face Up to That," originally published in *The New Yorker* as "Back Page" by Michael Gerber and Jonathan Schwarz, art by R. Sikoryak, July 1999.

The editors would like to thank Georgia Bassen for her help with technical and creative matters in putting this anthology together.

Nancy Holmstrom would like to thank Christine DeFranco for her assistance in finding sidebar material and Richard Smith for his never-wavering personal and political encouragement and support.

Anatole Anton
Milton Fisk
Nancy Holmstrom

Editors' Introduction

There is a spectacle of institutionalized greed being enacted across the world that at once alarms us and sucks us in. It promises prosperity in the new millennium, pointing to the mushrooming high-rises of Hong Kong, the superdome of Hartford, the Mercedes on the streets of Budapest, and the upscale malls of Mexico City. But while the spectacle is drawing our attention, its enactment is devouring resources and thereby intensifying misery. It mobilizes governments to cut back on welfare and social safety nets, adversely affecting in particular women, children, and the elderly. To service debts, it often pushes governments to impose austerity conditions including high unemployment, pension cuts, and a breakdown in the distribution of health care. It encourages crime, corruption, drugs, and a collapse of community. It encourages gender, race, and, national divisions among working people, damaging their ability to struggle together for their common interests. At the same time as it intensifies inequality within nations, the distribution of political, military, and economic power among nations grows more unequal. It creates unprecedented damage to nature and to the social and political fabric of all the societies it touches. It turns democracy into rule by corporations rather than people. And of course, it generates unnecessary arms buildups and hostile interventions both economic and military against dissenting nations.

The unregulated, institutionalized greed we confront today goes along with a conviction about the market. Human undertakings are judged in some way deficient when, to promote the good of society, the state shelters them from the workings of the market. Since this conviction about the progressive nature of the market resonates with a similar one behind nineteenth-century economic liberalism, it is commonly called neoliberalism, as is the global economic system that arises along with this conviction. There are both similarities and difference between the liberal economy of the nineteenth century and the neoliberal economy today. The nineteenth-century liberal economy was a response to feudal and mercantilist restrictions of a very different character from the restrictions neoliberalism set out to overcome. The earlier liberal economy eliminated guild restrictions on entry to trades, removed obstacles to starting a labor market arising from laws protecting the poor, and freed corporations from responsibility to operate for the common interest. The neoliberal economy has, though, done away with more recent restrictions, ones intended to prevent a repetition of the mass harm done by the very labor, trade, and financial markets that made up the nineteenth-century liberal economy. The similarities between the earlier and more recent versions concern the mobility and preeminent role of financial capital, the insistence on free trade by major producing countries as a means of penetrating others, and only limited protections for labor. Of course, neither the nineteenth century nor the more recent liberal economy has corresponded to its own ideology of a free market. The reality in both cases has been one of unequal power that allows for subordination through debt owed to international banks, through lack of sovereignty under political colonialism or neocolonialism, through the drain of profits by nineteenth-century trading companies or today's multinationals. If history teaches any lessons, we should be apprehensive lest the disasters liberalism led to in the first part of the twentieth century—world wars, dictatorships, and depression—might in the wake of neoliberalism have their twenty-first-century counterparts.

How, though, does one rein in the spectacle of unbridled greed? Ultimately it must be opposed politically. Majorities made up of people who have come to believe it is senseless, immoral, and dangerous will need to recognize and then exercise their political power. The philosophers and others who have contributed to this volume are intellectual advocates influenced by and in many cases part of larger existing social movements, such as the environmental, health care reform, women's rights, alternative media, human rights, computer scientists for social responsibility, and antiprison movements. Here they reflect critically on such general matters as privatization and individualism and also give reasons for public goods of specific forms. This is a vital part of the task of expanding the growing consensus against neoliberalism and formulating an oppositional vision.

There have been many ways people have already shown their opposition to the unregulated market. In France, Germany, and Denmark workers have demanded a thirty-five-hour workweek. In Mexico, the Zapatistas are in open revolt, and opposition to *maquiladoras* runs high. Part of the opposition to the North American Free Trade Agreement in the United States has been to develop international solidarity between American and Mexican unions. People have formed committees in many of the states of the United States to protest their treatment by corporate health care corporations. They have asked for state and national legislation for patient rights as a way to limit greed as it works its damage in health care. They have made their opposition to a sold-out and paid-for Congress known to their unresponsive sold-out and paid-for congresspeople. In addition, in numerous places people have shown determined opposition to continuing environmental degradation at the hands of multinational corporations. They have resisted vouchers in education and medicine. Increasing numbers are fed up with the sacrifice of content by media owners for the sake of profits from advertising. As local media are bought up by large chains, the role of profits in controlling content becomes even more pronounced. Finally, there is a growing movement against apparel sweatshops, whether they are located in the United States or abroad. By undermining the living wage, safe working conditions, and adequate housing manufacturers for apparel retailers engage in economic violence against workers in poor areas.

The energy of these movements needs to be put to work for a vision of a better way. Some say that vision need not abandon the program of unregulated capitalism but only graft onto it a program for protecting the unfortunate with a safety net. This so-called third way obscures the underlying issues. It cannot stop the national and international rise in inequality and the decline in democracy that unregulated capitalism generates. Even the safety net would become punier as the demand for more profit is backed by forces that deregulation has made increasingly powerful. What then might a feasible positive alternative be like? One answer is the story found in the essays in this volume as to why a system of public goods is called for. It is a story with a number of subplots—one is moral, another is social and economic, and still another is political.

The moral subplot focuses on changing ways of thinking about values and justice. It gives a central role to social goals, which are often called common goods. These goals are what people decide on to fix what they want their society to be like. For example, they may want it to be nondiscriminatory or to provide for those who are retired. Such goals are structural features of a society rather than simply goods individuals pursue merely for themselves. Of course, these structural features will make for the possibility of goods that go to individuals. In a nondiscriminatory society individuals will get job opportunities they otherwise might not have. In a society that provides for the retired, they will individually receive certain benefits, such as a pension. But even if everyone pursued a similar personal good, that wouldn't make it a social goal, since we strive for social goals precisely to back up individuals in their pursuit of certain personal goods.

For an actual or potential feature of a society to become a genuine social goal, it needs to be something that is not accepted just because of the weight of tradition or because of the manipulation of a leader. It has to be something people are willing to accept after meeting challenges to it. Pursuing a social goal involves people working together to create a society that offers stable expectations for something considered basic for themselves. It might offer a stable expectation for their education, health care, reading a reliable press, and living in a decent environment. We need to be sensitive to the diversity of our societies and not ignore the needs of particular groups in hastily declaring that accord has been reached on a certain social goal. We don't today live in communities where agreement is pre-given or where it is assured that agreement can be reached on all social goals. There needs to be plenty of room for struggles in the process of trying to reach broad agreement on social goals. When this process is short-circuited by manipulations, the result is often the adoption of a social goal that turns out to be destructive of others that in the long run are more important. Thus the neoliberal economy itself has provoked the adoption of extreme nationalist goals that lead to hostilities disrupting a society's ability to provide security, education, health care, nondiscrimination, and a free press. The existence of conflict over social goals should not then mean that only private goods are relevant in political morality, that is, in morality that concerns our life together.

The neoliberal push to make markets for more and more things fits a very different moral emphasis. In markets one tries to enhance personal, family, or corporate benefits, whatever may be the consequences for others or for the kind of society one lives in. The evidence is becoming compelling that behavior like this, that is "individualist" in relation to the wider society, will *not* bring us a more democratic, well-informed, healthy, or egalitarian society.

The socioeconomic subplot tells the story of the breakdown of networks of communication, with the recorded voice becoming emblematic of discourse in a cost-cutting world. It also tells the story of the decline of solidarity between races, genders, and nationalities, as differences are rubbed down so everyone can be treated as equal in a level market playing field. The socioeconomic subplot will have then to expose the unequal power relations that are in fact at work in the global economy. Powerful actors have a compelling edge, which they use to limit the free market both by cajoling the state to work on their behalf and by weakening competition through increasing market shares. Financiers dictate welfare and labor policies; free trade agreements threaten public goods as state monopolies. Neoliberalism enhances the freedom of the powerful to dominate the less powerful, allowing it to hide behind the rhetoric of the free market.

Finally, the political subplot tells of the necessity of open discussion in deciding on the kind of society a people want—the social goals they want. As diverse, they will have disagreements, though many of these can be resolved by compromises around which broad, if not total, consensus can form. But there is another crucial strand in the political subplot. To act on any such broad consensus on social goals calls for thinking about the system that will best realize it—a system for family assistance, schooling, health care, or media. A system that advances the realization of a social goal and organizes the distribution of its benefits for individuals is a public good. It is precisely any system of this kind that has been in the gun sights of the neoliberals. The new public goods to be built on what's left after neoliberalism has attacked the earlier ones will have to have some stringent new features. They will have to be genuinely universal. They can't just aim to provide means-tested benefits to the indigent. And they will have to be democratic rather than bureaucratic, which will mean that the public creating them will have to have a greater hand in running them. These new systems are the public goods around which the authors in this volume would hope to build a positive alternative to neoliberalism.

This volume is, without apologies, advocacy of the need for public goods. The authors were approached by the editors to write on the topic of the need for public goods as a step away from the depredations of neoliberalism. This topic became as the essays were being written the broad unifying theme of the volume. Nonetheless, there are important differences and nuances in the conceptions of public good with which the authors work, including the editors. As revisions were being made, the intention of the editors was not to insist on a common conception but to urge as much development of the various concepts as feasible so readers would have little trouble making comparisons and drawing their own conclusions. Still, it is possible to fit what many of the authors think about public goods into a common skeletal concept. This is the concept that allows us to say there is indeed the above unifying theme. The skeletal concept is that a public good gives the society a desired feature by being accessible for all to share. Though without apologies, the advocacy of the unifying theme is based, in the essays here, on a critical reflection on privatization and on the positive reasons for public goods. Most of the volume's contributors are not shy in expressing deep concern about the direction of neoliberalism as well as about the damage it has already done. They are equally frank about the need to turn that direction around by affirming a program of establishing public goods. Their reasons are often different but generally this results from their considering this need from the angle of different areas of neglected human interest. It is hoped that this rethinking of public goods will inspire others to continue in a politically relevant way what has just been begun here.

Far from all the areas is a need for public goods to be discussed. Still, one will find discussions here of the environment (Light), social diversity (Davis, Young), human rights (Syfers), family assistance (Exdell), intellectual property rights (Goldhaber), journalism (McChesney), mental health (Corlito, Lichtman), civilization (Ferge), the schools (Noddings), women's equality (Ferguson and Folbre), health care reform (Fisk), democracy (Nutting), and our cities (Resnick). The sheer number of such areas where a convincing case can be made for the existence of public goods shows that an adequate program for realizing social goods will affect great swatches of our social lives. The issue of public goods cannot then arise as a mere afterthought in an effort to organize society along market lines. Developing a program for public goods must, instead, be viewed as the central task in coming to grips with what living together in the early twenty-first-century society is to involve. In advocating the view that moving ahead with public goods is at this moment the central task, the contributors are setting themselves against the view of dominant elites that the central task is to deregulate and globalize markets. In fact, the dominant neoliberalism with its short-run point of view cannot be successful in regard to saving the environment and satisfying needs only public goods are addressed to. The plight of future generations being prepared by neoliberalism today will itself undermine neoliberalism.

The many facets of this volume are tied together by the overarching assertion against individualist ethics of the apparent truism that there can be no social life without social goals in the above sense. Social goals, both as theoretical concepts and as practical goals leading to public goods, run against the grain of the individualist tradition in ethics, which developed along with the market and provided a basis for decision theory in the social sciences generally and for the primacy of the market in economics in particular. There is, however, a tradition to back up the view that social goals are decisive in sustaining life together. It is not surprising that this social-value tradition had its Western origins in the classical

Greek period well before the triumph of the market. For, to realize social goals—ones that can be realized only by joint effort and once realized must serve all—the market must be stunted rather than full-blown. On the one hand, resources tied up in realizing social goals are as such placed outside the market in the running of public goods. The greater the number of social goals realized, the more the market shrinks. On the other hand, the dedication of individuals to realizing social goals is not measured, as it would be in a market, by their estimate of resulting personal benefits. Too many would find the expectation of purely personal benefits simply too small to justify their effort.

The basic fact in all this is that living together is not standing at the other end of a cash transaction. The individualist ethic that is used to justify the market—but that in fact has its roots in the market—is then not adequate as an ethic for living together. Values promoting personal or corporate gain may seem sufficient if the closest we get to others is at the other end of a market transaction. But they are not adequate for living together. This is because living together calls for a real concern that the well-being of others is realized. At the very least, one would like to see to it that certain of the basic interests of others don't get neglected. With concern, one doesn't want to leave those basic interests to chance or to one's own limited capacity. One wants, rather, the society to have features that give some assurance those interests will not be neglected. The society's having any one of those features becomes then a social goal. Such a goal is the kind of value referred to in a poster for a demonstration against the G8 governments and their proposed Multilateral Agreement on Investment which ran, "Join us in protesting against their world . . . where everything has a price and nothing has a value." More generally, as modern market societies continue to promote the commodity mode of need satisfaction, it becomes a matter of urgency to insist that increasing numbers of people will fail to have their most fundamental needs and wants satisfied.

A program around which those who find this volume pointing in a helpful direction might coalesce could then be sketched as follows: In view of the human and environmental costs of continuing with neoliberalism and its individualist ethic an alternative is to be pursued. It is an internationalist alternative to be pursued in conjunction with the majorities in many countries. Those majorities are desperate for an escape from neoliberalism resulting from their greater vulnerability as neoliberalism fragments and marginalizes them. This calls for a broad offensive, that, in opposition to further compromises with neoliberalism, promotes public goods, whether by creating or rebuilding them. Within this offensive there is need for an ethical and sociological reorientation that will emphasize both social values as the focus of ethics and solidarity as a basis for social structure.

A Call from Chiapas: "First Declaration of *La Realidad* For Humanity and Against Neoliberalism"

Subcomandante Marcos

I have arrived, I am here present, I the singer. Enjoy in good time, come here to present your selves those who have a hurting heart. I raise my song.
—Nahuatl poetry

To the People of the World:

Brothers and Sisters:

During the last years, the power of money has presented a new mask over its criminal face. Disregarding borders, with no importance given to races or colors, the Power of money humiliates dignities, insults honesties and assassinates hopes. Renamed as "Neoliberalism," the historic crime in the concentration of privileges, wealth and impunities, democratizes misery and hopelessness.

A new world war is waged, but now against the entire humanity. As in all world wars, what is being sought is a new distribution of the world.

By the name of "globalization" they call this modern war which assassinates and forgets. The new distribution of the world consists in concentrating power in power and misery in misery.

The new distribution of the world excludes "minorities." The indigenous, youth, women, homosexuals, lesbians, people of color, immigrants, workers, peasants; the majority who make up the world

(continues)

(continued)

basements are presented, for power, as disposable. The new distribution of the world excludes the majorities.

The modern army of financial capital and corrupt governments advance conquering in the only way it is capable of: destroying. The new distribution of the world destroys humanity.

The new distribution of the world only has one place for money and its servants. Men, women and machines become equal in servitude and in being disposable. The lie governs and it multiplies itself in means and methods.

A new lie is sold to us as history. The lie about the defeat of hope, the lie about the defeat of dignity, the lie about the defeat of humanity. The mirror of power offers us an equilibrium in the balance scale: the lie about the victory of cynicism, the lie about the victory of servitude, the lie about the victory of neoliberalism.

Instead of humanity, it offers us stock market value indexes, instead of dignity it offers us globalization of misery, instead of hope it offers us an emptiness, instead of life it offers us the international of terror.

Against the international of terror representing neoliberalism, we must raise the international of hope. Hope, above borders, languages, colors, cultures, sexes, strategies, and thoughts, of all those who prefer humanity alive.

The international of hope. Not the bureaucracy of hope, not the opposite image and thus, the same as that which annihilates us. Not the power with a new sign or new clothing. A breath like this, the breath of dignity. A flower yes, the flower of hope. A song yes, the song of life.

Dignity is that nation without nationality, that rainbow that is also a bridge, that murmur of the heart no matter what blood lives it, that rebel irreverence that mocks borders, customs and wars.

Hope is that rejection of conformity and defeat.

Life is what they owe us: the right to govern and to govern ourselves, to think and act with a freedom that is not exercised over the slavery of others, the right to give and receive what is just.

For all this, along with those who, beyond borders, races and colors, share the song of life, the struggle against death, the flower of hope and the breath of dignity.

(continued)

The Zapatista Army of National Liberation Speaks ...

To all who struggle for human values of democracy, liberty and justice.

To all who force themselves to resist the world crime known as "Neoliberalism" and aim for humanity and hope to be better, be synonymous of future.

To all individuals, groups, collectives, movements, social, civic and political organizations, neighborhood associations, cooperatives, all the lefts known and to be known; nongovernmental organizations, groups in solidarity with struggles of the world people, bands, tribes, intellectuals, indigenous people, students, musicians, workers, artists, teachers, peasants, cultural groups, youth movements, alternative communication media, ecologists, tenants, lesbians, homosexuals, feminists, pacifists.

To all human beings without a home, without land, without work, without food, without health, without education, without freedom, without justice, without independence, without democracy, without peace, without tomorrow.

To all who, with no matter to colors, race or borders, make of hope a weapon and a shield ...

Brothers and Sisters:

Humanity lives in the chest of us all and, like the heart, it prefers to be on the left side. We must find it, we must find ourselves.

It is not necessary to conquer the world. It is sufficient with making it new. Us. Today.

Democracy!

Liberty!

Justice!

Chiapas, 1996

PART ONE

Why Public Goods?

1

Public Goods as Commonstock: Notes on the Receding Commons

Anatole Anton

> The fault is great in man or woman
> Who steals a goose from off a common;
> But what can plead that man's excuse
> Who steals a common from a goose.
>
> —*The Tickler,* 1821

> The right not to be excluded from some use or enjoyment of some thing cannot, by its very nature, be marketed. So, of the two earlier kinds of individual property—the right to exclude others, and the right not to be excluded by others—the second virtually dropped out of sight with the predominance of this market, and the very idea of property was narrowed to cover only the right to exclude others.
>
> —C. B. Macpherson

Introduction

Economists since Adam Smith have proposed conceptions of public goods that are essentially bound up with a market society and the institutional underpinnings of such a society. This chapter argues for an alternative conception of public goods, one that does not presuppose either a market society or private property understood as entailing the right to exclude others. It proposes instead the notion of public goods as commonstock and suggests that the concept of commonstock provides a basis for the critical evaluation of the privatization, commodification, and the increasingly exclusive control of nature, communicative space, the social order, the political order, and the economic order that is characteristic of our time.

The notion of "commonstock" will be explained in some detail in Part 5, but, for our immediate purposes, suffice it to say that commonstock is social property from which, like a public park, we have a right not to be excluded. In our society, the use and enjoyment of the commonstock is typically administered by the state "in the name of the people" but, as we shall argue below in Parts 6 and 12, for democracy to have meaning, commonstock should be managed and administered in such a way as to be accountable to all stakeholders. To the extent that economic policies disregard the interests of stakeholders or regard such interests as "externalities" to the autonomous workings of the market, we shall call them "economistic." To the extent that political policies disregard the interests of stakeholders in the commonstock, we shall call them "statist."

My motives for writing this paper should be clear. Public goods are under attack throughout the world. The prevailing political philosophy of our time, neoliberalism, turns on arguments in favor of market efficiency as against the collective provision of public goods by the state or through communal means. Though there have been many clear, cogent responses to neoliberal arguments in defense of particular public goods such as health, education, and welfare, there has so far been little questioning of the very concept of public goods deployed by economists to discuss the issue. By initiating such questioning, this paper challenges political policies that are framed in terms of an economistic conception of public goods. I also write in the hope of articulating and encouraging an alternative, noneconomistic view of society implicit in the various social movements formed in opposition to the contemporary attack on public goods. Part of the challenge to an economistic view of society is the challenge to the statist view of politics, the idea that the economy (including—however implausibly—transnational corporations), civil society and the state are more or less distinct from one another and that the issues of political philosophy apply mainly to the relation between individuals and the state. My criticism of the twin fallacies of an economistic view of society and the statist view of politics is ultimately that they disempower oppositional social movements by both limiting consciousness of political possibilities and neglecting what has been referred to as the "non-decision making" process, the process that keeps potential political issues from becoming actual.

The Receding Commons

The implications of seriously considering public goods as commonstock are far-reaching. Not only do they call in question various direct and indirect schemes to privatize public goods in the area of health, education, criminal justice, and so forth, but they pose questions about high technology's headlong rush to commodify its products and the tilt away from public property in the law. Some examples are in order. Currently bruited voucher schemes for medicine and education are explicitly aimed at diminishing the status of those institutions as public goods. Similarly, the increasing rate of incarceration in the United States in combination with a flat crime rate speaks to prisoners as human commodities for newly emerging private-prison companies. The punishment industry has become a booming addition to the private sector.[1] Perhaps the best examples of the headlong rush to commodification, however, come from biotechnology. "... there has been a patent feeding frenzy going on, a mad scramble for chromosomes,"[2] as one observer, Josef Progler, recently noted. This feeding frenzy takes place in the absence of much serious reflection on the claims of the commons, although, as we discuss in following sections, there is certainly much about which to be concerned.

"The most ambitious of these endeavors is the human genome project, a mapping of genetic structure. Scientists, mostly in American universities or research institutions, aim to patent every genome they can lay their pipettes on, either at the behest of or in attempts to curry the favor of large medical and pharmaceutical corporations. At times, a genome is even modified, for example creating or inventing hybrid seeds that will grow under certain controlled conditions. The resulting new materials, which have been mathematically simulated ... can also be patented. In the case of seeds, one end result is that farmers have to pay royalties to multinational corporations for using seeds their own ancestors cultivated for centuries."[3]

When Iceland sold its genetic heritage to a company specializing in genomics, who in turn sold the human data to the Swiss firm, Hoffman LaRoche, for $200 million, the race to commodify began in earnest. It was spurred on by the extension of patentability in the United States both to the smallest unit of genetic variability, so-called SNPs (single nucleotide polymorphisms) and to large-scale sequencing programs and proprietary databases.[4]

This corporate enclosure upon the genetic commons is likely to be mirrored in the realm of culture. In the same recent article, Josef Progler warns of the rapid enclosure of "what was once musical commons": "Digitization allows researchers to parameterize human processes by way of mathematical operations known as waveguide simulation and motion capture."[5] As well as scores and melody lines, previously unique voices and cultural styles can now be captured technologically and, therefore, can in principle become intellectual property to be bought and sold. The notion of things "outside commerce," things beyond the reach of private ownership and subject therefore to special regulation, is ancient and still retains its importance in continental law.[6] Legal systems differ more on the extent to which they permit private ownership than whether they recognize private ownership at all. Thus, the civil code of both France and the former USSR defined ownership in roughly the same way but placed different limits on the range of things that can be owned.[7] What is now experienced as enclosures is a huge and largely unchallenged movement to stretch the limits of what can be privately owned at the expense of things which, by custom, law, or default, were assumed to be held in common. In a few cases, it is heartening to note, the selling off of public property has been challenged. Thus, for example, when New York City's Mayor Giuliani recently decided to sell more than 100 community gardens as though they were still the debris-strewn vacant lots from which gardens were originally created, he was prevented from doing so by a combination of a movement that raised money to buy the gardens in the name of a public trust and a court ruling that the city would have to show "there would be no environmental harm" resulting from its actions.[8] Yet in the larger picture of things, New York City's Greenthumb movement is an exception that proves the rule. The title of a recent book on public art, *Evictions: Art and Spatial Politics,* is probably closer to revealing the contemporary zeitgeist.[9] Consideration of common use—one basis for squatter's rights—has become a deeply troubling issue in the fast-moving economies of the rich countries of the world.

The Receding Commons in the World as a Whole

My focus here is primarily on issues internal to the United States, but this emphasis should not distract from the ubiquity of issues concerning the common-stock. With the demise of the former USSR, for example, the primary question in the former Eastern Bloc became that of "who should inherit the vast property that, in practice, has been run by the nomenklatura and, in theory, belonged to the people?"[10] The reason for the question is clear. "In Eastern Europe privatization was not, as in the Western world, the transfer of some enterprises to a dominant private sector. It was the creation of that sector almost from scratch."[11] And the answer to this question is equally clear. "Now privileges are personal and for keeps."[12] Mass privatization was implemented in 1992 by a nationwide voucher system together with the selling off of state enterprises as joint stock companies a few years later. The net effect of this privatization has led to debates about whether as few as fifteen big businesses now own half of Russia's wealth.[13] Similarly, in China, which is still nominally "socialist," the vast and impressive array of agricultural communes originally encouraged by the state and built up through tremendous collective effort have, with the support of a new regime, been, cannibalized by a few at the expense of the many, part of a situation sometimes cynically referred to as "market Stalinism."[14]

The issue of public goods crops up prominently in the so-called Third World as well, for example, in debt for nature (equity) swaps between poor countries and the lending institutions of the rich. Again, prior to the revolutionary change in government in the Union of South Africa, the African National Congress stated in its Freedom Charter that the country's resources, such as minerals, belong to all the people.[15] More recently, South Africa made clear its determination to authorize the manufacture of drugs to combat AIDS by its own national pharmaceutical companies, even though patents are held by American or European firms. "In a world where science is still the prerogative of the rich countries while the poor countries continue to die," as Philippe Queau remarks, "there can be no doubt that the niceties of intellectual property seem less persuasive than social reality."[16] After all, the price of medicines can be as much as thirteen times higher in Third-World countries that recognize patents on pharmaceutical products than countries that don't.[17] As symptomatic of the neoliberal mind-set toward public goods, a memo by Larry Summers, who was then the chief economist for the World Bank and is now secretary of the Treasury, was leaked to the press in favor of doing business on the assumption that "... countries in Africa are vastly *UNDER*polluted, their air quality is probably vastly inefficiently low compared to Los Angeles or Mexico City."[18] Meanwhile, throughout the Third World, communal institutions from *ejidoes* in Mexico to ordinary rural villages are crumbling under the pressure of massive urbanization and migratory labor markets. But the issue of public goods in the Third World are typically manifestations of our inability to recognize global public goods. A full page ad in the *New York Times* by a coalition of well-known environmental organizations informs us that "the next world war will be about water" and calls on us, among other things, to recognize that "Water should not become a commodity; it is part of the commons, owned by all of us forever. It should not be privatized or traded or globalized."[19] Arguably the political conflicts in the Middle East between Israel and its neighbors concern the inability to treat water in an arid, desert region as a common good to be shared equitably by the nations of the area and to be administered by a regional agency of some sort. One can speak of our failures with respect to the earth's oceans and atmosphere in a similar way. The situation is briefly summed up in a quote from a Global Intelligence Update.

> The United States remains at the center of the international system. It is the preeminent global military, economic and political power. Militarily, the U.S. Navy controls the world's oceans more completely than any empire in history. As important, the United States exercises almost complete control of space, enabling its intelligence apparatus to see deep and its military to shoot deep and with precision. Economically, the United States is experiencing an unprecedented boom, surging past all other regions of the world. This military and economic power yields unprecedented political influence. This is complemented by geography. As the only great power native to both the Atlantic and Pacific oceans, it can influence events globally with an ease that magnifies its inherent power.[20]

Finally, the global commons of preexisting human knowledge is as fundamental as the earth's oceans and atmosphere. Innovations, after all, draw on previously accumulated knowledge. "The international community could," notes economist

Joseph Stiglitz, "... claim the right to charge for the use of the global knowledge commons."[21] This is one—though not the only—plausible response to the privatization and patenting of local knowledge by the pharmaceutical industry. "In many cases," Stiglitz continues, "local people have long recognized the value of these local drugs, though they have not identified the particular chemicals that give the desired effects."[22] At any rate, local knowledge is typically, if unself-consciously, regarded as commonstock. To take a last example, the neem tree of India is the source of thirty-five patents related to its pesticide properties. Yet, as William Tabb notes, "local users who have long known and benefited from the trees' properties get nothing for the appropriation of this knowledge by European and U.S. firms."[23]

The Economic Concept of Public Good

My complaint about the way in which economists use the concept of public goods is that they take the concept of an unregulated market for granted and with it the legitimacy of the institutional framework of private property, which underlies the market. Indeed, their arguments for a capitalist market society presuppose a conception of property that is defensible only if one already accepts the market as the ideal form of social organization. In this way, arguments for capitalism from the supposed right of private property tend to be circular.[24]

The essence of private property is the right to effectively exclude others from what belongs to you. This right of exclusion is the institutional basis of the market; yet, the origin of this right defies moral justification. Much that was not private property became private property through forcible exclusion of ordinary people from what up to the point of exclusion had been traditionally held in common. We know from history and anthropology that, if anything, the norm for human societies includes common or shared property, and we also know that the development of the market means that the process of converting what is held in common to private property increases extensively, until it pervades the planet—part of the process now referred to as "globalization"—and increases intensively, until all features of social life—however intimate, sacred or ancient—fall under the sway of private ownership. Since some of the earliest and best known examples of this market process, the so-called Acts of Enclosure, date back to England under the Tudors, I will refer to "enclosures" of all sorts as part of the market process and think of the "commons" as not just a place for gathering firewood, recreation, grazing animals and the like but for all aspects of social life. The Acts of Enclosure applied to commonly held land that was turned over to the lords, but, metaphorically, enclosures can be thought of as applying to all that is held in common that is now being converted to private ownership. It is also well to remember in this era of neoliberalism the violence that accompanied the development of the market in the first place. "Enclosures have appropriately been called a revolution of the rich against the poor," Karl Polanyi tells us.

"The lords and nobles were upsetting the social order, breaking down ancient law and custom, sometimes by means of violence, often by pressure and intimidation. They were literally robbing the poor of their share in the common, tearing down houses which, by the hitherto unbreakable force of custom, the poor had long regarded as theirs and their heirs'. The fabric of society was being disrupted; desolate villages and the ruins of human dwellings testified to the fierceness with which the revolution raged, endangering the defenses of the country, wasting its towns, decimating its population, turning its overburdened soil into dust, harassing its people and turning them from decent husbandmen into a mob of beggars and thieves."[25]

Contemporary enclosures, being less obvious and more familiar, have largely gone unquestioned, if not unnoticed. To remind ourselves of the ever receding commons is an effort to carry further what John Dewey spoke of as "needed ... changes in patterns of mind and character."[26] We must first remember that our common humanity has had institutional form before we can fight effectively to restore it.

By contrast to the multifaceted concept of the commons in social life, economists, following Adam Smith, have thought of public goods as those that resist commodification, goods that resist the unspoken commandment: Thou shalt commodify whatever possible, for a good should be presumed a commodity until proven public. Smith argued that since a light house could not practically exclude some ships and not others from the benefit of its beams, it should be regarded as a public good. In Smith's world, technology to overcome the obstacles to commodification of light houses was unimaginable, and so it was easier to think of the distinction between public and nonpublic goods as natural and relatively fixed properties of those goods. In the contemporary world, however, where inventions, like synthetic fibers, can often be conjured up upon demand, it is a political decision, disguised as a simple market reality, whether to convert a public good to a private good. Since resistance to commodification can often be overcome by technological means, there is little that is natural about it. Whitehead was reputed to remark that the greatest invention of the nineteenth century was the invention of the method of invention.

In standard accounts of the subject, the economic concept of public goods concentrates on apparently natural features of commodities that make them "unmarketable" or at least not efficiently marketable and further requires that all significant externalities introduced by such commodities also be "unmarketable." One such feature of commodities is termed "nonexcludability" and another such feature is "nondepletability" (or the property of being what some economists have called "nonrivalrous"). Both of these textbook concepts take for granted the market norms of commodification and efficiency and then account for goods that can't be fit into the mold of commodification and efficiency as public. Both concepts presuppose the unquestioned results of history and, in that way, beg questions of political philosophy about the conditions for the legitimacy of markets in the first place. Economic textbooks don't mention enclosures, for example, even though there would not be a market of any significance without them.

Consider first the concept of excludability. It supposes clear and enforceable property rights, and the ability to monitor transfer and transport of such goods in a relatively costless way. The owner of such goods, as we have said, must be able to exclude others from the benefits of such goods. For Locke, in his "Second Treatise on Government," "the grass my horse has bit, the turfs my servant has cut, and the ore I have digged in any place ... become my property without the assignation or consent of anybody,"[27] but, in contrast to Locke's labor theory of property, as Bentham correctly noted, property "is entirely the work of the law."[28] How else can one understand contemporary intellectual property? Whether this excludability condition is met depends on an agency of enforcement (e.g., a state with a monopoly of force) as well as on the establishment of widespread social discipline, reasonable assumptions of intergenerational continuity, and the current state of technology. We might, for example, erect "fences" to exclude others from fish in a certain part of the ocean. Seemingly, the cost of doing so would be prohibitive, as Starrett suggests in his excellent book on public choice.[29] Yet, if fish farming were important enough to the interests of a state, resources might be expended for research and development aimed at finding technology capable of creating fish "fences" in the ocean and converting a seemingly natural public good into a private one. If such situations as the need to fish farm occurred frequently enough, the state might as a matter of political policy, promote the development of exclusion-enhancing technologies or patrol its territorial waters with great vigilance. It would certainly crack down on rogue fisherman and their ilk, who don't recognize the new norms, and would most likely teach children to resist the romantic appeal of fish pirates while at the same time they learn to value the heroic protectors of well-ordered sea-lanes. Surely, the decision to undertake or not undertake such policies might reasonably be called political. The labor of several generations of young people could conceivably be politically conscripted, under the banner of national competitiveness through economic efficiency, to labor in the ocean at the task of making fish a private resource. Such privatization is expensive, however, and would have to be paid for by the state and, one hopes, a willing populace. Once again, the economy and the state turn out to be far more intimately bound together than the statist conception of politics would lead us to believe.

For a market to work, there also must be public goods, such as roads, bridges, canals, and so forth, for which exclusion, though possible, is not desirable. These are not entirely public goods, the standard economic account tells us, since they entail maintenance and the amount of use they get does have a minuscule effect on their availability. They are in the long run depletable. Similarly, goods such as public monuments, parks, and museums all have attendant costs for dealing with congestion (as well as maintenance). By abstraction from such partially nonrivalrous goods, we may define an unconditionally public good as one for which there would be no depletion even in the case of unlimited public consumption. In the case of nonrivalrous consumption, one individual's consumption does not detract from another's. Aside from cases of knowledge (such as of a mathematical theorem), it is hard to find examples of such pure public goods and the better part of valor to recognize that our real concern is with partially nonrivalrous situations.

Even excluding transmission costs, there are only very rarely no marginal costs to sharing the benefits of a good. It thus becomes a political issue whether and how to pick up the costs of wear and tear and of congestion. Only given a commitment to the value of a market system for each does it become appropriate for all in some way to ensure the material, social, and technical conditions for its operations. Defenders of markets often will concede that such public goods as national defense, police, fire protection, and perhaps even health and education are suitable objects of collective provision to the degree that they both make the private goods of the market available and also provide commodities within a market system that would otherwise not be fully available to all within that system. Within this framework, national and international economic stability is a public good too, underlining the extent to which the economic conception of public goods itself presupposes market norms and values.[30]

Waiving consideration of the inevitable details and technicalities, we have said enough to show that there are issues of political policy behind the decision to promote a market economy. After all, market privatization has built in limits and public goods appear at these limit points. To commodify most things, it is desirable and often necessary to have some uncommodified (or public) goods. Indeed, feminists have pointed to the way in which societies with a market in labor depend parasitically on nonmarket institutions such as the family. In a similar spirit, those concerned with equity in the global economy have noted: "The market does benefit from the "global public goods" currently available, such as knowledge falling within the public domain or information or research financed out of public funds. But it is not its role to contribute directly to promoting and defending this public domain."[31] Even philosophical defenders of classical liberalism such as Nozick have to answer to the possibility, depending on circumstances, of the need for an extensive police state as the price for protecting and promoting a market economy and laissez-faire trade policies generally.[32] In another key, the Heritage Foundation stated in a report for the Reagan administration that: "It is axiomatic that individual liberties are secondary to the requirements of national security and internal order."[33] Whether we should collectively pay this price is not simply an economic question; it is also a political question that should be addressed in the terms of political philosophy. Radical critics of contemporary capitalism, for example, have challenged the socialization of costs of private production in all spheres of society, emphasizing that the high technology sector owes its existence to state funded R&D.[34] To mention only one example:

In 1985 all the data from the American publicly-funded programme of earth observation by the Landsat satellite were conceded to EOPSat, a subsidiary of General Motors and General Electric. As a result, the cost of access to the data increased 20 fold. Universities could no longer afford to buy the information, even though it had been obtained entirely using public money. It was used for the benefit of the big oil companies, who thus received a direct subsidy.[35]

To implicitly presuppose the overriding value of market efficiency or micro-order, as the economic concept of public good does, begs important questions of political philosophy. The division of society into three parts—economy, society, and state—is itself a political arrangement that, as our discussion of the commonstock in the following two sections aims to show, can only exist in tension with such political ideas as democracy, community, and equality.

Public Goods as Commonstock

There is a more basic conception of public good than that of the economists. This is the conception of a public good as a commonstock. From the point of view of political philosophy, it has the advantage of not begging the question of whether having a market (with its attendant enclosures) supersedes other nonmarket values (such as equality and community) or the question of whether markets really can be justified by their own standards in a noncircular way. For want of a better word, I have decided to call the notion of public goods as commonstock, the "historical" concept of public goods, reminding us of the times before the advent of enclosure. In doing so, I want to point to the concept's being both logically and temporally prior to the economist's notion of a public good. When a society considers the question of whether to commodify or not, of whether to privatize or not, that which they consider is a commonstock. Virgin land in the possession of a nation (such as the Louisiana Purchase) can be seen as a public good prior to any decision about whether or how to parcel it out to private owners or homesteaders and to disregard the claims of Native Americans. The defeated opposition to the acts of enclosure in England and the tradition of Gerard Wynstanley and the Diggers had this notion in mind in their opposition to the outcome of the English civil war. It is equally familiar in the context of European colonization. How to impose a European system of property on "the new world" once it had been conquered became a question for discussion and debate. As the following passage of a letter from Thomas Jefferson to James Madison brings out, there was a kind of presumption against commodifying or privatizing.

Whenever there are in any country uncultivated lands and unemployed poor, it is clear that the laws of property have been so far extended as to violate natural right. The earth is given as a commonstock for man to labor and live on. If for the encouragement of industry we allow it to be appropriated, we must take care that other employment be provided to those excluded from appropriation. If we do not, the fundamental right to labor the earth returns to the unemployed.[36]

Jefferson, of course, defended private property in land (and, sad to say, people), believing for reasons of political democracy, civic values, and economic efficiency that "the small landowners are the most precious part of the state."[37] But for all that, Jefferson never ceased to believe that the earth is given to us as a "commonstock" and can, therefore, be taxed. Rejecting the Lockean notion of tacit consent, he argued that a society has the right to revoke claims to excludability. Estimating in 1790 that a generation lasts nineteen years, Jefferson insisted that "no society can make a perpetual constitution, or even a perpetual law. The earth belongs always to the living generation" and, therefore, "every Constitution ... and every law expires at the end of 19 years."[38] Jefferson, of course, might have cited Mosaic legislation about the Jubilee year in defense of his views. According to one commentator: "The divine legislator viewed the land as the property of the invisible national God ... for thus spoke Moses in the name of God: 'The land shall not be sold forever, for the land is mine, for ye are strangers and sojourners with me'" (Leviticus 25:23).[39]

Madison's reply to Jefferson was Lockean in spirit. "If the earth be the gift of *nature* to the living, their title can extend to the earth in its natural state only. The *improvements* made by the dead form a debt against the living, who take the benefit of them."[40] But like Jefferson, he thought that this issue was not merely economic and legal. It is also political and concerns the political conditions for economic efficiency. "... most of the rights of property, would become absolutely defunct, and the most violent struggles ensue between the parties interested in reviving, and those interested in reforming the antecedent state of property."[41] Class warfare would be invited out into the open, and the distribution of property resulting from the workings of the economy would be subjected to political questions. At any rate, the right of eminent domain reminds us that the Jeffersonian conception of a commonstock is not totally absent in our legal system and that Madison's objections have not entirely won out over Jefferson's vision. Time limits on patents and copyrights are likewise Jeffersonian in spirit.

More generally, C. B. Macpherson has tried to draw our attention to "the demonstrable fact" that the concept of property has changed "not only as between ancient and medieval and modern societies but also within the span of modern society."[42] The modern concept of property as "an exclusive individual right to use and dispose of material things" evolved together with the predominance of the market. But this modern market conception is, in fact, "a drastic narrowing" of the meaning of property.[43] In historical perspective, Macpherson reminds us:

> From the earliest ideas of property, say from Aristotle down to the seventeenth century, property was seen to include both of two kinds of individual rights: both an individual right to exclude others from some use or enjoyment of some thing, and an individual right not to be excluded from the use or enjoyment of things that society has declared to be for common use—common lands, parks, roads, waters. Both were rights of individuals. Both rights were created and maintained by society or the state. Both therefore were individual property.[44]

The fact that we don't ordinarily think of public goods such as national parks as part of each citizen's individual property testifies to the questions that we have lost with the narrowing of our concept of property. Such questions would have been apparent to the ancients and medievals, who had a clear conception of common property, as well as to the early moderns who defined individual property

widely enough to include the commonstock. Indeed, the bulk of the world's population, like the Zapatistas in Chiapas, experience property as a right of exclusion, as an imposition upon them and their land.

Commonstock as a Condition of Democracy

Our discussion so far has suggested that rather than the presumption in favor of
commodification and private ownership implicit in the economic conception of
public goods, the presumption ought to favor the commonstock and place the burden of argument on the shoulders of those who would privatize rather than those
who would socialize. This view is not original. Defenders of a market perspective
such as Adam Smith or Thomas Jefferson did accept this presumption and then argued on grounds of efficiency that markets and hence the preconditions for markets, commodities, and private property would deliver consequentialist payoffs.
Similarly, Locke, though nothing of an egalitarian, recognized that he had to give
arguments for an unequal rather than an equal distribution of goods consistent
with his view of the social contract. Neoliberals today are so sure of the virtues of
the market that they seldom argue at much length that market solutions to education or the environment are better—on grounds of efficiency—than political solutions, but they take for granted that they have an efficiency argument at hand to
trump "bleeding heart" socializers if need be. In the seventeenth and eighteenth
centuries, with much social property still in evidence, the question of whether to
privatize or not naturally presented itself, but in the twenty-first century, with well-
developed systems of exchange and well-established rules of production for exchange appearing as a kind of second nature and the obvious failure of alternatives
such as the Soviet system, the question appears to be whether to socialize or not. It
is easy to forget that, logically speaking, market exchange already presupposes
ownership of that which is to be exchanged. Locke notwithstanding, such private
ownership depends on the prior existence of social rules. There are no commodities
in nature and thus for an item of nature to become a commodity, some social
process must have taken place. Appearances aside, the fundamental question, from
a historical and logical point of view, is that of privatization, not socialization.

If contemporary appearances partially obscure the reasons for placing the burden of argument on privatizers rather than socializers, there is another important
characteristic of contemporary reality that makes it clear. The early liberal states
of the eighteenth century became increasingly democratized in the nineteenth and
twentieth centuries. Taking something from a group and giving it to a single person (together with the right to exclude members of the group of original owners),
cries out to the democratic sensibility for reasons. Private property, from a democratic point of view, amounts to the surrender of democratic control of social resources to private individuals. Surrender might be the right thing to do, but
surely some good reasons ought to be given for so doing. Insisting on the claims
of the commonstock is thus a way of politicizing apparently apolitical economic
processes for the sake of democracy.

It is hard to exaggerate the extent to which what are regarded as public goods are economically motivated, are, in fact, part of a process of socializing some of the costs of private production. When Great Britain nationalized the coal industry after World War II, for example, it was because the profit had gone out of private coal production in England and dependence on foreign coal would hurt the remainder of English industry. Arguments for public education often turn on the need to have a pool of educated labor. If a private company were to train its own computer scientists, for example, they might easily lose their investment were their trainee to go to work for a higher-paying rival firm. Moreover, capital will gravitate to states with a large, educated labor force. Similarly, educating for what sociologists call "the social control professions" (such as teachers, social workers) assures the ongoing reproduction of a disciplined labor force in the future. Socialized health care relieves employers of paying for the health and retirement benefits demanded by the labor movement. In some situations, it might be better to sacrifice a particular industry, for example the health insurance industry, for the good of the industrial system as a whole. The decision to provide what economists simply call a "desirable" public good is obviously dependent on the political and social situation at the time. Bismark decided to provide such goods both to socialize costs and to forestall democratic pressures from below. In other cases; it was democratic pressures from below that forced the adoption of public goods such as compulsory education that could later be turned to the socialization of costs of private production.

What the economist would describe as public goods can also socialize the costs of private consumption. Notoriously, for example, Robert Moses, the master builder of roads, parks, bridges, and other public works for New York City, built overpasses that would discourage buses on his parkways. It is clear from Robert A. Caro's biography of Moses that doing so expressed his race and class biases. Poor people and blacks normally used public transportation, especially in the 1920s and 1930s. Moses wanted to limit access to Jones Beach, his widely admired public park, and ensure that it would be reserved for automobile-owning whites of the "upper" and "comfortable middle" classes.[45]

However problematic, public goods are not the result of a surrender of democratic control of social resources to private individuals. They are venues for democratic pressure and critique. They provide a legal and political framework for raising issues of democracy, equality, and community. An exclusively statist conception of managing the commonstock together with the various tensions buried within the associated conception of public ownership and administration cries out for a democratic conception of the commonstock and of public ownership. The claims of the commonstock here too have a presumption that has to be met by anyone who claims to govern in the name of the people. If public goods exist as a response to democratic pressures, then the administrators of those goods are accountable to show why they can go no further in the way of democracy than they have. Typically, of course, the answer to this challenge is spoken in the tech-

nical vocabularies of experts and appeals to considerations of efficiency and stability, but the challenges can have an effect. The requirements of the accumulation process can be overridden by demands for democratic legitimacy.[46] The limited but definite success of antitoxic movements testifies to this reality, for
example.[47] So what can be said is that what the economist would call the "desir-
ability" of public goods is in fact a contested terrain, a site of conflicted compromises between the requirements of capital accumulation and those of democratic
legitimacy. Since democratic legitimacy is often confused with a statist conception of politics, it is a particularly urgent task to explicate a conception of the
commonstock that is not exclusively statist, a conception that both transcends
the statist view of politics and can serve as a critical standpoint from which to
evaluate the successes and failures of public goods in terms of real democracy.

One way in which recognition of the claims of the commonstock can serve a
critical purpose is in the rejection of talk about the source of state legitimacy in the
correction of so-called market failures. My emphasis has been on the conditions
necessary to have a market in the first place (before it can fail or succeed), but it is
useful to remember that real markets in the real world are constrained in ways that
economists simply don't consider. The issues of governance present themselves in
practice, as Peter Brown notes in his book, *Restoring the Public Trust,* in noneconomic ways. "The question is not, as market devotees would have it, how we can
get the market to function at perfect efficiency. It is, rather, what subsidies and
other interventions in the market will serve humane and democratic purposes."[48]
Even in the absence of a democratic presumption, the commonstock makes its
presence felt, if you will, in the way in which we insist on social constraints on the
workings of real (as opposed to theoretical) markets. "... the more foundational
the classification of an item," Brown tells us, "the more it is protected from the
ravages of exchange. This explains the paradox that what a society values most is
what it keeps off the market."[49] We don't discount the future, as we do the time
value of money, when considering nuclear waste disposal, the ozone layer or top
soil conservation, for example, because if we did, we would not think beyond forty
years (when the future value of a present dollar virtually disappears).[50] More generally, we don't discount the future, because, in the words of Enrique Leff, "it is
not possible to establish discount rates that can actualize future preferences or
complex, uncertain and long-term ecological processes."[51] We don't yet allow markets in body parts or citizenship, and we have striven, with mixed results, to eliminate the market in certain kinds of pelts and drugs. We experienced qualms and
confusion as a nation over surrogate motherhood and the commodification of ba-
bies suggestive of deep concerns about opening up a formerly sacred area of life to
"the ravages of exchange." We still use criteria such as need and merit (rather than
dollars) to allocate food stamps and professional credentials, and finally we recognize what Brown calls fiduciary goods such as the items in the National Archives.
"What we actually do with respect to fiduciary goods ... cannot be understood in
terms of public goods," Brown reminds us, "... because they easily lend themselves
to exclusion. They do not fit the nonrivalness definition because they have low

congestion thresholds."[52] But they are part of the commonstock, and thus there is a strong, if not fully articulated, presumption against selling them. In sum, we do already recognize a partial presumption in favor of the commonstock. The problem is how both to defend and extend it.

The Contemporary Commonstock

The concept of the commonstock is of more than historical and conceptual interest. It provides us a way to frame a number of pressing contemporary issues and thus aids "in producing habits of mind and character ... that are somewhere near even with the actual movement of events."[53] To bring out the practical importance of framing these issues, I want to briefly sketch how the concept of the commonstock illuminates our present political situation. My aim is to urge that the right against exclusion from the commonstock and the need for democratic control over the commonstock are pressing political issues of our time. To take just one example, these issues were implicit in many of the recent critiques of the World Trade Organization that surfaced recently on the streets of Seattle at the dawn of the new millennium. The term "commonstock," then, gives us a way to talk about central issues of justice in our time. Contemporary political philosophy, which ignores this issue, is to that extent deficient. Though it is nameless, the issue of social property is all around us. The key problem in reaching a general formulation of the questions involved concerns the meanings of "exclusion" and "democratic control." When these expressions are understood broadly enough, "exclusion" from the commons and the "denial of democracy" are the order of the day and political struggles against these contemporary enclosures cry out for an appropriate political framework. The list of six "exclusions" below— exclusions from nature, communicative space, society, community, democracy, and the economy—will, hopefully, invest my claims with some plausibility and, perhaps, "a robust sense of reality." A seventh equally important "exclusion"— exclusion from knowledge as a social good—must await another book.

Nature as Commonstock

Natural conditions are a source of our being in the sense that undermining them is undermining our metabolic relationship with the earth established, in part, through several hundred thousand years of evolution. Yet the natural environment is treated as a dump as often as it is protected by the state. In the normal workings of the economy, the environmental and health costs of private production are shifted onto society. When social protest can successfully organize itself to make an issue of such cost shifting, the state takes notice and devises procedures—however flawed—to regulate the situation. Such measures are often described in terms of public goods. The economistic view of society and the statist view of politics conspire to justify not only the socialization of costs but also a shift in the burden of vigilance and responsibility. If an issue is to escape the non-decision-making process, it will typically come as a result of organized demands asserted by social movements. Yet when, as we argued above, the burden of responsibility should really rest on the shoulders of private property, a countervailing conception of social property is needed in a society organized around property. Mere principle, having no legal or political weight, is easily ignored. We have proposed a revival of the concept of "commonstock" to call attention both to the illegitimacy of the presumptions in favor of private property and the need to institutionalize a voice for those facing exclusion at the hands of private property or, as in the case of the construction of Three Gorges Dam in China ("which is expected to displace as many as 2 million people"), economistic public goods.[54] Given the likely preferences of the majority of stakeholders, serious commitment to the commonstock would institutionalize a presumption in favor of preservationism that would have to be met by private developers, state planners, and even conservationists.

In principle, the state is willing to acknowledge certain limits to the prerogatives of private property, but the list below of recognized, though selectively and haphazardly enforced, limits on the prerogatives of private property, as Langdon Winner has noted, artificially constricts the variety of reasons to question plans for growth and development.[55]

1. Threats to public health
2. Threats to exhaust a vital resource
3. Qualitative degradation of the environment (air, land, and water)
4. Threats to natural species and wilderness areas
5. Large, significant threats to social stability

Each of these potential limits have typically been recognized and realized as a result of popular pressure over an extended period of time. Of course, there is much backsliding on adherence to principle and these principles are typically recognized and applied in a selective and arbitrary manner. Moreover, they place a burden on those who would question plans for growth or technological development to adjust their complaints, which might after all be religious, philosophical, or aesthetic, to state recognized grounds for limitation. By insisting on the claims of all stakeholders in the commonstock, we are at the least opening discussion to advocates with widely differing worldviews. At first blush, it might seem that from the point of view of deep ecology, for example, insisting on social property is still anthropocentric and so not significantly different from private property in determining our relation to nature. But this impression is mistaken. Paying attention to the claims of stakeholders in the commonstock opens up a social space for practical consideration of the integrity of nature. The character of our relationship to nature in this way need no longer be relegated to the non-decision-making process and might become a political issue. The only practical alternatives to this democratic approach to consideration of the principles of deep ecology would be statist politics either "in the name of the people" or, at the limit, an eco-fascism or eco-anarchism ruling over or attacking the majority who are assumed to be hope-lessly benighted.

Recognition of the commonstock favors preservationism in another way. Commonstocks are bundled less tightly together than private property. Mineral rights, water rights, coastal access, air space, top soil, hunting and fishing rights, and rights to wild berries (as in Sweden) are parts of different and even cross-cutting commonstocks. Existing law tends to bundle them together in one piece of property, but from the point of view of the commonstock, the parts that are public might be routinely separated from those that are privately owned, rendering the complexities of the presumption in favor of preservationism harder to ignore.

The need to address such presumptions directly is urgent, and the force of this urgency itself provides a consideration in favor of the commonstock. The most ominous example of the destruction of the balance of nature concerns global warming. A scientific consensus is forming that average global temperatures are warmer than they were a century ago and that there are good indications that this warming trend is continuing. The evidence, in fact, shows that "the planet is heating at a rate faster than at any time in the last 10,000 years."[56] Since global warming is a direct result of industrialization and since industrialization is the path toward economic growth, the hope held out to the vast majority of the world's population for an escape from poverty, serious questions arise about the adequacy of market mechanisms "to serve as the co-ordinating mechanism of the social order," when "climatic conditions pose externalities of gigantic order."[57] The same then must be said for private property as the institutional underpinning of these market mechanisms. "If tomorrow," we are told, "the United States and the rest of the industrial world were to cut its emissions dramatically, that reduction would be overwhelmed by the coming pulse of carbon from China, India, Mexico, Brazil, and all developing nations who are struggling to keep ahead of the relentless undertow of chronic poverty."[58] Paradoxically, the historical moment of capitalist triumphalism is at the same time a moment that raises the most profound moral and political questions about the adequacy of capitalism to serve the human species. We are exposed to the epistemological irony that the very groups that express skepticism about the reality of global warming—often on the payroll of big oil—express little or no skepticism about the workings of an unregulated market and frequently express a kind of religious faith in the invisible hand that guides market mechanisms as regulators of social order.[59] Even the concerns of main-stream economists about the effects of imperfect information on an unregulated market encounter deaf ears.[60] If the various attempts to exonerate the free market from the charge of endangering the well-being of the human species will fail, handy divisions between issues that are economic, political, and social (consider, for example, the automobile as an element of civil society) lose in plausibility.

The natural way to see stable climatic conditions is as a commonstock, part of a biosphere to which every human being has a right. As one author remarks: "... the global environment is everyone's second home."[61] Causing floods or hurricanes or severe changes in climate has the effect of making parts of our commonstock uninhabitable. Thus, as Ross Gelbspan reminds us: "In 1995, a panel of more than 2,000 scientists from 100 countries reported to the United Nations that Earth has already entered a new period of climatic instability likely to cause widespread economic, social and environmental dislocations—including sea level rise of up to 3 feet, increases in floods and droughts, increasingly severe storms and temperature extremes."[62] The skeptic about global warming should have had to bear a burden of proof to convince us to put our "second home" at risk. From an economic point of view, global warming is just a huge externality, a way of passing off private costs of production and consumption to society as a whole. When scientific skeptics acknowledge that global warming, if true, would be a kind of tort against humanity, they acknowledge implicitly that stable climatic conditions are part of the commonstock. To assert unwillingness to pay the social and environmental costs of a free market is to assert rights that rival the rights of private property. Individuals who are harmed by global warming are, in effect, excluded without consultation from the commonstock quite independently of overall calculations of economic utility and the imperatives of economic growth.

Communicative Space as Commonstock

Social critics such as Herbert Schiller explicitly refer to "the corporate enclosure of public expression and cultural creativity" as well as "the corporate envelopment of public expression."[63] The scope of this enclosure is suggested by the following exclusions: exclusion from the sources of informed dialogue, exclusion from historic sites of dialogic communication, and exclusion from the technological means of dialogic communication. From such venerable institutions as the weather bureau to prominent agencies such as the U.S. Bureau of the Census, the maintenance of informational sources of public debate were until recently considered serious paradigms of public responsibility and data produced by such agencies was made available to the public at library depositories scattered around the country. Together with other public libraries, these depositories put into practice, if in a limited way, the democratic aspirations of the nation, embodying the principle of equal access for all to the nation's informational resources.[64] But in recent decades, the production and supply of information has become a major growth industry. "Decisions over the production, organization, storage, and dissemination of information," as Schiller notes, "are considered and decided upon without the presence of the public and its representatives."[65] His underlying point is that "transforming information into a salable good, available only to those with ability to pay for it, changes the goal of information access from an egalitarian to a privileged condition."[66] It also affects the functioning of the state. Following the neoliberal paradigm, states have farmed out public databases to subcontractors. In an amusing turn of events, for example, "the Securities and Exchange Commission ... has been obliged to buy back its own data from a commercial enterprise which now 'owns' it."[67]

The enclosure upon the sources of informed dialogue is matched by the enclosure upon the potential sites at which such dialogue might take place. From the point of view of communication theory, the suburbanization of U.S. society amounts to luring people into "depoliticized living spaces." The suburbanization of U.S. society resulted from conscious decisions to socialize the costs of highway construction (to encourage automobile transport) and cheap mortgages (to encourage the building and buying of private homes). In this sense, suburbanization results from political decisions to provide public goods such as highways and to give away public resources in the form of tax breaks. It is an unintended, privatizing consequence of these public policies. Since suburban life centers around privately owned shopping malls, "selling machines" (as one social critic referred to them), controlled environments to promote "a shopping mood," it lacks genuine public space.[68] When put to the test, courts have tended to uphold the private property claims of malls as against rights to free public expression and dialogue.[69] "Malls effectively insulate [masses of people]," Schiller tells us, "from seeing, hearing, or encountering expression and ideas that might, however slightly, disturb the mood, routines, and tranquility of daily shopping.... Distilled out are all conflicts seeking solution."[70] Looking at malls as social terrain or commonstock withdrawn from serving as a site of public dialogue brings out the political meaning of the fact that malls now outnumber post offices and secondary schools in the United States. It also provides the context for the ways in which malls get resocialized informally. Teenagers and old people use them for meeting and recreation with no intention of buying.

The growth of depoliticized suburban space has encouraged private enclosures on the city as communicative space. For at least the last 200 years, the public streets, parks, and neighborhoods of cities were places where people could gather to talk over or express grievances. And indeed zoning controls were placed in effect with at least some attention to these public interests. Out-migraton to the suburbs in the post–World War II years have transformed the space of cities. Downtowns are built "disregarding every notion of human scale" and "crowding out the possibility of street life."[71] Ironically, developers occasionally include small concrete parks and "gardens" that appear to be public even though they are privately owned and maintained. The urban poor are pushed to the fringes of the city while the homeless wander the streets or sleep in doorways. Shopping centers spring up on the model of suburban malls while boutiques and pricey restaurants make inroads on former centers of neighborhood life. As social distances grow in the city, communicative space shrinks. Public expressions such as parades and festivals are commercialized into tourist spectacles while the corporate sponsorship of museums and ballparks reshape and control the public purpose of these gathering places.[72] Throughout the global economy, historical and archaeological public treasures are used less for the people and more for purposes such as tourism, business incentives, and the like. That corporate professions of good citizenship are effective "public relations" shows that public values themselves are still alive even if they are disregarded.

Communicative space opened up by new technologies of communication such as radio broadcasting was initially seen as a commonstock also. Few people in the United States in the 1920s were aware of the money-making potential in the airwaves, and public debates about the proper use of broadcasting concerned the public goals that should guide their use. A public-spirited approach to the use of the airwaves persisted until the failure of organized opposition to the Communications Act of 1934 and the establishment of the Federal Communications Commission (FCC), when the question of the public use of technologies of communication as advocated by educators, religious leaders, labor, civic organizations, women's groups, journalists, farmers' groups, civil libertarians, and many intellectuals was converted into a nonissue.[73] Later arguments for public space in the airwaves were, as Robert McChesney tells us, "a far cry from the criticism of the broadcast reformers in the 1930's, who argued that the problem was not simply one of lack of competition in the marketplace, as much as it was the rule of the marketplace per se."[74] Since 1934, the United States has been unique among developed capitalist nations in turning the means of communication over to private industry as soon as commercial possibilities reveal themselves. This has been the pattern not only with AM radio in the 1920s but TV in the 1940s and UHF television in the 1940s and 1950s. Despite the socialization of costs implicit in the government-funded research and development that led to their existence, the same pattern has continued with the Internet, satellites, and digital communication technologies.[75] Given this context, it is not surprising that the Telecommunications Act of 1996, permitting the market and not public policy "to determine the course of the information highway and the communications system," encountered no serious resistance.[76] The fact that the 1996 law has not led to "the digital free-for-all" its proponents predicted but rather seems to encourage the direction of increased concentration, "downsizing," and consolidation of global markets raises questions about the legitimacy of enclosures once again.[77]

Commonstock and Social Equality

As well as bearing on the availability of public expression and the formation of what John Dewey referred to as "publics," the concept of the commonstock allows us to frame the question of social equality. What the familiar issues of racism, sexism, sexual preference, national chauvinism, and so forth are about, I suggest, is equal access to the social commonstock, the right not to be excluded from the use and enjoyment of common social resources. Following C. B. Macpherson, we assume that since property is of such overriding importance in our present scale of values, "... it is only if the human right to a full life is seen as a property right that it will stand much chance of realization."[78]

The term "commonwealth" is still in use and refers to the whole of a society's resources, its social as well as its tangible holdings. Arguably, then, we retain the concept of the social commonstock, but we rarely think out its implications. Public standards of health, education, and food security must be taken for granted as conditions no less fundamental than a "user friendly" biosphere for social functioning. However variable, such conditions have existed since the beginning of human societies and explain the possibility of society in the first place. The fact, for example, that human beings are relatively efficient processors of food energy and, over the last 10,000 years, have developed foods such as rice, wheat, maize, and potatoes that produce far more human energy than is required in their production is no less a part of the social commonstock than finely tuned human languages that enable subtle communication.[79] The development of mathematics in world culture, encompassing the Vedic concept of zero, Arabic numerals, Egyptian geometry (axiomatized by Greek mathematicians), and so on testifies to the extensive cultural inheritance of ordinary schoolchildren throughout the world. "Most innovations and inventions are based on ideas that form part of the common property of humanity," notes Philippe Queau. "It cannot therefore be right to restrict access to the information and knowledge that makes up this common property by making laws too keen to safeguard individual interests."[80] Repairing our relationship with the social commonstock is then comparable to repairing our relationship to nature as a source of our being.

One of the most persistent illusions of neoliberalism, illusions that fly in the face of the sociological concept of "cultural capital," is that individuals with the same talents and abilities would be equally productive independent of the social resources available to them and, thus, owe little to the society that provides the context for their achievements.[81]

If social equality, from this point of view, can be conceived of as the right of equal access to the commonstock, social rank becomes a mode of exclusion. Indeed, social rank is to the social commonstock what private property is to the natural and communicative commonstock. Possession of high social rank is comparable to a form of joint but exclusive ownership of the rewards and benefits of the social commonstock, since historically, access to the social commonstock has been limited by the hierarchical and class ordering of society. Rights to inclusion, from this perspective, point in the direction of social transformation, of the overcoming of those exclusions that accompany social rank. Enclosure upon the social commonstock in the form of the development of rank ordered societies has been a far more ancient and pervasive practice than the other enclosures. Reclamation of equality of access to the social commonstock points to the goal of social equality, the overcoming of remaining forms of social rank, a goal, as we have mentioned, that animates feminist, antiracist, anti-imperialist, and gay and lesbian movements. There is some empirical basis for the belief that such a reclamation would be a return to time-honored principles of the distant past, but, however that may be, more recent history suggests that such an overcoming is "civilizatonal." Pierre Bourdieu describes social entitlements in this vein as "among the highest achievements of civilization."[82]

Would anyone condemn as conservative the defense of the cultural achievements of humanity, Kant or Hegel, Mozart or Beethoven? The social entitlements ... such as the right to work, a health and welfare system, for which men and women have suffered and fought are achievements that are just as important and precious, and moreover, they do not only survive in museums, libraries, and academies, but are living and active in people's lives and govern their everyday existence.[83]

One main obstacle that confounds the realization of the right to inclusion in the social commonstock is the split, inevitable in the division of a society between economic and social parts, between rights of recognition in society and redistributive rights to social benefits. The Hegelian term "recognition" is here used to refer "to the wholesale transformation of societal patterns of representation, interpretation, and communication in ways that would change everybody's sense of self."[84] Distinctions of social rank are thus seen as presently dependent on a cultural apparatus and media that systematically misrepresents or fails to represent both those of high and low social rank. The overcoming of cultural misrecognition and nonrecognition of others on this view involves overcoming of one's own self-recognition together with the benefits that go along with such self-recognition. Given the enormous resistance such rights of recognition would encounter, it is hard to imagine their realization except in the context of a large social transformation. The contradictions of contemporary progressive politics that force us to choose between a social democratic politics of redistribution (without "recognition") and a politics of recognition (identity politics), lacking due attention to "redistributing income, reorganizing the division of labor, subjecting investments to democratic decision making or transforming other basic economic conditions" contributes to the strength of neoliberalism.[85] Pushing either set of demands generates backlash against the other and clearly indicates the extent to which the economic and social parts of society are placed in opposition to one another.[86]

The ultimate failure of the affirmative action policies in the United States to overcome racial exclusion (and to a lesser extent gendered exclusions) indicate the nature of these difficulties. Affirmative action policies could have been designed in such a way as not to intensify the competitive market relations between women and minorities, on the one hand, and white males, on the other. For example, in the case of *Vulcan Pioneers v. New Jersey Department of Civil Service,* Judge H. Lee Sarokin devised a way of administering layoffs so that minority firefighters would be given preference over white firefighters with more seniority. Sarokin ruled that since the more senior white firefighters would be giving up their jobs "in the name of the public good," the federal government should compensate them appropriately.[87] In effect, they would be given an attractive early retirement with the opportunity to enhance their income by getting another job if they so desired. Society as a whole would be assuming responsibility for past exclusions (in the form of racial discrimination) from the social commonstock and individual white firefighters would be freed of the burden of bearing the social costs of slavery, segregation, and the long history of racism in the United States. Had the Supreme Court not overturned Judge Sarokin's decision, it would have accepted a kind of social equality superfund comparable to such funds available to repair the environment. It would have recognized the need to repair our relationship with the social commonstock as comparable to our need to repair our relationship with nature.

The case of affirmative action in the United States mirrors some of the main issues with human rights laws generally. What are called human rights, particularly the rights enumerated in the International Covenant on Economic, Social, and Cultural Rights, can be seen as defining the issue of access to the social commonstock. The covenant has been signed by a large number of nations (including the United States) and specifies a long list of human rights. Included in the document is the right to the highest attainable standards of mental and physical health, gainful employment with a living wage and vacations, trade unions, nondiscrimination, social insurance, food security, all levels of education, access to the fruits of scientific progress, and the benefits of cultural life. Further, it is widely accepted that the Covenant on Civil and Political Rights, which has been ratified by the U.S. Senate, requires the economic, social, and cultural rights enumerated in its sister document to be meaningful. From this point of view, devices ranging from the threat of torture and arbitrary imprisonment to elitist language and culture are differing techniques of exclusion from the social commonstock. The point of asserting human rights is to assert that such exclusions are illegitimate. Commitment to these rights of inclusion can be measured by a society's willingness to establish a superfund and an appropriate institutional superstructure to implement them.

Commonstock and Community

I argued above that the concept of the commonstock allows us to frame the question of social equality, but we did not address the deeper question of human community, of the sort of "we-ness" and mutual awareness of needs, implied by the term "recognition" as used above. To do so, we must consider more deeply the relationship between the social and economic parts of society. What comes into question, then, is the commodity mode of need satisfaction, the way in which noneconomic staples of human community such as love and dignity get translated by unregulated markets into economic wants satisfiable in principle by purchases of various kinds. What human community calls for from the point of view of the social commonstock is a careful reconciliation between the social and economic parts of society. To satisfy the need to repair the relationship to the social commonstock, like our relationship to nature, one must consider the relationship between the social and economic parts of society. As things stand, market societies are in some sense parasitic upon this commonstock. They both depend crucially on the existence of the social commonstock and undermine it at the same time. Determinate levels of health and education are both required for contemporary society to function and also undermined by the social costs of the society's functioning. Whereas public goods such as bridges and highways are depleted slowly, human beings, like the soil, can be used up rather more quickly. To see parts of the social commonstock such as health and education as merely public goods in the economist's sense of the term, at worst, accepts the limitation of these goods to those of the smooth functioning of the market. At best, it simply ignores the presumption in favor of preservationism and so offers no serious justification for market externalities such as environmental toxins in relation to nature and the televised "distraction factory" in relation to society.

There is a special dialectical process in market societies between the social and the economic. It is clear that with the exception of the last two centuries, social values dominated or, at least regulated, the workings of markets. As Polanyi reminded us in 1943: "The outstanding discovery of recent historical and anthropological research is that man's economy, as a rule, is submerged in his social relationships. He does not act so as to safeguard his individual interests in the possession of material goods; he acts so as to safeguard his social standing, his social claims, his social assets."[88] The point is that for most of human history economic systems were run out of noneconomic motives. Psychologically, this situation, Polanyi tells us, "must exert a continuous pressure on the individual to eliminate economic self-interest from his consciousness to the point of making him unable, in many cases (but by no means all), even to comprehend the implications of his own actions in terms of such an interest."[89]

Principles of reciprocity, redistribution, and production for household use rather than for market gain dominate economic life at first.

Driven from the newly established economic sphere of life, the principles of community, reciprocity, redistribution, and production for household use live on in social institutions such as the family. The market in labor could not exist, as we have noted, without the noneconomic institution of the family regularly sending fresh supplies of laborers to the factory gates, often with the help of the church and the school. Ultimately, the prevalence of the commodity mode of need satisfaction, the idea that noneconomic needs of a loving family can be met through the purchase of commodities such as a station wagon and a large home signals how the social becomes submerged in the economy.[90] "The steady movement of such tasks as laundering, cooking, cleaning, and simple health care—not to mention recreation and entertainment," notes Robert Heilbronner, "from the exclusive concern of the private household into the world of business testifies to the internal expansion of capital within the interstices of social life. Much of what is called growth in capitalist societies consists in the commodification of life, rather than in the augmentation of unchanged, or even improved, outputs."[91] Public goods such as health and education also become submerged in the economic, so that health care is defined independently of obvious public health measures such as elimination of environmental toxins (for example, dioxin, PCBs), carcinogens in food, and occupational safety and is severely hampered by the refusal of pharmaceutical companies to share patented information.[92] Indeed, the original name of the field now referred to as "epidemiology" was "social medicine."[93] The fact that, for example, the medical syndrome of *karoshi* is defined as a result of having worked for "24 hours before death or at least 16 hours daily for 7 consecutive days" negates much that is excellent about health care in Japan. That mental health is effected by unemployment has been established beyond serious doubt.[94] The effects of consumerism on education have been much commented upon, and the contemporary dysfunctions of family life testify to the emotional effects of the submergence of the social in the economic. Thinking of health and education as parts of the social commonstock, as fundamentals of community rather than as public goods as defined by economists, allows us to raise a critical question that would otherwise be overlooked. Surgeon generals in the United States encountered enormous resistance in trying to promote even mild public health approaches in regard to smoking and sexual behavior related to the AIDS crisis. The clash between the requirements of public health and the market could instead be discussed in a systematic way. In sum, community requires a return to the time-honored principle of socially regulated markets.

Commonstock and Democracy

There is a critique of liberal democracy and of its main instrument, the liberal state, implicit in what we have said so far. In short, liberal democracy involves the idea that one can define democracy in a way that is independent of our relationship to the biosphere, communicative space, and society as commonstocks. Serious consideration of our connection to these commonstocks, after all, calls for serious consideration of the connection between the social ownership and social control of the commonstock. But the liberal definition of democracy is geared to private ownership and only requires certain prescribed limitations on the interactions between the state and individuals. At bottom, liberal democracy is a theory of how to draw the line between the private and public (in the sense of state-connected) areas of society. Since the private area of society came to be associated with the property requirements of a market society, the emergence of liberal democracy is bound up with the relatively recent historical emergence of an autonomous economic realm. Of course, the liberal state comes to us as a legacy of centuries of struggle to eliminate the arbitrary powers of absolute monarchies and the more recent legacy of struggles to democratize this liberal state (for example, through the struggles for universal suffrage) while at the same time liberalizing democracy (in the sense of excluding the power of the democratic state from the workings of the marketplace and the accumulation process). Yet, unlike the absolutist state that it replaced, the liberal state exists in a symbiotic dependence on the autonomous economic realm as a source of revenue. The theoretical context for our discussion of public goods is, then, that "... self-interest, not weakness, drives the [liberal] state to support and advance the accumulation of capital."[95]

Early aristocratic critics of liberal democracy—unable to imagine a genuinely social form of democracy—perceived the antagonistic connection between liberal democracy and the social commonstock. The question in their minds was whether a society founded on private property alone would result in the prevalence of antisocial individualism and thereby undermine civic life. "Egotism blights the germ of all virtue"; de Tocqueville tells us. "Individualism at first saps the virtues of public life; but in the long run it attacks and destroys all others, and is at last absorbed in downright egotism. Egotism is a vice as old as the world, which does not belong to one form of society more than another: individualism is of democratic origin."[96] A related question in the mind of aristocratic critics of liberal democracy was whether a society founded on private property must become ahistorical. "... not only does democracy make every man forget his ancestors, but it hides his descendants, and separates his contemporaries from him; it throws him back forever on his self alone, and threatens in the end to confine him entirely within the solitude of his own heart."[97]

Annette Baier has insightfully distilled the philosophical issue of shared responsibility out of de Tocqueville's reflections on the pitfalls of democratic individualism.[98] The issue is one that has been almost entirely ignored within the flawed framework of liberal democratic theory but finds a natural home as part of the political theory of the commonstock. Individualistic moral theory, Baier points out, "does not have much to say about the way individual responsibility of persons for their choices somehow sums in a democratic republic, to the states' and nations' responsibility for its choices ..." or even allows us to reflect on "our inherited schemes of cooperation" or, more important for our purposes, "can be geared to essentially collective rights or goods."[99] Thus, it has no account of really shared responsibility but only "pooled or passed along autonomy" and, since it can't end in sharing, it ends up in a division of society between a law-giving elite "accompanied by willing subjection of the rest."[100] By contrast, social ownership and control of the commonstock requires the sorts of deliberation that accompanies cooperative, shared responsibility. In such deliberation, Baier reminds us, it is implausible to think that "responsibility can divide without remainder into the bit that is mine and not yours, and the other bits that belong exclusively to specific individuals."[101] It is equally implausible to imagine that if we were to take shared responsibility seriously, we would not want to reform "our inherited schemes of cooperation for the better."[102]

De Tocqueville's equation of democracy with individualism shows one of the limits of liberal democracy and the liberal state detached from shared responsibilities for the commonstock. Clearly, if we jointly own the commonstock, then those who would damage it, as in the case of global warming, or sell it off in parcels, as in the case of the Telecommunications Act of 1996, or make it into an exclusive club, as in the case of good education, are accountable to all stakeholders in these commonstocks. Short of such public deliberations, shared responsibility for the management of the commonstock remains with the demos. Looking at the matter in this way brings out the point of John Dewey's view that democracy is more than a form of government; it is also a form of life centered on fulfilling our shared responsibilities. It is significant in this regard that in our present increasingly individualistic society, the strongest appeals to the need for public goods concern military defense and civil order (police, prisons, and so on). We are drawn together through shared fears rather than shared responsibilities.

Liberal democracy as opposed to real social democracy is then a mode of political exclusion or, at best, incomplete inclusion. It provides the institutional framework for the protection and promotion of ever-expanding private and corporate rights outside the reach of the state, a state that is at least subject to democratic pressures. At the same time, it attenuates the possibility of democratic pressures on the state by minimizing the place of the demos in the very definition of democracy, while in practice it largely controls the political agenda-setting process and sources of information relevant to political decision making. Modes of exclusion have varied but the aim of exclusion has remained constant. In the nineteenth century, advocates of liberal democracy such as Bentham, James Mill, and J. S. Mill argued for blunting the effects of universal male suffrage by plural voting schemes and other devices. In the twentieth century, once universal suffrage was an accomplished fact, liberal democracy has been redefined to incorporate the very aristocratic or elitist values that democracy was once invoked to challenge. To use Walter Lippman's phrase, the demos was regarded as "a bewildered herd" requiring the leadership of elites. Similarly, Joseph Schumpeter characterizes the popular will as "an indeterminate bundle of vague impulses loosely playing about given slogans and mistaken impressions."[103] Discounting the concept of popular will as unrealistic and of the common good as unworkable, Schumpeter proposed his famously and widely accepted redefinition of liberal democracy.

> The democratic method is that institutional arrangement for arriving at political decisions in which individuals acquire the power to decide by means of competitive struggle for the people's vote.[104]

Far from any notion of shared responsibility, democracy for Schumpeter means only that the electorate has the opportunity to choose their rulers in elections and reserves the right to select new rulers at regular intervals. Only such a view of democracy, Schumpeter insists, has a chance of realistically describing the system we call "democracy." A reworked and developed version of Schumpeter's conception of democracy was given the name "polyarchy" by Robert Dahl. As a new kind of "low intensity" democracy, William Robinson has argued in his study of recent politics in Nicaragua, the Philippines, Chile, and Haiti that "polyarchy" has been promoted in "the new world order" as the preferred mode of institutionalizing the enclosures that are inevitably associated with the development of the global market economy and its political correlate, the liberal state.[105]

Commonstock and Economic Justice

As we have seen, the existence of an autonomous economic realm is virtually synonymous with what we have called "enclosure." The damaging of our biosphere, the selling off of means of communication, the new ways in which social institutions and opportunities for political participation are maintained as exclusive are direct results of the ongoing submersion of the social and political in the economic. "Progress," as we have learned to talk about it, is a mixed blessing. Once the economy becomes autonomous, it grows at the expense of the environment, the dialogic as well as human and democratic rights to inclusion in the commonstock. These results follow directly from the fact that the institutional underpinnings of the economy are property rights of exclusion, transfer, and accumulation. Marx analyzed the dynamism of capitalist market societies as deriving from the ongoing socialization of the production process as organized for the purpose of the ongoing privatization of the process of appropriation. Even if Marx was wrong about many of the details of his analysis of capitalism, he was surely right in stressing that exclusion from the means of labor (whether in the form of land or capital) is a key condition for a fully developed market society, a society with a fully developed market in labor and land. The original enclosures were thus, according to Marx, historical preconditions for the development of capitalism. At bottom, Marx's critique of capitalism amounts to the assertion of workers' rights of access to the means of production as a commonstock, that he/she should not be in the position of having to compete for the privilege of paying a kind of rent to the owners of the means of production to exert productive energies and to utilize and develop productive capacities. The net transfer of the value of workers' productive powers entailed by the wage relation, being organized by the owners of capital, has the side effect of diminishing the workers access to the rest of the commonstock: nature, communication, the social and political order. It serves as a mechanism of exclusion in more ways than one. Marx used the concept of alienation to characterize these secondary exclusions.

What is not sufficiently emphasized in discussions of Marx is that enclosures are ongoing features of capitalist development. Thus, tendencies toward structural unemployment reflect this sort of enclosure. These tendencies are more evident in Western Europe than in the United States as I write, but they are partially disguised in the United States by the maintenance both of a huge and growing prison system as well as a large low-wage sector of the economy. At any rate, recent demands to shorten the workweek in Denmark, France, and Germany are about access to the economic commonstock. If the twentieth-century trend of severely reducing employment in agriculture has disrupted the life of much of humanity, then similar trends in industry have ominous long-term implications for the twenty-first century. If the sharply diminishing size of the peasantry throughout the world has been one of the developments of the twentieth century, the sharply diminishing size of the industrial workforce threatens to be one of the significant developments of the twenty-first century. From our point of view, this is a form of mass exclusion from the commonstock.

The capital side (as opposed to the labor side) of contemporary enclosure concerns the construction of the modern business corporation, a veritable engine of enclosure. So it is worth a moment to recount a few of the main steps by means of which corporations came to be assimilated into the autonomous economic realm. On the face of it, there are after all good reasons to think of corporations as part of the political realm. Theorists of deliberative democracy such as John Rawls, for example, have decried the extent of corporate influence in the political process. "In constant pursuit of money to finance campaigns," Rawls remarks, "the political system is simply unable to function. Its deliberative powers are paralyzed."[106] But lobbying and campaign contributions, like opinion-shaping influence on the media generally, are really only one aspect of corporate influence in the political process. Even more significant is the way in which corporations shape the political agenda, having preponderant influence over economic and foreign policy through foundations, roundtables, councils, corporate committees, corporate institutes, trade associations, consulting firms, and so on. Not only is public policy typically initiated and defined through the influence of these institutes, but it is often redefined in more corporate-friendly ways through corporate influence on public interest groups such as the big six environmental organizations. Some political scientists have gone so far as to speak of "the two American political systems," where each system (corporate, individual) is characterized by its own special set of rules and regulations.[107]

A second reason for thinking of corporations as part of the political realm—not just an autonomous economic realm—is sheer size. As early as 1970, a Library of Congress study found that corporations outnumbered nations fifty-one to forty-nine among the hundred largest entities in the world. GM, for example, was found by the conference board to be the twenty-third largest entity in the world in 1978.[108] A more recent study characterizes GM as follows: "With sales in 1993 of $133 billion, assets of $188 billion, and a global work force of 711,000 operating in 122 U.S. cities and 42 foreign countries, GM—producer of automobiles, jet and diesel engines, gas turbines, aerospace computers, telecommunications satellites, tanks and missiles"—cannot be readily thought of as just one more person in a democracy with assignable sets of rights and duties.[109] The sheer size of such an entity raises seemingly political issues about its internal organization as well as the political power it exerts on the nation as a whole.

Despite these obvious political appearances, political philosophy, like the legal system, treats the corporation as an element of the economy and civil society only. The word "corporation" does not appear, for example, in the index of either of Rawls's great works in political philosophy. But this is a result of arbitrary legal construction. Morton Horwitz has in fact brilliantly described the process whereby the natural entity view of the corporation (that is, the corporate person) was created in the twentieth century.[110] As we have said, it is not an exaggeration to say that the process of constructing the corporation was that of constructing what we have called an engine of enclosure, a device constructed to take over public goods. The process of constructing the modern corporation can be described as "judicial legislation."[111] By definition, almost, this process presented itself as apolitical. Equally important, a structurally antidemocratic entity was created and the way was paved to legitimate the ever-increasing swallowing up of public space within an already disempowered liberal democracy. The most far-ranging political decisions from the uses of technology to those concerning employment and the environment are corporatized and therefore privatized. This new kind of person begins to strut on the legal stage, claiming wider and wider constitutional rights, including rights under the First Amendment, the Fourth Amendment ("search and seizure" provisions), the Fifth Amendment ("self-incrimination"), and, of course, the Fourteenth Amendment ("equal protection," "due process"). Rather than being seen as part of the political order, the court has ruled them outside of politics.

In the early nineteenth century, corporations were understood as artificial entities dependent for their existence on state charters. Thus, the Supreme Court overturned New Hampshire's attempt to turn Dartmouth College into a public institution, because the legislature had failed to recognize that the college corporation was an "artificial being" created by contract out of a charter from the British Crown. The Court asserted that the college corporation provided for the maintenance of property rights by "a perpetual succession of individuals ... capable of acting ... like one immortal being."[112] On this view, corporations are fictions created out of charters from the state and, therefore, have only derivative political status and are subject, in theory, to political review.

But after the Civil War and the Fourteenth Amendment, the Court started to move away from the "artificial being" view of the corporation as a politically created and sanctioned entity. In opposition to populist efforts to tax the handsome profits of the railroads, to appropriate economic commonstock for social ends, in our language, the Court merely asserted without argument, much less democratic deliberation, in *Santa Clara County v. Southern Pacific Railroad,* that the corporation was a real person for the purpose of taxation. "The court does not wish to hear argument on the question whether the provision in the 14th Amendment to the Constitution, which forbids a state to deny to any person within its jurisdiction the equal protection of the laws, applies to these corporations. We are all of the opinion that it does."[113] In the succeeding years of the nineteenth century, the issue of whether to empower corporations to gain control of the commonstock was not fought out politically, much less democratically, but was fought out in the courts. In the twentieth century, with the rise of a national stockmarket, stockholders in corporations are also disempowered and ownership of corporations is increasingly separated from control. But most important, the corporate person's status as a natural entity, a being independent of the state, a being that has rights of access to all states and nations, has become definitively established. Contrast this situation with the earlier view, developed in *Bank of Augusta v. Earle:* Corporations "exist only in contemplation of law and by force of the law."[114] Since it is "a mere artificial being" of the state of its creation, "where that law ceased to operate, and is no longer obligatory, the corporation can have no existence."[115] The history of the twentieth century thus includes the legal disempowerment of democracy and the creation and empowerment of "a natural entity" specifically designed to privatize and expand the economy at the expense of the social and political commonstock. As John Dewey remarked: "the doctrine of "fictitious" personality has been employed under the influence of the "individualistic" philosophy ... in order to deny that there is any *social* reality at all back of or in corporate action. Hence the assertion of the simple fact that there is some social reality involved got bound up with the notion of a real, as distinct from fictitious personality."[116] The issue that Dewey's remark leaves open, however, is whether the social reality of the corporation should allow exclusive private control.

Conclusion

Herbert Marcuse coined the term "one-dimensional society" to refer to a society in which practical critical activity—what he called "praxis"—is blocked.[117] In such a society, practical opposition to exploitative, unjust, and inhumane conditions is self-limiting, since oppositional activity is rooted in the society's own uncritical self-consciousness. Critical theory is also self-limiting in such a situation, since, as a preliminary obstacle to informing practice, it must successfully bear the weighty burden of showing the bare possibility of an alternative society. Prevailing modes of thought, culture, and sensibility fail to acknowledge that noneconomistic alternatives are even worth talking about, so the project of identifying and challenging the hidden assumptions and implicit value commitments of the ruling order is disqualified in the name of objectivity, economic science, statist politics, or more recently, postmodern condemnations of "totalization." At the time he wrote *One-Dimensional Man,* Marcuse had in mind societies such as Nazi Germany, the former USSR, and the post–World War II United States in the period of the welfare/warfare state. He could not have imagined the sort of philosophical self-confidence and capitalist triumphalism that asserted itself with the doctrine for which Margaret Thatcher was nicknamed: there is no alternative (TINA). But with the emergence of neoliberalism in the 1970s as legitimation for the dismantling of the welfare state initiated by Thatcher and Reagan, the austerity conditions demanded of Third World countries by the International Monetary Fund (IMF) and the restructuring of the former Eastern Bloc in the 1990s, one-dimensionality has itself become self-conscious.

There is a close connection between one-dimensional consciousness and power. For to the extent that alternatives to a given kind of society are inconceivable within that society for long stretches of time, the intense psychological distress and rage generated by social evils cannot even be translated into gripes and complaints; similarly, gripes and complaints—however inflamed—cannot be accurately translated into organized demands. Yet, in liberal capitalist societies, it is only by way of carefully articulated and organized demands from below that popular wants and needs can be made into political issues. The movement originally led by Huey Long Sr., through his Share Our Wealth Clubs, for example, almost succeeded in making distributive justice into a political issue. Fortunately for those who set the political agenda for the New Deal, Long was assassinated and his great demand never became a political issue in the United States.

A few political scientists have begun to study the non-decision-making process by means of which potential political issues are prevented (for long periods of time) from becoming actual.[118] They have generally suggested that power in societies such as ours resides as much in the non-decision-making process as it does in the decision-making process. How the state sets the agenda and frames the issues on that agenda shapes the exercise of power in both the organized demands kept off the agenda and the framing of demands when they finally reach the political agenda. But those potential issues implicit in the unarticulated rage of the ruled as well as ordinary gripes and complaints of the unorganized are disqualified from being considered for a place on the agenda in the first place. Without the easy availability of the words to speak them, protests are often, in this way, diverted to prefabricated neoliberal nostrums recognized by the state and consciousness of needs is distorted, if not entirely inarticulate. Unfortunately, most political scientists simply take a set political agenda as given and devote themselves to the study of the decision-making process, the process by means of which groups contending for power prevail on policy issues, rather than the far more revealing process of how only certain issues get to be on the agenda in the first place. Conscious and unconscious psychological, cultural, social, economic, and ideological forces are all part of the agenda-setting process, but, unfortunately, that process itself is far from the object of careful study that real political self-consciousness would require. Our proposal is that issues concerning public goods be framed in term of the concept of the commonstock rather than economistically. For as J. S. Mill pointed out in criticizing Bentham, a preference for pushpin over poetry is not trustworthy unless the agent has had ample experience of both pleasures and sees both as, broadly speaking, realistic. To choose some voucher scheme without awareness of alternative remedies for the failings of public education or medicine is similarly defective. What is needed, to borrow language from John Dewey, is support for the production of "habits of mind and character, the intellectual and moral patterns, that are somewhere near even with the actual movement of events."[119] Only by so doing can we avoid the risk of becoming victims of our own obsolete consciousness, of unrecognized ideological scripts that live us rather than being objects of our own deliberation and actions.

A Final Clarification

Lest there be misunderstanding about the course of the above discussion, I want to distinguish my argument from that of an appeal to nostalgic primitivism. My claim isn't nostalgic, because it is in harmony with many presently existing appeals to the commonstock. Galarrwuy Yurupriju, leader of the Guratz people and head of Australia's Northern Land Office, for example, makes a contemporary point in discussing the meaning of current aboriginal painting. "We are painting, as we have always done, to demonstrate our continuing link with our country and the rights and responsibilities we have to it. We paint to show the rest of the world that we own this country and the land owns us. Our painting is a political act."[120] Arundhati Roy makes a similarly contemporary point when she writes of the struggle of the people of the Narmada Valley against the Sarda Sarovar Dam. "In India over the past ten years the fight against the Sardar Sarovar Dam has come to represent more than the fight for one river. Some years ago, it became a debate that captured the popular imagination. From being a fight over the fate of a river valley it began to raise doubts about an entire political system. ... Who owns this land? Who owns its rivers? Its forests? Its fish?"[121] Far from appealing to nostalgic primitivism, my aim is to offer philosophical support for these and thousands of similar counterhegemonic struggles against the ruling market conception of property and, as in the case of Arundhati Roy, the economistic conception of public goods associated with it.

But even if our appeal were entirely to the past, it would be no more nostalgic than Lord Keynes's vision of a future return to time-honored principles of the past "when the accumulation of wealth is no longer of high social importance."[122]

> I see us free to return to some of the most sure and certain principles of religion and traditional virtue—that avarice is a vice, that the exaction of usury is a misdemeanour, and the love of money is detestable, that those walk most truly in the paths of virtue and sane wisdom who take the least thought for the morrow."[123]

Our disagreement with Keynes concerns his view that a future return to the time-honored principles of the past should be postponed.

> For at least another hundred years we must pretend to ourselves and to every one that fair is foul and foul is fair; for foul is useful and fair is not. Avarice and usury and precaution must be our gods for a little longer still. For only they can lead us out of the tunnel of economic necessity into daylight.[124]

It is no longer plausible to think that foul is useful. To this extent, our view is similar to that of another economist, Karl Marx, who, like Keynes, could never plausibly be accused of nostalgic primitivism. Though Keynes despised Marx's views, Marx too had a vision of a future return to the time-honored principles of the past. This vision can be seen in Marx's early defense of the customary right of the poor to gather firewood fallen from trees growing on privately owned land and toward the end of his career, his careful defense of the Narodnik idea that a new socialist society might be built on the foundation of the mir, the ancient communal villages of rural Russia, without having to pass through the nightmarish stage of capitalism.[125] Without considering the question of whether Marx's conception of socialism entails, among other things, a restoration of the commonstock in the context of the material productivity developed by capitalism, it should be clear that in endorsing some of the moral principles and institutions of the past, neither Keynes nor Marx is endorsing all of the moral principles and institutions of the past, much less the savage, brutal, and hierarchical practices they both denounced. The relationship in this context between past, present, and future is what some commentators would refer to as "dialectical." Something is lost and something is gained in the present, and hopefully we can make present at a higher level some of the good that was lost. Doing so might be called "socialism." At the least, in this "postcolonial" epoch, we should be skeptical of self-serving, linear "histories" of how efficiency, rationality, and progress came to replace earlier inferior despotisms. What is being contested, after all, is the meaning of such terms as "efficiency," "rationality," and "progress." As Enrique Leff has formulated this point with respect to biodiversity as a paradigmatic case: "The issue cannot be solved through economic compensation. It is impossible to calculate the "real" economic value of biodiversity (the result of centuries and millennia of ethno-ecological coevolution) in terms of capital and labor-time invested in the conservation and production of genetic material, nor by the current market value of its products nor by estimating their future economic value."[126]

Notes

Thanks for helpful comments to the following: Glenna Anton, Kostas Bagakis, Georgia and Paul Bassen, Barbara Epstein, Fred Evans, Milton Fisk, John Glanville, Michael Goldhaber, Nancy Holmstrom, Kathy Johnson, Kurt Nutting, Barbara McCloskey, Osha Neuman, Peter Oppenheimer, Mike Pincus, Roberto Rivera, Richard Schmitt, Jim Syfers.

1. See Dyer, Joel, *The Perpetual Prisoner Machine: How America Profits from Crime* (Boulder, Colo.: Westview Press, 2000).

2. Progler, Josef, "Mapping the Musical Commons: Digitization, Simulation, Speculation," First Monday, peer reviewed journal on the Internet (http://firstmonday.org/issues/issue4_9/progler/, 4.

3. Ibid., 6.

4. Rural Advancement Foundation International, "News Release–21 January 2000" (www. rafi.org), 2. See also RAFI, "Phase II for Human Genome Research–Human Genetic Diversity Enters the Commercial," (http://www.rafi.org).

5. Progler, Josef, Mapping the Musical Commons.

6. Honore, A. M., "Ownership," in *Oxford Essays in Jurisprudence: A Collaborative Work*, ed. A. G. Guest (Oxford: Oxford University Press, 1961), 109.

7. Ibid., 110.

8. Stapleton, Richard M., "Bringing Peace to the Garden of Tranquility," Land & People 2, No. 2, fall 1999.

9. Deutsche, Rosalyn, *Evictions: Art and Spatial Politics* (Cambridge, Mass.: MIT Press, 1996).

10. Singer, Daniel, *Whose Millennium? Theirs or Ours?* (New York: Monthly Review Press, 1999), 35.

11. Ibid., 37.

12. Ibid., 41.

13. Ibid., 39.

14. I owe this formulation to David and Nancy Milton.

15. Arnove, Anthony, "Review of Hidden Agenda by John Pilger," Z 12, No. 12, December 1999, 64.

16. Queau, Philippe, "Defining the World's Public Property: Who Owns Knowledge?" *Le Monde diplomatique*, January 14, 2000, 5. Available on the internet (http://www.monde-diplomatique.fr/en/).

17. Ibid., 5.

18. Vallette, Jim, "Larry Summers' War Against the Earth," CounterPunch. Available on the internet (http://www.counterpunch.org/summers.html).

19. *New York Times*, December 6, 1999, A17.

20. STRATFOR.COM Global Intelligence Update, "Stratfor's Decade Forecast 2000–2010: A New Era in a Traditional World," December 20, 1999, 3. Available on the Internet (http://www.stratfor.com/).

21. Stiglitz, Joseph E., "Knowledge as a Global Public Good," in *Global Public Goods: International Cooperation in the 21st Century*, ed. Kaul, Grunberg, and Stern (New York: Oxford University Press, 1999), 316.

22. Ibid.

23. Tabb, William K., "The World Trade Organization? Stop World Take Over," *Monthly Review*, 51, No. 8, January 2000, 9.

24. I owe this formulation to Richard Schmitt.

25. Polanyi, Karl, *The Great Transformation: The Political and Economic Origins of Our Time* (Boston: Beacon Press, 1957), 35.

26. Dewey, John, *Liberalism and Social Action* (New York: G. P. Putnam's Sons, 1935), 61.

27. Locke, John, *Two Treatises of Civil Government* (London: Everyman's Library, J. M. Dent and Sons, 1966), 130.

28. Macpherson, C. B., ed., *Property: Mainstream and Critical Positions* (Toronto: University of Toronto Press, 1978), 51.

29. Starrett, David A., *Foundations of Public Economics* (Cambridge: Cambridge University Press, 1988).

30. Stiglitz, Knowledge as a Global Public Good, 310.

31. Queau, "Defining the World's Public Property," 4.

32. See Nozick, Robert, *Anarchy, State, and Utopia* (New York: Basic Books, 1974).

33. Schiller, Herbert I., *Culture, Inc.: The Corporate Takeover of Public Expression* (New York: Oxford University Press, 1989), 64.

34. For the classic discussion of the issues behind the socialization of costs, see James O'Connor *The Fiscal Crisis of the State* (New York: St. Martin's Press, 1973).

35. Queau, "Defining the World's Public Property," 4.

36. Jefferson, Thomas, "Letter of Jefferson to Madison, October 28, 1785" in *Jefferson Writings* (New York: Library of America, 1984), 842.

37. Ibid.

38. Jefferson, Thomas, "Letter from Thomas Jefferson to James Madison, September 6, 1789" in John Arthur, *Democracy: Theory and Practice* (Belmont, Calif.: Wadsworth, 1992), 22.

39. Avineri, Shlomo, *Moses Hess; Prophet of Communism and Zionism* (New York: New York University Press, 1985), 36.

40. Madison, James, "Letter from James Madison to Thomas Jefferson, February 4, 1790" in John Arthur, *Democracy: Theory and Practice* (Belmont, Calif.: Wadsworth, 1992), 23.

41. Ibid., 24.

42. Macpherson, C. B., *The Rise and Fall of Economic Justice and Other Essays* (New York: Oxford University Press, 1985), 76.

43. Ibid., 77.

44. Ibid.

45. For a discussion of these matters, see Langdon Winner, *The Whale and the Reactor: A Search for Limits in an Age of High Technology* (Chicago: University of Chicago Press, 1986), 23.

46. For a discussion of these matters, see James O'Connor, *The Fiscal Crisis of the State* (New York: St. Martin's Press, 1973).

47. See Andrew Szasz, "In Praise of Policy Luddism: Strategic Lessons from the Hazardous Waste Wars," *Capitalism Nature Socialism* 2(1), No. 6, February 1991, 17–43.

48. Brown, Peter G., *Restoring the Public Trust: A Fresh Vision for Progressive Government in America* (Boston: Beacon Press, 1994), 61.

49. Ibid., 65.

50. Ibid., 49–66.

51. Leff, op. cit., 93–94.

52. Brown, *Restoring the Public Trust*, 62.

53. Dewey, *Liberalism and Social Action*, 61.

54. Knight, Danielle, "New Corporate Welfare Wave: Backed by Tax Dollars, Export Credit Agencies Bankroll Project Other Funders Won't Touch," *Dollars and Sense* 226, November/December 1999, 30.

55. Winner, *The Whale and the Reactor*, 50–51.

56. Gelbspan, Ross, "History at Risk: The Crisis of the Global Climate," 1999, 2. Available on the Internet (http://www.heatisonline.org/htmloverview.cfm).

57. Heilbronner, Robert, *21st Century Capitalism* (New York: W. W. Norton, 1993), 116.

58. Gelbspan, "History at Risk," 2.

59. Ibid., 8.

60. Stiglitz, Joseph, *Economics of the Public Sector* (New York: W. W. Norton, 1986). See also Jonathan Chait, "Shoeless Joe Stiglitz: Renegade at the Top," *American Prospect: A Journal for the Liberal Imagination* 45, July-August 1999.

61. Gelbspan, "History at Risk," 14.

62. Ibid., 1.

63. Schiller, *Culture, Inc.*, 28–29.

64. Ibid., 75.

65. Ibid., 72.

66. Ibid., 75.

67. Queau, "Defining the World's Public Property," 5.

68. The quote is from Russell Jacoby, who is cited by Shiller, *Culture, Inc.*, 99.

69. Schiller, *Culture, Inc.*, 100.

70. Ibid., 101.

71. Ibid., 103.

72. Ibid., 101–106.

73. See Robert W. McChesney, *Corporate Media and the Threat to Democracy* (New York: Seven Stories Press, 1997).

74. McChesney, Robert W., "Corporate Media Versus Democracy" (manuscript for 1997 publication by Open Media and Seven Stories Press), 9.

75. Ibid., 8–10.

76. Ibid., 10.

77. Judis, John B. "K Street Gore," in *American Prospect: A Journal for the Liberal Imagination* 45, July–August 1999, 18–21.

78. Macpherson, C. B., *The Rise and Fall of Economic Justice and Other Essays* (New York: Oxford University Press, 1985), 84.

79. Debeir, Deleage, and Hemery, *In the Servitude of Power: Energy and Civilization Through the Ages*, trans. John Barzman (London: Zed Books, 1991).

80. Queau, "Defining the World's Public Property," 1.

81. For a discussion of these matters, see Pierre Bourdieu and Loic Wacquant, *An Invitation to Reflexive Sociology* (Chicago: University of Chicago Press, 1992).

82. Bourdieu, Pierre, *Acts of Resistance: Against the Tyranny of the Market* (New York: New Press, 1998), 60.

83. Ibid., 61.

84. Fraser, Nancy, *Justice Interruptus: Critical Reflections on the "Postsocialist" Condition* (New York: Routledge, 1997), 15.

85. Ibid.

86. Ibid., 11–33.

87. Ezorsky, Gertrude, *Racism and Justice: The Case for Affirmative Action* (Ithaca: Cornell University Press, 1991), 45.

88. Polanyi, *The Great Transformation*, 46.

89. Ibid.

90. See James O'Connor, *The Corporations and the State: Essays in the Theory of Capitalism and Imperialism* (New York: Harper Colophon Books, 1974), 1–15.

91. Heilbroner, Robert, *The Nature and Logic of Capitalism* (New York: W. W. Norton, 1985), 60.

92. Cimons, Marlene, and Paul Jacobs, "Sunday Report: Biotech Battlefield: Profits vs. Public," *Los Angeles Times*, February 21, 1999.

93. Greene, Gayle, *The Woman Who Knew Too Much: Alice Stewart and the Secrets of Radiation* (Ann Arbor: University of Michigan Press, 1999), 69.

94. Brenner, M. H., *Mental Illness and the Economy* (Cambridge, Mass.: Harvard University Press, 1973).

95. Heilbroner, *The Nature and Logic of Capitalism*, 90.

96. Baier, Annette, "How Can Individualists Share Responsibility?" *Political Theory* 21, No. 2, 1993, 232.

97. Ibid.

98. Ibid., 231–237.

99. Ibid., 234.

100. Ibid., 245.

101. Ibid., 244.

102. Ibid.

103. Arthur, *Democracy: Theory and Practice*, 90.

104. Ibid., 95.

105. Robinson, William I., *Promoting Polyarchy: Globalization, US Intervention and Hegemony* (Cambridge: Cambridge University Press, 1996).

106. Rawls, John, *Collected Papers*, ed. Samuel Freeman (Cambridge, Mass.: Harvard University Press, 1999), 581.

107. Froman, Creel, *The Two American Political Systems: Society, Economics and Politics* (Englewood Cliffs, N.J.: Prentice Hall, 1984).

108. Bowman, Scott R., *The Modern Corporation and American Political Thought: Law, Power, and Ideology* (University Park, Pa.: Pennsylvania State University Press, 1996), 288.

109. Ibid.

110. Horwitz, Morton J., *The Transformation of American Law 1870–1960: The Crisis of Legal Orthodoxy* (New York: Oxford University Press, 1992), 65–108.

111. Cohen, Morris R., "The Process of Judicial Legislation," in *Law and the Social Order: Essays in Legal Philosophy* (New York: Harcourt, Brace and Company, 1933), 112–147.

112. Horwitz, *The Transformation of American Law 1870–1960*, 104.

113. Ibid., 67.

114. Ibid., 79.

115. Ibid.

116. Dewey, John, "The Historic Background of Corporate Legal Personality," *Yale Law Journal* 35, No. 6, 673.

117. Herbert Marcuse, *One-Dimensional Man* (Boston: Beacon Press, 1964).

118. Bachrach, Peter, and Baratz, Morton S., *Power and Poverty: Theory and Practice* (New York: Oxford University Press, 1970). See also Steven Lukes, *Power: A Radical View* (London: Macmillan, 1974) and John Gaventa, *Power and Powerlessness: Quiescence and Rebellion in an Appalachian Valley* (Oxford: Clarendon, 1980).

119. Dewey, John, *Liberalism and Social Action* (New York: G. P. Putnam's Sons, 1935), 61.

120. This remark appeared as an explanation of a work shown at the California Palace of the Legion of Honor, San Francisco, California. The exhibition was entitled "Spirit Country: Australian Aboriginal Art from the Gantner Myer Collection," September 18, 1999–January 9, 2000.

121. Roy, Arundhati, "For The Greater Common Good," in *The Cost of Living* (New York: Random House, 1999).

122. Keynes, John Maynard, "Economic Possibilities for Our Grandchildren," in *Essays in Persuasion* (New York: Harcourt, Brace and Company, 1932), 369.

123. Ibid., 371–372.

124. Ibid., 372.

125. For a discussion of Marx's Wood Theft Articles, see Sherover-Marcuse, Erica, *Emancipation and Consciousness: Dogmatic and Dialectical Perspectives in the Early Marx* (New York: Basil Blackwell, 1986). For a discussion of Marx's views on the Narodniks, see Isaac Deutscher, "Marx and Russia" in *Russia in Transition*, rev. ed. (New York: Grove Press, 1960).

126. Leff, Enrique, "On the Social Reappropriation of Nature," in *Capitalism Nature Socialism: A Journal of Socialist Ecology* 10, No. 3, September 1999, 102.

2

Surviving with Dignity in a Global Economy: The Battle for Public Goods

Milton Fisk

The new name of injustice, slavery, usurpation: neoliberalism.
—EZLN Workers' Program,
May Day 1994

I propose to approach neoliberalism, which is the current underpinning of the global economy, as an issue of justice. I am thinking of neoliberalism here not just as an economic policy but as an economic system, specifically as a stage of capitalism that is characterized by greater control by financial institutions and large investors over the management of enterprises around the globe, by reduced regulation of the labor market, and by a commodification of goods and services that had recently been matters of public provision. The dominant attitude among those in and around policy circles in many nations reflects the view of Prime Minister Margaret Thatcher that there is no alternative to neoliberalism. Capital won't stay put; labor won't be protected; and public goods won't get funded. This fatalist attitude makes it no more sensible to confront neoliberalism with questions of justice than it would thundershowers on hot summer afternoons. I'm committed to showing that with the right sort of political will neoliberalism could have been prevented and can yet be ended, however, opening up the possibility of a global economy resting on new underpinnings with some promise of fairness.

Justice and Social Goals

Talking a bit about the nature of justice is unavoidable here. In measuring neoliberalism against the norm of justice, I am not appealing to a norm that needs to be discovered by a research program. Rather, I am appealing to something that our social practice delivers to us. In that practice we work out with others certain goals. These goals are not just private ambitions, but are what bind us together as a group. They are what *we* are all about. Fairness comes into the picture as a means whereby we maintain who we are, rather than falling into quarreling factions. We aren't then to fasten onto norms of justice through researching a text or a history in order then to run about measuring groups with those norms. Instead, once we know who we are and what commonalities exist among us, we know what justice must be designed to protect.

We can compress this into a three-stage elaboration. In the first place, norms of justice are about how best to handle conflicts. We look for justice in regard to what bothers people about what others are doing. In the second place, norms of justice, by the way they resolve conflicts, advance a set of goals a people pursues in order to give their group certain features. The people may want an educated and a secure community, and these would be the kinds of goals that would be advanced by the way justice resolves conflicts. Justice facilitates the realization of the goods these goals aim at by displacing obstacles to them. If the conflict is between people who are part of the same group, they are more likely to accept a just resolution since it advances goals they pursue together for their group. But justice emerges from only some such goals; which ones? In the third place, norms of justice, by the way they resolve conflicts, advance goals a people are likely, in their circumstances, to choose together as a result of extensive struggles and discussions over how to improve their group.[1] Adding this condition, that the goals be chosen together in struggle and discussion, emphasizes that the goals don't come from a small section of a group but are worked out within the whole group. Otherwise, there would be a possible one-sidedness that would be incompatible with justice.

The goals that justice tries to facilitate have two distinctive features, both implicit in the above elaboration. On the one hand, such a goal is something desired by each for all in a group. The process of struggle and discussion among the members of the group doesn't lead simply to each choosing the goal for his or her self. Such a process would be unnecessary for that. It is a process ending in clarity about what *we* want, and hence in solidarity. But what is the character of a goal each wants for all? To answer this I need to add, on the other hand, that what is aimed at is a feature of the group, and not directly a good for individuals. What we want is an educated society, a society with a sustainable environment, a society with an independent press, and so on. These social features, if desired by each for all, are what are called common goods. To have these common goods calls for capacitating the society for delivering to individuals certain individual goods. Thus we can get a healthy society, as a common good, only if there is a health care system capacitating the society to deliver health care to individuals. Such capacitating systems are called public goods, which are what I am trying to defend. Justice in a society is, then, about removing conflicts in a way that facilitates common goods, and hence the public goods needed for them.[2]

It might seem arbitrary to tie justice to social goals that are common goods rather than to other things, but doing so actually avoids arbitrariness. Imagine two people locked in a conflict who are not bound together by commitment to any good each of them wants for the other. There is then no common goal that can be appealed to as a standard for solving the conflict. One might object that there is a way out by appeal to common principles. This appeal is often involved when the right is said to be prior to the good. John Rawls appeals to tolerance among citizens as a principle prior to any goods they might adopt. And Robert Nozick appeals to entitlements to voluntarily transferred property as overriding social goods.[3] But it would seem quite arbitrary to appeal to common principles when there are no common goals from which they can emerge. I only sketch this argument against the appeal to principle in the absence of substantive common goods to show that the direction of my thinking is at odds with much liberal theorizing on the subject of justice.[4] In sketching an argument of this kind I am not espousing the view that justice reduces to common goods. Room has to be left for a reciprocal action between justice and common goods. Justice that may start out trying to ensure that common goods are realized may end up being a tool for modifying common goods that have shown themselves to be unrealistic, incompatible with a variety of other common goods, or manipulable by special interests. For example, the freedom appealed to against feudal restrictions promoted private enterprise, but ended up providing a critique of it.

On this common-good view of justice, it may happen that there are insufficient solidarities between certain groups to provide a basis for justice between them. Such breaks in justice always threaten class-divided and race-divided societies with a failure to achieve conflict resolution without resort to force. In such cases, the expedient on the part of groups in conflict of adopting partisan forms of justice may be unavoidable, leaving a more universalist justice as little more than a hope. Advancing beyond partisan justice would call for either an exhausting dialogue motivated by the futility of compromises in reducing a high level of conflict or a wrenching change away from the divided social structure itself motivated, perhaps, by solidarity in face of a common foe.

Divided Societies
and Public Goods

Ironically, the advance of the global economy highlights divisions. Think only of the division between established and industrializing economies or that between corporate and governmental elites and working people. Talk of common projects spanning these divisions is, in most cases, utopian at present. At Kyoto in 1997, industrializing nations were reluctant to accept targets for greenhouse gas reduction that might not let their economies catch up. Moreover, fossil fuel industries in the United States saw themselves as threatened even by the weak targets the U.S. government backed at Kyoto.[5] Neither international nor national public goods can thrive as competitiveness deepens divisions in the world and in its nations. To be sure, neoliberalism speaks in a universalizing way when it talks, say, of global capital markets. This does not mean it speaks for all. Indeed, it speaks for a minority, only pretending that deregulated labor, privatization, and unrestricted capital mobility are advancing a common goal that each wants for all. We can, though, speak of a partisan justice that points toward realizing common projects for the unemployed, most working people, and most retirees. Admittedly, such common goals are only partial, not being shared by all, but this is a limitation that needs to be accepted if we can hope for success in making inroads against neoliberalism.

Some—even some associated with social democracy—would doubt that we need to posit a partisan justice for the less well off. They would say that the universalizing stance of the apostles of neoliberalism, though perhaps exaggerated in some respects, is basically justified. For them, the neoliberal global economy is the hope for all classes, now that national welfare economies have shown their inability to avoid crises.[6] On this view, raising efficiency through competition will redound to the benefit of all. I shall have to respond to this view, but first it will be important to show there is indeed an alternative to neoliberalism that would be just in at least the partisan sense that it would promote the common goals of the great majority who are significantly less well off than the top few.

In the context of showing there is such an alternative, I make several assumptions. I assume, first, that we take to heart the view that justice points back to implicitly or explicitly agreed to common goals. Here common goals are not just goods everyone wants for him or herself but are features of a group each wants for all so that all can have a reasonable expectation of getting certain individual goods. Those group features give robustness to that expectation of individual goods, in the sense that the delivery of individual goods stems not from chance but from the group's having a certain character. I assume, second, that we take seriously, as applied to the current world, the idea that there may be breaks between the justice of different groups resulting from there being no common goals of the relevant sort that bind them together. The starting place will have to be a partisan justice based on partial common goals.

In the context of these two assumptions, I ask what steps a society's majority less well-off group would take to facilitate the realization of the common goals that bind its members in solidarity. The answer is, I think, that it would develop public institutions—institutions accountable to it as a whole—as the means for the realization of those common goals. This view of public institutions is a rough idea of what lies behind much of the more formal economic talk about public goods. Public goods are instrumental for realizing common goals, and are hence called for by justice, partisan though it may be. They give an institutional character to the demand that needs replace profits at the top of the political agenda

Why should the less well-off majority want such instruments for realizing common goals to be public? To leave these instruments to the market would bias them in favor of those who have market advantages.[7] And the less well-off are what they are since they are lacking certain market advantages. They have little or no capital, and the skills to get it with will be more readily available to those who already have capital. Common goals, being goals wanted by each for all, are not best advanced by means, like the market, that would favor those with market advantages for the individual benefits that realizing common goals would yield. Common goals are best advanced by institutions that, being accountable to all, provide equal access to all, rather than differential access based on private advantage. It is evident then why public goods are chosen for advancing the common goals the procedures of justice are devised to advance.

Destabilizing Neoliberalism with Public Goods

This leads us to a suggestion for action. Justice on our view is realized by establishing and maintaining public goods. But the theory and the practice of neoliberalism has been to attack public goods. An offensive to save what public goods are left and to create needed new ones would, if successful, undermine a key feature of neoliberalism, thereby destabilizing it as a whole. To survive in a global economy with dignity and justice calls for a concerted effort to change it from a neoliberal economy by an initial step of an offensive for public goods.

I am talking here both about national and international public goods, since the concept of a public good does not impose a restriction to national boundaries. As a practical point, some public goods will need to be national, though often embedded in international public goods whose primary concerns will then be with the results of interactions between nations. A national environmental body dedicated to a healthy and sustainable environment for members of that nation will, for obvious reasons, find it useful to work in conjunction with an international environmental body that is concerned with the global environment.

This call to action for public goods raises a host of questions, which I shall try to answer before I end. Neoliberalism, with its mobile capital, seems to have defeated or stalemated organized labor on a world scale. It has cowed socialist and

THIS MODERN

EVERYWHERE YOU LOOK, IT'S *PRIVATIZATION MANIA!* HOSPITALS ARE GIVING WAY TO *HMO'S*... PRISONS ARE BEING RUN BY *PRIVATE CORPORATIONS*... AND THANKS TO WELFARE REFORM, SOME STATES ARE EVEN CONTRACTING THEIR *WELFARE SYSTEMS* OUT TO FIRMS SUCH AS *LOCKHEED*...

--AND SO ACCORDING TO *MY* CALCULATIONS, THE ONLY WAY THIS COMPANY CAN POSSIBLY TURN A *PROFIT*--

--IS TO STOP GIVING ALL THESE DAMN *BENEFITS* TO THE *POOR!*

AND WHAT ABOUT *PUBLIC PARKS?* HOW ARE WE SUPPOSED TO INSTILL THE NOTION OF *PRIVATE PROPERTY* IN OUR KIDS IF THEY GROW UP THINKING THEY CAN RUN AROUND ON ANY PATCH OF OPEN SPACE THAT HAPPENS TO CATCH THEIR EYE? ANYBODY EVER THINK ABOUT *THAT?*

DAD--I WANT TO GO IN *THERE!*

SORRY, BOY--WE CAN'T AFFORD IT. NOW GO PLAY IN THE STREET, OKAY?

WORLD by TOM TOMORROW

NOW, SOME OF YOU BLEEDING HEARTS MAY FIND THIS TREND *OBJECTIONABLE* -- BUT AS FAR AS WE'RE CONCERNED, IT'S *ABOUT TIME!* THERE ARE *WAY* TOO MANY HANDOUTS IN THIS SOCIETY! FOR INSTANCE, IN EVERY CITY YOU'VE GOT *LIBRARIES*, JUST LOANING OUT BOOKS FOR *FREE!* WHAT'S UP WITH *THAT?* HAVEN'T THESE PEOPLE HEARD OF *BOOKSTORES?*

YOUR FREELOADING DAYS ARE OVER NOW, OLD TIMER! NO BUCKS, NO BOOKS -- *CAPICHE?*

BUT-- BUT--

YES, IF YOU ASK *US*, THIS COUNTRY HAS BEEN VEERING DANGEROUSLY CLOSE TO *SOCIALISM* FOR *TOO LONG*... AND THE SOONER ALL THESE KNEE-JERK GIVEAWAYS AND SOCIAL SERVICES ARE PRIVATIZED -- THE *BETTER!*

HELP! SOMEONE JUST STOLE ALL MY MONEY!

WELL, THEN, HOW EXACTLY DO YOU INTEND TO PAY US?

TAKE A HIKE, YOU DEADBEAT.

social democratic parties into accepting its basic premise that competitiveness is indispensable and can be achieved only by deregulating labor markets.[8] Is there, then, reason to think an offensive to support and strengthen public goods would itself escape a similar defeat or stalemate? Were such an offensive victorious, what reason is there to think neoliberalism would be destabilized by it? Why, to begin with, should there be a return to a welfare state that has been tried and seemingly failed? Instead of returning to a failed welfare state, wouldn't it be better to regulate the excesses of neoliberalism? I shall start with the question about public goods' potential to destabilize neoliberalism, leaving the questions about the feasibility of an offensive for public goods, the failure of the welfare state, and regulating neoliberalism's excesses till later on.

Almost all aspects of neoliberalism would suffer a blow if there were a successful offensive on behalf of public goods. To see this, consider briefly the origin and nature of neoliberalism. As an economic system, it grew out of the decline in rates of return to capitalist enterprise that began in the late 1960s and early 1970s. It was a throwback to the liberalism that emerged in the 1830s and lasted for the better part of a century.[9] Declining profit rates produced the crisis that put an end to the short-lived welfarist period of capitalism, a period both of relative withdrawal from the nineteenth-century global economy and of rapid advance in the construction of public goods. It was lower profit rates and not those public goods that generated the crisis of stagnant growth and higher unemployment.

In search of higher rates of return, employers tried, in the 1980s and 1990s, to find and to make cheap labor. Cheap labor could be found in abundance in places where industrialization was still developing; it could be made in those countries where the social contract—the postwar capital-labor partnership—had diminished labor's militancy. The decline in rates of return not only sent capital after cheap labor but also spurred an effort by creditors and investors to look with longing at areas that had not been capitalized. Public facilities for transportation, telephone, education, and energy were then to be turned over to private capitalists. They hoped windfall profits could be reaped in these virgin areas. The capitalization of health care from Chile, through Mexico, to the United States provides a striking example.

To take advantage of cheap labor and to capitalize public goods encouraged an end to national economies and a return to a global economy of mobile capital. To accelerate capital mobility an attack was mounted through trade agreements on both legal barriers discriminating against foreign investors and state monopolies in key sectors. Structural adjustment agreements with the World Bank and the proposed Multilateral Agreement on Investments threaten any state regulation for protection from global capital mobility. Nations with full-employment and welfare policies were urged to adopt austerity as a norm in order to avoid the inflationary consequences of those policies, which would make these nations unattractive to investors. The demand for greater capital mobility thus provided backing for the other neoliberal strategies, enabling thereby a rapid exploitation of opportunities for profits.[10]

Public goods are a threat to neoliberal efforts to secure profitability in these ways: (1) *Opposition to Privatization.* Public goods are provided by institutions that, in a number of countries, tend to be more highly and strongly unionized than private enterprises. Not only does this make it more difficult to conduct an all-out attack on wages in other sectors, but it also makes privatizations themselves more difficult since unions are anxious to avoid the drive to go nonunion by the typical privatizer. Consider for example the SNTSS—the Social Security Workers' Union—in Mexico, which conducted a valiant, but losing, battle against the PRI's privatization of pensions and health care,[11] the unionized public workers in France, who made a stand against Juppé's counterreform of social services,[12] and the unionized teachers in the United States who have fought contracting schools out to for-profit educators.[13]

(2) *Limiting Mobility of Capital.* Resources sunk in public goods are not directly profitable. They are only indirectly profitable insofar as they create demand for goods and services from the private sector. Public goods are then off-limits for capitalization, limiting thereby the mobility of capital. Privatizing these public goods makes fertile their "sterile" capital by releasing it for profit making.

(3) *Blocking Competitiveness.* A developed system of public goods can be supported only by high taxes, including high corporate taxes. Investors prefer areas of the world where taxes are lower. With lower taxes, firms can compete effectively against foreign competitors in regard to both imports and exports. A libertarian rhetoric then emerges that supports competitiveness and undermines public goods. According to it, people should be taxed less to give them more freedom to do what they want with their money.

(4) *Displacing Financial Control.* Public goods are to be under public control. In the welfarist hiatus of 1930–1970, managers were able to claim that they ran corporations, but with the advent of crisis in the welfarist period, neoliberals advocated making corporations responsive to the needs of investors and lenders. Their needs were not in resolving social problems, in product quality, or in long-term enterprise survival. They were narrowly financial, whereas managers could be distracted by other needs. With public goods under public management, they are not controlled by finance. They represent a limit on the dominance of financial control characteristic of neoliberalism.[14]

It would seem pretty clear, then, that to defend and expand the area of public goods would tend to destabilize the neoliberal program. There is every reason, though, to want a global economy to continue as public goods are expanded. Capital flows could still form a global network while being limited by keeping public goods healthy. Capital flows would work to develop both national and international public goods. In short, a global economy, instead of ignoring vast populations, would provide a basis for their dignity. It would cease being a corporate to become a social global economy.

Competitiveness and
Autonomous Capital

But it will be objected that, rather than undermining neoliberalism, public goods might only undermine the economies of countries that promote them. How can such an objection be dealt with convincingly? We are told the specter awaiting us is a drying up of private investment as the increased taxes needed for public goods diminish the incentive to invest. In the late 1990s, France suffers from just such a problem, whereas the Thatcherite attack on public goods has enabled Britain to escape it. Without investment, the export sector would suffer competitive failure. Investors would then look beyond their national boundaries for places to invest, with the result that domestic unemployment would boom.

It is assumed by this objection that capital is autonomous: it sets its own goals and when they are not realized in one place capital is free to make investments elsewhere. This, though, is far from the truth. In fact, capital's autonomy is an illusion based on falsely assuming state neutrality in its regard. We mustn't forget that the goals capital actually pursues are ones states have shown some willingness to defend. Not just that, but also most states have been instrumental in helping capital realize its goals. One need only think of the fact that structural adjustment programs, free trade agreements, and currency unions are crafted directly by or through pressure from powerful states.[15] The mobility of capital and the flexibility of labor, as enjoyed by capital today, are partly dependent on such arrangements. Forgetting that capital operates within the framework of the state can create the illusion that capital is setting its goals and moving where it will profit all on its own.

As a first step to seeing that capital's autonomy is an illusion, imagine the negative impact on the mobility of capital in states that would break ranks with neoliberalism by making public goods a priority. Prioritizing public goods would call for a cutback in the ways that states coddle capital. In particular, it would call for states to switch from promoting to limiting capital mobility. On the one hand, more of the nations resources would have to get locked up in public goods, thus limiting the amount of mobile capital. On the other hand, moving capital about couldn't be allowed to overburden public goods, as happens when capital flies elsewhere, leaving unemployment and reduced tax bases behind.

If capital is not autonomous but is conditioned by the state, political will can make a difference in what capital does. Of course, to make a difference there will have to be a reorientation of political will. Such a reorientation would take place if people were not just to formulate certain common goals but also to dedicate themselves to realizing those goals. I'm talking about goals such as full employment, democratic participation, universal comprehensive health care, socialized intellectual property, a sustainable environment, accessible education, and popularly controlled media. Some countries have come close to realizing some of these goals at certain times. Most countries have not come close at any time. Nonetheless, these are, by and large, goals for which there is already wide approval in many countries—they are popular demands today. This is true even where voters, overwhelmed by insecurity and recoiling in isolation, support neoliberal regimes. For popular demands in no way imply a political will to realize them. Here is where public discussion of shared grievances and public agitation against shared foes is decisive. Through discussion and agitation, those who now vote neoliberal can change from being overwhelmed by insecurity to being outraged by it and from recoiling in isolation to being motivated by solidarity. Then a new political will emerges to give effect to those demands. This political will is the force behind creating institutions that move us closer to common goals. Such institutions will be public goods expressing a political will that rejects the privileges the state gives to capital that make some think it is autonomous.

The Political Context of the Defeat of Public Goods

Creating the political will to form public goods resolves some problems but seems to give rise to others. We can learn from the history of the welfare state that once public goods are incorporated as part of the state a conflict arises between them with their goal of need-satisfaction and capital with its goal of enhancing competitiveness for profit making. Is it inevitable that this demand for creating the conditions for competitive advantage will win out over the demand for sustaining public goods? The history of the recent past might suggest that it is inevitable, and hence that capital gets its way in the end. Perhaps, though, the recent victory of capital over public goods is a result of the kind of political arrangement that developed along with those public goods and not a result of the autonomy of capital.[16]

There are, in fact, two special circumstances that made this recent victory over public goods by capital possible. The first was the bureaucratization of public goods. They were, that is, under public control only in the sense that those who made the decisions were sensitive to the criticisms of legislators, to opinion polls, and to business lobbyists. There was rarely control by local, regional, and national elected boards. Without genuine popular control, there was no sense of popular proprietorship. Public goods were, then, big government, and who wanted to come to the aid of big government?

The second circumstance was working people's reliance on a postwar social contract with capital: working people were to acquiesce in capital's expansion in exchange for capital's support for a higher standard of living and public goods. Entering into the contract had a profoundly corrosive effect. It led those who fought for public goods in the past to believe a permanent partnership with capital was possible in trying to get what they wanted. But within thirty years, the social contract of the postwar period came apart. Among other things, capital reneged on its support for public goods. By then the idea of a partnership for getting a better life had become entrenched among many working people. Despite the broken contract, the belief remained that, even with the wider range of freedom given it by neoliberalism, capital could still act as a partner in improving the lot of most working people.[17] What was to be the new basis for such a partnership? It was the acquiescence in the 1980s and 1990s in destroying or downgrading public goods in the hope that competitiveness might just work. A free-market strategy might just realize a prosperity so great that it would compensate for the lack of or degraded public goods.

As the old social contract came apart, labor unions—and the social democracy generally—were unable to fight for public goods because their acceptance of capital's demands persisted. The neoliberal view that the welfare state was antiquated triumphed, and union leaders and former social democrats accepted global competitiveness as the framework for a new prosperity that would make the welfare state unnecessary.[18] A key factor in this regard in the United States was labor's abandonment in 1991 of its support for national health insurance and its support in 1993 of President Bill Clinton's plan that made the promise of universal coverage and lower costs for health care dependent on competition between large medical corporations.

A new struggle for public goods must have new foundations, setting aside both bureaucracy and social contract. It must be a struggle for democratic public goods carried on with the awareness that unless there is a continual spreading and refining of public goods capital will defeat them again. Set on these foundations, a new struggle for public goods would advance us from competitiveness to solidarity. As we saw, the *inclusive logic* of public goods is that of pursuing goals each wants for all. And this is the opposite of the *exclusive logic* of competitiveness, which is that of pursuing goals one wants to prevent others from reaching.

This leads to the critical point about the alleged autonomy of capital. As the inclusive logic of solidarity takes root, there will be a reorientation of political will and hence a change in the political framework within which capital can act. A new public order of public goods will close down many of the incentives for capital flight. Otherwise, that new order will not be able to support its public goods. In a large and strong economy, measures to prevent corporate flight can be escalated gradually without great risk of economic disruption.

Leaving aside flows in all but capital for productive investment, consider the following sequence. The greater part of the productive enterprise of even such an economy is unwilling to move anyway. Either it is too small to have the economic resources to go elsewhere or it is still growing in a domestic market. Overall, there will be little effect on the ability to fund public goods during an early period in which only minor supports for the global competitiveness of capital are removed. In such a period the United States might, for example, decide to end its pressure on El Salvador to privatize its telecommunications system, a step that would open that system to U.S. corporate investment.[19] Soon thereafter stronger action would be needed, but this would be in a context of an even more developed solidaristic system of public goods. Decapitalizing profitable private plants without replacing them locally might at this point be subject to fines that would help support public goods. A surtax on goods imported into the United States from U.S. as well as foreign corporations to offset the cheap-labor advantage they enjoy might begin to shrink the labor gap. Corporations that allow free union elections, take their obligation for benefits seriously, and pay higher wages would enjoy a competitive advantage for their exports into the United States. Such strong measures would surely provoke a strong response, but these measures would come from within the context of a society moving toward the establishment of public goods. The gains from even incipient forms of these public goods would inspire popular support for measures that by limiting capital would help promote public goods even further. There would then be the political resources to meet the response of capital to these strong measures.

We can't, of course, expect such a new public order to take over everywhere simultaneously. Yet were the new order to be established in only a few countries, they would be vulnerable to exclusion from major financial markets and hence to a drop in their standard of living. Those countries would be in danger of repeating the Cuban experience of gradual impoverishment. The movement in the 1970s and 1980s toward neoliberalism took off over the span of a few years in various places—Britain, Chile, Mexico, and the United States. But it spread globally through the determined efforts of international finance. A new public order emerging from a movement for public goods would lack such an economically powerful unifying force. Still, there have already been impressive actions in a variety of countries against neoliberal austerity and in defense of public goods. This gives us hope that the isolation of the first few countries to adopt a new public order as an alternative to neoliberalism would be short-lived.[20]

Public Goods and
Public Consciousness

A new public order of public goods has an attraction that other proposals for radical social change lack. This attraction will hasten its spread among countries. The attraction is that this public order of public goods makes full use of the split consciousness of the citizens of most countries. On the one hand, people everywhere are largely in favor of public goods of the kinds already mentioned. They think they have rights that shouldn't depend on ability to pay. Education, health, and political participation are among them. Many have read the 1997–1998 international financial crisis as a warning that within neoliberalism they are personally more vulnerable economically. This has strengthened their desire for robust public goods—ones that don't collapse with the onset of crisis. On the other hand, people, wherever they are, are now unwilling to reject capitalism. There are different views as to why people want to introduce or to hang onto capitalism. Yet whatever theory about their consciousness is right, the fact is that, East or West, one doesn't get very far today with anticapitalism.

Given these two sides of popular consciousness, it makes sense to take advantage of current disgruntlement with the neoliberal downgrading of public goods to build a movement to strengthen and expand public goods. Such an effort can appeal to the sense of justice originating along with the elaboration of the social goals that these public goods try to realize. True enough, public goods will put certain enterprises off bounds to private entrepreneurs and will impose a tax on legitimate for-profit enterprise. These restrictions will limit competitiveness. Still, the vast numbers who favor public goods are willing to see capital subjected to these restrictions, for they are not viewed as aimed at the very heart of capital. If capital responds to a buildup of public goods with a tax strike, an investment strike, or massive capital flight, this will be taken by the public as a display of ill will and lack of civic virtue so serious that it calls for even further restrictions.[21] Such a radical response by capital will not be taken as a legitimate effort to save itself, for there was no bald-faced threat to do away with capitalism. If of course the hostility of capital escalates, then the strongly solidaristic political base for a society organized around public goods will be forced to escalate its restrictions. The future of capitalism may at that point come into question. But this was not where the movement we are talking about started. It started by calling into question only the neoliberal drive to downgrade and privatize public goods.

There are alternatives to our new public order that share more than it does with neoliberalism. For example, some social democrats have retreated from public goods to a defense of a scheme of equal basic income for everyone. The argument some of them give for a basic income program is from freedom. Having the freedom to do what one wants with a basic income is, on this view, more central to fulfilling justice than is welfare from preset public goods.[22] This jibes nicely with the neoliberal emphasis on individual choice. It turns that emphasis into a more credible ideological cover for the downgrading of public goods by ensuring equal opportunity for individual choice through equal basic income. It is assumed in all this that common goals are suspect, whereas individual goals are sacrosanct.

But under such an alternative I could choose to spend my basic income in irresponsible ways. I might choose not to educate my child, not to insure my family for sickness, and not to pay to participate in political deliberation. (Political participation instead of being a public good would involve a user fee.) These choices eventually place a heavy burden on others in the society, who are not going to let my uneducated child go hungry and my sick dependents go without health care, and who are not going to let political rule fall to a band of opportunists. The response of the defender of freedom will be that, even in a solidaristic society, consensus is never complete around public goods. Getting those few who are outside the consensus to go along will, they will object, involve an imposition. But this imposition will pale beside that brought on by a system based entirely on individual choice. Consider how many would have the consequences of selfish choices imposed on them where each is given a basic income to do with as he or she chooses. Since most people aren't brutes, they will let themselves be blackmailed into picking up the pieces after selfish individual choices. The children without education, the families without insurance, and political bodies abandoned to opportunists will impose responses. Basic individual income schemes are at bottom efforts to provide resources for individual solutions to what remain collective problems.[23]

Free Markets and Justice

I now turn to economic defenses of neoliberalism that if successful could be turned into defenses of its justice. The commitment to free markets derives from the conviction that in them supply and demand reach equilibrium, so that the market clears out the products brought to it by those who want to sell and satisfies the needs of those who come to it to buy. Neoliberalism is particularly interested in the implications of this conviction for labor markets and international trade.

According to this free-market view, restrictions on the *labor market* imposed by minimum-wage laws, social security taxes, and collective bargaining leave willing workers without jobs since there is only limited demand for workers with the high pay those restrictions create. Hence, to get full employment, it is necessary to deregulate the labor market and let wages spiral downward. From the point of view of neoliberalism's apparent concern for full employment, it is ironic that the struggle to make labor flexible—by removing legislated restrictions on the labor market—has focused in many places on employers' getting the right to dismiss labor without cause and the right to hire temporary workforces.[24]

According to the above free-market view, trade imbalances are created by restrictions on *international trade* imposed by a high exchange rate for currency, by enforcement of occupational health and safety legislation, and by state monopolies in oil, finance, or health care. The high price of exports from countries with such restrictions will depress their export sales and lead to their having to borrow to pay for their imports. To end these imbalances and avoid indebtedness, it is necessary, on the free-market view, for the affected nations to lift restrictions by devaluing currency, flexibilizing labor, and privatizing state monopolies. Whether this brings trade into balance or not, it makes life harder for consumers and workers. Imports become more expensive, the services and products previously subsidized by the state become more expensive, and workplaces come to approximate the "satanic mills" of William Blake's late-eighteenth-century England.[25]

Nonetheless, advocates of neoliberalism's global economy can contend that they offer a vision of a better future—one with full employment for workers and with harmony without domination among nations. In such a future, there will be freedom for all to do what they wish with their hard earned gains. The blights of individual unemployment and of national debt peonage will become things of the past. Of course, there is no guarantee of full equality of opportunity in such a future. But neoliberal apologists tell us that what counts is that there will be equality in the sense that each person and nation will be autonomous. Each will have the same freedom to acquire and use their own resources rather than being the slaves of those on whom they depend for their resources.[26]

What can we say of the merits of this neoliberal vision of a better future? A world in which individuals and nations have the resources to make free choices certainly can be a social goal. If the global free market were the only feasible way to realize this goal, then if there were a consensus that this should be a goal, the global free market would be a public good and implementing a global free market would then become a demand of justice. All of this follows from my view above of the relations between common goals, public goods, and justice. The question to be faced is whether in fact anything that might be called a global free market could implement the world of choice and harmony that is the common goal here. The global free market doesn't have to implement other social goals, such as a high level of welfare, to be a public good. It would suffice for it to implement the goal of choice without dependence. Can it do even this?

Collapse of the
Free-Market Defense

Nothing has changed in the past two decades to falsify the Keynesian critique of free-market economics. In brief, an unrestricted labor market, which keeps wages low, reduces demand for products; this in turn dries up investment, leading thereby to unemployment. But it is free-market economics from which the neoliberal vision of a better society and of justice springs.[27] This neoliberal vision is then vulnerable to the Keynesian critique, as I shall try to indicate.

Lowering the price of labor needn't reduce unemployment. Even with cheap labor available, employers may wait to hire it till sales pick up. But sales may not pick up; after all, the cheapening of labor implies a reduction of demand. There would, of course, be more demand if product prices were lowered along with wages. But this can't be guaranteed; product prices may be held high enough to guarantee a positive rate of return despite the lower wage bill. In a real-world competitive economy there will, then, be inflexibilities that trigger unemployment despite lower wages.[28] The importance of exports in neoliberalism need not offset this unemployment. In the current context, competition among exporting nations is accompanied by innovations that increase productivity. Once these innovations are spread through a national economy, the tendency toward unemployment need not be diminished by exports. So all things considered, the neoliberal vision of a better and more just society is in doubt.

In the international arena, the combination of currency adjustments, labor austerity, and privatizations have, with few exceptions, proven incapable of either pulling historically weak economies out of debt or strengthening them so they can afford to service their debt without harming their people. What then would make the weaker economies stronger? The most effective way would be reciprocity. The strong economies—the ones with either no deficit in their balance of payments or the productive power to afford to service their debt without harming their people—will need to reciprocate by both increasing the relative value of their currencies and having their corporations pay both their lower-wage domestic and foreign workers considerably more. If not, a nation with a strong economy would be subsidizing the strength of its economy at the expense of a lower standard of living for its corporations' workers. Also, insisting on devaluations and austerity for weaker economies that wouldn't altogether ruin them would still leave imports and loans from the stronger economies attractively cheap. But this would force them further into debt, which in the absence of reciprocity, would lead only to further austerity and devaluation. There is, though, no automatic market mechanism to push stronger economies—as Japan's was— to take such reciprocal measures. Of course, there may ultimately be political pressure and economic sanctions to try to get a stronger economy to value its currency upward and to bring its workforce up to a higher standard of living. But such threats are outside the free market. In a free international market, there will then be a tendency for imbalances to grow and for them to become structural sources of instability in the global economy.

So a neoliberal argument for the free market as a public good that implements choice among people through full employment and harmony among nations through trade balances simply collapses. Can the neoliberal argument be revived by adding nonmarket impurities to the market? I shall now show it cannot be revived. This will put me in a better position to argue that the global market economy is not a public good.

There are three possible nonmarket strategies that might provide relief from the consequences of unrestricted global competition.[29] One frequently talked about in the United States is the conscious shaping of a nation's advantage by the state's subsidizing the training of labor and the development of technology. A nation could then improve unit labor productivity in relation to others. This is not a strategy for general success but for the success of some nations—those not only with the resources for training and development but also with a better starting position in training and development. The successful nations will then export unemployment to the others—by drying up their export markets—and generate trade imbalances with them—by forcing them to borrow for imports.

A second strategy calls for the state to redistribute wages so that there is full employment. This is the strategy close to the hearts of those who advocate national basic income equality. Indeed, this strategy could protect the worst off from horrible poverty. Still, it does not address the issue of balances between surplus and deficit nations. Such a redistribution could, in some cases, mean only a redistribution of poverty.

The first two strategies don't set out to change neoliberalism but only to make it more palatable for some. There is no challenge to the fundamental neoliberal idea of unrestricted capital flows across the globe. And because of this those strategies don't change the inequality and poverty neoliberalism creates. The third strategy is more ambitious, attacking unrestricted capital flows.

The third strategy would control capital flows related to trade through international organizations aiming at balances and full employment. In the context of neoliberalism, however, any international organizations, whatever the intent in setting them up, would inevitably respond favorably to demands for free flows of capital, in the way the World Trade Organization does. Such demands would erode public monopolies and labor protections, leaving little room for trade balances and full employment. To have confidence that international organizations could hew to a progressive agenda, neoliberalism would already have to be locked in a losing battle at the national level with movements for public goods. Without such oppositional movements, the international arena would still be tightly under neoliberal control.

So a neoliberal global economy, with or without certain nonmarket adjustments, is not and will not be a public good. It will not provide individual autonomy through prosperity and international harmony through balances between economies. Yet these are what its claim to being a public good would rest on. Moreover, its inability to provide autonomy and harmony casts doubt on its ability to realize other important common goals. Intense competition will spark conflicts that feed militarism, will degrade the environment, will impede progress on gender and racial equality, and will put human rights second to profitability. Thus a neoliberal global economy will not be able to serve as a public good in relation to any of these other common goals.

The global market economy, then, joins ranks with numerous other pseudo-public goods.[30] I'm thinking here of the military, the prisons, and the police in today's world as belonging to one kind of pseudo-public good. Institutions of this particular kind derive their acceptance from an appeal to a perfectly valid common goal—security, both individual and collective. When they become, as they often have, instruments of imperialism, of population control, and of racially biased justice, they cease to serve the common goal of security, on which there is an unmanipulated consensus. The Cold War, the Gulf War, the War on Drugs, and the FBI Counter Intelligence Program (COINTELPRO) served, instead, many particular interests but not a common interest in security.

There are, to be sure, other kinds of pseudo-public goods. Air pollution credits get acceptance because of the common goal of a safe and sustainable environment. Are those credits then a public good? The U.S. Environmental Protection Agency, the institution that oversees air pollution credits, actually allows for unacceptable levels of air pollution in areas where a plant has bought enough credits to create such levels. Here we run up against the equal-access requirement for being a public good. Air pollution credits fail to give everyone equal access to clean air. The access one gets is less if local plants are buyers, rather than sellers, of credits.

Class Struggle and
a New Public Order

In rounding out this discussion, I want to point to the class nature of a movement for public goods. Habermas maintained that the shift from laissez-faire capitalism to a more interventionist state sounded the knell for the political importance of the working class.[31] With struggles around the state replacing those against owners, Habermas concluded that the important struggles cease to be class struggles. For two reasons, this seems to me quite wrong. First, I have emphasized that states are vital in supporting the goals of capital. From this I draw the conclusion, in opposition to Habermas, that attacks on state support for capital with the aim of defending public goods are indeed class matters. Second, I also emphasized that, as many traditional unions were accepting the idea of partnership, unions in the public sector were growing and becoming militant, as they had to, in order to cope with the tax reductions capital was winning. This aspect of the displacement of class struggle has provided one major reason for the neoliberal urge to privatize. In numerous cases, efforts to privatize have simply intensified public-sector class struggle. Thus, the move to a more interventionist state from laissez-faire did generate important class struggles, both within and around the state itself.

The struggle to defend public goods surely involves nonclass forces representing the interests of race, gender, and nationality. The same struggle involves in a massive way class forces representing the common interests of workers, whether in the private or the public sector. Those in the public sector are, to be sure, concerned about their conditions of work. But their conditions of work affect the quality of service they can render the public. Thus they have proven willing to join with those who receive such services in an effort to upgrade public goods. A vital element, then, of the struggle for public goods is the sense of many working people that their interconnected interests are not being served. There is a sense of being denied guarantees they view as entitlements—guarantees in regard to education, democracy, employment, health, and the media. Added to the class element are, to be sure, the elements of race, gender, age, sexual preference, and nationality. Underfunding and privatizing public education is a class matter that becomes more severe where racial discrimination in school districts enters as a factor. Lack of access to adequate health care is a class matter that becomes more pronounced for women where models for treatment are based on male anatomy. The lesson is not, as Habermas thought, that, as attention turned toward the state, class lost its importance in struggles. It is rather that within the context of a class struggle to establish a new public order there needs to be reciprocity between struggles based on class and those based in nonclass oppression.[32]

Admittedly, this view of class struggle alters a commonly held view of it as directed primarily at issues arising in separate workplaces. Different workplaces have different features and even different racial, gender, or ethnic mixes. This created the possibility of tensions between the demands coming from different workplaces.[33] Nothing in the workplace approach seemed to favor class unity. Workplace struggles are certainly not to be neglected, but they now need supplementation with struggles that have classwide relevance. These broader struggles pit working people not just against employers but also against the state in its role of promoting the classwide interests of capital. The demand for public goods fills the need here. It is a classwide demand with a potential for uniting the working class that the demands of different workplaces lack. An even stronger claim can be made for the demand for public goods. It is indeed a classwide demand, but it is also a universal demand that goes beyond class since public goods don't exclude anyone from access to them. Thus in struggling to realize the demand for public goods, a move is made from a struggle merely for one sector's benefit to a struggle for its hegemony in the whole society.

A Turn Toward
Classwide Demands?

There have been some encouraging recent examples of this broader concept of class struggle. First, Mexico. The weakening of official unionism in Mexico by neoliberalism has led to several efforts to set up working-class organizations with classwide demands. The Coordinadora Intersindical Primero de Mayo was one, made up of caucuses in official unions, workers' cooperatives, community groups, and parties of the left. It worked in alliance with the the Zapatistas of Chiapas, who have become an influence in the rural rebellion going on across Mexico. CIPM opposes the neoliberal project, though it is still searching for an alternative to it.[34] The independent union, Frente Auténtico del Trabajo, has contracts in a number of workplaces and also works within other unions to organize against neoliberal practices. Several organizations, including the independent labor federation, the National Union of Workers,[35] have formed recently with similar aims.

Next, France. French prime minister Alain Juppé wanted, in late 1995, to reform social services so spending on them could be cut. The response was 750,000 people in the streets on November 24. A railway strike, over plans to reorganize the railways, was extended as a protest over the threat to social services. This extension led to strikes by other public-sector unions. On December 12, 2 million took to the streets around France. The strike and its popular support were a rejection of the dogma that there was no alternative to the market. After three weeks the government was forced to back off. It got state control for social spending, but lost on revising pensions and the railways. Even without the private-sector unions, the struggle of the public-sector unions to save social services was based on a classwide demand.[36]

Finally, the South Korean general strike of late 1996 to protest neoliberal job insecurity got wide public support. The Kim Young-Sam regime tried to give capital greater freedom to lay workers off and to hire temporary workers. The rank and file pushed the new Korean Confederation of Trade Unions into a strike, which got the support of civic organizations and common citizens. After the government sweetened its stand with the addition of a proposal to remove earlier restrictions on trade union activity, the unions accepted modified forms of the proposal to give capital greater freedom over individual workers. Despite the disappointing results, the strike had raised issues that went beyond any given work sector and challenged the regime's neoliberal policies.[37]

These are only beginnings. They have been followed by the 1998 general strike in Indonesia which brought down the Suharto regime. Building on these struggles will involve going beyond defense to defining an alternative project. I have suggested that the alternative should be a new public order in which an extensive system of public goods takes many basic requirements of life out of the market and puts them under democratic control. People are already widely agreed on a number of the social goals such public goods would promote. In relation to this agreement, this system of public goods would be not just a new public order but a just public order.

Notes

1. For more on this view of justice, see Milton Fisk, "Justice and Universality," in *Morality and Social Justice*, ed. James P. Sterba (Lanham, Md.: Rowman and Littlefield, 1995), 221–244.

2. On the relation of social goals to public goods, see Milton Fisk, "Health Care as a Public Good," *Journal of Social Philosophy* 27, 3 (winter 1996): 14–40.

3. John Rawls, "The Idea of Public Reason," in *Political Liberalism* (New York: Columbia University Press, 1993), 212–254; Robert Nozick, *Anarchy, State, and Utopia* (New York: Basic Books, 1974), 149–172.

4. I have developed the connection between justice, social goals, and public goods in more detail in chapter 5 of a book in progress, *Health Care as a Public Good*.

5. Marc Breslow, "Can We Afford to Stop Global Warming?" *Dollars and Sense* (November/ December 1997): 20–24.

6. For a readable account of neoliberalism's corporate agenda, see Jeremy Brecher and Tim Costello, *Global Village or Global Pillage* (Boston: South End Press, 1994), chap. 3.

7. So-called market socialists are ambiguous about public goods since they prioritize the market. For market socialist John E. Roemer, public goods come in where the market fails; see his *A Future for Socialism* (Cambridge, Mass.: Harvard University Press, 1994), 21. Market socialists don't seem to worry too much about privatizing pensions and health care; see, for example, Hugo Fazio and Manuel Riesco, "The Chilean Pension Fund Associations," *New Left Review* 123 (May/June 1997): 90–100.

8. Even Sweden seems to have succumbed, where the welfare state has been cut back, labor made more flexible, state enterprises privatized, and restrictions removed from external capital flows.

9. Karl Polanyi, *The Great Transformation: The Political and Economic Origins of Our Times* (Boston: Beacon, 1957), chap. 12.

10. Financial flows have increased dramatically during the neoliberal period. International banking accounted for 1 percent of GDP of market economies in the 1960s. In the 1990s it has reached 20 percent. Speculation in equity, bond, and currency markets has exploded to $1 trillion a day, whereas trade volumes are only $3.5 trillion a year.

11. Asa Cristina Laurell, "La Nueva Ley del Seguro Social y el Viraje en la Política Social," *Acta Sociológica* 17 (May/August 1996): 11–37.

12. Daniel Singer, "The French Winter of Discontent," *Monthly Review* 49, 3 (July/August 1997): 130–139. This and a number of other articles I refer to here are in a special issue of *Monthly Review, Rising from the Ashes? Labor in the Age of Global Capitalism*, ed. E. M. Wood, P. Meiksins, and M. Yates.

13. Phyllis Vine, "To Market, to Market: The School Business Sells Kids Short," *The Nation* (September 8/15, 1997): 11–17.

14. Doug Henwood, *Wall Street: How It Works and for Whom* (New York: Verso, 1997), chap. 6.

15. Ellen Meiksins Wood, "Labor, the State, and Class Struggle,"*Monthly Review* 49, 3 (July/August 1997): 1–17.

16. William K. Tabb, "Globalization Is *an* Issue, the Power of Capital Is *the* Issue," *Monthly Review* 49, 2 (June 1997): 20–30.

17. On the persistence of partnership even after John Sweeney became head of the AFL-CIO, see Kim Moody, "American Labor: A Movement Again?" *Monthly Review* 49, 3 (July/August 1997): 63–79.

18. Thus, U.S. New Party leader Joel Rogers argues for "a new bargain between equity and efficiency" based on a restoration of Western capitalist competitiveness; see Joel Rogers and Wolfgang Streek, "Productive Solidarities: Economic Strategy and Left Politics," in *Reinventing the Left*, ed. D. Miliband (Oxford: Polity Press, 1994): 143.

19. Interview with Wilmer Erroa Argueta, "Fighting Phone Privatization in El Salvador," *Dollars and Sense* 212 (July/August 1997): 34–38.

20. There needs to be international solidarity among all those whose public goods are under corporate attack. Often they are under attack by the very same multinationals. For example, corporate medicine is threatening not just Canada's universal health care but also is pushing privatization of Medicare and Medicaid in the United States. Cross-border solidarity on health care is all the more relevant since the very same U.S. corporations are mounting the attack on both sides.

21. There will even be a "left-wing" of capital that finds certain restrictions on the capitalist market absolutely necessary for decent human life; see George Soros, "The Capitalist Threat," *Atlantic Monthly* (February 1997): 45–58.

22. This theme becomes the basis for Philippe Van Parijs's neolibertarian tract *Real Freedom for All: What (if Anything) Can Justify Capitalism?* (Oxford: Clarendon Press, 1995), chap. 1.

23. Van Parijs allows public goods, treating their benefits as part of basic income. But this clearly violates the primacy he gives to choice. You can choose to use money in many ways, but you can't substitute, say, education as a part of basic income for anything else. See his *Real Freedom for All*, 34–35, 42–44, 195.

24. In the United States, the successful 1997 Teamsters' strike against the United Parcel Service had as a primary issue temporary employment. In Holland, the neoliberals in government and labor have decided to permit temporary work contracts and laxer rules for firing (Marlise Simons, "Dutch Take Third Way to Prosperity," *New York Times* (June 16, 1997), A6. In contrast with the United States, both full-time and temporary work in Holland lead to full benefits.

25. In the United States, the workplace injury and illness rate in the first half of the 1990s was twice what it was in the first half of the 1980s. In Mexico in manufacturing, work accidents doubled between 1988 and 1995.

26. Conservative American columnist George Will put this philosophy of individual freedom eloquently in a syndicated article, "As Nation Becomes Wealthier, It Becomes More Free and Egalitarian," *Bloomington Herald Times* (August 21, 1997).

27. An accessible current critique of neoliberal labor policy of downward leveling of wages to get full employment is in Robert Kuttner, *Everything for Sale: The Virtues and Limits of Markets* (New York: Knopf, 1997), chap. 3. For a critique of the Keynesian idea of an "underemployment equilibrium," however, see Marc Blaug, *Economic Theory in Retrospect*, rev. ed. (Homewood, Ill.: Richard D. Irwin, 1968), 646–647.

28. I am relying here on ideas gleaned from Gregory Albo, "A World Market of Opportunities? Capitalist Obstacles and Left Economic Policy," in *Socialist Register*, ed. L. Panitch (London: Merlin Press, 1997), 5–47.

29. Gregory Albo develops this tripartite scheme in a more accessible way in his "The World Economy, Market Imperatives, and Alternatives," *Monthly Review* 48, 7 (December 1996): 6–22.

30. I do not intend to draw a sharp line here between public goods and pseudo-public goods. There is a whole range, with those serving a common goal at one end. For a sense of how extensive that range is, see Benjamin I. Page, *Who Gets What from Government* (Berkeley: University of California Press, 1983), chap. 4.

31. Jurgen Habermas, *Toward a Rational Society* (Boston: Beacon Press, 1970).

32. Milton Fisk, "A New Politics of Class," in *Marxism Today: Essays on Capitalism, Socialism, and Strategies for Social Change*, ed. C. Polychroniou and H. Targ (Westport Conn.: Praeger, 1996), 157–174.

33. Peter Meiksins, "Same as It Ever Was? The Structure of the Working Class," *Monthly Review* 49, 3 (July/August 1997): 31–45.

34. Richard Roman and Edur Velasco Arregui, "Zapatismo and the Workers Movement in Mexico at the End of the Century," *Monthly Review* 49, 3 (July/August 1997): 98–116.

35. Dan La Botz, "AFL-CIO Opens Up to Independent Unions in Mexico" *Labor Notes* 228 (March 1998): 1, 14.

36. Singer, "French Winter of Discontent."

37. Hochul Sonn, "The 'Late Blooming' of the South Korean Labor Movement," *Monthly Review* 49, 3 (July/August 1997): 117–129.

Privatization: Downsizing Government for Principle and Profit

Edward S. Herman

Privatization means the shift of activities from the government and nonprofit sectors to the market.

It may take the form of the sale of public (or nonprofit) sector assets to private companies or the contracting out of services previously supplied by public employees.

Privatization is not new. In France before the Revolution of 1789, the king farmed out tax collecting to individuals in a system notorious for corruption. Along with contracting out the provision of supplies for the French armed forces, private tax collecting was the basis of many great fortunes. Ending this system was one of the French Revolution's accomplishments.

Throughout the nineteenth century, the U.S. government engaged in massive privatization through the sale of millions of acres of public land (a domain greatly extended by the Louisiana and Alaska purchases and the seizure of Mexican territory). Many tycoons derived their fortunes from shrewd and sometimes fraudulent public land acquisitions. Abuses in the use and disposal of public property have continued throughout the twentieth century, manifested in both periodic scandals (such as the Teapot Dome) and the subsidized use of public property, which continues today through, for example, underpriced sales of national forest timber, bargain-rate use of mineral lands, and commercial broadcasters' free use of valuable air rights.

Western European and Third World governments have commonly owned airlines, railroads, telecommunications, and electric power systems, and sometimes banks, petroleum refining, and other industrial enterprises. But in the United States, government has been largely excluded from activities of interest to private business, and its periodic entry into these fields has been limited and often stripped away. The government did take over many private sector activities during World Wars I and II, but it speedily privatized them after the wars.

(continues)

(continued)

Since 1932, Congress, under the prodding of business, has made periodic surveys of government activities that compete with the private sector, with a view toward minimizing government competition. Ronald Reagan's Office of Management and Budget formalized the pressure on government agencies to minimize in-house production and ordered government managers to consider contracting out all functions, including data processing, janitorial services, and vehicle maintenance.

Despite this long-standing bias against public enterprise in the United States, with the rise of monopoly power in railroads, electric power, and telephones during the late nineteenth and early twentieth centuries the government created a regulatory apparatus. It grew with urbanization and the need for water supply and waste disposal, and the coming of the automobile and road building. The public sector grew further with the social democratization that accompanied the Great Depression and World War II, including the growth of organized labor and a new governmental health and welfare apparatus.

Privatizers from the early 1970s onward have been selling off government property—mainly water and wastewater facilities, parking garages, roads, airports, public lands and buildings, and mortgage portfolios. But privatization in the United States has focused mainly on the contracting out of government services, including the operation of government-owned facilities.

State and local governments carry out most public economic activity, and contracting out at these levels has soared over the past decade. The Mercer Group, an Atlanta consulting firm, estimates that between 1987 and 1995 the number of municipalities contracting out services increased as follows: janitorial from 52 percent to 70 percent, street maintenance from 19 percent to 38 percent, solid waste collection from 30 percent to 50 percent, and data processing operations from 16 percent to 31 percent.

This new wave of contracting out ignores historical lessons. A great deal of current government provision of services originated in the failures of contracting during the late nineteenth century and into the 1920s, under political systems that were often corrupt.

(continues)

(continued)

Ending such arrangements and turning them over to public agencies was a major accomplishment of the 1920s and later.

Although the privatizers claim that their objective is to increase efficiency, this is contradicted by their indiscriminate actions and the frequent disposal of public enterprises noted for efficiency. There is also evidence that they often respond to financial and political pressure. Furthermore, many bids for government property and contract services base their savings largely on shifting from union to nonunion and contingent labor.

Take, for example, contracting of the cleaning service for state buildings in Buffalo, New York, in 1992. Although initially claiming that the low contractor offer was based on efficiency improvements, state officials eventually admitted to the *Buffalo News* that the savings would come from the use of "more part-time workers at lower salaries and with fewer benefits." Study after study has shown that contractors offer lower wages and limited if any health and pension benefits. But gains from lower wages and benefits are not true "efficiency improvements," which implies a reduction in the use of resources such as labor and materials. They are actually income transfers from wage earners to employers and to government managers and taxpayers.

Even the nominal savings in privatization may be illusory or short-lived. A common phenomenon in contracting out was made famous in the weapons contracting formula "buy in, get well later." The contractor bids low, knowing that he can obtain cost adjustments after the government gets locked in to the contract and would find it difficult to cancel and locate another source, or to do the job in-house.

The most famous case was Lockheed's bid to produce the C–5A giant transport plane in the 1960s, which led to a huge cost overrun that doubled the price before a single plane was produced. Lockheed's contract had an automatic cost-based price escalation clause that was soon dubbed the "golden handshake."

Even fixed-price contracts could be raised through "improvements" offered by the contractor or demanded by the Pentagon—a process known as "gold-plating." One result of this abusive contracting system was that for decades the major contractors had

(continues)

profit rates on their Pentagon business roughly twice those in their commercial operations.

Many years ago the U.S. government did weapons research and produced many of its weapons in government arsenals. This was gradually phased out in favor of farming out research and production to private sellers. But without in-house production and research capabilities the government's bargaining position was reduced. It no longer had the option of producing for itself, and lacked the expertise to be a knowledgeable buyer, and so could be taken advantage of more easily. This point applies to other public functions—without a skilled body of managers and technicians the government is a ready victim in contract negotiations with knowledgeable private parties.

Contracting out is at an initial cost disadvantage compared to in-house production. It requires the additional expense of writing and evaluating contracts and then monitoring performance over their lives—the latter entailing a permanent bureaucratic apparatus on top of that deployed by the contractor. If that apparatus is skimped on, politicized, or corrupt, the road is open to massive cost escalation. Contracting out is often not able to overcome the disabilities of monitoring costs and potential corruption.

There is some truth to charges of inefficiency in public enterprises and nonprofit service activities. Many of these have become overbureaucratized, overstaffed, and politicized. Free-market proponents speak of "state failure" to counter claims of "market failure" by the private sector. But many state and nonprofit enterprises and services have done well, and when they have done poorly it is often the result of conservative macroeconomic and crippling state intervention. When macro policy is designed to keep a large reserve army of unemployed labor, labor strenuously resists staff cuts and public agencies find it harder to trim staff.

Underfunding, political appointments, and capture of regulatory agencies by corporate interests frequently undermine the function of government entities. Such damaging interventions are often deliberate, as in the case of the Reagan-era budget cuts and political appointments to the Environmental Protection Agency and the

(continues)

(continued)

Corporation for Public Broadcasting, both designed to demoralize and weaken the organizations. In these cases and others the damage inflicted reflects corporate efforts to undermine public bodies through the political process.

3

Rationality, Solidarity, and Public Goods

Nancy Holmstrom

Neoliberalism, a dominant ideology of our times, denies the importance of public goods or else maintains that all our goods are best achieved by individuals acting out of individual self-interest. On a social level it claims this is all best coordinated through the market. In this chapter I critique certain core assumptions of neoliberalism regarding rationality—unjustified assumptions that are obstacles to democracy and to people getting what they need.[1]

The Problem

There are various kinds of public goods, and several senses in which they may be public goods. But all public goods have certain things in common: Public goods are by definition goods for all or most of us and they can be satisfied for one only if they are satisfied for others. This may be for intrinsic or extrinsic reasons. Public goods are as a matter of empirical fact better than most people could achieve privately. The extent to which this is true varies, depending on what kind of public good it is. A good public education or medical care system provides better education and medical care than most individuals could achieve on their own.[2] Public parks provide what only very wealthy people can provide for themselves. For other public goods, economics makes little difference. If the air is polluted, the rich can try to keep moving to where it is clean, or get the best gas masks, but these are obviously very poor second bests. So clean air could be said to be intrinsically public because indivisible, whereas education is divisible. Another empirical fact about public goods is that most can be achieved only by collective action. Whether the good is a close community, a clean environment, a pleasant and efficiently organized city, a park, adequate medical care system, or a good educational system—none can be achieved individually, but only by coordinated collective action and usually, collective struggle. (An important exception to this is defense, the only public good that is immune to attack from even the most ardent opponent of public goods.)[3] Given the importance—even in some cases, the life-and-death importance—of these goods, it would seem to be the most rational thing in the world for individuals to engage in the collective action necessary to achieve them.

Yet, paradoxically, the dominant conception of rational motivation entails that this is mistaken—that it would not be rational to do so. This conception of rationality is called the individual utility maximization model or IUM. Though sometimes confused with the idea that people act for reasons, or that they engage in purposive behavior, IUM makes a more specific and technical claim about what peoples' reasons are when they are acting rationally. The claim is that when an individual's behavior is rational, she aims to maximize her own utility. She may be mistaken, of course, as to what will give her utility, and how much and what kind, but utility is always what she is aiming at. The theory has nothing to say about the rationality of her ends, that is, what will give her utility; the only restriction on ends is that they form a coherent set. Whatever the specific utility at which the agent aims, it is presumed to be open-ended, the more the better. The theory is descriptive in that it says that (normal) people act this way most of the time and also normative in that behavior that does not fit the model is judged irrational.

This conception of rationality is the basis of economics, of rational choice and game theory and of many ethical, social, and political theories as well, from libertarianism to Rawls's theory of justice. Though the view of human beings as utility maximizers has no necessary commitments regarding the nature of peoples' utility, the version of the theory that is dominant today in economics and the related field of public choice is more specific: The ultimate end of individual acts is always some (perceived) good of the agent. In the words of public choice theorist Dennis Mueller: "The basic behavioral postulate of public choice, as for economics, is that man is an egoistic, rational, utility maximizer."[4] Despite protests against "economics imperialism"[5] from some theorists, this model has been increasingly influential in other social sciences, and even in some Marxist circles.[6]

Whether we include egoism as part of the theory or not, this understanding of rationality generates problems regarding collective action—how it ever happens and how it can be rational. It might seem commonsensical that if something is in the interests of a group, for example clean air, it would therefore be rational for individual members of the group to contribute to that end—both by positive actions and by abstaining from detrimental behavior. But this is dismissed as a common fallacy by proponents of rationality as IUM (individual utility maximization), most famously by Mancur Olson in his book *The Logic of Collective Action.*[7] Written some thirty-plus years ago, it is still the classic work on the topic. On this view groups are just collections of individuals and group interests are the aggregate of individual interests. Hence it is only rational for a group to do something if it is rational for the majority of members individually. Now since achieving public goods does not depend on the efforts of a single individual and since individuals will get the benefit of success regardless of whether they contributed to the effort, it is not rational for an individual to contribute to achieving public goods. Yet if many act rationally, the result is that no one will get what would benefit them all. The problem of social coordination to which this gives rise is called the free rider problem.[8]

Olson claims that the free rider problem holds whatever the content of an agent's utility, specifically, whether it is selfish or unselfish. So even if an agent desired clean air for herself and everyone else, she would still calculate—insofar as she is rational—that since her individual action will make no difference to achieving it, she should not bother to work for it. She might participate anyway because she was manipulated or coerced into participating—but of course this would not count as rationally motivated behavior. More likely, she might participate out of strong emotions or moral conviction, but this too would be classified as irrational behavior by utility theorists. Participation in political movements and interest groups is rational for individuals only when the group is able to offer selective incentives, to reward individuals for joining or to punish them for not. A favorite example of selective incentives is labor unions' restricting employment to union members ("union shops"), to which Olson attributes the success of large-scale unionization in the United States.[9] Under these circumstances group participation is rational, but only because, for extrinsic reasons, it is individually rational.

Not only does the free rider problem apply to individuals; it also applies to groups that act as individuals to maximize the group's interests. Imagine an environmental group in conflict with a union over environmentally destructive work its members do. Both sides might benefit from uniting behind an alternative to the existing jobs, but if they think in individual utility maximizing ways they are unlikely to cooperate. The consequence is that either workers will lose their jobs, the environment will be damaged, or both. But even when there is no conflict of interest the same problem applies because on the utility maximizing view of rationality, it is rational for a group to free ride on the efforts of others if it can, even if they share common interests. Imagine several unions whose members would benefit from legislation strengthening occupational health and safety regulations. It would only be rational for an individual union to work for the legislation if it thought that its individual effort would make a difference to its passage. If it can presume that enough other unions will work for it to pass it, then it is rational for that union not to participate. Yet if each union thinks this way, it is unlikely the legislation will be passed and the unions' members will be less protected.

In these days when radical social movements are few and far between, it must be admitted that the theory has a lot of evidence in its favor. Much of the time people do seem to act just as the theory describes—as individual utility maximizers—which is to be expected in a competitive society where individuals' interests are often opposed to one another's. When people do engage in collective action, there are often selective incentives to do so and they are sometimes coerced. Groups often act the same way, which, again, is to be expected since group interests are often counterposed. I will argue that as a general theory of rational motivation and collective action, however, the theory is inadequate in fundamental ways. Even within the limitations of the theory, participation in collective action for public goods can still be shown to be sometimes rational. But there is no reason to accept the limitations of the theory. As a descriptive theory it fails; people do not act this way most of the time, even in their economic behavior. More important for my purposes here, the theory should be rejected as an implicitly normative account of rationality. It is an exceedingly narrow notion of rationality that fails to take account of the social character of individuals and their actions. Moreover, it obscures the nature of many of our most important goods. The claim that it is irrational for most people to engage in collective action for public goods is not defensible. Even if it is irrational from an individual point of view, it is rational from a collective point of view. And in cases of conflict I will argue that it is more rational to follow collective rationality. Perhaps the most fundamental flaw in the theory is its individualist methodology and metaphysics.

Are People Economic Men?

The most extreme version of the theory that is dominant in economics holds that all behavior is the expression of preferences, and that our preferences are always egoistic. Olson was not so arrogant as to make either of these claims. I shall ignore the issue of egoism, as I think that egoism as a general theory of human motivation was long ago shown to be either false or tautological.[10] People's behavior always reveals their preferences, these economists contend, so it follows, by definition, that people get what they want. Thus the market best serves our free choices and produces a general optimum. No distinction is made, nor can it be made by the market, between what consumers need and what they want, on reflection or on the spur of the moment.[11] As to why people form the preferences they do or why they change, proponents are agnostic; as two Nobel Prize–winning economists of the Chicago school, Gary Becker and George Stigler, explain in an article called "De Gustibus Non Est Disputandum," advertising merely helps consumers "differentiate products."[12]

It follows, then, that both smoking and quitting smoking, being expressions of preferences, are equally maximizations of utility and hence equally rational. As this example shows, the theory borders on self-parody. (Actually it gets worse; one of these economists demonstrated that committing suicide maximizes utility.)[13] The theory is also tautological, "a series of syllogisms," as critic Robert Kuttner calls it in a brilliant book called *Everything for Sale*.[14] One would think that this would invalidate it, but some of its proponents concede it is tautological but claim that it is useful nevertheless.

But once we acknowledge the complexities of genuine human choices, then the theory seems useful only as a justification of the market. As a number of philosophers, social scientists, and, recently, some experimental economists have shown, our choices do not fit the economic model of rationality. In actuality, they are often a function of ignorance rather than perfect information, or of manipulation.[15] Sometimes preferences are the result of unjust social conditions, so that preferences of oppressed people often reflect low self-esteem or are adaptations to unjust constraints.[16] Our preferences are usually changeable and often inconsistent. In part this is because when we prefer something it is always "in a respect," so we might prefer A in one respect, but we might prefer not-A in another respect.[17] Sometimes we have preferences about our preferences (so-called second-order preferences). That is to say, sometimes we care which of our preferences we act on; I want both to smoke and not to smoke, but I would prefer to act on the latter preference. Sometimes we even care which preferences we have. I might be deeply ashamed that I prefer violent trashy movies to all other kinds. So sometimes acting on a preference may violate other preferences that are more important to me.[18] Furthermore, many choices are simply the best of a bad lot ("the evil of two lessers" as someone called it). If we acknowledge all these complexities of human choices, then we have to recognize that the market is not necessarily the best way to give us what we want. I may choose to go to work by car, so that is my revealed preference, but only because it's the best of the available choices. What I would really prefer is to go by public transportation—but the market does not offer that choice. To get what I really want, I will have to go beyond the market and act politically in concert with others.

But there are different versions of IUM and I said that the one I just discussed, though dominant in economics today, is the most extreme. Not all are tautological and not all are egoistic. But even if we drop these aspects of the theory, the fact is that even in laboratory situations people do not always choose what is individualistically rational over what is best overall. In games like the Prisoner's Dilemma, where cooperation rather than individualist behavior will produce the best results, some people cooperate even in the first game and it begs the question to interpret this as game theorists tend to do, as due to the individuals' lack of intelligence.[19] Amartya Sen's critique of this view is summed up in the title of his classic essay called "Rational Fools."[20] So as a descriptive theory of how people behave, the IUM theory of rationality fails.

Cooperation and Individual Rationality

Whether or not it is rational—in IUM terms—for individuals to work for public goods depends in part on the size of the group involved. Utility theorists allow that free riding is not a problem for groups of a size where each individual's participation would be likely to make a difference. Since political movements are composed of many small groups working on many smaller issues over time, this reduces the free rider problem. But it does not eliminate it totally, since achieving public goods usually requires larger groups and coordination of groups, the more significant the change, the larger the group.

The fact that results that are best overall cannot always be achieved by individualistically rational action is hardly unique to collective action for public goods. As two well-known authorities on game theory put it, in certain situations, of which the Prisoner's Dilemma is the classic example, "two 'irrational' players will always fare better than two 'rational' ones."[21] Since most people find this conclusion unacceptable, various ways of avoiding it have been tried. Rather than abandoning the model altogether, as I will advocate, some wish to retain the identification of rationality with utility maximization but revise the individualist model for situations where the actions of individuals affect one another, and hence where some form of agreement and cooperation is in order. Game theorists attempt to devise formal models of such decision-making situations, but there is nothing at present that could be applied to the complex social issues I am concerned with.[22] One approach that could be applicable to our issue is David Gauthier's.[23] For interdependent action, he suggests, it is sometimes rational to agree not to act according to a policy of individual utility maximization in that this will produce an outcome with greater utility for everyone than acting individualistically. Although not rational in the traditional individualist sense, Gauthier argues that it follows from this sense. How would this apply to acting to secure public goods? It would be rational for me as an individual to throw out all my trash together rather than to recycle (because it would be easier, no one would have to know, and one person would not make any difference anyway ...). If everyone agreed not to do this, my utility would be greater than if they refused. So Gauthier's suggestion entails it would be rational for me to agree. However, wouldn't my utility be even greater if everyone else cooperated and I took a free ride? Although Gauthier wants to rule out this possibility he is unsuccessful because he stays within the individualist model. What would go further toward resolving the problem is if we worked to pass a law requiring recycling. Olson would agree that such measures are necessary but say that this is just because it is not rational for individuals to cooperate voluntarily and neither, though the laws are necessary, would it be rational to work for them.

Under certain limited conditions, however, the theory allows that cooperation is rational. Collective action for public goods sometimes fits these conditions— which would make such actions individually rational. In games like the Prisoner's Dilemma, if a player can be sure of the other's cooperation, then cooperation is individually rational. Experiments show that in repeated playings of such games cooperation increases and is more rational, because the possibility of communicating the intention to cooperate increases.[24] These findings apply to many ongoing activities in society such as participating in the PTA, which explains—in IUM terms—why people often cooperate when they could ride free. They also apply to large-scale and even dangerous political struggles. In her classic work, *The Mass Strike,* Rosa Luxemburg remarked, "The most precious, because lasting, thing in this rapid ebb and flow of the wave [of struggles] is its mental sediment: the intellectual and cultural growth of the proletariat."[25] One of the crucial changes brought by their collective activity is the trust workers develop that others will join with them, and not leave them out on a limb. The more experience they have of common sharing of risks, the more confidence—and more basis for confidence—each person has that acting collectively will produce the best results and hence that it is rational to take the risk. Organization can help to sustain this trust. Thus, even on individualist assumptions, collective action for public goods can sometimes be shown to be rational.

Joining together in collective action also gives people the recognition of themselves as a collectivity and the social power the collectivity has—from a neighborhood group that finally gets a traffic light to social movements that can topple a government. Outside of collective struggle, individuals have no sense of power because as individuals most people lack it. By coming to realize their power, individuals come to realize that their goal is more possible and their action less risky than they had previously thought. Hence it is more rational from an individual point of view. The rapid escalations of demands noted in revolutionary situations,—from "Bread and Peace" to "Overthrow the Czar" to "All Power to the Soviets"—is usually explained in emotional terms. Although emotions are undoubtedly involved, the rapid escalation can also be understood as a reflection of a changing calculation of what is possible and therefore what is rational to do.

Other factors affect cooperation as well. When individuals share a sense of identification, they are more likely to cooperate. Identification has several aspects. In part it involves taking others' concerns as one's own, aiming at a group utility rather than an individual utility. Some Rational Choice theorists have tried to broaden the model in this way. For example, German sociologist Karl-Dieter Opp has tried to explain political protest by showing that discontent with public goods can be a strong rational choice incentive.[26] But there is more to identification than an individual aiming at a group utility. A more adequate understanding of the phenomenon takes us beyond the individual utility maximizing model.

When people identify with others they think in terms of "we" rather than "I," of "what should we do?" rather than "what should I do?" Actions taken on the basis of this kind of identification may or may not be individually rational, but this is not why they are done.[27] The other aspect of identification is moral convictions. People feeling this kind of identification with others feel they ought to help if they are going to benefit, and they feel a sense of shame if they "let the others down." The concept of solidarity expresses both an identification and a moral commitment to others. Other moral principles may play a role too. People involved in a struggle for better public education most likely believe that a good education is a right and this conviction is important in explaining their actions. Moral convictions will be more motivating when it seems more possible to achieve them and the same is true of desires. If something seems impossible, a person may even be unaware he desires it—the "sour grapes" phenomenon. But such survival mechanisms disappear when the likelihood changes. What once was hard but could be borne becomes an intolerable weight; what once was a utopian fantasy becomes a marvelous possibility.[28] Collective action, by making the goals more possible, makes both moral convictions and desires more motivating.

From "I" to "We"

Sometimes people act out of solidarity, sometimes they act more individualistically. The question is how to understand cooperative behavior when it does occur and whether it is rational. Although IUM theorists have trouble explaining actions based on solidarity or explain it as irrational, within other political philosophical traditions, from Marxism to communitarianism[29] to feminist theory, it is to be expected and highly rational. Though less typical, this social perspective can also be found within analytic philosophy. In two recent books, *Social Facts* and *Living Together*, [30] Margaret Gilbert has developed the very fruitful concept of a plural subject. Though her locus of concerns is philosophy of language, game theory and the like (she criticizes individualist solutions to coordination problems), she notes the striking similarity between her formulation of the concept and some classical political theory. Two people taking a walk together, a committee (her examples) or an environmental justice organization, or a parents and teachers' group working for better public schools (my examples)—these constitute plural subjects in Gilbert's sense because in each case the participants have committed themselves to a goal, and they understand that there are obligations and entitlements entailed by that. Plural subjects can properly speak of "our" beliefs as well as "our" goals and they engage in collective action in accordance with their collective principles to reach their common goals—where none of this is reducible to actions by a collection of individuals. Gilbert contends, correctly, that plural subject concepts are "key to the description of human social life. [They] inform and direct a great deal of that life, in nations, clubs, families, and even in the taking of walks"(191).

Another recent work that goes further in the same direction is Richard Schmitt's *Beyond Separateness*.[31] Explicitly political in his concerns, bridging the analytic and Hegelian/Marxist traditions, Schmitt attempts to make the critique of individualism more precise than it often has been. A common assumption of mainstream philosophy for quite a while is that fundamentally we are all separate and distinct individuals—and various moral and political inferences are drawn from this assumption. Who could deny this, one might ask; it just seems a given—maybe a logical given or maybe one rooted in our biology. Well, Schmitt denies it—by distinguishing between being distinct and being separate. Being distinct is a fact of biology; each of us has a body we are connected to in ways no one else is. But being separate, he says, is a "posture" that we can choose to adopt or to reject in favor of a posture he calls "being-in-relation." We can share understandings and emotions, make joint decisions, and perform joint actions as individuals who are distinct but who are no longer separate, because we have chosen to bring our wills to some extent under the control of others. The "we" may be two persons or a very much larger group. Applying his analysis to two kinds of power, Schmitt distinguishes between power-over-others and power-in-relation, empowerment. Though individuals can and should choose to act in-relation, the efficacy of their choice will be limited by the fact that separateness "is embedded in the hierarchical institutions that govern all aspects of our lives." Thus fundamental political change is necessary if we are not happy being as separate as we are.

As he makes clear, Schmitt's work draws on feminist thinking, a central theme of which has been the critique of the abstract individualism of most Western philosophy. Feminists have challenged notions of self[32] and autonomy,[33] which are dominant in this tradition, as well as other distinctions central to this debate: the distinctions between reason and moral conviction and reason and emotion.[34] If a mother acts out of love for her child or a trade unionist out of solidarity with her fellow workers or an environmental activist out of commitment to the next generation, these motivations should not be counterposed to acting for rational reasons. Though characteristic of feminist approaches to moral theory, this critique is not unique to feminists. In fact it goes back to Aristotle, who maintained that in certain situations a proper understanding necessarily involved having certain emotional responses; failure to feel grief in certain circumstances would show that the person did not really understand the situation.[35]

The kind of "we" Gilbert and feminists speak of is mostly small groups, particularly family and friends. And in everyday life in capitalist society this kind of identification is certainly strongest within such small units; material interests as well as emotional bonds hold families together. But people sometimes act out in solidarity with much larger groups, even humankind as a whole. Research on individuals who saved Jews during the Holocaust shows that their unselfish actions on behalf of particular people were premised on just such a universalistic identification.[36] Between the universal humankind and families, there are social groups of all kinds and sizes and the likelihood of cooperation varies under different conditions. Within a very large and heterogeneous social group like the U.S. working class, there is ample basis for individualism and competitiveness, but there is also the basis for commonality. Objective material interests, culture and community, emotions, gender and ethnic identity—and the interactions thereof—all influence whether working people choose individualistic or cooperative survival strategies, and how broad or narrow these are.[37] People will often be moved into collective action to protect themselves from public evils, ills that befall every member of a group or many members indiscriminately, more readily than they will act to further public goods. In extreme cases, therefore, there is no conflict between individual and group utility because no individual "outs" are possible. Referring to the present desperate situation in Russia, Boris Kagarlitsky said recently, "People have either to organize themselves to carry out joint actions or to reconcile themselves to their fates."[38] It is especially in times of crisis like those to which Kagarlitsky is referring when people can protect themselves only through collective action, that the individualist side of their consciousness begins to break down and the collective side of their experiences and consciousness develops and deepens. Unlike economic behavior in the marketplace or political behavior in the voting booth (and critics like Sen question whether utility theory can even explain these),[39] people involved in radical economic and political struggles are not isolated atoms. Each individual's action will usually affect the actions (certainly the morale) of at least a few other people—family, friends, coworkers—and vice versa—and their actions will in turn affect the actions of a few others and so on. Because each action usually has these reinforcing and ripple effects, the individual cannot so readily imagine the result as independent of what she/he does. When people act as a collectivity they begin to think as a collectivity and in the process often begin to see one another as "brother," "sister," and "comrade." In actual struggles it seems it is not always easy to say when one's participation will make a difference and when it will not. Thus participation in struggles for public goods, and to prevent public evils, may in fact be rational in the individual utility maximizing sense, but then again it may not.

In any case, when people participate out of a sense of solidarity or identification or moral convictions, as they so often do, their actions do not fit the individual utility maximizing model. The IUM model fails descriptively because it portrays individuals as more individualistic or "separate" than they often are—and denigrates their action as irrational when it does not fit the model. The fact that the individual agent is part of the collectivity benefiting from public goods is obscured by the language used in these discussions. On the IUM model, those who benefit without contributing are "free riders"; those who contribute when they could free ride are "suckers."[40] Those are the only two options in this scenario. But the category of people who benefit from public goods without contributing is broader than the term "free rider" implies. Among those who benefit without contributing are some who could contribute but prefer to take advantage of others' cooperative behavior—true free riders—but also included are those who do not contribute because they can't contribute: children, the elderly, the disabled, who are not free riders in the ordinary sense. Rational people know that they were once children, will be elderly (hopefully), and could be disabled. So the categories of free riders and suckers may be distinct at a given time with respect to some given action, but over time, they are not. And most people realize that. Most people also have relationships with and commitments to people in both these categories. Thus people who contribute though they could get away with not contributing should not be called "suckers," which is defined by the

American Heritage Dictionary as "one who is easily deceived, a dupe." The rational man of the IUM model is indeed an odd bird. As one theorist put it: "... the isolated person equipped with a depersonalized vote ... resembles nothing so much as the anonymity of money."[41]

Kinds of Public Goods

The IUM account of rational action is also too narrow and too individualistic in its picture of peoples' values (their "goods"). First of all it assumes that all sorts of different ends can be compared meaningfully along a single, quantifiable and open-ended dimension of utility. But each aspect of this assumption can be challenged. Why reduce people's diverse and heterogeneous ends to one? Why assume all qualitative differences can be quantified? And why assume that whatever we want, we always want more of it? None of these assumptions hold up when we think of real people and what they want and how they choose. Utilitarianism has often been criticized on these points, but again the critique goes back to Aristotle.[42]

But amidst the diversity of peoples' goods, our focus here is on public goods. To a certain extent, what goods are public goods is a matter of decision. If the citizens in a society decide to provide a particular good, then it becomes a public good, even if critics argue that it could be satisfied better privately, on an individual basis. Even if the critics are wrong, this might be imaginable. Medical care is an example of a good we could at least imagine each individual satisfying on their own, even if in fact this cannot be done adequately for all. Before the collective decision is made to provide medical care for all, one might argue in favor of it by claiming that medical care is or ought to be a public good. On the other hand, some goods seem to be intrinsically public because they are indivisible, for example, clean air or national defense. And indeed, it would be impossible, or at least exceedingly difficult and inefficient, to try to satisfy the need on an individual basis (by supplying arms, gas masks, and such). This difference of divisibility could be said to be a matter of degree, rather than absolute, though it is not therefore unimportant.

Still other public goods, however, are public in an even stronger sense, in that it is not even imaginable that they be satisfied on an individual basis. Following Charles Taylor,[43] I will call these irreducibly social goods. That is because the very definition of the goods involves reference to more than one person and to relations between them. Before considering goods involving larger groups, consider first friendship and love. If Romeo loves Juliet, then he wants her to have certain feelings—feelings that are directed back to him. To say that Juliet loves Romeo is to say that she has certain feelings directed toward Romeo and wants Romeo to have certain feelings directed toward her. What is involved is a reciprocity of feeling, a reciprocity of awareness, and, moreover, an understanding common to both that this is something valuable. On a broader scale, I have in mind goods that might be grouped under the term "community." In *The Poverty of Liberalism* Robert Paul Wolff[44] distinguished three kinds of community that he suggested might jointly constitute a common good of community. One is affective community: the sharing of a common cultural experience, not as an outsider, a tourist, but as part of a group. This experience involves a reciprocity of awareness and a common understanding that it is a good thing. Anyone who has ever enjoyed some cultural event, a holiday, or some ritual that they have felt part of has shared in affective community. Productive community is the satisfaction that can come from working together on a common productive project. Building a house, making a quilt, working on a scientific project, or playing in a band often involve productive community. The satisfaction is not just the product, which could come by other means, nor is it in the activity per se, but the collective experience of working together and producing something of value. The experience involves a reciprocal awareness, a common appreciation that cannot be found working alone on a machine. The latter can be satisfying, but it is a different experience.[45]

The third kind of community Wolff discussed is rational community, which is like productive community, but the common project is political. People engaged in making some collective decision, deciding on goals, how to balance competing goals, and how to achieve their goals most effectively constitute a rational community. They discuss, debate, plan, make decisions … all the sorts of activities necessary to achieve public goods like education, clean air, and so on. But the process of collective political activity is not only necessary as a means to those goods, but rather, following philosophers like Aristotle, is a good in itself, one worthy of, indeed expressive of distinctly human capacities. A key aspect of it is a shared understanding that it is a valuable enterprise. What makes both productive and rational community a good to people might be, at least in part, the sense of power the collectivity gives them that as individuals they lack.

Participation in collective action for a public good often involves some or all these goods of community.[46] The civil rights movement, for example, aimed at the public good of racial equality, involved rational community, productive community and often affective community (I'm thinking of the importance of songs) as well. Certainly most people involved in the civil rights movement experienced it as a common good. All three modes of community distinguished by Wolff are irreducibly social in the strong sense I explained initially with Romeo and Juliet. What the good is cannot be explained without reference to other persons and shared understandings. And they cannot be reduced to separate acts by separate individuals. If two people are raising their hands, it does not count as "taking a vote" unless there are social conventions as to what a vote is, and how it is done, and unless those conventions are shared by those raising their hands. And if that vote comes after a process of discussion in which not only do many individuals take turns talking, but they also genuinely listen and learn from each other, then it is a collective decision. When people engage in this process and then carry out their decision, they constitute a plural subject of the kind explained by Gilbert.

If we think of all human action as motivated by the desire to maximize individual utility, then the fundamentally social character of many of our goods is obscured, distorted, or simply disappears. From friendship and love to the several kinds of community, people do care deeply about such goods and act to achieve them. When social goods are taken into account, when it is acknowledged that they are goods, and that people aim at them, then the inadequacy of the individualist account of rational action seems clearer. On that view, participation in collective action is always a cost, although sometimes offset by selective incentives. But what I am suggesting is that sometimes participation is itself valued. The process, as much as the effect of the process, is a good. This reveals another limitation of the IUM account of rationality: the assumption that rationality has solely to do with means, not ends. This consequentialist approach leaves out the fact that some means to an end can be a constituent of the end.

Collective Versus
Individual Rationality

Because individuals identify with others, from another particular individual to large groups, and because many of their goods are irreducibly social, the distinction between actions that are individually rational and irrational is not always clear-cut. But sometimes, of course, it is. My individual interests may conflict with the interests of the collective and hence what is rational from my point of view may not be rational from the point of view of the collective and vice versa. What action is rational in such cases?

Let's consider this example: A guidebook to Amsterdam, describing how pleasant and efficient it is to get around, states: "using cars in the city is frowned upon." Now suppose I, a resident of Amsterdam, feel no identification with others nor obligation, and since I like to drive and the streets are quite empty, I use a car regularly in the city. It's very convenient and lots of fun. Am I behaving rationally? According to the IUM model—of course my behavior is rational; in fact, not to drive in these circumstances would be irrational. But I think it is plausible to say that my action—if rational at all—is rational only from a very limited point of view; it is certainly irrational from a collective point of view since similar behavior by enough others would make the city less pleasant to everyone, including myself, and make it impossible for me to zip around town in my car. Since both points of view exist, then the IUM theory is simply wrong in saying that to refrain from driving would be irrational. From one point of view one behavior is rational and from the other point of view another behavior is rational. A relativist view of rationality would say that neither can show the other is irrational without circularity and that is all we can say.

This relativist position, it should be noted clearly, is enough to refute the IUM model of rationality—and relativism is the least we can say. But I would like to suggest some considerations in favor of giving priority to collective rationality when it conflicts with individual rationality. This would be uncontested if I were speaking about moral priority; except in certain cases (called rights), an individual's interests have to yield, morally speaking, if they conflict with the interests of the many. From the point of view of democracy, collective rationality has priority too; unless we give priority to collective rationality we cannot fulfill the will of the majority. But I want to argue now that the same is true from the perspective of rationality, without bringing in moral or political considerations. When something is rational from a collective point of view, though not an individual one, I want to say it is simply more rational—period—whether or not it conflicts with individual self-interest.[47] Suppose I, the Dutch driver, experience something like a Gestalt shift, and suddenly start to see things from the collective point of view. It seems to me it is plausible to describe this move from "I" to "we" as an advance in consciousness, just as we would if I moved from thinking only of the short term to thinking in a long-term perspective. After all, "short-sighted" is practically a synonym for "irrational," whereas a "far-sighted" person is one who is more rational than average. Since I (probably) will be around in the longer period that constitutes "the long term," that perspective should take priority if it conflicts with the short term. It's a more inclusive point of view. Similarly, I contend, since I (probably) will benefit along with the rest of the collectivity from satisfying collective interests, that is the more inclusive perspective and should take priority if the individual and collective interests conflict.

Certainly my behavior will influence others, probably encouraging others to do the same. But even if one can't show that my "free driving" behavior affects others enough to make the result different, to move so many others to drive that Amsterdam becomes congested and polluted, there is a psychological and symbolic inconsistency in saying it's rational for one individual to do what others should not—for I could not do it if others did it too. By my action I set an example; my action expresses symbolically how I want things to be. To knowingly act in ways that would be harmful, if everyone did the same, is to say I don't care about everyone else. To see me drive just for the fun of it is like seeing me make a rude gesture to the rest of the public. Saying it is rational for me but not for others is not an outright logical inconsistency, as Kant wanted to say regarding the moral dimension, but it is a psychological and symbolic inconsistency that ought to carry some weight.

Adopting a long-term perspective will often reduce the conflict between individual and collective rationality. Consider the loggers who are fighting with environmental groups over logging practices like clear-cutting. In the short run the loggers make more money by cutting down more trees, and environmentalist protests threaten their jobs. But in the long run if all the trees are cut down, loggers will lose their jobs anyway. So the long-run interests of loggers coincides with the collective interest of preserving the environment. This coincidence of interests is true in general, however, not for every particular logger. Some loggers will be gone before the trees are all gone, some will not be able to make the transition to other work, and so on. So a long-term perspective reduces the conflict between individual and collective rationality, but it does not entirely eliminate it. Still, if a logger switches from the short-term perspective to a long-term perspective, from a smaller "we" to a larger "we," I think we should say this is an advance in consciousness. Though it may or may not maximize his individual utility, a greater utility will be realized and hence he is acting more rationally when he acts to maximize collective utility.

For suppose we step back and ask what rationality is for, that is, what evolutionary role did it play? Clearly, the distinctively human capacity to act purposively is the principal evolutionary advantage our species has. It gives us control over the world, including ourselves, that we would otherwise lack. Our ability to think and plan for the future extends that advantage. Although IUM behavior is part of human rationality, consistently IUM behavior leads to socially destructive and even self-destructive results. At this stage of human and technological history it seems plausible to say that if we continue in our present antagonistic, competitive way, nuclear war and ecological disaster are inevitable or at least highly probable. Only social cooperation, social planning on a global scale, will prevent this. Only social cooperation will give us the control over our lives, which is the evolutionary function of rationality. But on the IUM conception of rationality,

this social cooperation cannot be achieved rationally. Thus behavior that is rational according to IUM will lead to the destruction of the species. Since this contradicts the function of rationality in the species, this ought to be a reductio ad absurdum of the IUM account of rationality.

A Social Perspective

That this even has to be argued shows how deep the individualist model goes, methodologically and metaphysically.[48] A basic assumption of those who accept the IUM account of rationality is that the concept of rationality is primarily ascribed to the individual and only in a derivative sense to an action or a society. Although this presupposition does not imply that our conception of a rational individual is of someone capable of existing independently of other persons or society, it does imply that the individual can be properly understood independently. Else how could that individual be the conceptual or analytical starting point? In my opinion, a social perspective, like that of Aristotle or Hegel and Marx, is more plausible, according to which human beings individuate themselves only in the context of society. The individualist model, indeed the very concept of the isolated individual—arose only at a certain stage in history, in the context of a particular kind of social organization and connectedness. This is lost sight of, however, and the isolated individual appears "not as a historic result but as history's point of departure."[49] And the point of departure for philosophy and economics as well. But just as Wittgenstein proposed starting from behavior and social practices, instead of starting "from the inside" or "one's own case," as the best way to understand concepts of language and mind, I would suggest that rationality first and foremost should apply to social practices, ways of life, and collective action. Only secondarily should it apply to individual persons and individual acts. Just as much as in the areas of language and mind, starting "from one's own case" in thinking about rational action leads to skepticism, inconsistencies, and conflicts. The free rider problem is an example of such conflicts.

All this may sound dangerous to individual freedom and autonomy. Each of us is an individual and we don't want to be submerged within and subordinated to a collectivity. Being able to think as an individual is a historic achievement—which has yet to be won for much of the world's population, particularly its women. But being able to think as part of a collectivity can be just as much a historic achievement. Nor need it conflict with autonomy. The plural subjects of which I spoke earlier are constituted by individuals who choose to bring their will to some extent under the control of others because they realize it is the best way to achieve their shared goals. This kind of choice is no more nor less free or autonomous than any other choice, the freedom and autonomy of which depends on many internal and external conditions. When individual and collective rationality conflict, social planning is the only way for people to achieve their aims. Thus, rather than conflicting with autonomy, collective action by plural subjects is the way autonomy is realized on a collective scale. Social movements and, to a lesser extent, the electorate can be such plural subjects. To work or to vote for mandatory recycling or restrictions on cars in the city is to agree to limit one's freedom in certain respects in order to expand one's freedom and well-being in others. To refuse to engage in the necessary collective action would be to limit one's autonomy as well as to limit democracy. Moreover, nothing I have said is inconsistent with putting constraints on the power of the collectivity, that is, recognizing individual rights.

The best way, however, to protect individual freedom and autonomy is to create the social conditions that are necessary for their realization, social conditions that facilitate individuals in formulating rational life plans and that minimize conflicts of interests within the individual and between the individual and collective, such as the free rider problem.[50] Social institutions that do this are more rational than those that do not. Unless this is the primary focus, attempts to resolve these conflicts will tend to fail because they are piecemeal rather than systemic. As Richard Schmitt pointed out, the individual choice to act in-relation can be hindered by hierarchical social relations. Or, as in the case of the loggers versus environmentalists, efforts to resolve the conflict, like retraining, often fail because of some other social problem: insufficient education, lack of jobs, and so forth. Thus again in deciding what is rational action a social perspective is primary, the individual perspective is secondary.

Summary and Conclusion

Coming back to rationality, collective action, and public goods—public goods are—by definition—goods for all or most of us and they can be satisfied for one only if they are satisfied for others. I explained that some public goods are social in an even stronger sense in that they intrinsically involve reference to social relationships and shared understandings. Public goods are as a matter of empirical fact better than most people could achieve privately. Another empirical fact about public goods is that they can be achieved only by collective action. The obvious conclusion that it would be rational to engage in such action is rejected by the dominant notion of rationality as individual utility maximization. I have argued that this is an exceedingly narrow definition of rationality that doesn't work even in the economic sphere and certainly should not be presumed to apply to social and political action. The most fundamental philosophical problem with the model, I argued, is its individualism.

At this point, someone might object that the whole debate is really just verbal. "Rational" sounds good so everyone wants to claim it. I think people ought to act for the collective good, not only individual good, so I want to claim that it's rational as well as right. Maybe that will help to get people to do it since people don't like to think their actions are irrational. Is that all the disagreement is about? No, but it is that in part. Like many of our most important concepts, "rational" is implicitly normative as well as descriptive, assuming it makes sense to distinguish the two. "Irrational" is pejorative, so to call an action irrational will make it more difficult to convince people they ought to do it, and make it less likely they will do it. Perhaps this is why students of economics, infused with the IUM paradigm, are more likely to act in IUM ways.[51] Since the only two alternatives on the IUM model of collective action are "suckers" and "free riders," who wants to be a "sucker"? Though it is fallacious, then, the IUM account of rationality can be a significant brake on collective action for public goods. And if people do not act collectively for public goods, they are left with just the market to satisfy their needs. To use good old-fashioned Marxist language, could one find a better example of bourgeois ideology?[52]

Notes

1. This paper overlaps slightly with Holmstrom, "Rationality and Revolution," *Canadian Journal of Philosophy* 13, No. 3 (1983): 305–325.

2. This, of course, is a claim that would be disputed by free market thinkers. My claim is supported by comparisons between the United States and countries of comparable wealth that invest more heavily in their education system and have universal medical care.

3. This fact suggests something about who are the principal beneficiaries of national defense in most countries and whether it really is a good for most people, but I leave all those questions aside.

4. Denies C. Mueller, *Public Choice* (Cambridge: Cambridge University Press, 1979), 1–2.

5. Kenneth E. Boulding, "Economics as a Moral Science," *American Economic Review* 59 (1969): 8.

6. Notable examples include John Roemer and Jon Elster. For the debate, see Terrell Carver and Paul Thomas, *Rational Choice Marxism* (University Park, Pa.: Pennsylvania State University Press, 1995).

7. Mancur Olson, *The Logic of Collective Action* (Cambridge: Harvard University Press, 1965). Olson applied his ideas to various macroeconomic phenomena in *The Rise and Decline of Nations: Economic Growth. Stagflation and Social Rigidities* (New Haven: Yale University Press, 1982).

8. Alternatively, the public goods problem, or the problem of collective action, sometimes distinguished but essentially the same problem.

9. This is disputed by, among others, Douglas Booth in "Collective Action, Marx' Class Theory and the Union Movement," *Journal of Economic Issues* 12 (1978).

10. The locus classicus of this critique is Joseph Butler, *Five Sermons* (Indianapolis: Bobbs-Merrill, 1950), especially Sermons 4 and 5. A contemporary discussion is Thomas Nagel, *The Possibility of Altruism* (Oxford: Oxford University Press, 1970).

11. For this and a number of other reasons, Elizabeth Anderson argues that "an adequate grasp of liberal commitments to freedom, autonomy, and welfare supports more stringent limits on markets than most liberal theories have supposed." "The Ethical Limitations of the Market," in *Value in Ethics and Economics* (Cambridge: Harvard University Press, 1993), 141.

12. George J. Stigler and Gary S. Becker, "De Gustibus Non Est Disputandum," *American Economic Review* 67 (March 1977), 76–90.

13. See Robert Kuttner, *Everything for Sale* (New York: Knopf, 1997), 44.

14. Ibid.

15. There are so many references here it would be pointless to try to enumerate them.

16. See Cass Sunstein, "Preferences and Politics," in *Philosophy and Public Affairs* 20, No. 1 (winter 1991): 3–34, who argues, for this and other reasons, that government should not be based on individual preferences. For related arguments, see Jon Elster, *Sour Grapes* (New York: Cambridge

University Press, 1983).

17. Thanks to Anatole Anton for this point.

18. Harry Frankfurt was the first to make this point in his "Freedom of the Will and the Concept of a Person," *Journal of Philosophy* 68 (1971): 5–20.

19. It is called the Prisoner's Dilemma because a commonly discussed example of it involves two prisoners confronted with the following options: If one confesses, he will go free and the other will get a very heavy sentence. If both confess they both get a heavy sentence. If neither confess, they both get a very light sentence. IUM dictates the first choice, but if they both choose it, they will do much worse than if they both choose the third.

20. Amartya Sen, "Rational Fools: A Critique of the Behavioral Foundations of Economic Theory," *Philosophy and Public Affairs* 6, No. 4 (summer 1977): 317–344.

21. R. D. Luce and H. Raiffa, *Games and Decisions* (New York: John Wiley and Sons, 1975), 112. For discussion of the Prisoner's Dilemma as showing the nonoptimality of individual utility maximization, see 94–102.

22. Luce and Raiffa, 115.

23. David Gauthier, "Reason and Maximization," *Canadian Journal of Philosophy* 4 (1974–1975). A later attempt at the same end is *Morals by Agreement* (Oxford: Clarendon Press, 1986).

24. Anatol Rapoport and Albert M. Chamman, *Prisoner's Dilemma: A Study in Conflict and Cooperation* (Ann Arbor, Mich.: University of Michigan Press, 1964); A. Rapoport, ed., *Game Theory as a Theory of Conflict Resolution* (Dordrecht: D. Reidel, 1974). Mathew Edel uses these results to explain how working-class actions can be individually rational in "A Note on Collective Action, Maximization and the Prisoner's Dilemma," *Journal of Economic Issues* 13 (1979).

25. Rosa Luxemburg, *The Mass Strike* (London: Merlin Press 1925), 35.

26. Karl-Dieter Opp, *The Rationality of Political Protest*, (Boulder, Colo.: Westview Press, 1989).

27. See Frederic Schick, *Having Reasons: An Essay on Rationality and Sociality* (Princeton: Princeton University Press, 1984), 115. Though his language and concerns are somewhat different from mine, his precise analytic account of these matters is very useful.

28. On the importance of this factor, see Barrington Moore Jr., *Injustice—The Social Bases of Obedience and Revolt* (White Plains, N.Y.: M. E. Sharpe, 1978), especially chap. 14. One might question how someone could say that they wanted it if they did not know they wanted it, but their response when they judge it to be at hand shows that they had wanted it all along. See Richard Brandt and Jaegwon Kim, "Wants as Explanations of Actions," *Journal of Philosophy* 60 (1969).

29. The positions I have defended in this chapter are social and in the broadest sense of the term "communitarian." However, they are different in important ways from the more specific perspective known as communitarianism, which feminists have pointed out is uncritical of oppressive relations within traditional communities. See Alasdair MacIntyre, *After Virtue: A Study in Moral Theory* (Notre Dame, Ind.: University of Notre Dame Press, 1981); Michael Walzer, *Spheres of Justice* (New York: Basic Books, 1983). For criticism see Nancy Holmstrom and Johanna Brenner, "Autonomy, Community, Women's Rights," in *The Year Led*, ed. Mike Davis, Fred Pfeil, and Michael Sprinker (London: Verso, 1985), Susan Molter Okin, *Justice. Gender and the Family* (New York: Basic Books, 1989).

30. *Social Facts* (London and New York: Routledge, 1989); *Living Together* (Lanham, Md.: Rowman and Littlefield, 1996).

31. Boulder, Colo.: Westview Press, 1995.

32. See Diana T. Meyers, ed., *Feminists Rethink the Self*, Boulder, Colo.: Westview Press, 1997.

33. See Christine Di Stefano, "Autonomy in the Light of Difference," in *Revisioning the Political: Feminist Reconstructions of Traditional Concepts in Western Political Theory*, Nancy J. Hirschmann and Christine Di Stefano, eds., Boulder, Colo.: Westview Press, 1996.

34. See, for example, Virginia Held's "Feminist Transformations of Moral Theory," in *Philosophy and Phenomenological Research* 1, supplement (fall 1990): 32144.

35. Aristotle rejected other features of the IUM account of rationality as well. See Martha Nussbaum, *Love's Knowledge: Essays on Philosophy and Literature* (New York: Oxford University

Press, 1990). Marx's views on these matters are similar to Aristotle's. See my "Rationality and Revolution" (1983).

36. See Norman Geras, *Solidarity in the Conversation of Mankind: The Ungroundable Liberalism of Richard Rorty* (New York: Verso, 1995).

37. The phrase "survival strategies" and a nice discussion of particular cases comes from Johanna Brenner, "On Gender and Class in U.S. Labor History," *Monthly Review* 50, No. 6 (November 1998): 1–15.

38. "The Unfinished Revolution," in *The Green-Left Weekly*, Sydney, Australia, 5 November 1997, cited in Colin Leys and Leo Panitch, "The Political Legacy of the Manifesto," in *The Communist Manifesto Now. The Socialist Register 1998*, Colin Leys and Leo Panitch, eds., New York: Monthly Review, 1998.

39. See Amartya Sen, *Collective Choice and Social Welfare* (San Francisco: Holden-Day, 1970), 195.

40. These specific terms are used by Anthony Jasay in *Social Contract. Free Ride* (Oxford: Oxford University, 1989) but the ideas conveyed by the terms follow from the IUM account of rationality. Jasay tries to argue that there is no inevitable public goods problem because enough people might contribute voluntarily to supply the public good. But his terms hardly make this likely.

41. David Reisman, *Theories of Collective Action: Downs. Olson and Hirsch*, (New York: St. Martin's Press, Inc., 1990), 10.

42. Aristotle, *Nicomachean Ethics*, trans. Terence Irwin. (Indianapolis: Hackett, 1985). For an important contemporary criticism, see Charles Taylor, "The Diversity of Goods," in *Philosophy and the Human Sciences*, 230–247 (Cambridge: Cambridge University Press, 1985).

43. Charles Taylor, "Irreducibly Social Goods," in *Philosophical Arguments* (Cambridge: Harvard University Press, 1995).

44. Robert Paul Wolff, *The Poverty of Liberalism* (Boston: Harvard University Press, 1968).

45. The experience of productive community may be the explanation for the otherwise very puzzling fact that some men report that their wartime experiences were a high point in their lives.

46. This is not to say, of course, that the action meets other tests of rationality. The same goods can come from collective action aimed at ends perceived to be public goods that are in fact evils, for example, joining the Nazi Party. Sidney Morgenbesser pressed this point on me when I presented the paper to the Columbia University Seminar on the Political Economy of War and Peace.

47. I state the point this way because the individual may or may not be part of the collective.

48. See Steven Lukes, *Individualism* (Oxford: Basil Blackwell, 1973); Andrew Levine, Elliott Sober, and Erik Olin Wright, "Marxism and Methodological Individualism," in *New Left Review* 162 (March/April 1987): 67–84, for critical discussion.

49. Karl Marx, *The Grundrisse* (Harmondsworth, Middlesex, England: Penguin, 1973), 83.

50. Mary Gibson argues that the basic institutions of capitalist society hinder the development and exercise of rationality even in the IUM sense by fostering inherently conflicting desires so that it is impossible to carry out a rational life plan, obstruct much of the knowledge necessary for such a plan, and often make it very difficult to successfully satisfy one's ends by requiring conflicting actions. The free rider conflict is an example of this. See "Rationality," *Philosophy and Public Affairs* 6 (1976–1977).

51. A fascinating article illustrating this point is Robert H. Frank, Thomas Gilovich, and Dennis T. Regan, "Does Studying Economics Inhibit Cooperation?" in *Journal of Economic Perspectives* 7, No. 2 (spring 1993): 159–171; reprinted in *Economics, Ethics and Public Policy*, Charles K. Wilber, ed. (Lanham, Md.: Rowman and Littlefield, 1998): 51–64.

52. A particularly powerful and accessible critique of this ideology is Noam Chomsky, *Profit Over People: Neoliberalism and Global Order* (New York: Seven Sisters Press, 1999).

A Genuine
Critical Internationalism

Pierre Bourdieu

Although globalization is above all a justificatory myth, there is one case where it is quite real, that of the financial markets. Thanks to the removal of a number of legal restrictions and the development of electronic communications that lead to lower communication costs, we are moving toward a unified financial market—which does not mean a homogeneous market. It is dominated by certain economies, in other words the richest countries, and more especially by the country whose currency is used as an international reserve currency and which therefore enjoys a greater scope within these financial markets. The money market is a field in which the dominant player—in this case the United States—occupies a position such that they can largely define the rules of the game. This unification of the financial markets around a small number of countries holding the dominant position reduces the autonomy of the national financial markets. The French financiers, the inspectors of finances, who tell us that we must bow to necessity, forget to tell us that they make themselves the accomplices of that necessity and that, through them, it is the French national state that is abdicating.

In short, globalization is not homogenization; on the contrary, it is the extension of the hold of a small number of dominant nations over the whole set of national financial markets. There follows from this a partial redefinition of the international division of labor, with European workers suffering the consequences, seeing for example the transfer of capital and industries toward low-wage countries. This international capital market tends to reduce the autonomy of the national capital markets, and in particular to prevent nation-states from manipulating exchange rates and interest rates, which are increasingly determined by a power concentrated in the hands of a small number of countries. National authorities are subject to the risk of speculative assaults by agents wielding massive funds, who

(continues)

(continued)

can provoke a devaluation, with left-wing governments naturally being particularly threatened because they arouse the suspicion of the financial markets (a right-wing government that acts out of line with the ideals of the International Monetary Fund (IMF) is in less danger than a left-wing government even if the latter's policy matches the ideals of the IMF). It is the structure of the worldwide field that exerts a structural constraint, and this is what gives the mechanisms an air of inevitability. The policy of a particular state is largely determined by its position in the structure of the distribution of finance capital (which defines the structure of the world economic field).

Faced with these mechanisms, what can one do? The first thing is to reflect on the implicit limits that economic theory accepts. Economic theory, when it assesses the costs of a policy, does not take account of what are called social costs. For example, a housing policy, the one chosen by Giscard d'Estaing when he was finance minister in 1970, implied long-term social costs that do not appear as such: Twenty years later, who, apart from sociologists, remembers that measure? Who would link a riot in a suburb of Lyon to a political decision of 1970? Crimes go unpunished because people forget. All the critical forces in society need to insist on the inclusion of the social costs of economic decisions in economic calculations. What will this or that policy cost in the long term in lost jobs, suffering, sickness, suicide, alcoholism, drug addiction, domestic violence, and so forth, all things that cost a great deal in money, but also in misery? I think that, even if it may appear very cynical, we need to turn its own weapons against the dominant economy, and point out that, in the logic of enlightened self-interest, a strictly economic policy is not necessarily economical—in terms of the insecurity of persons and property, the consequent policing costs, and so on. More precisely, there is a need to radically question the economic view that individualizes everything—production as much as justice or health, costs as well as profits—and forgets that efficiency, which it defines in narrow, abstract terms, tacitly identifying it with financial profitability, clearly depends on the outcomes by which it is measured, financial profitability for shareholders and investors, as at present, or satisfaction of customers and users, and, more generally, satisfac-

(continues)

tion and well-being of producers, consumers, and, ultimately, the largest possible number. Against this narrow, short-term economics, we need to put forward an economics of happiness that would take note of all the profits, individual and collective, material and symbolic, associated with activity (such as security), and also all the material and symbolic costs associated with inactivity or precarious employment (for example, consumption of medicines: France holds the world record for use of tranquilizers). You cannot cheat with the law of the conservation of violence: all violence is paid for, and, for example, the structural violence exerted by the financial markets, in the form of layoffs, loss of security, and so on, is matched sooner or later in the form of suicides, crime and delinquency, drug addiction, alcoholism, a whole host of minor and major everyday acts of violence.

At the present time, the critical efforts of intellectuals, trade unions, or associations should be applied as a matter of priority against the withering away of the state. The national states are undermined from outside by these financial forces, and they are undermined from inside by those who act as the accomplices of these financial forces, in other words, the financiers, bankers, and finance ministry officials. I think that the dominated groups in society have an interest in defending the state, particularly in its social aspect. This defense of the state is not inspired by nationalism. Although one can fight against the national state, one has to defend the "universal" functions it fulfills, which can be fulfilled as well, or better, by a supranational state. If we do not want it to be the Bundesbank, which, through interest rates, governs the financial policies of the various states, should we not fight for the creation of a supranational state, relatively autonomous with respect to international political forces and national political forces and capable of developing the social dimension of the European institutions? For example, measures aimed at reducing the working week would take on their full meaning only if they were taken by a European body and were applicable to all the European nations.

Historically, the state has been a force for rationalization, but one that has been put at the service of the dominant forces. To prevent this being the case, it is not sufficient to denounce the technocrats of

(continues)

(continued)

Brussels. We need to develop a new internationalism, at least at the regional level of Europe, which could offer an alternative to the regression into nationalism that, as a result of the crisis, threatens all the European countries to some degree. This would imply constructing institutions that are capable of standing up to these forces of the financial market, and introducing—the Germans have a wonderful word for this—a Regressionsverbot, a ban on backward movement with respect to social gains at the European level. To achieve this, it is absolutely essential that the trade unions operate at this European level, because that is where the forces they are fighting against are in action. It is therefore necessary to try to create the organizational bases for a genuine critical internationalism capable of really combating neoliberalism.

(SOURCE: Acts of Resistance, The New Press)

PART TWO

Equality and Justice

4

Women, Care, and the Public Good: A Dialogue

Ann Ferguson and Nancy Folbre

In their aim to highlight taken-for-granted aspects of women's lives, a number of feminist philosophers have argued that traditional approaches to ethics and economics have largely ignored provision for people's personal and emotional needs. Cross-culturally, the sexual division of labor in housework and wage work has assigned women greater responsibility than men for the direct care for children, the elderly, and other adults. This generalization holds even though the other content of women's and men's work has varied enormously in different modes of economic production and different societies.

Women's largely unpaid provision of caring labor is key to the survival of infants, the sick, and the elderly—as well as to the daily maintenance of adult workers. It is indispensable to society as a whole. For this reason we are intuitively attracted to the notion that the care of children and other dependents, and, indeed, care for people in general, is a public good and deserves public support. But as we explore this notion, we find ourselves stumbling over a big conceptual issue that neither philosophers nor economists (much less the two combined) agree on: What exactly are public goods? This conceptual issue may seem rather abstract, but it bears directly on concrete policy concerns such as the kind of support we should provide for the care of children, the elderly, and other dependents.

We offer our thoughts on this issue in the form of an interdisciplinary dialogue. In the first section, Nancy outlines a feminist economist's approach to care as a public good, and responds to Ann's comments and criticisms. In the second section, we reverse roles. Ann outlines a feminist philosopher's approach, and Nancy offers comments and criticisms. We both suggest ways that economists and philosophers could more systematically analyze the gendering (and de-gendering!) of human capabilities for care provision, and we close with a list of specific questions for further deliberation.

Economics and Public Goods

Nancy: In economics today, there is no well-developed concept of *the* public good that makes much sense in ethical or philosophical terms. There is simply a presumption that we all benefit by expanding the range of choices, and therefore, more is better. How do we measure "more"? We tend to revert to comparisons of the growth of gross domestic product, despite widespread recognition that it is not a good measure of human welfare.

Economists do, however, have a concept of public goods, which are technically defined as goods that are nonexcludable in consumption. In other words, some people can consume them without paying the price. It follows that prices are not a good means of allocating them. If you can't rely on prices, you can't rely on markets. Hence, a public good is something that must be produced by a nonmarket institution. Usually it is assumed that the community or the state is the relevant institution for producing public goods, and the examples usually given are bridges, highways, national defense, and education.

In my research to date on care I have focused rather narrowly on this economic concept of public goods, arguing that care tends to be undervalued and underproduced in the market economy (Folbre 1994a, 1994b, 1995a, 1997; Folbre and Weisskopf 1998; England and Folbre 1999a, 1999b). My coauthors and I argue that the weakening of patriarchal control over women generally may reduce both the quantity and quality of care supplied unless it is combined with generous and carefully designed public support for care provision. Patriarchal control generally forces women to specialize in care provision by limiting all economic opportunities that might compete with traditional family responsibilities. This provides a cheap supply of caring labor, because women generally lack the bargaining power required to demand greater remuneration and therefore are forced to simply accept whatever they get.

Capitalist development tends to destabilize traditional patriarchal families, opening up new opportunities for young women outside the home. The cost of care tends to increase (which is one reason why fertility tends to decline). The economic history of Europe and the United States reveals a process of capitalist development that pressures societies to redesign the organization of care. Welfare state policies are heavily influenced by economic inequalities based on nation, race, class, and age, as well as gender. But they do provide at least some public support for care, which is more than can be said for the capitalist marketplace.

Ann: Is this really happening? What do you have in mind? Welfare state services are being cut. Perhaps some families are reorganizing child and elder care, but I would argue that most of the reorganization, of necessity, still assigns the bulk of care provision to women rather than men. Indeed, the so-called transition from the laissez-faire state to the welfare state has really been a transition from private patriarchy, where men as heads of families controlled women's caring labor, to public patriarchy, where there still is an unequal gender division of labor but now it is controlled by male politicians and functionaries of the welfare state. For example, whether women receive maternity and family leave, affordable child care, and welfare benefits in the new situation where half the mothers are working in wage labor depends on the vagaries of public policy as enacted by male politicians (Hartman 1981; Brown 1981; Ferguson and Folbre 1981; Ferguson 1991).

Nancy: I'm not disagreeing with this point. I'm emphasizing the longer term. Despite a tremendous political and ideological assault on the very concept of the welfare state, it has not been reversed, merely modified. Even in the United States, the total percentage of government spending devoted to what might be broadly termed social welfare remains relatively high. And public patriarchy, however strong, is being contested by women whose political opinions differ sharply from those of men when it comes to social spending issues. Feminist theory can and should inform a major redesign of the welfare state.

We need to rethink the relationship between the family, the market, and the state, and to address a number of specific political problems. The welfare state is prone to bureaucratic inefficiencies and to capture by powerful interest groups.

Ann: Also, it is weakened by international capital mobility that allows investors to move out of countries with high wages and benefits and taxes and thereby reduce their share of the costs of creating a healthy and highly skilled workforce

Nancy: So, if we believe that the state should play an important role in supporting care for other people, then we need to do some serious thinking about how state support should be organized. I think this will require international democratic governance.

Ann: I assume you mean by this that there will have to be restrictions, in the form of taxes or ownership limitations, that keep multinational corporations from moving their operations without due compensation to the workforce that contributed to their profits. But before we go any further I want to focus on your definition of *a* public good (as opposed to *the* public good). The economistic definition that you gave does not account for valuable goods that are not produced or paid for by anyone yet meet individual and collective human needs. The air, the sea, and other aspects of our environment are valuable in the sense that they meet the needs of individuals, but individuals cannot easily own them. In fact, we should distinguish between goods that are produced by individuals in the market, goods produced by individuals but not in the market, and goods that are produced by nonmarket institutions. Although caring as a relationship produced by the work of individuals may not be a public good, the existence of more caring relations between individuals is a public good that is "produced" in some sense by many nonmarket institutions, such as the family and democratic culture, yet much of it is not paid for directly.[1]

Nancy: Good point. I should supplement the concept of care as a public good with the notion that some aspects of care may represent a "common property resource" that resembles natural resources that are not explicitly "produced." That is, people provide care for instrinsic or natural reasons, and not in response to some extrinsic incentive. Economists generally agree that since it is difficult to price these goods, there is a tendency to overexploit them—the so-called tragedy of the commons that must be addressed by establishing collective governance. If we set up an economy in which "nice guys and gals finish last" we end up with an economy in which nice guys and gals are exploited to extinction. Our economic system tends to waste natural human capabilities for care and love in much the same way that we waste free goods like air and water. Therefore, we can't continue simply to rely on the "natural" provision of care—we need to engage in specific forms of collective action aimed to protect, enhance, and expand it. I think we can describe the widespread lack of concern for individuals unjustly afflicted with poverty as a form of social pollution.

Ann: Nice metaphor, but it still seems to me that your definition of a public good rests on a contrast with private goods, which are commodities that can only be consumed by the individuals who own them. It also implicitly assumes that private goods are those that specific individuals have a right to, and hence those the state has an obligation to protect for individuals. This definition is based on a classical liberal understanding of rights as the basis of social values. Since rights are properties of individual persons, it is unclear on this definition of public good how governments, which are supposed to promote and defend the rights of their individual constituents, are justified in protecting and advancing public goods when doing so interferes with the rights of individuals.

Nancy: Yes, you're right. Economists don't usually think about the ethical principles that governments are supposed to follow. We (even we feminist economists) tend to think in terms of efficiency. So my argument is not that we have a moral or ethical obligation to provide public support for care, but that it is inefficient for us not to do so. The analogy with environmentalism works well here: in the short run an individual firm may benefit from polluting the environment. In the long run, however, pollution undermines the long-run sustainability of the economy and the ecosystem as a whole. "Fly-by-night" firms will still have an incentive to pollute, but capitalists as a class are eventually hurt if they soil their own nest. So the economic argument is kind of an appeal to long-run rather than short-run economic interests. Obviously, it is still very much based on economic interests, rather than political or moral principles.

Ann: I think you are relying too much on Rational Economic Man here. This model only works to explain human behavior in competitive economic situations. Even economists (including you, in your 1994 book *Who Pays for the Kids*) acknowledge that it really doesn't explain the altruistic behavior encountered in the family, or in economic cooperatives. In any case, you are making too sharp a distinction between economics and philosophy. As you know, all economic assumptions are dependent on prior philosophical paradigms. For example, the conservative argument that privatization increases efficiency in achieving the desired goals is itself based on the classical liberal assumption that allowing individuals to compete in their own self-interest in open markets will promote the general happiness. This is a utilitarian claim that is at once philosophical and empirical: general happiness is what should be promoted, and open markets will do a better job than planned public economic control.

Nancy: Let me separate out the two claims you make above. The conservative argument that privatization increases efficiency is an empirical one that progressive economists like myself need to address. It's not enough to just harp on distributional issues—the key argument that conservatives make is that it's better to have a small share of a big and growing pie than a big share of a small and shrinking one. My own thinking on this issue has changed considerably over the last fifteen years. Partly because I have a greater appreciation of the problems of centralized, bureaucratic forms of social organization, I am more optimistic about the potential role of markets than I used to be. If we distributed resources more equitably and provided a really good social safety net, markets could be a very good way of organizing some forms of production.

I am more concerned than market socialists like John Roemer (1994) about forms of production that involve public goods and common property resources, and cannot be efficiently organized on a market basis (Folbre, 1995b). In particular, the work that goes into producing people—health, education, and welfare— should not be privatized, because we cannot (and should not) put a price on the "output" of human capabilities. Roemer doesn't directly confront this issue, which is more central to the social democratic than to the Marxian tradition. But social democrats seem to have lost much of their conviction about it. Perhaps part of the problem is that the provision of public services like health, education, and welfare has suffered from bureaucratization. We need to go beyond the notion that we can measure "care" in terms of the amount of money we spend on various programs, or distribute to various groups, and focus more on the actual labor process of providing care both inside and outside the family.

Your more basic philosophical argument, that I'm implicitly relying on an efficiency-based approach based on utilitarian principles is exactly right. I confess! But what is the alternative?

Ann: I would begin with the claim that any broad concept of the public good must point out that economic arguments from efficiency fail to distinguish between promoting the good of the majority and promoting the good of all. Thus, marginalized populations, such as immigrants, the poor, people of color, and women may be worse off under a privatized public policy than under a social democratic welfare state. Indeed, if the only measure of increased efficiency is increased gross national product (GNP), then even the majority can be worse off if the rise is accompanied by an unequal distribution that makes the majority worse off.[2]

The broader conception of public good advocated by social democrats would include goods that meet the needs of the individuals in a society in a way better handled by a proactive program of the state than by private efforts. But part of this conception would have to include specifically the claims of justice and equality. At any rate, according to feminist social democrats, public goods are those that can only be distributed equitably and fairly to all, both majorities and minorities, by public programs rather than by private efforts.

Social democrats have argued that education of children, health care, and protection of the environment, though all conceivably could be achieved through individual efforts, such as private schools, individual health insurance plans, or donations by the wealthy to create national parks and clean up the environment, are better promoted by collective, hence state, action in the form of public schools, public health insurance, and laws protecting the environment.

You point out that the conservative critique of such arguments has some plausibility, given the historical inefficiencies of state planning and state welfare programs. But what conservatives neglect in their defense of privatization schemes is the persistent failure of such schemes to promote the well-being of minorities. For example, the persistence of a much greater percentage of people of color than their numbers in the overall population would warrant among those of low income in the inner cities, in sweatshops, as day farm laborers, and among the unemployed and on welfare shows the historical persistence of what Charles Mills calls the "racial contract" of white supremacy in this country (Mills 1997). Racial inequalities have not been mitigated by privatization. If we are concerned with justice as well as efficiency, I think we arrive at a different vision.

Nancy: I agree with you. It's not that I don't see the weaknesses of an efficiency-based approach. But sometimes it seems to me that every other philosophical approach has similar weaknesses, so I might as well just choose the assumption that makes it easiest for me to argue with other economists. How's that for economistic reasoning! Seriously, I think I really need help in moving beyond what I would call an efficiency-based argument about care as a public good. So you tell me how you think feminist philosophy can move us forward.

Philosophy and the Public Good

Ann: The labor of loving care for others, traditionally provided by women in the sexual division of unpaid labor in the family as well as in public service wage labor, ought to be classified as a public good because it is intrinsically valuable. We can define a public good as one that is tied to a fundamental agreement on which the society rests. Milton Fisk (1996) develops this argument in an article on health care as a public good. There are some goals that are valued by individuals as goals to be achieved not just for themselves, but for all others in the society.

Fisk claims that for something to be a public good rather than a private good, it must be a common good that ought to be provided collectively rather than by private efforts. To demonstrate this claim, we need to provide an empirical argument that not producing the good collectively (for example, by the government or by other means) will create more harm to individuals and possibly serious economic burdens than providing it collectively would.

There may seem to be a problem in using Fisk's concept of a public good to argue that caring work is a public good. His condition for a common good, hence one that could be a candidate for a public good, is that there needs to be an actual consensus that such values are desirable for all and are fundamental to the existence of public life as such. But would individuals in our society agree that receiving supportive and loving care is such a common good? Neither Hobbes nor Locke, the founding fathers of our democratic capitalist notion of the social contract, would have included the provision of loving care as necessary for public life. Rather this is assumed to be an optional perquisite of a private life where individuals make their own familial and love arrangements.

Cultures vary in the degree of destructive competition or solidarity that individuals in the society feel is acceptable. Our culture in the United States is particularly destructive in its competitive aspects, perhaps because of its excessive individualism and our history of imperialism, slavery, and union-busting owing to the heterogeneity of immigrant, slave, and indigenous populations. Thus, we can't rely on an actual consensus for maintaining a certain level of care provision as the deciding factor for whether it is a common good. We can argue, for example, that society ideally ought to accept health care as both a common and a public good, hence we ought to set up a nationally supported health care system. But unless we alter the conditions that keep people from feeling compassion with each other—for example, racism/ethnicism and the puritan ethic that the poor are undeserving—the majority of people won't be motivated to accept either health care or giving and receiving care as public goods.

I propose to argue for care as a public good along similar lines as does Fisk when he argues that the broad consensus that our society should be healthy can be used to try to argue for public health care as a means toward that end. We do not now have a consensus that care provision is a common good. But we do have a broad consensus as humans in promoting human functioning, not only of ourselves but at least some other loved individuals. If we can show that guaranteed public care provision (including government support for private care provision), rather than leaving private care up to the vagaries of individual resources, will better promote what most Americans find desirable human capabilities for themselves and their loved ones, then we can claim that caring should be a public good and not just a private one.

We can base this line of argument along the lines of Amartya Sen (1987), Martha Nussbaum (1993) and Nussbaum and Sen (1993) who argue that we ought to base the notion of common goods on what is necessary to promote human functionings and capabilities. This distinctively Aristotelian approach emphasizes the importance of providing a common public life as a means to allow individuals to achieve a sense of respect for others in the community, as well as goods such as freedom, democracy, and the rule of law.

To argue that maximizing the provision of loving care to all in society is a common good from this characterization requires one to make plausible the idea that receiving and learning how to give loving care is a distinctive human capability, not only for its own sake, but as a means to developing other capacities acknowledged as important, such as autonomy, the ability to make critical decisions, and the respect for others necessary for a democratic order. Empirical studies on early childhood development lend support to the claim that the lack of such care creates sociopathic individuals and is hence a public cost.

I want to take the valuing human capabilities approach, and to argue that receiving and giving care are important capabilities necessary for the provision of common goods. For example, though learning to think critically is a human capability, not everyone agrees that it is important to educate children to think critically. Those who have not been taught to value critical thinking don't usually feel either a need or a right to learn such a skill. But if we can mount a successful argument that individual freedom, something that is agreed to be a common good, requires the skill of critical thinking to be defended or exercised, then individuals could be persuaded that public school education in critical thinking is instrumentally necessary.

Is there a plausible analogous argument that can be made for defining the provision of adequate loving care to all as a public good? One line of argument could be to demonstrate the connection of such care provision to a society that develops more of a compassionate character in the bulk of its citizens and to argue that compassion connects to solidarity or fraternity. A society that raises citizens who care about their neighbors will be more likely to promote the acknowledged common good of public security of life in a more peaceful and less violent context.

Several feminist advocates of an "ethics of care" approach to public policy, that is, one that rejects narrow "ethics of justice" approaches that only guarantee values thought to be individual rights, would agree with this line of thought. Both Joan Tronto (1993) and Sara Ruddick (1989) use insights from Carol Gilligan's (1982) work to argue that a reorganization of caring labor would benefit both women and men. Such an approach would not supplant an ethics of justice, since we need to defend women's rights to a more reciprocal division of labor (Okin 1989; Delphy 1984; Ferguson 1991), but would allow us to discuss social ends and values that an ethics based on distributive justice doesn't address.

I would defend the idea of adopting the provision of loving care as a common good on the grounds that it will foster the kind of solidarity among members of society that will make the majority of people's lives better. I'm not arguing that individuals should be ordered by the central state apparatus to develop their abilities to provide care; rather, I am arguing that the rampant individualism of our society and the growing lack of compassion for the poor, particularly for single mothers who are care providers, will have effects that will make everyone's lives less secure (with increased crime) and less happy (with less care being provided to many). Hopefully if people are provided some evidence that this is true they will come through democratic means to prefer public policies that define care as a public good. The public debate could then be focused on means to achieve this good, for example, greater *emphasis* on training in care provision in public schools for boys and girls.

Nancy: I completely agree that caregiving is an important human capability. But what does "valuing human capabilities" mean? It implies that all human capabilities are good ones, and that more is better (sounds like GDP in this respect!). Obviously, the provision of care is indispensable to human society. But it is easier to agree with this general proposition than to argue that we need to put more emphasis and devote more resources to care. It seems to me that conservatives will argue two related points: we already provide enough public support for care, and if we provide more we will undermine private provision. And by the way, didn't you just make a utilitarian-consequentialist argument, that your proposal will "make the majority of people's lives better"?

Ann: I agree that we can't assume that developing all human capabilities is desirable, since human nature is capable of monstrous as well as wonderful things.

What I should have said is that we should try to maximize the opportunity for as many people as possible to develop those capabilities we agree are public goods. This means that each particular capability on our list has to be defended on both philosophical and empirical grounds as intrinsically valuable, and, if relevant, effective in promoting some other public goods already accepted as desirable. For the latter task (showing the social effectiveness of developing certain human capabilities) we can invoke utilitarian or consequentialist arguments without completely relying on them. I'm trying to make a case for the intrinsic importance of public provision of care, which we could then reinforce with specifics about how it should be organized.

Feminist theory can help us explain why care has historically been undervalued in patriarchal societies. Perhaps because of the general overvaluing of human skills and traits thought of as masculine, such as war-making, the human values involved in the skills of caring for and nurturing others, skills connected to women's work, have not been thought of as either rights or needs (Holliday 1978; Ruddick 1989). The sexual division of labor in which women do most of the caring labor is not thought of as unjust. In other places, you and I and others have argued that this common perception is mistaken on equity grounds, that is, that women's caring labor ends up being exploited by men, as well as by women who do not provide care but purchase it. (Ferguson 1991; Folbre 1994a; Delphy 1984; Okin 1989). What the feminist exploitation argument based on considerations of justice tends to ignore is that there are also some intrinsic costs to the exploiters in this arrangement: In such an unbalanced sexual division of labor, men don't get a chance to maximize their human capabilities of caring for others, and women are denied their abilities to be as independent as men. Indeed, empirical studies of dual wage-earning families who share child care provides evidence that many fathers providing care in these arrangements feel they have gained not only valuable skills but much greater intimacy with their children, and value this as an intrinsic good (Deutsch 1999).

Nancy: This raises another problem about capabilities—they may conflict with one another. For instance, capabilities for leadership may be achieved at the expense of capabilities for nurturance, which is exactly why different groups of people, such as men and women, often develop different sets of capabilities. I like the emphasis on capabilities as an end in themselves. But you are going beyond the simple prescription that we maximize human capabilities (which is problematic enough!) to a specific argument about the composition of capabilities. Specifically, you are proposing an androgynous solution: Men and women should develop equal capabilities for care.

I agree with this proposition. The economic rationale I offer is based on the characteristics of care as a public good: If care isn't shared, it will be underproduced, because the persons providing care will eventually respond to the fact that others are free riding on their efforts and will reduce their provision of care. This is related to your philosophical rationale that the current division of caring labor is unjust (which I agree with). Plus, you are emphasizing that capabilities for care are intrinsically valuable.

But I don't think either of us has answered some really difficult questions about the social provision of care or the social development of capabilities for care.

Ann: I don't care! Just kidding. You're right. Let's make a list of questions without being inhibited by the difficulty of answering them.

Questions About Care
and the Public Good

Contemporary Western capitalist societies assume a split between the public market values of self-interest and competition and the private family values of caring and sharing. We have argued that this public/private distinction ignores the possibility that caring and sharing are not just private family values but are public goods. Since masculinity and men are symbolically associated with self-interest and the public sphere, and femininity and women with altruism, care, and the private sphere, how do we find a way to revalue care so that it is not merely seen as a private, feminine value? As Judith Williamson writes, "Women, the guardians of 'personal life,' become a kind of dumping ground for all the values society wants off its back but must be perceived to cherish; a function rather like a zoo, or nature reserve, whereby a culture can proudly proclaim its inclusion of precisely what it has excluded" (1994:388). None of our utopian ideas for how to develop caring capabilities in both men and women will be realizable if we can't figure out a way to challenge the present ideological distinction between public goods (associated with the masculine) and private goods (associated with the feminine).

More specifically,

1. If we agree that men and women should develop equal capabilities for care, what should the level of this capability be? Equality could be achieved in a number of different ways: women could become more like men have been historically. Men could become more like women have been historically. Or, we could reject historical levels and aim for a higher—or lower—level of caring capabilities on the part of both. It seems like we would both prefer a solution that increases the overall supply of care, but how do we make a case for this?

2. What other capabilities do we need to balance with care? Feminist theory teaches us the value of autonomy as well as connectedness (Bartky 1990; Benjamin 1988; Ferguson 1991). We know that it is sometimes dangerous to care too much, as well as to care too little. How do we go beyond the notion of expanding human capabilities to a more specific vision of the larger set of capabilities we want to foster?

3. How do we develop caring capabilities? We would like to think that education could help achieve this. There is evidence that requiring young people to take more responsibility for providing care for others helps them develop the

norms, preferences, and skills of caring and eliminates differences between boys and girls in propensities to aggression (cf. Holmstrom, 1981). But because good quality care relies to a large extent on intrinsic motives, imposing requirements could backfire and simply create resistance.

4. What is the best way to reward caring labor? We both agree that care is currently penalized in both the family and the market. Yet we don't want to reduce this argument to a simple demand for "higher wages" for care, because we don't think care can be easily "priced." How do we honor and reward care without letting extrinsic rewards undermine intrinsic ones?

References

Bartky, Sandra. 1990. *Femininity and Domination*. New York: Routledge.

Benjamin, Jessica. 1988. *The Bonds of Love: Psychoanalysis, Feminism and the Problem of Domination*. New York: Pantheon.

Brown, Carol. 1981. "Mothers, Fathers, and Children: From Private to Public Patriarchy." In *Women and Revolution*, ed. Lydia Sargent, 239–268. Boston: Southend Press.

Delphy, Christine. 1984. *Close to Home: A Material Analysis of Women's Oppression*. Amherst, Mass.: University of Massachusetts Press.

Deutsch, Francine M. 1999. *Halving It All: How Equally Shared Parenting Works*. Cambridge, Mass.: Harvard University Press.

England, Paula, and Nancy Folbre. 1999a. "The Cost of Caring," *Annals of the American Academy of Political and Social Science*, forthcoming.

_____. 1999b. "Who Should Pay for the Kids?" *Annals of the American Academy of Political and Social Science*, forthcoming.

Ferguson, Ann, and Nancy Folbre. 1981. "The Unhappy Marriage of Capitalism and Patriarchy." In *Women and Revolution*, ed. Lydia Sargent, 313–338. Boston: South End Press.

Ferguson, Ann. 1991. *Sexual Democracy: Women, Oppression and Revolution*. Boulder, Colo.: Westview Press.

Fisk, Milton. 1996. "Health Care as a Public Good," *Journal of Social Philosophy* 27:3 (winter 1996), 14–40.

Folbre, Nancy. 1994a. *Who Pays for the Kids? Gender and the Structures of Constraint*. New York: Routledge.

_____. 1994b. "Children as Public Goods," *American Economic Review* 84:2, 86–90.

_____. 1995a. "Holding Hands at Midnight: The Paradox of Caring Labor," *Feminist Economics* 1:1, 73–92.

_____. 1995b. "Roemer's Market Socialism: A Feminist Critique," *Politics and Society* 22:4, 595–606.

_____. 1997. "The Future of the Elephant Bird," *Population and Development Review* 23:3 (September), 647–654.

Folbre, Nancy, and Thomas Weisskopf. 1998. "Did Father Know Best? Families, Markets and the Supply of Caring Labor." In *Economics, Values and Organization*, ed. Avner Ben-Ner and Louis Putterman, 171–205. Cambridge: Cambridge University Press.

Gilligan, Carol. 1982. *In a Different Voice: Psychological Theory and Women's Development*. Cambridge: Harvard University Press.

Hartmann, Heidi. 1981. "The Unhappy Marriage of Marxism and Feminism." In *Women and Revolution,* ed. Lydia Sargent, 1–42, 1981.

Holliday, Laurel. 1978. *The Violent Sex: Male Psychobiology and the Evolution of Consciousness.* Guerneville, Calif.: Bluestocking Press.

Holmstrom, Nancy. 1981. "Do Women Have a Distinct Nature?" *Philosophical Forum* 64, No. 1, 25–42.

Mills, Charles W. 1997. *The Racial Contract.* Ithaca and London: Cornell University Press.

Nussbaum, Martha. 1993. "Non-Relative Virtues: An Aristotelian Approach." In *The Quality of Life,* ed. Martha Nussbaum and Amartya Sen, 242–269. Oxford: Oxford University and United Nations University.

Nussbaum, Martha, and Amartya Sen, eds. 1993. *The Quality of Life.* Oxford: Oxford University and United Nations University.

Okin, Susan Moller. 1989. *Justice, Gender and the Family.* New York: Basic Books.

Roemer, John. 1994. *A Future for Socialism.* Cambridge, Mass.: Harvard University Press.

Ruddick, Sara. 1989. *Maternal Thinking: Toward a Politics of Peace.* Boston: Beacon.

Sargent, Lydia, ed. 1981. *Women and Revolution.* Boston: South End Press.

Sen, Amartya. 1987. *The Standard of Living.* Cambridge: Cambridge University Press.

Tronto, Joan. 1993. *Moral Boundaries: A Political Argument for an Ethics of Care.* New York: Routledge.

Williamson, Judith. 1994. "Woman Is an Island: Femininity and Colonization." In *Theorizing Feminism: Parallel Trends in the Humanities and the Social Sciences,* ed. Anne C. Herrmann and Abigail J. Stewart, 382–391. Boulder, Colo.: Westview Press.

Notes

1. This points comes from Nancy Holmstrom.
2. Thanks again to Nancy Holmstrom.

5

Difference as a Resource for Democratic Communication

Iris Marion Young

Recently, certain liberal and New Left writers have charged the politics of difference with bringing democracy to a new crisis. By a "politics of difference" I mean social movements that make a political claim that groups suffer oppression or disadvantage on account of cultural or structural social positions with which they are associated. To combat dominant stereotypes that construct members of such groups as despised and devalued Others, these movements have expressed uniquely situated understandings of members of society as arising from their group position. The perspectives of privileged and powerful groups tend to dominate public discourse and policy, these movements have asserted, and continue to exclude and marginalize others even when law and public rhetoric state a commitment to equality. The only remedies for these disadvantages and exclusions, according to these movements, require attending to the specific situations of differentiated social groups in politics and policy.

According to the critics, such assertion of group specificity has issued in nothing but confrontation and separation, resulting in the evacuation of the public space of coalition and cooperation. In the words of Todd Gitlin, the politics of difference is "a very bad turn, a detour into quicksand,"[1] and we had better pull ourselves out and get back on the main road of general citizenship and the common good.

Critics such as Gitlin and Jean Elshtain interpret the politics of difference as identity politics. According to these critics, the politics of difference encourages people to give primary loyalty to identity groups rigidly opposed to one another, instead of committing themselves to a common polity that transcends the groups.

People claim a victim status for these identities, and thus claim special rights for themselves without accepting any parallel responsibilities. The politics of difference produces a backlash, when those who previously thought of themselves as just "People" go looking for their group identities and then claim their own special rights. A cacophony of particular claims for recognition and redress soon fills the public sphere, and in disgust people turn away from public exchange and discussion as a means for solving problems cooperatively. So says Jean Elshtain:

> To the extent that citizens begin to retribalize into ethnic or other "fixed identity" groups, democracy falters. Any possibility for human dialogue, for democratic communication and commonality, vanishes as so much froth on the polluted sea of phony equality. Difference becomes more and more exclusivist. If you are black and I am white, by definition I do not and cannot in principle "get it." There is no way that we can negotiate the space between our given differences. We are just stuck with them in what political theorists used to call "ascriptive characteristics"—things we cannot change about ourselves. Mired in the cement of our own identities, we need never deal with one another. Not really. One of us will win and one of us will lose the cultural war or the political struggle. That's what it's all about: power in the most reductive, impositional sort.[2]

Thus these critics also reduce the politics of difference to the most crass form of interest-group politics in which people simply compete to get the most for themselves. This interest-group politics precludes discussion and exchange where people revise their claims in response to criticism and aim to reach a solution acceptable to all. For the critics, the politics of difference understood as identity politics removes both the motivation and the capacity for citizens to talk to one another and solve problems together.

Doubtless feminists, multiculturalists, and activists for gay liberation, indigenous peoples, people of color, migrants, and people with disabilities have sometimes been overly separatist, essentialist, and inward looking in their promotion of group specificity and its political claims. Attributing such excesses to the movements as a whole or to the very logic of their existence, however, and laying in their lap responsibility for an alleged crisis of democracy, in my view, greatly misrepresents their meaning. Regression and repression are the likely outcomes of a political position that dismisses these movements as a gross error, and seeks a renewed commitment to a mythic neutral state, national unity, and the proposition that we are all just human, simply individuals, and that social, cultural, and economic differences among us should be ignored in politics.

In this chapter I argue against the identification of a politics of difference with a politics of identity. Group differentiation is best understood as a function of structural relations rather than constituted from some common attributes or dis-

positions of group members. A relational interpretation of difference conceives groups less rigidly and exclusively, as more open and fluid. Individuals are not positioned as social group members because they have common identities or interests, I argue, that distinguish them entirely from others. Instead, the social positioning of group differentiation gives to individuals some shared *perspectives* on social life.

The idea that social perspective arises from group differentiation, I argue, contrary to the critics, helps us think of difference as a necessary resource for a discussion-based politics in which participants aim to cooperate, reach understanding, and do justice. Aiming to do justice through democratic public processes, I suggest, entails at least two things. First, democratic discussion and decision making must include all social perspectives. Second, participants in the discussion must develop a more comprehensive and objective account of the social relations, consequences of action, and relative advantage and disadvantage, than each begins with from their partial social perspective. Neither of these conditions can occur without communication across group-differentiated perspectives. Properly understood, then, and under conditions of mutual commitment to public discussion that aims to solve collective problems, expression of and attention to social group differentiation is an important resource for democratic communication.

Dilemmas of Difference

Some critics of group-differentiated politics write as though racial, ethnic, class, or gender conflict would not exist if it were not for the corresponding movements. Such attitudes reverse the causal story. These movements have arisen in response to experiences of oppression and disadvantage that are attached to group designation. Racist and xenophobic language positions people in groups and subjects them to invidious stereotypes. Racist and xenophobic behavior discriminates against them, treats them with disdain, avoids them, and excludes them from benefits. Culturally imperialist policies or attitudes devalue or refuse to recognize the particular practices of some people, or subject them to unfair social disadvantages because of their particular practices. Sexist assumptions about male proprietary rights over women make us vulnerable to physical, sexual, and psychological abuse and often enough to unwanted pregnancy. So it goes with many other groups of people—poor people, who are treated as lazy and stupid, people with disabilities, whose needs are often ignored and lives stereotypically misrepresented.

People speak and act as though social groups are real; they treat others and themselves as though social group affinity is meaningful. Social group designation and experience is meaningful for the expectations we have of one another, the assumptions we make about one another, and the status we assign to ourselves and others. These social group designations have serious consequences for people's relative privilege or disadvantage. The politics of difference arose from a frustration with exhortations that everyone should just be thought of as a unique individual person, that group ascriptions are arbitrary and accidental, that liberal politics should transcend such petty affiliations and create a public world of equal citizenship where no particularist differences matter to the allocation of benefits and opportunities. Oppressed groups found that this humanist ideology resulted in ignoring rather than transcending the real material consequences of social group difference, often forcing some people to devalue their own particular cultural styles and forms of life because they did not fit the allegedly neutral mainstream. Thus movements affirming group difference called for attending to rather than ignoring the consequences of such difference for issues of freedom and equality. For many, such affirmation also entailed asserting group solidarity and a positive group identity to subvert demeaning stereotypes.

We did not need to wait for recent critics of a politics of difference for its a priori and dilemmas to surface.[3] Much of the academic and political writing of these movements of the last ten years has explored problems with a politics of difference as the positive assertion of group identity, and has often itself argued against a politics of identity. While most people would agree that categorizations such as *women, Quebecois, African Americans, old people,* or *Muslims* are meaningful, they founder as soon as they try to define any one of these groups. Most reject an essentialism that would define a group by a particular set of attributes or dispositions that all members share and that constitutes their identity in some respect. The objections to such essentialism are fatal indeed.

Attempts to define the essential attributes of persons belonging to social groups, whether imposed by outsiders or constructed by insiders to the group, fall prey to the problem that there always seem to be persons without the required attributes but whom experience tends to include in the group. The essentialist approach to defining social groups freezes the experienced fluidity of social relations by setting up rigid inside-outside distinctions among groups. If a politics of difference entails such internal unity coupled with external borders to the concept of social group, then its critics are right to claim that such politics divides and fragments people, encouraging conflict and parochialism.

A politics that seeks to form oppositional groups on the basis of a group identity all members share, moreover, must confront the fact that many people deny that group positioning is significant for their identity. Many women, for example, deny reflective awareness of womanly identity as constitutive of their identity, and they deny any particular identification with other women. Many French people deny the existence of a French identity and will claim that being French is nothing particularly important to their personal identities; indeed, many of these would be likely to say that the search for French identity that constitutes the personal identities of individual French men and women is a dangerous form of nationalism. Even when people affirm group affinity as important to their identities, they often chafe at the tendency to enforce norms of behavior or identity that essentialist definitions of the groups entail.

Third, the tendency to conceive group difference as the basis of a common identity, which can assert itself in politics, would seem to imply that group members all have the same interests and agree on the values, strategies, and policies that will promote those interests. In fact, however, there is usually wide disagreement among people in a given social group on political ideology. Though members of a group oppressed by gender or racial stereotypes may share interests in the elimination of discrimination and dehumanizing imagery, such a concern is too abstract to constitute a strategic goal. At a more concrete level members of such groups usually express divergent and even contradictory interests.[4]

The most important criticism of the idea of an essential group identity that members share, however, concerns its apparent denial of differentiation within and across groups. Everyone relates to a plurality of social groups; every social group has other social groups cutting across it. The group "men" is differentiated by class, race, religion, age, and so on; the group "Muslims" is differentiated by gender, nationality, and so on. If group identity constitutes individual identity, and if individuals can identify with one another by means of group identity, then how do we deal theoretically and practically with the fact of multiple group positioning? Is my individual identity somehow an aggregate of my gender identity, race identity, class identity, like a string of beads, to use Elizabeth Spelman's image?[5] Such an additive image does not match my intuition that my life is of a piece. Spelman, Lugones, and others also argue that the attempt to define a common group identity tends to normalize the experience and perspective of some of the group members, marginalizing or silencing that of others.[6]

Many conclude from these arguments and uncomfortable feelings that a discourse of group difference is incoherent and politically dangerous. Groups do not exist; there are only arbitrary categories and strategic performances, fluid and pastiche identities. Or there are only interest groups that form associations to promote certain ends, whether the legalization of same-sex marriage, a raise in the minimum wage, or the right to wear a *hijab* to school. We are just only individuals, after all. This move, however, finds no way of accounting for or perhaps even noticing continuing patterns of privilege, disadvantage, and exclusion that structure opportunity and capacity in modern societies. Group difference is a political issue because inequalities that are structured along lines of class, race, gender, physical ability, ethnicity, and relationships can usually be traced between that group-specific situation of culture or division of labor and the advantages or disadvantages one has.

This, then, is one form of the dilemma of difference.[7] On the one hand, any attempt to describe just what differentiates a social group from others and to define a common identity of its members tends to normalize some life experiences and sets up group borders that wrongly exclude. On the other hand, to deny a reality to social groupings both devalues processes of cultural and social affinities and makes political actors unable to analyze patterns of oppression, inequality, and exclusion that are nevertheless sources of conflict and claims for redress. In the next section I will argue that the way out of this dilemma is to disengage the social logic of difference from the logic of identity.

Disengaging Difference from Identity

Critics are right to argue against defining groups in terms of essential attributes that all members share. They are wrong, however, to reject conceptualization of group differentiation altogether. Groups should be understood in relational terms rather than as self-identical substantial entities with essential attributes.[8] A social group is a collective of persons differentiated from others by cultural forms, practices, special needs or capacities, structures of power, or prestige. Social grouping emerges from the way people encounter one another as different in form of life or association, even if they also regard each other as belonging to the same society. A group will not regard itself as having a distinct language, for example, unless its members encounter another group whose speech they cannot understand. In a relational conceptualization, what constitutes a social group is not internal to the attributes and self-understanding of its members. Rather, what makes the group a group is the relation in which it stands to others.

For political theory the relations that most matter are structural relations of hierarchy and inequality. Social structures are the relatively permanent constraints and enablements that condition people's actions and possibilities in relation to others and in relation to the natural and built environment. Hierarchical social structures denote differential relations of power, resource allocation, and normative hegemony. Class, gender, and race are some of the most far-reaching and enduring structural relations of hierarchy and inequality in modern societies. Differentiations of class or racism often rely on cultural group differentiation as a mechanism for structuring inequalities of resource allocation, power, or normative hegemony, but such structures cannot be reduced to culture or ethnicity. In some societies, age, caste, or religion also serve as the differentiating factors for structuring social relations of hierarchy and unequal access to resources, power, or prestige. Insofar as structures enable some people to have significant control over the conditions of their lives and those of others, or to develop and exercise their capacities while the same structures inhibit others, leave them less free, or deprive them of what they need, the structures are unjust. Thus groups defined by structural relations of privilege are most important for political theory because they often generate political conflicts and struggles.

So far I have aimed to disengage group difference from identity by suggesting that social groups do not themselves have substantive, unified identities, but rather are constituted through differentiated relations. The other task of this disengagement concerns the relation of individuals to groups. Some critics rightly resist a politics of identity that suggests that personal identity is determined in specific ways by group membership. This interpretation of a politics of identity suggests that members of the "same" group have a common set of group-based dispositions or attributes that constitutes them as individuals. Such a notion of personal identity as constituted by group identity fails both to give sufficient force to individual freedom and to account for the multiplicity of group affiliations that intersect with people's lives. From these failings it does not follow, however, that groups are fictions, or have no significant relation to individual possibilities. It has been important for oppositional movements of subordinate social groups to reclaim and revalue the activities, cultural styles, and modes of affiliation associated with their social-group positions in order to subvert devaluation and negative stereotyping in dominant culture. This subversion has often encouraged cultivation of group solidarity by asserting a group identity. When the assertion of group identity is a self-conscious project of cultural creation and resistance, it can be positive and empowering, even though it corresponds to no preestablished group essence and inevitably involves some of those associated with the group more than others. Too often, however, this political use of group identity does indeed speak as though it represents a given group identity that all associated with the group do or ought to share. The relation of individual identities to social groups, however, is more indirect than this conceptualization allows. Social groups do indeed position individuals, but a person's identity is her own, formed in active relation to that social positioning, among other things, rather than constituted by it. Individual subjects make their own identities, but not under conditions they choose.

Pierre Bourdieu theorizes the social world as a set of fields, each of which is constituted by structural relations of power, resource allocation, or prestige.[9] Particular social agents can be understood in terms of their relative positions in these fields. Although no individual is in exactly the same position as any other, agents are "closer" or "farther" from one another in their location with respect to the structural relations that define the field. Agents who are similarly positioned experience similar constraints or enablements as produced by the structural organization of power, resource allocation, or normative hegemony. On this view, social groups are collections of persons similarly situated in social fields structured by power and resources, but this says nothing about their particular identity as persons.

The idea that language and social processes position individual subjects in structured social fields makes this positioning process prior to individual subjectivity, both ontologically and historically.[10] Persons are thrown into a world with a given history of sedimented meanings and material landscape, and interaction with others in the social field locates us in terms of the given meanings, expected activities, and rules.[11] We find ourselves positioned, thrown, into the structured field of class, gender, race, nationality, religion, and so on, and in our daily lives we have no choice but to deal with this situation.

In an earlier essay I suggested that Sartre's concept of "seriality" can be useful for theorizing this structural positioning that conditions the possibility of social agents without constituting their identities. In Sartre's theory, to be working class (or capitalist class) is to be part of a series that is passively constituted by the material organization of labor ownership, and the power of capital in relation to labor. In the earlier essay I suggest that being a woman does not itself imply sharing social attributes and identity with all those others called "women." Instead, "women" is the name of a series in which some individuals find themselves by virtue of norms of enforced heterosexuality and the sexual division of labor.[12]

Social processes and interactions position individual subjects in prior structures, and this positioning conditions who one is. But positioning neither determines nor defines individual identity. Individuals are agents: we constitute our own identities, and each person's identity is unique. We do not choose the conditions under which we form our identities, and we have no choice but to become ourselves under the conditions that position us in determinate relation to others. We act in situation, in relation to the structural conditions and their interaction into which we are thrown. Individuals can and do respond to and take up their positioning in many possible ways, however, and these actions-in-situation constitute individual identity.[13] Gloria Anzaldua expresses this active appropriation of one's own multiple group positionalities as a process of "making faces."[14] We are unique individuals, with our own identities created from the way we have taken up the histories, cultural constructs, language, and social relations of hierarchy and subordination that condition our lives. The gendered position of women, for example, continues to put greater obstacles in the way of girls achieving recognition for technical intelligence than boys experience. One girl may react to these obstacles by internalizing a sense of incapacity, whereas another may take them as a challenge to overcome, and each of these reactions will differently contribute to a girl's identity. Different people may experience and act in relation to similar positional intersections in different ways.

Complex societies position individuals in multiple ways, insofar as there exist multiple structures of privilege and subordination in respect to power, resource allocation, and normative hegemony. Which structures and positions intersect in an individual's life, and how they do so, conditions her particular situation. Kimberle Crenshaw theorizes this concept of the "intersectionality" of positioning for black women. Being located in a position where racist and sexist structures meet, she suggests, sometimes produces constraints, dilemmas, tensions, and indeed possibilities that are specific to that intersecting position, and cannot be understood simply as summing up the experiences of being female and white and being black and male.[15] Other intersectionalities—say, of being upper class, female, and old—produce other specific conditions of structural reinforcement or weakening of privilege. This concept of intersectionality retains a generality to each social-group position without requiring a merely additive approach to the fact that individuals are multiply positioned. Each person's identity is a product of how he or she deals with his or her intersecting social positions.

Disengaging group difference from identity thus addresses many of the problems of more essentialist understandings of social group I discussed above. For many, certain social group positionings are important to their identities, and they find strong affinity with others on the basis of these relationally constituted groups. Doing so, however, is an active project of the person and does not arise from essential group attributes. The disengagement of difference from identity also addresses the "pop-bead" problem. Since groups do not themselves constitute individual identities there is no problem of how to conceive of myself as a combination of several group identities. I have only my own identity, fashioned in relation to my multiple group positionings.

Social Perspective

Because they assume that giving importance to social group differentiation entails that fixed group identities make the groups entirely separate and opposed, critics claim that a politics of difference produces only division. I have argued, however, that group differentiation should be understood with a more relational logic that does not entail substantive and mutually exclusive group identities. The primary resource that structural positioning offers to democratic communication, I shall now argue, is not a self-regarding identity or interest, but rather a perspective on the structures, relations, and events of the society.

The idea of social perspective presumes that differentiated groups dwell together within social processes with history, present arrangement, and future trajectories larger than all of them, which are constituted by their interactions. Each differentiated group position has a particular experience of a point of view on those social processes precisely because each is a part of and has helped produce the patterned processes. Especially insofar as people are situated on different sides of relations of structural inequality, they have differing understandings of those relations and their consequences. Following the logic of the metaphor of group differentiation as arising from differing positions in social fields, the idea of social perspective suggests that agents who are "close" in the social field have a similar point of view on the field and the occurrences within it, and those who are socially distant see things differently. Though different, these social perspectives may not be incompatible. Each social perspective is particular and partial with respect to the whole social field, and from each perspective some aspects of the reality of social processes are more visible than others.

Each social group perspective offers what Donna Haraway calls a "situated knowledge." Individuals in each social location experience one another, their group relations and events, and the institutions in which they move in particular ways; their cultural and material resources afford them differing assumptions from which to process their experiences or different terms in which to articulate them. Among the sorts of situated knowledge people in each social location have are: (1) an understanding of their position and how it stands in relation to other positions; (2) a social map of other salient positions, how they are defined, and the relation in which they stand to their position; (3) a point of view on the history of the society; (4) an interpretation of how the relations and processes of the whole society operate, especially as they impact on their own position; and (5) a position-specific experience and point of view on the natural and physical environment. A social perspective is a certain way of being sensitive to particular aspects of social life, meanings, and interactions, and perhaps less sensitive to others. It is a form of attentiveness that brings some things into view and possibly obscures others. The insights each perspective carries are partial with respect to the whole society.

Thus a social perspective does not contain a determinate, specific content. In this respect perspective is different from interest or opinion. Social perspective consists in a set of questions, kinds of experiences, and assumptions with which reasoning begins, rather than the conclusions drawn. Critiques of essentialism rightly show that those said to belong to the same social group often have different and even conflicting interests and opinions. People who have a similar perspective on social processes and issues—on the norms of heterosexual interaction, for example—nevertheless often have different interests or opinions, because they reason differently from what they experience or have different goals

and projects. When Senator Robert Packwood was accused of sexual harassment, for example, nearly all the women in the U.S. Congress stood together to
say that this was a serious issue; many men were inclined to remain silent or even
joke. The women legislators did not agree on political values or even on what
course should be pursued in the Packwood case, but they nevertheless expressed
a similar perspective on the meaning and gravity of the accusations.

Perspective is a way of looking at social processes without determining what
one sees. Thus two people may share a social perspective and still experience
their positionality differently because they are attending to different elements
of the society. As sharing a perspective, however, each is likely to have an affinity with the other's way of describing what he experiences, an affinity that
those differently situated do not experience. This lesser affinity does not imply
that those differently positioned cannot understand the description of an element of social reality from another social perspective, only that it takes more
work to understand the expression of different social perspectives than those
they share.[16]

Social perspective as the point of view group members have on certain aspects
of social processes because of their position in them may be more or less self-
conscious, both between different individuals associated within a group and between groups. The cultural expressions of ethnic, national, or religious groups,
as well as groups responding to a history of grievance or structural oppression,
often offer refined interpretations of the group's situation and its relations to
others. Perspective may appear in story and song, humor and wordplay, as well
as in more assertive and analytical forms of expression.

As Linda Alcoff suggests, Paul Gilroy offers an extended example of group differentiation as providing social perspective in his book *The Black Atlantic*.[17]
Gilroy accepts antiessentialist critiques and thus denies that blacks of the diaspora are a homogenous group. He also confronts tendencies to treat social
groups as unified ethnic or national groups. But he strongly rejects the suggestion
that social groups are fictions. Instead, he aims to conceptualize the black experience as a particular structural location within modern history, a location initially
constituted by the enslavement of Africans and their transportation across and
around the Atlantic. The facts of slavery and exile produce specific experiences
whose traces remain in cultural and political expression even into the present, according to Gilroy. They give black Europeans, Americans, and many Africans a
distinct perspective on the events and ideas of modernity: "The distinctive historical experiences of this diaspora's populations have created a unique body of reflections on modernity and its discontents which is an enduring presence in the
cultural and political struggles of their descendants today" (45).

Gilroy argues that black experience and social location produce a black perspective on modernity. As with the concept of perspective I have developed here,
this does not mean a fixed and self-identical set of beliefs shared by group members, but rather an orientation on the ideas and events of modern Western history.

Blacks in the west eavesdropped on and then took over a fundamental question from
the intellectual obsessions of their enlightened rulers. Their progress from the status
of slaves to the status of citizens led them to enquire into what the best possible
forms of social and political existence might be. The memory of slavery, actively preserved as a living intellectual resource in their expressive political culture, helped
them to generate a new set of answers to this inquiry. They had to fight—often
through their spirituality—to hold on to the unity of ethics and politics sundered
from each other by modernity's insistence that the true, the good, and the beautiful
had distinct origins and belong to different domains of knowledge.... Their subcul-
ture often appears to be the intuitive expression of some racial essence but is in fact
an elementary historical acquisition produced from the viscera of an alternative body
of cultural and political expression that considers the world critically from the point
of view of its emancipatory transformation. (39)

Far from thinking of this black Atlantic perspective as homogeneous, self-
identical, and self-enclosed, Gilroy specifically articulates it as hybrid, in the
sense that it consists of multiple political and cultural expressions both differentiated from and influencing one another, and influenced by their internal relation to and differentiation from white bourgeois, democratic, and imperialist
culture and politics. Black intellectuals are a product of Enlightenment ideas,
but they query them in specific ways. Black social movement activists are cultural hybrids of African cultural experience and the experience of racial subordination with European-dominated culture and institutions that also form their
experience and identities. Black diasporatic music, literature, and political
rhetoric have traveled back and forth and up and down the Atlantic since the
eighteenth century, proliferating hybrid differentiations. One of the purposes
for theorizing a black Atlantic perspective, however, is to increase understanding of modern Western history generally, and not simply of the experience of
the black diaspora.

Suppose we accept this claim that individuals positioned in similar ways in the
social field have a similar group perspective on that society. What does this imply
for individuals who are positioned in terms of many group-differentiated relations? Since individuals are multiply positioned in complexly structured societies,
they interpret the society from a multiplicity of social group perspectives. Some
of these may intersect to constitute a distinctive hybrid perspective, a black
woman's perspective, perhaps, or a working-class youth perspective. But individuals may also move around the social perspectives available to them, depending
on the people with whom they interact or the aspect of social reality to which
they attend. The multiple perspectives from which persons may see society given
their social-group positioning may reinforce and enhance one another, or it may
be impossible to take one without obscuring another, as in a duck-rabbit figure.
The perspectives available to a person may be incommensurable, producing am-
biguity or confusion in the person's experience and understanding of social life;
or their multiplicity may help the person form a composite picture of social

processes. However experienced, the availability of multiple perspectives provides everyone with the resources to take a distance on any one of them, and to communicate in one way with people with whom one does not share perspectives. Thus, understanding what is shared by members of a social group as perspective rather than identity diffuses a tendency to interpret groups as fixed, closed, and bounded.

Group Difference as a Deliberative Resource

Critics of the politics of difference assume that the expression of group specificity in public life is necessarily and only the expression of a narrow and rigidly defined group interest, set against the interests of other groups in a win-lose relation. This inward-looking pressing of interests, according to them, is precisely why the politics of difference makes democracy or coalition unworkable. In contrast to this image of politics as war by other means, critics wish to promote a neorepublican image of politics as civic deliberation, oriented toward a common good in which participants transcend their particularist interests and commitments.

Thus, Jean Elshtain conceptualizes genuine democratic process as one in which participants assume a public mantle of citizenship that cloaks the private and partial concerns of local culture and familiar interaction. She is not alone among democratic theorists in setting up an opposition between the partial and differentiated, on the one hand, and the impartial and unitary, on the other. Either politics is nothing but competition among private interests, in which case there is no public spirit, or politics is a commitment to equal respect for other citizens in a civil public discussion that puts aside private affiliation and interest to seek the common good.

When confronted so starkly with an opposition between difference and civility, most people must opt for civility. But a conception of deliberative politics that insists that equal respect in public discussion requires putting aside or transcending partial and particularist differences forgets or denies the lesson that the politics of difference claims to teach. Where there are real group-based positional differences that give to some people greater power, material and cultural resources, and authoritative voice, social norms that appear impartial are often biased. Under circumstances of social and economic inequality among groups, the definition of the common good often devalues or excludes some of the legitimate frameworks of thinking, interests, and priorities in the polity. A common consequence of social privilege is the ability of a group to convert its perspective on some issues into authoritative knowledge without being challenged by those who have reason to see things differently. As long as such unequal circumstances persist, a politics that aims to do justice through public discussion and decision making must theorize and aim to practice a third alternative to both a private interest competition and one that denies the reality of difference in public discussions of the common good.

This third way consists in a process of public discussion and decision making that includes and affirms all particular social group perspectives in the society and draws on their situated knowledge as a resource for enlarging the understanding of everyone and moving them beyond their own parochial interests.[18] In this section I articulate this alternative meaning of politics as public discussion and decision making and argue that the particular social perspectives groups bring to the public are a necessary resource for making the wisest and most just decisions.

Gitlin mocks the perspectivism he sees to be typical of postmodernism. He interprets an account of social difference as positionality with perspective as a form of crass relativism and subjectivism:

> How you see is a function of who you are—that is, where you stand or, in clunkier language, your "subject position," the two nouns constituting an unacknowledged gesture toward an objective grid that prescribes where you stand whether or not you know it. (201)
>
> Perspective may lead to falsity or to truth, may be conducive to some truths and not to others. Perspective may be conducive to accurate observations or distorted inferences, may lead to promising notions or idiotic ideas—but to elevate the observations, inferences, or ideas, we need to do more than inquire into their origins.... To know whether the science is good or bad requires a perspective different from all other perspectives: a commitment to truth-seeking above all else. (20:v)

This interpretation of a theory of social perspective as relativist begs the question. For just what is truth in social knowledge, what is the truth about social justice, and how do we achieve them? Gitlin correctly suggests that perspectives can only be starting points and not conclusions, and that by itself no perspective is "Objective." Political discussion and debate can sort out the more from the less true, the better from the worse political judgments, however, only by encouraging the expression of all the particular social groups' perspectives relevant and salient to an issue. This is the argument I shall now make.

With the neorepublican position, I assume that the democratic process ought not properly to be an adversarial process of competition among self-regarding interests, in which each seeks only to get the most for himself, whatever the costs to others. Instead, democracy should be conceived and as far as possible institutionalized as a process of discussion, debate, and criticism that aims to solve collective problems. Political actors should promote their own interests in such a process, but must also be answerable to others to justify their proposals. This means that actors must be prepared to take the interests of others into account. With theorists of deliberative democracy, I define the democratic process as a form of practical reason for conflict resolution and collective problem solving. So defined, democratic process entails that participants have a commitment to cooperation and to look for the most just solution. These conditions of openness are much weaker, I believe, than what many thinkers mean by seeking a common good or a common interest.

If we understand democracy as a process of practical reason, then democracy has an epistemic as well as a normative meaning. Democracy is not only a process where citizens aim to promote their interests, knowing that others are doing the same, though it is that. It is also a method for determining the best and most just solution to conflicts and other collective problems. Though there is not necessarily only one right answer to political problems, some proposals and policies are more just and wise than others, and the democratic task is to identify and implement the best solutions. Ideally, this epistemic function of democracy requires a political equality that includes the expression of all perspectives equally and neutralizes the ability of powerful interests to distort discussion with threats or coercion.[19] Especially in the absence of such ideal conditions, acquiring the social knowledge needed to formulate the best solutions to conflict and collective problems requires learning from the social perspectives of people positioned differently in structures of power, resource allocation, or normative hegemony.

Elshtain correctly evokes a special status for democratic publicity. She rightly claims that workable democratic politics entails that people look beyond their own parochial and private concerns. She is wrong, however, to suggest that adopting a public-spirited stance entails leaving particular group interests and perspectives behind. On the contrary, decision making takes place under conditions of publicity only if it explicitly includes critical dialogue among the plurality of socially differentiated perspectives present in the social field. For this understanding of publicity as entailing group-differentiated social perspective I rely on recent interpretations of Hannah Arendt's idea of the public.

For Arendt, the defining characteristic of a public is plurality. The public consists of multiple histories and perspectives relatively unfamiliar to one another, distant yet connected and irreducible to one another. A conception of publicity that requires its members to put aside their differences in order to uncover their common good destroys the very meaning of publicity because it aims to turn the many into one. In the words of commentator Lisa Disch,

> The definitive quality of the public space is particularity: that the plurality of perspectives that constitute it is irreducible to a single common denominator. A claim to decisive authority reduces those perspectives to a single one, effectively discrediting the claims of other political actors and closing off public discussion. Meaning is not inherent in an action, but public, which is to say, constituted by the interpretive context among the plurality of perspectives in the public realm that confer plurality on action and thereby make it real.[20]

The public is not a comfortable place of conversation among those who share language, assumptions, and ways of looking at issues. Arendt conceives the public as a place of *appearance* where actors stand before others and are subject to mutual scrutiny and judgment from a plurality of perspectives. The public is open in the sense of being both exposed and inclusive; a genuinely public discussion is in principle open to anyone.

If differently positioned citizens engage in public discussion with the aim of solving problems with a spirit of openness and mutual accountability, then these conditions are sufficient for transformative deliberation. They need not be committed to a common interest or a common good; indeed, their stance of openness and mutual accountability requires them to attend to their particular differences in order to understand the situation and perspective of others. They share problems to be solved, to be sure; otherwise they would have no need for discussion. It does not follow, however, that they share a good or an interest beyond that.

Public critical discussion that includes the expression of and exchange between all relevant differentiated social perspectives transforms the partial and parochial interests and ideas of each into more reflective and objective judgment. By "objective" I do not mean a neutral point of view outside of and transcending those particular social perspectives. I mean only the contrary of subjective, that is, a reflective stance and substantive understanding that is not merely self-regarding. Judgment is objective in this sense when it situates one's own particular perspectives in a wider context that takes other perspectives into account as well. Objectivity in this sense means only that judgment has taken account of the experience, knowledge, and interests of others. Such objectivity is possible only if those particular perspectives are expressed publicly to everyone.[21]

If citizens participate in public discussion that includes all social perspectives in their partiality and gives them a hearing, they are most likely to arrive at just and wise solutions to their shared problems. Group difference is a necessary resource for making more just and wise decisions by means of democratic discussion owing to at least three functions dialogue across such difference serves.

1. Plurality of perspectives motivates claimants to express their proposals as appeals to justice rather than expressions of mere self-interest or preference. Proposals for collective policies need not be expressed in terms of common interest, an interest all can share. Especially where there are structural injustices—and these are everywhere today—at least some claims that correctly appeal to justice are likely not to express a common interest. Even without rectifying injustices, just solutions to many political problems can entail obligations on the part of the public to recognize and provide for some unique needs of uniquely situated persons. The presence of a plurality of social perspectives in public discussion helps frame the discourse in terms of legitimate claims of justice. Because others are not likely to accept "I want this" or "this policy is in my interest" as good reasons for them to accept a proposal, the need to be accountable to others with different perspectives on collective problems motivates participants in a discussion to frame their proposals in terms of justice.

2. Confrontation with different perspectives, interests, and cultural meanings teaches individuals the partiality of their own, and reveals to them their own experience as perspectival. Listening to those differently situated than myself and my close associates teaches me how my situation looks to them, what relation they think I stand to them. Such a contextualizing of perspective is especially important for groups that have power, authority, or privilege. Too often those in

structurally superior positions take their experience, preferences, and opinions to be general, uncontroversial, ordinary, and even an expression of suffering or disadvantage. Having to answer to others who speak from a different, less privileged perspective on their social relations exposes their partiality and relative blindness. Where such exposure does not lead them to shut down dialogue and attempt to force their preferences on policy, it can lead to a better understanding of the requirements of justice. Nor does the perspective of those less socially privileged carry unquestionable "epistemic privilege." They also may need the perspectives of others to understand the social causes of their disadvantage or to realize that they lay blame in the wrong place.

3. Expressing, questioning, and challenging differently situated knowledge adds to social knowledge. Although not abandoning their own perspectives, people who listen across differences come to understand something about the ways that proposals and policies affect others differently situated. They gain knowledge of what is going on in different social locations and how social processes appear to connect and conflict from different points of view. By internalizing such a mediated understanding, participants in democratic discussion and decision making gain a wider picture of the social processes in which their own partial experience is embedded. Such a more comprehensive social knowledge better enables them to arrive at wise solutions to collective problems to the extent that they are committed to doing so.

This account of democratic communication, which uses the differences in group perspectives as a resource for enlarging the understanding of everyone to take account of the perspectives of others, is of course an ideal. This ideal extrapolates from real elements and tendencies in public communication across differences present within the unjust and power-oriented politics we usually experience. This ideal can serve at least three functions: to justify a principle of the inclusion of specific group perspectives in discussion; to serve as a standard against which the inclusiveness of actual public communication can be measured; and to motivate action to bring real politics more into line with the ideal.

Notes

I am grateful to Linda Alcoff, David Alexander, Bill Rehg, and Steve Seidman for comments on earlier versions of this chapter.

1. Todd Gidin, *Twilight of Common Dreams* (New York: Henry Holt, 1995), 36.

2. Jean Elshtain, *Democracy on Trial* (New York: Basic Books, 1995), 74.

3. For some examples of critiques of essentialism and a politics of identity from within theories and movements that support a politics of difference, see Elizabeth V. Spelman, *Unessential Woman* (Boston: Beacon Press, 1988); Anna Yeatman, "Minorities and the Politics of Difference," in *Postmodern Revisionings of the Political* (New York: Routledge, 1994); Michael Dyson, "Essentialism and the Complexities of Racial Identity," in David Theo Goldberg, ed., *Multiculturalism* (Cambridge: Blackwell, 1994), 218–229.

4. Compare Anne Phillips, *The Politics of Presence* (Oxford: Oxford University Press, 1995).

5. Spelman, *Inessential Woman*, 15, 136.

6. Ibid.; Maria Lugones, "Parity, Imparity, and Separation: Forum," *Signs* 14, 458–477.

7. See Martha Minow, *Making All the Difference* (Ithaca, N.Y.: Cornell University Press, 1990), chap. 1, for the phrase "Dilemma of difference," and for some formulations of the dilemma.

8. Martha Minow proposes a relational understanding of group difference in *Making All the Difference*, especially in part 2; I have introduced a relational analysis of group difference in *Justice and the Politics of Difference* (Princeton: Princeton University Press, 1990), chap. 2; in the earlier formulation, however, I do not distinguish group affiliation from personal identity as strongly as I do in this essay.

9. Pierre Bourdieu, "Social Space and the Genesis of Groups," *Theory and Society* 14 (1985), 723–744.

10. See Rosalind Coward and John Ellis, *Language and Materialism* (London: Routledge and Kegan Paul, 1977), 49–60. See also Diana Fuss, *Essentially Speaking: Feminism, Nature and Difference* (New York: Routledge, 1989); Bill Martin, *Matrix and Line* (Albany, N.Y.: SUNY Press, 1993).

11. I refer here to Heidegger's concept of "thrownness," as the existential condition of not being one's own origin, of the facticity of history. See *Being and Time* (New York: Harper and Row, 1965), chap. 5. I have developed a more extended discussion of being "thrown" into group membership in *Justice and the Politics of Difference*, 46.

12. Young, "Gender as Seriality: Thinking About Women as a Social Collective," *Signs: Journal of Women in Culture and Society* 19, No. 3 (1994), 713–738.

13. I mean here to evoke Sartre's concepts of facticity and situation. In Sartre's early existentialism, agents are always free insofar as they choose to make of themselves what they are, but they always must do so within an unchosen historical and social situation.

14. Gloria Anzaldua, "Haciendo Caras, una entrada/an Introduction," in *Making Face, Making South/Haciendo Caras*, ed., Gloria Anzaldua (San Francisco: Aunt Lute Foundation, 1990).

15. Kimberle Crenshaw, "Mapping the Margins: Intersectionality, Identity Politics, and Violence Against Women of Color," *Stanford Law Review* 43 (July 1991), 1241–1299.

16. I develop this point more in my essay, "Asymmetrical Reciprocity: On Moral Respect, Wonder, and Enlarged Thought," *Constellations* 3 (1997), 340–363.

17. See Linda Alcoff, "Philosophy and Racial Identity," *Radical Philosophy* 75 (January-February 1996), 5–14; Paul Gilroy, *The Black Atlantic* (Cambridge: Harvard University Press, 1993).

18. James Bohman develops a version of this third alternative between the parochial and the unitary in *Public Deliberation: Pluralism, Complexity and Democracy* (Cambridge, Mass.: MIT Press, 1996), especially in chaps. 2 and 3.

19. For statements of this epistemic function of democracy, see Hilary Putnam, "A Reconsideration of Deweyan Democracy," *Southern California Law Review* 63, No. 6 (September 1990), 1671–1697; Joshua Cohen, "An Epistemic Conception of Democracy," *Ethics* 97 (October 1986), 26–38; David Estlund, "Making Truth Safe for Democracy," in Coop, Hampton, Roemer, eds., *The Idea of Democracy* (Cambridge: Cambridge University Press, 1993); and Estlund, "Beyond Fairness and Deliberation: The Epistemic Dimension of Democratic Authority," in *Deliberative Democracy*, ed. James Bohmen and William Relif (Cambridge, Mass.: MIT Press, 1997).

20. Lisa Disch, *Hannah Arendt and the Limits of Philosophy* (Ithaca, N.Y.: Cornell University Press, 1994), 80.

21. For such a meaning of objectivity I draw on feminist epistemologies. See, for example, Sandra Harding's notion of "strong objectivity," which relies on oppositional theories produced from the perspective of historically marginalized groups to produce objectivity in science, especially social science, in *Whose Science? Whose Knowledge? Thinking from Women's Lives* (Ithaca, N.Y.: Cornell University Press, 1991). See also Ismay Barwell, "Towards a Defence of Objectivity" in Kathleen Lennon and Margaret Whitford, eds., *Knowing the Difference: Feminist Perspectives in Epistemology* (London: Routledge, 1994), 79–94.

Disability Rights: Universally Accessible Environments as a Public Good

Ron Amundson

The disability rights movement contains a more diverse collection of activists than any other political movement. Members of the movement are defined by their divergence from an assumed "normal" human condition. The movement itself is recent. Disability activism prior to the 1970s was divided among impairment types, with separate groups of blind activists, paraplegic activists, and so on. After all, the problems of blindness seem very different from those of paralysis. The birth of the disability rights movement came with the realization that the disadvantages experienced by blind and paraplegic people, and people with any sort of impairment, can be traced to a common cause. That cause is the design of the physical and the social environment. The environment has been organized and constructed for the convenient use of only a circumscribed segment of the full range of human diversity. People who fall outside that segment find barriers that constitute the problem of disability. Disability is a social phenomenon. It is not merely a statistical aggregate of the pathologies of individuals.

Traditional views about disability are founded on the ideology of normality. This view supposes that the vast majority of humans are nearly identical in how they are able to function, and that this "normal" majority is objectively distinct from the "abnormal" minority. The reification of normality is imagined to be a simple biological fact. Surprisingly (or maybe not), scientific biology has found very little use for the distinction between normality and abnormality. The scientific basis for a reified normality dissolves on close examination, going the way of scientific racism and sexism. "Normal" people are actually very diverse in their modes of function. The breadth of diversity is hidden by the fact that a large number of us are able to get along in the particular environments we have built for our-

(continues)

selves. The "abnormals" among us fall on the wrong side of a socially negotiated but scientifically arbitrary boundary.

The segregation of people with impairments can be more subtly carried out than segregation based on race. A single stairstep entry to a building excludes a wheelchair user more efficiently than a sign saying "No wheelchairs allowed." A library that has no books in Braille, audiotaped, or computer-readable formats excludes blind users in the same subtle way. Bureaucratic procedures, such as complicated application forms, are barriers that can keep people with cognitive impairments from enjoying social benefits available to others.

The disability rights movement has had some success in arguing that disabling aspects of environmental design must be removed from market decisions. For decades the U.S. federal government jawboned the commercial sector with claims that it was good business to "hire the handicapped" and to create accessible business places. That project was futile. So long as decisions about environmental design were based on individual market choices, the public world was built only for the normals. In 1990 the Americans with Disabilities Act took the decision out of the marketplace (in theory if not yet in practice). Businesses and public places are now required to meet minimum standards of accessibility. It is revealing that the public world is now more accessible even to supposedly normal people. Many people who would have had to struggle up stairways now move easily on accessible ramps: children, parents with strollers, and workers moving large loads.

A great deal of economic injustice follows from the patterns of unemployment and underemployment. A disproportionate share of this burden falls on disabled people. At a time when the U.S. unemployment rate is 4.2 percent, the rate among disabled people is 75 percent. It would be not only just, but also economically productive to have an integrated and employed population, without the artificial distinction between the "normal" workers and the "abnormal" unemployed.

Those who oppose the public good of a universally accessible environment describe disability rights legislation as favoring a special interest group. On this view, market forces should control decisions

(continues)

(continued)

about environmental design, and the problems created by inaccessibility should be dealt with by private charity (the traditional capitalist response to market-imposed disadvantage). The view of disabled people as "the other" is alive even among some socialist thinkers. But the common bond that crosses the normal/abnormal boundary is more obvious even than the one that crosses race, class, and gender boundaries. Only the fantasy of our own invulnerability prevents us from seeing it. The line between normality and abnormality can be crossed in an instant. A slip on a stairway, a broken blood vessel in the brain, and a "normal" person will magically transform into an "abnormal."

A universally accessible environment is one in which the normal/abnormal boundary has no meaning, because it is possible to flourish no matter how unusual one's abilities. Everyone is a candidate for disability and (except for those who die first) everyone will eventually experience it. The disability rights movement is preparing the world for everyone.

6

The Prisoner Exchange: The Underside of Civil Rights

Angela Y. Davis

Thinking recently about the meaning of the phrase "the prison industrial complex" led me to Derrick Bell's short story, "The Space Traders," which opens with a description of the arrival on January 1, 2000, of a thousand spacecraft from a distant planet, whose mission is to exchange an immense supply of material resources for black bodies:

> Those mammoth vessels carried within their holds treasure of which the United States was in most desperate need: gold, to bail out the almost bankrupt federal, state, and local governments; special chemicals capable of unpolluting the environment, which was becoming daily more toxic, and restoring it to the pristine state it had been before Western explorers set foot on it; and a totally safe nuclear engine fuel, to relieve the nation's all-but-depleted supply of fossil fuel. In return, the visitors wanted only one thing—and that was to take back to their home star all the African Americans who lived in the United States.[1]

Within the story, however—and for my purposes, this is a crucial point—it is rumored that U.S. negotiators attempt to make a deal with the Space Traders that involves accepting the idea of the trade for all those in prison or in walled-off inner-urban environments but allowing other, more affluent black people to remain on Earth. The modern-day slave traders hold instead to a strict legal basis for inclusion, shunning almost all other category differentiation (save age and disability), and are set to deport all individuals whose birth certificates list them as "black," regardless of economic status and of their social or political prestige.

The exchange takes place on January 17, 2000, Martin Luther King Day, which, given the correlation of racial identity, interest, and historical memory that the story enacts, effectively eradicates the need for such a celebration:

> The dawn of the last Martin Luther King holiday that the nation would ever observe illuminated an extraordinary sight. In the night, the Space Traders had drawn their strange ships right up to the beaches and discharged their cargoes of gold, minerals, and machinery, leaving vast empty holds. Crowded on the beaches were the inductees, some twenty million silent men, women and children, including babes in arms. As the sun rose, the Space Traders directed them, first, to strip off all but a single undergarment; then to line up; and finally, to enter those holds which yawned in the morning light like Milton's "darkness visible." The inductees looked fearfully behind them. But, on the dunes above the beaches, guns at the ready, stood U.S. guards. There was no escape, no alternative. Heads bowed, arms now linked by slender chains, black people left the New World as their forebears had arrived.[2]

Bell's parable about the "permanence of racism"—the subtitle of the collection in which the story was published—raises important and disturbing issues regarding the material, ideological, and psychic structures of racism and specifically about the nation's willingness to pursue a strategy "in which the sacrifice of the most basic rights of blacks would result in the accrual of substantial benefits to all whites."[3] Predictably, this story has occasioned controversies, especially among scholars reluctant to criticize liberal ideas regarding the history of progress in U.S. "race relations," and who consequently criticize Bell for overly pessimistic and historically obsolete narratives of racism. There is another way, however, to critically examine the version of racism presented in Bell's parable, while also taking seriously his insistence on the permanence—or at least, the persistence—of racism and on the role of the law in achieving this permanence through the institutionalization of racist ideologies.

I should note that we might raise serious questions, as does Michael Olivas, about the relationship between the historical frame of Bell's story and the histories of Native American, Latino, and other nonblack populations of color that might also "mark them as candidates for the Space Traders' evil exchange."[4] In his response to Bell's "Space Traders," Olivas considers the Cherokee Removal and Chinese Exclusion laws as well as the Bracero program and Operation Wetback. He concludes with the argument that these abiding historical patterns of expulsion can also be discovered in 1990s U.S. immigration policy, which has created a scenario that ironically resonates with the parable of the Space Traders. Olivas points out that

> The *Chronicle of the Space Traders* is not ... too fantastic or unlikely to occur, but rather the opposite: This scenario has occurred, and more than once in our nation's history. Not only have Blacks been enslaved, as the *Chronicle* sorrowfully notes, but

other racial groups have been conquered and removed, imported for their labor and not allowed to participate in the society they built, or expelled when their labor was no longer considered necessary.[5]

By expanding Bell's ideas to include Latino, Native American, and Asian American populations in the scenario, as well as the class and gender axes that cut across the racial order, we can discover significant contemporary examples that increasingly involve the removal of substantial numbers of people from civil society.

If we focus specifically, nonetheless, on U.S. black history, even there we must ask if it is necessary for middle-class and politically conservative African Americans to be caught in the same web of racism as impoverished and working peoples for us to confirm the persistence of antiblack racism in the United States. I want to suggest that although the racial sacrifice all African Americans are compelled to make in Bell's story may help us to understand conventional historical features of U.S. racism, if we look further to note the exceptions to the mass transplantation and the rumored substitute proposal for the expatriation of prisoners and inner-urban dwellers, we find insights about the contemporary relationship between race and criminalization. Moreover, the Space Traders' plan confirms some of the most stereotypical thinking about labor and the capacity to work. The masculinized zones of the prison and inner city provide sites of raw potential profit but alone are insufficient to reproduce themselves. The feminization of the elderly and disabled condemn them to the zone of apparently benign neglect. The elderly and disabled, along with the 1,000 detainees delegated to hold black property in trust—in case the group is ever returned—are the only black people allowed to remain on Earth, useless to the Space Traders' purposes. In its division of the black population, Bell's story exposes the insidious conjunction of capitalism with what is ostensibly the realm of justice, as the Space Traders' logic is in fact ironically coincident with prison practice in its acknowledgment that prisoners and the un- and underemployed (who will soon be subject to arrest) are already an ideal laboring population. This contravenes media portrayals of lazy prisoners who receive free room and board and who apparently prefer the constant surveillance of police to substantial employment in legalized economies. The compassionate release of prisoners who are elderly or ill (and thus can no longer have their labor effectively extracted), though hard-won, is surely one of the great ironies of prison activism, since the victory must always be measured against the system that no longer finds the released prisoner cost-effective.

In fact, the prison industrial complex has given us a new scenario of removal and disappearance, which marks men and women, mostly of color, as the primary raw material for a profitable punishment industry. The imprisonment of substantial numbers of poor black, Latino, Native American, and Asian American people also results in the concealment of class-inflected structures of racism within the rapidly expanding spaces where the corporate economy is re-defining punishment for us and marketing it as public safety.

I am not, however, proposing a critique of the "Space Traders" for its failure to consider these historical and contemporary patterns of ostracizing communities of color from mainstream U.S. society. What interests me about the "Space Traders" is its compelling science fiction narrative, which, in negatively recapitulating slavery within the framework of constitutional law, clearly makes Bell's point regarding the role of a democratic legal system in sustaining racism. Bell, considered by critical race theorists as their pioneering legal scholar for his critiques of civil rights discourse,[6] constructs a story in which we confront the shocking possibility that such a proposition could become the law of the land. His point is not merely about the law as doctrine but about the ideologies imbedded in the law, however well disguised—the racism that preceded its instantiation in law and the failure, even inability, of the law to provide protections against the interests of the majority.

In the spirit of Bell's work, I want to briefly explore ways in which conceptualizations of racism that rely primarily on a narrow interpretation of legal principles of equality (and on the presumption that the law can protect) militate against an understanding of the relationship between the prison industrial complex and contemporary mutations of racism—tending to guarantee racism's permanence precisely at a time when dominant discourses insist on its having already disappeared. In Bell's parable, a constitutional amendment is required to provide a legal basis for the induction of all black people into this special sacrificial service for the nation. The referendum passes 70 percent to 30 percent.[7] It may be enough to pause here to ask, taking Lani Guinier's suggestions[8] a bit further, how this constitutes democracy, given that those who would be sacrificed could not even be said to constitute the dissenting 30 percent, and that the individualist framework of "one man/one vote" (which in its current antifeminist register already betrays its own insufficiency) does not and cannot account for group interests. But how are we to understand those structures of racism that do not require legislation or that cannot be contested through a deployment of the abstract juridical subject who putatively remains the same across class, gender, and other axes of social power? If racism can only be confirmed in legal terms, the most salient examples of which are those segregation-era laws that the civil rights movement succeeded in eliminating, and if we can assume that laws targeting black, Latino, or other subjects of color are not likely to reemerge, then it would be quite reasonable to accept the prevailing liberal discourse about the withering away of the racial order.

In Bell's parable, the fictional referendum for a new constitutional amendment requiring the conscription of all African Americans incites protests and engenders organizing efforts supporting the black community. On the other hand, the real forcible removal of more than a million people of color, presently incarcerated in a proliferating network of prisons and jails, has failed to incite widespread opposition and protest. Can this absence of activism be explained by the fact that no special legal procedures designating racial exclusion have been required to justify this "new segregation"?[9] The March 1999 Bureau of Justice Statistics report on "Prison and Jail Inmates at Midyear, 1998" revealed that more than 1.8 million people are incarcerated in the country's prisons and jails.[10] The incarceration rate is 668 per 100,000—more than twice the rate in 1985 (313 per 100,000). One in every 150 U.S. residents is in prison or jail. These figures are alarming on their face, but when one considers that approximately 70 percent of these 1.8 million prisoners are people of color,[11] one might meditate on the unacknowledged role of the law. Simultaneously enabling the racialization of punishment and rendering invisible its devastating impact on populations of color, the law constructs individual "criminals" about whom it can justly decide the question of guilt or innocence. The subject of the law is the abstract rights-bearing citizen and, indeed, the civil rights movement made great strides in deracializing the law and in extending its putative neutrality. However, the condition for the legal assimilation of racially marginalized communities is their conceptualization as aggregations of rights-bearing individuals who must appear separately before a law that will only consider their culpability and not its own. It has become increasingly difficult to identify the profound and egregious impact of racism, in and outside the law, on these communities. No racially explicit laws have facilitated the shifting of vast black and Latino populations from the free world to the universe of the imprisoned. Still, one wonders how the civil rights community might have responded thirty-five years ago had it been informed that by the year 2000 there would probably be (according to policy analyst Jerome Miller[12]) 1 million black men and growing numbers of black women behind bars. Ironically, it is their relatively new status as equal rights–bearing subjects that prepares them to be deprived of such rights in the arena of punishment and profit, for such an equality implies equal responsibility. This recapitulates, as I will later explain, the historical origins of the prison.

In another article, "Racial Realism," Bell proposes the following evaluation of the limitations of civil rights strategies:

> As a veteran of a civil rights era that is now over, I regret the need to explain what went wrong. Clearly, we need to examine what it was about our reliance on racial remedies that may have prevented us from recognizing that these legal rights could do little more than bring about the cessation of one form of discriminatory conduct, which soon appeared in a more subtle though no less discriminatory form. The question is whether this examination requires us to redefine goals of racial equality and opportunity to which blacks have adhered for more than a century. The answer must be a resounding yes.[13]

The emphasis in mainstream civil rights discourse on abstract equality and color-blindness (these principles have been abundantly analyzed by critical race theorists[14]) has rendered it extremely difficult to develop a popular understanding of the way—as Bell suggests we should move beyond the civil rights paradigm—imprisonment practices recapitulate and deepen practices of social segregation. Because it cannot be demonstrated that the people of color who have been herded into the country's prisons and jails have been convicted and sentenced under laws that explicitly identify them in racial terms, the vastly disproportionate numbers of black, Latino, Native American, and increasingly Asian American prisoners cannot be offered as material evidence of racism. The limitations of civil rights strategies of the past for considering the socioeconomic underpinnings of racism become even more clear when viewed in light of their contemporary deployment by opponents of affirmative action.

It may be more than a mere coincidence that the first state to abolish affirmative action in public education and employment has the largest prison population in the country.[15] The language used in the 1996 ballot measure known as the California Civil Rights Initiative (CCRI) was specifically designed to link this anti–affirmative action strategy to the civil rights movement of the 1950s and 1960s. Its advocates argued that by ending racial and gender preferences, quotas, and set-asides, it will be possible—evoking the oratory of Dr. Martin Luther King—to "realize the dream of a color-blind society,"[16] Yet, in California, a black man is five times more likely to be found in a prison cell than in a classroom at a public university.[17] Texas, which has the second largest prison population, has also abolished affirmative action. And at this writing, Florida, which has the fourth largest prison population (New York has the third) has been identified by Ward Connerly, the black regent of the University of California who chairs the CCRI, as the next state for the passage of a similar proposition eliminating affirmative action. The concurrence of anti–affirmative action efforts and the rising prison populations in California, Texas, and Florida would not appear accidental if we were willing to understand the historical link between the assertion of democratic rights for some and their guarantee by the deprivation of rights for others. In the debate around affirmative action, we should therefore examine the general failure, even by those who are genuinely interested in the extension of civil rights, to account for those who are clandestinely deprived of their rights (albeit legally) by the prison industrial complex.

The main clause of the CCRI contains the following language: "The state shall not discriminate against, or grant preferential treatment to, any individual or group on the basis of race, sex, color, ethnicity, or national origin in the operation of public employment, public education, or public contracting."[18] As implied here, a fundamental supposition of anti–affirmative action advocacy is that civil rights are now equally distributed among the citizenry *(any individual or group)* without regard to race. To account for the obviously inferior social and economic status of those who are putatively equal before the law, opponents of affirmative action tend to use an explanatory framework of social and cultural dysfunctionality. For example, Nicolas Capaldi's argument against affirmative action, which does not seriously consider its impact on any groups other than African Americans, is based on his assertion that as a set of policies, it cannot effectively deal with the problem it is designed to solve, namely, "the failure of African Americans to participate fully in American life."[19]

> What is meant by participating fully? To participate fully in our society means to be an autonomous and responsible individual—to be law-abiding, self-supporting, self-defining, and constructively active in one or more institutions. Any statistical survey will confirm that with regard to unemployment, welfare, crime, family breakdown, and other social problems, African Americans are *"overrepresented"* remarkably out of proportion to their percentage in the population. What these statistics show is that not only are African Americans as a group not participating fully but far too many of them are socially dysfunctional.[20]

Thus, pursuing the logic of Capaldi's argument, political figures like Ward Connerly dismiss the "overrepresentation" of people of color in the country's prisons and on the welfare rolls as an outcome of this dysfunctionality. Such logic, in turn, misapprehends the relationship between the structural equality of law on its face and the predictable and racialized outcomes it masks. In this instance, the narrow interpretation of civil rights principles is thus effectively deployed to exclude consideration of forms of discrimination and marginalization that disappear behind legal equality and spatial segregation in the prison. Precisely because mainstream civil rights discourse—with its conventional black/white framework—is predicated on such a narrow construction of citizenship, it fails to register not only the situation of prisoners but also those, like undocumented immigrants, who share similar status and often the same physical space in the prison. The Immigration and Naturalization Service in fact constitutes an important sector of the prison industrial complex, with the largest numbers of armed federal agents and an expanding network of detention centers, and detainees overflowing into the nation's jails and prisons. The irony of the shared status of the prisoner and the immigrant is not only in their racialized criminalization but in the fact that the pattern of their criminalization demonstrates a fundamental failure of the law: it cannot apprehend their individuality except on its own behalf. The paradigmatic immigrant and prisoner (read nonwhite) are marked in advance of appearing before the law as members of criminalized groups. The assertion of individual rights is only respected in the negative—the assumption of responsibility for illegality.

That prisoners might even possess civil rights is a relatively new notion. In 1871, several decades after the establishment of incarceration as the dominant mode of punishment in the United States, the Supreme Court of Virginia ruled that the convict had "not only forfeited his liberty but also his personal rights, except those which the law in its humanity affords him." In other words, the prisoner was "for the time being, the slave of the state."[21] Although various court decisions have reversed the ruling in *Ruffin v. Commonwealth of Virginia,* which stated that prisoners possessed no rights except those expressly extended to them by the state, in the United States and in those countries that have re- garded the U.S. criminal justice system as a model, democratic rights continue to have little meaning for those behind bars.

Citizens convicted of crimes are divested of rights on a constitutional basis. That these citizens are disproportionately citizens of color is attributed not to their racial targeting, but rather to individual and community dysfunctions. The historical stage was set for this ideological masking of the racialization of impris- onment with the passage of the Thirteenth Amendment to the Constitution, which, in abolishing the generalized slavery of black Americans, preserved the status of slaves for those "duly convicted of a crime."[22] That racist structures lurk within and behind the processes deployed to "duly convict" some "citizens" of crimes, leaving others relatively immune, cannot be uncovered by a narrow inter- pretation of legal discourse. It becomes impossible to argue that race is responsi- ble for the fact that some citizens are charged, "duly convicted," sentenced, and imprisoned with greater facility than others, even as the disproportions become more and more grotesque.

Racial differentials in sentencing practices have been a perennial feature of the criminal justice system at least since the end of the Civil War. But they have rarely been taken up by antiracist activists. Not even Frederick Douglass, who spoke out so eloquently against lynching, developed a critique of the convict lease sys- tem, which radically transformed the southern prison systems in the aftermath of the Civil War.[23] During the era of the civil rights movement, there were rare ref- erences to black people whom imprisonment had deprived of full citizenship. Even as the civil rights movement focused its energies on extending the right to vote to the black population, the disenfranchisement of prisoners was not as- sumed to present a serious problem. These blindnesses return us to Bell's assess- ment of the failure of civil rights activists and their reliance on legal principles and demonstrate the imperative of challenging such a limited view today.

Current prison activism has produced abundant evidence of the magnitude of the problem of the disfranchisement of prisoners. A 1998 report by the Sentencing Project and Human Rights Watch reveals that a total of 3.9 million people are currently or permanently disenfranchised by virtue of being felons or ex-felons.[24] As a result of state laws, 1.4 million black men—13 percent of all adult black men—have lost the right to vote. In the states of Alabama and Florida, 31 percent of all black men have been permanently divested of their right to participate in the electoral process.[25] It is a not entirely unpredictable irony that as prison populations expand under the conditions of an emergent prison industrial complex, civil rights principles have been appropriated by con- servative ideologists and have become unavailable for use in what might other- wise be a massive voting rights campaign.

This raises some larger questions about the evolution of democracy under conditions of capitalism. In what sense can we say that the measure of citizenship (or of rights available) has always been linked to the denial of rights to some? A brief discussion of prison history may be helpful here, particularly if we focus on the implications of the simultaneous emergence of imprisonment as the reigning mode of punishment and industrial capitalism, with its attendant discourses of individual rights within civil society. Just as the young United States of America furnished a model of political democracy to the Western world, it also provided a new model of punishment—imprisonment in penitentiaries. As an alternative to corporal punishment, the penitentiary was the supreme expression of bourgeois democracy as it negatively affirmed the citizen's status as a rights-bearing subject—criminalizing poverty, segmenting the population, and burdening the individual (read male) with the moral responsibility for social welfare, thereby liberating the state.

Based on their visits to numerous U.S. prisons in 1831, Alexis de Toqueville and Gustave de Beaumont conceded that

> The penitentiary system in America is severe. While society in the United States gives the example of the most extended liberty, the prisons of the same country offer the spectacle of the most complete despotism. The citizens subject to the law are protected by it; they only cease to be free when they become wicked.[26]

This observation, which was made in the coauthored work *On the Penitentiary System in the United States and Its Application in France*,[27] was based on research conducted during the same voyage to the United States that furnished Tocqueville with the material for *Democracy in America*. It is significant that discussion on imprisonment as a reverse image of democracy, and thus as a peculiarly "undemocratic" institution inextricably linked to the democratic process, is lacking in *Democracy in America*. The only reference Toqueville makes to prisons in that work is in the chapter on "The Unlimited Power of the Majority," where he refers to mobilization of public opinion for the reform of criminals. There he is critical of the power of the majority for having supported the new penitentiaries designed to reform and neglecting the old institutions "so that in the immediate neighborhood of a prison that bore witness to the mild and enlightened spirit of our times, dungeons existed that reminded one of the barbarism of the Middle Ages."[28]

But Tocqueville was impressed enough by the new American penitentiary to become a pivotal figure in the parliamentary debate on the reform of French prisons. He contended that American prisons—even the worst ones—were vastly superior to their French counterparts: "Our prisons are so inferior to American prisons, even to those they declared harmful to health, and mental balance, that to try to compare them is to abuse reason."[29] During the parliamentary debate,

Tocqueville argued in support of the Pennsylvania system—devised by Quaker prison reformers—of absolute separation and silence, which, he claimed, would prevent prisoners from further corrupting one another and thus result in the moral reformation of the individual convict.[30]

This reformation, however, could only be achieved through the most absolute repression of civil society. A democratic society in which freedom of assembly and free speech were the hallmarks could only be preserved by relegating its outlaws to solitude and silence—not only by banishing them from civil society, but by preventing them from engaging in any manner of social relations. Of course, Charles Dickens, another European who visited U.S. prisons, found the Pennsylvania system to be entirely incompatible with democracy. In an often quoted passage of his *American Notes,* Dickens prefaced a description of his 1842 visit to Eastern Penitentiary with the observation that "the system here is rigid, strict, and hopeless solitary confinement. I believe it, in its effects, to be cruel and wrong."

> In its intention I am well convinced that it is kind, humane, and meant for reforma-tion; but I am persuaded that those who devised this system of Prison Discipline, and those benevolent gentlemen who carry it into execution, do not know what it is that they are doing. I believe that very few men are capable of estimating the immense amount of torture and agony that this dreadful punishment, prolonged for years, in-flicts upon the sufferers.... I am only the more convinced that there is a depth of ter-rible endurance in it which none but the sufferers themselves can fathom, and which no man has a right to inflict upon his fellow-creature. I hold this slow and daily tam-pering with the mysteries of the brain, to be immeasurably worse than any torture of the body; ... because its wounds are not upon the surface, and it extorts few cries that human ears can hear; therefore I the more denounce it, as a secret punishment which slumbering humanity is not roused up to stay.[31]

Unlike Toqueville, who believed that such punishment would result in moral renewal and thus mold convicts into better citizens, Dickens was of the opinion that "[t]hose who have undergone this punishment MUST pass into society again morally unhealthy and diseased."[32]

The Pennsylvania system incorporated the English concept of "civil death," to which outlaws (and to which married women, who had no legal standing except through their husbands) were relegated. However, the prisoner banished from civil society was expected to reemerge phoenixlike through his own meditative exertions as a new citizen-subject. Yet, as Dickens predicted, insanity was the more likely consequence of years of isolation and silence. The notion of the pris-oner's "civil death" had obvious and intentional resonances with slavery, for slaves and their freed descendants were legally divested of a range of rights, in-cluding the right to vote. As slaves and their descendants were exempted from constitutional protection, so have imprisoned individuals found themselves be-

yond the pale of the Constitution. Although prisoners have periodically succeeded in winning certain rights (such as the right to proceed in federal courts
under a writ of habeas corpus for the purpose of bringing Eighth or Fourteenth
Amendment suits), these rights were drastically curtailed by the Reagan-Bush
Supreme Court. In California and other states, prisoners have recently lost the
right to be interviewed by the media. Since the majority of imprisoned individuals are people of color, the communities historically targeted by racism are the
same communities whose members continue to be disproportionately treated as
second-class citizens, and thus whose abilities to speak for themselves in legal
and public arenas have been severely restricted.

On the one hand, the racialization of imprisonment is taken for granted. Since
the abolition of slavery, black people have been incarcerated in discernibly excessive numbers. Today 49 percent of all state and federal prisoners are black and 17
percent are Latino.[33] Categories of blackness and criminality have mutually informed each other within dominant popular and scholarly discourses. In regions
of the country with substantial Latino and Native American populations, criminality is also racialized accordingly. Not only are undocumented immigrants from
Central America and Asia continually subject to arrest and deportation, but
Latinos and Asian Americans who are U.S. citizens as well. On other hand, legal
discourses—especially in the post–civil rights era—rely on racially neutral categories to explain the process of punishment. Thus, the historical divestment of
rights of people of color has merged with the historical treatment of criminals.

With these brief evocations of the historical connection between the rise of imprisonment as punishment and the rise of industrial capitalism, and of the attendant discourses of individual rights associated with bourgeois democracy, I want
to allude to the complexities of developing persuasive arguments against the
prison industrial complex and against the systematic and racist use of confinement in prisons and jails as the solution to what are perceived as social dysfunctions associated with racialized communities. Just as a historical analysis of the
emergence of the prison system necessitates a critique of early capitalism, an
analysis of the prison industrial complex today must be linked to a radical critique of the structures and values of global capitalism, including the strategic significance of racism and patriarchy. (In an earlier article,[34] I tried to suggest theoretical strategies for avoiding a masculinist approach to the prison industrial
complex in light of the overwhelmingly male population of the prisons by locating women's punishment on a continuum that includes both public and private
circuits of power.) I have intended here to suggest the radical potential of theorizing and organizing against the prison industrial complex. By locating the current prison crisis within an analytical context that is critical of limited understandings of civil rights, and that considers the class, race, and gender
implications of bourgeois democracy, Derrick Bell's parable of the Space Traders
can be reimagined in the everyday transactions of the corporations and government agencies that harvest colossal profits from the punishment industry and

consume the social resources needed to respond to the social problems that propel so many people toward prison. This work against the prison industrial complex can assist us in developing popular critiques of late capitalism and can potentially radicalize scholars and activists alike.

Notes

This is an edited version of a talk presented at the American Philosophy Association Regional Conference, Radical Philosophy Association Session, April 1, 1999. I thank Gina Dent for her invaluable suggestions.

1. Derrick Bell, "The Space Traders," in *Faces at the Bottom of the Well: The Permanence of Racism* (New York: Basic Books, 1990), 159–160.

2. Ibid. 194.

3. Derrick Bell, "Racial Realism—After We're Gone: Prudent Speculations on America in a Post-Racial Epoch," in Richard Delgado. *Critical Race Theory: The Cutting Edge* (Philadelphia: Temple University Press), 3.

4. Michael A. Olivas, "The Chronicles, My Grandfather's Stories, and Immigration Law: The Slave Traders Chronicle as Racial History," in Richard Delgado, *Critical Race Theory: The Cutting Edge* (Philadelphia: Temple University Press), 11.

5. Ibid.

6. See Derrick A. Bell Jr., "Serving Two Masters: Integration Ideals and Client Interests in School Desegregation Litigation" and "*Brown v. Board of Education* and the Interest Convergence Dilemma" in Kimberlee Crenshaw, Neil Gotanda, Garry Peller, and Kendall Thomas, *Critical Race Theory: The Key Writings that Formed the Movement* (New York, New Press, 1995).

7. Bell, "The Space Traders," 192.

8. See Lani Guinier, *The Tyranny of the Majority: Fundamental Fairness in Representative Democracy* (New York: Free Press, 1994).

9. I have borrowed this term from David Theo Goldberg. See his article "Wedded to Dixie: Dinesh D'Souza and the New Segregationism," in Goldberg, *Racial Subjects: Writing on Race in America* (New York: Routledge, 1997).

10. Darrell K. Gilliard (BJS statistician), "Prison and Jail Inmates at Midyear 1998," March 1999 NCJ 173414.

11. According to the Sentencing Project, in 1996, 49 percent of state and federal prisoners were black and 17 percent were Hispanic. "Facts About Prisons and Prisoners," March 1999.

12. Jerome Miller, director of the National Center on Institutions and Alternatives, analyzed the March 1999 Justice Department statistics and concluded that by the year 2000, there will be 1 million African American adults behind bars. Approximately one in ten black men will be in prison. "Number of Blacks in Jail Rising Toward One Million," *San Francisco Chronicle*, March 8, 1999.

13. Derrick Bell, "Racial Realism," in Crenshaw et al., *Critical Race Theory*, 307.

14. See Neil Gotanda's article, "A Critique of 'Our Constitution Is Color-Blind'" and other contributions of such scholars as Kimberl Crenshaw, Gary Peller, Cheryl Harris, and Kendall Thomas in Crenshaw et al., *Critical Race Theory*.

15. Gilliard, "Prison and Jail Inmates at Midyear 1998."

16. This slogan appeared on CCRI literature and can be found on their Web site.

17. Lea McDermid, Kathleen Connolly, Dan Macallair, and Vincent Shiraldi, *From Classrooms to Cellblocks: How Prison Building Affects Higher Education and African American Enrollment in California* (Washington, D.C.: Justice Policy Institute, October 1996).

18. The California Civil Rights Initiative, a proposed statewide constitutional amendment by initiative (authors and principals: Glynn Custred and Thomas Wood), passed in 1996.

19. Albert G. Mosley and Nicolas Capaldi, *Affirmative Action: Social Justice or Unfair Preference,* (New York: Rowman and Littlefield, 1996), 65.

20. Ibid, 65–66.

21. *Ruffin v. Commonwealth,* 62 Va (21 Gratt.) 790, 796 (1871). Quoted in Leonard Orland, *Prisons: Houses of Darkness* (New York: Free Press, 1975), 81.

22. "Neither slavery nor involuntary servitude, except as a punishment for crime whereof the party shall have been duly convicted, shall exist within the United States, or any place subject to their jurisdiction" (Section 1 of the Thirteenth Amendment to the Constitution, ratified December 6, 1965).

23. See Angela Y. Davis. "From the Prison of Slavery to the Slavery of Prison: Frederick Douglass and the Convict Lease System," in Joy James, ed., *The Angela Y. Davis Reader* (New York: Blackwell, 1998).

24. Jamie Fellner and Marc Mauer, "Losing the Vote: The Impact of Felony Disenfranchisement Laws in the United States," The Sentencing Project and Human Rights Watch, October 1998, 2.

25. Ibid., 8.

26. Gustave de Beaumont and Alexis de Tocqueville, *On the Penitentiary System in the United States and Its Application in France* (Carbondale and Edwardsville: Southern Illinois University Press, 1964 [original edition, 1833]), 78.

27. Apparently Tocqueville contributed little to the writing of this tract. However, it did reflect the collaboration with Beaumont. See Thorsten Sellin's introduction to the 1964 edition.

28. Alexis de Tocqueville. *Democracy in America,* vol. 1 (New York: Vintage Books, 1954), 268. Here he is probably referring to the two prisons in Philadelphia—Eastern State Penitentiary at Cherry Hill and Walnut Street Jail.

29. Seymour Drescher, ed. *Toqueville and Beaumont on Social Reform* (New York: Harper Torchbooks, 1968), 73.

30. "Consider a system in which the inmate is separated from those infamous but attractive pleasures that he finds in the company of other criminals, a system which leaves him alone with his remorse. Consider whether this system, after all, is not as repressive as what exists today. Consider, too, whether a system that absolutely separates the inmate from the gangrenous section of society and puts him completely in contact with its most honest portion, that perpetually opens the door toward hope and honesty and closes the door leading to crime and despair, whether . . . such a system must not be infinitely more moralizing than the one we now observe. In other words, let us ask whether the cellular system alone, among all others, necessarily leads to one great effect, the effect of absolutely preventing its inmates from ever being able to corrupt each other more than they were before, so that prison can never return men to the world more evil than those it received." Ibid, 88–89.

31. Charles Dickens, *The Works of Charles Dickens, Vol. 27, American Notes* (New York: Peter Fenelon Collier and Son, 1900), 119–120.

32. Ibid., 131.

33. See note 12.

34. Angela Y. Davis, "Public Imprisonment and Private Violence: Reflections on The Hidden Punishment of Women," *New England Journal on Criminal and Civil Confinement* 24, No. 2, summer, 1998.

7

Human Rights Versus Classical Liberalism: A Study in the Theory of Value

James Syfers

In 1976 two treaties came into force in international law that embody the highest ideals that have ever been expressed in law, let alone in international law. They are the Covenant on Civil and Political Rights and the Covenant on Economic, Social, and Cultural Rights.[1] The nations that have ratified these treaties—and that now includes the majority of nations on the earth—have in so doing surrendered a large measure of their sovereign powers over the populations of their countries, have committed themselves to making periodic reports to the United Nations on their progress in implementing the human rights established by the covenants, and have committed themselves to periodic public examinations by that body on their progress.[2] They have thus made themselves parties to the greatest collective project ever undertaken by our species. The success of this project over the next century will depend in part on the removal of many obstacles; some of these obstacles are entrenched political and economic interests, and some of them are ideas, attitudes, and habits of thought that are equally well entrenched. In the United States the most important obstacle of the latter kind appears to be the ideology of classical liberalism.

By the ideology of classical liberalism I mean the constellation of ideas and theories developed from the late seventeenth through the nineteenth centuries, and associated with John Locke, Jeremy Bentham, James Mill, Adam Smith, and many others. As an ideology classical liberalism has been the most powerful influence on the Western world since Christianity. Part of the explanation for this influence is undoubtedly the role it played in promoting the development of industrial capitalism.[3] But part of the explanation is also the fact that it was an ideology built upon the premises—already widely accepted—of modern philosophy. Since these premises include a metaphysics, or conception of the nature of reality, it is perhaps better to speak of classical liberalism as a full-fledged *Weltanschauung* rather than simply an ideology.

Part 1 will sketch those aspects of the classical liberal worldview that are inherently hostile to the implementation of important rights now held through the International Covenant on Social, Economic, and Cultural Rights and other international human rights conventions. The conflict is rooted in the classical liberal theory of value and associated moral principles. Part 2 will present an alternative to classical liberalism in the form of a systemic theory of value that is more compatible with human rights law. The following part considers some of the implications of the preceding parts for the institution of private property. And the last part returns to the subject of the International Bill of Human Rights as the blueprint for the common good in the twenty-first century.

Part 1: The Classical Liberal *Weltanschauung*

Modern philosophy rests on a philosophical premise that established itself in the period of the Renaissance, the premise that *only individual things exist or are real.*[4] Although the premise was stated as and appears to have been understood as an empirical and verifiable claim, it is in fact an a priori principle whose main function has been as a guide in the construction of theories in science, ethics, and law. The real "individual things" for many of the new scientists of the seventeenth century, for example, were the atoms (hard particles) out of which everything else was held to be composed. In theories concerning human society, including classical liberalism, the real "individual things" are individual persons, and society was seen as a mere aggregation of persons, having no reality beyond them. Thus any explanation of the characteristics and history of a society had to be found in the nature of its inhabitants or in the particular characteristics of particular individuals. This "reduction" of society to the individuals who compose it, however, is not the only aspect of modern philosophy relevant to classical liberal ideology. The premise that only individual things exist has two corollaries regarding value, referred to above as the classical liberal theory of value. If only individual things exist, then

1. Only individual things can possess value.
2. Only individuals are capable of creating value.

Both corollaries probably seemed very reasonable in the period in which the industrial revolution was gathering steam, where individual things capable of being bought and sold—raw materials, manufactured commodities, tracts of land, productive machinery, precious metals—were the sorts of things that had value, at least to those involved in market agriculture, commerce, manufacturing, and invention. And the notion that individuals were the sole or primary source of value was evidenced in the merchant adventurer, the inventor, and the entrepreneur, the class that was creating wealth and transforming the world.

At the same time, however, these new premises had profound implications. For example, if only individual things exist, then there can be no such thing as an ecological system in the sense of something greater than the mere sum of its individual constituents; and to one whose thought was habituated to these premises, it would seem irrational to look for or consider such a system. Again, if individuals alone can produce or create value, then *Nature* as such cannot be creative of value. Indeed, in early modern philosophy Nature was not regarded as creative of value for another reason as well: it was considered to be wholly mechanical. "Mind is active, Matter passive" was a formula taken for granted by proponents of early modern philosophy.[5]

In this intellectual framework value would have to be created by individuals expending labor on dead matter, that is, altering in some respect some part or aspect of a passive and mechanistic physical world. So the value of something produced would reasonably be commensurate with the amount of labor required to produce it. As labor was assumed to be painful, it was evidently regarded as moral common sense to require that the producer should enjoy the full value of what he or she produced. We have, then, two further principles:

3. The real value of a thing is the amount of labor required to produce it.
4. The individual should have the full value of the product of his labor.

Principle 3 is the labor theory of value, and 4 is one of the foundations of private property.[6] Both principles play an important role in the theory of the free market, which lies at the heart of classical liberalism.[7] Before stating the main thesis of that theory, one more principle needs to be added, that of utility:

5. What is right is whatever promotes the greatest happiness (or pleasure) of the greatest number.

This is a principle of many faces. It assumes that every person has a moral claim to be counted, and in this respect it was a powerful battering ram historically against feudalism and monarchism.[8] It asserts the primacy of worldly happiness, and so also confronted the moral hegemony of the Church. Unfortunately, it also assumes something that is commonsensically false, namely, that there is no such thing as a *common good* or *public good* apart from the sum total of individual goods. And the history of moral theory in the era of classical liberalism is virtually silent on any competing principle regarding the right as what promotes the public good. Last, the utility principle has been used and is still used to justify the sacrifice of the few in the name of scientific and/or industrial progress for the many. In this role it legitimizes the primary goal of the free market: maximizing the production of those things that would promote the greatest happiness of the greatest number, for example, food, clothing, shelter, and other manufacturable necessities of life.

The free market itself is envisioned by Adam Smith as a price-competitive economy with multiple individual producers of every commodity, in which everyone enjoys freedom of investment, freedom of exchange, and freedom of contract. I will refer to these freedoms as "economic liberties" to keep them separate from the economic rights that are accorded by the International Convenant, such as the right to a decent standard of living, the right to employment, and other rights.[9] Adam Smith's central hypothesis concerning the free market, then, is as follows:

(6) If there is a free market, then:

   (A) There will be the most efficient use of resources for the production of the necessities of life,
   (B) There will be a maximum increase over time in productivity, and
   (C) There will be a reasonably fair distribution of what is produced.[10]

What is meant by "productivity" here is output per man-hour. In the eighteenth and nineteenth centuries it may have seemed obvious that goals (A) and (B) should have priority over any and all other concerns; at the end of the twentieth century—confronted as we are with a host of environmental and ecological problems—it is no longer so obvious. In any case, a system that would maximize wealth in the form of exchangeable commodities and at the same time provide everyone with the full value of his or her labor must have appeared in the eighteenth century as a system inspired by angels. Indeed, trying to show that these results were truly sound has preoccupied more than a few nineteenth- and twentieth-century economists.[11] The following passage, for example, is from John Bates Clark's *The Distribution of Wealth:*

> It is the purpose of this work to show that the distribution of the income of society is controlled by a natural law, and that this law, if it worked without friction, would give to every agent of production the amount of wealth which that agent creates.[12]

The basic idea, first stated by Adam Smith, is that a free market will always tend to equalize the supply and demand for any commodity, and if the supply equals the demand, then the market price of the commodity will equal its real value, that is, the labor time required to produce it. Clark put it this way:

Normal prices are no-profit prices. They afford wages for all the labor that is involved in producing the goods, including the labor of superintending the mills, managing the finances, keeping the accounts, collecting the debts and doing all the work of directing the policy of the business. They afford, also, interest on all the capital that is used in the business, whether it is owned by the *entrepreneur* or borrowed from some one else. Beyond this there is no return. [13]

There is, of course, a problem in justifying the profits of capital within this schema, since capital expends no labor, and the problem comes out here in the evident contradiction between prices being "no-profit prices" on the one hand, and yet including the profit (interest) on capital on the other. Adam Smith dealt with the issue by saying the profit of capital would have to be a deduction from workers' wages.[14] But the deduction would be justified in his view, since over time rising productivity would cause the real value of commodities to decline, and thus the buying power of wages would increase. Whether this makes sense (if labor is itself a commodity) is another question, but it shows that Adam Smith took seriously the principle that "the whole produce of the laborer" should belong to the laborer.[15]

There are at least two main areas of conflict between classical liberalism and economic rights. One concerns the labor principle, Principle 4, and the other concerns the principle of utility and the primary goals of the free market. In what follows I will confine my remarks to a simple statement of the problem, without considering various qualifications of the principles that have been urged that might tend to mitigate but not eliminate the basic conflict.[16]

Assume, then, for the purpose of illustration the a priori principles of classical liberalism: (1) that there are only individuals, and (2) that only individuals are producers of value. The conflict arises when one class of persons is productive of value and another class, for whatever reasons, is not. The term "productive" here is highly tendentious, meaning engaged in the production of marketable commodities or services for profit; so "unproductive" means not so engaged.[17] If government intervenes in this situation to tax the former on behalf of the latter, on Principle 4 there would be a serious breach of ethics. Government is taking by force of law what rightfully belongs to productive citizens, who are deprived of the full value of their labor.[18]

Moreover, a further sin is committed by a government appropriating a share of an individual's labor for purposes of providing for the "nonproductive" class. The wealth that would otherwise be invested in creating new enterprises, improving existing ones, or upgrading productive skills will be reduced, so the economic growth rate of the economy will be slowed, interfering with the main purposes of the free market. And this is wrong on the utility principle, since the government is using its power to benefit a few today at the greater expense of the many tomorrow. The same objection would be made to the possibility of the government owning and operating sufficient profit-making enterprises to provide for the so-called unproductive class. So it would appear that within the worldview of classical liberalism it is morally problematic as to how a state could go about implementing the right to a minimum standard of living, medical care, and education; these would require continual "expropriations" of private property or "wastage" of capital on those who did nothing to earn it.

These same kinds of objections, urged by utilitarian radicals in the eighteenth century, are still being put forward by right-wing or neoliberal "conservatives" in the present. They make some sense if one accepts the a priori principles of the classical liberal theory of value; they make little or no sense from the perspective of a systemic theory of value.

Part 2: An Alternative View:
The Primacy of Systemic Value

A very different position on economic rights is made possible by the view that it is not individuals that are the primary source of value, *but the social system as such*. Before explicating the statement that the social system is the primary source of value, there are two preliminary comments, one on the existence or reality of social systems, the other on the meaning of the term.

That there are social systems is a matter of common sense; within the classical liberal perspective, however, a social system is regarded as being reducible to the individuals that make it up, so any and all social phenomena must be explained in terms of the nature or characteristics of those individuals. The counterclaim that social systems are not so reducible and exist in their own right does not entail postulating the existence of a mysterious and transcendent metaphysical entity (that would be to construe the category of system as if it belonged to the category of individual thing); nor does it require acceptance of the view that social systems exist independently of the individuals that make them up. It does require acknowledging that social systems may exist independently of any particular set of inhabitants, in the same way a corporation exists independently of any particular set of directors, officers, and employees.

Second, the term *social system* is being used here to include the legal, political, cultural, and economic systems of modern society, as distinguishable parts of one and the same overall system. All are thus subsystems interconnected to the point that none could or would be what it is without existing in the relational matrix of the whole social system, and all have both mental and material aspects. If this view is correct, and I believe it is, then any theory that treats one of these subsystems as if it were isolable from the rest would appear to have very limited usefulness in explanation or prediction. There could be, for example, no set of variables such that knowing their values and the relevant laws, one could predict future states of the economic subsystem, the way we can predict the future states of the solar system. Not only because the economic subsystem is part of a larger more complex system, but also because we are dealing with systems that are both material and mental, and the material and mental aspects of societies appear to interact in unpredictable ways. The same thing would be true of the social system as a whole, since it exists within the greater ecological system of the planet.[19]

Now the claim that the social system is the primary source of value does not entail that the labor performed by individuals is unnecessary or that it is illusory or has no value. What it does mean can, I think, be summed up in three points:

1. For virtually every kind of employment, it would not *exist* at all, or would exist only marginally, outside a particular social system and generally for a limited historical period. For example, the manufacture of square-head nails (ending in the 1870s), or the manufacture of glass radio tubes (ending after the invention of the transistor in 1948), or family farming (dying out in this century).
2. Further, it means that most kinds of products or services would have little or no *value* save within that particular social system.
3. Finally, it is the continuous operation of the entire social system that makes possible the individual contribution to the creation of value; stated in another way, it is a necessary condition for one's being engaged in a productive employment or service that the entire system be functioning on a more or less continuous basis. The reason for this is simply the fact that modern society is temporally, physically, economically, and administratively integrated into one system. If this social system "slows down" or "stops," individual production of goods or services slows down or stops. The integration of the social system, particularly the economic system, will be considered at length below, but there is first another principle regarding value and the social system that needs to be considered.

It will be recalled that the classical liberal perspective developed on the basis of the ideas that only individuals can produce value, and that only individual things can possess value. In like manner if social systems exist, *they may possess value in themselves as well as being a source of value*. In the case of a social system there would of course be no question that for its inhabitants it has value at least insofar as it is a life-sustaining system (although it may have other characteristics that are life-threatening as well). In either case, recognition of the existence of systems as such would make possible their protection in law and their modification by law.[20] Thus an ecosystem could be protected in its own right, rather than as a by-product of the protection of individual members of an endangered species.

That a social system may have great value in itself as well as being the primary source of value does not entail that the individuals who constitute it at any particular time must be subordinate to it; attribution of value to the one does not threaten the value of the other. This is a point that is often misunderstood and so requires some comment. Recall that under international law now in force, every individual has civil, political, economic, social, and cultural rights. This means that a principal criterion for the evaluation of any social system is now the degree to which the society has observed and implemented the International Bill of Human Rights.[21] Recognition of the reality, value, or causal role of social systems is thus in no way equivalent to a political philosophy that subordinates the individual to the needs or purposes of the state.

However, the protection in law of social systems, ecological systems, and even the human immune system will clearly require restrictions on economic liberties, that is, on the rights of private property. So will, of course, the implementation of the economic, social, and cultural rights of the Second Covenant; for example, under the covenant individuals have the right to security, employment, and a decent standard of living. Corporations therefore cannot be permitted to discharge them merely for the purpose of increasing quarterly earnings and/or temporarily raising the value of their stocks. An assessment of just what is involved in the conflict between private property rights, human rights, and ecological needs requires a close look at what has become of private property in the late twentieth century.

Part 3: The Theory of Systemic Value and Private Property

The economy of the United States is a highly organized system that is jointly administered in the main by two institutions, neither one of which is dealt with in classical liberal political or economic philosophy and neither one of which is addressed by the Constitution. The first is the corporation, which the U.S. Supreme Court brought to life in 1886 by the simple expedient of declaring that corporations were to be regarded as "persons" under the Fourteenth Amendment, and therefore would enjoy some of the same constitutional rights as those possessed by real persons.[22] The second is the federal agency that embodies all three powers of government in one institution: legislative, judicial, and executive. These agencies presently comprise the fourteen executive departments (as Agriculture, Defense, Commerce, or Energy) and the sixty-two independent institutions (as the Federal Reserve System, Central Intelligence Agency, or Nuclear Regulatory Commission); almost all of these are the work of the past century; 95 percent of federal law is enacted by these agencies, and although they are required by the Administrative Procedures Act of 1946 to conduct public hearings on proposed laws, these hearings are typically attended largely or solely by representatives of corporations.[23] That one agency should embody all three powers appears to violate the principle of the separation of powers, and indeed the Supreme Court ruled, in 1892, that Congress cannot delegate legislative power, as this "... is a principle universally recognized as vital to the integrity and maintenance of the system of government ordained by the Constitution."[24] In this century, however, the Court has stepped around this earlier ruling by distinguishing congressionally legislated laws from the "administrative rules" of agencies, and most recently the Court has made the federal agencies even more independent of Congress by eliminating the congressional veto power over agency legislation.[25] What has evolved over this century, then, is a political/economic system administered in the main by these two institutions, corporations and government agencies, in symbiotic relationship. It is a situation that lies outside the Constitution and outside classical liberal political theory in the sense that neither the corporations nor the triple-powered agencies were envisaged by either and do not appear to be justifiable by either. Let us now look at the institution of private property, one of the great foundations of classical liberal thought, to see how it has been affected by and fits into this system.

The concept of private property embedded in the classical liberal tradition— call this the classical conception of private property—has two aspects that are of particular interest here. Private property has been understood, first of all, as the *individual* ownership of things, tangible or intangible. Second, the meaning of ownership has been understood in terms of a set of rights held by the owner in relation to the things. These rights would include, following the analysis of private property by Honoré, the right to possess, use, manage, and receive income from the property, as well as the right to transfer, waive, abandon, or destroy it.[26]

The institution itself has been justified on the basis of the moral principles of classical liberalism considered above. We have considered one of the moral principles justifying private property in Principle 4: if the individual should have the full value of his or her labor, then the individual should have the rights that secure full value to the product of that labor. Closely connected with this justification is a further one also based on the individual, and that is the idea that private property is essential to the free development of the individual's personality and powers; the quotation following is from Thomas Hill Green, founder of the British Idealist movement of the 1860s:

> One condition of the existence of property, then, is appropriation, and that implies the conception of himself on the part of the appropriator as a permanent subject for whose use, as instruments of satisfaction and expression, he takes and fashions certain external things, certain things external to his bodily members. These things, so taken and fashioned, cease to be external as they were before. They become a sort of extension of the man's organs, the constant apparatus through which he gives reality to his ideas and wishes.[27]

The property envisaged here as an extension of the individual's person or personality was probably thought of as tangible property, as real property and chattels; it would be difficult to see how a securities portfolio or other similar intangibles could be conceived of as an extension of one's bodily organs or person or how any credence could be given to such a conception. The justification of most property of the intangible kind rests, therefore, on a second traditional argument based on the principle of utility.

The argument here is essentially the argument for the free market economy as promoting the greatest happiness; if the goals of the free market are accepted as having moral priority over all other concerns and policies, then the institution of private property is justified since it is a necessary condition for the existence of the free market. It is the legal foundation for the free market's economic liberties—freedom of investment, contract, and exchange. But if there is to be private property, is there no limit on how much property an individual may accumulate? The standard answer is that any such limit would interfere with the size of the capitals available for investment, and so would have the effect of retarding technological advancement and/or economic growth; and these ends, once again, have the highest moral priority.

This argument, however, lost its force for any practical purpose with the coming of the corporation, an exercise in the freedom of association that allows an unlimited number of individuals to pool their capital. And today, even the sale of stock by corporations is no longer a principal means of raising capital, since almost all investment in productive and service industries comes from funds raised internally.[28] Indeed, the problem in the late twentieth century is not that of raising more capital for investment in new technology, but the rate of technologically driven social change that we can tolerate without social and ecological destabilization and chaos.

In considering the nature and status of private property as it exists today, it will be useful to distinguish between *income-producing property*, and *income-reducing property*. This is a rough distinction, but still a useful one. Income-reducing property is, for the most part, tangible and personal property; for example, a person's dwelling, automobile, clothing, a pet, and so on. It is property that requires the expenditure of income over time in order to keep it in usable condition, to operate it, to keep it clean or in good health, and so forth. Income-producing property, on the other hand, is property of the intangible kind that provides regular income, as rental property, patents, stocks, bonds, and other securities. The distinction is not absolute; depending on its use, for example, a vehicle might belong to either category or both, and a professional license could be regarded as both.

More and more, over the past century or so, income-producing property has lost the attributes of private property as listed above; an owner of corporate stock has a very limited property right in the corporation: the right to receive dividends, to propose motions at annual meetings of stockholders, and in some cases to vote for directors (depending on the kind of stock held), but has no control over the operations and policy of the corporation or even over the portion of profits to be made available as dividends; indeed, the stockholder is even the last to be paid, after creditors and employees.[29]

Of the more than $8 trillion worth of stock held in 1995, the ownership of nearly half is even further removed from the classical conception of private property than the above. Some $2 trillion is held by private and public pension funds; here the individual investor is not the legal owner of any stock, but has only a beneficial interest—a limited property right—with little or nothing to say regarding the investments of the fund or its officers. Another $1 trillion is held in mutual funds, in which again the shareholder has no legal ownership of the stocks purchased with his or her money. Outside pension and mutual funds, $500 billion or $600 billion is owned by financial and nonfinancial corporations, legally and beneficially, and a great part of the remainder is held by nonprofit private foundations, nonprofit institutions such as charitable or educational corporations, and various kinds of trusts in which the trustee (often a bank or trust institution) is the legal owner. Thus, nearly half of the publicly traded stock in the United States is legally owned by corporations rather than individuals. This is again a state of affairs that lies entirely outside the classical liberal political or economic theory, made possible by the Supreme Court decision mentioned above that, with a wave of the judicial wand, made corporations into "persons."

Private property in the classical sense has thus virtually disappeared *as far as the category of income producing property is concerned.* In the classical sense private property involved a real owner, something owned, and a set of rights held by the owner over what is owned. As we have seen, much of the property in this category is not legally owned by individuals at all, and for what is so owned, the traditional rights do not obtain or obtain only in a severely limited sense. Thus the classical liberal arguments to justify property as a product of individual labor or as an extension of self or expression of personality are not applicable; corporations are really not individuals, and corporate stocks or mutual fund shares are really not private property in the classical sense.[30] The arguments would still apply, of course, in the case of personal property, the largely tangible property that is held by real individuals. Let us consider now how these two categories of property—income producing and income reducing—are distributed in the population as a whole.

Somewhat more than half of publicly traded stock is still held by individual owners, or by "households" in the terminology of the federal government. If households are ranked according to ownership of stock, the top one-half of 1 percent of the population held 58.57 percent of this stock in 1995. The top 5 percent held 94.49 percent of the stock; the top 10 percent held 99.11 percent. Eighty percent of U.S. households had none.[31] Ten percent of households, then, held 99 percent of the stock that is not owned by corporations, to which must be added a healthy percentage of bonds and other securities. In the case of stocks alone, this amounts to a bit over $4.114 trillion at 1995 market value.[32] In the case of the top one-half of 1 percent of households, this would amount to roughly $2,409,569,800,000, or $2.409 trillion. Much of this wealth is *dynastic,* that is, it is held and managed in such a way so as to increase from one generation to another. Here is one example of the magnitude of such holdings:

> Of some 1,600 living Du Ponts, only 250 constitute the inner circle. Of these, only about 50 make up the all-powerful inner core of the family. Together, these 50 Du Ponts control or share control over $211 billion worth of assets, greater than the annual Gross National Product of most nations. They own huge or controlling interests in over 100 multimillion-dollar corporations and banks, including some of the world's largest. [33]

The existence of dynastic fortunes requires that the transfer of property from decedent to heirs be permitted in law, and that the bulk of the property transferred escapes estate or inheritance tax. The classical liberal tradition was divided on the issue of passing such wealth from one generation to another.[34] Some took the view that there is a natural right to bequeath property; others, like Thomas Jefferson, took a diametrically opposite position:

> The earth belongs in usufruct to the living; the dead have neither powers nor rights over it. The portion occupied by any individual ceases to be his when he himself ceases to be and reverts to society.[35]

That there is no natural right to bequeath property is now the prevailing view in the law, as expressed here rather tersely by a California court:

> It is entirely immaterial whether the statutes relative to inheritance comport with the court's or counsel's idea of justice, morality, or natural right. The matter is in the plenary control of the state Legislature and depends entirely upon the provisions of the statutes.[36]

The issue, then, is the extent to which society should permit accumulated wealth to be passed on to heirs. I have argued that our economy is an integrated system and that this system is the primary source of value. From this standpoint, individuals who possess stocks and bonds possess *entitlements to future systemic value.* That is, they have a legal or beneficial interest in value to be produced in and by the economic system; the exact return depends on the particular investments, but primarily on the performance of the system as a whole. Now the economic system responsible for generating that value and the social system that sustains it required hundreds of years of thought, labor, and struggle by millions of persons to attain its present level of sophistication, complexity, and productive power; its continued operation requires the regular labor of millions of individuals carrying out myriad specialized tasks. Holders of stock, however, will receive regular shares of the value produced by this system in the form of dividends without the need to do or contribute anything. In this respect *entitlements to future systemic value* appear to be morally questionable; in the case of dynastic wealth there are good reasons for judging that inheritance to be entirely unethical.

An individual born into dynastic wealth inherits a portfolio of entitlements to part of the product of the labor of countless other human beings into the indefinite future; not only has the individual done nothing to earn this status, it is a violation of the basic democratic principle against special privileges by birth. It would also appear to be a violation of the Fourteenth Amendment to the Constitution, which requires that no one be denied equal protection of the law; those who are born into the position of having part of their future labor automatically appropriated by others are clearly not enjoying equal protection under the law.

Last, dynastic wealth is wealth that goes far beyond what any individual or family could ever use for any ordinary purpose of life, even allowing as ordinary purposes the possession of houses and apartments in a number of cities in this country, châteaus in France, castles in Spain, any number of vehicles, airplanes, yachts, fine art collections, and the income to keep up all these properties and the staffs they require. It is wealth that is not consumable. It has, therefore, only one purpose, a purpose that should never be among the ordinary purposes of property: it is a source of political power over other people and of political power over the operation and direction of the social system itself. We have considered one example in Part 3, where the controlling interests and boards of the largest corporations initiated or acquiesced in driving millions of fellow Americans off their farms to replace them with more "efficient" agribusiness corporations.[37] Those who inherit dynastic wealth are thus not only economically privileged to live off the labor of others, they are politically privileged with an inherited and illegitimate power over the lives of their fellow citizens.

After the American Revolution virtually all of the states abolished laws providing for primogeniture and entail, either by statute or constitutional provision. These were laws that made dynastic wealth possible in the form of land holdings, land being the principal form of wealth in the early states. It was believed by many that there was no place in a democratic society for an aristocracy perpetuated by inheritance.[38] The form of wealth has shifted in the last 100 years, land having given way to securities, but the belief is just as valid.

Part 4: The Common Good

We have reached a peculiar stage in the evolution of the political economy of the United States. We have developed an economic system of extraordinary technical complexity; its fundamental units of production, the corporations or corporate conglomerates, are themselves organized in a complex mosaic of trade associations and national and international policymaking bodies, and these organizations have in turn developed symbiotic relationships with quasi-sovereign governmental agencies. At the same time ownership of this system of production has been shifting slowly over this century from individuals to corporations, making possible an undreamed-of concentration of power in the hands of a few. The peculiarity is that none of this accords with the classical liberal political and economic theory that is supposed to constitute its moral foundations.

If the foregoing analysis is correct it appears that the worldview that has guided the developed nations since the Enlightenment—the classical liberal *Weltanschauung*—has helped to promote changes so profound as to undermine itself. We would therefore be approaching the next century with no generally accepted and applicable economic and political philosophy, were it not for another development of this century, and that is the emergence, worldwide, of the movement for human rights. By the human rights movement I mean the many and diverse struggles that have been and are in the process of crystallizing around the Universal Declaration of Human Rights and may be summed up in its language as the struggle for the dignity of the individual and the dignity of peoples. Among these are struggles to end slavery and colonialism, the struggle against racial discrimination, the struggle for equal rights for women, for freedom of speech and association, for basic security from starvation and homelessness, and many others. The declaration itself was an outgrowth of a seed planted in the charter of the United Nations, in the form of two articles:

Article 55

With a view to the creation of conditions and stability and well being, which are necessary for peaceful and friendly relations among nations based on respect for the principle of equal rights and self-determination of peoples, the United Nations shall promote:

  A. higher standards of living, full employment, and conditions of economic and social progress and development;
  B. solutions of international economic, social, health, and related problems; and international cultural and educational cooperation:
  C. universal respect for, and observance of, human rights and fundamental freedoms for all without distinction as to race, sex, language, or religion.

Article 56

All Members pledge themselves to take joint and separate action in co-operation with the Organization for the achievement of the purposes set forth in Article 55.

These articles became the basis for what I characterized above as the greatest collective project ever undertaken by our species. The third clause of Article 55

led to the adoption of the Universal Declaration of Human Rights in 1948. The
United Nations Human Rights Commission, chaired by Eleanor Roosevelt until
1953, began work immediately on turning the Universal Declaration into international law in the form of two covenants; that work continued for eighteen
years.[39] In the interim, sixty-six new nations had joined the United Nations, a
nonaligned nations movement had been organized (1961), and the General
Assembly declared the decade of the 1960s a decade of international economic
cooperation in accordance with the first and second clauses of Article 55.[40]
Human rights law, in other words, was being developed along with planning for
the international economic and political cooperation that would be necessary for
its implementation. These two aspects of the program of the United Nations, the
creation of the law and the effort to modify the global economy to implement
that law, continued through the 1960s and 1970s. Together they constitute a
global blueprint for the common good of all peoples, and they have been supported by virtually all of the 190-some nations that are currently members of the
organization. Only a minority of rich and powerful nations, such as the "Group
of Seven" (G-7), the United States, Britain, Germany, France, Japan, Italy, and
Canada have consistently stood in opposition.

International Human Rights Law

The international law concerning human rights may be divided into four categories, the first two of which are together referred to as the International Bill of
Human Rights:

I.   *The Universal Declaration of Human Rights* (1948);
II. The *Covenant on Civil and Political Rights* (1976), and *the Covenant on
     Economic, Social, and Cultural Rights* (1976);
III. A series of nearly forty independent supplementary conventions;
IV. A series of related declarations, principles, rules, standards, and guide-
     lines having an advisory status.[41]

In the main the above categories go from the very general statement of human
rights in the declaration to the more detailed statements of the covenants and
then to the still more specific law of the various conventions. For example, the
declaration states in Article 7: "All are equal before the law and are entitled
without any discrimination to equal protection of the law." The covenants are
more specific; each of them pledges states parties to the covenants not to discriminate on the basis of "race, colour, sex, language, religion, political or other opinion, national or social origin, property, birth, or other status." Still more specific
are, for example, the Convention Against All Forms of Racial Discrimination
(1969), or the Convention Concerning Discrimination in Respect of Employment
and Occupation (1958).[42] Last, it is expected that at the level of particular cases,

the judiciary of each country will have the task of interpreting international human rights law into the context of its own languages, culture, and tradition. Together the body of human rights law represented by all four categories now occupies over 900 pages in the 1993 compilation published by the United Nations.[43] That nations with different languages, cultures, political systems, religions, and traditions could all agree on so comprehensive a body of human rights law is probably the greatest moral and cooperative achievement in the most barbaric and destructive century in human history.

The Implementation of Human Rights Law

With the exception of war crimes and the crime of genocide, the United Nations makes no attempt to enforce international human rights law, if enforcement means the use of police power. First of all the organization is a voluntary association of politically sovereign nations, the governments of which are presumed to have joined this collective project in good faith. Thus in the main the role of the United Nations is properly that of being supportive of their efforts at implementation. Implementation means the creation of the political, economic, and social conditions that make possible the exercise or enjoyment of the rights that people now possess by law. This may require anything from internal changes in social practices or changes in law or administrative policy to changes in the economic relations between nations. Two principal means of implementation have been developed by the organization. One is a reporting process that is built into the various treaties, and the other is the project for what is referred to as the New International Economic Order (NIEO).

An example will illustrate the reporting process. Ratification of the Covenant on Economic, Social, and Cultural Rights requires a government to submit a report within two years on the measures it has adopted to give effect to the covenant rights and on the progress made in their enjoyment, and reports are expected to be submitted every five years thereafter.[44] Reports are reviewed by an eighteen-member Committee on Economic, Social, and Cultural Rights, made up of experts in the field of human rights nominated by states party to the treaty, elected by the United Nations Economic and Social Council and serving in their personal capacity rather than as official representatives of any government. Reports are reviewed by the committee in open public sessions, with the assistance of the various UN agencies whose work is intimately related to the implementation of specific treaty rights, such as the International Labor Organization, the Food and Agriculture Organization, the World Health Organization, and the United Nations Educational, Social and Cultural Organization (UNESCO).[45]

As important as the reporting process is in keeping governments in mind of and answerable to their treaty obligations, an enormous problem is posed by the limited resources that developing nations can devote to the implementation of human rights. World economic planning was therefore seen, very early on, as a necessary part of the implementation process. The first step in this direction was the formation of the United Nations Conference on Trade and Development (UNCTAD) in 1964. The final act of this conference, fifty-five pages in length, begins as follows:

> The States participating in the Conference are determined to achieve the high purposes embodied in the United Nations Charter "to promote social progress and better standards of life in larger freedom"; to seek a better and more effective system of international economic cooperation, whereby the division of the world into areas of poverty and plenty may be banished and prosperity achieved by all; and to find ways by which the human and material resources of the world may be harnessed for the abolition of poverty everywhere.[46]

This same conference saw the formation of the Group of 77, a caucus of developing nations representing the nonaligned movement; their joint declaration on international cooperation concluded:

> Such co-operation must serve as a decisive instrument for ending the division of the world into areas of affluence and intolerable poverty. This task is the outstanding challenge of our times. The injustice and neglect of centuries need to be redressed.[47]

A series of actions by the General Assembly to promote the aims of the charter and the first UNCTAD conference led to the adoption in 1974 of a Programme of Action on the Establishment of a New International Economic Order (NIEO).[48] Some of the goals of this ten-part program were bringing an end to all forms of foreign occupation, racial discrimination, apartheid, colonial and neocolonial domination and exploitation; establishing permanent sovereignty of the developing nations over their own natural resources; creating measures to eliminate the instability of the international monetary system (to prevent, for example, the currency fluctuations that can be devastating to developing nations); and regulation and control of the conduct of transnational corporations (proscribing, for example, "their collaboration with racist regimes and colonial administrations" and regulating "the repatriation of the profits accruing from their operations, taking into account the legitimate interests of all parties concerned").[49] Adoption of the NIEO was followed in the same year by the General Assembly's approval of a Charter of the Economic Rights and Duties of States, making clear the responsibilities of states in their internal affairs as well as in their relations with other states, and establishing a quinquennial review by the assembly of the progress made in its implementation.[50] The director of the United Nations Institute for Training and Research (UNITAR) commented on the magnitude of the NIEO undertaking in one of the seventeen volumes on the project produced by that organization:

Humanity's complex problems in the area of economics, the environment, disarmament, food production, the transfer of technology and other areas as well, have become so large, interrelated and urgent that they require the enormous efforts of thousands of international researchers and scholars at hundreds of international research institutions simply to survey the extent of the problem. Moreover, the recommendations of these experts on the various world problems must then be assessed at the many dozens of international forums, both within and without the United Nations, now dedicated to developing solutions to humanity's ever-growing dilemmas.[51]

Recognition of the interrelatedness of the world's social, economic, and political problems means understanding that they cannot be resolved in isolation from one another. The same interrelatedness exists for the implementation of human rights; no right or category of rights can be fully implemented or enjoyed in the absence of the rest. In 1993 the World Conference on Human Rights stated this clearly in the Vienna Declaration and Programme of Action:

All human rights are universal, indivisible, and interdependent and interrelated.

And the same document made clear that democracy was the only compatible form of government: "democracy, development, and respect for human rights and fundamental freedoms are interdependent and mutually reinforcing."[52]

It is, I believe, helpful to consider these developments in relation to the systemic theory of value, the theory that value is primarily a product of the social system. If value is systemically created, then the kind of value produced—as well as the moral value of the system—will depend upon the nature of the system. Call the primary institutions of a society those institutions concerned with production, communication, education, and governance; these institutions may be so organized and interconnected, for example, as to promote the ends and values of the International Bill of Human Rights. Or they may be so organized, as they are presently, to promote the ends and values of classical liberalism. But it is clear that the primary institutions of a society cannot be organized in such a way as to give priority to both. It was certainly clear to the governments of the Group of Seven developed countries and to transnational corporations, for since the 1970s they have worked on many fronts to undermine the UN project to implement human rights through the NIEO. This campaign has involved the World Bank, the International Monetary Fund (IMF), the General Agreement on Tariffs and Trade (GATT), the power of the UN Security Council, and even the overthrow of democratically elected governments.[53] It is too complex and extensive a history to review here, but the ideological foundation of the campaign is classical liberalism. In the late 1960s, George W. Ball, investment banker and undersecretary of state during the Kennedy and Johnson administrations, sketched the position in a talk before the International Chamber of Commerce in London that now seems prophetic:

Banker's Irony

In December 1991, Larry Summers, then chief economist for the World Bank, sent the following internal memo. When it was leaked to an outraged environmental community, Mr. Summers explained that the memo was meant to be "ironic."

The Memo

DATE: December 12, 1991
TO: Distribution
FR: Lawrence H. Summers
Subject: GEP

"Dirty" Industries: Just between you and me, shouldn't the World Bank be encouraging MORE migration of the dirty industries to the LDCs [Less Developed Countries]? I can think of three reasons:

1) The measurements of the costs of health impairing pollution depends on the foregone earnings from increased morbidity and mortality. From this point of view a given amount of health impairing pollution should be done in the country with the lowest cost, which will be the country with the lowest wages. I think the economic logic behind dumping a load of toxic waste in the lowest wage country is impeccable and we should face up to that.

2) The costs of pollution are likely to be non-linear as the initial increments of pollution probably have very low cost. I've always thought that under-populated countries in Africa are vastly UNDER-polluted, their air quality is probably vastly inefficiently low compared to Los Angeles or Mexico City. Only the lamentable facts that so much pollution is generated by non-tradable industries (transport, electrical generation) and that the unit transport costs of solid waste are so high prevent world welfare enhancing trade in air pollution and waste.

3) The demand for a clean environment for aesthetic and health reasons is likely to have very high income elasticity. The

(continues)

As *The New Yorker* saw it ...

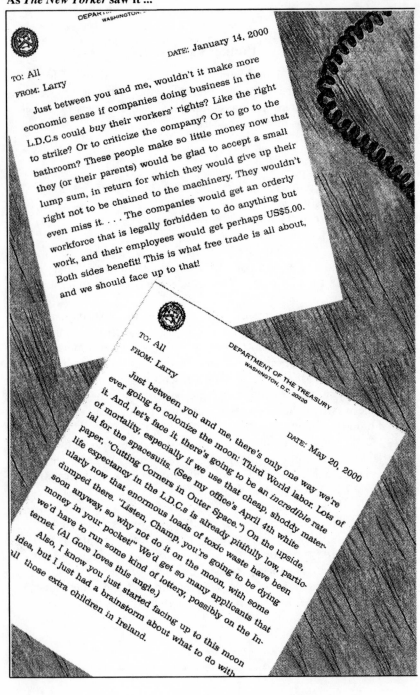

DEPARTMENT
WASHINGTON

DATE: January 14, 2000

TO: All

FROM: Larry

Just between you and me, wouldn't it make more economic sense if companies doing business in the L.D.C.s could *buy* their workers' rights? Like the right to strike? Or to criticize the company? Or to go to the bathroom? These people make so little money now that they (or their parents) would be glad to accept a small lump sum, in return for which they would give up their right not to be chained to the machinery. They wouldn't even miss it. . . . The companies would get an orderly workforce that is legally forbidden to do anything but work, and their employees would get perhaps US$5.00. Both sides benefit! This is what free trade is all about, and we should face up to that!

TO: All

FROM: Larry

DEPARTMENT OF THE TREASURY
WASHINGTON, D.C. 20220

DATE: May 20, 2000

Just between you and me, there's only one way we're ever going to colonize the moon: Third World labor. Lots of it. And, let's face it, there's going to be an *incredible* rate of mortality, especially if we use that cheap, shoddy material for the spacesuits. (See my office's April 4th white paper, "Cutting Corners in Outer Space.") On the upside, life expectancy in the L.D.C.s is already pitifully low, particularly now that enormous loads of toxic waste have been dumped there. "Listen, Champ, you're going to be dying soon anyway, so why not do it on the moon, with some money in your pocket." We'd get so many applicants that we'd have to run some kind of lottery, possibly on the Internet. (Al Gore loves this angle.)

Also, I know you just started facing up to this moon idea, but I just had a brainstorm about what to do with all those extra children in Ireland.

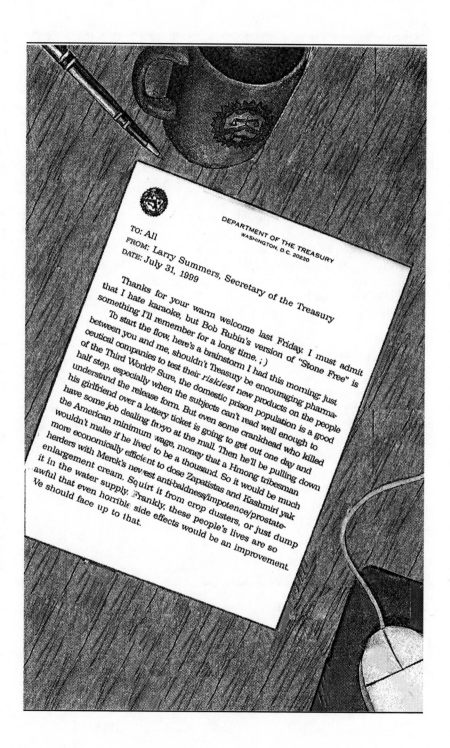

DEPARTMENT OF THE TREASURY
WASHINGTON, D.C. 20220

TO: All

FROM: Larry Summers, Secretary of the Treasury

DATE: July 31, 1999

Thanks for your warm welcome last Friday. I must admit that I hate karaoke, but Bob Rubin's version of "Stone Free" is something I'll remember for a long time. ;)

To start the flow, here's a brainstorm I had this morning: just between you and me, shouldn't Treasury be encouraging pharmaceutical companies to test their *riskiest* new products on the people of the Third World? Sure, the domestic prison population is a good half step, especially when the subjects can't read well enough to understand the release form. But even some crankhead who killed his girlfriend over a lottery ticket is going to get out one day and have some job dealing froyo at the mall. Then he'll be pulling down the American minimum wage, money that a Hmong tribesman wouldn't make if he lived to be a thousand. So it would be much more economically efficient to dose Zapatistas and Kashmiri yak herders with Merck's newest anti-baldness/impotence/prostate-enlargement cream. Squirt it from crop dusters, or just dump it in the water supply. Frankly, these people's lives are so awful that even horrible side effects would be an improvement. We should face up to that.

(continued)

concern over an agent that causes a one in a million change in the odds of prostate cancer is obviously going to be much higher in a country where people survive to get prostate cancer than in a country where under-five mortality is 200 per thousand. Also, much of the concern over industrial atmosphere discharge is about visibility impairing particulates. These discharges may have very little direct health impact. Clearly trade in goods that embody aesthetic pollution concerns could be welfare enhancing. Although production is mobile the consumption of pretty air is a nontradable.

The problem with the arguments against all of these proposals for more pollution in LDCs (intrinsic rights to certain goods, moral reasons, social concerns, lack of adequate markets, etc.) could be turned around and used more or less effectively against every Bank proposal for liberalization.

As Brazil's secretary of the environment saw it
[Jose Lutzenburger, reply to Mr. Summers, 1991]:

Your reasoning is perfectly logical but totally insane.... Your thoughts [provide] a concrete example of the unbelieveable alienation, reductionist thinking, social ruthlessness and the arrogant ignorance of many conventional "economists" concerning the nature of the world we live in.... If the World Bank keeps you as vice president it will lose all credibility. To me it would confirm what I have often said ... the best thing that could happen would be for the Bank to disappear.
Mr Lutzenburger lost his job.

We recognize that we live in a world whose resources are finite and whose demands are exploding. To avoid a Darwinian debacle on a global scale we will have to use our resources with maximum efficiency and a minimum of waste ...

This can be achieved only when all the factors necessary for the production and use of goods—capital, labor, raw materials, plant facilities and distribution—are freely mobilized and deployed according to the most efficient pattern. And this in turn will be possible only when national boundaries no longer play a critical role in defining economic horizons.

However, "corporate persons," as the undersecretary calls them, are impeded in carrying out these tasks, as developing countries are fearful their economies will fall under foreign domination and so impose obstacles to the entry of foreign firms; moreover,

A greater menace may come from the actions of governments addicted to a regime of planning, who see in the global corporation a foreign instrumentality that may frustrate their economic designs. The basis for their concern is easy to understand, especially in countries where a world company, if allowed in, would become the largest employer of national labor and consumer of national materials.

A solution favored by undersecretary Ball was the establishment by treaty of an international companies law, administered by a supranational body:

An international companies law could place limitations, for example, on the restrictions nation-states might be permitted to impose on companies established under its sanction. The operative standard defining those limitations might be the quantity of freedom needed to preserve the central principle of assuming the most economical and efficient use of world resources.[54]

It would appear at the present time that Ball's supranational body may be the United Nations, as transnational corporations are in the process of carrying out a palace revolution in the United Nations, negotiating a framework with UN leadership for their regular involvement in UN decision making, including the disbursement of development funds to developing nations.[55] They are also in the process of composing international treaty law that would give them virtually unimpeded access to any nation's economy that wants to participate in the world market.[56] It would be very difficult—given the materialization of these developments—for any nation to control the nature or direction of its own economy, eliminating the possibility of giving priority to the implementation of the International Bill of Human Rights.

This attack by transnational corporations and the governments of developed nations on an international project for the common good of humanity, however, is hopefully the last phase in a period characterized by the philosophical hegemony of the classical liberal worldview. For even though its proponents are attempting to arm-twist the rest of the world into accepting its narrow and anachronistic articles of faith, they are now faced with a powerful moral alternative that has been enacted into international law and is backed by the majority of the nations on earth. The struggle between these two philosophies will very likely be a protracted one, and will surely be as turbulent and confused as the long struggle that ended the Middle Ages and produced the modern world.

Notes

An expanded version of this chapter will be published in a collection of essays by the author entitled *Law Subversive of Democracy*, in the San Francisco State University Series "New Directions in Philosophy."

1. *Human Rights: A Compilation of International Instruments*, vol. 1, United Nations, 1993, 1–49. In pamphlet form, *The International Bill of Human Rights*, Department of Public Information, DPI/797–40669, United Nations, 1985.

2. Reporting requirements are required by each of the treaties; Article 40 in the case of the ICCPR, and Article 16 of the ICESCR.

3. Distinguishing industrial capitalism from the earlier commercial capitalism, with its mercantile ideology.

4. The principal figures here, of course, are William of Ockham and his school. A useful account is Gordon Leff's *The Dissolution of the Medieval Outlook: An Essay on Intellectual and Spiritual Change in the Fourteenth Century* (New York: New York University Press, 1976).

5. The formula was challenged in the mid-eighteenth century by French materialists, but did not disappear until much later.

6. There are several ways of connecting Principle 4 with private property. Locke argued that we have private property in ourselves and our labor, so anything we join our labor to becomes our private property (*The Second Treatise of Government*, chap. 5.). This, however, is ambiguous. Locke appears to have included as "his" labor under the principle the labor of family, that is, wife, children, servants, and slaves (chap. 6)—thereby allowing for unlimited accumulation of property—whereas if "his" labor is interpreted as including only the labor of the individual laborer, this would justify only limited property.

7. In what follows I will be concerned with the theory of the free market (as a part of classical liberal ideology), and not with the actual workings of contemporary capitalism. If the theory ever had a substantive connection with reality, it was most certainly prior to the Civil War in the United States.

8. Another influential philosophical idea favoring democracy in the eighteenth century was John Locke's theory of the mind as a tabula rasa. Compare Kenneth MacLean, *John Locke and English Literature of the Eighteenth Century* (New York: 1962), book 1.

9. The Universal Declaration of Human Rights included a right to own property alone and in association with others (Article 17). However, neither covenant includes a right to own property, nor any of the rights I have referred to here as economic liberties.

10. How the free market is supposed to accomplish these goals is spelled out by Adam Smith in book 1 of *An Inquiry into Causes of the Wealth of Nations*, 1776, esp. chaps. 2, 5, 6, and 7.

11. Compare Gunnar Myrdal, *The Political Element in the Development of Economic Theory* (Cambridge, Mass.: Harvard University Press, 1954), for an extended examination of the conflation of morality with science in the history of economic theory.

12. John Bates Clark, *The Distribution of Wealth* (New York: Augustus M. Kelly, 1965), 111.

13. Ibid. *v*.

14. Op. cit., book 1, chap. 6, 7, 1776.

15. Various attempts to justify the return on capital as having a different basis than that proposed by Smith are critically examined in the first chapter of David Schweickart's *Against Capitalism* (Boulder, Colo.: Westview Press, 1996).

16. Compare, for example, the discussion in Stephen R. Munzer, *A Theory of Property* (Cambridge: Cambridge University Press, 1990), chap. 10.

17. Rosa Luxemburg long ago pointed out the moral absurdity of this idea: ". . . the dancer in a café, who makes a profit for her employer with her legs, is a productive working woman, while all the toil of the woman and mothers of the proletariat within the four walls of the home is considered unproductive work. [This] sounds crude and crazy but it is an accurate expression of the crudeness and craziness of today's economic order." Quoted in Hal Draper and Ann Lipow, "Marxian Women Versus Bourgeois Feminism," *Socialist Register*, 1976.

18. James Mill, in his *An Essay on Government*, part 1, 1820, put it this way: "It is impossible to attach to labor a greater degree of advantage than the whole of the product of labor. Why so? Because if you give more to one man than the produce of his labor, you can do so only by taking it away from the produce of some other man's labor."

19. This is not to say that one cannot discern and characterize various tendencies and their possible interactions; but that is far from the quantitative prediction of future states of a system.

20. The U.S. government has endeavored to manage the economic system since the establishment of the Federal Reserve System, and particularly since the passage of the Full Employment Act of 1946.

21. The UN assesses the implementation of human rights treaties through a periodic and public reporting process; compare part 5. The U.S. government has tied aid to human rights, as in the 1974 Foreign Assistance Act, section 502B, advising the president to withhold security assistance from countries that are gross human rights violators.

22. The case was *Santa Clara County v. Southern Pacific Railroad*, 118 U.S. 394, 1886. The decision was made without hearing argument and without explanation by the Court. It was perhaps considered the most expedient thing to do at the time, since corporations were becoming increasingly important to the economy and the Constitution, of course, said nothing about them.

23. Barbara H. Craig, *Chadha: The Story of an Epic Constitutional Struggle* (Oxford: Oxford University Press, 1988), 40–41, citing 1975 House Committee hearings on administrative rule making.

24. *Field v. Clark*, 143 U.S. 649, at 692 (1892).

25. Compare Craig, *Chadha Immigration and Naturalization Service v. Chadha* (1983) was the case that led to the setting aside of over 200 legislative veto provisions in congressional statutes.

26. A. M. Honoré, "Ownership," in A. G. Guest, ed., *Oxford Essays in Jurisprudence, First Series* (Oxford: Oxford University Press, 1961), 107–147.

27. T. H. Green, *Principles of Political Obligation*, in *The Works of Thomas Hill Green*, vol. 2, ed. R. Nettleship (London: 1885–1888), 335ff.

28. Henwood, Doug, *Wallstreet* (New York: Verso, 1997) 12.

29. Of course a stockholder who has millions of shares and thus a controlling interest in a corporation may have a seat and/or one or more representatives on a board. The classic study of the rise of the corporation as well as its challenge to the classical theory of private property is that of A. A. Berle and Gardiner C. Means, *The Modern Corporation and Private Property* (New York: Macmillan, 1934).

30. Compare Berle and Means, *The Modern Corporation*, book 4. This is still a useful study of the classical theory; the dissolution of private property, they wrote, "destroys the very foundation on which the economic order of the past three centuries has rested" (8).

31. Percentages are from James M. Poterba and Andrew A. Samwick, "Stock Ownership Patterns, Stock Market Fluctuations, and Consumption," in *Brookings Papers on Economic Activity* 2, ed. Brainard and Perry, Brookings Institution, 1995).

32. This figure is based on the Federal Reserve Board's "Flow of Funds Accounts" showing stockholdings of households, minus the 4 percent of this category that is represented by nonprofit institutions.

33. Gerard Colby, *Du Pont Dynasty: Behind the Nylon Curtain* (: Lyle Stuart, 1984), 30.

34. For a survey of various positions on the question, compare William J. Schultz, *The Taxation of Inheritance, Part 2, Inheritance Tax Theory* (Boston: Riverside Press, 1926).

35. Letter to James Madison, September 6, 1789, in William J. Schultz, *The Taxation of Inheritance* (Boston: Riverside Press, 1926).

36. *Estate of Guthman* (1954), 125 C.A.2d 408, 413. Compare *U.S. v. Perkins*, 163 U.S. 628, 1986.

37. Quote marks because they are *not* more efficient in energy use, in providing wholesome and nutritious food, in preventing the pollution of groundwaters and rivers, in preserving the genetic heritage, and so on.

38. J. Franklin Jameson, *The American Revolution Considered as a Social Movement* (Princeton: Princeton University Press, 1926), chap. 2; and Richard B. Morris, *The American Revolution Reconsidered* (New York: Harper and Row, 1967), 77–81.

39. The day before Eleanor Roosevelt resigned, the U.S. secretary of state—John Foster Dulles—announced that the United States would not sign or ratify the covenants. President Carter signed the covenants in 1977, and the ICCPR was ratified on June 8, 1992.

40. Resolution of the sixteenth session, 1961/61: United Nations Development Decade: A Program for International Economic Co-operation, *A New International Economic Order: Selected Documents 1945–75*, undated, vol. 2, 831.

41. Instruments of categories II and III have the status of international law; those of category IV have an advisory status, as the declaration on the Rights of Disabled Persons, or the Code of Conduct for Law Enforcement Officials.

42. Of the major human rights treaties the United States has ratified the Covenant on Civil and Political Rights, the Convention Against All Forms of Racial Discrimination, and the Convention Against Torture and Other Cruel, Inhuman or Degrading Treatment or Punishment. By Article 6, section 2 of the U.S. Constitution, this law has the same status in the United States as any statute passed by Congress.

43. *Human Rights: A Compilation of International Instruments, Vol. 1, Universal Instruments*, parts 1 and 2, (New York: Center for Human Rights at Geneva,1993).

44. United Nations Center for Human Rights, *Manual on Human Rights Reporting* (1991), 40.

45. Op.cit., 70, 72. On the relation of UN agencies to the reporting process, compare A. G. Mower, *International Co-operation for Social Justice: Global and Regional Protection of Economic and Social Rights* (Greenwood Press, 1985), chaps. 4 and 5.

46. *Proceedings*, vol. 1: *Final Act and Report*. UNCTAD I (Geneva: UNCTAD I, 1964).

47. *Proceedings*, Annex B: Observations and Delegations. A history of the nonaligned movement may be found in A. W. Singham and Shirley Hume, *Non-Alignment in an Age of Alignments* (Lawrence Hill and Co., 1986).

48. UN General Assembly, Sixth Special Session, May 1, 1974; Moss and Winton, *A New International Economic Order*, vol. 2, (UNITAR), 893.

49. Ibid., Articles I1(a), I11(b), and V(a).

50. UN General Assembly, Twenty-ninth Session, December 12, 1974; Moss and Winton, *A New International Economic Order*, 901–906.

51. J. Lozoya, J. Estevez, and R. Green, *Alternative Views of the New International Economic Order: A Survey and Analysis of Major Academic Research Reports* (Pergamon Press, 1979), vii.

52. Vienna Declaration, UN GAOR, World Conference on Human Rights, Forty-eighth Session, UN Document A/CONF. 157/24 (Part) 1, 1993.

53. Much of this history may be found in *50 Years Is Enough: The Case Against the World Bank and International Monetary Fund*, ed. Kevin Danaher (South End Press, 1994).

54. George W. Ball, "Cosmocorp: The Importance of Being Stateless," *Atlantic Community Quarterly*, Summer 1968, 163–170.

55. "The United Nations and the Corporate Agenda," attachment to a memo by David C. Korten to the President of the UN General Assembly, communicated to the author via E-mail, July 1997.

56. This is the Multilateral Agreement on Investments (MAI), which is being negotiated in great secrecy by the twenty-nine richer nations that belong to the Organization for Economic Cooperation and Development (OECD).

8

Failed Prophecies,
Glorious Hopes

Richard Rorty

Failed prophecies often make invaluable inspirational reading. Consider two examples: the New Testament and the *Communist Manifesto*. Both were intended by their authors as predictions of what was going to happen—predictions based on superior knowledge of the forces that determine human history. Both sets of predictions have, so far, been ludicrous flops. Both claims to knowledge have become objects of ridicule.

Christ did not return. Those who claim that He is about to do so, and that it would be prudent to become a member of a particular sect or denomination to prepare for this event, are rightly viewed with suspicion. To be sure, nobody can prove that the Second Coming will not occur, thus producing empirical evidence for the Incarnation. But we have been waiting a long time.

Analogously, nobody can prove that Marx and Engels were wrong when they proclaimed that "the bourgeoisie has forged the weapons that bring death to itself."[1] It may be that the globalization of the labor market in the next century will reverse the progressive bourgeoisification of the European and North American proletariat, and that it will become true that "the bourgeoisie is incapable of continuing to rule, since it is unable even to assure an existence to the slaves within their slavery." Maybe the breakdown of capitalism and the assumption of political power by a virtuous and enlightened proletariat will then come to pass. Maybe, in short, Marx and Engels just got the timing a century or two wrong. Still, capitalism has overcome many crises in the past, and we have been waiting a long time for the emergence of this proletariat.

Again, no scoffer can be sure that what evangelical Christians call "becoming a New Being in Christ Jesus" is not a genuinely transformative, miraculous experience. But those who claim to have been reborn in this way do not seem to

171

behave as differently from the way they behaved in the past as we had hoped. We have been waiting a long time for prosperous Christians to behave more decently than prosperous pagans.

Analogously, we cannot be sure but that some day we may catch sight of new ideals that will replace those that Marx and Engels dismissively called "bourgeois individuality, bourgeois independence, and bourgeois freedom." But we have waited patiently for regimes calling themselves "Marxist" to explain to us exactly what these new ideals look like, and how they are to be realized in practice. So far, all such regimes have turned out to be throwbacks to pre-Enlightenment barbarism rather than the first stages of a post-Enlightenment utopia.

There are, to be sure, still people who read the Christian Scriptures in order to figure out what is likely to happen a few years or decades down the road. Ronald Reagan did, for example. Up until quite recently, many intellectuals read the *Communist Manifesto* for the same purpose. Just as the Christians have counseled patience and assured us that it's unfair to judge Christ by the mistakes of his sinful servants, so the Marxists have assured us that all the "Marxist" regimes so far have been absurd perversions of Marx's intent. The few surviving Marxists now admit that the Communist Parties of Lenin, Mao, and Castro bore no resemblance to the empowered proletariat of Marx's dreams, but were merely the tools of autocrats and oligarchs. Nevertheless, they tell us, someday there will be a genuine revolutionary, genuinely proletarian, party—a party whose triumph will bring us a freedom as unlike "bourgeois freedom" as the Christian doctrine that love is the only law is unlike the arbitrary dictates of Leviticus.

Most of us can no longer take either Christian or Marxist postponements and reassurances seriously. But this does not, and should not, stop us from finding inspiration and encouragement in the New Testament and the *Manifesto*. For both documents are expressions of the same hope: that someday we shall be willing and able to treat the needs of all human beings with the respect and consideration with which we treat the needs of those closest to us, those whom we love.

Both texts have gathered greater inspirational power as the years have passed. For each is the founding document of a movement that has done much for human freedom and human equality. By this time, thanks to the rise in population since 1848, both may have inspired equal numbers of brave and self-sacrificing men and women to risk their lives and fortunes in order to prevent future generations from enduring needless suffering. There may already have been as many socialist martyrs as Christian martyrs. If human hope can survive the anthrax-laden warheads, the suitcase-sized nuclear devices, the overpopulation, the globalized labor market, and the environmental disasters of the coming century, if we have descendants who, a century from now, still have a historical record to consult and are still able to seek inspiration from the past, perhaps they will think of Saint Agnes and Rosa Luxemburg, Saint Francis and Eugene Debs, Father Damien and Jean Jaures, as members of a single movement.

Just as the New Testament is still read by millions of people who spend little time wondering whether Christ will someday return in glory, so the *Communist Manifesto* is still read even by those of us who hope and believe that full social justice can be attained without a revolution of the sort Marx predicted: that a classless society, a world in which "the free development of each is the condition for the free development of all" can come about as a result of what Marx despised as "bourgeois reformism." Parents and teachers should encourage young people to read both books. The young will be morally better for having done so.

We should raise our children to find it intolerable that we FAZ *(Frankfurter Allgemeine Zeitung)* readers[2] who sit behind desks and punch keyboards are paid ten times as much as people who get their hands dirty cleaning our toilets, and a hundred times as much as those who fabricate our keyboards in the Third World. We should ensure that they worry about the fact that the countries that industrialized first have a hundred times the wealth of those that have not yet industrialized. Our children need to learn, early on, to see the inequalities between their own fortunes and those of other children as neither the will of God nor the necessary price for economic efficiency, but as an evitable tragedy. They should start thinking, as early as possible, about how the world might be changed so as to ensure that no one goes hungry while others have a surfeit.

The children need to read Christ's message of human fraternity alongside Marx and Engel's account of how industrial capitalism and free markets—indispensable as they have turned out to be—make it very difficult to institute that fraternity. They need to see their lives as given meaning by efforts toward the realization of the moral potentiality inherent in our ability to communicate our needs and our hopes to one another. They should learn stories both about Christian congregations meeting in the catacombs, and about workers' rallies in city squares. For both have played equally important roles in the long process of actualizing this potentiality.

The inspirational value of the New Testament and the *Communist Manifesto* is not diminished by the fact that many millions of people were enslaved, tortured, or starved to death by sincere, morally earnest people who recited passages from one or the other text to justify their deeds. Memories of the dungeons of the Inquisition and the interrogation rooms of the KGB, of the ruthless greed and arrogance of the Christian clergy and of the Communist nomenklatura, should indeed make us reluctant to hand over power to people who claim to know what God, or history, wants. But there is a difference between knowledge and hope. Hope often takes the form of false prediction, as it did in both documents. But hope for social justice is nevertheless the only basis for a worthwhile human life.

Christianity and Marxism still have the power to do a great deal of harm, for both the New Testament and the *Manifesto* can still be effectively quoted by moral hypocrites and egomaniacal gangsters. In the United States, for example, an organization called the Christian Coalition holds the Republican Party (and thus the Congress) in thrall. The leaders of this movement have convinced millions of voters that taxing the suburbs to help the ghettos is an un-Christian thing to do. In the name of "Christian family values," the coalition teaches that for the U.S. government to give a helping hand to the children of unemployable and unwed teenage mothers would "undermine individual responsibility."

The coalition's activities are less violent than those of the now-moribund Sendero Luminoso movement in Peru, but the results of its work are equally destructive. Sendero Luminoso, in its murderous heyday, was headed by a crazed philosophy teacher who thought of himself as the successor of Lenin and Mao, as an inspired contemporary interpreter of the writings of Marx. The Christian Coalition is headed by a sanctimonious televangelist: the Reverend Pat Robertson—a contemporary interpreter of the Gospels who will probably cause much more suffering in the United States than Abiel Guzman managed to cause in Peru.

To sum up: it is best, when reading both the *Manifesto* and the New Testament, to ignore prophets who claim to be the authorized interpreters of one or the other text. When reading the texts themselves, we should skip lightly past the predictions and concentrate on the expressions of hope. We should read both as inspirational documents, appeals to what Lincoln called "the better angels of our nature," rather than as accurate accounts of human history or of human destiny.

If one treats the term "Christianity" as the name of one such appeal, rather than as a claim to knowledge, then that word still names a powerful force working for human decency and human equality. "Socialism," similarly considered, is the name of the same force—an updated, more precise name. "Christian Socialism" is pleonastic: nowadays you cannot hope for the fraternity that the Gospels preach without hoping that democratic governments will redistribute money and opportunity in a way that the market never will. There is no way to take the New Testament seriously as a moral imperative, rather than as a prophecy, without taking the need for such redistribution equally seriously.

Dated as the *Manifesto* is, it is still an admirable statement of the great lesson we learned from watching industrial capitalism in action: that the overthrow of authoritarian governments, and the achievement of constitutional democracy, is not enough to ensure human equality or human decency. It is as true as it was in 1848 that the rich will always try to get richer by making the poor poorer, that total commodification of labor will lead to the immiseration of the wage earners, and that "the executive of the modern state is but a committee for managing the common affairs of the whole bourgeoisie."

The bourgeoisie-proletariat distinction may by now be as outdated as the pagan-Christian distinction, but if one substitutes "the richest 20 percent" for "the bourgeoisie" and "the other 80 percent" for "the proletariat," most of the sentences of the *Manifesto* will still ring true. (Admittedly, however, they ring slightly less true in fully developed welfare states like Germany and slightly more true in countries like the United States, in which greed has retained the upper hand, and in which the welfare state has remained rudimentary.) To say that history is "the history of class struggle" is still true, if it is interpreted to mean that in every culture, under every form of government, and in every imaginable situation (for example, England when Henry VIII dissolved the monasteries, Indonesia after the Dutch went home, China after Mao's death, Britain and America under Thatcher and Reagan) the people who have already gotten their hands on money and power will lie, cheat, and steal to ensure that they and their descendants monopolize both forever.

Insofar as history presents a *moral* spectacle, it is the struggle to break such monopolies. The use of Christian doctrine to argue for the abolition of slavery (and to argue against the American equivalent of the Nuremberg laws—the racial segregation statutes) shows Christianity at its best. The use of Marxist doctrine to raise the consciousness of workers—to make it clear to them how they are being cheated—shows Marxism at its best. When the two have coalesced, as they did in the Social Gospel movement, in the theologies of Paul Tillich and Walter Rauschenbusch, and in the most socialistic of the papal encyclicals, they have enabled the struggle for social justice to transcend the controversies between theists and atheists. Those controversies *should* be transcended: we should read the New Testament as saying that how we treat each other on earth matters a great deal more than the outcome of debate concerning the existence or nature of another world.

The trade-union movement, which Marx and Engels thought of as only a transition to the establishment of revolutionary political parties, has turned out to be the most inspiring embodiment of the Christian virtues of self-sacrifice and of fraternal *agape* in recorded history. The rise of the trade unions is, morally speaking, the most encouraging development of modern times. It witnessed the purest and most unselfish heroism. Though many trade unions have become corrupt, and many others have become ossified, the moral stature of the unions towers above that of the churches and the corporations, the governments and the universities. For the unions were founded by men and women who had an enormous amount to lose—they risked losing the chance of work altogether, the chance to bring food home to their families. They took that risk for the sake of a better human future, and we are all deeply in their debt. The organizations they founded are sanctified by their sacrifices.

The *Manifesto* inspired the founders of most of the great unions of modern times. By quoting its words, the founders of the unions were able to bring millions of people out on strike against degrading conditions and starvation wages. Those words buttressed the faith of the strikers that their sacrifice—their willingness to see their children go without sufficient food rather than to yield to the owners' demand for a higher return on investment—would not be in vain. A document that has accomplished that much will always remain among the treasures of our intellectual and spiritual heritage. For the *Manifesto* spelled out what the workers were gradually coming to realize: that "instead of rising with the progress of industry," the worker "was in danger of "sinking deeper and deeper below the conditions of existence of his own class." This danger was avoided at least temporarily in Europe and North America, thanks to the courage of workers who had read the *Manifesto* and who, as a result, were emboldened to demand their share of political power. Had they waited for the Christian kindness and charity of their superiors, their children would still be illiterate and badly fed.

The words of the Gospels and of the *Manifesto* may have provided equal quantities of courage and inspiration. But there are many respects in which the *Manifesto* is a better book to give to the young than the New Testament. For the latter document is morally flawed by its otherworldliness: its suggestion that we can separate the question of our individual relation to God—our individual chance for salvation—from our participation in cooperative efforts to end needless suffering. Many passages in the Gospels have suggested to slave-owners that they can keep right on lashing their slaves, and to rich people that they can keep right on starving the poor. For they are going to Heaven anyway, their sins having been forgiven as a result of having accepted Christ as Lord.

The New Testament, a document of the ancient world, accepts one of the central convictions of the Greek philosophers who urged that contemplation of universal truths was the ideal life for a human being. This conviction is that the social conditions of human life will never change in any important respect: We shall always have the poor with us—and perhaps the slaves as well. This conviction leads the writers of the New Testament to turn their attention from the possibility of a better human future to the hope of pie in the sky when we die. The only utopia these writers can imagine is in another world altogether.

We moderns are superior to the ancients—both pagan and Christian—in our ability to imagine a utopia here on earth. The eighteenth and nineteenth centuries witnessed, in Europe and North America, a massive shift in the locus of human hope: a shift from eternity to future time, from speculation about how to win divine favor to planning for the happiness of future generations. This sense that the human future can be made different from the human past, unaided by nonhuman powers, is magnificently expressed in the *Manifesto*.

It would be best, of course, if we could find a new document to provide the children with inspiration and hope—one that was as free of the defects of the New Testament as of those of the *Manifesto*. It would be good to have a reformist text, one that lacked the apocalyptic character of both books—that did not say that all things must be made new, or that justice "can be attained only by the forcible overthrow of all existing social conditions." It would be well to have a document that spelled out the details of a this-worldly utopia without assuring us that this utopia will emerge full-blown and quickly, as soon as some single decisive change has occurred—as soon as private property is abolished, or as soon as we have all taken Jesus into our hearts.

It would be best, in short, if we could get along without prophecy and claims to knowledge of the forces that determine history—if generous hope could sustain itself without such reassurances. Someday perhaps we shall have a new text to give to our children—one that abstains from prediction yet still expresses the same yearning for fraternity as does the New Testament, and is as filled with sharp-eyed descriptions of our most recent forms of inhumanity to each other as is the *Manifesto*. But in the meantime we should be grateful for two texts which have helped make us better—have helped us overcome, to some degree, our brutish selfishness and our cultivated sadism.

Notes

1. The *Manifesto of the Communist Party* by Karl Marx and Friedrich Engels is the source of this and subsequent quoted passages in the text.

2. This article was first published in 1998 in the *Frankfurter Allgemeine Zeitung* commemorating the 150th anniversary of the February 1848 publication of the *Manifesto of the Communist Party*.

PART THREE

Environment
and Welfare

move forward

9

What Are the State Functions that Neoliberalism Wants to Eliminate?

Zsuzsa Ferge

An Outline and
Summary of the Argument

The necessity of rethinking and reshaping the role of the state that involves, inter alia, the far-reaching reform of social policy, is everywhere on the agenda. The reasons and arguments are manifold. The debate is unfortunately often highly ideological. Thus there is the challenge of finding less loaded arguments. History seems to offer a mine of less ideological approaches.

There is a neoliberal agenda that, in its extreme form, would like to get rid of the welfare state as it evolved in Western Europe. A milder variant of this agenda emphasizes individual responsibility but accepts the responsibility of the state in case of the destitute. In this chapter I address some of the issues connected with the neoliberal project. It focuses mainly on Europe. Even this restricted framework will be badly treated: The huge variations within the Continent will be hardly touched upon.[1] Western Europe will be differentiated only from Central and Eastern Europe.

My main thesis is that the functions of the state as they have evolved in Europe tend to describe a bell curve. In the early period of state formation the military function dominated, soon complemented by the policing function for inner troubles. State coercion was based on the gradual and always contested monopolization of violence, legislation, taxation, and (a little-mentioned issue) coinage.

The coercive functions proved to be insufficient in handling the major new problems of the modernizing world. Industrialization, urbanization, and the increasing social density required the active participation of a central agency in the creation of the regulatory frameworks and the infrastructure promoting the expansion of the capitalist market (Polànyi 1944). In addition, the new forms of poverty needed alleviation in order to avoid the physical, social, and even moral dangers connected with them (Swaan 1988). Thus the state was forced to take on "proactive" functions alongside continued repression and policing.

All the above and the following categories of state duties are well known in political science from—let us say—Adam Smith on. The only "innovation" is that I somewhat enlarge the well-known list. Over and above the military, the policing, and the regulatory-administrative functions one usually adds the so-called welfare functions. I propose splitting the welfare functions in two. I shall define on the one hand activities termed *civilizing functions* that promote the adjustment of people to rapidly changing conditions, and enable them to live together in a relatively peaceful way. The civilizing attempts will be distinguished from the "helping functions" or welfare functions in the strict sense of the word that are meant to promote directly the well-being of people.

The frontier between these two functions—or, for that matter, between all the functions—is admittedly unclear. Many of the civilizing acts, the expansion of literacy, for instance, may have been first forced on the "victims," the children of the lower strata. At a later stage literacy could become instrumental in improving the living conditions or the life chances of the early victims. However, the happy outcome was more an indirect consequence rather than the *explicit* aim of these efforts. Or to give another example, the workhouses in England had been an instrument of poor relief and hence may qualify as belonging to the welfare functions. However, since they produced more "ill-fare" than welfare, their policing function was more than manifest. Yet they may have had some sort of civilizing impact through their strict disciplinary practice.

The central and eastern part of Europe followed suit promptly regarding the military, the policing, and perhaps to a lesser extent the proactive regulatory duties of the state. They remained more reluctant regarding the other ones.

The near-consensus reached after World War II in Western Europe about the multiple functions of the state started to dissolve in the seventies. The state began to "withdraw" at least from the civilizing and welfare fields. Central-eastern Europe is following suit in this instance, too. However, the process seems to be relatively slow in the majority of the western countries of the Continent probably because it meets with strong resistance, whereas the slashing of the "welfare state" seems to be rather rapid in the so-called new democracies.

The conclusion of the paper is that the demand for a "minimal state" is a selective one: Not all state duties come under attack. It threatens primarily the civilizing and welfare functions that promoted relatively peaceful and relatively integrated national coexistence. The deterioration of the situation that follows may legitimate the strengthening of the policing functions. These processes may trigger a trend toward decivilization threatening important gains of (Western European) civilization.

The Positions in the State-Versus-Market Debate: A Series of Examples

The attack on the big state has indeed become predominantly an attack on the welfare functions of the state. The tone of the arguments may differ but their essence is uniform. The ubiquitous theme is the—probably more alleged than real—contradiction between the coveted economic growth and exaggerated social spending. The underlying motif is the conviction that the supreme value is economic growth to be attained by unfettered free trade equated with freedom *tout court*. A surprising feature of the free trade believers is the contradiction between their rhetoric about freedom and pluralism and their monolithic attachment to the neoliberal value system, which is utterly intolerant toward views sharing the "incorrigibly old-fashioned ideas" *("indécrottable archaïsme")* that Robert Castel (1995b) attributed to himself.

The conservatives come from different traditions. Their arguments are not particularly original either, but at least they show some variety or some pluralism in the intellectual traditions they endorse.

In what follows, both stances will be illustrated by some examples. All positions are present in the West and in the East of Europe alike. Yet I shall quote whenever possible from the Eastern authors who may be less well known to Western readers.

The Supporters of the Market

1. The most extreme promarket, antistate position claims (to quote an author from the West) that "The phoney help on offer from the Welfare State is no help at all. It is a lethal threat to our freedom. We should get rid of it at once and for all ... "(Marsland 1996, xii). A Czech economist, J. Kinkor, is not less zealous. He rejects the validity of such concepts as the public interest or the public good; he maintains that the state has to stop interfering not only with the economy, but also with education, health care, culture, housing. All this has to be regulated by free market exchange. He has crowned the argument by qualifying unemployment as a purely individual problem, in regard to which "the foolish battle of governments with unemployment is nothing other than a distortion of this extremely valuable information source" (Kinkor 1996: 119).[2]

2. Another pure example of neoliberalism may be found in the writings of Leszek Balczerowicz, the Polish politician and economist. He has theoretically elaborated the underpinnings of his shock therapy. In a relatively recent book, he expressed his aversion to the concept of social justice and his predilection for private, as against public, "solidarity" (Balczerowicz 1995a). He has also taken a strong position in favor of formal market rationality as the dominant social rationality, and the reliance on economic growth as the unique criterion of social success. This last argument is worth following. He started by reducing the role of social policy to that of an adjunct to the economy.

> Social policy—SP in what follows—should be defined by its instruments and not by its proclaimed goals (reducing inequality, alleviating poverty, reducing individual economic risk), as intentions do not necessarily become reality.

This claim is then translated into the formal language of economics. According to Balczerowicz the relevant question is

> how various states or types of SP affect the rate of economic development, or—in other words—which states of SP are incompatible with the rapid rate, (SP_{inc}), and

which can coexist with fast and sustained economic growth (SP$_c$). (Balczerowicz 1995b)

In other words, economic growth is the only valid social objective. Social policy may be tolerated if it promotes this objective, without having relatively autonomous objectives about social coexistence. The views of the two above authors are apparently insensitive to the social consequences of the operation of the economy. Also, they fully ignore the ethical dimensions of economic or other actions.

3. János Kornai, the Harvard professor and Hungarian economist, thus representing both worlds, seems recently to have enriched the economist's argument. Kornai coined the expression a "premature welfare state" to describe the social policy of state socialism. He implied thereby that the Hungarian state in the eighties was overdeveloped in proportion to its economic development. He has suggested (in 1992) another "pure" model. In this model the responsibility of the state for public welfare should be strictly limited. "[The state] gives financial help from the taxpayers' money only to the needy." Otherwise everybody should find individual solutions to solve their problems through nonprofit and for-profit insurance companies or other marketed services.

In his later writings economic considerations seem to give way to ethical ones. In a paper written in 1996 and rewritten several times since, the moral dimension and some social considerations are explicitly taken onboard.

> Although I am an economist, I do not base my argument here on economic principles, or advocate reform because the welfare sector is too costly or cannot be financed over the long run. Rather, this study embodies a set of ethical principles ... that represent also a *credo*—the set of values I espouse.(1997, 277)

Two ethical principles are in fact spelled out—with a slightly changing vocabulary, though. The first principle is about

> *The sovereignty of the individual: Reforms should maximize the sphere within which individuals make decisions. The state's sphere should be correspondingly curtailed....* Principle 1 not only ensures the individual's right to make his/her own decision, but also requires that individuals be *responsible* for their own life.[3] (1997, 278, emphases in the original)

The second ethical principle is about *Solidarity*, a key concept in European social thought and practice. It has acquired many meanings. It may refer to the "brotherhood of men" in general; or to mutual and reciprocal help not in line with the market logic; or as "justice defined in terms of rights" (Baldwin 1990, 31), or as "the outcome of a generalized and reciprocal self-interest" (229). Less often it is understood as help offered to the weak. Kornai uses it only in this last sense:

Principle 2—Solidarity: Help should be provided to the suffering, the troubled and the disadvantaged.... Implementation of the solidarity principle requires only *targeted* state assistance [going] only to those who are truly in need. (Kornai 1997, 278–279, emphases in the original)

The extremely individualistic approach that characterizes this ethic justifies the diagnosis of many that neoliberalism is about the "individualization of the social." The individuals responsible for their and their families' futures, who are engaged in saving for the future and for "unforeseen eventualities," undermine the status quo from another perspective as well. For the above ethic offers arguments against "the old solidarities, against the reserves of social capital protecting a large part of the present social order from plunging into anomie" (Bourdieu 1998, 118). Thus the "ethical" approach gives additional support to "the program of the destruction of the collective structures that could create an obstacle to the pure market logic" (110).

Arguments for the State

Let me make a cautionary note. The "partisans" of the state are all aware that the "state" may come in all forms, and may be the source of all evils. What is meant by "the state" in the following arguments is a state built on democratic principles without being impervious to many "state failures."

1. The most widespread of the counterarguments is probably that the negation of the "common good" and of public responsibility for public well-being is in stark contrast with a European tradition that is at least 2,000 years old. After all, "it was Aristotle who maintained that while states originate in the need to safeguard life, their *telos*—their ultimate goal—is the morally Good Life" (Avineri 1997, 26). The "common good" was one of the important leitmotifs of politics throughout European history, though one might wonder how often it was taken seriously. The ethical dimension is manifest in this argument. Most recently it was George Soros who revived this tradition, with the advantage of a most intimate knowledge of the market.

Laissez-faire capitalism holds that the common good is best served by the uninhibited pursuit of self-interest. Unless it is tempered by the recognition of a common interest that ought to take precedence over particular interests, our present system is liable to break down. (Soros 1997, 48)

2. Those attentive both to current developments and to the political dangers of impoverishment have misgivings about the current welfare cuts. They ask whether this is a good time for the welfare cutbacks and rapid marketization of social policy schemes. One does not need too much imagination to realize that the consequence has to be the rapid fragmentation of society, and the inability of various

groups to satisfy their most basic needs. The escalation of the costs of housing, of medical expenses, of the schooling of children are particularly threatening, and so are the dangers connected with the large-scale deprivation of children.

The destitution and the anxieties stemming from these trends as well as from the threat of unemployment are increasing, and may cause long-term social, physiological, and psychological damage. The political dangers (for instance of right-wing populism) are not to be ignored either. As George Soros has put it:

> By ... declaring government intervention the ultimate evil, laissez-faire ideology has effectively banished income and wealth redistribution.... Wealth does accumulate in the hands of its owners, and if there is no mechanism for redistribution, the inequities can become intolerable. (52–53)

3. The political analysts dealing with the countries "in transition" add a further consideration to this argument. According to them, the slogan of the "minimal state" may be dangerous under the present conditions. A strong state may be exceptionally important when all the institutions are undergoing basic change, when laws must be passed for everything, when the new laws have to be enforced, and when self-restraint is at its weakest everywhere. The absence of a strong state may lead to total chaos as in Russia (Holmes 1997, Kende 1997).

4. Economists (and philosophers) repeatedly formulated moral arguments against unfettered individualism. They enriched the meaning of (individual) freedom by distinguishing between negative and positive freedom (Berlin 1969, Sen 1990). This interpretation of freedom—perhaps more implicitly than explicitly—argues for social redistribution. The economic argument is sharpened when the analysis turns to the inevitable failures of the market (Barr 1987). Przeworski (1997) carries the well-known arguments beyond the usual limits.

> When some markets are missing, as they inevitably are, and information is endogenous, as it inescapably is, markets need not clear in equilibrium, prices do not uniquely summarize opportunity costs and can even misinform, externalities result from most individual actions, information is often asymmetric, market power is ubiquitous, and "rents" abound. These are no longer market "imperfections." ... The economics of incomplete markets and imperfect information allows room for a much greater role for the state [than allowed by the neoliberal agenda]. The neoclassical complacency about the market is untenable: markets simply do not allocate efficiently. Even if governments have only the same information as the private economy, some government interventions would unambiguously increase welfare." (414)

5. The "new progressives" or "new social democrats" try to find a way between the old left and the new right. They accept the idea of an activist state but with many caveats. Redistribution—the encouragement of a policy of "handouts"—should be limited, and investment in human capital, in high technology,

or in the environment may be seen as a priority. This approach shows concern for human suffering by allowing for help for the poor, but it is not unduly preoccupied with problems of social integration or social exclusion (Ladányi and Szelényi, 1997).

6. This line of thought leads us to the new endeavors in the European Union to find a new public philosophy. A growing number of citizens are concerned about the deteriorating quality of public life. Hence the new approach takes as its central concept the quality of society. The group of European scholars involved suggest that social quality rests on the degree of economic security, the level of social inclusion, of solidarity, and of autonomy or empowerment (Beck et al. 1997). These objectives require a strong, if reformed, state involvement and large-scale public debates about the kind of society worth having. This approach has had a sympathetic response in Hungary. (Over a hundred social professionals signed a slightly modified version of the Amsterdam Declaration endeavoring to attract the attention of politicians to the conditions instrumental in promoting social quality under the Hungarian conditions.)

7. A last approach—mine as it were—tries to turn to history, particularly the relationship between the "welfare state," and the problems of social coexistence or civilization. It endeavors to think through the present consequences of the reversal of a historical trend. The argument will be briefly summed up here, only some conclusions will be spelled out.

Unfolding State Functions

The state "is a being which cannot be liked"—wrote József Eötvös, the Hungarian liberal thinker, in the middle of the last century. I guess that most of those participating in the current passionate debates about the state would agree on this point. I certainly do—even if the state in question is not of the totalitarian, dictatorial, or authoritarian variety. (In fact, as already mentioned, if not specified otherwise, I understand by the state a modern parliamentary democracy.) Despite this aversion, nobody—with the possible exception of extreme anarchists—thinks about its abolition. The differences between the attitudes toward the state do not depend so much on the emotions toward it: as I said, most of us dislike it. But there are different reasons, values, and interests behind this apparently collective dislike. Consequently, there are large differences concerning the functions that are thought to belong to the proper realm of the state, and concerning the agencies that could or should replace it in performing some or most of its tasks.

The ensuing attempt to give an overview of the changing duties and functions of the state is utterly overgeneralized. The story is different in different countries. It has to be reemphasized that all state actions have always been heavily opposed usually by groups that feared the curtailment of their privileges or their power. The resistance to a growing state varied from country to country, and among the states. Apparently in the nineteenth century "statism," or at least the increasing bureaucracy, was more strongly rejected for instance in England than in the absolute monarchies of Central Europe. Also, once established, state bureaucracies have often strongly resisted further changes, seeking "rents" and wanting to maintain privileges. Hence the utter importance of the role of civil society in requesting transparency and accountability from the state. Needless to add, these civil efforts often fail or succeed only partially—but this is already another story.[4]

Military and Policing Duties

Most analysts agree that in the last two to three centuries first absolutist states (Anderson 1974) and then in most if not all cases so-called nation-states emerged in Western Europe alongside the evolution of a predominantly capitalist society (Mann 1993). This process reached most other parts of Europe, too, albeit with many delays and differences. The historian Jenô Szûcs was probably right in suggesting that one could distinguish at least "three Europes," the west, the east, and east-central Europe in between. State formation is not the *differentia specifica* of Europe, though.

Even the great pre-European states have been sooner or later affected by European influence. "Europeans created a system that dominates the entire world. We live within that state system today. Yet the world outside Europe resembles Europe no more than superficially" (Tilly 1992, 191). The states created under very different circumstances and built on altogether different traditions and cultures may indeed adopt the formal traits and the institutional arrangements of (Western) Europe. Yet the essence of "modern European statehood," the relationship between the state and the citizens as well as the role and functions endorsed by, or forced upon, the state may not always follow the original patterns.

Tilly is no doubt right to connect war-making and state making. The (European) nation-states emerged after a protracted chain of clashes and combats between feudal (or similar) minor powers that continued their enmities even after the establishment of the new centralized powers. Thus one of the first functions of the state was, to quote Hobbes, to assure "mutual ayd against the enemies abroad" (quoted in Pierson 1996, 9), to protect subjects against attacks from outside. No less important was, in the words of the early theorists, the protection of the safety of the subjects, the prevention of their own destruction through civil wars or strifes, and the protection of their property. To quote Eötvös again (though without being able to render the charm of his mid-nineteenth-century Hungarian prose):

> What may be the aim which makes the majority see it as necessary to support the state, to defend it with their arms, to accept taxation, to endure all the irritating stints of public administration? ... The aim of the state is security. When the state cannot assure this for each individual, its citizens may think it the greatest evil. (Eötvös 1902, 2, 94, 95)

Security did not mean for Eötvös what we understand by it. He himself emphasized that its meaning varies with time and different nations understand by it different things. But on the whole the early state was needed essentially for warmaking in all its forms, and for assuring outside and inside peace. These activities implied at that time mainly coercive, that is, military or policing functions. Throughout this process the state gradually acquired, to quote Max Weber, "the monopoly of the legitimate use of violence." These functions required huge resources so that the state slowly obtained also the monopoly of tax collection (called extraction by Tilly). All these monopolies were acquired in long struggles with the other former important agencies of power, including the Church, the feudal princes or lords, the towns, and sometimes various oligarchies.

The policing duties were increased with the changing character of poverty. The poor "had always been there" in European history and it was never quite comfortable to live together with them. Depending on the spirit, on the "ethos," on the resources of the times, and also on the number and characteristics of the poor, society tried to "cope'—either by oppressing them, or by alleviating their plight, or both (see for instance Castel 1995a; Geremek 1987; Mollat 1978; Swaan 1988). Whether regulation or help, the handling of the poor was the duty of the smallest available helping unit—be it the family, the lord, the parish, the guild, or the locality. After all, "subsidiarity" is not a new idea.

The evolving market economy changed the face of poverty. With increasing social density and mobility, the scattered poor had changed their geographic and social position. They had become more visible in the fast-growing cities. Their miserable conditions certainly caused concern for them among their "betters," who had become more sensitive or refined than before—hence the strengthening of the welfare functions to which we shall come back. However, the poor had also become more dangerous and more endangering than before. They represented a danger for the bodily safety, for the property, for the morality, and even for the health of the better-off (Swaan 1988). Meanwhile those better-off were gradually deprived of the means of self-defense because the state monopolized the instruments of violence.

The first reaction of the state—empowered with the authority to maintain order—was certainly to respond with oppression or violence to this challenge. The cruel punishment of those belonging to the first waves of the "new poor," for instance under Henry VIII in England or Louis XIV in France, is common knowledge. Hence the strengthening of the policing function of the state. This function was time and again reinforced when, for instance, the movements of the emerging working class had to be fought back (Thompson 1963), or when the escalation of poverty prompted in England the Poor Law of 1834, a particularly nasty disciplinary act. With the formation of the working class the problems had become more acute.

Regimes now (in the middle or second half of the nineteenth century) had a broader "policing" problem. Capitalism and urbanization had weakened local-regional segmental control over the lower classes. Propertyless laborers, subjected to capitalist markets, periodically were rendered destitute, migratory, and rebellious. Peasants were burdened by debts as commercialization swept the countryside. Because capitalism conferred new powers of collective action on workers and peasants, more universal forms of social control were required, especially in the burgeoning towns. (Mann 1993, 500)

All in all, the new economic and social order and the upkeep of public safety under the new conditions required the state to further strengthen its policing functions. The pressure came as much or more from the middle and upper strata as "from below."

Administrative and Regulatory Functions

Of necessity the role of the state in administration unfolded along with its policing and tax collecting roles. Also from the earliest days it had to take on a role of "adjudication," the "authoritative settlement of disputes among the subjects" (Tilly 1992, 97). This role became effective with the monopolization of the right to promulgate binding laws and to enforce them. The monopoly of violence was obviously instrumental in promoting this role.

The emerging market society imposed further duties on the state. One of the threads of the story of state-building is the increasing density in many realms of society in the last centuries (a topic first developed by Durkheim). This development is related to the evolution of the capitalist economy, to the unfolding of industry, trade, and communication, paralleled by urbanization and population growth.

With the differentiation of production, the monetization of an increasing part of transactions as well as with a broadening network of industry and communication the need for adequate infrastructure support (roads, railways, urban planning, public buildings) increased. Many of those investments were forced upon or taken over by the state for more than one reason. As Swaan (1988) pointed out in a different context, the free rider problem created obstacles to the private production of many widely used facilities. In the majority of cases the building or planning activity also served either strong industrial interests, or military and policing aims, or both. (The most familiar example of the relationship between town planning and policing is the redesigning of the boulevards of Paris by Hausmann.) Once the need for them arose, the use of roads, of land, of seas, or the air had to be regulated in a uniform way. Also the emerging industry and trade needed state regulation or legal underpinning. As Polányi put it:

There was nothing natural about laissez-faire; ... Just as cotton manufactures were created by the help of protective tariffs, export bounties, and indirect wage subsidies, laissez-faire was enforced by the state. The thirties and forties saw [alongside with the repeal of restrictions] an enormous increase in the administrative functions of the state." (1944, 139)

The multiplication of commercial transactions went hand in hand with the intensification of communication and social networks. They developed into ever longer "chains of human interdependence" conducive to the "generalization of interdependency" (Swaan 1998, 2). As the chains of human interdependencies lengthened and multiplied, as the complexity of the transactions relating to objects and of social relationships grew, the danger of confusions or disorders increased. Local or regional regulations became inadequate. A gradual upward shift took place in the power centers entrusted with the regulation of the emerging chaos. In other words, the state grew. State regulation, administration, and "accounting" spread to people, to money matters, and to innumerable other phenomena, strengthening state bureaucracies further. The story is well known. The examples above just serve to justify the separation of the regulatory from the policing function, which may not be self-evident.

Most of these actions promoted mainly, if not exclusively, what was called by David Lockwood (1964, and later by Habermas and Luhmann 1971) system integration. This implies the relatively smooth operation of the institutions and mechanisms—such as the market, the communication system, and public administration itself—assuring the reproduction of the system.

One may add that all the above functions, the military, the policing as well as the administrative and regulatory functions have characterized every known state, albeit the extent of the bureaucracy and the instruments used may have varied widely.

Welfare Functions

The policing of poverty did not offer a lasting and satisfactory solution. The massive and cruel oppression or punishment of the poor came into conflict with the ideas of the Enlightenment, the increasing sensitivity of the "established" strata, the idea of the nation-state, and also with sheer economic rationality. The subduing of the poor was always costly. Also the overexploitation of children and young women led to the waste of lives that could be put to use more profitably if handled differently. With the spreading of "modern" ideas and with growing resources, it became increasingly difficult and increasingly costly to handle the conflicts only by coercion. Quiescence seemed to be easier to reach by means of compromises that dealt with some of the causes of discontent or conflict.

In truth, the "helping" duty of the state appeared from the earliest days of state intervention, alongside its cruel sanctions. Section 2 of the Act for the Relief of the Poor (Elizabeth I, 1601, 43) declares:

> It is agreed and ordered by the present Assembly that each town shall provide carefully for the relief of the poor, to maintain the impotent, and to employ the able, and shall employ an overseer.

But poor relief was insufficient to answer the new needs. The "spirit of the times" was changing. The idea of human dignity slowly gained ground. It led to the recognition of the indignities inflicted on the poor both by the procedures of traditional poor relief and by their miserable living and working conditions. The efforts to improve the lot of the poor started at various points of society. Self-help groups or mutual funds survived from before or were created anew. "Scores of philanthropies," initiatives of "private individuals," the helping efforts of "philanthropic" capitalists gained ground (Himmelfarb 1991, 12). All in all, the belief spread that "it could and should be better than it was." However, the scattered efforts were often weak (the free rider problem was an obstacle here too) and they were not ubiquitous.

The story mentioned in regard to other state functions repeated itself in regard to welfare. Various interest groups of society forced the central power to take over responsibility for improving the living standards and the "existential" security of the more vulnerable groups. Factory acts limiting the exploitation of children and women and defining standards of occupational safety paved the way for a more acceptable, not to say a more dignified status of the workers (Castel 1995a). Haphazard and demeaning social assistance was slowly transformed either into statutory state social assistance or into social insurance schemes covering at the beginning only the workers (Hatzfeld 1971).

Better hygiene, slowly improved housing, more accessible health services—all of which were part and parcel of the civilizing process—also had an immediate "welfare dividend." Mass education, which was at first forced on the children of the poor, was gradually accepted as a means that could perhaps help to improve their lot. It may be conjectured that social insurance helped to reduce the sufferings caused by the anxieties related to unpredictable and fateful events.

In the twentieth century, and particularly after World War II, the welfare functions of the state have spread gradually to the whole of society. (We shall come back to this point, which is closely intertwined with the civilizing process.) Services of improved quality reduced the resistance of the middle classes so that income redistribution achieved relatively high levels in quite a few countries. The opinions about this development are very much divided. From our perspective, though, it meant the reduction of poverty in general, and of deep poverty in particular. It also meant a reduction in the inequality of physical and social life chances. In short, it reduced the level of anxiety all around, and also the potential for conflicts between the rich and the poor, the insiders and the outsiders, those on the top and those at the bottom of society.

Civilizing Functions

"Civilization" is a concept with many different meanings. In Elias's approach it is related to the "self-consciousness" of the Occident as it evolved from the fifteenth century on. In his analysis it covers a wide range of phenomena from the most common everyday behaviors like nose cleaning to changing norms in manners, attitudes, patterns of communication, and perception of self and others, to affect in the end the psychological makeup of people, "the formation of a more complex and secure 'superego' agency" (Elias 1978, 248).[5] This process may lead to replacing external by internal constraints, to greater self-restraint and greater foresight (Elias and Scotson 1994, 152), and ultimately to the pacification of everyday life. Swaan has filled out this picture on two accounts. He analyzed in detail and by country the evolution of the involvement of the state with education, public health, and income maintenance programs to prepare people for new public duties, to defend the better-off against the dangerous poor, and also "to cope with inefficiencies and adversities" affecting the less well-off (Swaan 1988. In a later book he drew attention to changes in interpersonal relationships such as the decrease of social distances between groups of different rank, between genders, generations, "superiors" and "inferiors" within organizations, and between governments and their subjects (Swaan 1990, 150–151). In what follows I would like to emphasize some elements of the above story or to complete it with some considerations.

It should be repeatedly underscored that civilization is about social coexistence. A common language may be an important means of living together, but shared codes, ethical and (later) legal norms and rules may further promote "social integration." This last is a difficult concept whose content and meaning varies with space and time. It seems to me, though, that Habermas and Luhmann are right in suggesting that system integration in itself is arid. The "life-world" means more than the undisturbed functioning of basic social mechanisms and institutions. Part of the life-world is "a normative integration" which is evolving through a common sense of "belonging." If there are no shared norms and values, the rules of coexistence lose their credibility and legitimacy. I suggest that "system integration" and civilization are related but separate concepts.

It follows that at least in the modern world system where the market brings into contact practically everybody, social integration and civilization have to reach all the strata and all the members belonging to a given community recognized as a society. However, the codes, rules, norms emerge usually at the top of society. Spontaneous trickling-down processes do occur, but they usually go only "halfway," and many elements of the complex are left out altogether from the spontaneous processes. The successful spread of civilization requires at least two conditions: civilizing agents on the one hand, and the adequate "preparation" of the strata far removed from the top on the other.

The emergence and the mode of operation of the various "civilizing agents" would need a minutely detailed country-by-country analysis. Here only two aspects would be briefly mentioned.

One is the wide variety of the agents. Some of the earliest agents were the churches. In western Europe the role of Christianity is hard to overestimate. The feudal estates, the guilds, later the factories also fulfilled important civilizing functions. This is partly explained by the growing pluralism of modern societies. But most early agents were particularistic or partial. They fulfilled only a limited role (for instance the Church contributed to spread literacy but not numeracy), or they served particular clienteles (for instance, the workers of the factory). To reach the large masses and to spread a more complex common culture, more resources, more institutionalized solutions, and more ubiquitous agents were needed.

The state qualified for this role. From the onset of enlightened absolutism it deliberately took over the steering and also the implementation of many aspects of the civilizing process, taking over, for example, regulations referring to behavior in public places. It did this via the educational system, but also via the military and other services.

The other condition of the success of the civilizing efforts was indeed the adequate "preparation" of the strata far removed from the top. They had to be enabled to absorb the "blessings" of civilization: if and when children did not have shoes or decent clothing, they could not attend school (particularly in wintertime). They had also to be convinced by changing conditions that these blessings could be useful. Sheer coercion could not be effective. It may be shown probably everywhere, for instance, that children who were taught to read and write lost literacy if it could not be put to use.[6]

In other words, if the real and symbolic distance between the top and the bottom of society is too large, the civilizing process will remain defective. These distances are never reduced "spontaneously"—rather, their reduction requires the resources that perforce have to come from the better-off.

The early civilizing efforts of the state were restricted to those who were not "spontaneously" affected. Initially the compulsory institutions of health, education, and income-saving to deal with spells of bad fortune "affected workers, peasants and poor people more than the higher strata in society, who may have helped initiate these arrangements but have alternative resources to rely on for coping" (Swaan 1988, 475–476). The "higher strata" already had the use of these institutions or at least their functional alternatives.

Gradually, however, the compulsory institutions became increasingly collective. Thus their compulsory, policing, and constraining character could weaken, and the interactive and integrative features could strengthen. The widening of the clientele and the inclusion of more vocal groups with higher expectations led to a "virtuous circle." The more affluent groups gradually realized that it was in their own interest to profit from their own taxation. The history of the "welfare state" after World War II is the history not only of the spreading of the all-encompassing compulsory institutions, but also of the gradual improvement of their quality. The collective arrangements, just because they could appear as less discriminatory and enforced, could become more effective in changing interpersonal relations. The informed self-interest of the taxpayers has been an important factor in accepting "enforced solidarity" leading to the spreading of good-quality institutions of a universal character.

Whether the civilizing process makes people and societies better or worse—is a question I am not prepared to answer. It is certainly a double-faced process. On the negative side it curtails freedoms (by enforced solidarity) and makes people more vulnerable in the face of aggression, for instance. I only suggest that the civilizing process is instrumental in preparing people to adjust to changing social conditions. Applied to a society as a whole, or to different groups within a given society, being "more" or "less" civilized means, among other things, that one is more or less well prepared to exploit the opportunities offered, to cope with reality. If this is true, then one aspect of the process may be looked upon in value terms. If the civilizing process helps people survive in a given society, then it is a crucial question whether it reaches everybody, or whether many remain outside its grasp. The components of the civilizing process are indeed constituent parts of the social or cultural capital. If many are denied access to these resources, they will inevitably move downward or stay down in any given society.

I suggest that the main achievement of the by-and-large fully fledged "welfare states" was the inclusion of the vast majority into the mainstream. This was achieved by ensuring access to many important civilizing assets (including jobs with a fair wage surrounded by rights). Obviously these societies were not perfect. I think, however, that the level of human suffering was reduced with spreading rights and resources. Also, "social integration" could become a more meaningful concept than heretofore.

The Case of Eastern Europe

The extent to which the above processes reached Central and Eastern Europe is another long story. Before World War II the majority of those countries had a more rigid and more hierarchized social structure than their Western counterparts. They were also laggards in terms of the civilizing and welfare functions of the state. After the war "authoritarian state socialism" did not offer a fertile soil for many ingredients of the Western civilizing process. The political culture was nipped in the bud under the conditions of totalitarian politics. The contractual culture of the market disappeared in an economy that tried to abolish the market. Still, there were strong efforts to promote the civilizing and welfare functions of the state.

The "collective, nation-wide and compulsory arrangements" spread literacy, self-care, a change in manners. The "thresholds of shame and embarrassment" were advancing. Although various external constraints were heavier than ever before and in many cases were not even meant to become self-constraints, self-constraint was strengthening in many spheres with the changing economic conditions and social relations. Income security, combined with the expanding and free (or available) educational opportunities, motivated people to plan a future for their children, at least in the majority of families.

The civilizing and integrative impact of all these changes had to be weaker than in the West for a number of reasons. First, because of nondemocratic politics there was much less participatory involvement between the users of the institutions and the state. Without active involvement the identification with, or the sense of belonging to, the institutions was probably weaker, and therefore the messages emanating from them had to be less effective. Second, time for these changes was too short. It is sometimes assumed that it takes at least three generations for the civilizing impact to become effective (Fletcher 1997)—and the period in this case was much shorter. Third, the huge prewar social distances were politically declared void and were factually reduced. Yet the real distance between the most down-and-out and the models of civilization on offer in schools, hospitals, and so on remained too large. The kindergartens, for instance, made huge efforts to inculcate in children "civilized" ways of behavior such as washing hands—but the effect was dubious when even in 1980, 10 percent of the homes lacked basic amenities.

Despite these obstacles and adverse circumstances, I maintain that a civilizing process in the Western sense took place. One set of reasons is historical-political. The welfare arrangements were not artificial inventions forced upon the country by an alien power. Most of them had historical roots, and the improvements could be sensed as the fulfillment of age-old requests. Thereby a process was started enabling large strata to acquire some "civilizing capital." And in most cases the impact was reinforced by the changing social relations.

In short, I suggest—knowing that the position may be contested—that there was a civilizing process under state socialism. The process was not unequivocal; there were all sorts of obstacles owing to dictatorship, to the short time span, and so forth. Nonetheless, there were gains, and I think the most positive outcome of "socialist dictatorship" was the reduction of the civilization gap both between East and West, and between the higher and lower echelons of society. Many civilizing acquisitions spread through society, even if the very bottom may have been hardly touched.

The Weakening of
Some State Functions

With neoliberalism the expanded role of the state has begun to be questioned. The civilizing and welfare functions of the state have come under heavy attack. This does not seem to meet with the preferences of the majority of taxpayers (Svallfors and Taylor-Gooby 1999). Yet the interests adverse to state redistribution in favor of both weaker groups and social integration are successfully defeating mass expectations—a very paradoxical fact in democratic regimes. The strength of the opposition to the withdrawal of the state depends in fact on a number of factors. It is relatively strong in (some Western European) countries where civil society has been instrumental in forcing the state to serve "the common good"; where the major and better-off segments of society have also visibly profited from these functions; and where civil society is strong enough to fight back the mighty new financial interests.[7]

In the latecomer, poorer, and more vulnerable countries of central-eastern Europe the withdrawal of the state seems to meet less resistance. The above factors are weak or missing, and also the pressures of supranational monetary forces are stronger and more difficult to resist. The countries in question are economically weak, often indebted, and have to prove that they have overcome their "statist," "communist" and "paternalist" past. In many countries of the former Third World the welfare and civilizing functions appeared so late that they could not take root while "the going was good." The chances do not seem too good for their further growth except perhaps in some countries of Far Asia. Their economic takeoff has coincided by and large with the unfolding of economic globalization.

There seems to be, then, an apparent convergence at least between former Second World and former Third World countries. This is not pure coincidence: international pressures push the Eastern countries in this direction. Many analyses assess

> "the post-communist countries in Eastern Europe" as having "the most generous social welfare budgets in the world" with 15 to 30 percent of the GNP spent on it. This compares badly "with the outlays of East Asian countries at similar income levels, which average between 5 and 10 percent of GNP for similar social programs." (J. Sachs, 1991, 2, quoted in Vecernik 1996, 206)

No doubt, the living conditions of the people in Central Europe are not among the worst in a global perspective. The majority of the poor are still probably better off than many poor in the Far East or Latin America, let alone Africa. But the situation is graver if social dynamics are taken into account. It is not the same thing to have never had something and to lose something. That is why a static comparison with Asia à la Sachs is completely misleading.

Meanwhile the global economy appears, at least for the time being, to need neither a global civilization nor a global appeasement of the conflicts over the extremely unequal distribution of resources. There are no countervailing forces to bring it to realize the troubles and conflicts that may ensue. Neither are there international agents to promote efforts in this direction.

A Vicious Circle?

One could gather the impression from the previous arguments that the civilizing process—at least in the West—was cumulative and followed a direct line. This is clearly not the case. Even though it is only a footnote in the work of Elias written in the thirties, he explicitly suggests that

> The armor of civilised conduct would crumble very rapidly if, through a change in society, the degree of insecurity that existed earlier were to break in upon us again, and if danger became as incalculable as it once was. Corresponding fears would burst the limits set to them today. (1939, I., 307)

Revolutions, wars, grave natural or social calamities and crises, and then in an unprecedented way Fascism and Bolshevism all entailed various anticivilizing effects.[8] The onset of a new decivilizing process cannot be excluded on the level of (some) nation-states, or on the global level.

The pessimistic scenarios are all related to the assumption that the neoliberal recipe will spread, involving wholesale deregulation, individual competition, and state retrenchment. The decivilizing process, even if it does not go the whole way, may take two forms, both connected to the reversal of historical processes. One of them implies that those elements may crumble first that were the last to be built up. This means that the process may not start with thinning social density or shortening chains of interdependency, but with changes in affect management or self-imposed constraints. The other partial process means that those will be the first victims of decivilization who had been the last ones reached by the civilizing process.

Out of the many historical processes of capitalist development, we hinted at three at least that seemed to have been particularly instrumental in propelling the growth of the civilizing and welfare functions of the state: increasing density and longer chains of interdependence; the increase and the increasing visibility of the dangerous and endangering poor; and the need for the containment of inequalities for the sake of social integration and for bridling social conflicts.

Apparently, none of these tendencies has subsided. On the contrary, density is increasing at an astronomic speed. Inequalities within and between countries seem to be increasing (World Bank data, 1997). The number of the poor is growing even in the rich countries, producing alarming phenomena like the emergence of an underclass, or marked tendencies of social exclusion. Indeed, in the last one or two decades growing unemployment, other major changes on the labor market like the destabilization of jobs, declining earnings, weakening rights, and eroding "social solidarity" have all contributed to the expansion of poverty, to the accentuation of problems such as homelessness, hopelessness, criminality, and other forms of anomic behavior.

Similar phenomena prompted the state a century and a half ago to complete its policing functions with civilizing and welfare functions. By contrast, we currently witness the institutionalized weakening of the collective, all-encompassing and compulsory arrangements. The first direct consequence of the cuts is the downgrading of the institutions: either their coverage may shrivel, or their standards may decrease, or both. Their attractiveness is weakening. This triggers the vicious circle of a sort of tax revolt: people are less and less willing to pay taxes for deteriorating services that, in addition, are increasingly "targeted" only to the poor.

We have come full circle. The main function of the early modern state was the defense of society against attacks from inside and outside. Within the country this meant the defense of private property and the "war against the poor." Gradually "helping" and "civilizing" functions were added to the policing functions. Welfare redistribution has become an important instrument. The current revolt against it may not really want to minimize the state.

The attack on the big state has become predominantly an attack on the welfare and civilizing functions of the state. This seems to be the price exacted by those who are profiting the most from the globalization of the economy, the free movement of capital, the exacerbated competition within and between countries and companies. With increased income and wealth, the winners are able to spend much more on services of which they are the exclusive users. The former common institutions are destroyed. Of necessity what remains at the service of the losers becomes impoverished and of low quality.

Some other consequences of these movements may also be conjectured. With the replacement of former public services by market or pseudo-market solutions, huge sums are sacrificed from the state budget—that is, from taxpayer money— to give incentives (through tax breaks) for individuals to participate in these new market programs; to popularize the new formula of marketization; and to strengthen and to regulate these incomplete markets since they are particularly prone to market imperfections and failures (like the health or pension "industries"). And as an ultimate irony, the state guarantees at least a minimal level of those services. Thus if the market solution fails, it is not the entrepreneur but the general taxpayer who will pay the price of defective business management. (The newly reformed Hungarian pension system shows all these characteristics of enforced marketization and privatization.)

The balance between the regulatory and the oppressive functions, on the one hand, and the enabling functions of the state on the other, is changing. The dangers of social polarization, of an increasing level of resentment and violence, of a decreasing level of "civilization," of the spread of lawlessness are in the offing. If society wants to maintain peace, policing forces have to be strengthened. (The peace dividend created by the end of the Cold War may be used partly to this end.) With this switch it increasingly serves those who have the most to lose and to fear. Thus the weakening of the "welfare state" may, or indeed must, go together with the strengthening of the policing state.

In short the functions of the state in the last centuries seem to describe a "bell curve." The ascending side promised a "virtuous circle," forcing the state to complete its self-serving and coercive functions with more responsibility for the "common good." The descending side may lead to a vicious circle giving free rein to a process of decivilization.

Notes

The study of the historical role of the state and its connection with the civilizing process is a project I am working on. Some of the preliminary results have been presented in Ferge 1997a. However, the whole project is yet in an embryonic stage, and the results are more hypothetical than final. The people I have to thank for valuable, critical, and/or encouraging comments are by now almost too numerous to list. Let me mention, though, at least some of them: Shlomo Avineri, Nicholas Deakin, Herbert Gans, Don Kalb, Károly Kecskeméti, S. M. Miller, Pál Léderer, Frances Fox Piven, Agnes Simonyi, Adrian Sinfield, Stefan Svalford, Abram de Swaan, Peter Taylor-Gooby, and the doctoral students in Budapest.

1. I have described the social policy changes in the "transition countries" in detail in some other papers, e.g., Ferge 1997b, and had a cursory glance on the other parts of the world in Ferge 1998, where I also tried to map the relevant literature.

2. The quotation is taken from M. Potucek, 1996, 6.

3. As explained in this and other papers of Kornai, one's responsibility extends not just to old age, illness, disability, death of the breadwinner, and unemployment, but also to the housing and schooling of the children.

4. The comparison between the market, the local state, the central state, and the NGO sector in terms of transparency and accountability is a slowly emerging topic. Because of the *par excellence* political nature of their exercise, the instruments for control of the state seem to be somewhat more developed and more efficient (at least in mature democracies) than those for control of the market or of the voluntary sector.

5. The very idea of civilization as a process of imposing self-control goes back of course to Freud as widely acknowledged by Elias and Swaan. The super-ego is not only an individual phenomenon—it is one of the connecting links to society. Freud explicitly says that *some* curtailment of individual freedom seems to be the price of civilization (1951: 59–60).

6. For instance Kálmán Benda, a Hungarian historian, showed that at the end of the eighteenth century the ability of the peasants to write and to count remained functionally alive only in the centers of trade and commerce, and only in case of those involved in trading (Benda, 1978).

7. For the strengths of resistance of different countries to marketization see Altenstetter and Bjorkman, 1997.

8. There is a new body of research centered on the decivilizing processes that I cannot handle here in depth (Duclos 1993, Fletcher 1995 and 1997, Mennel 1990).

References

Altenstetter, C., and J. W. Bjorkman, eds. 1997. *Health Policy Reform, National Variations and Globalization.* Basingstoke, Hampshire: Macmillan.

Anderson, P. 1979. *Lineages of the Absolutist State.* London: Verso.

Avineri, S. 1997. "Towards Zionism's Second Century." *Jerusalem Review,* April 1997: 23–26.

Balczerowicz, L. 1995a. *Socialism, Capitalism, Transition.* Budapest-London: Central European University Press.

Balczerowicz, L. 1995b. "*Economic Development and Social Policy (an Outline.)*" Address delivered at the Fourth Central European Forum: Providing Social Welfare Under Conditions of Constraint, Vienna, December 15–16.

Baldwin, P. 1990. *The Politics of Social Solidarity. Class Bases of the European Welfare State 1875–1975.* Cambridge, New York: Cambridge University Press.

Barr, N. 1987. *The Economics of the Welfare State.* London: Weidenfeld and Nicholson.

Beck, W., L. van der Maesen, and A. Walker. 1997. *The Social Quality of Europe.* The Hague, London, Boston: Kluwer Law International.

Benda, K. 1978. "A felvilágosodás és a paraszti műveltség a XVIII. századi Magyarországon" (Enlightenment and peasant culture in eighteenth-century Hungary). In BK. *Emberbarát vagy hazafi? Tanulmányok a felvilágosodás korának hazai történetéből,* 287–308. Budapest: Gondolat.

Berlin, I. 1969. *Four Essays on Liberty.* Oxford: Oxford University Press.

Bourdieu, P. 1998. "Le néolibéralisme, utopie (en voie de réalisation) d'une exploitation sans limites." In *Contre-feux. Propos pour servir a la resistance contre l'invasion néolibérale,* 108–119. Paris: Liber.

Castel, R. 1995a. *Les métamorphoses de la question sociale. Une chronique du salariat.* Paris: Fayard.

Castel, Robert 1995b. "Élargir l'assiette." *Projet,* 242, 9–16.

Duclos, D. 1993. *De la civilité. Comment les sociétés apprivoisent la puissance. Éditions de la découverte,* Paris.

Elias, N. 1978. *The Civilizing Process.* Vol 1, *The History of Manners.* 1982. Vol 2, *State Formation and Civilisation.* Oxford/New York: Blackwell (first published 1939).

Elias, N., and J. L. Scotson. 1994. *The Established and the Outsiders.* London: Thousand Oaks; New Delhi: Sage Publications.

Eötvös, József. 1902. A XIX. század uralkodó eszméinek befolyása az álladalomra. I - III. (The Impact of the Dominant Ideas of the Nineteenth Century on the State) Révai. Testvérek Irodalmi Intézet R. T. 1902, (first published between 1851 and 1854).

Ferge Zs. 1997a. "And What If the State Fades Away—The Civilising Process and the State," in Stefan Svallfors and Peter Taylor-Gooby, eds., *End of the Welfare State? Public Attitudes to State Retrenchment,* 235–264. London: Routledge, 1999.

Ferge Zs. 1997b. "Social Policy Challenges and Dilemmas in Ex-Socialist Systems. The Need for Social Policy Reforms." In Nelson, Tilly, and Walker, eds., *Transforming Post-Communist Political Economies.* Washington, D.C.: 299–321.

Ferge Zs. 1998. *The Changing Functions of the State—A Virtuous or Vicious Circle?* (Unpublished manuscript).

Fletcher, J. 1995. *Towards a Theory of Decivilizing Processes. Amsterdams sociologisch Tijdschrift* 22, nr. 2 (okober 1995), 283–297.

Fletcher, J. 1997. *Violence and Civilization. An Introduction to the Work of Norbert Elias.* Cambridge: Polity Press.

Freud, S. 1951. *Civilisation and Its Discontents.* London: Hogarth Press.

Geremek, B. 1987. *La potence et la pitié. L'Europe et les pauvres du moyen age a nos jours.* Paris: Gallimard.

Gombár C., E. Hankiss, and L. Lengyel, eds. 1997. *És mi lesz, ha nem lesz? Tanulmányok az államról a század végén* (And What if it Fades Away: Essays on the State at the End of the Twentieth Century). Budapest: Helikon-Korridor.

Habermas, J., and N. Luhmann. 1971. *Theorie der Gesellschaft oder Sozialtechnologie?* Frankfurt am Main: Suhrkamp Verlag.

Hatzfeld, H. 1971. *Du paupérisme à la Sécurité Sociale.* Paris: Librairie Armand Colin.

Himmelfarb, G. 1991. *Poverty and Compassion. The Moral Imagination of Late Victorians.* New York: Albert A. Knopf.

Holmes, Stephen 1997. *"When Less State Means Less Freedom." Transitions* 4, No. 4 (September 1997): 66–75.

Kende, Péter. 1997. "Erős, republikánus állam nélkül ki fogja egyben tartani a magyar társadalmat?" (Who will hold together Hungarian Society Without a Strong Republican State?) In C. Gombár, E. Hankiss, and L. Lengyel, eds., *És mi lesz, ha nem lesz? Tanulmányok az államról a század végén.* (And What if It Fades Away: Essays on the State at the End of the Twentieth Century). Budapest: Helikon-Korridor, 358–380.

Kinkor, J. 1996. *The Market and the State. Why Do We Need Philosophy?* Prague: Svoboda, in Czech, 119.

Kornai, J. 1992. "The Postsocialist Transition and the State: Reflections in the Light of Hungarian Fiscal Problems." *American Economic Review, Papers and Proceedings* 82(2):1–21.

Kornai, J. 1997. "Reform of the Welfare Sector in the Post-Commmunist Countries: A Normative Approach." In *Transforming Post-Communist Political Economies,* ed. Nelson, Tilly, Walker, 272–298.

Ladányi, J., and I. Szelényi. "The New Social Democrats?," *Social Research* 64, No. 4 (winter 1997): 1532–1548.

Lockwood, D. 1964. "Social Integration and System Integration" In *Explorations in Social Change,* G. K. Zollschan and W. Hirsch, eds. Boston: Houghton Mifflin Company.

Mann, M. 1993. *The Sources of Social Power.* Vol. 2, *The Rise of Classes and Nation-States 1760–1914.* Cambridge: Cambridge University Press.

Marsland, David. 1996. *Welfare or Welfare State? Contradictions and Dilemmas in Social Policy.* Houndmills, Basingstoke, Hampshire, and London: Macmillan.

Mollat, M. 1978. *Les pauvres au Moyen Age.* Paris: Hachette.

Nelson, J. M., C. Tilly, and L. Walker, eds. 1997. *Transforming Post-Communist Political Economies.* Washington, D.C.: National Academies Press.

Polányi, K. 1944. *The Great Transformation.* Boston: Beacon Press.

Pierson, C. 1996. *The Modern State.* London and New York: Routledge.

Potucek, M. 1996. "Theory and Practice of Czech Social Policy." Paper prepared for the seminar on the Future of the Welfare State in Post-Communist Europe, orgnanized by Central European University and the Friedrich Ebert Stiftung. Prague, 1996.

Przeworski, A. 1997. "The State in a Market Economy." In *Transforming Post-Communist Political Economies,* ed. Nelson, Tilly, Walker, 411–431.

Sachs, J. D. "Crossing the Valley of Tears in East European Reform." *Challenge,* (September-October 1991).

Sen, A. 1990. *"Individual Freedom as Social Commitment." New York Review of Books,* June 14, 1990.

Soros, G. "The Capitalist Threat." *Atlantic Monthly,* (February 1997): 45–58.

Svallfors, Stephan, and Peter Taylor-Gooby, eds. 1999. *The End of the Welfare State? Public Attitudes to State Retrenchment.* London: Routledge.

Swaan, A. de. 1988. *In Care of the State: Health Care, Education and Welfare in Europe and the USA in the Modern Era.* New York: Polity Press/Oxford University Press page numbering is based on the multigraphed edition of Amsterdam University of 1987).

Swaan, A. de. 1990. *The Management of Normality. Critical Essays in Health and Welfare.* London and New York: Routledge.

Szûcs, Jenõ. 1983. *Die drei historischen Regionen Europas.* Frankfurt: Verlag Neue Kritik.

Thompson, E. P. 1963. *The Making of the English Working Class.* London: Penguin Books.

Tilly, Charles. 1992. *Coercion, Capital and European States,* A.D. *990–1992.* Oxford: Cambridge University Press; New York: Blackwell.

Vecernik, Jiri. 1996. *Markets and People. The Czech Reform Experience in a Comparative Perspective.* Aldershot, Brookfield, USA, Hongkong, Singapore, Sidney: Avebury.

Social (In-)Security

What precisely about the current Social Security "reform" debate makes it so hateful and repellent? Why—to quote Brookings economist Henry Aaron, normally a temperate establishment figure—are we headed toward "the My Lai of American social policy" if "partial privatization" reforms go through?

Make no mistake: As President Clinton plays television talk show host to a series of "Town Hall" meetings and then convenes a White House conference later this year on "retirement security," he will—all earnestness and concern—ask Americans to "think" with him about "what we need to do" to "fix" the system. But Americans need to think first about several crucial facts before they buy one more "big-picture" policy reform from the Man from Hope:

(1) Social Security isn't broke—and doesn't need the fixes Washington will propose.

A government advisory commission last year produced "exact" dates and dollars that gave apparent concreteness to the dimensions of the Social Security "crisis." Starting in 2029, it calculated Social Security won't have enough income to cover more than 75 percent of the benefits it must pay to aging baby boomers. But the specificity is illusory, all lever-pulling and smoke-blowing from the Wizard of Oz. The projections aren't economic (no even semi-sane economist does decades-long projections) but actuarial extrapolations based on assumptions that Social Security's own actuaries know are fictitious at best. Tweak them ever so slightly—lift real wages by a quarter- or half-percent per annum, or immigration by a little—and the same actuarial "crisis" disappears entirely. Federal law has mandated these projections for years, but—as the actuaries know well—they're redone every time they're revisited because the methodology is so poor. Until recently, apart from a handful of Washington technicians, nobody paid attention to them—knowing what they were worth. (Just a few weeks ago, we got an example of the slipperiness of these projections: Last year's economic growth moved Social Security's projected crisis date three years, to 2032.)

(continues)

(continued)

But amid Washington's bipartisan passion for "marketizing" America—the capital's new "anti-Communist" consensus for our post-Communist era—you might think the numbers have come down from Moses. They haven't.

(2) But—just for a moment—let's pretend there is a crisis. What should we do?

Fairness, you might think, is the place to start. Most Americans pay more into Social Security than they pay in income tax. Yet polls show most Americans don't even know that contributions to Social Security are "capped" at $68,400 in individuals' wages. By excluding wages above that line—those earned by the top 6 percent of U.S. households—and by excluding all nonwage income (dividends, interest, capital gains, rents, and so on) from Social Security taxation, guess what the effect is? It's enormously regressive.

Senators and representatives, who each make $136,673 a year, effectively pay at just half the rate of those earning below $68,400 yet receive the same maximum benefits as a middle-class worker at retirement—plus, of course, a hefty congressional retirement package. Bill Gates likewise will get the same maximum benefits but pays FICA only on his first ten minutes of income each year. Gates, of course, has $40 billion to tide him over; but 60 percent of U.S. workers retire without a private pension, and 66 percent of retirees count on Social Security for more than half their income.

At his first town meeting on Social Security in Kansas City, President Clinton—neatly forgetting that Medicare has no similar cap—took "lifting the cap" off the table. It must be put back on, at the center of the table. Social Security officials forthrightly admit that raising the cap alone would remove two-thirds of their projected actuarial crisis—something that somehow largely escaped the president's, and the press's, attention.

(3) But what about putting some of Social Security's money into the stock market—doesn't everyone agree that over the long term markets outperform Social Security returns?

(continues)

(continued)

This is tricky but must be understood: First, there's an "apples and oranges" problem—Social Security provides disability benefits, survivor benefits, and other features apart from just retirement income; factor these in, and the performance "advantage" of equity markets gets razor-thin at best. Second, Social Security benefits are already moderately progressive, meaning that the bottom 60 percent of retirees get more back than the affluent relative to their contributions.

Third, markets are subject to gravity—what goes up comes down, in both long and short waves. Since the Little Crash of October 1987, U.S. markets have been on a nonstop charge; but if you'd gone into the same markets in 1970, you were worse off by 1980— not to mention where you'd be today if you'd bet on Japan in the mid-eighties or Southeast Asia's "sure thing" markets a couple of years ago. Forget hyper-collapse 1929-style for a moment; think instead about retiring to find that your income's eroding each year as you grow older. Will you do all right in the long term, as brokers and economists insist? Well, probably yes—but that gives a new and nasty twist to Keynes's caustic observation that "in the long run, we're all dead."

Fourth, market averages aren't the same as individual returns. Turn 120 million workers loose to bet the markets (40 million of whom are marginally literate or numerate), and guess how many will beat the averages? The mutual fund industry's dirty little secret is that three-fourths of funds underperform market indexes. Yet such funds have millions of naive investors in them; in one recent survey, a majority of mutual fund investors couldn't even distinguish between a "load" and a "no-load" fund.

Here's where the income and wealth distribution effects of privatization turn very ugly: Some will do well—but not surprisingly, they're mainly the ones already well insulated against the financial vagaries of retirement. For millions of Americans—who bet on Kaypro instead of Microsoft (oops), Pan Am instead of American (sorry), or cattle futures without the skill and connections of Hillary Clinton (smile, please), life at seventy-five could mean not "golden years" but working for the folks at the golden arches, or even being out on the street.

(continues)

(continued)

There is a fifth issue that connects Social Security privatization to what has so far been undiscussed in the debate. Right now, Americans are delighted that, for the first time in nearly thirty years, the federal budget's in balance. But it's in balance because each year the Treasury borrows $80 billion from the Social Security Trust Fund surplus, and "covers" the deficit in the rest of the federal budget. If a big piece of Social Security contributions goes into private accounts, the trust fund surplus will disappear and the federal budget will plunge back into deficit—launching gleeful Republicans on another round of "cut, cut, cut." And which federal programs are likeliest to be cut by a Republican Congress? You fill in the blanks.

(4) What we could—and should—be doing.

First, we should strengthen the existing Social Security system. Single and divorced women fare poorly under the existing system: As a group, they're twice as likely to be poor as the senior population as a whole. That should be fixed forthwith.

Second, we should help Americans acquire real wealth—but not at the expense of Social Security. Social Security is only one leg of the three-legged retirement stool. The other two legs are private pensions and personal savings.

Only 40 percent of workers today get private pensions (and, increasingly, those are risky defined-contribution, not defined-benefit, plans). With corporations earning record profits, now's the time to expand corporate responsibility for helping workers create real personal wealth. Mandate that all employees share in those profit-payouts to senior executives; vest workers early; make plans fully portable; let workers draw from them for a first-time home purchase, lifelong learning, and major medical expenses.

On increasing personal savings, the issue grows politically more difficult—yet it is the core political and economic challenge of our time. The richest 1 percent of Americans have more wealth than the bottom 80 percent. The solution is simple: Most Americans should be earning more, and the richest should be paying more taxes. Period. The politics of getting there are hellish.

(Source: Editorial, *The Nation,* June 1, 1998)

10

Public Goods, Future Generations, and Environmental Quality

Andrew Light

In the past few years North Americans have seen a change in the approach of their governments to a variety of economic and policy matters based in part on an ideological shift that favors more libertarian approaches to public policy. Foremost in importance among these changes has been a transition in many governments' attitudes to fulfilling their role as caretaker of environmental quality. A question remains, however, concerning the propriety of managing a publicly provided good, such as the regulation of water and air quality, through market mechanisms such as optimal taxes and transferable quotas.[1]

But to claim that many governments have changed their economic philosophy toward publicly provided goods over the past few years is nothing new. Some governments, like Premier Ralph Klein's Progressive Conservative provincial government in Alberta, Canada, would welcome an acknowledgment of their approach. Klein has been lauded for his moves to scale back the size and scope of government involvement in everyday life through increased deregulation. In that respect, according to the Klein government, the Tories have responded to the wishes of its constituency—people want less interference by governments in their lives, first and foremost, by discontinuing interference that they feel is unwarranted. Gauging from the success of policies like Klein's and the popularity of similar policies in the United States, a claim could be made that most North Americans would rather see the market assume responsibility for the distribution of some goods rather than pay for the maintenance of these goods through their taxes.

Take, for example, the decision by the Klein government following closely on the heels of its first electoral victory to get out of the business of retail alcohol sales. Up until then, Alberta, like most Canadian provinces, managed government-run liquor stores. Most citizens of the province have approved the change out of this system. After all, is it not clear that first, the government has no business in regulating the provision of a need not shared by the population as a whole, and second, that the market is more efficient in providing this service than the government ever could be? Based on the success of policies like these the Klein government has moved aggressively to propose privatization of other goods, including those that we might loosely describe as dealing with environmental quality.

But moving from the gradual deregulation of liquor stores to broader issues involving the effective and efficient distribution of goods begs several questions. Is there not a difference between deregulation of the good represented by government retail alcohol sales and deregulation of a good like maintenance of water quality? If so, how do we describe this difference? Is that difference sufficient to warrant a claim that the propriety of deregulation can be challenged in some cases because of the sort of good under consideration? Further, have we citizens expressed a desire for privatization in all areas? Clearly, no. There appear to be few serious calls for other publicly provided goods, like police protection, to be regulated through market mechanisms rather than a government. Almost no one in North America is clamoring to scrap community police departments in favor of privately hired security forces, subject to the highest bidder. So what about the environment?

There are a number of options open to us if we wish to object to the privatization of the regulation of environmental quality from an ethical perspective.[2] Here, I will claim that the shift to privatization of environmental regulation can be challenged closer to its own economic ground, a move considered somewhat unusual by many environmental ethicists. I will argue that inside the economic definition of a "pure public good" resources already exist for challenging the privatization of environmental regulation. A sound philosophy of economics may be the first line of defense for the environmental community against the claim that regulation of environmental quality ought to be privatized. Such an argument may also be more persuasive to policymakers and policy analysts, for whom the appeal to an ethical criterion outside of the economic evaluation of nature as a set of resources may be quite foreign.[3] Important for this consideration in particular, my argument here is anthropocentric, or human-centered, and so outside the bounds of most work in environmental ethics today. I am not arguing that a nonanthropocentric environmental ethic is philosophically flawed, only that it is most likely that an anthropocentric argument here will be more intuitively plausible to the anthropocentrists who make the policy decisions that I will discuss.[4]

Now, a straightforward answer to the propriety of using economic criteria to determine how the environment should be governed could be given simply by checking the record. Clearly, direct regulation and enforcement with command and control policies is costly in terms of tax dollars spent. If both direct regulation and privatization result in the same environmental quality overall, then all other things being equal, we should allow the market to regulate the environment where possible and restrict government interference to the minimal task of setting quality goals. After all, this would be consistent with current economic and political trends. Accordingly, the presumption of many regulators today is that the burden of proof is with those who want to preserve the status of a good like environmental quality as a publicly provided good. Defenders of regulations have to give a compelling reason why we should not privatize where possible.

But outside of such efficiency criteria, is there anything else that we might want to consider? My answer will be that there are other considerations to take into account, and that many kinds of environmental quality should be considered and therefore regulated as publicly provided goods. The burden of proof should be on those who would privatize the maintenance of environmental quality, and the specific burden that they must overcome is one involving the normative status of such goods rather than simply the efficiency of their delivery. I will focus my discussion here on issues like water and air quality, even though I believe it can be applied to other areas of environmental regulation as well, such as access to public land and parks protection. Additionally, nothing in this argument will give an answer to the question of what the content of environmental quality should be. I will only address the broader question of how environmental quality should be treated, assuming its content is determined by other means. I have no philosophical argument to offer here that would help determine, for example, minimum standards for safe drinking water. Nonetheless, I believe a framework for discussing these issues can be set prior to their more precise determination.

Pure Public Goods and Publicly Provided Goods

Before continuing, we need to clarify the differences between publicly provided goods and pure public goods. I do not want to confuse the terms *public good* and *publicly provided goods* with a broader notion of the "good of the public." Here, such goods will refer to a restricted class of goods and services, which, though related in a broader sense to the community good, have traditionally expressed more distinct economic ideas, and are not historically treated as moral categories.

Publicly provided goods are goods that may not be traded as commodities, as determined by a public policy. These goods represent the package of benefits that a government decides to provide equally to all of its citizens, such as police and fire protection. Economists, following Paul Samuelson, define a specific subclass of these goods as "public goods," or "pure public goods," in a technical sense. These entities are those goods that are "nonrival," that is, the quantity consumed by one person does not limit its consumption by others, and "nonexcludable," meaning that the good *cannot* be provided for some and excluded from others.[5] A classic example of such a good is a lighthouse, which materially meets both of these conditions.[6] The marginal cost of adding another user to the provision of such a good is zero. The market fails in providing the efficient production and distribution of these goods because their benefits and costs cannot, as a matter of fact, be fully captured. Public goods must be ensured by a tax-collecting government.

It is difficult, however, to find examples of pure public goods, and many goods that are publicly provided do not fall into this category. A simple test is whether the marginal cost of providing any particular good increases with additional users. For most goods, like police protection, fire service, health care, public schools, and so forth, additional users do increase the costs of provision. But many of the particular goods provided by these institutions may appear to meet the criteria of a public good, as for example when an increased number of members of a community do not require an increase in the expenditure for delivery of a good because it already exists in amounts adequate to serve the demand. This is the case when some aspect of police protection exists to a degree that it can absorb an increased demand without necessitating increased expenditures. In such cases economists may speak of these goods as "quasi-public goods."

What is important for me here are not such marginal cases, but the fact that we model standards for delivery of publicly provided goods on the nonrival and nonexcludable criteria of pure public goods. Our goals for the provision of publicly provided goods are generally for there to be enough to go around for everyone (nonexcludable), and that one person getting access to the good does not limit another person's access (nonrival). Publicly provided goods are legislated so that, for the latter criterion for example, the goods *ought not* to be provided for some and excluded from others. The identifying criteria of pure public goods thus become the provision goals of publicly provided goods. For many publicly provided goods it is impossible to meet these criteria (for example, in the case of organ transplants in a country with a national health service and an organ shortage). Nonetheless, these are the ideal standards by which we measure the provision of these goods, in order to ensure their equal distribution for all who have a right to them.

Police protection, for example, benefits all members of a community regardless of whether each user has paid for the service through taxes. Hopefully, the supply of adequate police protection through government provision is not limited by the quantity demanded at any given moment. Anyone calling a police station for help should expect to get a response regardless of the demands of other citizens for similar service. Although it is common for police protection not to be available on demand, citizens have a just cause to complain that the good has not been adequately provided when they cannot get it, even though technically police protection is not a pure public good.

Because of their connection, unless specifically noted, for the remainder of this argument I will use "publicly provided goods" and "public goods" interchangeably, acknowledging that most publicly provided goods are not pure public goods. But this usage will help to remind us that publicly provided goods share the standard criteria of public goods as ideals for the former's provision. Whatever goods a community decides to publicly provide will therefore include a commitment to attempt to treat those goods as if they were pure public goods. Those goods that we think should be provided as if they were nonrival and nonexcludable are those goods that we believe deserve a special guarantee for their provision, not found in their delivery by the market. There is however still something important to notice in this distinction between pure public goods and publicly provided goods that I will return to soon.

First, however, we should note that, when looking at the differences between many of the goods provided by different governments, the public goods definition is not sufficient to explain the public provision of some goods and not of others. Whether something counts as a public good or as a commodity is often a matter of dispute embroiled in a number of issues. The social and political climate of a country, for example, may influence whether a particular service is identified as either a commodity or a public good. Consider, for instance, that in the United States health care has predominantly been treated as a commodity rather than a public good. Patients go to doctors and purchase a certain amount of care as they would any other service. The health consumers with more money will get more, or better, care in return for their outlay, just as the automobile buyer can get a better car with more money. In contrast, Canada has treated health care as a public good for some time. All Canadians are entitled to the same health services provided by state-regulated health facilities and staff. At times these respective philosophies of health care have been called into question. In the last few years, both in Canada and in the United States, national discussions have been held aimed at rethinking their respective approaches to health care. But clearly in each case, the discussion of the status of health care is shaped by the different political cultures and histories of the two countries. It is worth noting, though, that we can expect relatively more Canadians to be upset at moves to privatize health care than Americans would be at the defeat of a proposed public health care system in the United States. Why? Because Canadians have come to see health care, like police protection, as something they have a right to expect will be delivered equally to everyone—it is treated as a public good. Taking away that right seems anecdotally more difficult than failing to fulfill a promise to institute it anew.

But the fact that people have come to expect a service to be guaranteed by the government is not enough to explain why its loss would be resisted. Some government services are not missed, as the Alberta experience indicates from the privatization of liquor stores. What accounts, then, for cases where tensions run high over moves toward privatization?

Goods as Needs

I want to suggest that the key to understanding the choices involved in the public distribution and guarantee of a good can be found in understanding how publicly provided goods represent a community's expression of which goods it considers meet human needs that should be assured equally for everyone, or, which goods satisfy common needs. My claim is that publicly provided goods have the normative status of publicly recognized needs. A public good meets a need that we think everyone has, such as protection of their person and property, as provided by the public goods of police and fire service. The idea that some goods represent generalizable needs is part of the implicit rationale for the claim that there is a class of goods that ought to be treated as if they are nonrival and nonexcludable, when actually they are not. Because we think everyone needs these goods we want to make sure that everyone has them, or has equal access to them.

Now, to thicken the concept of a publicly provided good by articulating its fulfillment criteria as satisfying commonly accepted needs will help to make sense of my intuition that the loss of environmental quality as a public good is a problem even if the market alternative results in equal environmental protection. But this claim will take some unpacking. First we have to understand how justifying the abandonment of the provision of a need requires more than proof that the market can efficiently distribute a good that was publicly provided. What exactly is lost in the privatization of a public good?

If the provision of a good as if it were nonrival and nonexcludable really means that the good represents a need as I have described it, then questions of equal distribution, fairness, and other moral considerations come into play in discussions of policies regarding these goods. Such goods cannot simply be made available as such; they must be guaranteed equally for everyone at the same level of quality. Why? By the analysis so far, the extension of the pure public goods criteria to publicly provided goods requires us to recognize that the goals for the provision of publicly provided goods rest on strong normative claims. Adopting the criteria of pure public goods for publicly provided goods is a move from a simple description of a kind of good—here the ontology of pure public goods—to the rather strong normative claim that another class of goods should be treated as if they were the same thing because they represent a commonly perceived need. We have moved from claiming that some good X has the characteristics A and B, to saying that some good Y ought to be treated as if it has the characteristics A and B. Because publicly provided goods are really not pure public goods, we cannot simply ignore this normative shift in their treatment when we consider changing their disposition to the market.

The shift in the status of a publicly provided good to a commodity is completed at the expense of crossing a normative line, the line drawn when the good was treated as if it were a pure public good. It is not sufficient, then, to justify such a transition in the status of a publicly provided good by only appealing to efficiency criteria. An additional argument is also needed for why this transition in the treatment of the good is permissible, since the application of what would otherwise be purely descriptive elements of a specific kind of good to this class of goods was a normative one. The specific hurdle that the privatization claim has to overcome is that it is permissible for some people not to have access to the good, while others have access to the good, a common occurrence when the distribution of a good is privatized. Here, claims to fairness and equity come into play. Note that this argument would not apply to goods that really are pure public goods, but only to those we wish to treat as if they were. In the case of environmental quality, such as air or water quality, we have a good that is clearly not a pure public good: it does cost more to maintain with more users, even though its public provision tries to absorb this cost. Like all publicly provided goods, a normative standard has been set with its public provision. This good must be provided equally to everyone at the same level of quality. Such a normative description of the kind of good represented in environmental quality could count as a good reason to reject a claim to determine the propriety of privatization efforts on efficiency grounds alone.

But an initial problem with this redescription of publicly provided goods as publicly recognized or common needs is that different communities still recognize that different kinds of goods are needs. This is clear from the health care example. How, then, does expressing the definition of publicly provided goods as publicly recognized needs help us to form an argument that some goods should be publicly provided even in places where they are currently left up to the market? If the base of the normative criteria is relative between different communities, is not efficiency a better measure of the propriety of the provision of a good? The central question is how strong the normative standard is for the public provision of a good as it is derived from the descriptive criteria of a pure public good: Is there any rationale for a claim that such goods must be publicly provided as a matter of right to all people? This is a fair set of issues to try to understand if only because within a community there is often disagreement over which goods should be publicly provided. Not every good expressed as a need is provided. In the industrial democracies, at least, we tend to endorse a system that privatizes the provision of some goods that some individuals, or even whole communities, might describe as an important need for everyone. But because there is also resistance to the privatization of all goods, there may exist some intuitive rationale for deciding which needs should be publicly provided for and which can be left to the market. If this is true, then the question becomes whether that rationale carries between communities rather than only applying within a community. A still thicker characterization of public goods is needed than simply recognizing their representation as common needs to provide a better answer to the advocate of the efficiency criterion.

Needs can be roughly understood as human requirements and desires. Normally we only express human needs in terms of the desires of currently living people, sometimes even acknowledging them as only the expressed preferences of those people. Certainly, this connection between needs and expressed preferences is one important source of relativity among the recognition of public goods by different communities. Because preferences can be very different between communities there is little basis for critique of any given society for not fulfilling needs that are expressed as preferences in another society, but not in its own. But sometimes, certainly within communities, some needs are recognized that are not contingent on expressed preferences. Some needs are thought to be crucial for everyone equally, including future generations. If publicly provided goods are publicly recognized needs, and if there is some rationale for determining which needs must be publicly provided, then a good candidate for that rationale is the class of needs we think are important for everyone, regardless of whether they are in a position to recognize that importance. Future generations in principle cannot express preferences, even though we regularly ascribe needs to them. For example, future generations cannot recognize the importance of maintaining their own personal security, and are not able to express their preferences concerning its provision. Nonetheless, we recognize that they have this need, and would do our best to ensure that they are born into a society that has preserved the public provision of that good as inviolate. If we fail to ensure this need we may even be blameworthy for failing to fulfill a moral obligation to the future.

Certainly, there are many ways in which obligations to future generations can be justified. And of course there are many interesting philosophical objections to recognizing these obligations. Without getting too much into these debates, though, it is probably true that obligations to future generations can be validly justified. Further, it turns out to be the case that obligations to future generations have been widely used in the past as the grounds for progressive environmental policies (see, for example, Federal Title 16, §1 of the U.S. National Parks Service Authorization Act). If we are inclined to such justifications, the question seems not whether to endorse the claim to obligations to future generations but rather how to justify and extend the appeals to future generations already in use.

Avner de-Shalit has done one of the better jobs of justifying these obligations in an environmental context.[7] Here, de-Shalit specifically justifies these obligations through a communitarian framework for the purpose of grounding better environmental policies. De-Shalit's framework is based on the extension into the future of the values and obligations assumed to be important for contemporary communities as these obligations are conceived by most communitarians. We exist, therefore, not only in communities, with concomitant sets of obligations to those communities, but also in transgenerational communities that include explicit obligations involving environmental goods. De-Shalit's version of communitarian obligations to future generations could serve as a framework for the kind of claim I am suggesting for maintaining environmental quality as a publicly provided good. The argument would be that the normative delivery standard at work in treating a good as a publicly provided good entails not only the assurance of equal distribution of the good for present generations but for future generations as well. Certainly, other frameworks for obligations to future generations could also serve this argument, so my overall claim does not depend on the strengths of any particular grounding of such obligations. Important, though, the analysis here so far is consistent with some of the better schools of thought on this issue.

Certainly, the ascription of needs to future generations is an expression of the preferences of currently living people. In that sense, one could claim that, no matter what justifications for obligations used, ascribing needs to the future is just another case of a preference that is no less susceptible to the relativism charge than any other expressed preference. In fact, for de-Shalit, expressions of obligations to the future are an extension of how we would like ourselves to be remembered in the future and hence do represent the current state of our preferences. But surely there must be something to the view that the act of expressing a preference for those who cannot express preferences is a different kind of normative claim than only expressing one's own preferences. Does this difference matter? If it does not in practice, then I think that sustained reflection on our intuitions would reveal that this difference should matter. We are at least making the claim here that something ought to be guaranteed as a need for reasons not restricted to our own preferences and that can in principle be defended as important to those who might someday disagree with our judgment.

The description of public goods as needs of present and future citizens is particularly strong. Because such goods are treated as important even to people who cannot express preferences about their needs, they are in some sense an articulation of basic human needs. To express such needs is to claim that we cannot imagine someone having a full life without their guarantee. This seems to be a fair way of characterizing a class of needs that gets around the claim that publicly provided goods are always relative between different communities, or within communities between individuals. On this account, there is at least a difference between goods that we can reasonably claim ought to be provided for people regardless of their preferences, and goods that cannot meet this requirement. As there is a class of goods not necessarily provided because of actually expressed preferences, the fact that such goods are not expressed as preferences by some people and in some places is inconsequential to determining their importance.

Certainly, it is difficult to identify such basic needs. Intuitively, however, we ought to be able to come up with some pretty clear candidates for such needs, and consequently for public goods that guarantee the maintenance of those needs.[8] This argument takes care of the issue of the relativity of needs within a community: At least needs are relative between individuals only if those needs depend on expressed preferences of those who will benefit from their maintenance. As to the issue of the relativity of the public provision of goods between communities, the issue is more complex but not insoluble. Certainly we have a basis now for an argument that some goods ought to be publicly provided for all people, given a defensible argument that a particular good is important for future generations who cannot express any preferences on that good. All future generations, regardless of which community they will eventually belong to, will have this need. Perhaps more concretely to the issue I started out with, the argument I have made here can be used to criticize a community's policy to not guarantee the delivery of a good that community had in the past delivered according to the extended criteria of pure public goods. Such a community is violating a normative standard that it has set for itself. This claim strengthens the argument that a normative burden of proof lies with those who would privatize the delivery of those goods currently provided by regulations. Such an argument would depend, however, on a claim that the good in question is arguably a basic human need.

Combining the normative burden of the decision to publicly provide a good with the description of some of these goods as basic needs gets us a very strong argument against the assumption that regulated goods should be privatized solely on grounds of increasing efficiency. My intuition is that environmental quality is one of these basic needs and as such ought to be preserved as a publicly provided good. An attempt to privatize the maintenance of environmental quality that would either (1) risk the guarantee of its equal delivery or (2) diminish its quality, would thus have to overcome the normative burden of the status of this kind of public good no matter what other benefits of privatization were gained. When governments move to privatize the delivery of all goods regardless of their particular character, based on an efficiency claim, and without an acknowledgment of the normative aspects of such decisions, a broader conception of a public good is violated. Such polices threaten the "good of the public," or, the aggregate sense of what is good for the community. Though I do not have an argument to offer at this time on this issue, I believe this greater good is violated when we abandon public goods most clearly identified as representing basic human needs. When basic human needs are in jeopardy, the pursuit of private goods and individual goals becomes impossible. Such a situation, if widespread, cannot be good for the public.

But the specific argument concerning the status of the environment as a public good is not yet complete. Clearly, regulations may be kept in place to ensure the minimal delivery of a public good, as a minimal guarantee of a basic need, even when the good itself is subjected to the play of the market through deregulation. The challenge is to carefully decide which specific changes are consistent with our description of a public good, and which steps take us too far away from the greater good of the public. But even given a case-driven practical method, which I prefer, we need a more explicit argument for the general importance of environmental quality for everyone, including future generations, than has been provided so far. Although such a claim is implicitly made in the statutes regulating water and air quality, it is not yet adequately defended. Still, outlining the ground for the claim that environmental quality, broadly construed, is a basic need, increases the burden of proof on those who would seek to privatize or simply diminish the maintenance of environmental quality.

The Distributive Burden
of Environmental Quality

To further test my argument on the basic needs status of environmental quality, we need to narrow the discussion. Take, for example, the proposals for transferable quotas for pollution rights whereby governments are asked to shift away from a policy of setting minimum standards for each polluting firm to achieve toward a policy where the firms in an area must collectively reduce emissions to the standard for that community. Under some such schemes it is permissible for a firm that produces less pollution than mandated to sell its "right" to pollute more to another firm that is producing more pollution than allocated. Is this transformation of the treatment of environmental quality desirable? I think not. But why not, especially if market mechanisms such as transferable quotas could get us comparable levels of, for example, emission control? How strong is the normative requirement attached to the treatment of environmental quality as a basic need through its provision as if it were a pure public good?

To answer this question we must first acknowledge an even more fundamental sense than we have so far, in which environmental quality, especially as it is instantiated in air and water quality standards, is a basic need. It is conceivably one of the foundations for other basic human needs, specifically those related to health and welfare. If environmental quality decreases, then human health problems increase. Although concern about human health is certainly not the only reason to insist on strong environmental protection, from the perspective of the public goods argument, it may be the most important reason. Anthony Cortese summarizes this connection:

> We have known for centuries that a healthy environment is essential for human existence and health, and that contamination of the environment with heavy metals, microorganisms, physical agents, and certain organic compounds can cause serious illness and death. Improved water, food, and milk sanitation; reduction of physical crowding, better nutrition; and central heating with cleaner fuels were the intervention strategies most responsible for the marked improvements in public health that were achieved during the twentieth century.[9]

If this crudely drawn relationship is true between environmental quality and human health (and though I will not adequately defend it here there seems little reason to doubt it), it is clear that a threat to environmental quality is a threat to the fulfillment of other basic needs for current and future generations. It is also importantly a threat to the fulfillment of all private needs as well, since the ability to select those needs is parasitic on personal health maintenance.

Some environmental ethicists might object that the reduction of environmental protection to considerations of environmental health is overly anthropocentric. This is probably true. But without engaging the debate over anthropocentrism versus nonanthropocentrism, a clear argument can be made for the importance of making a sound argument for the protection of environmental quality only in human terms, especially given a starting point in economic analysis. Such claims may be more morally motivating for those who control such policies and who may find the ascription of nonanthropocentric value to nature incoherent. Although this claim is consistent with other philosophical arguments for the validity of pluralism in environmental philosophy, it is also importantly different.

Philosophical arguments for pluralism are usually based on philosophical premises. So when Gary Varner provides one of the most cautious arguments for pluralism in environmental ethics, it is because he believes it best fits the prerequisites for the successful articulation of holism in environmental axiology (the dominant view in the field today, which holds that the focus of an environmental ethic should be on the value of whole ecosystems rather than individuals).[10] That is to say, any theory that seriously argues for moral consideration of entire ecosystems rather than individual entities must accept pluralism as the only way to make sense of how that valuing is to take place.

In contrast, my pluralism is more pragmatic. It is not necessarily because of the philosophical prerequisites of one form of environmental valuing that I advocate this anthropocentric model of the value of the environment. Instead, I believe that the first line of defense against the privatization and commodification of environmental quality (and hence of nature) should come from an attempt to work within the dominant forms of economic analysis. As mentioned at the beginning of this paper, if it can be proven that a strong argument exists within a sound economic argument to challenge privatization moves, then surely that will be the most persuasive argument to those who hold this view. I can defend a form of environmental pragmatism that allows me to make this argument and to consistently hold the position that environmental quality (and nature itself) ought not to be treated in reductionist economic terms.[11]

Therefore, more rigorously defended argument on the role of environmental quality in maintaining human health ought to be enough to provide us with sound reasons for why environmental quality should be protected as a publicly provided good. But even the importance of environmental quality in meeting basic needs, as suggested by Cortese, is insufficient for making this claim without a firmer grasp of how the importance of needs drives our sense of their public disposition. An understanding of the obligations involved in meeting needs is provided partly by the argument offered above, concerning the normative structure of basic needs embedded within our commitments for the delivery of publicly provided goods. But in addition to the positive argument for why the set of goods represented in environmental quality responds to some basic needs, we still need an account of why it is permissible to privatize some goods that were previously publicly provided. If there is a good reason to claim that a certain class of public goods are basic needs, and hence ought to be protected as such in every community, then it should also be true that some goods that are publicly provided do not meet these criteria. Important, though, if such goods cannot be described as basic needs, then this is not a reason alone to discontinue their public provision. It only means that the claim to privatize them does not need to answer the normative component of the basic needs criterion. Still, there would be less reason to worry about the equity concerns involved in the treatment of non-basic needs as goods.

Let us return to the Alberta liquor store case mentioned at the beginning of this chapter. If public goods sometimes provide basic needs, then we should approach decisions on changing the disposition of this particular good by asking what need for the community was provided by government-owned liquor stores. Although it is difficult to ascertain now, the need being provided involved public regulation of a controlled substance thought to be of moral consequence for everyone in the community. But our views (and evidently those of Albertans) on alcohol consumption, for better or worse, have changed as a society. Most communities in North America now believe that alcohol consumption is the fulfillment of a personal (or private) need only, and so it is no longer regulated as a publicly provided good. Regulation of the substance is still needed, but at least the retail side is no longer considered a necessary part of

that regulation. Whatever good for the community that may have been preserved by the regulation of retail sales is now captured by other laws concerning zoning, drunk driving, and so on.[12] Some may even argue that the service
provided by governments in maintaining liquor stores was never a public good
to begin with.[13] And because, as mentioned above, there does not seem to be a
future generations claim to justify the provision of these goods, such an argument is on solid ground.

But environmental quality is not like this case. We have no doubt, for example,
that a clean environment—and particularly the health consequences associated
with it—is something that we all need. Although we may all do risky things with
our lives from time to time, none of us reasonably desires to be unhealthy. At
least we certainly do not want to be unhealthy through no fault of our own. The
public goods maintained in the preservation of environmental quality meet the
clear overlapping desires of us all, rather than catering to our individual (perhaps
unshared) preferences. It is also clearly important for all future generations.
Considered thus, environmental quality is like police protection: It is something
that we all have an interest in whether we recognize it or not, simultaneously
meeting our overlapping desires. Ensuring environmental quality is, in other
words, an assurance of environmental protection for us all.

One thing more, returning us to the burden-of-proof issue raised at the beginning. Although it is consistent with my pragmatism that a case needs to be made
for the preservation of each public good as an inviolate basic need, there are still
starting points for the assessment of public goods in general. The burden of
proof should always be on the market rather than on the state as the best
provider of the good. Why? One answer could be that it seems contradictory to
expect private institutions to provide something that is needed by all of us. But
there is a more specific reason that follows directly from the analysis of the normative content of publicly provided goods given so far: Ignoring the normative
burden that accompanies the public provision of a good can result in real inequalities among beneficiaries of a good.

Environmental protection, like police protection, is something that is regulated
to provide equal delivery of the good; assurance of equal distribution is part of
the burden assumed by a government when the good is treated as if it were a
pure public good. According to the description of some public goods as basic
needs, considerations of equal distribution are certainly also important. Good
environmental quality must be assured no matter where we live, just as protection of our person and property must be assured no matter where we live.
Certainly, when it comes to personal safety, we know that for various reasons,
some parts of a community are more dangerous than others. But what we do not
expect is that the legal standards for safety will vary from one place to another.
We do not, as a matter of law, allow a greater number of robberies in one part of
a city rather than another. A crime is a crime wherever it is committed.

We expect no less from our environmental protection. We know that some places are cleaner than others, but we expect all places to have the same standards for quality. But privatization measures, such as pollution tax credit schemes, can challenge this expectation in a peculiar way. Some pollution tax credits allow corporations to own the right to produce a certain amount of pollution. This amount represents their share of a burden on environmental quality. But because it is a credit, this burden may be traded. As mentioned above, if one company needs to pollute more, it is allowed to buy the right to pollute from another company which in consequence must pollute less in order to sell its share of its burden on the environment. In theory then, nothing prevents this system from protecting the same aggregate amount of environmental quality of, for example, clean air, as a strict state regulation applied to every polluter equally.[14]

But the distribution problem here should be clear. Although the total amount of pollution may remain at the same level overall as with a direct regulation, the amount of pollution in different areas will vary from place to place. If one is unfortunate enough to live close to a factory that can (or must) buy more of a right to pollute from another factory, then environmental quality will be lower in that area. If one lives near a cleaner factory, rich enough to afford to pollute less and sell its excess environmental burden, then one will reap the benefits of access to better environmental quality. Environmental protection as the mechanism of assurance of the publicly provided good of environmental quality is on such a plan, not equal. Important for this example, such risks to equal distribution are legally permitted to be unequal. By analogy to the police protection example, it is like allowing as a matter of law more crimes to be permitted in one part of a city, as long as fewer crimes are committed in another. Clearly, this is not an acceptable disposition of a public good that is distributed as if it were a pure public good because it is construed as a basic need.

Of course, the best versions of pollution trading plans ban trading of emissions that can accumulate at their point of origin. Trading is restricted only to emissions that do not cause increased harm to the communities closer to the point of production. So, a clever advocate of market mechanisms can design a plan to redistribute environmental protection more equitably through the market without risking the equal distribution of harm. But what is important to recognize in such plans is that in making such concessions they acknowledge the prior fundamental principle that environmental quality is a public good that must be assured equitably and fairly for all citizens, and I would argue, for future citizens. When we combine this principle with a strong precautionary principle, also justified by the common needs represented in environmental quality, then the burden of proof on those advocating shifts away from state control is quite high.[15] This does not mean that this burden cannot be overcome. One can even imagine cases where markets could lead to increased environmental protection, which would count as a strong reason to shift away from state regulation (a shift that I would endorse following my pragmatist convictions). But the beginning point for all such discussion is still that because environmental quality is a public good with strong normative expectations for equal provision, it must first be managed publicly. Increased savings cannot justify shifting from such provision if there is any risk that equal distribution will be diminished or quality decreased.[16]

Notes

1. The general consensus of economic thought argues that market-based regulation of source and point-based pollution is more efficient compared to command and control policies. See Thomas Tietenberg, *Emissions Trading, an Exercise in Reforming Pollution Policy* (Washington, D.C.: Johns Hopkins University Press, 1985). There is, however, a growing literature that suggests that market-based regulation of the environment may be less efficient than command and control policies, using a moral calculus. See, for example, Bruno Frey, "Pricing and Regulating Affect Environmental Ethics," *Environmental and Resource Economics* 2, 1992, 399–414.

2. The traditional approach in the environmental ethics literature is to offer an ethical argument that suggests that there is some nonanthropocentric value that we can ascribe to nature, according to which it should not be treated like other kinds of goods. For example, Mark Sagoff argues that environmental policy should be governed by "ethical, aesthetic, cultural, and historical considerations," as opposed to being treated only for its economic value. The unique character of natural objects demands a qualitatively different kind of policy. (Mark Sagoff, *The Economy of the Earth* [Cambridge: Cambridge University Press, 1988], 125.) Sagoff argues that "economistic" approaches to environmental quality can be opposed for their incommensurability with the respect for nature embedded in American culture. Compared to such a claim, the argument presented here will be more modest in scope. Although I agree with this approach in general, and even Sagoff's argument in particular, I think that rather than offering only one approach to the economic challenge to environmental policy, we should instead come up with as many possible arguments as we can against policies that seek to privatize environmental regulation. I discuss the strategic rationale for pluralism in environmental ethics in "Callicott and Naess on Pluralism," *Inquiry* 39:2, June 1996, 273–294. I will return to this issue in the last section of this chapter.

3. This compatibilism between the ethical account and the social science account, including the appeal to the claim that the latter argument may be more persuasive for public policy, is a consequence of my form of environmental pragmatism. See, for example, the introduction to *Environmental Pragmatism*, by Andrew Light and Eric Katz (London: Routledge Press, 1996), 1–18. My view assumes that pluralist, pragmatic answers to environmental questions are always to be preferred on methodological and metaethical grounds. This view is echoed in the "practical philosophy" of theorists like Bryan Norton, Jon Elster, and Kristin Shrader-Frechette. See Bryan Norton, "Why I Am Not a Nonanthropocentrist: Callicott and the Failure of Monistic Inheritism," *Environmental Ethics* 17:4, 1995, 341–358; Jon Elster, "The Idea of Equality Revisited," in *World, Mind, and Ethics: Essays on the Ethical Philosophy of Bernard Williams*, ed. J. E. J. Altham and Ross Harrison (Cambridge: Cambridge University Press, 1995), 4–18; K. S. Shrader-Frechette, "Practical Ecology and Foundations for Environmental Ethics," *Journal of Philosophy* XCH: 12 December 1995.

4. It is fair to say that most environmental ethicists embrace some form of nonanthropocentrism. The pursuit of such a kind of theory was after all part of the original justification for the field. See, for example, Richard Sylvan's (then Routley) seminal early article in the field, "Do We Need a New, an Environmental Ethic," originally delivered at the fifteenth World Congress of Philosophy in Varna, Bulgaria, in 1973, reprinted in *Environmental Philosophy*, ed. Michael Zimmerman, et al. (Englewood Cliffs, N.J.: Prentice Hall, 1993), 12–21. I will refer throughout this paper to a number of authors who embrace a weak anthropocentrism as the basis for their environmental ethics. As a realist I think there is an answer to the question of whether environmental ethics must be nonanthro-

pocentric. As a pluralist I do not think that we need to worry about that issue now and instead should articulate as many convincing answers to bettering environmental conditions as we possibly can.

5. See Paul A. Samuelson, "The Pure Theory of Public Expenditure," *The Review of Economics and Statistics*, 1954, 387–389; "Diagrammatic Exposition of a Theory of Public Expenditure," *Review of Economics and Statistics*, 1955, 350–356; and "Pure Theory of Public Expenditure and Taxation," in *Public Economics*, ed. J. Margolis and H. Guitton (London, 1972).

6. Certainly there are many objections in the economics literature to Samuelson's lighthouse example. I do not think, however, that those objections to that particular example will mitigate the point I will hang on the articulation of the idea of a public good.

7. See Avner de-Shalit, *Why Posterity Matters* (London: Routledge Press, 1995).

8. I will make the case that environmental quality in general is such a need but will not answer for now the question of what other needs fit this description. My intuition is that as a good practical philosopher, I would argue that each basic need must be identified on a case-by-case basis. But this is a question that I want to consider at greater length on another occasion.

9. Anthony Cortese, "Human Health, Risk, and the Environment," in *Critical Condition: Human Health and the Environment*, ed. Eri Chivian et al. (Cambridge, Mass.: MIT Press, 1993), 1. The rest of the papers in the volume provide exhaustive and elaborate proofs of Cortese's general intuition.

10. Gary Varner, "No Holism Without Pluralism," *Environmental Ethics* 13:2, 1991, 175–179. Varner's claim is that "It is because an ecosystem has no welfare of its own, that a holistic environmental ethic must be pluralistic. If it is plausible to say that ecosystems (or biotic communities as such) are directly morally considerable—and that is a very big if—it must be for a very different reason than is usually given for saying that individual human beings are directly morally considerable (and, perhaps, higher animals or all individual living organisms)" (179). Certainly a more robust defense of pluralism is needed than this one to ameliorate the relativist worries about pluralism by theorists such as J. Baird Callicott. I have attempted such a defense in "Callicott and Naess on Pluralism."

11. See Andrew Light, "Materialists, Ontologists, and Environmental Pragmatists," *Social Theory and Practice* 21:2, 1995, 315–333. I am currently completing a book that more adequately defends a methodological form of environmental pragmatism, tentatively titled *Pragmatism and the Reconstruction of Environmental Philosophy*.

12. I would suggest a substitution test for determining if it is permissible to privatize a public good: If the good for the public represented by a particular public good may be captured through the provision of other public goods then it may be permissible to privatize the good in question.

13. Laws like those governing retail alcohol sales are often referred to as "blue laws," meaning statutes designed to enforce a certain form of religious-based morality. Government-run liquor stores made it easier to ensure that the good folk of Alberta did not drink on Sundays, and so on. But many of these laws have now been abolished throughout Canada and the United States, and there is a growing consensus in some regions that they are unsupportable. This helps to explain why such laws are often the first to go in a push toward privatization of government services.

14. See Tietenberg *Emissions Trading*, for a more in-depth discussion of emissions trading through transferable discharge permits.

15. For a good summary of the literature on the precautionary principle and its applicability to environmental questions see Jenneth Parker's entry, "The Precautionary Principle," *Encyclopedia of Applied Ethics* Vol. 1, 1998.

16. I am particularly indebted to the critical responses provided by Mathew Humphrey, Avner de-Shalit, the Honorable Bruce Collingwood (former MLA, Sherwood Park, Alberta), Anatole Anton, and Milton Fisk.

11

Family Assistance
and the Public Good

John Exdell

If we hope to build political support for a more ample provision of public goods in the United States, we have to come to grips with widespread convictions about the evils of welfare. The political currents that ended family assistance entitlements in 1996 under the guise of "welfare reform" reflected the new prominence of libertarian conceptions of civic virtue and national character. A resurgent individualism has declared New Deal and Great Society policies a failure. From this standpoint the nation's half-century experience with welfare entitlements proved that dependency on state programs is morally corrupting, unfair, and socially harmful. Instead, Americans should assume greater personal responsibility for their own well-being, depending when necessary on friends, family, church, and local charity.

Such ideas are fast becoming the new common sense on welfare policy. I will argue that we find a viable response to them in the system of family assistance established in France and other European social democracies. I will also relate the popular debate on welfare policy to recent developments in liberal political philosophy. I contend that contemporary liberalism—as we see it in the work of John Rawls, Ronald Dworkin, William Galston, Will Kymlicka, and Thomas Nagel—does not provide us with the framework we need for justifying a social democratic alternative to American-style welfare. That is, the main current in contemporary liberal philosophy lacks both the ethical vision and the identification of a broad class interest that could win popular support for such measures in the United States. My aim is to distinguish the French system of family assistance from the theory and practice advanced by the authors above, and to argue for its political and ethical superiority.

This essay has four parts. The first part reviews the nature and origins of the pre-1996 U.S. system of welfare assistance to single mothers. I show that in contrast to a system based on the provision of universal public goods, such as that in France, the established U.S. welfare policy generated popular political opposition to redistributive programs and support for individualist ideas of civic virtue. Part 2 shows how the theories of justice in the work of John Rawls and Thomas Nagel fail to see this consequence and hence justify policies that are politically unstable. Part 3 highlights further weaknesses in much contemporary liberal theory. I argue that the idea of neutrality in Rawls and later theorists lends itself to the judgment that many of the poor are undeserving of public assistance, and also prevents us from seeing a unifying class interest in the reduction of labor time as the fruit of collective action. In Part 4, I suggest that a social democratic welfare system structured around universal public goods advances an oppositional vision of human ends. If I am right, a comprehensive program of this nature is politically tenable, and in radical conflict with the ethical and empirical axioms of today's resurgent capitalism.

Welfare Policy and Working-Class Unity: Comparing the United States and France

In recent years I have devoted some time to the debate over welfare policy in political philosophy classes. I did not choose to do so unprompted. Rather, I found that student resistance to any proposal for creating a more equal society was invariably influenced by their hostility to state assistance to mothers on welfare. Unless I put the welfare question on the table, it seemed that students could not seriously entertain egalitarian ideas of justice and attendant proposals for institutional change.

Several times I invited a single mother on public assistance to speak to the class about her background and experience in the system. Karen was a white woman in her late twenties with two children whose need for welfare support arose after a divorce. She had received AFDC income, food stamps, and Medicaid for about five years while attending college, and was now close to finishing a bachelor's degree in social work. Karen offered her story to the class as a sympathetic case study of a single mother in the welfare system who is working hard, struggling on meager benefits, contending with bureaucratic suspicion and stupidity, and at times psychologically drained by the moral judgment of a hostile society.

On one occasion she told my class about buying a ready-made salad for her two kids, with her food stamps, at one of our town's upscale supermarkets. Her purchase provoked a contemptuous comment from a man behind her in the checkout line, who declared to all within earshot that "*she* is why this country is in such a mess." In telling the story Karen tried to convey the moral vulnerability of welfare mothers and the strain of defending oneself against the general assumption that one is an irresponsible freeloader and a primary source of social pathology.

Most of my students are from working-class backgrounds or middle-income professional strata. They are full-time students who also typically work at least twenty hours a week, and they incur a sizable debt by the time they graduate after five years at the university. It soon became clear that Karen had misjudged her audience. Here are some representative responses:

I can see why people get mad when they see welfare people buying things with their food stamps that some people without welfare cannot afford. I would enjoy a salad as much as the next person, but the cold hard fact is that I do not have the money to splurge for a salad. I feel that if people are that poor and have to have welfare to survive in this world then they need to be more cautious about what they are spending other people's money on. People on welfare should be trying to save every penny that they can, even though the money they are spending is mostly not theirs to begin with.

One might argue that those on welfare are free individuals and can spend their money however they choose. This is not the case. Though they are free individuals, they do not have the right to spend governmental aid on items not essential for subsistence. Since the aid was given to them by others, they lose the right to determine how they can spend it. As *receivers*, they are responsible to the *givers* to spend aid in a way the *givers* deem appropriate.

I remember when I was younger my parents would tell my brothers and me stories of how poor they were. They would have to sit on the floor on evenings and count out pennies to buy food for that week. They saved every chance they could for the few extra pennies to make ends meet. In addition my dad worked as many jobs as he could to help out. Slowly he worked his way up to the top mechanic in this area. We as college students can't go buy salad at Dillon's because we do not have the money, so why should someone who we are giving this money to from taxes be able to. It just doesn't seem fair.

I still had a hard time feeling that all of the problems she faced in her life to get her where she is now were beyond her control. I saw Karen fitting the situation of not taking responsibility for her own actions. I think her divorce played a very big role in her economic situation. She should have looked a little bit further ahead in her life and at the person she was committing to.

I feel cheated in some respects that certain people are given help just because they made a poor decision. I agree there are certain circumstances that are unavoidable and do deserve help from the government, but in many instances (as with our speaker Karen) people simply made the wrong choices and now it is *our* (the tax-paying American citizens') responsibility to help them. Why is it justified in giving people money just because they had a child? I feel as if we are punishing those who actually are working hardest and doing the right thing.

I just have one question: How does one get into such a position? How did she become so subservient and helpless that her life was destined for this outcome?! A lot of the outcomes in our lives stem from poor choices made early on. I feel the answer is to do everything in your power to eliminate the .001 percent chance of failure by means of education and life preparation and basically look out for "number one." Hopefully her children can learn from her experiences.

I feel that going to the government for money should be the last step after all other options have been tried. I think that if a person has children and wants to go to college they should look for help from their family.

Now these comments reveal assumptions and judgments that are widely held in the United States of America today, and that together have made many working-class people suspicious of redistributive programs.[1] In some of the statements above we find a hard-line libertarian conception of civic virtue. We should be self-reliant. To be in need of public charity is shameful. The model citizen shows foresight, perseverance, and infinite pluck in the face of adversity. She must be willing to work hard for very little and for many years if necessary to find an honorable escape from poverty.

Others reflect not a wholesale libertarian rejection of taxpayer support, but rather a distinction between who is and who is not *deserving* of public assistance. On this view society is divided between an improvident few and a conscientious majority. The welfare system gives money to women who have made irresponsible choices, while it ignores those who have chosen wisely and who are themselves struggling to make ends meet. The system is therefore inherently unfair in its distribution of benefits. It rewards people who make poor decisions and does nothing for those who do the right thing. The former are meritless supplicants whom we provide with a subsistence income for a time only for the sake of the children they take care of. Since their condition of need is the result of voluntary choices, it is appropriate that we limit their consumption to bare necessities.

These are the perceptions and convictions that begin the debate, like it or not, and we must be ready to engage them directly if we are to win popular support to the side of social democratic policies. A philosophical theory of justice in any way useful for our society at this time must respond to this individualist ethos of hard work, self-reliance, personal desert, and the conception of fairness to which these ideals are joined. In so doing it will also respond to working-class resentments directed against those perceived to be living parasitically off the labor of others. As I will argue, these resentments are not altogether the creation of right-wing political rhetoric. On the contrary, they have been nurtured by the U.S. welfare system itself. The institutional design of aid to single mothers with children in this country, from its inception in the New Deal to the present day, has actually fostered this hostility.

We can begin by showing how the old AFDC system generally made it irrational for single mothers on welfare to support themselves with full-time jobs. For most women, going to work meant losing ground. In 1993 the typical American mother with two children on public assistance got welfare and food stamp benefits at about $7,500 a year, plus free medical coverage for the entire family. If she found a minimum-wage job, her after-tax income was only about $3,900 more than her welfare and food stamp allotment. That was her net cash reward for a year of labor in what is likely to be a dead-end, monotonous, dirty, insecure job, lacking in benefits and medical coverage and requiring special expenses for child care and transportation. Once employed, she lost her Medicaid coverage and child care allowance. Although she needed more cash for job-related expenses, government assistance dropped to only 10 percent of what she received as a welfare mother.[2] Meager as her welfare benefits were, her life with a full-time job would be more difficult, and her standard of living lower. It follows that to escape poverty through full-time employment she needed to break out of the unskilled labor market, probably on the strength of a college degree, and land a job paying over $20,000 per year. Lacking this good fortune her choice was between (a) poverty on welfare, with medical care and some child care provided, and (b) poverty in an unstable and probably difficult low-wage job with even less government support.[3]

Thus our system of public assistance for single mothers actually discouraged recipients from working outside the home, and in so doing created a segregated caste of nonworking poor women who appeared to prefer a life of parasitic dependency on the labor of others. The rationale for this seemingly irrational system had its historical roots in the New Deal. At that time policymakers consciously designed welfare support to keep women out of the wage labor force, except as marginal, part-time contributors. From the outset the American welfare system was constructed to confine women within domestic roles. In the words of New Deal policymakers, the program was "designed to release from the wage-earning role the person whose natural function is to give her children the physical and affectionate guardianship necessary not alone to keep them from falling into social misfortune, but more affirmatively to rear them into citizens capable of contributing to society" (*Report to the President*, Committee on Economic Security, 1935).[4]

This "maternalist" view was the foundation of the New Deal system of support for single mothers. That system was not conceived as another form of support for working people, because it was thought that women were meant to be domestic caregivers, and not "workers." Hence the New Deal welfare state programs covered men and women in very different ways. The depression was seen as a crisis of male employment. Unions needed to be strong enough to get fair wages for men. Social Security and unemployment insurance were supposed to help the male wage earner through hard times. Women's dependency on wage-earning men was assumed and encouraged, and for that reason most women in the workforce were actually excluded from work-based entitlement programs, including Social Security and unemployment insurance. New Deal policy assumptions were quite explicit. Wage labor was a temporary status for single women in need of support before marriage, or a stopgap measure to assist women enduring the unfortunate and hopefully temporary lack of a husband. Women (this applied at the time only to *white* women) generally ought not to work, although sometimes they needed to. Mothers, on the other hand, were simply not supposed to seek wage employment at all, and Aid to Dependent Children was crafted to sustain the maternal ideal of full-time domesticity, given the absence of a male provider. It would offer single mothers and their children only a subsistence income sufficient to avoid homelessness, starvation, and the orphanage.[5]

For all the changes that have taken place since the New Deal—both in the welfare rules and in women's employment—the structure of aid to single mothers remained fundamentally unaltered, and did a fair job of keeping unskilled single mothers out of the wage labor force, or confining them to part-time, short-term marginal roles. By the time of the 1996 repeal of AFDC, it did little to lift its clientele out of poverty. By this means the system itself stigmatized its beneficiaries, generated in the public a sense of futility and failure, divided society between workers and slackers, and fueled the resentment expressed by my students in the comments excerpted above.

Barbara Bergmann's recent study of the French welfare system shows us a workable alternative that gives single mothers a reason to be employed. The centerpiece of the French system is ample government help for all working parents sufficient to ensure provision of all basic needs. These benefits are available to both one- and two-parent families, regardless of income, with a larger share for working parents with low wages. French families, for example, enjoy free day care for toilet-trained kids continuing to first grade, roughly ages two and a half to six, just as with our kindergarten, only for full days. The service is provided by the Ministry of Education, in real school buildings and with well-paid trained and committed professionals. For parents with infants and pretoddlers, a combination of subsidized public day care, tax breaks, and state-assisted private care makes child care available to all parents who want it.[6] French parents, whether they work or not, will also get full health care coverage, child allowances, and housing assistance, the latter graduated by income and the number of dependent children. Transplanted to the United States, the total public cost for the full package of services would be $16,000 a year for a three-person family, or about $5,000 more than government laid out in AFDC, food stamps, and Medicaid for a family of three in 1993. The extra $5,000 per family in the United States would buy top-quality developmental day care programs for children, health care, and an escape from poverty. Most important, it would give single parents a reason to work, because it guarantees that work will bring significant economic benefits.[7] In France, Bergmann notes, only 23 percent of French single mothers receive American-style welfare benefits, compared with 67 percent of American single mothers. The other 77 percent of single French mothers are working or looking for work. The explanation is not that French women are more responsible, but that for them work actually brings significant rewards rather than penalties.[8] The total net additional cost in the United States for a French-style system of public assistance would be about $86 billion per year, most of this for additional child care and health care benefits.[9]

The French system has broad public support for two reasons. First, it offers significant benefits to a wide segment of the population.[10] Assistance is not restricted to homebound mothers, or even to mothers coming off welfare, but extended to all those in the paid workforce, including those we would here call "the working poor." Second, and more important, because universal programs reward paid labor, they do not fuel resentment that "responsible" people get less help than those who "make mistakes." The French approach does not isolate and stigmatize a sector of the population; it does not generate a division between those perceived as the idle poor and citizens of good standing, but makes it likely that its recipients will gain the sense of social membership that comes with the status of workers. In short, unlike American welfare, French welfare fosters the political and social unity of the nation, and more particularly the working-class majority.

The American welfare system, in contrast, has played an important role in blocking the development of social democratic politics in the United States. It has created a breeding ground for the exaggerated individualist ethos of personal responsibility. Especially when joined to the cleavage of race, the system's design fosters division within the American working class and stifles the formation of a political majority backing state action for more equal access to wealth and well-being.[11] These political and ideological consequences, I suggest now, are manifested in the argument of several influential liberal political philosophers, and render their theory useless for a movement seeking alternatives to the ethical and political norms of resurgent capitalism.

Pessimism in Liberal
Political Philosophy

John Rawls's theory of justice was written with the Johnson-Nixon war on poverty programs as fresh illustrations of what appeared to be its main redistributive strategy. The war on poverty assisted the least advantaged, increased eligibility and benefits for welfare mothers, and designed its other major initiatives in housing, education, and job training to attack deeply rooted forms of racial discrimination.[12] We find these priorities reflected in the dominant political theory emerging from this historical context.

Thus, according to Rawls's Difference Principle, the state will use its powers of taxation to transfer resources to the least advantaged members of society, up to the point where further redistribution would make this group materially worse off. Who are the "least advantaged"? Rawls admits the "serious difficulty" of defining this group, but suggests what he takes to be two reasonable criteria. We might focus on the social category of unskilled workers and then "count as the least advantaged all those with the average income and wealth of this group, or less." Or we might designate the least-favored segment as "all persons with less than half of the median income and wealth." Either definition, says Rawls, "has the merit of focusing attention on the social distance between those who have least and the average citizen."[13]

On either option the least advantaged are not all of the working class, or even all of the unskilled members of the working class. They will comprise less than a majority of society, and probably a small minority identified by its relative social and economic inferiority to "the average citizen." So defined, Rawls's Difference Principle reflects the liberal politics of his day, which was focused on the poor and not the working class as a whole.

In Rawls's focus on redistribution to the least advantaged we find another parallel between policy and philosophy. Just as liberals could not sustain majority support for the war on poverty, Rawls's theory of justice cannot easily explain why the policies most handily justified by his theory will sustain support for the redistributive Difference Principle. Rawls indeed sees the need for such an explanation when he advances his theory as the practical basis for what he calls a "well-ordered society." By this he means that the basic principles and institutions of society will generate in citizens a sense of justice enabling them to accept and apply these principles for the most part and generally to comply with them. Indeed, Rawls makes this a critical test for the validity of his theory. A theory of justice must generate "its own support" and is "seriously defective if the principles of moral psychology are such that it fails to engender in human beings the requisite desire to act upon it."[14] To this we should add, a theory of justice is defective if its implementation generates popular support for contradictory ideas of justice.

Now the question is whether the implementation of the Difference Principle, giving redistributive assistance to the least advantaged, will be self-sustaining and stable in this sense.[15] Again, the historical evidence on U.S. welfare policy suggests a negative answer. Certainly single women with children can sensibly be classified as among the least advantaged members of our society, suffering both low social status and high rates of impoverishment. Yet redistributive policies targeted specifically for their benefit have been met with steadily diminishing political support. They have instead fueled resentment in the hearts of the working poor, broken down class solidarity, and stigmatized the intended beneficiaries as irresponsible freeloaders. Moreover, insofar as the American welfare system has fostered a division between the deserving and undeserving, it prompts adherence to one of the very concepts of justice that Rawls's theory seeks to discredit, and undermines the moral consensus on principles crucial to a stable, well-ordered society.

Rawls contends that the institutions outlined in his theory will generate the requisite supporting sense of justice among citizens subject to them. He notes that his contractarian theory of justice is founded on the idea of reciprocal obligation for mutual benefit. Unlike utilitarian or perfectionist theories, it does not exaggerate the capacity for sympathy with the good of others, or require citizens to sacrifice themselves for alien ends. It is therefore psychologically possible for citizens to develop the ties of civic friendship that naturally evolve among human beings who cooperate for mutual benefit. In this sense Rawls sees his theory of justice as consistent with known "principles of moral psychology," a doctrine that "elicits men's natural sentiments of unity and fellow feeling" and the cohesive sense of justice essential for stability in the long run.[16]

To be sure, a sense of fellow feeling must be strong and widespread if people are to support a society significantly more equal than ours is today. The challenge is to construct institutions that will cultivate such sentiments in the natural course of people's lives. A society based on market competition, where the majority get their subsistence from wages and salaries, while the least advantaged rely on means-tested public assistance, is not likely to do so. In this context we have no reason to believe that redistribution to the least advantaged will be understood as a manifestation of cooperation for mutual benefit, rather than as coercive sacrifice of some for the ends of others.

It should therefore come as no surprise that philosophers adhering to Rawls's principle of focusing exclusively on the worst off would arrive at pessimistic conclusions about the human prospect. Thomas Nagel's *Equality and Partiality* is a clear case of updated Rawlsian theory suffering from political inertia generated by its own premises.[17] For Nagel, however, the problem is not located in the historical failure of liberal theory and practice, but in a universal human moral predicament. Absent in Nagel is Rawls's confidence in the human disposition to civic friendship in associations for mutual benefit. As he puts it, "on the motivational viability of an egalitarian position ... I find myself unable to share his psychological expectations."[18] We have instead "the stubborn realities of human nature" that consistently obstruct the development of a just society.

Human nature, in Nagel's theory, consists of a division in each individual between two standpoints, the personal and the impersonal. The impersonal standpoint produces in each soul a "powerful demand for universal impartiality and equality," based on the truth that everyone's welfare is of equal value. From this

COMPETITION: KEEPING AMERICA GREAT

central truth two obligations follow. First, we must achieve the "alleviation of urgent needs and serious deprivation" and "the elevation of most of our fellow human beings to a minimally decent standard of existence." That is, impartiality requires a basic minimum for the least advantaged. But we cannot confine our concerns to the worst off. The impartial standpoint leads us to recognize the justice of a more "comprehensive equality." The demand for equality does not "cease to apply above the level of basic needs."[19] We must give "preferential weight to improvements in the lives of those who are worse off as against adding to the advantages of those better off" even at higher levels of income, status, and wealth. That means that even distinctions in material wealth between the skilled and unskilled working class, between middle class and upper class are morally questionable. We should aspire to eliminate all inequalities flowing from differences in talent and productivity, insofar as they are unrelated to individual choice. They are morally undeserved and unfair. Hence, the "first requirement of any social or political arrangement would seem to be its likelihood of contributing to this goal."[20]

What stands in the way is the force of the personal standpoint, "individualistic motives and requirements which present obstacles to the pursuit and realization of such ideals."[21] We are individuals driven to satisfy our private interests. We cannot escape the preference we give to ourselves, our families, and our friends, and so we find ourselves torn between the pull of such concerns and the simple truth of conscience giving absolute priority of the needs of the worse off. As things stand, egalitarian public values collide with inegalitarian personal aims. We cannot mandate equality by political means without demanding that the better off sacrifice more than they are willing of what is presently dear to them. It follows that to achieve the principled equality required of the impersonal standpoint we must transform people's existing personal ends so that these are consistent with the obligation of impartiality. This is what we do not know how to do. Thus, the reconciliation of the two standpoints through nonutopian and sustainable institutions is a challenge for political theory so daunting that "pessimism is always in order."[22]

For Nagel, even the more limited goal of meeting the basic needs of the worst off is politically dicey. Once the poor are no longer a majority, establishing even a social minimum requires that a "quantitatively larger middle class" be willing to surrender some of their wealth for the benefit of a minority. We should expect then that meeting basic welfare needs of the poor will have a "hard time in modern democracies."[23] Since providing for the less numerous poor is not something we can count on majorities consistently doing, nations may need to "constitutionalize" their welfare system, putting the provision of public funds for basic welfare needs "beyond reach of ordinary political bargaining and the calculus of interests," just as we now guarantee rights of free speech, religious freedom, and so on in the U.S. Constitution today.[24]

In Nagel's analysis, the establishment of such a social minimum by moderate redistributive means is the hallmark of European social democracies. Although clearly a move in the direction of impartiality, it falls far short of the comprehensive equality required by our disinterested sense of fairness. It does not stop the formation of social classes, "since the priority of gains to the worse off would cease once they reached the social minimum."[25] For the same reason it does not touch the differences in reward separating skilled and unskilled labor above the poverty level. And, finally, it does "nothing to damp down the acquisitive motives that drive a competitive society."[26] The pull of the personal standpoint, the motivation that puts us on the side of our private interests and against comprehensive equality, is left largely untouched. The equality required by unalloyed impartiality, by fairness pure and simple, requires "some as yet unimagined change either in the motivation of economic actors or in the design of economic systems, or both."[27]

The analysis underlying this pessimism is flawed in three respects. First, Nagel's lack of trust in democratic majorities is not justified by the empirical experience of social democratic nations. Perhaps Nagel is influenced by the political weakness of traditional liberal programs in the United States during the past twenty years. But the nature and history of American welfare policies must not be confused with the social democratic tradition in Western Europe. There powerful electoral majorities have constructed a system of universal programs that still enjoy broad public support even as they are attacked by global financial markets, imported free-market ideology, and plutocratic political elites. The continuing solidity of popular support contradicts Nagel's assumption that majorities can't be trusted and that egalitarian measures must somehow be "hardwired" into a constitutional structure. Human nature is the same on both sides of the Atlantic. The extent to which we can rely on majority support for redistribution and equality depends greatly on the nature of the principles and programs we advance to bring it about. If these programs, following Nagel's principle of impartiality, give "preferential weight to improvements in the lives of those who are worse off as against adding to the advantages of those better off,"[28] if they are means-tested to help only the poor, if they foster resentment against the beneficiaries of public assistance, then indeed they will be politically vulnerable. On the other hand, if they provide free access to resources for meeting the needs for all citizens—for example, in health care, child care, old-age pensions, long-term nursing care, education through college, and so on—they will enjoy solid support against the entreaties and machinations of the business class and their political representatives.[29]

Second, it is a mistake to characterize European social democracy as guaranteeing only a "social minimum," or as achieving a merely statistical reduction in income inequality, with no impact on the general nature and quality of life or the values and motivation of the agents within it. Consider the social democratic provisions now enjoyed in Denmark. The legal minimum wage is $14 per hour, the average hourly wage of unskilled female workers $18 per hour, and for unskilled males $20 per hour. Most health care and child care is free. The average workweek is thirty-seven hours and a political movement is organizing to reduce it to thirty. Unemployed workers get an annual after-tax income of $14,000 to $15,000, paid continuously up to seven years if necessary. Every employee is guaranteed six weeks of paid vacation, and all people in the workforce have the right to one year's paid leave from the labor market in order to get adult education, take care of small children, or simply to have a sabbatical year for any reason they wish. (Pay for child care and education is 90 percent of unemployment benefits, and for a sabbatical, 80 percent.) Thirty percent of postsecondary students go to college or technical schools at government expense—they pay no tuition and receive an annual living allowance of $6,000 for up to five years, plus housing assistance. If they need more, they can get loans from the state. Not only social security pensions, but free domestic help for the elderly and nursing home care are available to all at public expense.[30] This package of public goods requires much higher levels of taxation than we have in the United States—48 percent of GDP compared with 30 percent[31]—yet is supported by parliamentary majorities.

Admittedly, this is not a society that has eliminated class inequalities, unemployment, and the other afflictions of capitalism. But the system of universal public goods and legal guarantees has ensured that all citizens have access to the basic resources needed for a good life from childhood through old age. Prominent among these are a stable and nurturing environment for children, lifelong education, health care, and abundant free time. Consequently daily existence in Denmark is much more secure, less harried, and more leisured than it is here.

This has further implications. To the extent that the lust for high incomes is itself fueled by the fear of falling into a state of deprivation, both for oneself and one's children, then acquisitiveness can indeed be diminished by the provision of a high level of free public goods. We know that in our society many people desire higher incomes as a hedge against future ruin.[32] When we reduce anxieties over material need by social means, and simultaneously expand free time, we create the space for other values—for cultural interests, devotion to family and friends, recreation, education, and community involvement. Along with security and leisure, these interests emerge within a social democratic "personal standpoint," as Nagel would put it, and reinforce a commitment to maintain a more equal society. When people see that vital satisfactions are made possible by collective means (and indeed by a higher general rate of taxation), the origin of majority support for a comparatively more equal society is no deep mystery. This is not to deny the role of a sense of fairness, or of simple sympathy for the disadvantaged, as elements in a commitment to social equality. But these aspects of civic character must be supported by a general understanding of how the quality of life for a large majority can be raised through the cooperative provision of universal public goods.

In belittling the egalitarian impact of social democracy Nagel also fails to see how universal access to public goods—in particular to health care and child care for infants and toddlers—is the key condition for equality between men and women. It should be settled as beyond dispute that the role of housewife is the foundation of male supremacy in contemporary society. When women are consigned to reproduction, domestic nurturing, and household chores, they will be economically dependent on male providers, and socially vulnerable. It is crucial, therefore, that they be freed from these responsibilities, and the only sure basis for this emancipation is the public provision of the requisite health and child-care services. This gives women greater freedom to choose their male partners and to escape abusive or unsatisfying relationships, as well as the time and energy to develop their talents as equals to men in the world of public work. As a political bonus, we have one more plain demonstration of the enormous human benefits flowing from the collective provision of basic needs, and a numerous and potentially powerful constituency behind it.

Third, it is remarkable that in explaining antiegalitarian politics in modern democracies, Nagel has so little to say about the interconnected influence of budgetary constraints generated by global trade and capital markets, the power of corporate and financial elites to block progressive policy ideas in the political process, the decline of union representation in the United States, the legacy of racism in limiting class consciousness and solidarity, and the role of plutocratic and antifeminist ideology in shaping resistance to a broad egalitarian agenda. It is not possible here to elaborate on these factors. In light of their powerful role in pushing politics to the right, however, both here and abroad, Nagel's focus on "the personal standpoint" as a universal obstacle to human equality, expressed in the preferences of a political majority, should strike us as a scandalous abstraction from empirical reality. If we wish to highlight the role of prevailing appetites and interests in blocking progress toward equality, then we should recognize that these do not arise spontaneously within the human soul in modern society. As the contrast between French and American welfare policy suggests, they are themselves the outcome of public choices and political and cultural struggle.

Liberalism, Neutrality, and Class Struggle

According to numerous empirical studies, the views of my students quoted above are by no means anomalous. The values of nineteenth-century liberalism have long contended against popular support for the welfare state in the United States.[33] This tradition of belief manifests itself not as strict adherence to abstract libertarian principles, but in the widely affirmed civic ideals of hard work and personal responsibility.

Models of good character are found among our most deeply rooted moral convictions. We seldom give up our beliefs about good character as a result of reflection on complex arguments concerning justice in the abstract, and this is certainly true about individualist norms noted here. An effective challenge must direct people's attention to the real social world, and the material impact of their ideas in it. It is here that an empirically well-founded, unsentimental class analysis can play a subversive role. We have to ask people whether a society based on these cherished and familiar moral ideals will function in the interests of people like them. The positive examples of collective responsibility in providing health care, child care, free college education, and so forth is of course critical in this effort. On the negative side, we need to link the idea of self-reliance and individual responsibility to a sobering critique of unfettered labor market competition.

We can first point to the facts about the actual performance of American capitalism in the past twenty years: increasing wealth and declining wages, more work and rising profits, general insecurity and growing inequality.[34] We can link these developments to increasing competition among individual workers and local communities for capital and scarce jobs, and to the fact of unequal dependency and unequal power between capital and labor. We can show that unemployment and fear of job loss are normal and pervasive in the capitalist world left to its own devices, and that competition for scarce opportunity is an essential means by which owners of capital increase their power to extract more labor from working people. The greater the competition among workers for jobs, the more workers are dependent on employers, the lower are their wages, and the greater are the profits reaped by those who own. When workers compete against each other as individuals in a capitalist society, they maximize this power of employers over labor, with the result that people will work harder for less, even while the productivity of their labor is steadily increasing. The performance of American capitalism during the past twenty years is a textbook illustration of these realities.[35]

In this context the ethic of self-reliance and hard work induces people to accept a competitive society where each relies on her own assets and talents in the struggle against others for the means of security. It follows that the more working people buy into individualist ideals of good character, the less they are able to resist efforts of capitalists to maximize profits at their expense. Self-reliant individuals accept all the risks and dangers workers face in a capitalist market system as a personal challenge that they should meet with courage and tenacity. In as much as one seeks to be self-reliant, one avoids cooperation and collective action for common gain. To affirm self-reliance is therefore to acquiesce to the pressures of competition, and to render ourselves even more vulnerable to the demands of the few who reap the rewards.

Finally, we can explain the importance of unity and collective action. Workers must seek ways to reduce their dependency on private capital and their competition against each other, which work to erode wages and increase workloads. This means, for example, joining labor unions and enlarging the provision of public goods, which make workers less dependent on private employers and more able to demand higher pay, less labor, and better working conditions for themselves. Workers will benefit together from the ethic of solidarity and collective action; most will lose together through the ethic of self-reliance.

These are simple verities, and the historical record—for example, the rise and decline of the U.S. labor movement, the weakening of our social insurance provisions, the impact of intensified global competition—provides ample verification of them. Yet among students of a large public university in the heartland these truths are not native knowledge. They are rarely more than dimly perceived. When set out in plain view, however, many find them sensible, empirical, and persuasive. From this vantage point many students are able to reconsider their attachment to the libertarian ideal of the self-reliant citizen.

Our aim is to connect the ethic of self-reliance and the ethic of collective responsibility to the opposite sides of an enduring class struggle. In this endeavor we will find much of the theoretical writings of contemporary liberal social philosophers unhelpful, even as they argue for redistributive measures to create a more equal society. Indeed, it should come as no surprise that conventional ideas about self-reliance, the work ethic, and personal responsibility have found their way to the writings of academic philosophers who still think of themselves as egalitarians.

Since Rawls's *A Theory of Justice,* contemporary liberal philosophers have focused on the following question about distributive justice: What institutions and policies can in some sense correct for inequalities caused by the undeserved advantages and disadvantages affecting people's life prospects in modern society? Individuals do not deserve their natural endowments or the inherited and circumstantial differences in their access to resources. But, say some, perhaps they are entitled to reap the higher rewards that flow from effort, sacrifice, and hard work. A fair society recognizes this distinction between the two origins of inequality, and seeks to rectify the effects of the former without undoing the results of the latter. Furthermore, the principles and policies designed to meet this challenge must not pass judgment on the validity of the various conceptions of the good life that arise in a free society. Even as we acknowledge that some inequalities are deserved, we must avoid any official or collective judgment that some ends are intrinsically more valid than others, considered as conceptions of human well-being. This much discussed doctrine of neutrality has become a central if not a defining feature in contemporary liberal political philosophy.[36]

Thus in recent years a number of prominent liberal philosophers have argued that John Rawls's theory of justice obscures the empirical and moral significance of individual choice as a generator of unequal outcomes. The problem, on their view, is that Rawls's theory appears to assume incorrectly that inequality is caused entirely by the combined effect of natural differences and social institutions. In Rawls's theory undeserved biological and institutional sources of unequal life prospects are causally decisive. Hence, "Even the willingness to make an effort, to try, and so to be deserving in the ordinary sense is itself dependent upon happy family and social circumstances."[37] The intent of the redistributive Difference Principle is therefore to remedy the dominant influence of morally arbitrary factors in a market society.

William Galston (an adviser to President Clinton on welfare and family policy) challenges Rawls's determinism in his book *Liberal Purposes.* According to Galston, liberals must concede the validity of popular convictions about individual responsibility. If they deny that individual choice does make a difference, they undercut their own fundamental commitments to liberty and equality. Determinism would contradict the idea of equal respect for all persons as beings capable of rational choice. The reality and efficacy of choice in human life is also assumed in all liberal defenses of individual freedom. Once choice is acknowledged, however, we cannot avoid the conclusion that "working versus shirking is a great moral divide in a liberal society," and we must admit the need for a "thoroughgoing critique of individuals who are physically and mentally able to make a contribution but nonetheless fail to do so."[38] Galston argues for these points in part as a way of bringing liberal social philosophy back in harmony with the convictions of "the American working class," which "clings most fervently to ... desert as the basis of distribution, to ability, effort, and self-denial as the bases of desert."[39] Prominent among "liberal virtues" we therefore find "independence" and "the work ethic" on Galston's list.[40]

Ronald Dworkin rejects Rawls's theory in part because the Difference Principle wrongly equalizes inequalities in income caused by differences in ambition.[41] Will Kymlicka concurs. The Difference Principle, he notes, does not differentiate between inequalities caused by morally arbitrary differences in endowment and those caused by individual choices. To illustrate the point he contrasts a hardworking gardener who earns a living from selling her produce with a man who avoids labor to spend his days enjoying recreational tennis. Because of their different work/leisure priorities the gardener earns a higher income, an inequality that is reduced by standard redistributive measures. By applying the Difference Principle the state transfers income from the gardener to the tennis player. Kymlicka objects, "She has to pay for the costs of her choice—i.e., she forgoes leisure in order to get more income. But he does not have to pay for the costs of his choice—i.e., he does not forgo income in order to get more leisure.... Rawls requires that she pay for the costs of her own choices, and also subsidize his choice."[42]

To the extent that the Difference Principle equalizes inequality caused by such lifestyle choices—for example, differences in freely chosen ends regarding leisure, labor, and education—then it "does not promote equality, it undermines it."[43] The state fails to treat individuals equally in the sense that it does not show equal respect for their choices of ends. It requires some to sacrifice to support the ends chosen by others; it allows others to achieve their goals with no sacrifice at all. The unfairness in this policy consists of the state's failure to remain neutral between differing individual conceptions of the good. Neutrality—an essential feature of justice in the liberal state—thus requires that all individuals be held equally responsible for the costs incurred in their choices of ends. In the case above, redistribution is not neutral in this sense. It requires those who work hard to bear the costs of other people's preference for leisure.

This conception of fairness can be directly applied to justify my students' objections to the welfare system. Women on welfare have made choices about ends. Some have chosen to have children early in life without acquiring the means of supporting themselves, or as in the case of Karen they have chosen to marry and have children before acquiring the education necessary for independence in the event of divorce. These choices of ends entail costs. By requiring others to bear these costs, the state relieves welfare mothers of the responsibility for the choices they have freely made. Liberal neutrality is abandoned: The state subsidizes the ends chosen by some and imposes a penalty for the ends chosen by others.

Let us put the issue of welfare aside for the moment. I think a response to this argument should begin first by noting that Kymlicka's example misrepresents the context of labor/leisure choices in the real world. We need to ask whether most participants in a society such as ours are acting on their various preferences for work or for play on the model of his hypothetical gardener and tennis player. The differences between example and reality are quickly apparent. First, in the capitalist world most people must seek employment in a competitive labor market where the number of job seekers usually far exceeds the number of jobs, and certainly the number of desirable jobs. In Kymlicka's example, however, the two parties do not in any way compete against each other, and the choices made by one do not limit the opportunities for the other. Second, in the real world labor market businesses—owners for the most part—will decide who is employed and who isn't, and they typically make this decision from a position of market power. They need the services of any particular job seeker much less urgently than any particular job seeker needs the position they offer. Employers are therefore more often in a position to be choosy about who they hire than employees are about where they work.

Third, employers will often decide which workers to hire, promote, or retain in their businesses on the basis of their employees' willingness to work very hard for long hours (for example, to agree to "voluntary overtime" for wage workers, or evening and weekend work for salaried professionals). In this context those most willing to exert themselves to the maximum win the competitive game for money, security, and status, and those less willing are the losers. The choices made by the former to labor extra hours in effect raises the bar for all, and allows employers to make greater demands as a condition for having any work at all. Finally, the game itself has certain general consequences for the participants. For most workers it means more hours, days, or weeks of labor than they would like, and probably more than is good for them. For employers as a class it means higher profits, since the benefits of their workers' surplus exertion show up mainly on their side of the ledger.

Once we place this labor/leisure choice in the context of class struggle, we see that this choice is rarely made by individuals for themselves, but is the outcome of relative bargaining advantage between workers and owners. The proposal made by Dworkin and Kymlicka, that we allow the market to reward the ambitious, is thus by no means a neutral one. Given the realities of unequal class power, we should see it as a policy favoring the aim of owners to extract as much labor as possible from their employees. That is not to say that workers will have no choices as individuals, but rather that their options are likely to be all undesirable. For many it would mean a choice between too much work and too little work, between sixty hours a week at the office or plant and half-time minimum-wage work at a convenience store, or between poverty as one option and neglect of one's children, friendships, and marriage as the other. We know how in the real world people have sought to avoid such dilemmas. They have acted collectively—either through unions or through legislation—to limit the working day, to increase vacation time, and to slow down the pace of labor required of them on the job. Collective decisions of this nature in effect limit the choices of individuals about how hard they will work. Individual decision is replaced by a social judgment about how hard we ought to work, or about how much work is good for us. When working people have fought for such limitations, either through unions or legislatures, they have themselves rejected the doctrine of liberal neutrality. They have decided something together about what constitutes a good life for human beings. To put it another way, they have rejected the idea of accepting a principle of justice that is "ambition sensitive" in favor of a judgment about how much ambition we ought to allow in our world as consistent with the human good.

This point brings us to the final reason why the main current in contemporary liberal philosophy fails to provide the basis for an egalitarian political movement capable of winning majority support. Such a movement must be motivated by the confidence that political action can change human life fundamentally for the better. It must therefore be moved by a vision of concrete ends attainable only through unity of action for a common cause. One key element of this ideal involves an unavoidable collective judgment about labor and leisure. We should aim to create a society in which people have less work—and hence more time for friends, families, recreation, hobbies, art, meditation, politics, or community. This is a flexible but definitely nonneutral vision about human purpose, one that explicitly rejects a cultural value fundamental to capitalist civilization from its origins to the present day—that is, the identification of virtue with a life of arduous labor and ever-increasing quantities of private consumption.

A movement with such a goal, however, rejects the premise by which much of contemporary liberal political philosophy has defined itself—that individuals alone are responsible for choices about what makes a good life, whereas our politics remains neutral between rival ideas about ends. A successful political struggle for greater equality cannot be about justice or fairness in isolation from some shared conception of the human good. The collective goal of reducing work time can be realized only through a social democratic politics aiming to enlarge the sphere of universal public goods. Strict adherence to liberal neutrality, on the other hand, would make it impossible to organize a political majority united by a general class interest in less work and a substantive idea of a good life for all.

Old Truths and New Visions

Belief in the virtues of self-reliance, personal responsibility, and hard work is a powerful barrier to progressive social policy in the United States. I have argued that a philosophical argument for social democracy must respond effectively to this ideological screen, and furthermore to the specific working-class resentments that are aroused by what is experienced as a system of unfair subsidies for those who have made irresponsible choices, paid for by the wages of the responsible majority. By this criterion the main current of contemporary liberal social philosophy fails decisively. To recapitulate, this is so for three reasons.

First, the ethical commitment in liberal theory to assist the least advantaged has lent support to means-tested redistributive policies, rather than to a comprehensive program of free public goods guaranteed to all citizens. This approach erodes the ethic of solidarity so badly needed by working people to advance their interests against the owning class, and to build a social democratic imagination as an alternative to the current mania for free markets. Instead, it fosters and reinforces social divisions that have blocked the formation of a working-class political majority in the United States. Much of liberal theory lead us into this political dead end, and those like Nagel who have taken this route are naturally led to pessimistic conclusions about prospects for social equality in a democratic society. This pessimism is unjustified. From France and Denmark we learn at least that the human capacity for solidarity is real and effective, that it does infinitely more good than punitive appeals to self-reliance and individual responsibility, and that it generates interests on which we can build demands for further advances in social equality.

Second, the most effective critique of the libertarian ethos is to expose its empirical role as ideology in a system of exploitation and class struggle. Liberal theory, however, actually steers us away from this analysis. Starting with Rawls, its primary objective is to correct for inequalities caused by undeserved differences in endowment and resources. This leads us to the corollary that inequalities caused by "preferences"—that is, by differences in ambition—must be preserved. The liberal legitimation of deserved inequalities flowing from individual choice is in effect a philosophical endorsement of the very doctrine that a social democratic movement must combat. The approval of market rewards for supposed individual choice between labor and leisure deflects our attention from the dynamic of class struggle, and the effort of the owning class to increase the burden of labor as the means of maximizing profits. Indeed, the new liberal doctrine offers an ethical blessing to the class that generally holds the upper hand in this struggle.

Third, since the issue of balancing labor and leisure must be decided collectively, we cannot avoid making a social, that is, political, choice about ends. Unfortunately, the liberal doctrine of neutrality seeks to remove judgments about the human good from the political sphere. If we accept this boundary line, we exclude the working-class interest in less labor from the central role it must play in motivating a majoritarian movement for social democratic reform.

I wish to show now how this argument applies directly to the case of welfare policy. Let us consider first where we end up if—following Galston, Dworkin, and Kymlicka—our point of departure is the distinction between undeserved inequalities of endowment and deserved inequalities of choice. On this view, welfare mothers neatly illustrate the difference between workers and shirkers. Many have made the pleasures of childrearing a higher priority than education or paid labor. Our commitment to neutrality entails that we will not ask others to subsidize their freely chosen ends. We must hold single mothers responsible for the special risks and costs associated with having a baby out of wedlock, or becoming dependent upon a husband before they have acquired the means of living independently. Since it is unfair to require others to bear these costs, we should demand (consistent with the humane treatment of their blameless children) that the mothers themselves shoulder the burden of the choices they have made and the sacrifices entailed by the ends they have voluntarily selected. As I argued above, this reasoning is perfectly exemplified in the stern comments of my students reacting without sympathy to the story of a welfare mother eager for their support.

We come to a very different understanding once we recognize that popular support for egalitarian social policy requires the organized provision of basic goods for all members of the national community outside the sphere of market competition. Liberal neutrality is clearly not possible for us. Political choice guided by a conception of the human good is imperative, debate about comprehensive ends unavoidable. A successful social democratic politics must enter this debate, and articulate a persuasive vision of essential elements of human well-being, and the collective means to achieve them.

We can begin with some obvious facts about the nature of human life. No one can reasonably deny, for example, that as a general practice childrearing makes an indispensable contribution to the social good. It cultivates the nurturing and pedagogical capacities in human nature, with the many joys and satisfactions this affords. It produces new minds and bodies that will carry on our traditions, complete our unfinished projects, and bear the burden of supporting those who have advanced to the end stages of their lives. Anyone who expects to grow old will with luck depend on the capacities of the presently young. It follows that an individual's decisions to have and care for children does not have the status of a consumer purchase, a merely personal act for private ends that others may not fairly be asked to subsidize. Raising children is a socially productive undertaking, insofar as each of us hopes to benefit from the contributions made by those who are bringing along the next generation of working citizens. Indeed, it is hard to imagine any activity that is more deserving of public support and collective interest. The fact that individuals may choose to reproduce for personal reasons is therefore irrelevant to the question of who should bear responsibility for the costs involved.

We also know that those costs can be very high. Raising children is arduous work, and in our society often entails significant sacrifices for the mothers who perform it inside the private household. Their labor is unpaid, tedious, invisible, and unrecognized. Too often it requires accepting a position of unequal dependency on a male provider, with a consequent loss of opportunity to develop skills and assume responsibilities in other areas. The resulting vulnerability and low status of women consigned to unpaid child care and domestic labor is well-documented and in no need of elaboration here. Suffice it to say that raising children is not labor we should ask anyone to make an exclusive sphere of activity. We should instead organize social institutions so that it is easy for mothers to include public labor at all times in their lives, just as they please, through which they may develop a wider range of rational powers, social ties, and clear standing as productive contributors to the larger society.

This will require a system of public subsidies, as exemplified by the French provision of free child care, child allowances, housing subsidies, and so on, which are well within the capacity of any modern industrial society. In virtue of these resources it would not be necessary for anyone to choose between raising children and assuming responsibilities in the wider public world. We can make it possible for individuals to readily include both in their life plans, and to cultivate a great variety of skills that are socially useful and personally enriching.

Picturing a social democratic welfare policy in this way may help articulate an ethical goal now within reach of modern societies organized on principles of collective action and public goods. On the basis of universal programs providing access to basic well-being, we can make it possible for single women to both parent children and perform public labor without great personal sacrifice. In this example it should be easier to see how social control over resources enables us to become, as Karl Marx put it, many-sided individuals who "cultivate their gifts in all directions."[44] By these means and others we can revive the hope that a community "in which the free development of each is a condition of the free development of all"[45] is a credible nonutopian possibility for our civilization. Actually existing social democracies show us societies that understand certain elemental truths—for example, that a generation of healthy and productive children will soon provide security for the generation of elders ahead of them, that reducing workloads and labor time requires social choice and solidarity, and that the good of each of its members can be visibly linked to the good of most others through a system of public goods. When measured against these concrete accomplishments, the pursuit of individual success through self-reliance, personal responsibility, and a lifetime of hard work may finally lose its appeal.

Notes

1. William Julius Wilson, *When Work Disappears: The World of the New Urban Poor* (New York: Alfred A. Knopf, 1997), 158–162.

2. Barbara Bergmann, *Saving Our Children from Poverty: What the United States Can Learn from France* (New York: Russell Sage Foundation, 1996), 93–94. At this writing Bergmann is president elect of the International Association for Feminist Economics. During the Kennedy administration she served as a senior staff member of the President's Council of Economic Advisers.

3. Ibid., 12–13.

4. Gwendolyn Mink, *The Wages of Motherhood: Inequality in the Welfare State, 1917–1942* (Ithica, N.Y.: Cornell University Press, 1995), 132.

5. Ibid., chap. 6, "Maternalism in the New Deal Welfare State: Women's Dependency, Racial Inequality, and the Icon of Welfare Motherhood," 126–136.

6. Bergmann, chap. 3, "Government Child-Care Programs in France."

7. Ibid., 125.

8. Ibid., 14.

9. Ibid., 128. This figure is based on 1994 programs and estimates. In that year U.S. federal and state programs helping working families with children totaled $121 billion. Bergmann's predicted in-

crease of $86 billion assumes that about 60 percent of those currently on welfare would be enabled by the program to become labor force participants. She defends that assumption on 133–136.

10. Ibid., 69.

11. At this writing the conversion from AFDC to the new Temporary Assistance for Needy Families (TANF) is still incomplete and uncertain in its results. According to its supporters, welfare reform will foster a new "philosophy of work" rather than "welfare dependency." In those states that provide free child care, transporation subsidies, and medical coverage for families moving from welfare to work, TANF may indeed succeed in helping many welfare families out of poverty. Such an approach would be a move in the direction of the French system described below. The preliminary evidence suggests that in many states such help will not be available, and in states who do offer this support it will be available only on a temporary basis. To the extent that such support is absent or only temporary, "welfare reform" will prove to be only a means of expelling more single mothers and their children from the welfare system and into the ranks of the working poor. Moreover, even where child care, medical coverage, and other assistance is made available to former welfare clients holding jobs, it is puzzling why this help should be available *only* to them, rather than to all the working poor.

12. See Jill Quadango, *The Color of Welfare* (New York: Oxford University Press, 1994) for comprehensive analysis of the major policy initiatives of the War on Poverty.

13. Rawls, *A Theory of Justice* (Cambridge: Harvard University Press, 1971), 98.

14. Ibid., 455–456.

15. For another critical treatment of this issue see Walter Glannon, "Equality, Priority, and Numbers," *Social Theory and Practice* 21, No. 3, fall 1995, 427–455.

16. Rawls, *A Theory of Justice*, 502. For the principles of moral pyscology see pp. 490–491.

17. Thomas Nagel, *Equality and Partiality* (New York: Oxford University Press, 1991). Although Nagel avows optimism in the opening page of his introductory chapter, the general drift of his analysis supports a much more negative message, which is found in numerous passages in the remainder of his text. For another critique of the political viability of Rawls's Difference Principle, see Walter Glannon, "Equality, Priority, and Numbers," *Social Theory and Practice* 21, No. 3, fall 1995, 427–455.

18. Nagel, 63.

19. Ibid., 70.

20. Ibid., 12–13, 69.

21. Ibid., 4.

22. Ibid., 7.

23. Ibid., 80.

24. Ibid., 87.

25. Ibid., 125.

26. Ibid., 124–5.

27. Ibid., 123.

28. Ibid., 12.

29. Popular resistance in Europe to proposed cuts in such public programs is now a cause for dismay among right-wing pundits. For example, see Jim Fralick's commentary on the June 1997 French parliamentary election, "Europe: The Tyranny of the Middle Class Electorate," *Global Economic Forum*, June 20, 1997.

30. Andreas Jorgensen, "Efficiency and Welfare Under Capitalism: Denmark vs. the United States, A Short Comparison," *Monthly Review*, February 1997, 34–42.

31. Larry Mischel and Jared Bernstein, *The State of Working America, 1994–95* (New York: M. E. Sharpe, 1994). The difference in taxation devoted to human well-being is even greater than these figures indicated, given that a large portion of the discretionary budget in the United States is wasted on needless military spending.

32. Barbara Ehrenreich, *Fear of Falling: The Inner Life of the Middle Class* (New York: Pantheon Books, 1989).

33. See Stanley Feldman and John Zaller, "The Political Culture of Ambivalence: Ideological Responses to the Welfare State," *American Journal of Political Science* 36, No. 1, February 1992, 268–307; and Stanley Feldman, "Economic Individualism and American Public Opinion," *American Politics Quarterly* 11, No. 1, January 1983, 3–29. The classic work on this thesis is Louis Hartz, *The Liberal Tradition in America* (New York: Harcourt Brace Jovanovich, 1955).

34. For a sample of recent literature documenting these trends see Larry Mischel and Jared Bernstein, *The State of Working America, 1994–95* (New York: M. E. Sharpe, 1994); Juliet B. Schor, *The Overworked American: The Unexpected Decline of Leisure* (New York: Basic Books, 1992); Edward Wolff, *Top Heavy: A Study of the Increasing Inequality of Wealth in America* (New York: 20th Century Fund, 1995); and Nancy Folbre, *The New Field Guide to the U.S. Economy* (New York: New Press, 1995).

35. See Mischel and Bernstein; also Andrew Hacker, *Money: Who Has How Much and Why* (New York: Scribner's, 1997).

36. Neutrality as a central doctrine in liberal theory is the view that conclusions about justice should not depend on prior commitments to a particular vision of the good life, and that the state should favor a particular idea of the good only if logically independent reasoning about justice leads us to affirm it. This understanding of neutrality characterizes the views of the liberal theorists discussed in this essay. Rawls's commitment to neutrality in this sense is strongly reaffirmed in his most recent book, *Political Liberalism* (New York: Columbia University Press, 1993).

37. Rawls, *A Theory of Justice*, 74. See also 104. The dominant role of institutional structure is asserted in many places. For example, p. 7: "Major institutions . . . influence their life-prospects, what they can expect to be and how well they can hope to do. The basic structure is the primary subject of justice because its effects are so profound and present from the start. The intuitive notion here is that this structure contains various social positions and that men born into different positions have different expectations of life determined, in part, by the political system as well as by economic and social circumstances. . . . These are especially deep inequalities . . . yet they cannot possibly be justified by an appeal to the notions of merit or desert."

38. William Galston, *Liberal Purposes: Goods, Virtues, and Diversity in the Liberal State* (New York: Cambridge University Press, 1991), 185.

39. Ibid., 161–162.

40. Ibid., 222–223.

41. Ronald Dworkin, "What Is Equality? Part 2: Equality of Resources," *Philosophy and Public Affairs* 10, No. 4, 1981, 311.

42. Will Kymlicka, *Contemporary Political Philosophy: An Introduction* (New York: Oxford University Press, 1990), 74.

43. Ibid.

44. Karl Marx, *The German Ideology: Part I* in *The Marx-Engels Reader: Second Edition*, ed. Robert C. Tucker (New York: W. W. Norton, 1978), 197.

45. Karl Marx and Friedrich Engels, *Manifesto of the Communist Party* in *The Marx-Engels Reader*, 2d ed., ed. Robert C. Tucker (New York: W. W. Norton, 1979), 491.

Profits or People? Challenging the Privatization of Public Welfare Services

Kim Diehl, Laura Stivers, and Keith Ernst

As a hardworking mom, Jennifer* was glad to learn that the court had ordered her daughter Julia's father to pay child support. He wouldn't be paying a lot—only $80 a month—but it would help with the bills, as it would for most families in Davidson County, Tennessee, home to Nashville and country music.

Despite the court order, Jennifer didn't receive many payments, so she asked the child support agency in her county to enforce it. After hounding the agency, Jennifer thought she had received a response when a representative from the agency told her they were going back to court for her. When the court date arrived, Jennifer took a day off work, only to find that the father had not been given notice of the hearing.

The child support agency wrongfully told her that it was "her duty to locate the noncustodial parent"—a man who had abused their daughter—and that she had "failed in this duty." To add insult to injury, the agency representative had scolded Jennifer in front of a packed courtroom.

There's also the case of Gina, who hit a similar brick wall when she tried to get support for her son Carl. Not a small task, Gina says, considering that the agency's phone lines are always busy, she's been denied access to the worker who first took the information on her case, and the agency employees don't identify themselves on the phone.

More examples of a bloated government agency, clinging to an outdated system? Not quite. Jennifer's and Gina's cases—detailed in a lawsuit that accuses the state of providing such poor quality child support as to violate federal law—weren't handled by a public agency, but by a private corporation. Tennessee has contracted with Maximus, Inc., for child support enforcement services. Under the contract, Maximus is responsible for fulfilling a federal requirement

(continues)

(continued)

to establish paternity for children entitled to support, locate noncustodial parents, and obtain consistent support from those parents.

Established in the 1950s, the goal of child support enforcement programs is twofold. First, the program seeks to collect child support owed to families receiving public assistance. The federal and state governments keep these funds to recover part of the cost of that assistance. Second, for a small fee, the program will help families who are not receiving public assistance to collect child support. The latter service is provided, in part, to prevent more families from needing public assistance.

Maximus, Inc., derives its name from the company's original specialization—helping state and local governments develop strategies to maximize federal revenues. Today, however, private corporations such as Maximus are more focused on "maximizing" their own revenues from public funding of social services.

One good example of this behavior occurred in Connecticut, where Maximus threatened to walk away from a contract until the state agreed to a 50 percent increase in the per-client fee it paid Maximus to run a child-care assistance program, a state program to find child-care placements for families in the welfare system. This demand came after Maximus had won the contract by undercutting a bid from a nonprofit organization. Maximus, with its vast resources, could afford to bid low, knowing it could improve profits after holding the contract; the nonprofit could not.

Although privatization may be politically expedient, the experiences from Tennessee and Connecticut clearly challenge the notion, sweeping statehouses across the country, that privatization is the answer to solving the problems that have often plagued public welfare services: insufficient funds and inefficient services (with the former likely causing the latter). Moreover, the experiences of Jennifer and Gina raise key questions: *When public services are provided by private corporations to whom are these corporations accountable? What are the long-term effects on families and taxpayers when inexperienced companies take over the provision of services that the government has managed and operated for over four decades?*

(continues)

Had Jennifer's and Gina's complaints involved a public child-support enforcement agency, they might have requested a fair hearing or sought to appeal to an agency head—one who would have to answer to the people of Tennessee. With a private for-profit corporation such as Maximus having the sole contract for the provision of child support enforcement services in Davidson County, the lines of accountability are unclear.

What's worse, according to Vicki Teretsky from the Center for Law and Social Policy, is that with privatized services like child support, private contractors have an incentive to provide less service to very low-income families. This incentive arises because most child-support contracts pay the corporate contractor a percentage of the total amount collected. This means that low-income women like Jennifer and Gina, who need support most, are out of luck when companies pursue more profitable claims.

As services are contracted out to private companies who promise cost-efficiency, community and worker groups are increasingly demanding that governments focus not only on cost savings but on the quality of services. These groups are helping clients of the public welfare system assert their rights, but they are also demanding that county and state governments, which are backing away from serving clients (that is, citizens) directly, take responsibility for setting standards and regulating private contractors.

In Tennessee, for example, a welfare rights group named Manna is trying to minimize the damage done by the privatization of Davidson County's child-support enforcement agency. They are organizing and supporting low-income single mothers who are outraged by the low-quality services offered by Maximus. One Manna board member says, "Maximus doesn't have the manpower to find fathers. There is no 'enforcement' because the word gets around that [noncustodial parents] won't be punished for not making the payments."

Beverly, a woman who has worked with Manna to pressure Maximus to fairly provide quality services, relates that "things were much better when child support was under the [public] juvenile court. You could call up and talk to a human being and things

(continues)

(continued)

would get done. They could have used more people, but you always felt like they were trying."

Manna's goal is to make Maximus accountable to all of the families it is supposed to serve. The group is developing a long-term strategy to improve the child-support collection program by pressuring the state to cancel the contract or put pressure on the Maximus corporation to be more responsive to its clients. For now, it is building a base by informing these women of their rights and referring them to agencies such as Legal Aid to help them weave through the private company's complicated system.

*The names of women trying to obtain child support enforcement have been changed to preserve their anonymity. Their problems and concerns are real and unaltered.

12

Reconstructing Cities, Restoring the Environment: New Urbanism Versus Mobile/Agile Capital

Bill Resnick

Summary

The American Dream is changing fast. Midcentury's secular creed—the quest for a pastoral suburban home—didn't last long. The suburb is now synonymous with sprawl, social disconnection, and environmental degradation. Suburbanites are now demanding growth boundaries, greenbelts, and land trusts. And search for a replacement dream is under way, with sole candidate for both city and suburb a "new urbanism"—housing and neighborhoods that are more compact, walkable, diverse, neighborly, close to necessary shopping, accessible by public transit—that stresses human connection and life patterns with less environmental damage.

But new urbanist reconstruction requires extensive public action: expanded public regulation of economic development and land use (like growth boundaries); and increased taxation to create public goods including open space, transit, parks, town centers, historic and environmental restoration, access to the "specially abled," poverty reduction, and more, which arouses fierce elite and corporate opposition, indeed overpowering threats by global/mobile firms to relocate or take other measures lethal to workers and community should increased regulation or taxation be imposed. So up to now growth limitation measures and the new urbanism have had no teeth and meager funds. The United States is still suburbanizing, indeed leapfrogging out, but no longer from conviction and sense of grace, but rather because commercial power immobilizes the popular forces necessary to gain the resources to reconstruct.

But if mobile/agile capital has the upper hand, its ecologically and socially destructive trajectory will intensify. Critique, yearnings, and search for alternatives will not be extinguished, and many of the experiments provide inspiration for what could be done. Thus, for the foreseeable future, struggles to save the cities—actually whole regions—will generate local activism and starkly and vividly raise progressive alternatives requiring public goods to the rule of wealth and market.

The New American Dream
Requires Reconstructing
Metropolitan Areas—The Big Package

This is a big, rich, diverse, urbanized country with traditions in many cities of extensive public works and investment. As the suburban dream withered, support grew for experimentation and action toward renewing "livability" in metropolitan areas. Although this sentiment and willingness to spend was mostly exploited by business and bureaucratic interest for narrow gain, still some succeeded, enough to demonstrate what would work and what could be done. This chapter leads with what has been learned, synthesized into a big vision and package, itemizing the many public goods and controls—like transit, growth boundaries, design standards, parks, and so forth—needed to reconfigure cities in democratic and sustainable directions. For each component, like transit and growth, it also shows how reliance on market forces decimates land and undermines community.

Component 1.
A Growth Boundary and
Attractive Affordable In-Fill Development
Creating Higher Population Densities

A metropolitan growth boundary is necessary to stop suburban and exurban flight and concentrate investment (material and emotional) in the city and already existing suburbs. But growth boundaries and greenbelts, the mechanisms to stop sprawl, won't retain public support unless higher density development inside the boundary is beautiful, pleasing, and affordable. Thus, growth boundaries must be combined with a set of public initiatives: Land-use laws and zoning induce better use of land and smaller lot sizes.

- Design standards maintain neighborhood character and avoid the cheap and ugly. Many wonderful projects no more expensive than the truly degrading ones have been built, and these must be promoted, indeed made into shrines, for neighborhoods and builders to emulate and prospective homeowners to seek.
- The "growth lobby" effectively argues that eliminating growth boundaries and relaxing land-use regulations reduces land and housing costs. Of course housing costs are rising in every growing city, including those without growth boundaries. But pointing this out will not be enough to convince the public. Meaningful steps to keep housing affordable include: replacement ordinances, inclusionary zoning, requirements on builders, subsidies to builders, and public construction. Necessary monies (call it a Housing Trust Fund) can be accumulated through a progressive real estate transfer tax (a higher percentage as the houses get more luxurious) and the Vermont system of taxing speculative gains, that is, the profits gained on rapid turnover. The speculation tax slows increases in housing prices by discouraging quickie investment and raising considerable sums for building new affordable housing.

Component 2.
Reducing Congestion by Reducing
Car Use and Providing Transit Options

Greater population density can mean more street life and more vibrant public and commercial districts; it can also mean intolerable traffic congestion, noise, and fumes. Reducing the deadly crush of autos requires several public initiatives:

- Throughout the region town centers, satellite small retail and "mixed-use" residential and commercial projects can be designed and built closer to people and transit and as community gathering places, thus satisfying the "Orange Juice Rule" of city planning: that every home be close enough to small stores so a ten-year-old can bike to buy a newspaper and milk.
- Many transit modes (rail, buses, jitneys) must be designed to work together to make a fast convenient comfortable system pleasant for reading and small talk.
- Neighborhoods and shopping areas can be redesigned, to be not just pleasant but positively inviting for walking and biking.

Component 3. Creating
Parklike Neighborhoods

Unlivable cities feature parking lots. Great cities are parklike with a pervasive grace and beauty; this reduces car use (people walk for pleasure), reduces crime and vandalism, increases public commitment to neighbors, neighborhood, city maintenance, and public goods, and inspires voluntary contributory acts of stewardship and beautification. To create a parklike and ecologically sound city requires both public initiatives and the humanization/socialization of private space:

- Remaining open space can be purchased and appropriately developed by the public, as in Minneapolis, Minnesota, where every home is within six blocks of a well-kept park.
- Residential and commercial areas can be enhanced through traffic calming, more walking paths and pedestrian ways, more sheltered places to sit, better design and landscaping, and protection of historic and scenic places.
- Since the great bulk of real estate in U.S. cities—factories, stores, offices, apartments, homes—is privately owned and maintained, neighborhoods can become parklike only if most owners make their "private property" pleasing and beautiful, symbolized by the small homeowner's front garden.
- Restoration of the region's natural elements (lands, streams and wetlands, public and private) can be accomplished through enforcement of industrial waste standards, better sewers, reduced chemical use on lawns and streets, replanting with native plants, and, strikingly, renaturalizing what had become storm drains and culverts. The relatively natural reproduction of fish, birds, and native plants becomes a dramatic symbol of the new city with the "built environment" part of nature.

Component 4. Reducing Poverty
and Building Expectations that
Social Contribution Will Lead
to a Dignified Life

No region will be safe, comfortable, compact, and democratic if income and opportunity keep polarizing. Income polarization leads to inner-city or inner-suburb decay, and drives suburban flight. And those confined to the bottom, when denied realistic hope, can be every bit as antisocial as those at the top. Even within the neoliberal world, U.S. regions can partially ameliorate poverty, and can also challenge the system generating increasing income inequality.

- Local action can raise wages to the working poor through a regional Earned Income Tax Credit, increased public contract standards and minimum wage, creating public work at decent wages, supporting unionization, providing child care and medical care.
- Training and education are socially beneficial, but they can not compensate for an economy in which 25 percent of the people are unemployed, underemployed, or employed in very low-wage jobs, and where the wage structure is becoming bipolar, with the middle disappearing. The first priority is to raise the pay of all the jobs the economy/society requires and people actually perform, like cashier, truck driver, child and elder care, restaurant work, and on and on.
- Distressed communities can be assisted by supporting Community Development Corporations and directing resources for infrastructure, park, transit, and enterprise development.
- No city can succeed on its own. These partial and ameliorative efforts must be part of larger campaigns in which city leadership and local organizations join counterparts in other cities to shape national policy through a national "Living Wage Campaign," progressive tax initiatives, fair trade enactments, controls on capital mobility and financial speculation, and other measures to ensure wealth is equitably shared.

Component 5. Maintaining and Enhancing the Public Spaces and Democratic Activities that Create a Rich, Stimulating, Democratic Public Life

Tin Pan Alley had the right idea: "The best things in life are free."[1] More accurate, "The best things in life require public control and taxes." But the latter does not scan very well, and everybody knows "there's no free lunch." Love, friendship, solidarity, community, those most meaningful connections and identities (personal and private, communal and broadly social), cannot be achieved through purchased experience in private markets. Indeed, the market, with its graded offerings per consumer wealth and its veneration of money, undermines community and solidarity. In an age of market expansion with ever more studied and diabolical means aiming to seduce people to seek satisfaction and pursue life through purchase and commodities, it becomes ever more important to enhance public and democratic space and institutions against those who have demonized the city, sown fear, and generated a culture of privatism, defensiveness, and resentment, especially targeting black and Hispanic youth. This requires a set of public controls, initiatives, and taxes:

- Public education and the parks, squares, libraries, theaters, meeting halls, and low-rent commercial districts and their pubs and coffeehouses—all generate solidarity, respect for history and diverse contributions, and confidence in common humanity and democratic prospects. These places can be protected and strengthened.
- So must public events and gatherings—entertainments and parades, as well as hearings, neighborhood forums and public meetings, social and political—which also produce identity, community, and responsibility.
- Citizen participation needs to be enhanced in schools, including teaching, governance, and community education.
- Ensuring access to the handicapped, elderly, and infirm symbolizes inclusiveness, respect, and community commitment to ensuring full public lives to all.
- Public life can feature more intensive participation and engagement, with forums for democratic decision making embedded in daily life, including local decision making in neighborhood and workplace, which means strong democratic unions and meaningful workplace participation and self-managing activity.

Once under way, this process could gain momentum, inspiring efforts to cut the workweek, otherwise gain free time, and generally democratize daily life, shifting the focal quest from the personal to the mutual, from private aggrandizement (whether the tidy suburban bungalow or mansion wealth) to the collaborative and contributory pursuit of nonmaterial goals, including the healing of nature.

Component 6.
Democratic Governance

Planning, implementation, funding, and enforcement of growth boundaries, transit, environmental and public space restoration, and affordable housing will not occur without public democratic decision, action, and administration. Some variant of metropolitan government with the power to plan, decide, and gain minimal cooperation of local governing bodies must be established. Of course this powerful planning/implementation body must be responsive to local planning efforts and work to forge consensus and protect minority positions. Within this system the massive variety of creative, intellectual, cultural, and spiritual options would preserve spheres of autonomy within a community with strong enforceable democratic and environmental values.

If the many city struggles and initiatives have made it possible to imagine and synthesize this big package, and be confident of its success, the big package is not on any city's agenda nor being promoted on the federal level. Still, all the pieces are in many places being fought for and sometimes implemented, if mostly in compromised disappointing ways. The bulk of this chapter, following, discusses the background of these struggles, the reasons for the generally disappointing results, yet the continued popular desire and ferment, and thus the great political potential these metropolitan reconstruction struggles offer.

The New American Dream Runs into Mobile/Agile Empowered Capital

The Rise and Fall of the Suburban Dream

Today the suburb is in disrepute, in elite and popular cultures portrayed in terms of empty materialism, alienation, and ecological destruction. Conversely, parts of the city—not those where the poor live—have renewed appeal for their diversity, charm, richness, and excitement.

But for the working class who fled city for suburb in postwar America, meanings were very different. The city was dirty, noisy, and dangerous. Factory whistles pierced the neighborhood and structured daily life and time. The city was ruled by industrial, political, and religious bosses, and haunted by ethnic/religious hatreds and unhappy memories (one's own, one's parents or grandparents) of dingy lives, poverty, and insecurity.

The suburban pilgrimage was to fresh air, tranquillity, cleanliness, self-government, independence, and community. The suburb meant escape from the shadow of the factory and fear of want,[2] and embodied the new relation between labor and capital. Earning a family wage for an eight-hour day, men had time for family and home. Separate from factory and traditional church and their disciplines, that home had greenery, private play space, often a home workshop, a car offering freedom and mobility, and meat on the table at nearly every meal. It was the latest version of yeoman democracy, with all its failings: women subordinate in the home and racial minorities need not apply.

That was then. City, suburb, economy, women's lives, and meanings have changed. Though its circulation is mostly suburban, *Time* magazine summarized: "New American suburbs tend to be disappointments, if not outright failures. Traffic jams are regularly as bad as anything in the fearsome loathsome city. Waste problems can be worse. Boundaries are ill defined; town centers are non-existent. Too often there's no there there." *Newsweek*'s article on sprawl slightly distanced itself from the critique: "As anyone who reads the fiction in the *New Yorker* knows, Americans mostly live in banal places with the souls of shopping mall, affording nowhere to mingle except traffic jams ..." Then the article affirmed the critique, offering "Fifteen Ways to Fix the Suburbs." In 1966 the construction industry's slickest journal put it: "Millions of Americans in our sterile suburbs allow themselves to be robbed of a human necessity that our European counterparts enjoy day to day: a balanced social/environmental upbringing."[3] And contemporary film and literature are filled with these bleak suburban landscapes.

This critique is overblown and misplaced. The alleged meaninglessness, materialism, and sterility of the suburb—where most U.S. people live—is just one cliché among many characterizing the American working class in moral, intellectual, spiritual, and characterological free fall. This whole story of narcissism, self-indulgence, irresponsibility, divorce, AWOL parents, drugs, and declining work ethic ad nauseam is the contemporary equivalent of midcentury's "working-class authoritarianism" indictment. It's an ideology that explains national troubles in terms of working-class character and moral deficiencies, and thus undermines working-class confidence and legitimates elite rule. And it conceals the real story: that in nearly every sphere of social life—child rearing and male-female and race relations, for examples—people are struggling toward more democratic lives, to be sure in much turmoil and difficulty.[4]

Still, if not emotional and social hell, the suburb that was to give harmony with nature, abundance, free time, respite from work, even serene community can no longer deliver. Why not?

As to environmental degradation, that's largely a function of the development pattern and spatial dispersal: nature got paved and culverted; single-family homes on large lots meant much driving and ultimately congestion. City troubles moved out, and many inner suburbs got old and poor,[5] spurring flight by their middle class, industry, and business, with job loss and decay comparable to the inner cities. This pattern then, of the urban edge constantly expanding, eating the countryside, leaving in its wake squalor, congestion, abandoned neighborhoods, and ruined land, is not just unattractive but ecologically unsustainable and potentially catastrophic. Metropolitan growth patterns demonstrate how capitalism's "creative destruction" became "malignant creation."

The social failings are rooted in the two great twentieth-century revolutions: capitalist-driven economic recomposition that forced all family members into wage labor; and the rising of the subordinate, especially women. For as Gans has shown, the postwar suburb was not similarly afflicted; early suburbanites created rich, lively, if unequal and women-confining societies, with the wives supervising kids after school, building community, and making social life.[6] Of course back then one eight-to-four unionized working-class job earned enough for house and car and reasonably secure comfortable living; the commutes were relatively short; and there was plenty of time for ferrying kids, leisurely shopping, bowling leagues, and community life based in mostly women's unpaid effort.[7]

When that era ended, so did the allure of the suburb. Women want to and must work outside the home, and want a richer, more varied public life. So fertility declined and most homes were without children. Even in compact cities people are sorely pressed for time for community life, and in dispersed suburbs with more travel time and fewer options, it's even tougher. Isolation from the city seems a bad bargain.

So the souring of the suburban dream comes from the recognition of ecological limits and the added difficulty caused by suburban housing patterns for people seeking to fulfill contemporary economic and social demands and desires.

The New Urbanism Hijacked

The failure of the suburb has profound implications. For people don't do well without goals and a sense of a larger purpose, and the American Dream has traditionally taken spatial form. John Winthrop's shining "city upon a hill, the eyes of all people upon us" was Calvinist collectivist under divine discipline exercised by Winthrop and the elders, with individual expression and taste forbidden. With royalty and theocracy overthrown, village and small-town America, serving a natural resources and agricultural economy, provided the center for community life for a people prizing independence and yeoman democracy. As industrialization proceeded, first the "streetcar suburb," and for the second half of the twentieth century the dispersed suburb, gave life meaning and symbolized deliverance. Certainly for most people that drive for the good life in the suburb, denigrated as materialist but in fact political and spiritual, surpassed religion for most heartfelt and central commitment. And the withering of that dream forced search for alternatives, for ways of life offering purpose and the reconciliation of the two great contemporary conflicts: comfort/abundance versus nature, and autonomy/independence versus community.

As in any great public quest, the pilgrims have gone off in many directions; some get lost, some waylaid, some get "sold a bill of goods," some near succeed, many keep searching. The next three sections—on the commercial response and the "new urbanism," on publicly subsidized urban reconstruction, and on legislated growth limitations—detail the limitations of contemporary commercial and political response.

The Commercial Response and the New Urbanism.   In a civilization devoted to business, with easy market entry and great and small pools of capital pursuing return, every impulse and desire brings forth commercial offerings. What the people want, that is, the people with disposable income, business will sell them—if it can be shaped into profitable product.

For harried suburbanites, with time a precious commodity, fast food sells, as do microwavable three-minute prepared meals. Drive-through cleaners and banking have done well; funeral parlors haven't. And for parents who cannot afford full-time child care, Kinder Care and others offer drop-off service.

Early on in U.S. suburban development, community nostalgia became a hot product, pioneered by Disney. Thus Disneyland's entrance, Main Street U.S.A., offered an absence of cars and the comforting reassurance, tidy cleanliness, and democratic feel of small-town life before entering the thrills and chills, now dated, of that archetypal amusement park. Later, older cities and traditional residential areas around the country came to spiff themselves up for tourism with early-twentieth-century flourishes, with new ballparks, for example, being designed retro after the great success of Baltimore's Camden Yards. All are selling community and roots, or a taste of them, to starving suburbanites.

When gentrification became big business, when the hottest-selling and most expensive (by square foot) real estate was in the old streetcar suburbs and refurbished older neighborhoods, it became clear that people would pay a premium to live in more convenient, neighborly, citified surrounds. Thus, many developers, including the Disney Corp/ABC, came to embrace "new urbanist" or "neotraditional" design.

Most of it is long on promotion, short on product, and superficial, particularly the new towns and big developments. The critique of Kentlands (Maryland) and Laguna West (Sacramento) applies to them all:

> [They] ... have a stronger sense of public structure than conventional suburbs; more interesting and cohesive streetscapes.... But neither achieves the ease of access to retail and office uses, mix of housing types, pedestrian access to daily needs, and overall connectedness found in many small towns or in the early-twentieth-century streetcar suburb that the neotraditional designs emulate.... They represent modest improvements over most conventional suburban planned unit developments. ... There is little urbanity in the new urbanism.... In reaction to the anonymous sprawl of suburbia, the tendency has been for designers to superimpose an image on a development before it is even occupied, providing a "scenographic" setting that is fixed and unchangeable.... Often this image, though strong, is a fraudulent one, like Disneyland, that ignores tradition and context.[8]

Disney/ABC's "Celebration" city in Florida, near Disneyworld, is mostly derivative and superficial, and just a bit less segregated, securitized, and auto dependent than standard suburban development.

"They are sprawl under another name ... and as restrictive as any suburban development."[9] To truly change the standard suburban style of living, with its dependence on the car and the heartbeat of the Beltway, you have to make more fundamental changes, and more politically difficult ones, than altering a few front porches or setback rules. You have to use distasteful words like growth controls, parking restrictions, and more investment in mass transit." [10]

Peter Calthorpe, a prominent new urbanist who designed Laguna West, responded to this sort of criticism: "Planned communities must be judged in contrast to suburban sprawl, not idealized urban environments."[11] Even granting Calthorpe his point, even if planned communities are better than the old suburbs, even if they keep urban ideas alive (though also cheapen and delegitimize them), genuine efforts are few and far between, with little presence in the suburban housing market.

Very little, very late also describes suburban initiatives to create town centers. Schaumburg, the archetypal Chicago suburb (nothing but malls and big lawn McMansions spread across the prairies, all connected to the freeway) is building "a ready made downtown—shops, restaurants, a library, ponds, parks and waterfalls," that officials call "Olde Schaumburg."[12] But suburban densities are too low to support either transit or small shopping districts, and the fate of Olde Schaumburg is to become another up-scale mall, with "civic" trappings.

But the new urbanism is not just commercial exploitation. Indeed, many of the architects produce full, progressive visions; if to get them built they make deadly compromises, the initial designs can be attractive, even inspirational. And the new urbanism has fared better in the city; some mixed-use development (residential above, commercial ground level) not only looks good but demonstrates the feasibility of intentional town centers, with child-care facilities and services closer to people. If designed to permit noncommercial interaction, they do generate more community life.

Publicly Subsidized Urban Reconstruction. The failure of the suburbs and popular desire for city renewal has led to much activity trumpeted as urban reconstruction initiated by commercial interests mostly for private advantage. Transit and rail builders, office complex developers, inner-city multiple dwelling developers, hotels and tourist destinations, specialist architects and business associations, the lawyers and bond sellers who organize the financing—all are pushing public spending and regulation that spruces up their location or otherwise creates economic benefit.

Downtowns, at least salvageable parts with powerful corporate residents, have done best. To reverse "blight and flight" the businesses advance publicly subsidized downtown development packages. These include office building for high-end professional, administrative, and business firms; university and hospital upgrade and expansion; convention and sports centers; trendy retail, entertainment, museum, and restaurant districts; river, lake, or oceanfront tourist attractions; stylish low- and high-level apartments and condominiums; old neighborhood gentrification.

And they have sought transit investment to match, gaining support from the urban antifreeway citizens lobby (which originated in opposition to superhighways devouring the city). This coalition now advocates Transit Oriented Development (TOD): a necklace of high-density new urbanist beads connected by high-speed, high-capacity transit links, so cities "grow up, not out." These advocates point to many successful transit examples: the excellent systems in many European cities; the clean and popular new light-rail and subway systems in San Diego and Washington, D.C.; the older renovating systems in New York, Philadelphia, Boston, and Chicago; and the novelties like San Francisco's cable cars and Seattle's Monorail.

These projects—downtown, transit, convention centers, and trendy districts—are designed to appeal to people hungry for lively cities, sense of place, and community. All come with architectural embellishment representing "community," and all promote themselves as creating jobs and saving the city by avoiding sprawl and environmental degradation. Indeed, all exploit these decent popular impulses for the greater glory and profit of various elite owner and commercial interests, and channel scarce monies from more pressing needs, like maintaining schools and current bus-based transit systems that serve the lower working class.

By century's end localities began to go beyond mere subsidies to cede large public spaces (streets, parks, and plazas) to corporate control through nonprofit corporations and special tax-assessment districts. These then employ high security measures to sanitize and remove unsavory elements and construct urban mall cultures for high-end consumers.[13]

Still, if corporate welfare, some of the big projects have created decent public areas. A good deal of historic renovation and preservation has succeeded. Waterfront and riverfront development has helped rejuvenate sectors of many cities. And the better projects, like some light-rail, do show what could be done.

In this redevelopment game, the big interests do best. But neighborhood groups, small business and developers, and homeowners are not entirely absent. They also seek public help and monies. Some of this is gentrification, led by developers who take areas with attractive housing and other assets, redevelop, and sell to the affluent. But in some areas working-class residents cooperate to stop blight, rebuild, restore services, and sometimes create livable communities, again demonstrating what can be done with sufficient resources.

Legislated Growth Limitations.   Though big suburban developers strongly resist, many substantial monied interests have come to support growth limitation. Some of it is NIMBYist (Not In My Back Yard): privileged city or suburban residents fighting to preserve the comfort, cleanliness, views, and amenities threatened by the next high-rise or next suburb out. More important civic elites and local politicians are coming to recognize that the costs of providing infrastructure (roads, sewers, schools, and so on) to new areas is greater than any tax gains. And banking, agribusiness, and farmers' associations are seeking to protect their investments against the costs of sprawl. In California the Bank of America, the godfather of suburban expansion, with huge portfolios of agricultural and city-suburban business and residential loans, has now concluded that sprawl "now threatens to inhibit growth and degrade the quality of life.... We can no longer afford the luxury of sprawl."[14]

In combination with environmentalists, these interests can exert sufficient power to challenge and force the developer/construction lobby into compromise. Thus, growth limitations are being considered and enacted in fast-growing affluent areas all over the country, cities like Seattle, Portland, Oregon, Boca Raton, Petaluma, California, and Boulder. In California over a dozen cities from 1996 to

1999 adopted urban growth boundaries, including San Jose, Santa Rosa, Napa, and Novato.[15]

Most outlying suburbs are now considering growth controls through quotas on new building permits or by raising permit costs to reflect the real cost of new roads, water, sewers, schools, police and fire protection, and the rest. Other anti-growth measures have also been enacted, depending on the threat, with some, for example, opposing Wal-Mart expansion, and others banning drive-throughs, as a way of keeping people walking downtown.[16]

As of 1995 thirteen states had comprehensive growth legislation (California, Florida, Georgia, Hawaii, Maine, Maryland, Massachusetts, New Jersey, New York, Oregon, Rhode Island, Vermont, Washington); all but Hawaii were state mandates on localities to plan. Every state has some type of right-to-farm law protecting farmers from legal actions by residential neighbors. And nearly every state has mechanisms to protect farmers from increases in property taxes when nearby development begins raising land prices.[17] Oregon's land use laws have survived developer attack through a coalition of urban environmentalists and rural farmers.

New Jersey, led by Republican Christine Whitman and a Republican legislature, is now supporting growth boundaries, increasing mass transit subsidies, and buying ex-urban land for greenbelts, parks, and nature preserves, which the *New York Times* pointed out was "only the latest in a series of nation-wide grass-roots efforts to protect farmland and other open areas from commercial development."[18] Colorado and twenty-eight of its cities and counties in the fast-growth vacation home areas levy taxes to buy open space or conservation easements; others require developers to cluster development to avoid chopping the landscape into thirty-five-acre lots.[19] In Idaho 78 percent of the population expressed serious concerns about growth, and "don't Californicate Idaho" sentiment is high.[20]

By early 1999 suburban anger and desire for relief seemed so potent that Al Gore made it an early feature of his presidential campaign, proposing a new federal program, a "Livability Agenda," with monies for land protection and greenbelts. "Plan well and you have a community that nurtures commerce and private life. Plan badly and you have what so many of us suffer from first-hand—gridlock, sprawl, and that uniquely modern evil of all, too little time." Gore noted that in the 1998 elections more than 200 jurisdictions had growth initiatives on the ballot, "and most of them passed." And the article noted that New Jersey governor Whitman had "focused on the issue in her annual address to the Legislature."[21]

Since most Americans and an even larger majority of the voters live in the suburbs, all politicians hear the suburban pain. But on the local level where land use decisions are made and where applications for plan "variances" and zoning changes are heard, local developers still mostly win. Thus, growth limitation measures have by and large been gestures to placate people but do not really control development interests that colonize local government. Thus the major assessment of California's growth limitation measures found "little effect in reducing construction activity, though they may redistribute growth." Translated, this means that some privileged areas have saved their views, but at the expense of others.[22]

Nelson, the chronicler of growth management measures, concluded: "Unfortunately, we find that most cities and urban regions do not have the will to craft truly effective growth management plans that include the necessary urban containment component."[23] No one reports that growth management plans have been accompanied by builder contribution or support for tax policies and public works (transit, parks, and so forth) necessary to build livable cities. Nor have they led to radically changed patterns of investment, particularly not to blighted areas. On the other hand, Portland's growth boundary, the national model, has stopped leapfrog development, though it was initially drawn so far out in the countryside that developers hardly raised a fuss. Now the crunch has arrived, land is in short supply, and a fierce struggle has begun.

The Metropolitan Future and the Struggle to Control Capital

So growth limitation, urban reconstruction, and new urbanist development, happening across the country, has had limited, disappointing impacts that mostly benefit the powerful, but they have shown some promise. And research and reporting are now sufficiently advanced that it is pretty clear what works, what doesn't, and what must be done. Although no region approaches a complete package, even the embryonic bits and pieces confirm that city reconstruction, a very different urban regime, is feasible and desired.

As noted in the first section of this essay, this model would require a metropolitan growth boundary, huge investment in public transit, public improvements to encourage walking and biking, more parks, environmental restoration, historic preservation and street reconfiguration, encouragement of private beautification, town centers and satellite shopping areas in the suburbs, more child care, subsidies of dense affordable housing, access for all including the "handicapped," and reduction of poverty.

If almost nobody can articulate this big vision, nearly everywhere there are signs of popular support for the pieces. That's why the interests who sponsor them can get people to support and vote for downtown development and gold-plated transit projects. And why suburbs and "edge cities" across the country are trying to refashion themselves, as Schaumburg's mayor explained, to: "give people a place to gather ... to bump into each other ... to share."[24]

Joel Garrow, who first named and celebrated the "edge city"—the big shiny suburban strips of shopping centers, hotels, office parks, landscaped parking lots, and suburban housing only reachable by car, near airports—assessed their prospects: "What's going to determine success for an edge city in the future? There has to be civilization, soul, identity. Is this going to be a good place for me to grow old? For my kids to grow up? Could you imagine a Fourth of July parade here?"[25] Disneyland can: Their latest attraction, "as nostalgia loses its edge," will be to "celebrate generic seasonal rituals—Christmas candlelight tours, harvest festivals, spring floral shows ... "[26] A Chicago urban planner discussing Schaumburg commented: "People want a sense of place, a feeling that they are part of a bigger whole."[27]

Actually, they want to be part of a meaningful community. In visual preference surveys people are shown pictures of: (1) traditional urban streetcar neighborhoods with dense, well-kept single-family homes and Main Street shopping patterns, (2) new urbanist development mimicking the old dense patterns, (3) big lawn suburban and mall development. Majorities now report they would rather live in the first two.[28] This should not be dismissed as popular nostalgia or consolation. People have seen enough of the suburbs and enough new urbanist development and restored city neighborhoods to make informed choices.[29]

In this sense all the experimentation and hoopla around it have had positive impacts, and maintained desire for and visions of rebuilt cities. And so nearly every region has a big array of activist organizations that educate, lobby, and generally promote the elements of the reconstructed city: transit, bicycling, parks, land use, child care, historic preservation. Environmental concerns have spawned not just protest or clean-up groups but also local ameliorative work such as tree plantings, stream cleanings, trash pickups, and all manner of neighborhood groups dedicated to saving their area. And people take much personal action like recycling, natural gardening, and even green investing.

But all this is so limited, more personal witness than political movement. Thus nationally there is no thrust toward exposure, education, program, and action ambitious enough to challenge the many processes that threaten apocalypse: toxic buildup and the chemical time bomb, water degradation, soil erosion, climate change, metropolitan sprawl, or unsustainable agriculture, forestry, and industrial production. And though it is metropolitan consumption, production, and sprawl life patterns that generate the apocalyptic processes (captured by the slogan "Save the City, Save the Planet"), there are no local/regional movements that seek the combination of growth limitation and public investment necessary to reverse urban decline and reconstruct sustainable democratic cities.

This same disproportion also characterizes the income and opportunity component of the democratic city. There is widespread support for health care, job support, and measures to raise the income of the working poor.[30] For example, the furiously probusiness House of Representatives, over the objections of its religiously free-market leadership, voted to raise the federal minimum wage just before the 1996 election, afraid of public response if it didn't.

But near century's end, although campaigns to reverse income polarization and create more public services had revived, their goals were limited (to raise the minimum wage or raise public contract standards), hardly enough to even slow the intensification of inequality. As in the environmental and civic movements, popular organizing and action was mostly devoted to personal and local amelioration—charitable efforts to help others and mutual efforts to help a small group, as in cooperative child care.

Thus, although it is easy to conceive the full program, and though there is considerable public concern and multiple bits and pieces of action reflecting that concern, still in no city is the big reconstruction package even visible, much less being fought for. If the sentiments are majoritarian, the movements are weak with very narrow goals. Most activism is individual, expressive, local, and barely political.

Metastatic Suburbanization Continues

So by century's end the forces that generated urban decline and suburban growth were operating unabated. The general direction of public policy remained as it has been for the last twenty years: to reduce aid to cities, to polarize income (by allowing unions to get eroded and the minimum wage to fall, making taxes less progressive), and to subsidize suburban edge development. Cities were hard-pressed to maintain existing infrastructure (transit, roads, parks, schools), much less invest in the transit and the rest necessary for urban reconstruction.

Thus with all the talk, conferences, and agitation and even considerable legislation directed to growth management and urban reconstruction, the cities and inner suburbs kept declining and metastatic suburbanization continued, in some few places in new urbanist veneer. What's new and widespread is that blight and flight is no longer just from city to suburb but also from inner to outer suburb. Even cities deemed to have done well—Portland, Charlotte, Seattle, San Diego, Miami—mostly succeeded in rearranging metropolitan trouble and squalor, developing glitzy affluent districts surrounded by decaying central core and inner suburbs, then the ever-expanding new suburbs.

Global/Mobile/Agile Capital
Intimidates People and Dominates Politics

Why is there so much concern, action, groups, and movements, but so unambitious and to so little end? How is it that popular desire for democratic and sustainable cities can get so easily manipulated by profiteering place interests? Why is the comprehensive package not on the agenda?

Because, as this essay has detailed, stopping sprawl and reconfiguring metropolitan areas as people want requires public planning, a legislative framework, and investment. This means increasing control and taxation of business, which is impossible to achieve within contemporary politics dominated by local elites.

This domination is not principally the result of the political finance system (politicians need rich people's money to run campaigns) nor corporate ownership and control of media. Even with the most radical program of campaign finance and media access, local movements to control and tax business would have a nearly impossible uphill struggle.

That's because business controls the livelihoods of people and communities. And as business has become more mobile, agile, and powerful over the past thirty years, competitive forces have required every firm to pursue a universally and irresistibly successful strategy: to threaten to relocate or otherwise adversely change operations unless workers accept concessions (wages and the rest) and localities create a "good business climate" (reducing regulation and taxes).[31]

Since many plants have moved and many communities have been decimated, fear of loss of jobs and community economic base is now so pervasive and powerful that people cannot afford to vote their ideals or even recognize them. The electorate's bottom-line demand on local political officials is to maintain and grow the economic base. Those who fail this test or antagonize local business do not get elected.

Politicians who campaign to tax the rich and raise corporate taxes, or ballot initiatives in these directions, get vociferously attacked by local business and media as threatening the economy by forcing business to leave, downsize, or sell out. And people heed the warning. Corporate power is so intimidating that there is little room for traditional populist demands, and even less for a program of regulating growth and land while taxing companies to rebuild the city. Popular ideals for home and community have changed, the suburb has lost allure, and new urbanism is attractive, but supporting and voting for local taxes and land use policy is another matter.

Indeed, progressivism has been driven from contention[32] and the choices people get are not progressive but from the right, which get increasingly accepted. That's because economic polarization and insecurity continue to increase, public benefits, public services, and wages continue to decline, and their former defenders, the Democratic Party and unions, offer little help. What remains are privatistic and defensive tactics and strategies to protect self and family. These tactics include tax avoidance, attacks on weaker groups like the poor and immigrants, making sure your kids and your friends' kids get the best jobs opening up in your workplace, and of course flight to the suburbs and their lower taxes.

Once gaining momentum this system tends to institutionalize in a dreadful class politics. The privatistic life choices come to commit people to more of the same and to accepting a rightist set of ideas. When the only way offered to preserve income is to cut taxes, then it becomes easy to believe that government is the enemy and that welfare has debauched the poor, who need a kick in the ass. Those who have fled the city and chosen big mortgages and the big expense of two cars become more vulnerable to rightist, antitax, antigovernment, anticity, prosuburban politics. And those in the inner suburbs cling to their relative privilege even as it disappears.

Indeed, local movements and groups may avoid coalitions, systematic critique, or broader goals in favor of getting something done in their locale. Even groups that reject NIMBYism and have broader purposes become very "pragmatic," being careful their ideas, visions, and goals don't offend the increasingly conservative rich people, foundations, and state legislatures who control the money.

Thus, the market prevails, trumping democratic and community yearnings, which if not extinguished get corrupted, submerged, and denatured. People hungry for democracy and community get to briefly rent the illusion at Disneyland or buy it at Disney's Celebration, Florida, and other "new urbanist" tracts, or at a gated securitized development camouflaged with gingerbread flourishes and other "community" artifacts. Popular desire to save the cities is exploited by corporate-sponsored transit, housing, park, public plaza, and greenbelt measures.

But the necessary policy package—tough public land use controls and higher taxation on wealth to create the public goods that would make sustainable democratic cities—is not visible or proposed in conventional politics or popular media. And if it or its elements were put to a vote, they would likely be decisively rejected by popular majorities intimidated and convinced by corporate opposition charging it as extreme, dangerous, and threatening economic disaster.

Conclusion—A Long Continuing Struggle and Democratic Potentials

But even as the market triumphs as an ideology and business power is nearly unchallengeable in conventional politics, the yearnings, the knowledge of possibilities, and the movements and struggles will live on and strengthen, for many reasons:

- Because the environmental and social consequences of relentless growth will keep generating less satisfaction and more resistance.
- Because those same yearnings that brought the many pilgrims to this country and carried them to the suburbs—that desire for comfortable free independent democratic lives in healthy nature (trying to reconcile autonomy/community and abundance/sustainability)—do not go away. Indeed, these have strengthened by midcentury's (the sixties) democratic tide in U.S. life, with struggles in homes, families, schools, workplaces, and government challenging arbitrary and imperious authority and generating appreciation and support for more respectful and democratic conduct.
- Because in this very urban country (80 percent of people live in the top 330 metropolitan regions and over half in areas with populations over 1 million), the agitation, activism, and movements, mostly of and speaking

to the grass roots, will concern and reach most Americans and keep movements well supplied with adherents and activists.

- Because all this can culminate in that most powerful of processes, where common situation leads people to talk to neighbors; consider what has worked elsewhere; evaluate what makes sense in their area; meet others from other localities; and thus come to see each neighborhood reconstruction as part of what must be a regional and national solution.
- Because alternatives exist. Even today some city-saving projects are attractive; some cities do work better (especially in Canada and Europe), and these inspire and provide confidence in the larger model combining some old and some new, even as the limited impact of many efforts and experiments demonstrates the necessity of larger systemic change.

Perhaps contemporary reform movements will explosively grow, build coalitions, take control of politics, stop market-compelled metastatic suburbanization, and reconstruct production, consumption, and life patterns in metropolitan areas. More likely the destructive trajectory will continue and approach economic-environmental bankruptcy, when it will become clear that momentous steps must be taken and the corporate leviathan put under control and the system reorganized. This surely will trigger intense high-stakes conflict, with rightist authoritarian and left democratic solutions in fierce struggle.

To the extent that progressives work successfully to raise democratic possibilities and build commitments in today's and tomorrow's movements, people will be prepared to choose and battle for the democratic. The point then is not so much to win every battle but to operate in local "reform" movements, however partial, in ways that help people come to their own conclusions about the need for systematic change, be able to appreciate the big vision including the democratic and sustainable core, and realize their personal capacities and collective power.

Notes

1. Song from *Good News*, the 1927 Broadway musical by Bud De Sylva and Lew Brown (book and lyrics) and Ray Henderson (music).

2. See Robert Fishman, *Bourgeois Utopias: The Rise and Fall of Suburbia* (New York: Basic Books, 1987).

3. "Old Fangled New Towns; Replacing Charmless Suburban Sprawl with Civilized Familiar Places that People Love," *Time*, May 20, 1991, 52(4). "Paved Paradise," *Newsweek*, May 15, 1995, 42–53. John Henry, "What Is Disney Celebrating? Is Celebration Mayberry or a Stepford Village?" *Professional Builder*, September 1996, 46–48.

4. This is my controversial but pretty easily demonstrable hypothesis in a book in process relying on diverse studies, such as Murray A. Straus, *Beating the Devil Out of Them* (New York: Lexington Books, 1994), on corporal punishment of children; Sharon Hays, *The Cultural Contradictions of Motherhood* (New Haven: Yale University Press, 1996), on parenting practices; Scott Coltrane, *Family Man: Fatherhood, Housework, and Gender Equity* (New York: Oxford University Press, 1996, on male-female negotiation of family responsibilities. Each of these includes longitudinal data

that indicate slow and halting change toward more respectful, egalitarian, humane practices, though the authors, especially Straus, hesitate to emphasize this in books dedicated to exposing the continuity and damage of oppressive practices. Additional evidence comes from the many challenges to arbitrary authority and dominating practice, where, if slow and contested, real gains have been made, as, for example, in struggles around sexual harassment, or professional responsibility to inform clients, or racial discrimination. "While one should not forget the continued conservatism of America on certain questions involving law and order (for example, drugs and capital punishment), school prayer, pornography, the flag, and other matters, the great story about social issues in the mid–twentieth-century United States remains the gradual, sweeping liberalization that occurred over several decades: the strong trends toward increased support for civil rights, civil liberties, women's rights, and the legal tolerance of diversity." Benjamin I. Page and Robert Y. Shapiro, *The Rational Public: Fifty Years of Trends in Americans' Policy Preferences* (Chicago and London: University of Chicago Press, 1992), 115. And not just more tolerant and willing to grant rights to others, people are seeking more democratic and fulfilling relations, slowly and painfully with much backlash to be sure, in child rearing, mating, and racial and work relationships.

5. *New York Times,* "Becoming Unstuck in the Suburbs," October 19, 1997, News of the Week in Review, 4. The older close-in lower-working-class suburbs are literally falling apart, built fifty years ago with plywood sheathing, flooring, and roofing whose glues hold well for about forty years.

6. Herbert J. Gans, *The Levittowners, Ways of Life and Politics in a New Suburban Community* (New York: Pantheon Books, Random House, 1967).

7. In his study of suburbanizing auto workers in the late 1950s Bennett Berger describes workers who make $5,000 a year with $12,000 tract houses, two cars, two kids, wife in the home, many appliances, and a TV. Bennett M. Berger, *Working-Class Suburb, A Study of Auto Workers in Suburbia* (Berkeley: University of California Press, 1960). Of course this life was confined to the mostly white families in the industrial working class able to overcome employer resistance and form unions.

8. Michael Southworth, "Walkable Suburbs? An Evaluation of Neotraditional Communities at the Urban Edge," *APA Journal,* winter 1997, 28–44.

9. *New York Times,* "A Cure for the Rootlessness of Modern Suburban Life?" August 1, 1998, A15.

10. Alex Marshall, "Putting Some 'City' Back in the Suburbs," *Washington Post,* September 1, 1996, C1.

11. Sim Van Der Ryn and Peter Calthorpe, *Sustainable Communities: A New Design Synthesis for Cities, Suburbs and Towns* (Sierra Club Books, 1991), 234.

12. *New York Times,* "Town Sired by Malls Seeks Soul Downtown," August 7, 1996, A7.

13. Sharon Zukin, *The Cultures of Cities* (Cambridge, Mass.: Blackwell, 1995).

14. *Beyond Sprawl,* Bank of America, 1994. It is discussed by Neal R. Pierce, "A MegaBank Joins the Critics of Urban Sprawl," *Nation's Cities Weekly,* March 6, 1995, 18.

15. *Landmark,* the magazine of 1,000 Friends of Oregon, spring 1998, 10. For differing analyses of Portland's growth management efforts see Jay Walljasper, "Portland's Green Peace: At Play in the Fields of Urban Planning," *Nation,* October 13, 1997, 11(5) (supportive and optimistic); Tim W. Ferguson, "Down with the Burbs! Back to the City," *Forbes,* May 5, 1997, 142–152 (free market critical); "The Big Experiment in Big Trouble, *Portland Alliance,* November 1997, Special Supplement, (supportive but pessimistic).

16. *The Portland Oregonian,* "Drive-Through Ban Seeks to Restore Small-Town Feel," August 3, 1998, A9.

17. Arthur Nelson and James Duncan, *Growth Management Principles and Practices* (Washington, D.C.: Planners Press, American Planning Association, 1995).

18. *New York Times,* "New Law Stresses Conservation and Growth," February 18, 1996, R11, and editorial: "Conservation Close to Home," May 31, 1998, News of the Week in Review, 16.

19. *New York Times,* "Rare Alliance in the Rockies Strives to Save Open Spaces," August 14, 1998, A1.

20. Gayla Smutny, "Legislative Support for Growth Management in the Rocky Mountains: An Exploration of Attitudes in Idaho," *APA Journal,* summer 1998, 311.

21. *New York Times,* "Gore Offers Plan to Control Suburban Sprawl," January 12, 1999, A16.

22. Madelyn Glickfeld and Ned Levine, *Regional Growth . . . Local Reaction: The Enactment and Effects of Local Growth Control and Management Measures in California* (Cambridge, Mass.: Lincoln Institute of Land Policy, 1992). See also Kee Warner and Harvey Molotch, "How Development Persists Despite Local Controls," *Urban Affairs Review,* January 1995, 378–406.

23. Nelson and Duncan, *Growth Management Principles and Practices,* 92.

24. *New York Times,* "Town Sired by Malls."

25. William Fulton, "Are Edge Cities Losing Their Edge? To Stay Competitive Outlying Developments Should Take a Clue from Downtown," *Planning,* May 1966, 4–7.

26. *New York Times,* "Tale of Two Main Streets' Search for Magic," October 1998, B1.

27. *New York Times,* "Town Sired by Malls."

28. Anton Nelessen, *Visions for a New American Dream: Process, Principles, and an Ordinance to Plan and Design Small Communities* (Washington, D.C.: Planners Press, American Planning Association, 1994).

29. For more on consumer preferences including citations see Reid Ewing, "Is Los Angeles Style Sprawl Desirable?" *APA Journal,* winter 1997, 107–125.

30. Page and Shapiro summarize years of opinion polling, "The high and generally stable public support for government action on Social Security, education, jobs, medical care, the cities, the environment, consumer safety, and the like—and willingness to pay taxes for these purposes—is especially striking." "Throughout the Reagan years and on into the Bush years, Americans favored more, not less, spending and action on virtually all these economic welfare programs." Page and Shapiro, *The Rational Public,* 169–170.

31. For discussion of urban dependency, the competition among cities, and the bargains corporations demand, see Paul Kantor, *The Dependent City Revisited: The Political Economy of Urban Development and Social Policy* (Boulder and San Francisco: Westview Press, 1995). A left exposé with policy proposals is *No More Candy Store; States and Cities Making Job Subsidies Accountable* (Washington, D.C.: Grass Roots Policy Project, 1994). George E. Peterson, ed., *Big-City Politics, Governance, and Fiscal Constraints* (Washington, D.C.: Urban Institute, 1994), discusses the unhappy fate of the black mayors who were elected on populist promises, with no option to retain jobs but to satisfy mobile/agile capital and cut corporate taxes and thus local services.

32. This is a very different assessment of the failure and prospects of the Democratic Party than a host of books from the pundits, politicians, and academics, who see the problem as mostly being too close to the "interest groups" (blacks, women, labor) and counsel disengagement. See, for example, Thomas Byrne Edsall and Mary D. Edsall, *Chain Reaction: The Impact of Race, Rights, and Taxes on American Politics* (New York: Norton, 1991); Stanley Greenberg, *Middle Class Dreams, the Politics and Power of the New American Majority* (New Haven: Yale University Press, 1996); E. J. Dionne, *They Only Look Dead: Why Progressives Will Dominate the Next Political Era* (New York: Simon and Schuster, 1996); Barney Frank, *Speaking Frankly: What's Wrong with the Democrats and How to Fix It* (New York: Random House, 1992).

PART FOUR

Education and Public Expression

13

Education
as a Public Good

Nel Noddings

Public schooling in the United States today faces the largest challenge since its inception. Significant numbers of people are now repeating the charges that were initially thrown at Horace Mann's proposals: Public schools are not really "public" at all. They serve the interests of some and work against the interests of others. Among those dissenting today are members of the Christian right and various Protestant sects who were once staunch supporters of public schools. I want to examine their case here and consider how advocates of continued public education might respond. I will start with a discussion of cases that raise grave concerns about the wisdom of allowing a separation of state and school, follow this with an examination of the case made by advocates of separation, and then suggest how defenders of public schooling might respond. Throughout the discussion, I will be concerned with the effects of our responses on teachers, students, and what is taught about democratic life.

Before launching into the main arguments, however, I want to remind readers that compulsory education has always posed a peculiar problem for liberal states. On the one hand, from a Millian perspective, it is absolutely essential. It spells the difference, as Mill described it, between happiness defined in Socratic terms and the purely sensual wallowing pleasure of the pig. It should ensure the intellectual virtues required of a liberal citizenry. On the other hand, it requires coercion and, although Mill was willing to use coercion on children, the dependent young, and "barbarians," later liberals expressed deep concern about this.[1] I want to be clear also that what follows is not meant as a defense of liberalism. When I speak of life in liberal democracies, this is an acknowledgment of the widespread belief that we do in fact live in such a society and that the dilemmas we encounter can be resolved within a liberal framework. I am not at all sure this is true. It may well be that the state we should strive for is better described in Deweyan terms as a *social* democracy.

A second point to be made by way of preliminaries is that the matter under discussion is especially important for women. Some of the groups desiring separation have very conservative traditional views about the role of women. Girls educated by these groups might well be deprived of the knowledge and opportunities they need to make genuine choices. Second, although I will not be able to discuss it here, the increasingly vigorous campaign of the dissenters makes it difficult for feminist theorists to advance the project of valorizing women's traditional tasks and virtues, to talk seriously about the importance of home and home life. Whereas we want to educate both boys and girls for a universal caregiver model,[2] valorizing the virtues associated with caregiving seems to give support to the separatists. Thus we must exercise great sensitivity in promoting the care orientation.

What Should Worry Public School Defenders

In his introduction to Sheldon Richman's *Separating School and State,* Jacob G. Hornberger writes:

> It is time for the American people to rediscover and move toward the principles of individual liberty and free markets of their ancestors—and to lead the world out of the socialist darkness of the twentieth century. The best place to begin is to liberate America's families through the separation of school and state.[3]

The attack on public schools is broad-based and contains strange bedfellows: members of the Christian right who condemn the secularism of public education, entrepreneurs who see economic possibilities in the big business of education, libertarians who put their faith in free markets for everything, inner-city parents who despair of obtaining a decent education for their children, parents who are appalled and frightened by increasing violence in the schools, and citizens who have been persuaded (often by badly slanted news stories) that the schools are doing a poor job in academic studies. All of the reasons for challenging public education should be given attention, but here I will confine the discussion to what should worry us in the religious attack.

More than a few Christian schools advocate traditional patriarchal gender roles. Alan Peshkin reports the following comments made by a twelfth-grade teacher in a Christian school, after reading Ephesians 5:

> Relationship of man to wife—I'm the head of my wife and my kids come under her. That's God's order. If a wife doesn't submit, the doors are wide open to Satan. Wives learn to submit, husbands learn to love. If there's a problem, we talk it out. I allow her her say. If I make a wrong decision, then she's not responsible.[4]

If these comments were unusual, it would be unfair to point to them as a source of worry for educators in a liberal democracy. But they are not unusual. In

Bethany, the school Peshkin studied, girls are advised: "Make sure the guy you're interested in is on a higher spiritual plain than you are, that he's someone you can look up to as a spiritual leader." And boys are advised to lead. They are told that girls respect men as leaders: "They need leaders; they need to be led. God didn't put them in a position to lead. He put them in a position to follow."[5]

Peshkin admits that he fears "those who know they have the Truth and are convinced that everyone else would do best to hold this same Truth,"[6] but he also strongly defends their right to exist without harassment. Indeed, a liberal democracy must, by its own principles, allow illiberal groups to survive so long as they do not threaten the state itself. But their existence does create a paradox. What threats must the state take seriously, and how can it protect citizens who may fall under the control of such groups without consciously deciding to do so? In particular, a liberal state must be concerned with the education of its young for life in a pluralistic society.

From a feminist perspective, the worry is not so much that all women will be affected by a revival of patriarchal religion, but that girls who are trained from an early age in schools espousing such views will not gain either the knowledge or the opportunity to make the free choices a liberal democracy tries to ensure for its citizens. In agreement with Peshkin, most of us would still prefer to keep hands off the Christian (and other illiberal) schools. Providing public moneys for them, however, crosses the line of constitutionality, and so we have to look carefully at arguments for vouchers that contend that voucher money would support *parents,* not institutions. But the worry goes well beyond the issue of using public money for religious schools.

Parents in the United States are already free to choose (at their own expense) nonpublic schools for their children, but how much control should they have over what is taught in the public schools? Consider the 1987 case *(Mozert v. Hawkins)* in which a group of Christian fundamentalists brought suit against a school board for denigrating their religious views in a required reading program.[7] I'll discuss here just one component of the complaint. One of the stories in the required reader depicts a boy cooking while his sister reads to him. The parents complained that this reversal of gender roles contradicts biblical teaching and that exposing their children to such views threatens the group's free exercise of religion. They did not insist that the reading program be eliminated but only that their own children be excused from it. Now, putting aside the nightmare of control that a multiplicity of such cases might induce, how should a liberal state respond? I will consider an answer to this question a bit later, but for now it should be noted that the decision of the appeals court did not put aside issues of control. On the contrary, the court majority noted that accommodating the parents' request "will leave public education in shreds."[8]

This conclusion, that responding positively to parents' requests would leave public education in shreds, is at least debatable. Critics regularly complain that the American school system has become both an unwieldy bureaucracy and an arrogant monopoly. There is some foundation for such a complaint. At the early stages of the Mozert conflict, some school people were willing to respond positively to

THIS MODERN

WORLD by TOM TOMORROW

the parents' request. Older reading texts were available, and parents volunteered to come in and teach their children at the designated time. The pervasive notion that professionals know best and that everything "educational" must be handled by certified personnel gets in the way of a caring response. The American tendency to settle all things great and small by litigation doesn't help either. One might argue that some things should not be settled once and for all but should be left open for continuing discussion. At least, law should not make it impossible for schools to respond positively to parents if such a response is not inordinately expensive. The alternative to increased responsiveness is deepening distrust and separation. At its worst, growing distrust and dissatisfaction may destroy the public schools entirely.

The *Mozert* decision stands in some contrast to the earlier *Yoder* decision in which the court decided that the Amish could remove their children from high schools entirely on the grounds that attending such schools would expose their children to lifestyles likely to undermine the Amish religious community.[9] The Court recognized that high school attendance put a special burden on the Amish's "free exercise" of religion. Allowing the Amish to opt out of secondary schooling did not, however, put any burden on the schools, and the Amish made no moves to influence public education. The *Mozert* complaint, in contrast, was much more modest, but it opened the door for further requests that might have involved significant accommodation on the part of schools. It is an open question, however, whether a positive response will lead to further demands or, instead, to an increase of trust and cooperation. If we approach these issues with a "give them an inch and they'll take a mile" attitude, we violate the precepts of associated living that John Dewey described as the essence of democracy.[10] In education especially, we should reject processes that work against the free interaction of differing groups.

Missing from most of the legal discussion (Justice Douglas's dissent in *Yoder* is an exception)[11] is any consideration of children's rights. Should parents control the education of their children as suggested by the separatists? Should government, through public schools, control that education? Here, whichever decision is made, we run into a liberal paradox. If parents control the education of their children, many children will be deprived of the legitimate choices offered in a liberal society. If government controls education, the perceived rights of parents are put into question. The only answer seems to be a parent-school partnership that until recent years has been largely taken for granted. That partnership which, in effect, has operated as a check on the power of both groups and thus as a protection for children is now at serious risk. Why do powerful groups want to dissolve it?

The Religious Case
Against the Schools

A general case against the public schools—their bureaucratic sluggishness, monopolistic power, and lack of responsiveness—has been made by a great variety of critics. The more specialized case brought by the religious right against the public schools is usually expressed in two phases. In the first, schools are criticized from a religious perspective; in the second, a recommendation is made for public funding of religious schools. It may be that the criticisms raised in phase one could be answered in a way that would make the recommendation of phase two unnecessary. That should be the first line of response. If no reasonable and caring reconciliation can be reached, defenders of public schooling should still resist the separation called for in phase two.

Phase one arguments typically take one of two forms. One deplores the loss of God in schools and cites an antireligious school environment that tends to undermine the free exercise of religion; the other, less frequently heard but powerfully articulated by Christian intellectuals, charges that the schools are already soaked in religion—the religion of secular humanism. In a sense, this second form of critique charges violation of the Establishment Clause, whereas the first depends for its force on the Free Exercise Clause. Both draw heavily on evidence of changes in school structure, classroom behavior, and curriculum that they regard as the pernicious effects of secular humanism.

In 1963, the Supreme Court ruled in *Schempp* that required Bible reading and school prayer are unconstitutional.[12] Since then, there have been many court cases involving religious practice in public schools and the relations between public and parochial schools. One might indeed argue that God has been dismissed from the public schools, and although this seems right and proper to many Americans, it represents a genuine loss to many others. One might also point out, however, that after some of the initial fear and attendant extreme decisions, there has been something of a rapprochement between those who would keep the wall of separation tall and solid and those who would open gates and windows for the sake of better educating children and allowing them freedom of speech.[13]

Some of the most interesting and worrisome arguments go well beyond technical claims to free exercise. Extremism on both sides has made it hard for citizens to assess the situation in public schools fairly. In the late 1970s and again in 1988, for example, Mel and Norma Gabler led a blistering attack on the public school curriculum. Humanism was identified as the villain and was accused of promoting "situational ethics; evolution; sexual freedom, including public school sex education courses; and internationalism." Their later publication went further and said that humanism promotes "a Darwinian, anti-biblical, individualistic, relativistic, sexually permissive, statist, materialistic, and morally dissolute mindset."[14] On the other side, as Gilbert Sewall fairly points out, "evangelicals and fundamentalists have suffered great disrespect in the educational and popular press."[15] Called "'paleolithic spear throwers' and many other unpleasant names," they have also been accused of complicity with various racist groups and racist agendas, and these accusations are often (although not always) unfair.

None of this name-calling is helpful. Fundamentalists are not alone in noting and deploring what seems to be a general moral deterioration or at least malaise in our schools. The sticking point is identification of the cause. Fundamentalists are too quick to blame humanism. The truth is that many humanists also deplore the school's reluctance to discuss moral issues and make a commitment to moral education. But when educators in public schools try to do something in the line of moral education, they are often opposed by the very people who complain most loudly about moral bankruptcy. Complaints against programs such as Values Clarification have been around for a long time, and come from every sector, including humanist philosophers, but fundamentalist opposition to newer character education programs has been vociferous as well. Why do people object to the inculcation of virtues that they themselves advocate? The reasons vary but usually fall along the following lines: the principles or rules are not made absolute; the teaching of tolerance may include tolerance for that which should not be tolerated (for example, homosexuality); character formation is not properly a function for government; and the recommended virtues are not traced to their authority in God.

Opposition of this sort places the schools in a classic "damned if you do—damned if you don't" situation. They are called on to encourage traditional virtues such as honesty, courage, loyalty, compassion, and the like, but when they do so without crediting God (which they cannot do constitutionally), they are attacked. This dilemma hit me forcefully in an exchange with Richard Baer at an annual meeting of the American Educational Research Association. Baer spoke eloquently of the values his group espoused and, as he named them, I objected that these values were not "his" but were, in fact, widely shared. After considerable debate, I understood his point. For him and those who share his religious perspective, the values we share are *secondary*. What counts most is the worldview that sustains and justifies the values. My heart sank at this disclosure, for how would we ever succeed at moral education if we had first to agree on a worldview? Worse, if we are allowed only one worldview on which "to agree"—no compromise—how could further discussion be conducted? John Goodlad, too, points out that the best moral values of secular and religious thinkers have much in common. He quotes W. Warren Wager:

> This much, at least, is clear: If we descend from the mountain peaks of theology to the plateau of ethics, all the formulas for the spiritual unification of man converge in perfect harmony ... about these four final values—life, personality, transcendence, and love—there is no disagreement whatever in nearly the whole range of contemporary prophetic literature.[16]

I think Wager exaggerates the agreement, but he is close to what I was feeling as I listened to Baer's talk of values and virtues. One difficulty is that those who value the mountain peak over the plateau will not settle on the plateau. Another difficulty is that those of us who see this as narrow absolutism will not listen without prejudice to those who cling to the mountaintop.

The case brought by Baer and others is not easily dismissed. There is no constitutional proscription against discussing worldviews in public schools so long as students are not required to accept or affirm them. Would it satisfy the dissenters if curricula were amended to include discussion of the sources of virtue and moral law? Such a move would be in keeping with a recommendation that many of us have made to "teach the conflicts."[17] Schools would be far more interesting and educative places if we shared with our students the underlying beliefs and conflicts that have shaped the curriculum. At no point in these discussions need any teacher say, "Here is the truth," but rather, "This is a position espoused by X." It is not outlandish to suggest that high school students hear the words of great religious leaders and of secular thinkers on religion. With the inclusion of religious worldviews in the curriculum, dissenters could not claim that only a secular worldview is presented in the schools.

My guess is that this solution will satisfy neither the dissenters whose case I am considering nor the people who adamantly oppose them. The dissenters will likely object to having their view presented as one among many when they believe it is the only true view. The charge will be relativism. Opponents, who often want to avoid even the mention of religion in public schools, will object (and have objected) that teachers are not adequately prepared to teach this subject matter. Of course, if we were to take this objection seriously, we would have to abandon most of the subjects we now teach in schools. However, I want to leave open the possibility that further discussion might produce a viable compromise. The dissenters are right in complaining that the schools give short shrift to the great existential questions and almost no attention to what might be called metaphysical longing.[18]

The second prong of the attack addresses not the lack of religion in schools but what is seen as a religious monopoly. Baer and James Carper, for example, write that "it is fair to say that public schools today are saturated with religion, but of a secular and humanistic variety."[19] Using a functional definition of religion—one that defines religion in terms of "how ultimate commitments and world view convictions actually operate in the lives of individuals and communities"[20]—they claim that secular humanism is a religion. To give this claim credibility, they note that sociologists and anthropologists frequently use a functional definition, but in fact this is a matter of some dispute. Sociologists Rodney Stark and William Bainbridge give a powerful argument against using such a definition. They caution that the inclusion of antisupernatural, political creeds in religion

> makes it needlessly difficult to explore conflicts between these contrary systems of thought or to identify the rather different capacities present in each.... We are prepared to assert that there can be no wholly naturalistic religion; that a religion lacking supernatural assumptions is no religion at all.[21]

Stark and Bainbridge have a powerful argument, but Baer points to the words of John Dewey to further his claim. It is true that Dewey wanted to retain use of the adjective "religious" to describe a secular faith and commitment—faith in the capacity to better human life through inquiry and commitment to this betterment. I think Dewey was wrong, and wrong in at least two ways to do this, but it is crystal clear that he did not regard secular humanism as *a religion:*

> I should be sorry if any were misled by the frequency with which I have empha-sized the adjective "religious" to conceive of what I have said as a disguised apol-ogy for what have passed as religions. The opposition between religious values as I conceive them and religions is not to be bridged. Just because the release of these values is so important, their identification with the creeds and cults of religion must be dissolved.[22]

Dewey himself recognized the risk he was taking when he tentatively defined *God* as "this *active* relation between ideal and actual." He immediately noted that he had been warned by sympathetic critics that "the associations of the term with the supernatural are so numerous and close that any use of the word 'God' is sure to give rise to misconception and be taken as a concession to traditional ideas."[23]

It would have been better, for reasons cited by Stark and Bainbridge, if Dewey had not used the language of religion to refer to his humanism. Further, and this is the second way in which he was wrong, there is something insensitive about appropriating the language of believers to launch a scathing attack on their cen-tral beliefs. Now we in education are faced with the task of clarifying and modi-fying the words of one of our most powerful thinkers.

The strategy of Baer and others in classifying secular humanism as a religion is to argue for the protection of the Establishment Clause. But the strategy does not work well for them. It puts them in the embarrassing position of demeaning a worldview they themselves have called a religion. They would not denigrate the religion of Catholics, Jews, or Muslims. Yet, Baer writes:

> Under the banner of secular neutrality, sex education curricula and home economics texts simply assume and implicitly teach that rational behavior is self-interested be-havior. Public schools routinely indoctrinate school children with humanistic beliefs like those found in values clarification; ... these "secular" courses teach (implicitly if not always explicitly) that self-fulfillment and satisfying one's personal needs are the goals of human existence. They insist that all value judgments are subjective and matters of personal opinion. They view tradition and traditional wisdom as a hin-drance to achieving the good life.[24]

Much of this is simply untrue. Most schools today are trying hard to develop ideas of cooperation, caring, and civility, although the current demand for un-precedented levels of academic achievement is getting in the way of such human-istic purposes, and this worries many secular humanists quite as much as it does fundamentalists. Where the schools are promoting the values Baer accuses them of, they are not following the ideas of "secular humanism," certainly not the hu-manism of Dewey. There simply is no real philosophy—religious or secular—

guiding the public schools. Many who identify ourselves as humanists also deplore the fact that the schools do not address the great existential questions, ignore the great religious traditions, and fail to address metaphysical longing in constitutionally acceptable ways. But it will not do to trace all the bad things that occur in public schools to secular humanism, and if critics really believed that secular humanism is a religion, they would not make such a move.

What Might Be Done

Baer and other critics of public schools ("government" schools) want "to get the state out of the business of operating schools."[25] As part of their campaign, they refer to public schools as *government* schools. This change in language is deeply disturbing, first, because the designation "public" applied to schools has long been a term of some approbation in contrast to anything associated with government and government control. Even more disturbing, however, is the implication that the schools no longer serve a recognizable public and that, therefore, citizens need no longer concern themselves with education as a public good. Even if it is true that the schools are in a period of unparalleled struggle to serve many publics, the continued search for a solid public must remain a high priority. Dewey recognized a problem that has only grown more complex since he wrote this:

> We have the physical tools of communication as never before. The thoughts and aspirations congruous with them are not communicated, and hence are not common. Without such communication the public will remain shadowy and formless, seeking spasmodically for itself, but seizing and holding its shadow rather than its substance. Till the Great Society is converted into a Great Community, the Public will remain in eclipse. Communication can alone create a great community. Our Babel is not one of tongues but of the signs and symbols without which shared experience is impossible.[26]

What I am arguing for here is that we maintain the search for a Great Community, that we keep trying to communicate across the lines created by different worldviews. In the continued search for a Great Community, the public school plays a central role.

Baer and Carper (and many others in the broad-based campaign to reduce the hegemony of the public schools) recommend a voucher system that would enable parents to choose their children's schools. It is beyond the scope of this chapter to address the many problems with vouchers, but two are pertinent here.

First, vouchers should not be instituted in response to the "double taxation" argument. In recent months, countless speeches at public meetings have begun with the words, "Why should I pay for ... [schooling that does not affirm my beliefs]?" The answer to this question must be that we all pay for public schools, whether we use them personally or not, because education is a *public good,* and we care about the education of all children, not just our own. Parents who believe that public schooling undermines the free exercise of their religion must either work together to finance alternative schooling or (better) work with the schools to find a satisfactory compromise.

There is a parallel here to tax-supported health plans. Some people argue strenuously against these, too, not only on the grounds that such plans tax many citizens for services they will never use but that state-run medicine leads inevitably to mediocrity. This widely expressed objection to "socialized medicine" echoes Mill's early concern about state-run schools. The claim about mediocrity in medicine is an empirical one and seems, on present evidence, to be false, but pursuing the matter here would take us too far afield. Few would argue that a healthy citizenry is *not* a common good, but many differ on how this goal is to be achieved.

Similarly, most people agree that education is a public good—that is, that an educated citizenry benefits everyone. But why can't individuals be left free to choose forms of schooling consonant with their own deepest beliefs? The answer here has to be that public schooling serves the best interests of a liberal democracy and its individual members. It provides the sites for demonstration of democratic life in miniature; it brings together people and views that might otherwise remain outside the domain of public communication.

There is another way in which public schools serve the public good. In design at least, they are committed to the fullest education of every individual. Speaking of the purpose of public institutions, Dewey wrote:

> That purpose is to set free and to develop the capacities of human individuals without respect to race, sex, class or economic status. And this is all one with that the test of their value is the extent to which they educate every individual into the full stature of his possibility. Democracy has many meanings, but if it has a moral meaning, it is found in resolving that supreme test of all political institutions and industrial arrangements shall be the contribution they make to the all-around growth of every member of society.[27]

I'll return to this important theme a bit later.

But what if the public schools do not live up to the purpose described by Dewey?

Rejection of the double taxation argument does not imply rejection of all voucher plans. A means-tested program that would allow poor parents to escape demonstrably bad schools might still be entertained.[28] But all able citizens would have to pay for this. The good achieved would be a public, not a private good. The need to provide such plans should be taken as a heavy reproof of the existing public schools and should trigger serious reform.

A second set of arguments that must be rejected is ideological. As noted above, parents who object to the worldview projected by public schools must avail themselves of alternatives already available. Even this method of escape from public schools has been questioned in the past, but the right of parents to choose nonpublic schools (at their own expense) was firmly established in 1925.[29] However, it is still appropriate to ask on what grounds this should be allowed. Amy Gutmann has argued that a "democrat must reject the simplest reason for sanctioning private schools—that parents have a 'natural right' to control the education of their children."[30] She believes, as I do, that education is a task for both parents and state. The state, parents, and children all have interests that must be protected.

Even if the claim to a "natural right" is rejected, however, a recognition that many citizens believe in this natural right cannot be brushed aside. In a community composed of many differing beliefs, no majority or powerful minority should ignore the deeply held beliefs of others unless they are so harmful that the community must be protected against them. Gutmann would protect against the loss of democratic values by insisting that all schools—public and private—teach these basic values.

But there may be ways in which the public schools could be more responsive to the concerns of parents who have religious objections to some of what is taught. Baer and Carper, although expressing a preference for separation of school and state, suggest a "released time" plan that might be workable. Under such a plan, children would be taught during school day released time some of the ethically charged subjects (for example, sex education, values, worldview) by religious leaders in groups chosen by their parents. This kind of plan would be very like one that seems to work in much of Europe. Children might elect a secular ethics course or a religious one. There should be a way to work out such a plan, and its great merit would be to keep as many children as possible in public schools.

Keeping as many children as possible in the public schools is in the interest of a liberal democracy; allowing the inclusion of explicitly religious worldviews in public education (strictly by choice) might satisfy the legitimate concern of parents who want to take primary responsibility for the education of their children. But the needs and rights of the children must also be considered. This is the concern I expressed at the outset and again in quoting Dewey on the purpose of public education—one that is too often overlooked in liberal thinking.

Public education has served as a check on the power of parents, and this is another powerful reason for maintaining it. Feminists are right to be concerned about the deprivation of rights many girls would suffer if they were schooled entirely in some religious settings. Further, by its very nature, a liberal democracy depends for its legitimacy on the continuing and voluntary affirmation of a critical citizenry. This means, and Dewey was clearly right on this, that students must be encouraged to inquire, to object, to think critically.[31] Thus, the state has a compelling interest to enforce forms of education that will produce such a citizenry. It also has an obligation to see that all of its young citizens are well informed about their rights as well as their responsibilities.

In exploring ways in which a liberal state might accommodate illiberal groups, William Galston has acknowledged that the state must educate for tolerance:

The state may establish educational guidelines pursuant to this compelling interest. What it may not do is prescribe curricula or pedagogic practices that require or strongly invite students to become skeptical or critical of their own ways of life.[32]

I think that this rather extraordinary recommendation has to be rejected. The whole notion of liberal democracy requires that we "strongly invite" students to examine their ways of life, but it also requires that they have a fair chance to understand both their own and other ways of life. The publicly controlled part of schooling need not engage in the explicit criticism of religious belief, but it must promote critical thinking, and it would be disingenuous on the part of advocates to deny that critical thinking might "spill over" into areas not explicitly addressed. Of course, it might. Such spillover is the great hope of liberal education, and too often we are disappointed that it does not occur.

It need not, and should not, be the purpose of schooling in a liberal democracy to support some groups and undermine others (assuming the legitimacy of all), but as Will Kymlicka has suggested, it is not a violation of neutrality if some practices, chosen for compelling reasons, have the unintended effect of weakening some groups.[33] Critical thinking widely adopted (at the secondary school level) might indeed weaken some religious groups. But without it, the public schools really will have given up their central mission in a democracy. That mission has long been to support the health of democratic communities and to do so by promoting the "all-around growth of every member of society."

Responsible school people, together with parents, should decide at what ages critical thinking will be strongly encouraged. My own sense is that children of all ages, engaged in age-appropriate discussions, should be encouraged to ask, "How, why, and on what grounds?"[34] But serious discussion of the great existential questions should probably occur at the secondary school level—probably in grades ten to twelve. By then, students should have a fair understanding of the basic teachings in their own religious or secular framework and, if they have been educated earlier to ask for reasons on less controversial matters, they should be ready to join the "immortal conversation."

It is important for both educators and students to understand that critical thinking does not involve only analysis and criticism or, if it is so limited, it is not enough. If we are committed to a search for community, then the best thinking must also include appreciation and caring. The purpose of critical thinking need not be destructive. Students should learn about commitment that survives criticism and doubt and come to appreciate well-considered positions very different from their own.[35]

In conclusion, I think public school advocates can concede much to religious dissenters. The schools have largely abdicated their role in examining the great existential questions, and they do not give fair and appropriate respect to our religious traditions as powerful answers to existential questions. I would, of course, favor a curriculum that presents a full range of responses to existential questions. Discussion should continue on ways to reconcile secular and religious views without denying the very differences that separate them. Finally, any plans advanced to accomplish this reconciliation should provide adequate protection not only for state and parents but also for children, and that's a powerful reason for keeping children in the public schools and teaching them to think critically.

Notes

I wish to thank Milton Fisk, Chris Higgins, Nancy Holstrom, and Charlene Haddock Seigfried for helpful comments on an earlier draft.

1. See John Stuart Mill, *On Liberty* and *Utilitarianism* (New York: Bantam Books, 1993). In *On Liberty*, Mill contends that the harm principle does not apply to children. He also says that the liberal state has a right to insist on education, but he expresses concern about state-run schools. The Socrates/pig comparison appears in *Utilitarianism*, p. 148. In contrast to Mill, Bertrand Russell expressed great reservations about compulsory education and felt that liberalism probably could not justify such coercion. See Alan Ryan, *Bertrand Russell: A Political Life* (New York: Hill and Wang, 1988), 13.

2. See Nancy Fraser, "Social Justice in the Age of Identity Politics: Redistribution, Recognition, and Participation," Tanner Lecture on Human Values, Stanford University, 1997; also Nel Noddings, *Caring: A Feminine Approach to Ethics and Moral Education* (Berkeley: University of California Press, 1984).

3. Jacob G. Hornberger, Introduction to *Separating School and State* by Sheldon Richman (Fairfax, Va.: Future of Freedom Foundation, 1994), xii.

4. Alan Peshkin, *God's Choice: The Total World of a Fundamentalist Christian School* (Chicago: University of Chicago Press, 1988), 127.

5. Ibid., 150.

6. Ibid., 298.

7. *Mozert v. Hawkins County Public Schools*, 827 F. 2d 1058 (6th Cir. 1987). For a comprehensive discussion of this case and its effects on a community, see Stephen Bates, *Battleground: One Mother's Crusade, the Religious Right, and the Struggle for our Classrooms* (New York: Poseidon Press, 1993).

8. Quoted in Louis Fischer, David Schemmel, and Cynthia Kelly, *Teachers and the Law*, 5th ed. (New York: Longman, 1999), 444.

9. *Wisconsin v. Yoder*, 406 U.S. 205 (1971). For a thoughtful discussion of both this case and *Mozert*, see Stephen Macedo, "Liberal Civic Education and Religious Fundamentalism: The Case of God v. John Rawls?" *Ethics* 105 (3), 1995, 468–496.

10. See John Dewey, *Democracy and Education* (New York: Macmillan, 1916), 87 and passim.

11. For a discussion of the Douglas dissent, see Macedo, "Liberal Civic Education."

12. *Abington School District v. Schempp*, 374 v.s. 203 (1963).

13. See the discussion in Leonard W. Levy, *The Establishment Clause: Religion and the First Amendment* (New York: Macmillan, 1986); see also Fischer, Schimmel, and Kelly, *Teachers and the Law*.

14. Quoted in Gilbert J. Sewall, "Religion and the Textbooks," in *Curriculum, Religion, and Public Education*, ed. James T. Sears with James C. Carper (New York: Teachers College Press, 1998), 76.

15. Ibid., 74.

16. Quoted in John I. Goodlad, "Democracy, Education, and Community," in *Democracy, Education, and the Schools*, ed. Roger Soder (San Francisco: Jossey-Bass, 1996), 102.

17. See Nel Noddings, *Educating for Intelligent Belief or Unbelief* (New York: Teachers College Press, 1993).

18. I have discussed the metaphysical longing shared by believers and unbelievers in Joan Montgomery Halford, "Longing for the Sacred in Schools: A Conversation with Nel Noddings," *Educational Leadership*, December 1998–January 1999, 28–32.

19. Richard A. Baer and James C. Carper, "Spirituality and the Public Schools: An Evangelical Perspective," *Educational Leadership*, December 1998–January 1999, 34.

20. Ibid.

21. Rodney Stark and William Sims Bainbridge, *The Future of Religion* (Berkeley: University of California Press, 1985), 3.

22. John Dewey, *A Common Faith* in *The Later Works, Vol. 9: 1933–1934* (Carbondale, Ill.: Southern Illinois University Press, 1989), 20.

23. Ibid., 35.

24. Richard A. Baer, "A Functional View of Religion," in *Curriculum, Religion, and Public Education*, ed. Sears, 108, 109.

25. Baer and Carper, "Spirituality and the Public Schools," 35. The same call is made by Richman, *Separating School and State*. For an earlier argument along the same lines, see Stephen Arons, *Compelling Belief: The Culture of American Schooling* (New York: McGraw-Hill, 1983).

26. John Dewey, *The Public and Its Problems* (Chicago: Swallow Press, 1927), 142.

27. John Dewey, *Reconstruction in Philosophy*, vol. 12, *The Middle Works* (Carbondale: Southern Illinois University Press, 1988), 186.

28. For a discussion of democratically defensible voucher plans, see Kenneth R. Howe, *Understanding Equal Educational Opportunity* (New York: Teachers College Press, 1997).

29. *Pierce v. Society of Sisters*, 268 U.S. 510 (1925). See the discussion in Fischer, Schimmel, and Kelly, *Teachers and the Law*.

30. Amy Gutmann, *Democratic Education* (Princeton: Princeton University Press, 1987), 116.

31. Dewey was not alone in this recommendation. Countless philosophers including Socrates, Cicero, John Stuart Mill, Israel Scheffler, and Harvey Siegel have argued for self-examination and critical thinking.

32. William Galston, "Two Concepts of Liberalism," *Ethics* 105 (3), 1995, 529.

33. See Will Kymlicka, *Liberalism, Community, and Culture* (Oxford: Oxford University Press, 1989).

34. See the discussion of "manner" in teaching in Israel Scheffler, *The Language of Education* (Springfield, Ill.: Charles C. Thomas, 1960).

35. For an excellent and moving example (the commitment of a Mormon feminist), see Judith Dushku, "The Mormon Caregiving Network," in *Caregiving*, ed. Suzanne Gordon, Patricia Benner, and Nel Noddings (Philadelphia: University of Pennsylvania Press, 1996), 278–291.

The Color of "Choice"

Bob Peterson and Barbara Miner

Conservatives use the rhetoric of "choice" to portray vouchers as a vehicle for leveling the educational playing field for communities of color. Nothing could be further from the truth. Just ask Wisconsin state representative Polly Williams (D-Milwaukee).

Williams, who is African American, became a national spokesperson for vouchers in 1990 when she spearheaded a much-publicized, but very limited, voucher initiative for low-income students in Milwaukee. But recently Williams told the *Boston Globe* that "I knew that once they [white Republicans and right-wing foundations] figured they didn't need me as a black cover, they would try to take control of vouchers and use them for their own selfish interest."

In the last eight years, Williams has seen how Republicans and other conservative power brokers use the rhetoric of equal opportunity to mask their real goal of privatizing Milwaukee's public schools and removing schools from public oversight, predominantly to the benefit of white families with money and privilege.

Why the Right Loves Vouchers

Just about every group on the right loves vouchers, a system in which the government gives students a "voucher" that can be used to pay for their education at any private or public school that will accept them. The religious right sees vouchers as a way to batter down the separation between church and state and to make the public pay for fundamentalist religious schools. Free-marketeers see vouchers as a way to privatize public education—opening up a $600 billion market and removing education from the messy realm of democratic control. For the libertarians, vouchers are a way to dismantle the biggest and most important public institution in this country.

All love the fact that vouchers transfer money away from public schools into private schools. Private schools are not subject to hard-

(continues)

(continued)

won antidiscrimination or accessibility laws, educational quality standards, separation of church and state mandates, or public safety and environmental safeguards. They are accountable only to their owners.

Take the case of Tenasha Taylor. Tenasha, an African American student at University School, a private high school in Milwaukee, criticized the school as racist in a speech assigned by her English teacher. The school suspended her and asked her not to return the following fall. Tenasha sued on the grounds of free speech. The court ruled against her, saying: "It is an elementary principle of constitutional law that the protections afforded by the Bill of Rights do not apply to private actors such as University School. Generally, restrictions on constitutional rights that would be protected at a public high school ... need not be honored at a private high school."

Contrary to the claims of its supporters, privatization of schools through vouchers would greatly aggravate the existing problems of racial inequality and poor standards in the public schools.

Milton Friedman and Vouchers

Conservative economist Milton Friedman, infamous for his free-market economic blueprints for the Chilean dictatorship of August Pinochet, initiated the concept of vouchers in the 1950s. At the time, only white segregationists rallied to his support. They established the first publicly funded school vouchers in the United States in Georgia in 1956 for the explicit purpose of circumventing the historic *Brown* desegregation decision of the same year by helping white people attend private academies.

Eventually, the Virginia program and similar plans passed by segregationist southern legislatures in the 1950s were ruled unconstitutional. But following the rightward drift of national politics in recent decades, vouchers were resurrected. This time, voucher supporters have tried to appeal not only to their traditional white conservative base, but to people of color who are, not surprisingly, also dissatisfied with public education. As voucher advocate Daniel McGroarty put it in a strategy paper for the Milton and Rose D. Friedman Foundation, limited voucher programs targeting poor families

(continues)

(continued)

should be used as a "beachhead; a way to win and hold new ground in the long march to universal school choice."

The Milwaukee Proving Ground

The Milwaukee-based, right-wing Bradley Foundation and other well-heeled voucher advocates chose the Milwaukee public schools as the proving ground for this strategy.

In 1990, the Wisconsin state legislature passed a limited voucher program for Milwaukee that was tailored to gain support from minorities. The program allowed a few hundred low-income children in Milwaukee to use publicly funded vouchers to attend a specified handful of nonreligious private schools. The principal argument for this program was that it would allow low-income African American students to attend good private schools. And, indeed, the program has been quite popular in black Milwaukee.

Having established this "beachhead," voucher proponents are now moving to implement their full agenda. Recently, the program was opened to religious schools and was expanded to include up to 15,000 students. In June 1998, the Wisconsin Supreme Court ruled that the expansion does not violate the separation of church and state and the U.S. Supreme Court refused to hear the appeal, thereby leaving it intact. The ink was barely dry on the Wisconsin Supreme Court decision when Milwaukee mayor Ken Norquist called for an end to the income cap for those receiving vouchers, currently set at about $23,000 a year for a family of four.

14

Voting, Democratic Political Action, and the Public Good

Kurt Nutting

Voting is at the heart of modern democracy.[1] Whether the vote is cast for candidates seeking executive and legislative offices in a representative democracy, or on a legislative proposal directly, the people's will is expressed through their votes.[2] Not only is voting the basis for the sort of democracy we experience in modern political life, but proposals for extending the scope of democratic decision-making beyond the liberal state to other arenas of life, or for making existing political practices more thoroughly democratic, themselves typically presuppose voting mechanisms[3] in all but the smallest and most homogeneous groups.[4]

It is perhaps not too strong a point to say that voting and elections, and thus democratic politics more generally, are in a state of crisis in the United States. By the late 1990s, the proportion of the eligible population that cast a vote in elections for national, state, or local office had been declining for thirty years and was at a historically low level, the lowest since the period immediately following the extension of the suffrage to women in 1920 or even, on some measures, since the suffrage was extended generally to the white male population during the Jacksonian period, in the 1820s and 1830s.[5] Voter turnout is consistently lower in the United States than in any other economically advanced democracy.[6]

These low levels of voting do not express satisfaction or contentment, however; in scientific surveys for thirty years, for example, more than half of those polled have said that they believe the government is run for the sake of a few big interests and not for people generally,[7] at a time when economic inequality has risen, poverty levels seem resistant to the effects of economic growth, parts of the welfare state created from the 1930s to the 1960s are being dismantled,[8] and more and more of the government's economic policies are being made by the agencies most resistant to democratic pressures, like the Federal Reserve System.[9]

The nonvoters are, moreover, disproportionately of lower socioeconomic class; this "class skew" of voter turnout in the United States is the greatest of any advanced democracy. The class skew of the U.S. electorate contributes to the class skew of U.S. public policy; it cannot be a coincidence that the only government in the industrial world that does not guarantee health care to all its citizens is chosen by the most disproportionately affluent electorate in the industrial world.[10]

The sources of this crisis are, no doubt, multiple. But one of them may be a failure of understanding. Despite its centrality to both our democratic practices and our democratic aspirations, and despite its familiar and seemingly simple role, we don't fully understand voting and other forms of political action at a theoretical level, and this lack of theoretical understanding leads to adverse consequences in practice.

In this chapter I want to begin to develop a richer theoretical and normative understanding of electoral democracy, with the ultimate aim of using that richer theory to help expose those problems in our current practices that are caused or exaggerated by our theoretical misunderstandings.

My central contention is that voting has a dual nature; intrinsically, it is simultaneously both an individual, and a social or collective, action. When we overlook one or the other of these two aspects, we are apt to misunderstand our own political action. In particular, in the United States there has been a persistent tendency, by conservatives, liberals, and radicals alike, to focus only on the individual aspects, and to overlook the social or collective aspects, of voting. By failing to see that voting and other political action in a democracy constitute a public good, which in turn creates a further set of public goods, we denigrate the potential in democratic politics and acquiesce in an insufficiently democratic way of life.

In particular, I want to defend the idea that democratic political action is the basis of an important public good—the creation of shared understandings and meanings regarding political institutions and policies—and that this good does not, and cannot, exist except as the result of collective action. That is, when it votes an electorate acts collectively in a meaningful way; it creates a set of shared understandings about its action that ordinarily is understood by voters and candidates alike. In a healthy democracy this socially created and socially shared meaning shapes and guides the formation and execution of public policies. In arguing this I reject what I take to be the dominant understanding of democracy in liberal social science and political philosophy, an understanding of democracy and democratic politics that is at its core individualistic, instrumentalist, and, paradoxically, antipolitical.

My argument begins in Part 2 with a sketch of the multiple interests, both individual and social, implicated by a right to vote. I then use the political scientists' notions of critical elections and partisan realignments to illustrate the sense of an election having a "social meaning." In Part 3 the complex account of voting is contrasted with the narrower account, familiar in theories of politics that draw on neoclassical economics, which presupposes an account of human rational action based on instrumental individualism. In Part 4 I show that individualism and instrumentalism, despite their significant theoretical drawbacks, have been unspoken but powerful components of recent U.S. Supreme Court decisions interpreting the constitutional doctrines of the right to vote.

The Varied Social Functions of Elections and the Complexity of Electoral Rights

In a representative government, those who make policy are, directly or indirectly, chosen through the means of popular elections. Electoral rights, thus, concern the rights people have in regard to this process of electing the government. In the classical theories of representative government, elections are the central (though by no means the exclusive) means by which the ruled are (potentially and, sometimes, also in actuality) able to control the rulers. The set of electoral rights structures the process of popular election, and so in any particular political system the ability of the ruled to control the rulers depends upon how the electoral rights have been formulated and how they can be exercised.

To determine the appropriate content of the electoral rights in a democracy, I begin with a truism of political theory—ultimately, that the function of elections in a genuinely representative government is to provide a mechanism through which the ruled can exercise control over the power of the state. Only by winning an election can at least the most important officials secure the legal title to exercise the powers and privileges of office; in legal and political theory, the election serves to transfer legal and political power from the electorate to the officials, and without an election that power may not be exercised.

In what ways is it possible, through the process of elections, to bring the delegation of power from electorate to officials potentially and actually under the effective control of the electorate? How can the voters use elections to control the officials and policies of the government? An election in a modern polity is an enormously complex social phenomenon, but we can identify at least some of the aspects of electoral politics that operate to make popular control of the government possible.

At a minimum, control of the government through a system of popular elections presupposes that the conditions under which the people form their judgments about policy and administration are relatively favorable to free and rational thought, so that the judgments made can be the best possible given the limitations of available knowledge, time, and energy; that the (actual and potential) lawmakers and administrators are able to make proposals in response to popular judgments; and that there are moral or material incentives for the (actual and potential) lawmakers and administrators to make such proposals. Voting rights should be (though they too often are not) structured to create conditions under which these presuppositions are true. The right to vote, as the right that protects the people's ability to use elections to control the power of the state, is more than the bare "right to mark a piece of paper and drop it in a box,"[11] it is a right protecting the entire electoral process through which popular control over the state is exercised.[12]

The Interest in Rational Deliberation

How do elections (in the ideal if not in the actual case) produce these beneficial results? First, an election serves as the occasion for heightened public discussion, debate, and deliberation about the past and future course of public policy; the campaign preceding the actual vote gives shape and meaning to that act of choice. An election without a campaign beforehand is, in a very real sense, not a legitimate election at all. In a genuine campaign, voters and candidates participate in a many-sided examination of the state of public affairs. The importance of this discussion and deliberation underscores the function of free speech and a free press in a representative government, as Meiklejohn[13] and others have emphasized; without wide opportunities for discussion, debate, and deliberation the election will not be an expression of the electors' considered judgments but (all too often) of top-of-the-head prejudices and whims (whose moral claims over the content of public policy, as a matter of democratic theory, are presumably less weighty). In one respect, then, electoral democracy is (or ideally ought to be) educational. It is worth mentioning that deliberation, debate, and discussion are intrinsically social activities; they cannot take place at an individual level but require the participation of an entire group. We will refer to this function as deliberative[14] or rational, and American constitutional law has formally recognized its importance.[15]

The Interest in Political Competition

Second, an election serves to force candidates for public office to seek the electorate's votes on a competitive basis with other candidates, before they can exercise public power. That is, a candidate may exercise power only if the electorate judges that the operations of the government will be better with that candidate exercising power than they would be with any available alternatives, all things considered. Just as consumer sovereignty in a free and competitive product market is said, by neoclassical microeconomic theory, to lead to continued improvements in the consumer's well-being through a ceaseless process of innovation spurred by competition for the consumer's money, so is popular sovereignty in a free and competitive electoral "market" said, by the theorists of public choice, to lead to continued improvements in the public's well-being through a ceaseless process of policy innovation spurred by competition for the people's votes. We will refer to this function, for short, as instrumental or competitive,[16] and as with the deliberative function, the courts have explicitly recognized its importance.[17]

The Interest in Popular Consent

Third, in addition to the creation of a forum for popular discussion and deliberation on matters of public policy, and the creation of a competitive struggle for political power, a system of popular campaigns and elections is itself the public representation, in a somewhat ritualized form, of the status of the government as periodically legitimized by the participation of the people, on the one hand, and of the status of the voters, recognized as full and equal members of the polity, on the other.[18] Consent occurs on at least two levels: we consent (or not) to the authority of the government generally, and we consent (or not) to the specific policies proposed and adopted by particular elected officials at a given time. Voting implicates consent at both of these levels. These public recognitions of the moral status of the government and its policies as ultimately resting on the wills of the members of a free and equal electorate are a further way in which elections are a popular mechanism for exercising popular control over the policies of the government. We will refer to this political function, for short, as legitimizing, and this too is firmly a part of American constitutional law.[19]

The Interest in Self-Expression

And fourth, in voting people may have various noninstrumental goals in mind, which we may for brevity refer to as symbolic. They vote to make a point, send a message, or express a moral conviction; to express solidarity with their class or ethnic group or co-religionists; to defy those in authority; and so on. Furthermore, campaigns and elections are diverting and entertaining as well as educational. We will refer to this function (or set of functions), for short, as expressive[20] or symbolic, and note that expression has also merited recognition by the courts as a constitutionally weighty interest in voting.[21]

The Relation Between
Electoral Rights and Elections

I make no suggestion here that this listing is by any means an exhaustive one, but only that these four aspects of electoral politics are in fact significant and that paying attention to each of them will help us understand in greater depth what we do when we hold elections or set up a political system employing elections, and therefore what is the role of voting rights in the legal system of a representative democracy.[22] If the rough outline of this account is correct,[23] then the content of legal voting rights should be (at least in part) explicable in terms of the social and political functions of electoral politics. That is, political rights should at a minimum serve to protect and guarantee the deliberative/rational, instrumental/competitive, legitimizing, and expressive/symbolic aspects of popular voting.

"Critical Elections"

The deliberation, debate, and discussion inherent in an electoral campaign are not just the colorful preliminaries to the voting, but give it meaning. What we (collectively) say about our votes, what reasons are offered or rejected for voting as we do, give our votes a social meaning.[24] Despite the often issueless character of American elections, in at least the so-called critical elections[25] both contemporaries and historians have a fairly good idea about what I am terming the social meaning of the votes cast in an election. In the context of American politics in 1860, for example, a vote for Abraham Lincoln was a vote in support of the political agenda offered by the new Republican Party, which emphasized restricting the scope of slavery in the western territories; that is, it was at least in some general sense an antislavery vote. It had, in other words, a fairly coherent meaning in the political context of the time.

Similarly, in 1896, a vote for William McKinley had the meaning of rejecting the anticorporate demands of the southern and western agrarians; in 1936, a vote for Franklin D. Roosevelt had the meaning of endorsing the general thrust of the New Deal. Sometimes political analysts and historians refer to this process of an election having or lacking a particular meaning in terms of a "mandate"—sometimes it is generally agreed that a winning candidate or party has a mandate to carry out a particular sort of innovative agenda, to make certain sorts of policy initiatives, but on other occasions no such mandate is conferred because the shared understandings of the campaign and the vote are too divergent or too limited.

Social Meaning ...

The shared meaning of a political campaign and an election is created by what people write and say and do about it, and the extent to which these understandings motivate or affect the actual distribution of votes on election day. Public speakers, especially candidates for public office, play a crucial role in this process. But the discussion that gives rise to shared understandings is not confined to candidates or public officials (or to their agents, such as those who write and produce campaign advertising or those who canvass door to door on their behalf). Religious leaders, business and labor leaders, educators, and the news media, as well as ordinary voters, are part of this process. We also look at the pattern of votes cast to determine an election's meaning—a shift by some group of voters from one party to another, or an unusually large or small vote for minor parties, are all part of what we understand of an electorate's action.[26]

If, adapting the venerable tradition of the social contract, we analogize voting to contracting, for a vote to count as some sort of consent it must be understood, or understandable, as such by the parties to the contract (the citizenry, on the one hand, and the elected officials they choose with their votes, on the other). Voting legitimizes the exercise of governmental authority because the vote authorizes the public official, once elected, to act in particular ways that are (more or less) understood beforehand.[27] On the contractarian model, a vote doesn't simply elect a person to office; to some extent it also directs that person as to what they may or may not do while holding that office. Of course, it doesn't follow that office-holders always do what they are expected to do, nor that voters don't sometimes change their minds about what they want their elected officials to do; and, of course, changed circumstances sometimes make it inappropriate to act in accordance with such prior expectations. But it is ordinarily taken as a serious criticism of an elected official that their actions depart significantly from the expectations held by the citizenry prior to the election.

A recent example of this can be seen in the midterm congressional elections of 1998. The Republicans, as the party "out" of the White House, were expected to significantly increase their numbers in the House of Representatives as the out party historically had. Immediately prior to the election, the Republican House began to hold hearings in preparation for impeaching President Clinton. When the election results were in, the Republicans had lost several House seats rather than gained any; most commentators understood this result as the electorate refusing to agree to the House Republican agenda of impeaching the president. The fact that when the lame-duck House did vote for articles of impeachment it aroused a storm of public opposition, and that the president's approval in public-opinion surveys actually rose to record highs following the House vote, supports this understanding of the 1998 election's "meaning."

The Rational Choice
Theory of Voting

It may be helpful to contrast the view of electoral politics sketched above with a more explicitly individualist and instrumentalist one, an account of electoral politics that in one way or another has become quite influential in empirical political science and in the law. This theory sees voting as having only one function—to maximize the voter's individual self-interest, or what I referred to above as the instrumental or competitive function of voting—and this presents theorists with a puzzle about the nature of democratic government. The puzzle is familiar in the literature of rational choice; there it is known as the "paradox of voting."

Popular voting in a democracy is often conceptualized by social scientists as a species of rational choice, on a parallel with the behavior of buyers and sellers in a market. Theoretical discussion of democratic collective choice is thus dominated, in this tradition, by the individual rational-choice paradigm familiar from neo-classical microeconomic theory. On this account, rationality consists in maximizing one's (expected) individual welfare, or acting in such a way as to satisfy as many of one's preferences as possible;[28] collective rationality is aggregated from the individual cases. Derived from our understanding of rational behavior in a market economy, this account of rationality presupposes, at a deep level, a theory of human action that is individualist.[29]

As a way of understanding such collective actions in a democratic society as marching, picketing, striking, joining a reformist or revolutionary movement, or even simply voting, the sort of self-interested instrumental rationality familiar from microeconomics and rational-choice theory is incomplete at best and positively misleading at worst. Normative democratic theory, for example, has traditionally emphasized the role of the public interest in shaping collective decisions, and rather than being wholly assimilated to economic life, political life (at its best, anyway) is contrasted with self-interested commerce. At least prima facie, moral considerations are prominent (if not always dominant) in the ways people make political decisions, much more than in the making of economic decisions.[30]

To put the point somewhat differently, it is notorious that the rational-choice paradigm has a very difficult time explaining, not only why particular people act collectively as they do, but more generally why anyone ever bothers to act collectively at all.

For the moment, let's use the act of voting to stand for a wider range of democratic actions.[31] Given plausible assumptions about the likelihood of a single vote being decisive in a particular election and the expected utility to be gained or lost as a result of one candidate or another winning, it seems that for almost anyone behaving as rational-choice theory predicts, it will be rational to do something else besides vote on election day.[32] As rational-choice theorists sometimes put it, for most people in most elections the expected utility of voting is, given the tiny odds of having one's individual vote decide the outcome of the election, much less than the expected utility of not voting, given the odds of being struck by a car and killed going to or from the polling place.

And yet, of course, millions and millions of people in democratic societies do in fact vote, sometimes in the face of threats to life or limb aimed at them specifically as voters.[33] Either voting is a sort of massively irrational action on the part of many or most adults,[34] including many of the best-educated ones, or the theorists have made a mistake.[35] Like neo-Ptolemaic astronomers adding epicycles to their original model of planetary motion,[36] rational-choice theorists have been quite inventive in recasting their theories so they will conform to observed reality and our ordinary beliefs about political action.[37] But, of course, there is another possibility—that the premises of rational-choice theory are not the best place from which to start in developing a theory of rational action in electoral democracies.

Instrumentalism and Individualism
in the Constitutional Theory of Voting

Many of the faults of the U.S. electoral system, and hence of the public policy that the elected government creates, can be traced to deep-seated structural features, many of them a direct result of the ways the legal system organizes political participation. Ultimately, the ways the Constitution is understood by the Supreme Court has a profound influence on the structure of the electoral system. In a wide range of cases about voting and elections, the Supreme Court has presupposed that when people campaign and vote, they are acting as individuals with fixed beliefs and desires employing instrumentalist reasoning, and not also as members of larger social collectivities who sometimes act noninstrumentally, seeking ends other than or in addition to the maximization of their own utilities, and whose beliefs and preferences are open to revision and change upon education and reflection. That is to say, that in deciding whether regulations affecting the right to vote are constitutionally valid, the Supreme Court frequently has employed the rational-choice account of voting, a theory which, as I noted above, cannot even make sense of why people vote in the first place. As a result, the Supreme Court has reduced the level of protection afforded to voting rights.

To illustrate this contention, I will discuss a series of court decisions regarding voter registration, the regulation of political parties and candidate nominations, and the regulation of spending on political campaigns. I argue that the existing individualist and instrumentalist understanding of voting unnecessarily narrows the scope of voting rights and, hence, narrows the political possibilities of our democracy.

Voter Registration and the
Individualist Conception of the Vote

In forty-nine of the fifty states,[38] plus the District of Columbia, a legal precondition for casting a valid ballot is that the person casting that vote first be registered to vote, now typically a month in advance of election day. The all-but-universal practice in the United States is that registering to vote is done personally by the prospective individual voter, a direct contrast to the practice in many other democracies, where registration of the entire electorate is the responsibility not of the individual voters but of some public authority. Political scientists are in general agreement that so-called personal rather than impersonal voter registration of the U.S. variety reduces voter turnout substantially, though the precise extent of the reduction is disputed.[39]

Although now taken for granted in the United States, personal registration was adopted only after a long period of political struggle. When compulsory personal registration was originally introduced—in most states, between about 1890 and 1920—it was seen as a device for reducing voter turnout, especially along class and ethnic lines. Since voting, like the freedoms of speech and press, has long been held to be a fundamental right under the Constitution[40] the extraordinary character of personal voter registration requirements can be seen by noting that requiring people who wish to speak or publish on political matters to register in advance with the state would clearly be in violation of the First Amendment as an "abridgment" of our free-expression rights;[41] but advance voter registration is seen as a mere "regulation" of the right to vote that does not thereby "abridge" it.[42]

In the early days of compulsory personal registration, some state courts did in fact strike down the requirement as an abridgment of the state constitutional right to vote, and in some cases state constitutions had to be amended specifically to allow for the practice.[43] In this century, however, the courts have not seen even very restrictive voter registration laws as violating the constitutional voting rights of the people; these laws must satisfy only the weakest test of constitutionality, a test of "reasonableness," rather than pass the stronger test of "strict scrutiny," the test usually applied to state actions or regulations impinging on constitutionally protected fundamental rights.[44]

Personal registration requirements are individualistic in that they require that each individual, rather than the collectivity (e.g., an agency of the state) assume the burden of registering to vote. The effect of this individualistic requirement is a significantly smaller active electorate: that is, it functions in such a way that where it operates, many fewer people vote.[45] Moreover, in the context of modern U.S. society, these "missing" voters are disproportionately nonwhite and of lower socioeconomic status. With a less-individualistic analysis of voting rights, the courts could see existing voter-registration systems for what they are—a state-instituted device for keeping millions of people from exercising their rights to vote and, as such, an abridgment of that right. A state institution whose operation discourages some people from exercising a fundamental constitutional right should, ordinarily, be subject to a constitutional challenge under the equal protection clause of the Fourteenth Amendment, but such challenges to personal voter registration requirements have not succeeded because of the courts' individualistic assumptions about the vote.[46]

Write-In Voting and the Instrumentalist Conception of the Vote

Until the late nineteenth century voting in the United States was on an unofficial ballot, a ballot printed and distributed to voters by the political parties and, occasionally, by independent candidates, or was sometimes a ballot prepared by the individual voters themselves. It was perfectly legal to add names to these unofficial ballots by scratching out one candidate's name and writing in a replacement. When the unofficial ballot was replaced by the official or "Australian" ballot, there were concerns that the official ballot would eliminate this possibility of write-in voting.[47] When lawsuits challenged the constitutionality of the Australian ballot acts under state constitutional provisions protecting the rights to free and equal elections, or to the right to vote, some courts cited the continued availability of the write-in vote on the official ballot as one of the grounds for upholding the constitutionality of the new system.

All the states now use official ballots, and in most of them the ballot still contains spaces for casting write-ins. In several cases in the past thirty years, following the lead of the turn-of-the-century state courts deciding on the constitutionality of state official ballot laws, the U.S. Supreme Court has cited the availability of write-in voting in turning down challenges to state restrictions on the access of minor parties and independent candidates to the official ballot.[48]

Ironically, however, in the early 1990s, a hundred years after the official ballots were introduced on the condition that they continue to permit voters to write in their own preferred candidates, the Supreme Court rejected a federal constitutional challenge to one of the few state election laws that does not allow voters to cast a valid write-in vote, in part by denying that expressive, as distinct from instrumental, interests are even an aspect of what is protected by the right to vote. In *Burdick v. Takushi*,[49] the Court said that

> ... the function of the election process is "to winnow out and finally reject all but the chosen candidates," not to provide a means of giving vent to "short-range political goals, pique, or personal quarrel[s]." Attributing to elections a more generalized expressive function would undermine the ability of States to operate elections fairly and efficiently.[50]

Put simply, the Burdick Court saw any but strategic interests in voting as trivial and unworthy of constitutional protection. Even the dissenting justices agreed on this point: "the purpose of casting, counting, and recording votes is to elect public officials, not to serve as a general forum for political expression,"[51] and the dissent agreed with the majority that there is no constitutional protection for the casting of a "protest vote." Beginning from that premise, the Court then balanced the voter's interest in making "free choices and to associate politically through the vote"[52] against the state's interest in the efficient operation of its election system, and decided that efficiency was weightier. The harm to free political expression by being denied the ability to vote for the candidate of one's choice, the harm to electoral competitiveness in a state where many candidates have no opponent on the official ballot, and the harm to the political legitimacy of a government that refuses even to allow the casting of the occasional protest vote are all minimized or ignored by the court. The emphasis on efficiency is worthy of Mussolini, but not of judges sworn to "promote the blessings of liberty."

Political Parties and the
Instrumentalist Conception of the Vote

Political and legal practice in the United States have traditionally been quite ambivalent toward the institution of political parties; the framers of the Constitution warned against "factions" and many of the reformers of the Progressive Era were convinced that parties were at the root of much corruption and short-sightedness in public affairs. But parties have existed since Washington's administration, and as the political scientist E. E. Schattschneider remarked, "modern democracy is unthinkable save in terms of the parties."[53] Parties seem indispensable to any serious effort at social and economic reform in the United States, as is suggested by the role of the Republican Party during the Civil War and Reconstruction or of the Democratic Party during the New Deal.[54] Political parties have long had explicit protection under the Constitution, in the nineteenth century as a necessary condition for effectively exercising the suffrage and more recently also under the doctrine of "freedom of association."[55]

Political Party Ballot Access

Echoes of the old hostility to political parties as mere self-interested "factions" still emerges in judicial opinions, however, especially when the Court is considering a claim by a minor political party. The Democratic and Republican parties, having had presidential nominating conventions since 1832 and 1856 respectively, and being the means through which every president since Andrew Jackson was elected, have a preferential status in constitutional jurisprudence, while third parties are often suspect.[56] Only the nominees of the Democratic and Republican parties have automatic access to the official ballot in every state and the District of Columbia; other parties must prove their legitimacy.

The favored position of the two major parties is reinforced by state laws regulating access to the general-election ballot. Typically, a minor party must show that it has some minimum level of support among the voters before its nominees will automatically be granted a space on the official general-election ballot. Since the Supreme Court first decided (in 1968) that state ballot–access laws implicated federal constitutional rights, much litigation has centered around how high the constitutionally permissible threshold of voter support may be drawn. The question is not an abstract one; a high threshold means that fewer parties will appear on the general-election ballot to compete for votes.

Ballot-access laws have historically been used to eliminate parties of protest, like the Populists, Socialists, and Communists, from general-election ballots.

Raising thresholds has often had the effect (whether intended or not) of removing existing parties from the ballot.

For example, in 1935 New York State raised the threshold for a recognized political party from receipt of 25,000 votes in the preceding gubernatorial election to receipt of 50,000 votes in that election. The Communist Party, whose gubernatorial candidate had received 45,778 votes in the 1934 election, thereby lost its automatic access to the New York state ballot. The Socialist Party, which had run a candidate for governor in each biennial New York election beginning in 1900, lost its ballot status when it fell below the 50,000-vote mark in the 1938 election. These voters thereafter presumably stopped voting or, in the main, voted for Democratic gubernatorial candidates. Is this the sort of effect the Supreme Court has in mind when it refers to ballot-access laws approvingly as having "the effect of channeling expressive activity at the polls"?[57] Is it desirable to channel all expressive activity into the Democratic and Republican parties?

In answer, the Supreme Court has justified some restrictions on ballot access as necessary to eliminating "frivolous" candidates and parties from consideration. The Supreme Court's understanding of the concept of "frivolity" demonstrates the underlying instrumentalism of its doctrines of voting rights.

The concept of "frivolity" in these contexts is not apolitical or viewpoint-neutral. A party is not judged to be frivolous according to the plausibility of its proposals for public policy; this might well be a test that many major-party candidates would fail along with the minor-party candidates at whom it is aimed, and, in any event, such a judgment is supposed to be the function of the voters, not of judges or even of incumbent legislative majorities. Typically, rather, a candidacy is judged to be frivolous by the Supreme Court if it has no chance of electoral success,[58] and (on this criterion), most minor-party candidacies will be "frivolous." In tacitly defining frivolity in terms of unlikelihood of gaining power, the Supreme Court is acting to restrict the possible functions of voting to the most narrowly instrumental—picking people to hold certain government offices.[59]

Antifusion Laws

The favored status of the major parties vis-à-vis their minor competition was underscored by the Supreme Court's 1997 Timmons decision upholding Minnesota's "antifusion" statute.[60] "Fusion" is a joint nomination of a candidate by two or more parties; it was widely used in the late nineteenth century, especially by smaller parties of economic protest, like the Greenback and Populist parties, in forming alliances with one of the two major parties while retaining their own distinct identities. In general, fusion nominations were used by minor parties and the weaker of the two major parties; therefore, permitting fusion nominations typically made elections more competitive. Despite (or, more likely, because of) this pro-competitive effect, between the mid-1890s and about 1920 fusion nominations were outlawed in most states, in large measure to discourage the protest parties.[61] However, it continued to be employed in some states, notably New York, where from 1936 through 1998 the votes provided to major-party candidates by their minor-party nominations have been the margin of victory in four of the sixteen presidential elections, three of the seventeen gubernatorial elections, and six of the twenty-three U.S. Senate elections; fusion nominations have also been decisive in five of the eighteen regular elections for mayor of New York City from 1933 through 1997.[62]

Since with a fusion nomination several parties' names will appear next to the candidate's name, fusion nominations allow the voter to cast a more expressive vote. The voter who can choose party as well as candidate is able to send a more discriminating message.[63] On the analysis given above, in which expression is a distinct interest protected by the right to vote, there should be a serious argument to the effect that the right to vote should protect the rights of parties to make fusion nominations. Moreover, since fusion nominations have a strong tendency to increase the competitiveness of election campaigns in which they are used, and since an electoral system serves the voters better if it forces candidates to compete vigorously for the voters' ballots, we have a second right-to-vote argument for fusion nominations based on the voters' interest in having a highly competitive electoral system.

In rejecting the minor party's challenge to the state antifusion law in the Timmons case, the Supreme Court relied upon the strength of the state's interest in the "stability" of its political system, an interest that allows states (the Court held) to "enact reasonable election regulations that may, in practice, favor the traditional two-party system, ... and that temper the destabilizing effects of party-splintering and excessive factionalism."[64] This actually understates the implications of the Court's decision, for by allowing the states to restrict the activities of existing third parties, it allows a freezing of the political status quo, which (since the Democrats and Republicans are the current beneficiaries of the two-party "system") in effect favors the two existing parties, not merely the two-party system (which in theory might well be open to replacing one or both of the existing major parties with others).

In this context as in others, the Court's decision rests upon an explicit claim that there is a single, instrumental function of elections in the United States[65]—choosing candidates[66]—which rules out other, even complementary functions.[67] As noted above, allowing fusion nominations tends to make elections more competitive. In principle, more-competitive elections should make the elected officials who win those elections pay closer attention to the needs and desires of the voters who choose them; this much follows even from an instrumentalist analysis of elections. But if the function of the election is only to make sure that some candidate or other is selected to hold office through some sort of electoral mechanism, then it is of relatively little significance whether the candidates for office closely reflect popular needs, or not. The narrowness of the Court's understanding of democracy is seldom made so explicit.[68]

Campaign Spending Doctrine:
Individualism, Instrumentalism, and
the Static Conception of the Vote

These themes of an individualist, instrumentalist, and static conception of voting converge in the leading Supreme Court decision on campaign spending, *Buckley v. Valeo*.[69] In *Buckley*, the Court addressed (among other issues) the question of whether Congress could, constitutionally, place a ceiling on campaign spending by candidates for federal office; the answer was that it could not. A candidate's spending on behalf of his/her own campaign is, according to the Court's ruling, analogous to the candidate's speaking on behalf of the campaign,[70] and (therefore) cannot be restricted any more than speaking could be.

The Court's reasoning has been much-criticized, and those criticisms will not be repeated here.[71] For present purposes, we can note the following three features of the *Buckley* decision. First, the Court conceptualized the legal issues at stake in the spending-limits statute as a matter of the rights of the individual candidate to speak (i.e., to spend money campaigning), rather than as a matter of the (collective) right of the members of the electorate, or the (collective) right of the candidates for office, to participate in a free and equal electoral process; this indicates the deeply individualist nature of the Court's reasoning.[72]

Second, the Court conceptualized the function of campaign spending in instrumentalist terms—it is legitimate for a candidate to spend money in whatever manner might be thought necessary to win election (short of outright bribery of the voters), regardless of whether the money so spent contributes in any way to a sensible discussion of relevant issues, public policy, and the respective merits and demerits of the candidates themselves. In fact, the instrumentalism of *Buckley* is so radical that the Court saw it as applying regardless of whether such a competitive spending race might in fact create a sort of "prisoners' dilemma," in which the instrumentally rational behavior of each individual becomes collectively irrational.[73] That is, in a competitive situation each candidate will, in self-defense, raise and spend more and more money, but at the end it's quite possible that all candidates (to say nothing of the electorate itself, and the state of public policy) will be worse off than if the amount of money raised and spent had been much lower.

And third, as it had in other election-law cases,[74] the Court conceptualized the electoral campaign itself in static rather than dynamic terms—it is acceptable, under the *Buckley* decision, for a candidate to win by outspending the opposition by 10 to 1, or 100 to 1, or even 1,000 to 1, because for the Court the ability to outspend merely reflects the preexisting division of support for the wealthier campaign,[75] regardless of whether a more even pattern of spending might have made it possible for the less-wealthy candidates to engage the wealthier candidate in a debate that might have changed voters' minds about the relative merits of the candidates.[76]

The results of the *Buckley* logic have been little short of disastrous. Election campaigns have grown more and more expensive, and political candidates must spend an increasing share of their time and attention simply finding wealthy supporters from whom to solicit contributions. In approximately 90 percent of the cases in recent elections, the winning candidate for a seat in the U.S. Senate or the U.S. House of Representatives is also the candidate who has spent the most money. One candidate in a 1994 U.S. Senate race in California spent nearly $30 million; this means that a competitive candidate for such an office in California must raise $5 million per year for each of six years, or something like $100,000 a week fifty weeks a year for six years. It would be little short of amazing if this level of fund-raising did not affect the sort of legislation considered by elected officials; while it may be relatively rare for an individual contributor to bribe a candidate to support or oppose particular legislation, it seems that this system virtually guarantees that the class interests of the wealthy will be given priority over the general interests of the community as a whole.[77]

These results are not required by the Constitution. If the Constitution protects the right to vote, then (on the analysis I offered above) the Constitution protects the collective right of the electorate to participate together in a deliberative process concerning the parties and candidates seeking public office. And this deliberative process need not—in fact, must not—be dominated by great accumulations of wealth, but must be equally open to those without great material resources.

Conclusion

I have argued that voting is a complex action, both individual and social in nature and done for a variety of reasons. From the viewpoint of democratic theory, the complex set of interests advanced by voting are all weighty, and from the viewpoint of constitutional theory they should all be protected by the right to vote. Some of the interests I mention are deeply social in their nature, and require a healthy public debate about public matters and a public concern for the participation of all in democratic decision-making. In particular, I have argued that debate, discussion, and free expression create a public good, a shared social meaning about our votes, that helps to guide and control the government. To the extent that political expression is stifled, or that debate and discussion are desultory, focussed on trivia, or dominated by narrow elites, the vote loses its ability to guide the policies of the government. An appreciation of the social aspects of elections would help reorient our theoretical and political understanding of voting, which well might, in turn, help reinvigorate our democracy.[78]

Notes

1. Portions of an earlier version of this essay were delivered to the third national conference of the Radical Philosophy Association, held at San Francisco State University in San Francisco, California, in November 1998. Anatole Anton, Nancy Holmstrom, and Richard Lichtman were cosymposiasts. Earlier drafts of this essay benefited from the extensive and helpful comments of W. Sarvasy and A. Anton; for the failure to take all the good advice I was offered, I take full responsibility.

2. Article 21(3) of the Universal Declaration of Human Rights states that "The will of the people shall be the basis of the authority of government; this will shall be expressed in periodic and genuine elections which shall be by universal and equal suffrage and shall be held by secret vote or by equivalent free voting procedures." *United Nations General Assembly Resolution 217 A (3)*, December 10, 1948. See also Article 25 of the *International Covenant on Civil and Political Rights,* adopted by United Nations General Assembly Resolution 2200 A (21), December 16, 1966; entered into force March 23, 1976.

3. See Marx's favorable comments on the role of universal suffrage in the Paris Commune, in *The Civil War in France: Address of the General Council [of the International Working Men's Association]*, § 3, in *Karl Marx, Political Writings, vol. 3: The First International and After,* ed. David Fernbach (Vintage Books ed.; New York: Random House, 1974), 209; see also 210–211. (Originally published 1871.)

4. See Jane J. Mansbridge, *Beyond Adversary Democracy* (New York: Basic Books, 1980), in which she argues that consensual decision-making works well only in groups whose members share the most significant interests in common.

5. Turnout in the 1996 presidential race was 53.5 percent of the voting-age citizenry, while in the U.S. House elections that year it was 49.8 percent of the voting-age citizenry. In the midterm congressional elections of 1998, it was 35.3 percent of the voting-age citizenry. A general discussion of these issues is in Steven J. Rosenstone and John Mark Hansen, *Mobilization, Participation, and Democracy in America* (New Topics in Politics series; New York: Macmillan Publishing Company, 1993).

6. Cross-national comparisons are not precise, but rough figures are possible. In 153 elections between 1968 and 1989 in twenty-four economically advanced democracies other than the United States, voter turnout for elections to the lower house of the national legislature averaged 82.48 percent of the eligible electorate. The countries are Australia, Austria, Belgium, Canada, Denmark, Finland, France, Germany, Greece, Iceland, Ireland, Israel, Italy, Japan, Luxembourg, Malta, The Netherlands, New Zealand, Norway, Portugal, Spain, Sweden, Switzerland, and the United Kingdom. See Thomas T. Mackie and Richard Rose, compilers, *The International Almanac of Electoral History,* 3d ed.(Washington, D.C.: Congressional Quarterly, 1991). The comparable U.S. figures are 51.85 percent (six presidential election years) and 39.48 percent (five off-year elections). Ibid., at tables 25.15b and 25.16b. A general discussion is in G. Bingham Powell Jr., "Voting Turnout in Thirty Democracies: Partisan, Legal, and Socio-Economic Influences," in Richard G. Niemi and Herbert F. Weisberg, eds., *Controversies in Voting Behavior,* 2d ed. (Washington, D.C.: CQ Press, 1984), 34–53.

7. Between 1975 and 1995, the share of total household income received by the top 5 percent rose from 16.6 to 21.0 percent, while the share received by the lowest 80 percent declined from 56.4 to 51.3 percent. U.S. Department of Commerce, Bureau of the Census, Money Income in the United States: 1995, *Current Population Reports,* (Washington, D.C.: U.S. Government Printing Office, 1996), 60–193, table B-3, B-6. The percentage of individuals living in poverty was 12.3 in 1975 but 13.8 in 1995. Historical poverty tables, accessed on the Internet February 1999 at http://www.census.gov, table 5.

8. See William Greider, *Secrets of the Temple: How the Federal Reserve Runs the Country* (New York: Simon and Schuster, 1987).

9. In 1998, 64 percent of those surveyed agreed that the government "is pretty much run by a few big interests looking out for themselves" while 32 percent said "it is run for the benefit of all the people." In 1964, 29 percent agreed the government was run for a few big interests while 64 percent thought it was run for the good of all. In all 14 surveys since 1970, 50 percent or more has agreed with the "few big interests" view. National Election Studies 1964–1998, accessed on the Internet October 1999 at http://www.umich.edu/~nes, Table 5A.2.

10. "One is indeed inclined to suspect that the large hole in voter participation which developed after 1900 roughly corresponds to the area in the electorate where a viable socialist movement 'ought' to have developed but ... did not succeed in doing so." Walter Dean Burnham, "Party

316 Kurt Nutting

Systems and the Political Process," a 1967 paper reprinted in Burnham, *The Current Crisis in American Politics* (New York: Oxford University Press, 1982), 92–117; the quote is from p. 110.

11. *South v. Peters,* 339 U.S. 276, at 279 (1950) (Justice Douglas, dissenting), quoted in *Reynolds v. Sims,* 377 U.S. 533, at 555–556, n. 29 (1964).

12. As the Supreme Court has said, approvingly quoting the words of the 1965 Voting Rights Act, "voting includes 'all action necessary to make a vote effective.'" *Allen v. State Board of Elections,* 393 U.S. 544 (1969), citing the Voting Rights Act of 1965, Pub. L. 89-110, title I, § 14, 79 Stat. 445, current version codified at 42 U.S.C. § 1973l (c) (1).

13. That the protection of political speech is at the core of the free-speech and free-press clauses of the First Amendment is the argument given its classical form in Alexander Meiklejohn, *Free Speech and Its Relation to Self-Government,* a 1948 book reprinted in *Political Freedom: The Constitutional Powers of the People* (New York: Oxford University Press, 1965). See also *New York Times Co. v. Sullivan,* 376 U.S. 254, especially at 269 and 273 (1964) and *Red Lion Broadcasting Co. v. Federal Communications Commission,* 395 U.S. 367 (1969).

14. For recent theoretical discussions, see the essays in James Bohman and William Rehg, eds., *Deliberative Democracy: Essays on Reason and Politics* (Cambridge, Mass.: MIT Press, 1997), and in Jon Elster, ed., *Deliberative Democracy* (Cambridge Studies in the Theory of Democracy; Cambridge, England: Cambridge University Press, 1998).

15. See *Buckley v. Valeo,* 424 U.S. 1, at 92–93 (1976), and *Illinois State Board of Elections v. Socialist Workers Party,* 440 U.S. 173, at 186 (1979) ("an election campaign is a means of disseminating ideas as well as attaining political office").

16. The emphasis on permanent competition among self-interested individuals as a crucial element in maintaining the institutions of a republic goes at least as far back as Madison's discussion of factions. See James Madison, "The Federalist No. 10," in Jacob E. Cooke, ed., *The Federalist* (Middletown, Conn.: Wesleyan University Press, 1961), 56–65 (originally published 1787).

17. "Competition in ideas and governmental policies is at the core of our electoral processes and of the First Amendment freedoms." *Williams v. Rhodes,* 393 U.S. 23, at 32 (1968); see also *Storer v. Brown,* 415 U.S. 724, at 735 (1974), *Davis v. Bandamer,* 478 U.S. 109 (1986), and *Burdick v. Takushi,* 504 U.S. 428 (1992).

18. For a brief introduction, see Michael Lessnoff, ed., *Social Contract Theory* (Readings in Social and Political Theory series; New York: New York University Press, 1990); for a discussion of voting rights as a recognition of the status of the citizen, see Judith N. Shklar, *American Citizenship: The Quest for Inclusion* (*The Tanner Lectures on Human Values*; Cambridge, Mass.: Harvard University Press, 1991), 25–62.

19. The legitimizing aspects of electoral politics are emphasized in the reapportionment cases, such as *Wesberry v. Sanders,* 376 U.S. 1, at 17–18 (1964), and *Reynolds v. Sims,* 377 U.S. 533, at 555 (1964). The need to avoid corruption and to assure the integrity of the government, which is presumably closely connected to political legitimacy, is acknowledged in *Buckley v. Valeo,* 424 U.S. 1 (1976).

20. See, for example, Morris P. Fiorina, "The Voting Decision: Instrumental and Expressive Aspects," *Journal of Politics,* vol. 38 (May 1976), 390–413, and Richard Rose and Ian McAllister, "Expressive Versus Instrumental Voting," in Dennis Kavanagh, ed., *Electoral Politics* (Oxford, England: Clarendon Press, 1992), 114–140.

21. The expressive aspects of the vote are acknowledged in, for example, *Socialist Labor Party v. Rhodes,* 290 F. Supp. 983 (S.D. Ohio 1968), modified and affirmed sub nom. *Williams v. Rhodes,* 393 U.S. 23 (1968), and *Illinois State Board of Elections v. Socialist Workers Party,* 440 U.S. 173, at 184 (1979), in which the Supreme Court remarked that "By limiting the choices available to voters, the State impairs the voters' ability to express their political preferences."

22. I do not offer a unified "theory" of voting that identifies the necessary and sufficient attributes of a valid vote in a system of electoral politics. The goal here is much more modest: to offer a set of descriptions and normative claims that are part of our more naive understanding of voting and elections; this phenomenology of voting and elections identifies some of the interests that should be ac-

commodated or protected by a legal right to vote. See generally Ludwig Wittgenstein, *Philosophical Investigations*, G. E. M. Anscombe, trans., 3d ed. (New York: Macmillan, 1958); and also the discussion of the method of "reflective equilibrium" in ethical theory, especially in John Rawls, *A Theory of Justice* (Cambridge, Mass.: Belknap Press, 1971).

23. My account is in some respects parallel to the political scientists' discussion of the several functions of democratic political parties. See, for example, Burnham's "Party Systems and the Political Process," cited in n. 10, supra, especially at p. 93.

24. For concrete examples, see Wilson Carey McWilliams, *The Politics of Disappointment: American Elections, 1976–94* (Chatham House Studies in Political Thinking; Chatham, N.J.: Chatham House Publishers, 1995); and Wilson Carey McWilliams, "The Meaning of the Election," in Gerald M. Pomper et al., *The Election of 1996: Reports and Interpretations* (Chatham, N.J.: Chatham House Publishers, 1997), 241–272.

25. The notion of a critical election comes from V. O. Key Jr., "A Theory of Critical Elections," *Journal of Politics* 17 (February 1955), 3–18; see also Walter Dean Burnham, *Critical Elections and the Mainsprings of American Politics* (New York: W. W. Norton 1970); the essays reprinted in Jerome M. Clubb and Howard W. Allen, eds., *Electoral Change and Stability in American Political History* (New York: Free Press, 1971); and James L. Sundquist, *Dynamics of the Party System: Alignment and Dealignment of Political Parties in the United States*, rev. ed. (Washington, D.C.: Brookings Institution, 1983). The basic notion is that at intervals approximating thirty years or so, the partisan balance in American national elections shifts; this affects which party holds power, what issues are raised or suppressed, and so forth. The election that precipitates this shift, or during which this partisan realignment of the voters becomes manifest, is known as a "critical election." A critical election, Key believed, is one in which "voters are ... unusually deeply concerned, in which the extent of electoral involvement is relatively quite high, and in which the decisive results of the voting reveal a sharp alteration of the pre-existing cleavage within the electorate." Key, "A Theory," reprinted in Clubb and Allen, supra, 28. The classic episodes are the rise of Lincoln and the Republicans to national power with the 1860 election, the defeat of the Democratic-Populist revolt under Bryan by McKinley's Republicans in 1896, and the coming to power of the Democrats under Roosevelt in 1932. See also Byron E. Shafer, ed., *The End of Realignment? Interpreting American Electoral Eras* (Madison, Wisc.: University of Wisconsin Press, 1991).

26. In the U.S. context, where the single-member district, ballot-access laws, and the engrained habits of voters often make third-party campaigns difficult and third-party voting pointless, a large vote for a third party is typically taken as quite significant. See generally Steven J. Rosenstone, Roy L. Behr, and Edward H. Lazarus, *Third Parties in America: Citizen Response to Major Party Failure*, 2d ed. (Princeton, N.J.: Princeton University Press, 1996).

27. On representation generally, see Hanna Fenichel Pitkin, The *Concept of Representation* (Berkeley: University of California Press, 1967), especially 168–189 (on Burke).

28. "The basic behavioral postulate of public choice, as for economics, is that man is an egoistic, rational, utility maximizer." Dennis C. Mueller, *Public Choice II: A Revised Edition of "Public Choice"* (Cambridge, England: Cambridge University Press, 1989), 2.

29. On its own terms, and even in the domain of economics narrowly construed, the economic account of rationality has had difficulties explaining what we might call the rationality of groups, in particular "the firm" or "the household." See Herbert A. Simon, "From Substantive to Procedural Rationality," and Amartya K. Sen, "Rational Fools," both reprinted in Frank Hahn and Martin Hollis, eds., *Philosophy and Economic Theory* (Oxford Readings in Philosophy; Oxford: Oxford University Press, 1979).

30. See Mueller, *Public Choice II*, supra n. 8, Ref459891120 28 chap. 18.

31. These actions would include joining with others to march or picket; joining with others in a union or political party; to strike; joining in "sit-down" strikes or "sit-in" demonstrations; joining with others to resist unjust or tyrannical authority, through civil disobedience, resistance, or revolution; and the like.

32. See Mueller, *Public Choice II*, supra n. 28., 348–350.

33. To take the most famous instance, the marchers beaten, whipped, and tear-gassed by the police on the Edmund Pettus Bridge in Selma, Alabama, on March 7, 1965, were specifically protesting the denial of the right to vote. David J. Garrow, *Protest at Selma: Martin Luther King, Jr., and the Voting Rights Act of 1965* (New Haven, Conn.: Yale University Press, 1978), 35.

34. Mueller, for example, does conclude that voting is usually irrational. But this "irrationality" is such only on the economic characterization of rationality. Perhaps nothing would turn on labeling the voter as irrational, if it weren't that the economic and ordinary senses of rationality are apt to be confused, that the ordinary sense of rationality includes a normative aspect—irrational is not how people should act—and if the economic and ordinary senses of rationality weren't at odds with one another in contexts such as this one. See Mueller, *Public Choice II*, supra note 28, 350; C. Dyke, *Philosophy of Economics* (Foundations of Philosophy Series; Englewood Cliffs, N.J.: Prentice-Hall, 1981), 1–20.

35. The American blacks who marched at Selma in order to vote were (on the ordinary moral understanding of human action) extraordinarily courageous; for public-choice theorists, extraordinarily irrational. A theory of human action in which the concept of rational prudence has so displaced such concepts as heroism or cowardice has purchased simplicity and predictive strength at the cost of utter implausibility.

36. See Thomas S. Kuhn, *The Copernican Revolution: Planetary Astronomy in the Development of Western Thought* (Cambridge, Mass.: Harvard University Press, 1957).

37. One risk of adding epicycles in this way is, of course, that the explanation will ultimately be vacuous. If rational egoism is redefined to include, in an ad hoc fashion, altruistic behavior as well, then the explanatory power of rational-choice theory has been sacrificed. See Mueller, *Public Choice II*, supra note 28, 362.

38. The exception is North Dakota.

39. See generally Raymond E. Wolfinger and Steven J. Rosenstone, *Who Votes?* (New Haven, Conn.: Yale University Press, 1980), 88. A recent examination of the system and its effects is in Frances Fox Piven and Richard A. Cloward, *Why Americans Don't Vote* (New York: Pantheon Books, 1989).

40. See *Yick Wo v. Hopkins*, 118 U.S. 356, at 370 (1886), and *Reynolds v. Sims*, 377 U.S. 533, at 561–562 (1964). Congress has also expressed this view of voting rights; see the National Voter Registration Act of 1993 ("Motor Voter"), Pub. L. 103-31, 107 Stat. 77, now codified at 42 U.S.C. § 1973gg (a) (1) (1994), which states that "The Congress finds that—(1) the right of citizens of the United States to vote is a fundamental right."

41. See *Bantam Books, Inc. v. Sullivan*, 372 U.S. 58, at 70 (1963), in which prior restraint on speaking or publishing is said to face a "heavy presumption against its constitutional validity," for which the state would need to show both that it is attempting to avoid a serious harm and that it has no less restrictive means for avoiding that harm. The analogy between the protections afforded to speaking and voting was noted by the judge striking down the Texas poll tax for participation in state elections; taxing voting is no more acceptable than is taxing speech, he concluded. *United States v. Texas*, 252 F. Supp. 234 at 254 (W.D. Tex. 1966), aff'd mem. 384 U.S. 155 (1966).

42. The leading case is *Capen v. Foster*, 29 Mass. (12 Pickering) 485, 23 Am. Dec. 632 (1832).

43. See *Page v. Allen*, 58 Pa. (8 Smith) 338 (1868), holding unconstitutional a Pennsylvania voter registration law.

44. In *Reynolds v. Sims* the Court held that "any alleged infringement of the right of citizens to vote must be carefully and meticulously scrutinized." *Reynolds*, 377 U.S. at 562. *Reynolds* concerned apportionment of seats in state legislatures. In the context of voter registration laws, however, strict scrutiny has not been applied; see *Marston v. Lewis*, 410 U.S. 679 (1973), in which the Supreme Court employed the "rational basis" test in upholding a fifty-day durational residency requirement for voting in state or local elections in Arizona.

45. For example, Canada has impersonal voter registration, in which a list of eligible voters is compiled by official registrars at their own initiative. In Canada, turnout for Parliamentary elections from 1968 through 1989 averaged 74.3 percent of the voting-age population; over the same period turnout for U.S. House elections averaged 46.2 percent of the voting-age population. See Mackie and Rose, comps., *The International Almanac of Electoral History*, supra n. Ref459890545 6. In 1997, turnout in Canada was about 67 percent of the total electorate. See Federal Election Commission, "International Voter Participation Figures," accessed on the Internet in January 1999 at http://www.fed.gov .

46. That is, the Supreme Court conceptualizes the twentieth century's low voter turnout outside the South not structurally, as the result of the states' systems of personal voter registration laws, but as the result of the apathy, laziness, or irresponsibility of individual voters. According to the standard constitutional doctrine of fundamental rights, if the state's action (that is, its laws) operate in such a way as to abridge the fundamental rights of any person (that is, keep an eligible citizen from casting a vote in an election), the equal protection clause has been violated and a remedy may be sought in the courts. See Deborah S. James, "Note—Voter Registration: A Restriction on the Fundamental Right to Vote," *Yale Law Journal* 96 (June 1987), 1615–1640.

47. See, for example, *Eaton v. Brown*, 96 Cal. 371, 31 P. 250 (1892); *State ex rel. Lamar v. Dillon*, 32 Fla. 545, 14 So. 383 (1893); *Sanner v. Patton*, 155 Ill. 553, 40 N.E. 290 (1895); *Bowers v. Smith*, 111 Mo. 45, 17 S.W. 761 (1891); and *People ex rel. Bradley v. Shaw*, 133 N.Y. 493, 31 N.E. 512 (1892). An early discussion of the legal issues is by the distinguished legal scholar John Wigmore, "Ballot Reform: Its Constitutionality," *American Law Review* 23 (1889), 719; see also John H. Wigmore, *The Australian Ballot System as Embodied in the Legislation of Various Countries*, 2d ed. (Boston: Boston Book Company, 1889), esp. 53–56.

48. See, for example, *Jenness v. Fortson*, 403 U.S. 431, at 438 (1971), and *Storer v. Brown*, 415 U.S. 724, at 736 n. 7 (1974). Since then, however, the Supreme Court has apparently rejected the idea that the availability of write-ins is sufficient to avoid all constitutional challenges to ballot-access restrictions; see *U.S. Term Limits v. Thornton*, 514 U.S. 779, at 828–832 (1995) (striking down state attempts to place limits on the number of terms served by federal legislators via state ballot-access restrictions, even while allowing write-in election of legislators exceeding the limit on number of terms served, as contrary to the "qualifications clauses" of the Constitution, in article I, § 2, cl. 2, and article I, § 3, cl. 3).

49. 504 U.S. 428 (1992).

50. Burdick, 504 U.S. at 438. Internal citations omitted; emphasis added. Since the Supreme Court required that the state satisfy only a weak standard of review rather than "strict scrutiny," the state did not actually have to provide evidence that its ban on write-in votes was "necessary" for it to achieve its legitimate interests in operating its election system fairly and efficiently. It is difficult to see how the state could have done so, since most states seem to operate their election systems efficiently despite their allowing write-in voting. In the 1996 general election, write-ins for president were counted and reported in at least thirty-two states and the District of Columbia, according to the Federal Election Commission. See Federal Elections 96, supra note _Ref460048962 _5_, 17–28.

51. Burdick, 504 U.S. at 445 (Kennedy, J., dissenting) (emphasis added). Justice Kennedy's phrasing is especially noteworthy for its question-begging character; the lawsuit challenging the Hawaii write-in ban was brought by a voter who maintained that his purpose in casting a vote was to protest the available choice of candidates, but Kennedy's opinion suggests that the voter was mistaken about his own purposes.

52. Burdick, 504 U.S. at 439.

53. E. E. Schattschneider, *Party Government* (New York: Rinehart and Company, 1942), 1.

54. As Burnham says, "mobilization of the mass electorate is and always has been contingent on the existence, competition, and organizational vitality of political parties." In Walter Dean Burnham,

"The Appearance and Disappearance of the American Voter," a 1978 paper reprinted in *The Current Crisis in American Politics,* supra note Ref459883482 10, pp. 121–165, at 121.

55. See *Kusper v. Pontikes,* 414 U.S. 51 (1973), *Cousins v. Wigoda,* 419 U.S. 477 (1975), and *Democratic Party v. Wisconsin ex rel. LaFollette,* 450 U.S. 107 (1981).

56. See the discussion of the constitutionality of the public funding scheme for major-party presidential candidates in *Buckley v. Valeo,* 424 U.S. 1, at 97–98 (1976).

57. Burdick, 504 U.S. at 438.

58. The state of Washington required that for general-election ballot access, a candidate from a minor party must have received at least 1 percent of the vote in the preceeding direct primary election. The Supreme Court upheld this requirement as reasonably aimed at ending frivolous candidacies in *Munro v. Socialist Workers Party,* 479 U.S. 189 (1986).

59. But by the same criterion, the label of "frivolous" should also apply to major-party candidates in many congressional and state legislative races. The median victory margin in the 435 House races held in 1996 was 27.8 percent of the total vote cast; in 1998 it was 36.7 percent of the total vote cast. The traditional threshold for a "safe" seat, a 10 percent margin of victory over the second-place finisher, was attained by 355 candidates (82 percent of the total) in 1996 and 386 candidates (89 percent of the total) in 1998. See Federal Election Commission, Federal Elections 96, supra note Ref460048962 _5_, and Federal Election Commission, Federal Elections 98 (Washington, D.C.: Federal Election Commission, 1999). Yet the Supreme Court has not ruled (and will not) that a Republican running in a safely Democratic district, or vice versa, is running a "frivolous" campaign and so need not be granted access to the ballot. Perhaps the fact that the Supreme Court has explicitly approved the gerrymandering of congressional and legislative districts to maximize the partisan advantage of the party in power plays a role here. It has proved difficult, in practice, to apply the strictly instrumental criterion.

60. *Timmons v. Twin Cities Area New Party,* 520 U.S. 351 (1997).

61. See Peter Argersinger, "'A Place on the Ballot': Fusion Politics and Antifusion Laws," in Argersinger, *Structure, Process, and Party: Essays in American Political History* (Armonk, N.Y.: M. E. Sharpe, 1992), 150–171 (originally published 1980).

62. Minor-party votes for the winning major-party candidate were decisive in the presidential elections (for New York's electoral votes) in 1940, 1944, 1960, and 1980; in the gubernatorial elections of 1938, 1954, and 1994; in the regular U.S. Senate elections of 1944, 1950, 1980, and 1992, plus the special elections of 1938 and 1949; and in the New York City mayoral elections of 1933, 1937, 1941, 1965, and 1993. In addition, minor parties sustained by fusion arrangements under New York law were successful in the U.S. Senate race in 1970 and in the New York City mayoral race in 1969. The success of the minor parties in New York suggests that the ballot-access and antifusion laws in other states may well "channel" political expression in ways not preferred by the voters whose expression is being channeled.

63. For example, in 1996 New York voters could decide whether to vote for Bill Clinton as the nominee of the Democratic Party or as the nominee of the Liberal Party; and whether to vote for Bob Dole as the nominee of the Republican Party or as the nominee of the Conservative Party. To the extent that the minor parties have identities and platforms distinct from the major parties, the minor-party vote for a fusion nominee is a more nuanced vote.

64. *Timmons,* 520 U.S. at 367. The Court did not require the state to actually provide evidence showing that states allowing fusion were more subject to political instability, party-splintering, or factionalism, however.

65. If a complex social institution such as electoral politics in a democracy had only a single function, that fact would itself be quite remarkable; but that this function is so narrowly understood as to allow states to permanently institutionalize the roles of the two existing major parties and then protect them against all but the most extraordinary minor-party attacks, is truly extraordinary.

66. See *Burdick,* 504 U.S. at 438.

67. Such as the ones I outlined earlier, which I labeled "deliberative/rational," "expressive/symbolic," and "legitimating," including educating the voters, expressing voters' views, protesting the actions of the entrenched majority, and demonstrating that the policies of the government genuinely reflect the popular will.

68. The view is highly reminiscent of Joseph A. Schumpeter. See his *Capitalism, Socialism and Democracy,* 3d ed. (New York: Harper Torchbooks; New York: Harper and Row, 1950), especially chap. 22; and the criticisms of it by Carole Pateman, *Participation and Democratic Theory* (Cambridge, England: Cambridge University Press, 1970); and C. B. Macpherson, *The Life and Times of Liberal Democracy* (Oxford, England: Oxford University Press, 1977).

69. 424 U.S. 1 (1976).

70. In the Court's summary of the constitutional issues at stake, "... contributions and expenditures are at the very core of political speech ..." *Buckley,* 424 U.S. at 15.

71. See J. Skelly Wright, "Politics and the Constitution: Is Money Speech?" *Yale Law Journal* 85 (July 1976), 1001–1021, who begins his critique of the reasoning in *Buckley* by citing Meiklejohn; and see also Marlene Arnold Nicholson, "Campaign Financing and Equal Protection," *Stanford Law Review* 26 (April 1974), 815–854.

72. The Court explicitly declared that the "interest in equalizing the relative financial resources of candidates competing for elective office" was "clearly not sufficient" to justify expenditure ceilings. *Buckley,* 424 U.S. at 54. Why this was "clear" to the Court is, in fact, quite unclear.

73. Rejecting the claim that spiraling campaign spending justified placing limits on candidate outlays, the Court said that "... the mere growth in the cost of federal election campaigns in and of itself provides no basis for governmental restrictions on the quantity of campaign spending." *Buckley,* 424 U.S. at 57.

74. In the write-in case discussed above, *Burdick v. Takushi,* the Court explicitly gave "little weight" to the interests of voters whose minds might have changed during the final two months of the campaign. See 504 U.S. at 436–437.

75. As the Buckley Court said, "... the financial resources available to a candidate's campaign, like the number of volunteers recruited, will normally vary with the size and intensity of the candidate's support." *Buckley,* 424 U.S. at 56. This conclusion depends upon the distribution of wealth not being too different from the distribution of votes. Votes, however, are distributed equally ("one person, one vote," as the Court said in *Gray v. Sanders,* 372 U.S. 368 [1963]); wealth is very highly concentrated, so that in 1989 the wealthiest 1 percent of the population owned 39 percent of the wealth and the wealthiest 20 percent owned 85 percent of the wealth. Edward N. Wolff, *Top Heavy: The Increasing Inequality of Wealth in America and What Can Be Done About It* (New York: New Press, 1996), 10–11.

76. Where the "marketplace"—of ideas or anything else—is monopolistically (or oligopolistically) structured, the "successful" ideas will tend to be those backed by the dominant "seller" (or sellers) of ideas.

77. See generally Jamin B. Raskin and John Bonifaz, *The Wealth Primary: Campaign Fundraising and the Constitution* (Washington, D.C.: Center for Responsive Politics, 1994).

78. I would like to thank Stephanie Kay for her support in the writing of this essay.

From *Savage Inequalities*

Jonathan Kozol

I stand at the door and look at the children, most of whom are sitting at a table now to have their milk. Nine years from now, most of these children will go on to Manly High School, an enormous, ugly building ... that has a graduation rate of only 38 percent. Twelve years from now ... fourteen of these twenty-three boys and girls will have dropped out ... Fourteen years from now, four of these kids, at most, will go to college. Eighteen years from now, one of those may graduate from college, but three of the twelve boys in kindergarden will already have spent time in prison (45).

On an average morning in Chicago, 5,700 children in 190 classrooms come to school to find they have no teacher ... the city's dropout rate of nearly 50 percent is regarded by some people as a blessing. If over 200,000 of Chicago's total student population of 440,000 did not disappear during their secondary years, it is not clear who would teach them (52–54).

After lunch I talk with a group of students ... (who) seem not just lacking in important, useful information that wouid help them to achieve their dreams, but, in a far more drastic sense, cut off and disconnected from the outside world. In talking of some recent news ... they speak of Moscow and Berlin, but ... are unaware that Moscow is the capital of the Soviet Union or that Berlin is in Germany. Several believe Jesse Jackson is the mayor of New York City (70).

15

Language as a Public Good Under Threat: The Private Ownership of Brand Names

Michael H. Goldhaber

"Of all the laws that bind us to the past, the names of things are the stubbornest."
—Robert Haas, poet laureate of the United States, 1996–1997

Prologue

In early 1997, if you were watching television news, you might well have run across a scene very much like this:

[The setting—outdoors somewhere near Beijing] The camera faces a huge pile of audio cassettes, videocassettes and compact discs, containing work (we are told) mostly by American artists. A bulldozer enters the frame, then another, smashing into the pile, riding over it, in each pass reducing countless hours of music and video to useless plastic scrap. All this is done, the announcer reports, his voice strangely complacent, under the direct orders of high Chinese government officials.

Except for the announcer's tone, this scene is strikingly reminiscent of the dreaded past, the legendary destructions of books (and their authors) by the first Qin emperor, a parallel to the book burnings of the Inquisition or Nazi Germany. At this point in the broadcast, you might have expected to hear of the U.S. government expressing outrage at this act by the "Red Chinese." You would have been very much mistaken.

> The announcer goes on to report tempered praise from the White House and Congress alike. They have only one reservation: Not enough has been pulverized so far. But the basic attitude is relief: Finally the roguish Communist Party-run government of China is in compliance with U.S. demands—demands to clamp down on the "piracy" of intellectual property.

Large American corporations were the chief promoters of the diplomatic efforts behind this extraordinary event. Is this orgy of destruction to be taken as purely a business matter, correctly preserving private property rights? Or is it, in fact, what it appears to be, in essence a book burning, an act of censorship that assures that many members of the Chinese public will be denied a chance to experience what they otherwise would have chosen to hear and see? Many—though undoubtedly not all—of the artists whose expression was erased backed the action; yet does that free it from concerns over censorship? And is it at all worrisome or surprising that no public outrage whatsoever was registered here in the United States?

The event I describe may be unusually dramatic, but the fact that it took place underlines the level of determination and seriousness with which the business world now takes the enforcement of intellectual property laws, which include patents, copyrights, trademarks, and others and which cover inventions, stories, pictures, movies, music, logos, and words—language. That very determination suggests the need for careful scrutiny. So does the vast extent of the claimed rights and their novelty. But that scrutiny, or any vigorous public debate, has been quite lacking.

We as members of the public have been too ready to accede to the growing chorus of claims to this basically new and strange kind of private property right. In the process we lose a great deal that we can ill afford to give up. A large proportion of entities in the sphere of mental productions that are now undergoing privatization—or have already been categorized as private—simply should not be so.

This chapter thus focuses on the contrast between intellectual property rights as a form of private property, and the need in any well-run society, even a market-based one, to have a set of goods that remain public. I use the term "public goods" in the sense in which even market-oriented economists normally use it, namely to mean those goods that either cannot usefully be owned, or if owned must be subject to public control for even economic life to be able to proceed.[1]

Copyright's Commons

Copyright's Commons is a coalition devoted to promoting a vibrant public domain. It is a group of students, teachers, authors, filmmakers, archivists, publishers, and other members of the public who believe in widespread access to creative works.

THE IMPORTANCE OF THE PUBLIC DOMAIN

Public access to literature, art, music, and film is essential to preserving and building upon our cultural heritage. Many of the most important works of American culture have drawn upon the creative potential of the public domain. Frank Capra's "It's a Wonderful Life" is a classic example of a film that did not enjoy popular success until it entered the public domain. Other icons such as Snow White, Pinocchio, Santa Claus, and Uncle Sam grew out of public domain figures.

PROJECTS

Copyright's Commons seeks to invigorate the public domain through a number of projects:

PROMOTING ACCESS TO THE PUBLIC DOMAIN: The public domain grows richer as it becomes more accessible. Copyright's Commons provides links to sites that provide widespread dissemination of public domain materials.

FIGHTING AGAINST UNLIMITED COPYRIGHTS: Last May, Copyright's Commons joined as a plaintiff in the Eldred v. Reno lawsuit challenging the recent Copyright Term Extension Act. The statute has restricted access to thousands of works that helped define twentieth century and that had been at last slated to enter the public domain.

FINDING OPEN SPACE: Cyberspace greatly expands the boundaries -- and the creative potential -- of the public domain. In conjunction with the Berkman Center for Law and Society at Harvard Law School, Copyright's Commons seeks to insure free access to cyberspace. The "open code" and "openlaw" projects are pioneer efforts to expand the public domain into cyberspace.

LAUNCHING A COUNTER-COPYRIGHT CAMPAIGN: By marking their works with a [cc] and a link to the Copyright's Commons website, authors invite others to use and build upon their works. A counter-copyright does not replace a copyright, but strips it of its exclusivity.

PROVIDING A DISCUSSION SPACE: The Copyright's Commons site itself is a part of the public domain. It maintains a forum for discussions and welcomes all comments.

Copyright's Commons maintains this website as a forum for (public domain, of course) discussions. We welcome all comments.   http://cyber.law.harvard.edu/cc/

My favorite example of such a good is the sidewalk. It would be perfectly possible for each bit of sidewalk to be under the complete control of the owner of the abutting property, but that would make ordinary social and economic life impossible, so much so that we could hardly recognize the resulting stretches of land as the sidewalk as it is commonly understood. Often, sidewalks technically are privately owned, but in these cases they can only remain sidewalks when their different owners are required to allow essentially unrestrained and open public use, as is in fact the case in those jurisdictions that permit private ownership.

No matter how much one might favor private control of property as a matter of principle, it would be difficult to quarrel with its sharp restraint in such cases as sidewalks, and hardly anybody does. When it comes to other forms of property, however, such as intellectual property—which is in fact much more difficult to maintain as property than ordinary material things without vast protective efforts by the state and the international order—arguments about why and how these private rights should be limited remain seriously underdeveloped—to everyone's detriment, I believe.

To avoid confusion, I want to emphasize that this definition of public goods is not the only one in use, even in this volume as a whole. Rather than using the word "goods" as synonymous with possessions, one can use it, and philosophers typically do, in a much more abstract sense as more or less the plural noun form of the adjective "good." In that sense, the more public goods there are, the better, regardless of whether that permits a functioning market or not. My reason for focusing on the economists' definition is simply that it seems more helpful in argument at the present, when the benefits of markets and the private property they seem to entail are so widely taken to be beyond question. It seems to me it is worth making as clear as possible that even within the market framework, more goods should be held as public than currently are. Arguments of the sort I want to try to make cannot simply be countered by a general skepticism about whether socialism works, for example, since they are constituted around the question of how markets themselves must work. I don't in fact know how to show that socialism in the widest sense could work, regardless of my abstract attraction to it. I do know how to begin to show how utter privatization cannot work, and doing so seems the most fruitful way to proceed now.

I must immediately qualify this, however. The economists' definition, when applied to the real world, can hardly fail to encompass situations where what is at stake seems closely tied to issues of political or moral necessity rather than to purely economic ones, since economic life itself could hardly proceed in a political or moral vacuum. Specifically, a quite common assumption by economists is "perfect information" on the part of buyers, that is consumers, as well as sellers. This information surely must include knowledge about the possible meanings and effects of possessing, or even desiring, certain kinds of goods, and such knowledge necessarily can only be garnered through public discussion and debate, which therefore connects with political rights. So the distinction between the philosophers' sense and the economists' cannot be ironclad and I won't take it to be.

Whether mental productions are best taken to be public goods or private intellectual property is not a static question. The possible arguments depend on what is possible and also on how important particular kinds of potential intellectual property are. Thus, more or less in the shadows, a series of practical "debates"—more precisely, struggles—are in progress between the two sides in many areas of intellectual property. For example, take the case of computer operating-system software. The powerful Microsoft corporation and its flagship Windows is increasingly seen as pitted against Linux, the brainchild of a twenty-something programmer named Linus Torvalds and the legion of programmers who openly and continually modify and update Linux while making it available at no charge for anyone who wants to use it. Even though this contest is taking place outside the legal sphere, what is at issue is the appropriateness of different concepts of property and public goods.

A different sort of struggle involves the efforts (so far successful in Congress and the courts) to patent the following: genes—including the naturally occurring genes that, when they mutate, cause human breast cancer; genetically engineered seeds; drugs; surgical procedures; and other biological entities—including live animals or plants that have long been used as parts of the herbaries of indigenous peoples. Also newly patentable are business methods and mathematical models. The list keeps growing despite some attempt for just about every item on it to remain unowned and in the public arena.

Meanwhile, the battles over the correct means to publish music, video, and other expressive forms continues. One of the latest skirmishes involves a standard known as MP3. As anyone in contact with moderately affluent teenagers must know firsthand by now, an MP3 player, based on memory chips, can quickly be filled with music downloaded over the Internet, often after having been copied by other teenagers and made available over their own websites. The major music publishers fight against this, although at present they are not winning. Musicians who often resent the artistic control enforced in record company contracts are increasingly embracing MP3 as offering them more opportunity to be heard. No bulldozers are likely to be used in this instance, since here music (and presumably books and videos eventually) can be distributed over the Internet; interventions to protect private property can only take the form of suppressing certain Internet traffic by constant monitoring.

As these examples perhaps suggest, anything approaching an adequate plea for the role of public goods in the entire area encompassed by the concept of intellectual property would be well beyond the scope of a book chapter (though I have addressed it in condensed form elsewhere).[2] My focus here is thus on a more limited domain: trademarks, which encompass insignia, logos, brand names, mottos, and slogans, concentrating on the purely linguistic aspects, that is, the last three items. Of all intellectual property issues, those involving trademarks are the most ignored from a broad standpoint of public policy. Yet trademark claims turn out to be nothing less than a straitjacket tightening around the construction of social meaning, in the process strangulating the very possibility of public discourse and threatening free speech, as well as free economic choice. The restrictions may seem slight today, but they are rapidly accelerating. Now is the time to wake to the danger.

Language as a Public Good

Language is perhaps the quintessential public good. Without the free flow of words, indeed there can be no public. It is only because in public discourse meanings are continually in flux, always open to new shadings and redefinitions, regardless of what quarter they come from, that society can navigate the continual changes it itself undergoes and still retain any semblance of communal coherence, even the minimal sort needed for a functioning market.

At first thought it might seem that words as such inevitably escape any possibility of private ownership, for, as Wittgenstein argued, a purely private language is impossible. New words, new phrasings, new colorations of meaning, and new grammatical patterns, even though individually introduced or invented, require acceptance and adoption by others in a continual public interchange if they are to have any communicative value, that is, if they are to be part of language at all. Or, to put it in slightly different terms: The play between signifier and signified is necessarily constructed socially, rather than individually.

Even your "own" name has meaning only because others may use it to refer to you; you do not control exactly what they mean when they say your name, nor what hearers hear when they recognize it. Nor could you. The dance of overtones and implications are part of everything said, tingeing each utterance. To own a word would imply a control over acceptable meaning and usage that quite apparently is unachievable.

Apparently—but what seems impossible on philosophic, scientific, or logical grounds is not necessarily so from a legal standpoint. Laws have a reality of their own, and even if the ends they ostensibly seek prove to be well beyond their actual grasp, as, for instance, in the case of antidrug laws, they still can have powerful shaping (or distorting) effects on public life. For this to happen, of course, the laws in question cannot simply be on the books; they must be invoked. Once they are, even when they are not ultimately enforced, or when the invocations are wildly exaggerated, they can exert an enormous pull.

That, I suggest, is exactly the case when it comes to the sorts of property rights over the uses and meanings of words that are codified in the trademark and related laws. The problem is not that speech or thought can be directly coerced but rather that we have too readily accepted a diminution of our rights to free coinage or development of the meanings of protected words. Further, we do that because of deliberate efforts, on the part of the holders of those supposed rights to convince us of the power of their claims, all the while carefully camouflaging what is at stake.

One way in which trademarked words influence language is simply by cluttering up our attention with new terms we must learn just to maintain an understanding of life around us. Often these are completely invented words that had no prior meaning at all: the newish Netscape, Prozac, Pentium, CNN, iMac, or Viagra alongside the more established Shalimar, Levis, 747, Xerox, Jeep, Kodak, and so on. Were these no more than new words for new concepts they would be relatively unproblematic, but as trademarks they are specifically restricted in meaning, forcing us to master generic terms as well: Netscape is a kind of "browser," Prozac is a "serotonin-uptake inhibitor," Xerox is a "photocopier," a 747 is a "jumbo jet," a Jeep is a "sports-utility vehicle" or perhaps "an all-terrain vehicle," and so forth. Although the tendency of users of language would be to slide between specific and generic terms, trademark owners do everything they can—including obtaining legal injunctions—to force the use of the generic term while at the same time, largely through advertising, hardly allowing us to forget the brand names. Thus a university may have a copying department, but the Xerox corporation makes sure it does not have a xeroxing department.

Difficult as it is to navigate these branded and generic terms, trademarks are by no means restricted to newly minted words. Standard, well-used terms can also be trademarked for specific products. Thus "Philosophy" is a foot cream, "Contradiction" is a perfume, "Biography" is a trademark of the A&E Television Networks; then there are Windows, Word, Office, all emanating from Microsoft, along with Accord, Civic, and thousands of others. (Even the Communist hammer and sickle is now the trademarked logo for a brand of vodka.)

It might seem that these terms also are unproblematic, merely adding new meaning to old, while creating little confusion. But trademark owners themselves often don't see it that way, and act to wall off usage in their own favor.

Consider this letter to the editor appearing in *Motorland,* the magazine of the California State Automobile Association (and therefore with a circulation in the millions):[3]

"Motorland's" article "Sniffing Out Drunk Drivers" (Nov/Dec) refers to the "Sniffer" as a device that quickly measures the alcohol in the surrounding air. This use may cause confusion. Network General Technology corporation is the owner of the trademark "Sniffer," a computer program for use in analyzing and testing digital traffic operations in local area networks. . . . Network General, owner of the mark, has the exclusive right to use the mark and has registered this mark with the U.S. Patent and Trademark Office as well as other government agencies.
  —Jill E. Fishbein, Vice President and General Counsel, Network General

Note the subtleties here—and the gross threat they hold. "Sniffer" is of course a noun formed from the verb "to sniff"; it is a very common colloquialism meaning nose, and also, in slang dating back to the 1920s, a cocaine user. Or is it? Can it be used these ways any more, now that Network General has claimed it as a "mark"?

In her letter Fishbein nowhere actually states that it was legally impermissible for *Motorland* to use the word in the completely reasonable and comprehensible sense it had. Most likely the courts would finally reject such a claim, should it come to that. But it doesn't have to. Although in fact threatening nothing, Fishbein leaves a strong implication, backed by her weighty references to ownership and exclusive rights, that the word, when capitalized at least, is now to be restricted to a meaning that would only be of concern to a rather select group of information-systems managers. The success of the tactic is evident: It was enough to scare some presumably professional editors into devoting scarce letters-column space for her recondite remarks. Further, it was very probably enough to make them look over their shoulders with a bit of concern from now on whenever a remotely similar sort of usage—of any word—crops up again.

Inevitably, some of this concern is passed on to *Motorland*'s many readers and even more to its writers, and is clearly not limited to the word "Sniffer." Who but a few lawyers know what limitations are implied by someone's ownership of a trademarked word? When in doubt in this litigious society, it often feels best to be cautious. Sticking to the olfactory, if you innocently should happen to refer to "the scent of contradiction," might you be infringing on Calvin Klein's perfume trademark? If you put your remarks in print will you and your publisher receive a warning as stern as Fishbein's? Or what about planning a conference on the peripatetic school, entitled "Philosophy on Foot." Will the foot cream people get you?

If that possibility seems remote, consider this:

A couple from the state of Montana decided to open a knitwear business, logically enough calling their new little company "Montana Knits." They soon fell under the gaze of the protectors of French fashion-designer Claude Montana's trademark rights, and were duly sued to prevent their use of their logical name. It apparently was not germane to the suit whether or not Claude Montana actually designs knitwear or has any intention of starting. It is just that the westerners might be appropriating a bit of his good (trademarked) name.

Or this: Since 1981, Key West, Florida, has "honored" its onetime resident, Ernest Hemingway, now dead for thirty-eight years, with a "Hemingway Days Festival," of amusements vaguely connected to the author. In 1997 it canceled the festivities after a company called Fashion Licensing of America told them "Hemingway, Ltd." a partnership of his descendants, owns the rights to "exploit" his "name and likeness."[4]

Could George W. Bush, Jesse Jackson, Madonna, or Bill Gates bar public conferences on themselves? Could it become illegal to "exploit" their images by writing articles, for pay, about any of them? Could some "Dewey Society" claim such rights relative to the thought of John Dewey? Again, probably not if it went all the way to the Supreme Court, but still, comparable ownership rights of some sort have been supported by courts, and such examples once again indicate a general chilling effect in the air. The Hemingway event was canceled; how many comparable events will never reach the stage of serious consideration for the same reasons?

Perhaps even these examples seem marginal to you. Consider then the doll that originated as a mini-version of a prostitute for the amusement of German men in the post–World War II era. Brought over to America and slightly altered, it was rechristened Barbie, and the rest is history.[5] The Barbie doll's ubiquity and its influence on the imagination of young girls make it as much the legitimate object of serious social and even political scrutiny as, say, violence in the movies. Indeed, some serious researchers believe that Barbie's ludicrously thin figure has helped lead to the current epidemic levels of female anorexia and bulimia, either of which, untreated, can be fatal. And that is only one of the social implications ascribed to the doll.

Thus it is no wonder that there are, for example, several prominent websites devoted to Barbie, some in homage, some in challenge, some in satire (for instance the site for the "Klaus Barbie" doll, referring of course to the war criminal of that name). In addition there are books, museums, popular songs, magazine articles, and much else.

Currently, Matell Inc., owner of the name, has decided that the Barbie brand is so valuable it wants to make sure that only websites and music approved by the company can use the name. To achieve this, it has mostly been using strongly worded legal letters, relying, as Fishbein's did, on the fact that the mere hint of a lawsuit by a large company is often intimidating. In some cases, such as that of a Danish group's extremely popular song about Barbie, it has gone much further, suing against what is argued to be trademark infringement. Evidently only Mattel has the right to permit a song about Barbie to appear.

If songs and websites can be threatened, why not much else? Why not books, movies, newspaper articles, or any prominent mention of Barbies or of any other controversial trademarked item or service whatsoever? Can there still be any doubt that the mere exercise of plausible rights stemming from the ownership of trademarked names can have a chilling effect on politically important intercourse?

All the examples I've given imply restrictions on the smooth operations of markets as well. For a still clear instance of deleterious economic impact, consider this: For nearly a century, operating from a factory in the Bronx, employing about a thousand people, the Farberware company had been turning out a line of well-regarded, moderately high-priced, functional but not stylish, very sturdy pots and pans. Having not made much money of late, the business was sold in 1996. The new owner, in turn, promptly sold an exclusive 200-year license for the use of the brand name "Farberware" to a businessman in Asia, at a price well exceeding the amount he had just paid to buy the entire company. Thus enriched, this able entrepreneur then decided to close the now nameless factory.

The Farberware name could go on, presumably leading customers falsely to believe they were getting the same good products as ever. The new licensee could also produce completely new products—or have them produced—and identify them with the same reliable name. The loyal Farberware workers were simply left out of the equation: They could no longer benefit from association with the name they had made so valuable over the years. This sale would almost certainly have been fully approved by the courts. A public outcry about closing the factory may have delayed that, but the name does seem lost.

There is nothing uncommon about this basic pattern. Brands are sold or merged, and factories are partially or wholly closed down while the trademark survives, all the time. Sometimes nothing but the brand name remains, to be bought and then applied to products wholly different from anything that went under that name before. Thus, Packard-Bell was once a distinguished brand of radio. After manufacture had entirely ceased the name was bought so that the new owner could clothe his low-cost computers with unearned repute, a transaction the business community found entirely kosher.

Together, these scattered examples hint at the magnitude of the distortion of language that can come about when thousands of different firms, many very large, start taking their trademark ownership more and more seriously. Each time a company acts to protect what it views as its inalienable turf, the domain in which the public at large has free rein over language is narrowed, though more by self-inhibition than actual force or legal ruling. But no alarms go off. Each action is separate, with the cumulative effect unnoticed.

Because language, by its very nature, is diverse and variable, that is likely to remain true. We cannot expect any single instance of overwhelming magnitude, or any single moment when we suddenly can feel a crisis at hand. Far from justifying complacency, this bespeaks the danger of death by a thousand cuts. The quickening pace of events adds to the urgency of a thoroughgoing effort to rethink the laws that control how language is owned, and how we react to them.

Why Trademarks?

I now want to trace the kinds of arguments that can be advanced for the kinds of rights now accorded to trademark "owners," in comparison especially with the rights adhering to ordinary proper names. I shall show that there is no reasonable justification for the laws as they are now. Yet, as I shall also indicate, the current emphasis on trademark rights is an outgrowth of the evolution of "late capitalism," putting this entire system increasingly at odds with the kinds of flexibility of language a social order needs if it is to survive.

Trademarks have been in use for centuries, though their importance in economic terms has grown markedly of late, and as a result, trademark law has become far more active than it used to be. A brief review of their history will help explain why.

In their origins trademarks and brands had nothing to do with anything resembling a free market. They were among the many signs used in a basically preliterate society, including coats of arms, banners, icons, and so forth. Brands were of course marks burned into slaves, cattle, and other "goods" to indicate ownership. Trademarks arose in guilds, as markings that denoted each separate master worker, and were owned only in the sense that they adhered to the workshop when the master willed that to heirs, or more rarely, sold it. The primary function of the marks was probably to ensure that taxes and license fees were properly paid, and that guild monopolies, standards, and limits on production, when these existed, were observed. The marks were generally small and inconspicuous, befitting their unimportance for buyers.

As long as commodities were mostly fairly simple, and generally traded in bulk, the names of their originators would rarely be known to, nor have any great importance for consumers. Even today, direct inspection tends to be adequate when it comes to choosing fresh produce or meats, nails and screws, pads of lined paper, potted plants, hammers and similar tools, yards of cloth, bulk gravel, and much else of the kind. For other items such as concert-quality musical instruments, fine furniture, and handmade glassware, the hand of the specific maker has certainly long been relevant—Amati and Stradivari, the stringed instrument makers, were at work and admired in the seventeenth century—but the quality of a particular piece of craft work could still be detected by a discerning buyer without having to rely on the maker's mark. If you're a good enough player to benefit from having one, you just have to pick up the violin, for instance, and try it out.

Only well into the nineteenth century, and only for items that did not reveal themselves directly and therefore could not be directly assayed, did brand names assume a much larger weight. That condition came to hold true for two major classes of products: complicated technological ones such as watches, cars, or computers; and goods that come prepackaged in sealed containers, whether opaque boxes, cans, bags, cartons, or even transparent but sealed bottles. The brand became especially relevant when such items originated in distant factories, so that the consumer could neither observe the manufacturing process directly nor have a familiar face to complain to when something fell below expectations. Brand relevance rose further when the distant factories' output had become highly standardized and uniform, for otherwise past experience of a branded product would indicate nothing about present possibilities.

Once commerce began to operate on a national level, in the late nineteenth century, buying a known brand could afford several benefits to consumers. It offered a sense of assurance that the product was reliably designed and made, that someone would stand behind it if problems arose, and especially in the case of packaged foods that the contents would have the same consistency, flavor, and nutritive quality as the last time. If you love Coca-Cola, Stolichnaya vodka, or Nabisco Oreo cookies or depend on Bayer aspirin or Elmer's glue, you expect exactly the same substances in the same form to appear whenever you open a pack or container.

How Brand Names
Referred, Formerly

This value of the brand rested on a set of assumptions that were left unstated but implied. One was the continuity of the company producing the product and affixing the brand. At first the brand name was usually the family name of the proprietors, and the assumption was that under the same family's leadership the same assiduousness of control would be handed down through the generations, and that family respect for tradition and reputation could be relied upon.

A second implicit assumption was the continuity of the production process itself. New machinery might be introduced from time to time, but only to improve upon and perfect the methods already in effect. Behind that was yet another assumption—the continuity of knowledge, skillfulness, and trustworthiness of workers and forepersons in the factory, who would keep turning out the product through the same operations and to the same specifications time after time, and who would have ample opportunity to train successors to proceed with the same craft and care through the same routines.

Thus—and this point is critical—the actual referent of the brand name was not so much the product itself as the specific proprietors, factories, and collectivity of workers who kept turning it out, along with the shared values, methods, and traditions that held them to the task.

One thing that presumably keeps all engaged in making a product keen to continue traditions of the past is the very knowledge of the value of the reputation it has previously garnered. This reputation is granted, in effect, by the public, through awareness of what the brand name designates, and thus the name's value and meaning is circular, self-reinforcing, and self-referential through the continued will of that public itself. A worker turning out a product of high repute can take pride in being connected to this name, and that pride is reflected in the dedication she brings to her task. Whatever is designated by each particular brand name, then, the ultimate validator of this designation, the ultimate definer of the term, thus remains society as a whole.

Were it the case that brand names continued to obtain their meanings in a similar fashion, the proliferation of products might lead us to fill an awkwardly large portion of our personal vocabularies with such terms, which might cause problems, but the more serious problem of who is permitted to control meaning itself would probably not arise.

How Names Are
Owned, and Why

In effect, brand names represent a new part of speech, intermediate between proper and common nouns or adjectives. With a person, town, or region designated by proper name, one expects the referent to alter over time, as the person ages and changes in habits or attitudes and as the town develops or decays; but one counts on there being only one Paris, France, with its location remaining fixed; likewise one expects that each person, though moving about the globe, will always be in only one place at one time, remaining singular and unique. For the traditional brand-name good to the extent that the brand is taken to refer to the product itself and not to its origins, the opposite is the case; the product does not alter in time, but remains fixed by its ideal type, while it is to be found, if not everywhere, then in a huge number of places at once. It takes on the characteristics of an Aristotelian natural kind, which normally would be designated by a common rather than a proper noun; yet proper—and owned—it is supposed to remain.

But proper names, as such, are not in fact owned. In general, each proper name distinguishes just one individual in the community in which the name is used to refer. Thus, "John the smith," or "John Smith" might well have picked out exactly one individual in a typical, small, or even medium-sized village a century or two ago. Even today, it is a nearly universal rule that a first name is only used once within a nuclear family, and neighbors do not commonly designate different children with the same first and last names. This is the sense in which a name may be said to belong to a specific person.

Nonetheless, these limitations remain purely conventional rather than legally mandated. They are frequently breached in practice. No matter how hard you may have worked to build and secure your personal reputation, nothing prevents someone else from having exactly the same name yet acting entirely unlike you.

Further, in the normal course of events, the existence of more than one person with the same name is not much of a problem. The usual procedure used to repair this present-day lack of specificity is to add additional characteristics such as place and date of birth or aspects of individual biography (for example, "John Smith, the late head of the British Labour Party") narrowing down the designations until only one biological person is singled out by the reference. We do not have much trouble, in such cases in keeping reputations separate in our minds, though on occasion embarrassments resulting from mistaken identity do occur.

Despite these dangers of mix-up, however, the point is quite clear. You do not own your name, nor have exclusive right to designate only yourself with it, however convenient that might be. If you happen to have an "evil twin," that is your tough luck, to manage as best you can, without the law's intervening. Only when someone goes beyond claiming the same name, pretending to your specific identity, can you can have legal recourse (against fraud).

As I have already mentioned, you also have no control over the overtones attached to the words that designate you. To be useful to you, your name remains a word available to anyone who knows of you, a part of language, though a special part. Others can take it and turn it into an adjective or a portion of some more complex compound, such as "Reaganomics," "Aristotelianism," "Castroist," "Yeltsin-like." The more you are in the public eye, the more this will happen, and the less your control over the usages, friendly or unfriendly, or the precise forms of your name that appear in talk or print.

There is another sense in which you do not own your own name. You cannot normally sell it to anyone else, as you can anything that is normally considered to be your property. (True, you could agree to change your name in return for a payment from someone else who wanted to use it, but that wouldn't mean that they would acquire exclusive use of it, any more than you have that for sure now.) The more famous you are, the more people are likely to change their names to resemble yours or to name a child in your honor, and that too is beyond your control, as a rule.

To return to brand names, though they began mostly as the proper names of local craftspeople or proprietors, they have long since developed quite different characteristics insofar as legal ownership is concerned. Claude Montana the designer has no exclusive ownership of his name as a personal name, but he can still successfully claim exclusive ownership rights to designations vaguely relating to his business, just about anywhere in the world. Likewise, if "John Smith" were the name of a soft drink, the current legal trend in brand names is that there could be only one owner of the rights to that designation in the world.

Presumably, this difference between personal names and brand names stems from the fact that single corporations have grown to supply their products first to whole countries, and then to the entire world. The argument would be that if a firm is active everywhere, there can be one and only one ultimate reference (or proprietor) for each brand name it relates to. Clearly, today this separate treatment makes little sense, since a sufficiently famous person is also, in effect, everywhere, yet does not and should not have comparable exclusive name rights.

One argument in favor of exclusivity of brand-name assignment is that without it the buying public might be dangerously confused and too readily cheated. But if, whenever they want, owners of brands can legally make any changes at all in their branded products or even sell off the names to whomever they choose, that argument fails to hold.

A Shift in Capital Leads
to a Shift in Meaning

One thing both Karl Marx and any recent MBA would agree upon is that in the long term profits will be low or nonexistent in any industry where pure price competition holds sway. In contemporary business parlance, the products of such industries are known as commodities, and producing them is to be avoided. This is because increasing profits in this situation involves increasing sales by either ratcheting up production or lowering prices or both, and in combination, when carried out by all competitors, these mean that a market is soon saturated. At that point prices drop until manufacturers at best recoup their costs.

The way out of this dilemma is to make sure that pure competition doesn't hold for what you produce. National brands themselves arose in reponse to this, but more or less as a by-product of the fact that one way to beat competition is to produce at such a high volume and at such low costs per item that cometpitors cannot match you. In other words, successful manufacturers took advantage of what are known as returns to scale, the fact that very large production operations could be more efficient than small ones, usually through the use of very large factories. Since huge amounts of capital are needed for production on a national or international scale, that fact in itself limited competition. The barriers to entry were just too great.

That era is largely past. Flexible methods of production limit the advantages of scale in many industries. Almost any given category of thing, from complex computers to four-wheel-drive automobiles to perfumes or baked goods can now be turned out successfully by many possible producers located somewhere on the globe. Even distribution channels are no longer difficult to obtain. Other methods to avoid price competition are required.

For a while, patents played a pretty large role in this. General Electric managed to maintain a lightbulb monopoly by having essentially the same patents reissued to it over and over, until the courts in the midfifties struck down the maneuver. Today, even though patent life has been extended to twenty years, with our current level of science-based technology, patents no longer offer much in the way of working monopoly. Prescription drugs are a good example.

Whenever the type of disease to be treated suggests a large market, potentially valuable drugs currently emerge from laboratories at a rapid clip. Any significant breakthrough almost always points the way to a whole class of similar yet distinct drugs, not covered by the same patent. Prozac, the antidepression drug, was followed to market in just a couple of years by Zoloft, and then by others with different formulae but the same function. Were the drug approval process less lengthy and costly, the flow of new drugs of comparable performance would be greater yet.

In these circumstances, advertising, combined with other methods of public relations and marketing, have become practically all-important. If they are to work effectively, all these means of generating profits rely on recognizable brand names, which have therefore become absolutely central to the success of almost every large business. Further, in this highly competitive environment, companies naturally seek to "leverage" familiar brand names by affixing them to as many (loosely) related products as possible.

To facilitate this, advertising agencies devote great efforts toward attempting to define the essence of each brand name in the most vague possible terms that still can have any meaning. Consider how the meaning of the phrase "IBM" has evolved. Originally the three letters stood for the imposingly global "International Business Machines, Inc.," its products being such things as punched-card sorters, addressing machines, and other specialized office tools for large to midsized firms. Then came electric typewriters. Later, by 1960, "IBM" became virtually synonymous with what are now known as mainframe computers.

As computer technology advanced, however, IBM could no longer dominate all branches of this market. First "mini-computers," then "supercomputers," and finally micro-computers or personal computers broke free from IBM's hold. The mainframe itself seemed an endangered species—too expensive, gigantic, and difficult to use, and no longer necessary. If the company were to continue to survive and prosper, the name "IBM" could no longer stand for "mainframe computers." PCs had meanwhile pushed electric typewriters and all IBM's other precomputer products into oblivion.

With its ad agencies, IBM discovered in the midnineties that, in truth, its name stood for "solutions"—as in solutions to problems. You or I may not think of IBM whenever a problem needs solving, but IBM's advertising is now geared to just such a response among business executives. The very vagueness of the concept is part of its appeal, at least to IBM. Any state of affairs may be viewed as a problem, and therefore under almost any conditions, presumably, one might think "IBM." Of course, the thought would be altogether too vague were it not that IBM's prior computer connotation continues to lurk in the mind.

Identifying itself as the "solution" company turned out to be highly profitable for IBM. Even in the relatively rational field of management, the unconscious, irrational processes that lead executives to think of calling IBM to find a "solution" are plainly at work. How much more important, then, are similar vague connotations and feelings when it comes to ordinary consumer goods and services, where the constraints of careful management and accounting rarely enter at all?

Defining Desire

Some thoughts due to the French psychoanalyst Jacques Lacan[6] afford insight here. One has to do with desire. When infants cry, their parents take it for granted that the cry has meaning attached to it. In trying to stop the crying, they think they are finding out what the meaning is. Does the child want to be fed, to sleep, to be rocked, to be sung to, to have her diaper changed? These questions and a few more are all that are likely to come up, at least in our culture. The baby's wishes aren't necessarily that specific, however, or if they are, not in exactly these categories. In effect, the parents' responses force infantile wishes into certain preexisting pigeonholes, teaching the child in the process what is meaningful to want or to express. Desire comes to have definite meanings attached to it, when quite possibly, some desires or pains are much more nebulous, and may not have any definite object in advance at all.

Another Lacanian observation concerns the way we are mentally and emotionally structured by the exigencies of language. In English, at least, "I want," is not a possible sentence until an object is supplied. A state of simple desiring is not an emotional condition we are taught to recognize in ourselves; to exist, desire has to have some focus. I suggest it is in the lacunae created by this unacceptable indefiniteness that advertising operates as a kind of surrogate parenting. As an infant you learn that you are supposedly hungry-thirsty (that is, want the breast or the bottle), and then later that you are hungry or thirsty. Hungry for what? Thirsty for what? Food? Drink? Too unspecific. Why shouldn't you be thirsty for a Coke, so that as soon as the vague desire wells up in you, obtaining a glass, bottle, or can of Coca-Cola comes instantly to mind? Why shouldn't you be "hungry for Burger King" (to quote an old jingle), even though that implies not a specific item of food but a place of business?

What advertising now does, obviously with some degree of success, and especially so for the young, is to add to and shape language, supplying us with the words, words that happen to be brand names, by which to know the meanings of our own vague and unnameable sensations, to know as well, in fact, just who we are. The greater the range of inner feelings that end up corresponding with the desire for some particular brand-named object, the greater the success of the company that owns the brand.

Unhitching Referents

Maximizing the power of brands entails not only adding meanings, but also sub-tracting them, when that works more favorably. The older references to propri-etary families, specific factories in definite locales, stable groups of production workers, or even particular, unchanging products or pseudo-natural kinds are now all secondary. They are to be cast aside when they no longer suit the ends of the controlling body of shareholders of the moment and the top executives they put into place. Further, as factories can be sold, and as brands are now even more important than those factories, it is natural for businesses to take seriously the impression that the control they have over brands should amount to ownership that can be transferred by the same kind of selling process. The arbitrariness and illogic of this presumed right is neglected or denied.

The New Sources of Community and Identity

It is no coincidence that advertisers and the developers of brand names find their most opportune targets in many of the very groups who have in the past been among the most fecund remakers of language and, thus, of thought. The young especially are in their sights, and, as more traditional determiners of identity, such as family, religion, local loyalties, political party loyalties, occupational traditions, and the like continue to lose their grip, self-definition through full acceptance of the Lacanian chains of commercially created meanings obtains new leverage. Kids, in other words, seek brands and the meanings supplied by brands as sources of their own authenticity as never before.

Surrounded by advertising and consumer goods, but otherwise often part of a huge, undifferentiated crowd, consumers in general and children—teenagers especially—increasingly attempt to strengthen their own chances at achieving belonging or recognition through linking themselves with major brands. Corporations eagerly exploit this. Thus, there is a Coca-Cola store in Times Square that sells not the drink so much as the logo, emblazoned on T-shirts, sweatshirts, mugs, and just about any other item, just as college names and mottoes have been for some time, or in the manner of baseball teams' caps and jackets.

Although one might well bemoan the contemporary absence of deeper attachments for providing context, there is something commendable about this search for common symbolism. Membership in a community of this type is open to anyone, anywhere on earth. Further, in comparison with other forms of community, the costs of entry and the barriers to be overcome are very low. Kids around the world can wear Nikes, or failing that, Nike knockoffs, close imitations that cost less. Superficial as such items may be as indicators of identity, they may be preferable to a situation in which every ethnic group, or indeed every subgroup or caste, has its own distinctive costumes, or when clothes clearly demonstrate gender, class membership, and the like.

The more corporate identity is connected with brand names, the greater the reason to try to domesticate these names, to sublty alter and redefine meanings, to incorporate them in metaphors, and to find still other ways to control the mental processes they evoke. Thus, if the corporations involved were to achieve total brand-name penetration, along with their delight at such a takeover of language, would have to come dread as well.

Corporate profitability would at once be tied up in maintaining their carefully chosen vague connotations, yet utterly exposed to unexpected linguistic creativity. In these circumstances, for them, exercising the greatest possible control over meaning becomes a prerequisite for sheer survival. Even the most enlightened of businesses will be increasingly tempted to police meaning with an ever greater rigor, doing everything possible to keep their brands on every lip, and yet at the same time keeping them immune to the vagaries that beset unowned, common nouns and adjectives.

Consider some simple examples of what their exercise of control already can mean in limiting linguistic options. A generation ago, it was not uncommon to feel some fondness for eating in "beaneries," "dives," or "greasy spoons," but in using these terms of familiarity, a certain contempt necessarily showed through.

Were McDonald's the homey place it pretends to be, such attitudes would be expected in regard to its name or nickname as well.

But no matter how seedy or divelike an actual McDonald's may be, the generic one is always to be regarded as neat, sanitary, and cheerful. One can expect any usages that contradict this to come under swift and heavy corporate attack. Furthermore, every speaker and writer must be at least slightly aware of the threat of such verbal policing, and thus inclined to shy away from threatened constructions.

The vaguer the connotations a corporation wants associated with its brands, the greater the temptation to police for subtle misuses that will inject different meanings into consciousness. This implies thought control that nothing at present prevents from rising to odious levels.

Taking Language Public Again

If language is to retain its central value as a public medium of expression and communication, we cannot allow meanings that creep into all aspects of life to be treated as private property, to be subjected to legal restraint, threats of such restraint, or even implications of such. A clear rule to insist on is that all words be under the minimal possible public constraint, including trademarked words. Like a person, a company should have the right to identify itself, and to prosecute anyone else who falsely claims to be them or to speak for them. Any other rights of trademark should be granted only under the most careful showing that the public good or the workings of truly free markets would be injured were these rights not granted, and then for as limited a time as possible, and certainly not in perpetuity.

If the justification for restrictions on the completely free use of brand names as labels is to avoid consumer confusion, and to allow well-behaved companies to reap the rewards of their past integrity, then the restrictions are misused when they are treated as property to be bought and sold, which leads to their utterly misleading use. It should not be possible for a firm's owners to decide to get rid of its workers and keep its name, because the name stands for workers too as a rule, if it has any value.

The Farberware example, which in basic outline is a quite common one, offers nothing to the public except for the shareholders, and there is no reason to reserve such a right for them. If Farberware's name may be sold, to be used by a previously unconnected manufacturer then, as in the case of a personal name, anyone else who wants to should be allowed to use the name. The different Farberwares, like the different John Smiths, would just have to distinguish themselves by other characteristics, such as "Farberware of the Bronx, the Original, Century-Old Makers."

We could reasonably go even beyond that standard. When, in a rash move in the 1980s, Coca-Cola changed its formula and flavor, it apparently did so in a conscious effort to make its product more like Pepsi, which it thought at that time had greater appeal in "emerging markets" around the world. Suppose, instead, it had introduced a new product, called, for instance, "Imitation Pepsi-Cola by Coca-Cola" or "Coca-Cola's Pseudo Pepsi,"or simply, "Coke's Pepsi." The meaning of that would have remained quite evident, certainly as clear as "Diet Coke" and numerous other modifications of well-established products.

Why should such usage be forbidden? What valid public interest is served? Anyone who cared about the difference could soon distinguish Coke's Pepsi from, say, Pepsi's Coke, among other permutations that might turn up. Instead of restricting and limiting, such a move would allow brand names to enrich language. In this case, both the companies in question have prospered for years despite having to share with each other and other competitors, the otherwise uncommon word "Cola" in their names.

By the same set of standards, of course, companies would not be allowed to protect their names or the meanings they wish to associate with their brands from anything other than intentional, malicious libel. Network General would have no cause to pretend that its trademark was being infringed by the utterly different usage cited above. Anyone could run an Ernest Hemingway festival, or even a Thomas Pynchon festival (Pynchon being alive) without having to ask for any sort of authorial or familial permission, as long as in announcing and advertising they don't falsely pretend to have such an imprimatur.

Of course, such changes would affect corporate profits. But why should the benefits of public language be sacrificed to prevent that? Why should the power of the state be invoked? If companies derive their profits essentially through using government-sanctioned and -enforced monopolies over brands, in effect browbeating the world into accepting whatever meanings they wish to apply to words, then the standard arguments in favor of pure free enterprise don't apply.

In truth, the exclusive registration of trademarks is a very strict form of government regulation, so it is mere hypocrisy to claim that the restrictions involved do not affect competition or free trade. This is not to mention the additional restraints on meaning, restraints that other kinds of government regulation quite often manage to steer clear of. On the other hand, if the justification for free enterprise is that it helps give us, as consumers, the goods and services we want, it is absurd to accept restraints on our abilities to define what we want, or to have our desires shaped for us in a process in which we are not permitted to intervene.

Disobedience

Quite obviously current realities of corporate power prevent these reforms occurring anytime soon. In the meantime, supporters of language as a public good can and should conduct a form of civil disobedience. Words, including brand names, should be used in a manner that seems most communicative and comfortable, with no bow to implied threats that the trademarking of words confers control of meanings on their putative owners.

Even this step will not be easy. It entails overcoming repressive habits of speech and writing. Intellectuals and academics, for instance, will have to change our very common avoidance of brand names. We may think we eschew these words, which are most often perfectly familiar to us, precisely so as not to give way to corporate power or the banalities of Madison Avenue and so as not to "plug" particular products. But in assuming that to use these words freely we must do any of these things, is to accept their "owners'" power to control their definitions. A use or a mention of a word is only a plug when it completely conforms to the meanings the trademark holder insists on. As it is, when we feel comfortable with the canonical meanings, we almost certainly hesitate less over employing the terms in question; that simply reinforces the status quo. To reestablish language as a public good, therefore, we can start by resisting our own misguided attitudes.

There is no point that is above the fray.

Notes

1. See, for example, Paul A. Samuelson, *Economics*, New York, McGraw-Hill, 1973, 159–161.

2. Michael H. Goldhaber, *Reinventing Technology*, New York, Routledge, 1984, 182–200.

3. *Motorland, Magazine of CSAA*, San Francisco, January-February 1997, 7.

4. Maureen Dowd, "Liberties," *New York Times*, April 12, 1997, 19.

5. M. G. Lord, *Forever Barbie: The Unauthorized Biography of a Real Doll*, New York, Avon, 1995.

6. For a relatively clear account of this see Bruce Fink, *The Lacanian Subject*, Princeton, Princeton University Press, 1995, especially chaps. 1 and 3.

16

Communication as a Public Good

Robert W. McChesney

Public good theory is an especially useful manner to approach the issue of media and, especially, journalism. On the one hand, nearly all U.S. media are privately held, operated for profit, and dependent to a large degree upon advertising for a significant amount of their revenues. On the other hand, media play a central role in providing the basis for culture and civic life. That there is a conflict between these two objectives—to serve owners and advertisers and to serve citizens—has been a recurring theme in media criticism throughout the twentieth century. The criticism has only intensified at the dawn of the twenty-first century as corporate concentration and commercialization of media content have reached unprecedented levels. Increasingly, the United States is experiencing the paradox of "rich media, poor democracy," as a recent book put it.[1] Although criticism of the antisocial and antidemocratic implications of commercial media can be made in numerous areas, I will concentrate specifically on the subject of journalism, as it is with news and public affairs that the importance of media for a viable democracy is paramount. I argue that journalism has embodied the contradiction of media's role in capitalism and democracy more than any other institution. Public good theory not only points to the limitations of market-driven journalism, it points to the necessary solutions.

Journalism has been regarded as a public service by all of the commercial media throughout this century. In particular, commercial broadcasters displayed their public service through the establishment of ample news divisions. These were largely noncommercial during broadcasting's early years and did not become a "profit center" until the 1970s. Historically, public service is something that newspapers, magazines, broadcasters, and journalism schools regarded as an activity directed toward the noncommercial aims that are fundamental to a democracy—aims that could not be bought and sold by powerful interests. Professional journalism was predicated on the notion that its content should not be shaped by the dictates of owners and advertisers or by the biases of the editors and reporters, but rather by core public service values. For much of the twentieth century the media corporations have brandished their commitment to the high ideals of journalism as their main explanation for why they deserve First Amendment protection and a special place in the political economy.

Professional journalism did not develop in the early twentieth century as the result of a philosophical effort to improve the caliber of journalism for democracy. To the contrary, professional journalism emerged as a pragmatic response to the commercial limitations of partisan journalism in the new era of chain newspapers, advertising support, and one-newspaper towns. In such an environment, partisanship only antagonized much of the market, upset advertisers, and called into question the legitimacy of the news product. As Badgikian has shown, professional journalism is severely compromised as a democratic agency in numerous ways.[2] To avoid the controversy associated with determining what is a legitimate news story, professional journalism relies on official sources as the basis for stories. This gives those in positions of power (and the public relations industry, which developed at the same time as professional journalism) considerable ability to influence what is covered in the news. Moreover, professional journalism tends to demand "news hooks"—some sort of news event—to justify publication. This means that long-term public issues, like racism or suburban sprawl, tend to fall by the wayside, and there is little emphasis on providing the historical and ideological context necessary to bring public issues to life for readers. Finally, professional journalism internalizes business as the proper steward of society, so that the stunning combination of ample flattering attention to the affairs of business in the news with a virtual blackout of labor coverage is taken as "natural." In combination these trends have had the effect not only of wiring pro–status quo biases directly into the professional code of conduct, but also of keeping journalists blissfully unaware of the compromises with authority they make as they go about their daily rounds. Professional journalism is far from politically neutral or "objective."

It is arguably at its worst when the U.S. upper class—the wealthiest 1 or 2 percent of the population that owns most of the productive wealth, as well as the top corporate executives and government officials—is in agreement on an issue. In such cases (for example, the innate right of the United States to invade another nation, or the equation of private property and the pursuit of property with democracy), media will tend to accept the elite position as revealed truth and never subject the notion to questioning. The classic example of this phenomenon today is the virtual blackout of media coverage of the CIA, to be discussed below, and the military budget. There is no known explanation for the $250–$300 billion annual military budget in the post–Cold War world, and, interestingly, the media never press politicians to provide one. Why is this? Military spending is the one form of government largess that directly harms no notable upper-class interests, at the same time actively promoting some elite interests. So although the media on occasion will analyze school budgets, public broadcasting proposals, and health care and welfare spending in detail to see if the monies are being spent wisely, there is barely any media examination of the military budget, which is in effect a cash cow for powerful elements of the corporate community.[3] Members of the press, to the extent they even recognize the problem, defend their lack of interest in military spending by noting that the dominant political parties are not debating the matter so therefore it is not a legitimate issue. But such a defense points exactly to the limitations of professional journalism as a democratic force, particularly in a society where commercial forces dominate the political culture.

Professional journalism is arguably at its best, then, when elites disagree on an issue—such as whether a specific U.S. invasion was tactically sound or not—or when the issue does not affect upper-class interests directly (for example, abortion rights, school prayer, flag burning, gay rights, affirmative action). In some circumstances, too, domestic nonelite constituencies like organized labor can be so strong as to have some mitigating effect on elite pressures and the logic of the system. In instances like these, professional journalism has thrived and produced exemplary coverage. Indeed, after World War II this caliber of professional journalism prospered and developed a certain amount of autonomy from the dictates of owners and advertisers, and the corporate sector as a whole. But journalism has always been a struggle, and even in the best of times journalists have had to contend directly and indirectly with powerful corporate, commercial, and government forces that wanted to neuter or corrupt their enterprise. By the 1990s, traditional professional journalism was in marked retreat from its standards of the postwar years, owing to the tidal wave of commercial pressure brought on by the corporate media system.

The decline, even collapse, of journalism as a public service is apparent in every facet of the media. For network and national cable television, news has gone from being a loss-leader and a mark of network prestige to being a major producer of network profit. At present, NBC enjoys what is regarded as "the most profitable broadcast news division in the history of television," with annual advertising revenues topping $100 million.[4] NBC is renowned not so much for the quality of its news as for its extraordinary success in squeezing profit from it. NBC uses QNBC, a high-tech statistical service, to analyze its news reports to see exactly how its desired target audience is reacting to different news stories, and to the ads. Its goal is to have a "boundaryless" flow across the program so as to satisfy those paying the bills.[5] Arthur Kent, NBC's correspondent who gained notoriety for his coverage of the 1990–1991 Gulf War, left the network and published a damning exposé of GE's ongoing efforts to cheapen, degrade, and censor the news. "The people who constitute the conscience of the broadcast news discipline—working journalists—now have less real influence on the daily news agenda than ever before," Kent wrote, "and they face harsh treatment from management if they speak out."[6]

Nor is Kent alone in his assessment. Whereas only ten or fifteen years ago prominent journalists were the staunchest defenders of the commercial media system, today, in what amounts to almost a sea shift, journalists have emerged among its foremost critics. "Our big corporate owners, infected with the greed that marks the end of the 20th Century, stretch constantly for ever-increasing profit, condemning quality to take the hindmost," observes Walter Cronkite. They are "compromising journalistic integrity in the mad scramble for ratings and circulation."[7] "In any honest appraisal of the state of the press," David Broder, legendary *Washington Post* columnist, noted in a eulogy for journalist Ann Devroy in 1998, "the values that defined Ann Devroy's life are increasingly in jeopardy. Media companies—especially those which are part of megacorporations—show little respect for that responsibility and professionalism Ann demonstrated every day in her work."[8]

Of course, many working journalists remain dedicated to providing a public service independent of the commercial needs or political aims of their owners and advertisers. And even in the horrid context we are describing some superb journalism is produced. Disney's ESPN, for example, which counts Nike and Reebok among its major advertisers, aired an extraordinary exposé of Asian shoe manufacturing sweatshops in 1998. CNN and CBS's *60 Minutes* periodically do investigative reports that remind one of what journalism is supposed to be as well. But regrettably these are the exceptions that go against the trajectory, and most journalists who remain in the commercial news media come to internalize the dominant values if they wish to be successful and if they wish to be at peace with themselves.

Indeed, the overriding commercialism of contemporary journalism has been adapted as well by the leading editors and reporters. As James Fallows chronicles in depressing detail, the superstars of journalism are increasingly those who do fairly mindless TV shows, give lectures for exorbitant fees, and generally earn annual incomes approaching seven figures.[9] One almost had to feel sympathy for the CNN correspondent who was reprimanded in 1997 after he did a television commercial as a spokesperson for Visa USA; his role in the commercial had been originally cleared by CNN and it certainly seemed in keeping with the commercial thrust of television journalism. His crime, it would seem, was being caught, or being a small fry.[10] In 1998, recently retired ABC news anchor David Brinkley began doing advertisements for the Archer Daniels Midland corporation that ran on his old *This Week* program.[11] ABC stopped running the spots only after controversy erupted, after having aired them initially so as not to antagonize one of its most important sponsors.[12] (Archer Daniels Midland is the agribusiness firm that had to pay a $100-million fine for price-fixing and that has shown a distinct self-interest in the outcome of environmental, regulatory, and agricultural policy debates.[13]) *Advertising Age* captured the irony of the Brinkley situation:

"Journalists have raised the biggest racket about Mr. Brinkley's new job, even as they solicit paid speeches from groups they could be reporting on."[14]

Sometimes the media giants use their control over journalism to promote their other media holdings. In 1996, for example, the news story that NBC gave the most time to was the Summer Olympics in Atlanta, an event that did not even rank among the top ten stories covered by CBS, ABC, or CNN. What explains NBC's devotion to this story? NBC had the television rights to the Olympics and used its nightly news to pump up the ratings for its prime time coverage.[15] According to the *New York Times,* "various shows on ABC, now owned by Disney, have devoted a great deal of time to several movies produced by Disney, although the network has maintained in each instance that there was justified journalistic interest in the films."[16]

But the main concern of the media giants is to make journalism directly profitable, and the best way to do that is to have fewer reporters, concentrating on inexpensive and easy stories to cover, like celebrity lifestyle pieces, court cases, plane crashes, crime stories, and shootouts.[17] It is also good business because this caliber of journalism rarely offends people in power. Because such trivial topics do not require serious investigative work, they are cheaper to cover and air, and they hardly ever enmesh the parent corporation in controversy, as do "hard" news stories. Consider network TV news. There has been a decline in international news from 45 percent of the network TV news total in the early 1970s to 13.5 percent in 1995. Most of this drop took place in the 1990s after the end of the Cold War, but this was also the time of the rise of the global economy, so one might reasonably expect TV's international coverage to remain at earlier levels if not increase.[18] What replaced the expensive international news? The annual number of crime stories on network TV news programs *tripled* between 1990–1992 and 1993–1996.[19] In one revealing example, CNN addressed a decline in ratings in the summer of 1997 by broadcasting a much-publicized interview with accused murderer O. J. Simpson.[20]

As bad as this seems, local television news is considerably worse. One recent detailed content analysis of local TV news in fifty-five markets in thirty-five states concluded that the news tended to feature crime and violence, triviality, and celebrity, and that some stations devoted more airtime to commercials than to news.[21] In the winter of 1998, local TV news programs in Los Angeles turned the airwaves over to the live coverage of several prolonged car chases à la O. J. Simpson, but where the significance of the chases eluded even the broadcast news anchors.[22] In 1998, California's local TV news broadcasts effectively stopped covering the primary campaign for state governor, or gave brief mentions of the race well after running through a litany of trivial stories. As one political reporter put it, this left all campaign information to TV advertising, making it the first truly "all-commercial political campaign."[23] A writer for the *New York Times Magazine* concluded in 1998: "Most anyone in the press and academia who has given it much thought has concluded that while there are exceptions, local television news is atrocious."[24] Besides making it ever more difficult, even impossible, to have an informed citizenry, this lame local news can have stark material consequences. A 1998 study of local television news in Baltimore concluded that the extreme focus on crime stories, with a strong racial twist, was an important factor in declining opinion of the quality of life in Baltimore, leading to business exodus and job loss.[25]

The attack on journalism is every bit as pronounced in the nation's newspapers. Newspaper coverage of international news, for example, declined by an even greater percentage than that of network TV news between the 1970s and 1990s.[26] The concentration of ownership into local monopolies that are part of large national chains gives the media corporations considerable power to reduce the resource commitment to journalism, thus fattening the bottom line. Gannett showed the genius of this approach as it built its empire over the past thirty-five years. Since purchasing the *Des Moines Register* in the 1980s, for example, it has slashed the paper's once-extraordinary coverage of state affairs to the bone.[27]

To cut costs, these corporate giants increasingly use temporary labor to serve as reporters and photographers.[28] In addition, there is implicit pressure on editors and reporters to accept marketing principles and to be "more reader friendly."[29] This means an emphasis on lifestyle and consumer issues that strongly appeal to sought-after readers and advertisers.[30] "Marketing," one reporter stated in 1997, "these days means spending more time focusing on the things that concern the people who have all the money and who live in the suburbs."[31] In 1998 the massive Times-Mirror newspaper chain asked three of its most prominent reporters to write portions of its annual report, a task usually assigned to accountants and public relations officials.[32]

In perhaps the most publicized new measure, the Times-Mirror's flagship *Los Angeles Times* in 1997 appointed a business manager to be "general manager for news" and directly oversee the editorial product to ensure that it conformed to the best commercial interests of the newspaper.[33] *Times* publisher Mark Willes informed *Forbes* magazine that he intended to tear down the "Chinese wall between editors and business staffers" with "a Bazooka if necessary." A sense of what this leads to came in 1998 when Willes wrote a memorandum to his editorial staff saying the paper could attract more women readers by offering more emotional and less analytical articles. He later apologized for the stereotyping of women, but not for his attitude toward journalism.[34] Investors are wild about Willes and his plans for journalism; "Wall Street has loved Willes from the first," *Forbes* notes.[35] The editor of the trade publication *Advertising Age* applauded Willes's reforms wholeheartedly: "Is it a sin to try to come up with ideas advertisers respond to? Are editorial people selling out when they work with ad people to ... attract more advertisers? I don't think so; in fact, that's their job."[36] It may say a great deal about the state of journalism that among publishers Willes sometimes is held up as the "liberal" protector of journalism values, in contrast to the

CEO of Cowles Media, who argues that newspapers should have no qualms about writing favorable pieces about major advertisers.[37]

What is happening at the prestigious *Los Angeles Times* in fact only makes explicit a growing trend in journalism: the need to serve commercial needs first and foremost. On balance, magazine journalism has had less concern with keeping a formal separation between advertising and editorial content for years; in 1997 the *Wall Street Journal* reported that some major national advertisers demanded to know the contents of specific issues of magazines before they would agree to place ads in them.[38] In the immediate aftermath, reports described numerous other incidents of advertiser scrutiny, implying censorship of magazine editorial content.[39] This caused a public outcry, with magazine editors and publishers formally denouncing the practice.[40] By the end of the 1990s major magazine publishers like Time Warner and Newhouse's Condé Nast had "corporate marketing departments." Their purpose is to help their magazines work with advertisers so that the magazine becomes "an integral part of the [advertising] message," and helps "advertisers adjust their image in hopes of increasing their sales."

The logic is such that major advertisers are increasingly in a position to demand favorable treatment. "Let's be honest," the president of Chanel confessed. "I think you want to support those magazines which—from an editorial point of view—support you."[41] But even if advertisers are not officially vetting the contents of magazines, and even if publishers are not explicitly ordering their editors to serve advertisers first and foremost, the message has been underlined and bold-faced: what they do will directly affect their magazine's and their own personal fortunes.

Perhaps some sense of the general commercialization of editorial content came in 1998 when Tina Brown quit her position as editor of *The New Yorker,* perhaps the most respected U.S. commercial publication, to go to work on a new magazine and other projects for Disney's Miramax subsidiary. "I feel the kind of movies [Miramax] makes are the kind of journalism we try to do," Brown stated. They "have this incredible gift for making good things commercial." Brown's partner in the new venture is Ron Galotti, former publisher of *Vogue.* Galotti and Brown will produce a magazine explicitly designed to produce synergies; that is, to generate stories that will turn into good TV programs and movies.[42] And the synergies extend to advertisers. As Galotti put it, he and Brown will be able to help major magazine advertisers get their "tentacles into the Hollywood area." "I think clients are looking for out-of-the-box ideas and ways to position products and brand their products." Galotti said that advertisers in Brown's new magazine could look for product placements in Miramax films, among other things. But there is no need to worry, according to Galotti, because "the editorial aspect of the magazine will have no commercial overtone at all."[43] This, then, would seem to be the nature of editorial integrity in the era of commercialized journalism.

There are some who argue that this turn to trivia and fluff masquerading as news is going to ultimately harm the media corporation's profitability. As more and more people realize they no longer have any particular need to read or watch news and as news competes with the entire world of entertainment for attention, its readership and audience may simply disappear. Whether that is true or false is impossible to say, but the media corporations, by their actions, have made it clear that they prefer to take their profits now rather than make a lot less money now for a chance at pie-in-the-sky profits far down the road. In fact, it would be highly irrational business conduct for the dominant media firms to approach journalism in any manner other than the way they presently do.

The case of James Fallows provides depressing evidence of this. As mentioned above, Fallows's 1995 *Breaking the News* was a stinging critique of contemporary journalism practices, although he tended to avoid structural explanations for the problem. In 1996, based to large extent on the ideas raised in *Breaking the News, U.S. News & World Report* hired Fallows to be its editor, luring him from the *Atlantic Monthly,* where he had served as Washington editor. Fallows made sweeping staff changes and instituted longer and better researched stories on public affairs. It is worth noting that *U.S. News & World Report* has never been confused with the *National Enquirer* or even *Entertainment Weekly;* its focus has traditionally been serious journalism about politics. In 1998, after nearly two years in which *U.S. News*'s weekly circulation held steady at 2.2 million, Fallows was fired. Although advertising had slumped 7.7 percent from 1997 to 1998, it was unclear if that was in response to Fallows's editorial imprint or even if that had anything to do with his firing.

The explicit reason for Fallows getting fired was his ongoing conflict with *U.S. News* owner Mortimer Zuckerman and Zuckerman's acolytes throughout his tenure. One cause of tension was Zuckerman's insistence on reducing staff and closing foreign bureaus. Zuckerman also wanted to devote extended coverage to the shooting death of fashion designer Gianni Versace, a story Fallows believed had been sufficiently covered elsewhere. Most important, Zuckerman kept a tight rein on the magazine's politics. When Fallows prepared a cover story on health maintenance organizations with the headline, "The Patient Is the Enemy," Zuckerman killed it. "Any coverage that wasn't pro-business ran into trouble with Mort," a *U.S. News* senior writer said. Zuckerman also spiked an article suggesting that real estate developers pay a tax on the land they developed. He also fired Tom Tomorrow, the gifted left-wing political cartoonist Fallows had brought onboard. Until hired by Fallows, Tomorrow's work appeared in some 100 "alternative" newspapers, but Tomorrow could never get picked up by a big circulation publication. "I am pro business," Zuckerman said. "I plead guilty to that."[44] The point is not to skewer Zuckerman; he was perhaps the only major media owner who would even give someone like Fallows a shot at editing a major publication. There is no evidence that any corporate owner would ever dare to give editorial power to someone who had not internalized the dominant commercial journalism values. Fallows's replacement as editor immediately announced he would "run more boxes and shorter stories—that way I think we can better gain the attention of our readers."[45]

Few defend the new journalism, except to say half-heartedly that the media are now "giving the people what they want," as if the people have had any particular choice or as if what generates the best market for advertisers was ever a satisfactory determinant for journalism. This defense smacks of apologia. A recent examination of TV news concludes that consumption of this "distorted diet of information has profound side effects, contributing to public cynicism, desensitization, alienation, ignorance, and the American culture of violence."[46] Some also defend commercial journalism, arguing that the threat of libel suits from powerful interests makes it unfeasible to conduct investigative journalism. This may explain the shyness toward some sorts of stories (though it does not necessarily justify it), but it hardly explains the lack of ideological diversity, the lack of public affairs coverage, and the emphasis on crime, celebrity, advertising fare, and fluff.[47] Indeed, the track record for the media giants is to shy away from hard-hitting stories on their corporate brethren; it caused barely a ripple when a News Corp. station fired two television reporters in December 1997 for refusing to water down and create a misleading impression for their investigative report on Monsanto. The report never aired.[48] In a world where the business and commercial orientation of journalism is increasingly accepted as the norm, investigative forays on corporate misconduct or hostile to the interests of affluent consumers are starkly out of place.

Several other incidents surrounding major news stories and journalists in 1998 point to the severe limitations of contemporary journalism as a democratic agency. On the one hand, the corporate sector is increasingly exempt from any sustained critical examination from a public-interest perspective. (Serious examination of certain aspects of corporate behavior to provide information to the investment community, of course, is one of the main functions of the business press.) In May 1998, for example, the *Cincinnati Enquirer* ran an eighteen-page investigative report on Cincinnati-based Chiquita Brands International that chronicled in detail the unethical and illegal business practices of Chiquita overseas. The factually based story seemed a potential Pulitzer Prize winner. Chiquita, however, determined that one of the reporters had gleaned some of the information for the report from illegally obtained voice-mail messages, and sued the newspaper. The *Enquirer* folded, giving Chiquita $10 million, formally retracting the series, and firing the reporter in question. It is worth reiterating that the truth of the story itself has never been disproven.[49]

On the other hand, in 1998 the corporate news media faced—and failed—their moment of truth with regard to how they cover government activities that primarily serve elite interests—the CIA and the military. This is not a new development, as I noted above, and the media have had a distinct double standard as they investigate the affairs of state. Government activities that serve primarily the poor or the middle class (for example, welfare and public education) are often subject to close scrutiny, and operations that serve some powerful interests and harm others can also receive vigorous coverage (such as tobacco subsidies and regulations against smoking). But intelligence, foreign policy, and military operations are conducted primarily to serve the needs of the elite, and while some powerful interests may not benefit as much as others, none are penalized by these activities and all benefit from having the government commissioned to act in defense of corporate power abroad. Debate on these issues historically has occurred only when the elite itself was split over specific military actions, such as the Vietnam War after 1967 or 1968. During the Cold War this clear double standard that journalists applied toward different types of government activities was justified—for better or, in my opinion, for worse—on grounds of national security. It was fueled by an intense anticommunism that made it "natural" to apply vastly different standards to the U.S. government and to its official enemies. But since the demise of the communist "threat," this justification for treating with kid gloves what some call the national security state has evaporated. It was only a matter of time until some principled mainstream journalists began applying the same standards to the CIA and to the military that they were encouraged to apply to welfare spending and onerous business regulations.

That moment came in 1996 when the *San Jose Mercury News* ran Gary Webb's exposé of the CIA's connection to drug dealing in U.S. inner cities. The balance of the media ignored the story, until pressure from the African-American community forced a response. The main gatekeepers—the *New York Times, Washington Post,* and *Los Angeles Times*—all published attacks on the *Mercury News* story. After all, if a story like this was true, it called into question the entire "free press" that had been asleep at the switch for decades while all of this was going on. Finally, the *Mercury News* published a retraction of the story. Webb was demoted and ultimately forced to leave the *Mercury News.* What received little attention, however, was that extensive subsequent research effectively supported the thrust of Webb's allegations, and, indeed, suggested they were only the tip of the iceberg.[50] Moreover, due to pressure from the Congressional Black Caucus, the CIA agreed to do an internal investigation of Webb's charges. The in-house report did not disprove and, indeed, effectively supported Webb's claims, acknowledging that the CIA had relations with drug dealers throughout the 1980s. Yet, aside from brief mention, the matter was ignored in toto in the commercial news media.[51]

Another 1998 incident was also revealing of this trend. In June Time Warner's CNN formally retracted an investigative story it had run concerning the use of sarin, a nerve gas, by the U.S. military on deserters in the Vietnam War. Although the exact truth of the story has yet to be determined, what was striking was how quickly the CNN executives folded to pressure from the military-industrial complex. The story that took nearly a year to produce, was reviewed by scores of CNN officials along the way before being broadcast, and was the work of several of CNN's most respected and experienced producers was shot down in two weeks without the producers having a bona fide chance to defend themselves. The producers, April Oliver and Jack Smith, refused to resign, insisting on the report's truth, and were fired.[52] As the *Times of India* noted, the incident "raises troubling questions about press freedom" in the United States. "While U.S. journalists routinely speculate about the crimes of other governments on the flimsiest of evidence, they are evidently not free to point fingers at their own."[53]

There is no reason to believe the corporate news media will reverse course and begin conducting journalism toward corporate or national security state activities. In fact, the way these examples from 1998 played out—with journalists fired, demoted, or pressured into resignation in every case—almost assures that few journalists will venture down this path in the future. This is the classical "chilling effect," much talked about in First Amendment law when the issue is government, not corporate, intervention in the affairs of the press. Journalists who wish to do investigations of corporations or the national security state will have to use all their leverage and then some to get clearance from their bosses, while they build up their leverage by doing the tried-and-true formula pieces that cost little, mesh well with the commercial aims of the news operation, and do not antagonize elite interests. Over time, successful journalists simply internalize the idea that it is goofy and "unprofessional" to want to pursue these controversial stories that cause mostly headaches.[54] In addition, journalists will find it ever more difficult to get the go-ahead for these types of stories from their editors and bosses. Time Warner's largest shareholder, Ted Turner, insisted that the CNN story lacked "evidence to convict."[55]

In the future, it would seem, prospective stories on the military and intelligence agencies (or powerful corporations with the resources to make a counteroffensive) will require "evidence to convict" before they are even opened to journalistic examination, a preposterous standard. "By this standard," April Oliver noted, "there would have been no Watergate."[56]

The 1998 incidents also highlight something perhaps even more insidious, the lack of any follow-up for critical investigative journalism. For journalism to be effective, a single reporter or story cannot be the extent of treatment of an issue. The initial report can only open up an area of inquiry, into which some other journalists must pour their attention, unleashing a very healthy journalistic competition. A good example of how it can work was Watergate, where several top journalists followed up the *Washington Post* revelations with their own important exposés. In the 1998 episodes, however, there was no follow-up, no echo, so the stories floundered while the journalists were flame-broiled. This is now pretty much standard operating procedure in journalism toward controversial investigative reporting, especially when the target is a powerful corporation. Former *Washington Post* reporter Norman Mintz counted five major news stories that were published about corporate malfeasance in the summer of 1998, but he noted that the stories were rarely reprinted in other media, especially the elite media, and certainly not investigated further. The stories died on the vine.[57] Moreover, in 1998 journalists themselves, like Howard Kurtz of the *Washington Post*, emerged as the primary attackers on journalists like Webb, the *Cincinnati Enquirer*'s Mike Gallagher, Oliver, and Smith. "Aggressive reporting always has been risky business, but most disgusting about recent assaults are not the predictable onslaughts of corporate lawyers," one observer noted, "but the venom with which other journalists have turned on their colleagues." As Daniel Schorr put it, "Attack a government agency like the CIA, or a *Fortune* 500 member like Chiquita, or the conduct of the military in Southeast Asia and you find yourself in deep trouble, naked, and often alone."[58] In sum, time-consuming and expensive investigative journalism into subjects that raise any questions about the ultimate legitimacy of our ruling institutions is not welcome in the domain of corporate media and the professional journalism it spawns.

It is tempting to say that all Americans suffer as a consequence of this lame journalism, and in an abstract sense that is true. But some people and some sectors of society benefit and benefit mightily from these developments, in addition to the shareholders in media corporations. Those include the powerful corporate and political forces that have less and less fear of critical examination of their activities. Moreover, it includes anyone who benefits from the status quo and finds the prospect of a depoliticized citizenry more comforting than the prospect of an informed, aroused, and active populace. Hence there is a clear political dimension to the decline of journalism; it is ever more a product in service to the political agenda of business and the wealthy few. As the notion of journalistic autonomy from owners and advertisers weakens, the journalistic product will necessarily more closely reflect the interests of the wealthy few who own and advertise in the news media. This is the main reason why U.S. conservatives are so obsessed with taming the "liberal" news media; what they desire is for journalism to more closely reflect the political agenda of the business class. As Newt Gingrich informed a meeting of the Georgia Chamber of Commerce in 1997, business and advertisers ought to take more direct command of the newsroom.[59]

Some corporate media barons maintain their holdings not merely to make profit but also to promote their probusiness, antilabor view of the world. Rupert Murdoch, for example, is an outspoken proponent of the view that the main problems with the world are the prevalence of taxation on business and the wealthy, and the regulation of business, government bureaucrats, and labor unions.[60] He subsidizes the right-wing *Weekly Standard* in order to see that those views get a constant plug before the political elite. As Liberty Media (and former TCI) CEO John Malone stated, Murdoch would be willing to keep his Fox News Channel on the air even if it was not profitable because Murdoch wants "the political leverage he can get out of being a major network."[61] Both Murdoch and Malone are board members of the Cato Institute, one of the leading right-wing probusiness think tanks in Washington, instrumental in advancing deregulation and privatization policies.[62] "It is curious," the famous graphic designer Milton

Glaser wrote in 1997, "that after the triumph of capitalism, American business is embracing the politburo practice of censoring ideas it deems unacceptable."[63]

Two other points merit consideration. First, the commercial media system has played a central role in the degradation of electoral politics. An assessment of recent U.S. elections provides some indication of just how absurd our electoral system has become. It is ironic that back in the 1950s and 1960s, commentators bemoaned how commercial television had turned "political candidates into commodities."[64] By the 1960s many considered it troubling that candidates were more concerned with getting a two- or three-minute segment on a television newscast than with getting out and dealing directly with voters and constituents. Those seem like glory days in comparison to what exists today, much as the Lincoln-Douglas debates evoked nostalgia in the 1950s.

After three decades of deevolution, the political campaign is now based largely, arguably entirely, upon the paid television advertisements. The vast majority of the money spent on political campaigns goes toward these ads. It is nearly unthinkable for a legitimate candidate to be without a massive war chest to produce and run TV ads. This favors candidates who appeal to the richest one-quarter of 1 percent of Americans who give most of the money and candidates who themselves are extremely rich, since they can spend as much as they wish on their own campaigns. Hence people like Steve Forbes and Ross Perot can buy their way into the political process, while dedicated public servants like Ralph Nader, who refuse big money contributions, are shut out altogether. The laws also mean that vested interests like corporations can spend as much money as they want on political ads—what is called "soft money"—as long as the ads do not formally endorse a particular candidate.[65]

What is the nature of the content of these TV ads that are the political lingua franca of our age? Except to those who cannot see that there might be alternatives to what currently exists or to those who have a vested interest in the current electoral system, the content of these ads is uniformly understood to be, at best, troubling. It is often said that TV ads are dreadful because they have the same ambiguous interest in truth that commercial advertising has, but it is worse than that, and the stakes are higher. Political ads are protected from regulation by the First Amendment, unlike most commercial advertising, so basically any half-truth, decontextualized and misleading fact, or even outright lie is fair game. The subjects of the ads are sometimes completely irrelevant to the main policy issues the candidate who wins the election will face. I share the view of Robert Spero, the high-ranking ad executive at Ogilvie & Mather who spent a year analyzing the content of presidential TV ads to see how their accuracy compared to commercial advertisements. Spero concluded that in 1976 "few if any" of the Carter and Ford TV spots "would have been allowed on television" if they had been required to meet the standards the government then placed on commercial advertising. "They could not have met the standard that network television imposes on the most trivial product commercial."[66] Political ads also diverge from product ads in the widespread use of purely negative ads, generally with standards for honesty that would make Spero cringe. It does not make sense for Coca-Cola, say, to spend a fortune merely trashing Pepsi—saying, for example, that Pepsi workers urinate in the bottles—because what matters to Coke is ultimately that people buy Coke, not that they not buy Pepsi. It is different in politics. If candidate A can run down candidate B enough that people leaning toward candidate B opt not to vote altogether, it very much improves candidate A's chances of success. For this and other reasons, negative advertising, deployed prudently, is an indispensable weapon in the candidate's arsenal.

Political advertising, and the expensive electoral system it generates, therefore, has a cause-and-effect relationship with voter cynicism, apathy, and overall depoliticization. On the one hand, in a highly aroused and informed political culture, the sort of material that gets placed in these ads would be dismissed as insults to people's intelligence and never fly. Depoliticization is due, ultimately, to deeper causes than campaign spending or political advertising. On the other hand, this expensive electoral system demoralizes the body politic well beyond what existed prior to the age of the TV political ads. As one report on the 1998 congressional elections noted, "people are gagging on negative ads."[67] In this climate, people increasingly attempt to tune out electoral politics altogether, which makes political advertising all the more important. The only way to reach reluctant voters effectively, then, is to bombard them with ads during entertainment programs and sports events. Most voters are not seeking out the information voluntarily. This is the classic case of both a vicious cycle and a downward spiral.

This leads to the crucial role of the corporate media—especially the commercial television networks and stations—in creating and perpetuating the campaign spending crisis. In the 1998 elections, well over $1 billion was spent on political advertising in broadcast and print media. More then $500 million was spent by candidates to buy airtime on local broadcast stations, not including national networks and cable channels, up some 40 percent from the total for 1994. As one analyst put it, political advertising "saved the quarter" for stations' earnings.[68] This biannual financial windfall is why the commercial broadcasters steadfastly oppose any viable form of campaign finance reform, or any system that would allocate broadcast time for free to candidates. They claim that it is their First Amendment right to do whatever they want to maximize profit. (It also points to the conclusion that if we did not have a commercial broadcasting system, we would probably not have a campaign spending crisis.) But the complicity of the corporate media runs far greater than this. Survey after survey shows that by 1998 the commercial broadcasters had reduced, almost eliminated, any meaningful coverage of electoral campaigns in their newscasts. By any calculation, TV viewers who looked to the news would have found it nearly impossible to gather enough information to assess the candidates or the issues.[69] Broadcasters have little incentive to cover candidates, because it is in their interest to force them to purchase airtime to publicize their campaigns. As TV ads become the main form of information, broadcast news has little or no interest in examining the claims made in these ads, since that might antagonize their wealthy benefactors.[70]

Is it possible that the blackout in electoral information on television news is compensated for by the print media, especially by daily newspapers? Even though an increasing number of Americans, especially younger Americans, do not use newspapers for political information on a regular basis, print journalism still is the pacesetter for what and how serious issues get covered. Campaign coverage tends to provide a dissection of strategy and considerable emphasis on polling data. There is often considerable reporting on candidates' TV ad campaigns, but mostly to discuss the strategy and tactics, and not to assess the ideas in the content.[71]

Consider the highly publicized 1998 U.S. Senate race in Wisconsin between incumbent Russell Feingold and Republican challenger Mark Neumann, for example. Neumann was able to cut Feingold's substantial lead in the polls by using soft money to saturate the airwaves with ads attacking Feingold on a number of issues. Many of these ads were dubious in character, attacking Feingold on issues like flag burning and partial birth abortion. What was striking was the lack of press coverage in the state's newspapers (and, of course, television and radio stations) investigating the allegations in Neumann's ads, or even attempting to clarify what these issues entailed. Instead, Feingold was left, in effect, to spend his limited budget (he refused to accept soft money on principle) to counter the charges. He narrowly won in a race that, had the spending been equal, most observers suspect he would have won in a rout. In short, candidates with the most money who run the most ads have the inside track to set the agendas for their races. It does not mean that they will always win, but it means that a candidate without a competitive amount of cash will almost always lose. Most prospective candidates without gobs of money or ready access to those who have it will rationally opt not to participate, regardless of their qualifications.

Second, in the 1990s the consolidation of media in the United States has been accompanied by the development of a global commercial media system, dominated by a handful of U.S.-based transnational media conglomerates. As in the United States, journalism worldwide is deteriorating, since it has become an important profit source for the media giants.[72] Because investigative journalism or coverage of foreign affairs makes little economic sense, it is discouraged as being too expensive.[73] On the one hand, there is relatively sophisticated business news pitched at the upper and upper-middle classes and shaped to their needs and prejudices. CNN International, for example, pitches itself as providing advertisers "unrivalled access to reach high-income consumers."[74] But even in "elite" media there is a decline. *The Economist* noted that in 1898 the first page of a sample copy of the *Times of London* contained nineteen columns of foreign news, eight columns of domestic news, and three columns on salmon fishing. In 1998 a sample copy of the *Times,* now owned by Rupert Murdoch, had one international story on its front page: an account of actor Leonardo DiCaprio's new girlfriend.

"In this information age," *The Economist* concluded, "the newspapers which used to be full of politics and economics are thick with stars and sport."[75] On the other hand, there is an appalling schlock journalism for the masses, based on lurid tabloid-type stories. For the occasional "serious" story, there is the mindless regurgitation of press releases from one source or another, with the range of debate mostly limited to what is being debated among the elite. "Bad journalism," a British observer concluded in 1998, "is a consequence of an unregulated market in which would-be monopolists are free to treat the channels of democratic debate as their private property.[76]

At times the media giants generate first-rate journalism, but this is a minuscule fraction of their output and often causes just the sort of uproar that media firms prefer to avoid. It is also true that some well-organized social movements and dissident political views can get coverage in the world of commercial journalism, but the playing field is far from level. And, as John Keane noted, "in times of crisis"—meaning when antibusiness social movements gain too much political strength—"market censorship tends to become overt."[77]

Just how bogus this commercial journalism is, when measured by any traditional notion of the communication requirements necessary for a democracy, becomes especially clear when one looks at China. There, a full-scale dictatorship with a long tradition of suppressing dissident or prodemocratic political viewpoints has no particular problem with business news or tabloid journalism, the two main products of the so-called free press.[78] The Chinese government media has lost most of its subsidy, and has turned to advertising as its primary means of support, with all that that suggests about content. So far the marriage of commercial media and communism has been considerably less rocky than most analysts had anticipated.[79] Indeed, it appears increasingly that the Chinese government can coexist with the corporate media giants quite comfortably. Chinese Communist Party chief Jiang Zemin went so far as to praise the 1997 U.S. film *Titanic* in a speech before the National Peoples Congress. "Let us not assume we can't learn from capitalism."[80]

The relationship of the media giants to China is highly instructive about their commitment to democracy as well. In 1997, when Disney had the temerity to produce *Kundun,* a film biography of the Dalai Lama, Disney's numerous media projects in China were "frozen" by the Chinese government.[81] Disney responded by working with the Chinese government to show them how to use public relations to ride out the controversy. Disney even hired superlobbyist Henry Kissinger to go to China and "to keep China open to the Walt Disney Company."[82]

The advertising that Disney was contractually obligated to provide for *Kundun* virtually eliminated any reference to Disney.[83] In the summer of 1998, Disney appointed a special executive, John J. Feenie, to coordinate its Chinese activities. Feenie observed that Disney had made "great strides toward smoothing things over with the Chinese" and it hoped to distribute more films and even build a theme park in China. Disney CEO Michael Eisner "is very serious about wanting meaningful progress in that market," Feenie stated.[84] The message is clear: Disney, and any other firm that is attempting to maximize profit, will never again produce a film like *Kundun* concerning China. Nor will such a firm countenance the caliber of journalism that could significantly undermine the firm's capacity to maximize profit.

Far more striking have been the activities of Rupert Murdoch and News Corporation in China. Since Rupert Murdoch fell into the Chinese leadership's bad graces by suggesting in 1993 that it would not survive the rise of satellite communication, he has bent over backward to appease them. In 1995 he eliminated the BBC from his Star Television bouquet because the Chinese leaders thought the BBC too critical of their activities. Then, in 1996, he launched an Internet joint venture with the Chinese *People's Daily* newspaper. He also published what one critic termed a "fawning biography" of Chinese leader Deng Xiaoping, written by no less an authority than Deng Xiaoping's youngest daughter.[85] Then in 1998 Murdoch's HarperCollins canceled its contract to publish former Hong Kong governor Chris Patten's book, which was expected to be highly critical of the Chinese government. Murdoch, terming the Patten book as "boring" and beneath his standards, personally ordered the cancellation—leading the HarperCollins editor to resign in protest. (Those standards had apparently been determined after the publication of the Deng Xiaoping biography.) After an extraordinary public brouhaha, Murdoch and News Corporation apologized for the cancellation and reached a settlement with Patten; his book would be published, but by another press.[86] (It may be worth noting that this incident was ignored in the newspapers and news media owned by News Corporation.[87])

But Murdoch will hardly be deterred by a little bad publicity. Mandarin-language Phoenix Television, in which News Corporation has a 45 percent stake, signed major deals to gain clearance on Chinese cable television systems in 1997 and 1998, with the tacit approval of the Chinese leadership.[88] And industry observers claim Phoenix "has made significant progress in capturing advertising."[89] As the *Financial Times* put it, Phoenix "enjoys rare access into China, which has been denied to other foreign broadcasters."[90] In May 1998 Murdoch won another major victory when his Chinese partners in Phoenix Television won effective control of Hong Kong's second (of two) terrestrial broadcast stations.[91]

Some sense of Phoenix's "journalism" came when a Phoenix reporter prefaced a question to Chinese premier Zhu Rongii with the words: "You are my idol."[92] In December 1998, Murdoch had a well-publicized visit with Chinese president Jiang Zemin, worthy of a head of state. As a result, observers noted that Murdoch's fortunes were "rising fast in the East."[93] In stunning contrast, at the exact moment Murdoch was breaking bread with the Chinese leadership, three of China's foremost prodemocratic activists—who advocated free elections, new political parties, free speech, and independent trade unions—were given long prison sentences in the toughest crackdown on political dissidents since 1989.[94]

Compare this corporate behavior with that of Baruch Ivcher, the Peruvian whose TV station's numerous exposés of the Fujimori government's corruption and criminal activity led to the seizure of his station and caused him to flee Peru.[95] Or compare Murdoch and Eisner to Jesus Blancornelas, the Mexican newspaper editor who has faced assassination attempts for refusing to back down on his investigation into that nation's drug trade, and its links to the highest echelons of Mexican society.[96] Or compare Murdoch and Eisner to Larisa Yudina, the Russian editor savagely murdered in a contract killing, whose crime was reporting the corruption of her local government.[97] Across the world there are numerous examples of heroic journalists, risking life and limb to tell the truth about the powers-that-be. The Brussels-based International Federation of Journalists reports 41 journalists murdered worldwide in the line of duty in 1997, and 474 since 1988.[98] The U.S.-based Committee to Protect Journalists reported 26 journalists murdered worldwide in 1997, with another 129 cases of journalists wrongly imprisoned for going about their work.[99] But only in rare instances are these murdered and imprisoned journalists in the direct employ of the media giants. One might posit that thugs and tyrannical governments are afraid to mess with reporters from powerful media corporations, so they concentrate on hassling the small fry. But if that was the case, why don't the types of stories that these martyrs were investigating get sustained attention in the corporate giants' media? The truth is that Baruch Ivcher, Jesus Blancornelas, Larisa Yudina, and their ilk may be courageous journalists valiantly advancing the public interest, but they lack what it takes to become successful in the brave (new) world of commercial journalism.[100]

The current media system is set up to serve the needs of a small handful of wealthy investors, corporate advertisers, and transnational media conglomerates. The journalism that is produced by this system is one that best promotes the economic interests of these wealthy few. It is a journalism that by nearly any standard is disastrous for generating or contributing to the development of a participatory democracy. The public good represented by journalism has shriveled through private control and domination. Democracy requires a communication system that provides a fair hearing for a wide range of positions on all significant public issues, as well as a strict accounting of the activities of the powers-that-be and the powers-that-want-to-be. If the problem is structural, so must be the solution. What is necessary are any number of measures to reduce the domination of Wall Street and Madison Avenue over U.S. (and global) media. Measures along these lines include: antitrust; genuine public broadcasting; strict public service requirements for commercial broadcasters; and subsidies for nonprofit and noncommercial media, among other things. Unless there is a political effort to reform the media system, all indications suggest that journalism will continue on its merry path of asininity, triviality, banality, irrelevance, and, ultimately, service to the powerful.

Notes

1. See Robert W. McChesney, *Rich Media, Poor Democracy: Communication Polifics in Dubious Times* (Urbana: University of Illinois Press, 1999).

2. For classic treatments of these hypotheses, which to my knowledge have never been disproven, see Edward S. Herman and Noam Chomsky, *Manufacturing Consent: The Political Economy of the Mass Media* (New York: Pantheon, 1988); Noam Chomsky, *Necessary Illusions: Thought Control in Democratic Societies* (Boston: South End Press, 1989).

3. William Greider, *Fortress America: The American Military and the Consequences of Peace* (New York: Public Affairs, 1998).

4. Jon LaFayette, "The Most Powerful Person in Television News," *Electronic Media*, September 15, 1997, 21.

5. Diane Mermigas, "GE Brings Quality Control to NBC," *Electronic Media*, October 13, 1997, 15.

6. Arthur Kent, "Breaking Down the Barriers," *The Nation*, June 8, 1998, 29. His book is *Risk and Redemption: Surviving the Network News Hour* (Tortola, British Virgin Islands: Interstellar, 1997).

7. Jon LaFayette, "Journalists Hash Out Trust Issue," *Electronic Media*, September 22, 1997, 35.

8. David Broder, "Whose Values Rule Journalism Today?" *Wisconsin State Journal*, May 1998, 7A.

9. James Fallows, *Breaking the News* (New York: Pantheon, 1996).

10. Stuart Elliott, "CNN Orders Its News Staff to Avoid Ads," *New York Times*, June 16, 1997, C3.

11. Bill Carter, "David Brinkley, Now an Archer Daniels Spokesman, Returns to Network Television," *New York Times*, January 6, 1998, C5.

12. Jennifer Nix, "After ABC Blinks, CNN Winks at Brinkley Ads," *Variety*, January 19–25, 1998, 3.

13. Maureen Dowd, "Good Night, David," *New York Times*, January 7, 1998, A21.

14. Rance Crain, "What I Don't Understand: Huizenga, Huff over Brinkley," *Advertising Age*, January 19, 1998, 25.

15. Tyndall Report, December 31, 1996.

16. James Sterngold, "Journalism Goes Hollywood, and Hollywood Is Reading," *New York Times*, July 10, 1998, C5–C6.

17. Kyle Pope, "How Many TV News Magazines Are Too Many?" *Wall Street Journal*, May 30, 1997, Bl.

18. Edward Seaton, Keynote Speech to IPI World Congress, Moscow, Russia, May 26, 1998, 1.

19. Jon LaFayette, "Crime Wave Hits Network News: Study," *Electronic Media*, August 18, 1997, 6.

20. Mark Landler, "CNN Ratings Head South. Calling O.J., Calling O.J.," *New York Times*, July 14, 1997, Cl, C7.

21. Paul Kite, Robert A. Bardwell, and Jason Salzman, *Baaad News: Local TV News in America*, (Denver: Rocky Mountain Media Watch, 1997); see also Lisa Bannon, "In TV Chopper War, News Is Sometimes a Trivial Pursuit," *Wall Street Journal*, June 4, 1997, Al, A10.

22. Christopher Parkers, "Felons Provide Freeway Freak Show," *Financial Times*, February 17, 1998, 24.

23. Todd S. Purdum, "Race for California Governor Is Not Necessarily the News," *New York Times*, May 6, 1998, Al.

24. Michael Winerip, "Looking for an 11 O'clock Fix," *New York Times Magazine*, January 11, 1998, 33.

25. Mark Crispin Miller, "Crime-Time News in Baltimore: The Economic Cost of Local TV's Bodybag Journalism," released to public in June 1998; Dan Trigoboff, "Study Blasts Baltimore News," *Broadcasting & Cable*, July 8, 1998, 33.

364 Robert W. McChesney

26. Seaton, 1.

27. Richard Gibson, "Minneapolis Publisher Awaits Suitors, Looks in Mirror," *Wall Street Journal*, September 12, 1997, B4.

28. Sheila P. Calamba, "At Big Dailies, More News Jobs Are Temporary," *Wall Street Journal*, August 26, 1997, Bl, B6.

29. Iver Peterson, "Newspaper Owners Proselytize Business Sense to Their Reporters and Editors," *New York Times*, June 9, 1997, C23.

30. Iver Peterson, "Rethinking the News: Papers Seek More Personal Connection with Readers," *New York Times*, May 19, 1997, Cl, C8.

31. Iver Peterson, "Editors Discuss Their Frustrations in the Age of Refrigerator-Magnet Journalism," *New York Times*, April 14, 1997, C9.

32. Iver Peterson, "New Issue for Journalists: Corporate Writing Duties," *New York Times*, January 12, 1998, C13.

33. James Sterngold, "Editor of Los Angeles Times Quits amid News Shake-Up," *New York Times*, October 10, 1997, C5; Iver Peterson, "At Los Angeles Times, a Debate on News-Ad Interaction," *New York Times*, November 17, 1997, Cl, Cll.

34. Felicity Barringer, "Publisher of Los Angeles Times Apologizes for Gaffe on Women," *New York Times*, June 3, 1998, Al9.

35. Ann Marsh, "Rewriting the Book of Journalism," *Forbes*, June 15, 1998, 47, 48.

36. Rance Crain, "Conservative Editors Need to Heed Radicals Like 'L.A. Times' Willes," *Advertising Age*, May 4, 1998, 30.

37. Ann Marie Kerwin, "New Doors Cut in Wall Between Business, Edit," *Advertising Age*, April 27, 1998, 62.

38. G. Bruce Knecht, "Magazine Advertisers Demand Prior Notice of 'Offensive' Articles," *Wall Street Journal*, April 30, 1997, Al, A8.

39. Alicia Mundy, "The Church-State Dodge," *Mediaweek*, May 12, 1997, 24–2s; Constance L. Hays, "Titleist Withdraws Advertising in Dispute with Sports Illustrated," *New York Times*, April 28, 1997, C10.

40. Robin Pogrebin, "Magazine Publishers Circling Wagons Against Advertisers," *New York Times*, September 29, 1997, Cl, C6; G. Bruce Knecht, "Magazine Groups Reject Early Disclosure," *Wall Street Journal*, September 24, 1997, Bl2; Constance L. Hays, "Editors Urge Limits on Input by Advertisers," *New York Times*, June 23, 1997, C7.

41. Robin Pogrebin, "Magazine Marketing Raises Question of Editorial Independence," *New York Times*, May 4, 1998, C9.

42. Lisa Granatstein and Betsy Sharkey, "The Talk of the Town," *Mediaweek*, July 13, 1998, 4–5.

43. Felicity Barringer and Geraldine Fabrikant, "Tina Brown Edits Her Career to Match the Zeitgeist," *New York Times*, July 13, 1998, C1, C7.

44. G. Bruce Knecht, "Amid Slump in Ad Pages, U.S. News Fires Its Editor," *Wall Street Journal*, June 30, 1998, Bl, B8.

45. Robin Pogrebin, "U.S. News & World Report Decides to Replace Its Editor," *New York Times*, June 30, 1998, A14.

46. Paul Klite, Robert A. Bardwell, and Jason Salzman, "Local TV News: Getting Away with Murder," in *Harvard International Journal of Press/Politics* 2, No. 2: 102–112.

47. Jennifer Nix, "Hard-Hitting News Harder to Air," *Variety*, April 20–26, 1998, 5.

48. "Two Fired for Trying to Tell the Truth," *Journalist*, June 1998, 24; Steve Wilson, "Fox in the Cow Barn," *Nation*, June 8, 1998, 20.

49. Peter Phillips,"Corporate Media Sells Out Journalists for Profits," *Censored Alert*, Summer 1998, 2.

50. See Gary Webb, *Dark Alliance* (New York: Seven Stories Press, 1998); Alexander Cockburn and Jeffrey St. Clair, *Whiteout: The CIA, Drugs and the Press* (London: Verso, 1998).

51. James Risen, "C.I.A. Reportedly Ignored Charges of Contra Drug Dealing in '80s," *New York Times*, October 10, 1998.

52. April Oliver and Jack Smith, "Smoke Screen," in *In These Times*, September 6, 1998, 10–13.

53. Siddarth Varadarajan, "CNN's Capitulation: No Freedom to Accuse U.S. of War Crimes," *Times of India*, July 11, 1998.

54. Barbara Bliss Osborn, "Are You Sure You Want to Ruin Your Career?" *Extra!* March-April 1998, 20–21.

55. Varadarajan, "CNN's Capitulation: No Freedom to Accuse U.S. of War Crimes."

56. Victoria Calkins, "CNN Reporters Casualty of Corporate and Military Fire," *Censored Alert*, Summer 1998, 3.

57. Norman Mintz, "Where Is the Outrage?" *Nation*, October 26, 1998, 10.

58. Alexander Cockburn, "The Press Devours Its Own," *Nation*, August 24–31, 1998.

59. Kevin Sack, "Gingrich Attacks the Media as Out of Touch," *New York Times*, April 23, 1997, A16.

60. Christopher Parkes, "Murdoch Rails Against Regulators," *Financial Times*, June 28–29, 1997, 2.

61. Chuck Ross, "From the Top of TCI," *Electronic Media*, September 29, 1997, 50.

62. Norman Solomon, "Media Moguls on Board," *Extra!* January/February 1997, 19–22.

63. Milton Glaser, "Censoring Advertising," *Nation*, September 22, 1997, 7.

64. Dallas Smythe, *Counterclockwise: Perspectives on Communication*, ed. Thomas Guback (Boulder, Colo.: Westview, 1994), 107.

65. Sheldon Rampton and John Stauber, "Keeping America Safe from Democracy," *PR Watch 5*, no. 3, Third Quarter 1998, 1–6.

66. Robert Spero, *The Duping of the American Voter* (New York: Lippincott and Crowell, 1980), 3.

67. Jeff Mayers and Rick Barrett, "In Your Face," *Wisconsin State Journal*, October 31, 1998, 1A.

68. Michael Freeman, "Hot Air Lifts Second Half," *Mediaweek*, November 2, 1998, 6.

69. Dan Trigoboff, "Political Ads Outnumber Election Stories, Study Finds," *Broadcasting & Cable*, November 2, 1998, 26.

70. Ira Teinowitz, "Paid Ads Looming Larger on the Political Landscape," *Advertising Age*, October 1998, 28.

71. See, for example, Richard L. Berke, "G.O.P. Begins Ad Campaign Citing Scandal," *New York Times*, October 28, 1998, Al, A21; Francis X. Clines, "Democrats Launch Counterattack Ads," *New York Times*, October 30, 1998, A26.

72. Jane Birch, "Package Deal," *Television Business International*, November 1997, 31–32.

73. Louise McElvogue, "Not in My Back Yard," *Television Business International*, November 1997, 16–22.

74. CNN International advertisement, *Ad Age International*, June 29, 1998, 6.

75. "Here Is the News," *The Economist*, July 4, 1998, 13.

76. Nick Cohen, "The Death of News," *New Statesman*, May 22, 1998, 20.

77. John Keane, *The Media and Democracy* (Cambridge, Mass., and Oxford: Polity Press, 1991), 91–92.

78. James Harding, "Gang of Four Found on Mars," *Financial Times*, December 6–7, 1997, 7; Robert S. Greenberger, "Interim Pact with China Is Reached on Access for Financial-News Providers," *Wall Street Journal*, October 27, 1997, B10.

79. Elisabeth Rosenthal, "A Muckraking Program Draws 300 Million Daily,"*New York Times*, July 2, 1998, A8.

80. Alan Riding, "Why 'Titanic' Conquered the World," *New York Times*, April 26, 1998, 1, 28.

81. Joyce Barnathan, Matt Miller, and Dexter Roberts, "Has Disney Become the Forbidden Studio?" *Business Week*, August 4, 1997, 51.

82. Bernard Weimraub, "Disney Hires Kissinger," *New York Times*, October 10, 1997.

83. Dan Cox, "Disney Trumps Sony with China Card," *Variety*, December 8–14, 1997, 3.

84. "Disney's Appointment of a China Executive Signals a New Thrust," *Wall Street Journal*, June 8, 1998, B2.

85. Eric Alterman, "Murdoch Kills Again," *Nation*, March 23, 1998, 7; Ken Silverstein, "His Biggest Takeover—How Murdoch Bought Washington," *Nation*, June 8, 1998, 29.

86. "Harper/Collins Settles Row with Patten and Apologizes," *Wall Street Journal*, March 10, 1998, A13.

87. "Murdoch Hunt," *Financial Times*, March 2, 1998, 19.

88. Craig S. Smith, "China Television Appeals to Beijing as Broadcaster Nears End of Its Funds," *Walll Street Journal*, February 27, 1998, S6.

89. John Gapper, "News Corp Joins Hong Kong Book Row," *Financial Times*, February 28/March 1, 1998, 5.

90. Louise Lucas, "Hong Kong's ATV Won by Pro-Beijing Interests," *Financial Times*, May 27, 1998, 4.

91. Janine Stein, "ATV Sale Prompts Censorship Fears," *Television Business International*, June 1998, 1.

92. James Kynge and John Gapper, "Murdoch Mends Fences with Beijing," *Financial Times*, December 12–13, 1998, 1.

93. Don Groves, "Star Shines Bright in East," *Variety*, December 21, 1998–January 3, 1999, 37.

94. Erik Eckholm, "Beijing, Toughening Crackdown, Gives 2 Activists Long Sentences," *New York Times*, December 22, 1998, A1, A6; James Kyuge, "Third China Dissident Gets Jail Sentence," *Financial Times*, December 23, 1998, 4.

95. Andrew Paxman, "TV Mogul Out to Retake Peru Broadcast Empire," *Variety*, March 23–29, 1998, 68.

96. Sam Dillon, "After a Murder Attempt, an Editor Is Unbowed," *New York Times*, March 7, 1998, A4.

97. Celestine Bohlen, "Slain Editor Makes Moscow Take Notice," *New York Times*, June 12, 1998, A1.

98. "Killing the Messengers," *The Economist*, July 4, 1998, 41.

99. Committee to Protect Journalists, *Attacks on the Press in 1997* (New York: Committee to Protect Journalists, 1998).

100. Sally Bowen, "Peruvian TV at Centre of Legal Drama," *Financial Times*, September 23, 1997, 8. Calvin Sims, "Crusading TV Station Is the City's Daytime Drama," *New York Times*, July 22, 1997, A4.

Proposed Declaration
of the Rights of Netizens

Michael Hauben and Ronda Hauben

We Netizens have begun to put together a Declaration of the Rights of Netizens and are requesting from other Netizens contributions, ideas, and suggestions of what rights should be included. Following are some beginning ideas.

The Declaration
of the Rights of Netizens

In recognition that the Net represents a revolution in human communications that was built by a cooperative non-commercial process, the following Declaration of the Rights of the Netizen is presented for Netizen comment.

As Netizens are those who take responsibility and care for the Net, the following are proposed to be their rights:

Universal access at no or low cost
Freedom of electronic expression to promote the exchange of knowledge without fear of reprisal
Uncensored expression
Access to broad distribution
Universal and equal access to knowledge and information
Consideration of one's ideas on their merits
No limitation to access to read, to post, and to otherwise contribute
Equal quality of connection
Equal time of connection
No official spokesperson
Uphold the public grassroots purpose and participation

(continues)

(continued)

Volunteer contribution—no personal profit from the
  contribution freely given by others
Protection of the public purpose from those who would use it for
  their private and money making purposes

The Net is not a service, it is a right. It is only valuable when it is collective and universal. Volunteer effort protects the intellectual and technological commonwealth that is being created.

DO NOT UNDERESTIMATE THE POWER OF THE NET AND NETIZENS.

Inspiration from: RFC 3 (1969), Thomas Paine, Declaration of Independence (1776), Declaration of the Rights of Man and of the Citizen (1789), NSF Acceptable Use Policy, Jean-Jacques Rousseau, and the current cry for democracy worldwide.

This article is a draft chapter from the Netbook by Michael Hauben and Ronda Hauben titled *The Netizens and the Wonderful World of the Net*. Commercial use of this writing is prohibited and this draft is being made available for comment. Please send comments to both of us at hauben@columbia.edu and rh120@columbia.edu.

17

Higher Education as a Public Good

Stanley Aronowitz

For the first time since the late 1960s, when student demonstrations and occupations forced open admissions in many public colleges and universities, higher education has become a major public issue. There are three questions that define the debate: The first concerns the commitment of legislative and executive authorities to maintaining public higher education at a level of funding adequate to enable institutions to offer a high-quality education to students. The second concerns who should be admitted and who should be excluded from higher education, the so-called access debate. Put another way, should higher education be a "right" like elementary and secondary schooling? Or should it be, like European counterparts, a privilege reserved for those who have a requisite level of academic achievement? In this conversation we hear comments like: "After all, not everyone should be in college; what about the millions who work in factories or offices?" Third, especially in recent years, curriculum has been thrust closer to center stage. The chief bone of contention is whether the liberal arts should be available to every college student. Indeed, should every student regardless of discipline be required to imbibe at least a sampling of literature, philosophy, history, and the social sciences? Or as some have urged—and many institutions have agreed—should students in technical and professional areas like computer science, engineering, and even natural science largely be exempt from such encumberances? Of course this argument applies to both high-level technical universities such as Carnegie Mellon, RPI, and Case and to the large number of community colleges whose "mission" is now almost exclusively confined to preparing trained workers for the corporations with whom they have developed close relationships.

Higher education has become prominent on the political screen as the widespread perception that earning a bachelor's degree is the absolute precondition for obtaining a better niche in the occupational structure. But as postsecondary credentials have become a necessary qualification for nearly every technical, let alone professional job, higher education costs—both tuition and living expenses—have skyrocketed. At the same time, more than ever students and their families are seeking places in private colleges and universities. And they interpret failure to secure admission to leading private schools (with the exception of a handful of elite public research universities) as a major personal and economic defeat. For the bare truth is that in the last decade of neoliberal economic and social ideologies public postsecondary schools are taking a severe beating in the commonweal. In the current environment budget cuts and downsizing are prescribed by policymakers as the zeitgeist has shifted to the view that only the marketplace represents quality and anything connected to public goods that does not submit itself to the business environment is a second-rate article.

The effect of this persistent and merciless attack on public higher education has been to demoralize faculty and to prompt conservative-dominated legislatures to impose a regime of permanent austerity. With the exception of a handful of public research universities, notably those of the University of California and of the Big Ten, this has resulted in sharpening the distinction between the two research tiers of the academic system on the one hand and the "third tier" of public teaching institutions, both senior and community colleges, on the other. Former Berkeley Chancellor Clark Kerr's notorious proposal, first announced in 1958 and inscribed in the Calfornia state systems in the early 1960s, that the research tiers be fiercely defended from the horde by establishing a clear cleavage between those institutions that produce knowledge and those that transmit it has succeeded beyond his and his critics' wildest expectations. Today this mantra has been advanced by the proposition that only certain teaching institutions, some private four-year colleges, are "excellent" enough to qualify for the transmission task.

For the Kerr plan was no mere speculation; it contained a detailed program to ensure the separation. Research university faculty were to teach one or two courses a semester, even be able to purchase their teaching time with research grants. In contrast the third-tier universities and colleges would oblige faculty to teach three or four courses, and community colleges as many as five. The reward systems in the two tiers would be different insofar as publication would play a distinctly subordinate role in the third tier. At the same time Kerr envisioned substantial salary differentials. The only means for moving upward in the new academic system would be through research and writing and, of course, administration.

Yet the tiering of higher education hit a snag in the 1960s. Two distinct movements for university reform gained momentum. The first was the insistent demands by black, Latino, and working-class students for access to the institutions as a sign of equality as well as equality of opportunity; the second was the profound dissatisfaction of mostly white, middle-class students in elite universities with the growing trend toward focusing on technical/scientific knowledge production in what Kerr called the "multiversity." At Berkeley, and elsewhere, in the early 1960s they came together in a mass student movement in which these two quite different thrusts were merged in the struggle against the emergence of the corporate university. The success of the demand for extending higher education access to virtually any high school graduate depended, in part, on the authority of the civil rights movement, which undergirded student protest, and of the crisis of legitimacy of the national government in the wake of its unpopular Vietnam War policies. It was made feasible, as well, by the relative buoyancy of the war-suffused U.S. economy, which enabled federal and state governments to supply the funds needed to expand the public university system.

Students made their protest on questions of curriculum and, for a time, forced faculty and university administrations to give some ground. Although the Berkeley Free Speech Movement was detonated by the policy of the technocratic Kerr administration barring "outside" political groups from the campus, its apogee was in the achievement of significant curricula reforms. In the UC system, Berkeley, San Diego, and Irvine students wanted the right to select their own courses and choose instructors to teach them. In some places they demanded and won exemption from course requirements and from large introductory classes and protested the the authoritarian pedagogical styles of some professors, which prompted the most obdurate among the latter to resign and go elsewhere. These struggles, which dominated many campuses until the emergence of the antiwar movement in the late 1960s, succeeded in changing higher education's culture for the next twenty years. Aided by Harvard's reimposition of the core curriculum in 1979 and the ebbing of the student movement, faculty and administration slowly regained the upper hand in the following two decades.

With the triumph of market principles in higher education (in which everything from student enrollments, curriculum, and tuition costs were determined by the sales effort and the job market) and with the ebbing of the black freedom movement and mass antiwar movement, the astounding expansion of public colleges and universities came to a screeching halt. Suddenly in this most advanced of advanced industrial societies, corporate and government economists announced a "fiscal crisis" in public goods, including higher education. The "public"(read business, professional, and corporate farm interests) were simply unwilling to pay the bill for education, health, and other elements of the social wage. They suggested that the way out of the crisis was that user taxes be imposed on public goods; students and their families should be required to substantially pay for public higher education. If enrollees in the private schools were willing to pay large tuition fees, why not those in public universities?

Conservatives in and out of higher education never accepted open admissions. By their lights the democratization of access to public colleges as well as the elite and private schools degraded the value of the degree. There was a sea change in public higher education, brought about by the entrance in the late 1960s into colleges and universities of perhaps a million additional blacks, Latinos, and other racialized minorities who, absent the civil rights movement, would never have reached their gates. On the heels of these events there was considerable pressure on the Ivys and other private schools to undertake policies which, in effect, modified their traditions of cronyism and nepotism and their meritocratic bias. Contrary to popular myth, neither the public nor the private sector was indiscriminate in their admissions policies; open admissions never applied to public senior colleges, let alone the private elite colleges and universities. Although these schools often provide remediation services to students, especially to those who failed the math sections of the SAT or did not take enough math to qualify, admission policies remain selective. In most states open admissions has been confined to community colleges and some third-tier senior colleges.

Abetted by the media, which seems to swallow almost any attack on public higher education emanating from conservative education think tanks like the Hudson and Manhattan Institutes, the educational right has mounted what may be the most concerted and coordinated attack against public goods in this century. With the possible exception of the widespread belief that charter schools and vouchers are needed to radically issue a wake-up call to public elementary and secondary education, in recent educational history educational policy is more than ever driven by the conservative ideology of hierachy and privatization.

The rise of mass public higher education in America was a result of several influences, chiefly those that resulted from the problems associated with the post–World War II era. Perhaps the most important piece of social engineering after the war was the Servicemen's Readjustment Act of 1944, popularly known as the GI Bill of Rights. At the urging of President Franklin D. Roosevelt, who feared mass unemployment in the postwar period, Congress passed a bill providing returning veterans with income support for a one-year period and funds to enter educational programs, including higher education. Between 1945 and 1952 a million veterans entered mostly private colleges and universities, armed with the price of tuition and modest living expenses. All manner of institutions, including the Ivys and other elite schools, gladly accepted these veterans and the government money that accompanied them.

Actually, public higher education has a long history. Founded in 1847 by Townsend Harris, the City College of New York was intended to provide an opprortunity for "talented" young people of modest means to gain the benefits of a college education on a tuition-free basis. The municipal college movement spread slowly and never really embraced a large number of communities, but its example inspired parallel efforts at the state level. After the founding of City College, the most substantial event in the emergence of public higher education was the Morrell Act of 1862. Under this act, the government supplied large tracts of federal land to states who were willing to found universities for the purpose of providing general education in all areas of learning, but chiefly scientific and technical research and assistance to agriculture and industry.

Within a half century states in the Midwest, the Northeast, and the South established so-called land grant colleges. Despite the intention of the Morrell Act, many of them remained glorified teachers colleges, but some, like the Universities of Michigan, Wisconsin, Illinois, and Indiana, took on characteristics identified with the modern research university. Together with the University of California at Berkeley and Cornell University and with Harvard, MIT, and Princeton among the private sector, they constituted the basis for the development of the modern research university, which came into its own with the government's rearmament program on the eve of World War II.

After World War II the state universities and public municipal colleges also benefited from the largesse of the federal government. In fact, the GI bill was extended under the imperatives of the Korean War, which drafted more than a million men and women. And the Cold War provided a substantial boost to the research programs of public state universities. Having exploded a nuclear device by 1949, the Soviet Union accelerated its military nuclear and space programs. Among other windfalls, this prompted the U.S. government to support higher education in a concerted attempt to stem the "Sputnik" effect, the alleged Soviet superiority in space exploration and its perceived nuclear parity. By the late 1950s the federal government had committed itself to long-term support for postsecondary schooling, especially to students seeking careers in natural science and technology, but also in the humanities and social sciences. States were pouring substantial funds into higher education as well. By 1960 the public sector was larger than the private sector and a decade later accounted for more than 70 percent of student enrollment.

After more than sixty years of public colleges and universities gradually supplanting private schools as the dominant sector of higher education, we are now witnessing the return of tradition. The private sector of postsecondary education is growing faster than the public and, perhaps more to the point, is widely perceived as superior. For all practical purposes, since the measure of quality is equivalent to a school's ability to exclude students because of its prestige, elite private schools have gained substantially on similarly placed public institutions. To be sure, some public systems such as the Big Ten and the University of California schools are still highly competitive, but private institutions such as Brown, Harvard, and Yale, for example, reject more than four of every five applicants; many others, such as the "little" Ivies, have similar records of exclusion.

The economic reasons for this state of affairs are not difficult to discern: Faced with deregulation and the threat of globalization, Congress and state legislatures hurried to court the favor of business interests. They deprogressivized taxes, made it difficult to raise public funds for public education by raising the standard by which such bills would be passed, and removed authority for new taxes to the voters. In California, Massachusetts, and many other states the initiative and referendum, whose origin was in the Progressive Era's skeptical response to the "bought" politicians of those years, were used to provoke what Richard Elman has called "The Poorhouse State." In California, the Northeast, and the Southwest, for example, annual budget cuts, either in monetary or real terms, have been imposed by many state legislatures. In consequence, systematic replacement of full-time professors with adjuncts, teaching assistants, and temporary professors in teaching the undergraduate curricula is rife. Salaries for full-timers have declined so that those with some lateral mobility are inclined to move on to private institutions, And witness the drying-up of funds for construction and maintenance of aging physical plant.

But money tells only part of the story. Private colleges and universities have mounted a huge public relations effort to persuade those parents and prospective students who have the resources to pay that the advantages they offer are worth the price of exorbitant tuition, especially in comparison to the costs of public education. They brazenly attempt to capture disaffected students from public education and shed no tears when their appeal results in huge debt for families that can ill afford the price of private tuition. Needless to say, getting a good education is only part of the consideration. Above all, the privates, especially the elite schools, offer prestige that leads to effective job placement in the corporate world, valuable contacts among peers for future jobs, and a more comfortable student life exemplified in better facilities such as dorms, sports, and recreation centers.

Beyond these trumpeted advantages is the systematic attack against public higher education emanating from right-wing think tanks and conservatives whose views find a receptive ear in the media. For example, the New York media gave enormous and favorable publicity to a recent report on City University of New York by a mayoral commission headed by former Yale president Benno Schmidt, among whose members were conservatives of all stripes and employees of the mayor. The commission found the 200,000-student CUNY "adrift" and in need of reform. It recommended major changes, among them further administrative centralization, to assure that the reform program would be effective; erosion of faculty governance, since the faculty was judged a leading obstacle to changes anticipated by the report; provisions to undermine its professional autonomy; "mission differentiation," a code term for creating several new tiers in the system to assure that the top tier was protected against the community colleges; and a hard look at tenure with a view to abolishing or severely restricting it. Schmidt is currently the leader of the Edison Project, a for-profit corporation that organizes and consults with public schools in search of privatization around the country. Schmidt's commission included Heather McDonald, a fellow of the Manhattan Institute (a conservative think tank), and an array of members who were similarly oriented. Shortly after issuing the report, which has become a blueprint for the administration that took office at the end of 1999, Schmidt became vice chair of the CUNY Board of Trustees.

The prospective transformation of CUNY from a beacon of open admissions for the city's minority and working-class population to a genuine competitor in the elite game that has swept through higher education would be a step into the pre-

1960s, when New York City's four colleges were held to a higher standard than nearly all of the area's higher education institutions. To gain entrance to tuition-free schools, students were required to earn grade-point averages of 85 or higher from a secondary school system that was second to none in the entire country. In fact the four original city colleges and Baruch, the system's business college, still require high GPAs as well as passing grades on each of three "placement"(that is, admission) tests. The difference in the intervening forty years is that these grades are held in the majority by blacks, Latinos, and Asians and for this reason are considered by CUNY's detractors to be "inflated."

Curiously, the charge of grade inflation, which has been made and tacitly acknowledged by several Ivy League schools, has failed to diminish their prestige. Having recently abolished its A-plus grade, what counts for schools such as Princeton is that it rejects many more applicants than it accepts and has a sumptuous endowment and accordingly retains its elite standing. Similarly, in an article on the alleged revival of Columbia University, reporter Karen Aronson pointed out that one of the major indicators that the school enjoys a revived reputation is that it admitted only 13.7 percent of applicants last year, a figure that places it second only to Brown, whose rejection rate is 87 percent. In none of the recent reports of the booming private college industry has the question of educational quality figured in the evaluation of their successes. The measure of quality seems to rely heavily on whether school admission is considered a valuable commodity to prospective students. In other words, is it a product that can command high tuition and many applicants?

In fact, as a grim report in 1999 from the University of Chicago attests, this paragon of the vaunted Great Books curriculum was having trouble in its recruitment campaign precisely because, according to the university administration, in the face of the zeitgeist pointing in the opposite direction, it retained too much academic rigor. Consequently the board and the administration announced a new emphasis away from its classical educational focus toward a more lenient academic program, with added sports facilities and stronger placement services. Appalled members of the faculty and student body protested the shift, after which the university's president announced his resignation to take up teaching duties. But the board has neither retracted its program nor expressed any intention of modifying it. Despite its prestige, many faculty at the University of Chicago have discovered that even in matters of curriculum, the heart of faculty sovereignty, their powers are limited.

In the sciences, technologies, and in graduate professional education the two dozen or so leading public research universities are holding their own in this competition. Despite budget constraints imposed by state legislatures eager to reduce taxes for their business and upper-middle-class constituents, many have retained their ability to raise substantial research grants. For example, UC-Irvine and UC-San Diego are major recipients of grants for bioengineering from agencies such as the National Institutes of Health and the Centers for Disease

Control; Cornell, Berkeley, and Illinois are leading research institutions in physics; and Penn State and Pittsburgh are among the most important of the technical science research institutions. Where the legislature has cut back on operating funds, the proceeds from research activity often keep many programs in the humanities and arts alive.

Institutions that face the most severe problem in public higher education are those in the tiers below the two categories of research universities. Departments and schools of teacher education, although not prospering in this age of academic austerity, have substantial social utility, even by conservative lights. Apart from them, many universities and community colleges are scrambling to find a "mission" sufficiently attractive to convince skeptical legislators that they have an economically viable role. The new mantra of higher education is that postsecondary schooling makes significant contributions to local and regional economies by training technically competent labor, and also by providing income to a large number of blue-collar, clerical, and professional workers. Consequently, schools are making agreements with private corporations to provide curricula and teaching staff for dedicated skills training. Even when specific deals do not drive the curriculum, vocationalization does. As students get the message that in this global economy a higher education credential is necessary for survival, many feel they do not have the luxury to indulge their artistic, critical, or literary interests and must, instead, keep their collective noses to the technical grindstone. As a result, many social sciences departments are relegated to providers of "breadth" requirements or are encouraged or forced to adopt vocational majors to prevent being dropped. When majors have declined steeply, English departments are often little more than composition mills.

For the time being there is no imminent threat of school closings in most state systems. But university and college administrations in the third (nonresearch) tier are admonished by regents and state commissions of higher education to find ways to close budget shortfalls by raising tuition, to make alliances with corporations or otherwise turn their predominantly liberal arts institutions into vocational schools, or to add more research capacity to their faculty and facilities. A history professor tells me that the third-tier Illinois public university in which he teaches, once a broad general education school with a few scientific and technical programs, now consists largely of business and technical majors. Similar trends are evident in New York, New Jersey, Colorado, and California. The separation between the "flagship" schools and the largely undergraduate and master's-level institutions is widening. For the latter, the message is clear: sink or swim. Needless to say, few administrators in public higher education are willing to risk the severe penalties of smaller enrollments and diminished income by retaining their liberal arts focus. The brute fact is that undergraduate humanities majors are few. Only in fields like economics, because of its predominant business ties, political science, because it is seen as a good prelaw major, and sociology, because of the still lively student interest in the social services as a profession, has there been some growth.

Even some private school students exhibit anxiety about the future. As we have seen, they are demanding better placement services and are sticking more closely to fields that have direct occupational outcomes rather than using their undergraduate schooling as a time of exploration and creative uncertainty. Some elite schools, public as well as private, remain beacons for English and other language majors and some, like Pittsburgh, have attractive undergraduate philosophy and history programs. But major state schools such as the four SUNY research universities, Rutgers, and many in the UC system report a decline in undergraduate majors in history, philosophy, and literature. Although most of these are in no imminent danger of becoming composition factories for technical majors, even as they retain their highly rated Ph.D. programs, the so-called economic boom has failed to produce a new era of relaxation. Students remain enervated because, I suspect, they know what the media has ignored: There is a lot of work but few jobs, if by jobs we designate work that is accompanied by the amenities of security, benefits, and a career ladder that enables one to gain income and authority along with experience. Moreover, students know from their own parents' experience that corporate downsizing has affected middle management and professionals as well as blue-collar workers.

The economic and social environment of the late 1990s is inimical to the development of a system of public higher education in which the goals are defined beyond the utilitarian uses of credentials and acquisition of job skills. Far from education, many public colleges and universities are constituted not as public spaces where adults of all ages can take non-credit-bearing courses in world affairs, craft and art classes, and participate in forums and conferences of all sorts, but as labor exchanges. One of the historic aims of public higher education has been the development of citizens able to participate in key decisions affecting the polity. This role has been consigned to one of the "distribution" requirements of the first two years of a bacalaureate degree. The hard fact is that continuing and citizenship education is now conceived by administrators as a money-making activity and is most effective in private institutions. Threadbare, many public schools are bereft of these programs or offer only a limited range of skills-oriented courses.

Having succeeded in reimposing a core curriculum in most colleges and universities, leaders in higher education are in the throes of a second stage in curriculum "reform," one that has provoked considerable debate. Its central issue is education for whom and for what? The dispute over the curriculum takes many forms. Feminist, black, Asian, and Latino educators have responded to the imposition of core curricula that resusitates the traditional literary canon as a site of privileged learning by insisting on the inclusion of global, postcolonial, and otherwise marginalized literatures and philosophy. But the so-called multicultural or diversity curriculum only peripherally addresses the central problem that afflicts public universities: the command from executive authorities in and out of the institution that public schools justify their existence by proving their value to the larger society, in most cases read business interests. In turn, educational leaders such as presidents and provosts are inclined to seek a "mission" that simultaneously translates as vocationalization, which entails leasing or selling huge portions of its curriculum and its research products directly to companies.

As a result, the public research universities are dusting off one of Kerr's most important suggestions: Undergraduates as well as graduate students should be recruited to participate in the research activities of the professoriate, especially in the sciences. Research, like sports, demands a considerable time commitment from the practitioner. Some schools, notably UC campuses such as San Diego and Irvine, are reducing the obligation of science and technology majors to the humanities and social sciences so they can more accurately mimic the practices of the great private technical universities. Which, of course, raises the question of whether public universities as public goods should maintain their obligation to educate students for citizenship as well as job skills.

In this connection as a professior in UC Irvine's School of Social Sciences, I can recall legislative hearings in the 1970s conducted by the chair of the higher education committee of the California State Assembly. The chair and other committee members were concerned that faculty were avoiding undergraduate teaching in the service of their research and the state universities were slighting programs aimed at educating for citizenship. The university administration appeared to bow to the legislators' stern warning that if they did not alter the situation their budgets would feel heat. But as with all attempts by legislatures to micromanage education, it did not take long for the administration and the faculty to regain lost ground. Today most UC campuses are monuments to technoscience and, with a few exceptions at the undergraduate level, the humanities and social sciences are gradually being relegated to ornaments and service departments.

In the third tier the forms of privatization and vocationalization are far more explicit. So, for example, the New York telephone company Bell Atlantic has developed relationships with public community and senior colleges throughout the state in which the schools agree to enroll and train students for specific occupations needed by the company. Although in most cases no money changes hands, the school benefits by additional enrollment and the college gains because it shows the legislature and other politicians that it is playing a role increasing worker productivity and enhancing economic growth and for these reasons should be rewarded with funds. In addition to a degree, employees gain occupational skills that often lead to job upgrading and the company transfers the costs of training it would have to do anyway to the public. Ironically, the Communications Workers of America, the collective bargaining representative, takes credit for the program by including the right of certain high seniority members to an "education" in the contract—read here as upgrading opportunities—without assuming the cost of tuition.

The question at issue is whether schools should forge direct corporate partnerships and in effect sell their teaching staff, let alone the curriculum, to voca-

tional ends. Needless to say, in the occupational programs I have examined the liberal arts, especially English and history, play a service role; at Nassau Community College in Long Island students are required to take a course in labor history and their English requirement is confined to composition. Otherwise the remainder of the two-year curriculum is devoted to technical subjects of direct applicability to the telephone industry. Put more broadly, third-tier public colleges and universities are under pressure to reduce their humanities and social sciences offerings to introductory and service courses to the technical and scientific curriculum. In effect, the prospective English or sociology major faces a huge obstacle to obtaining a degree in their chosen discipline, because there are often not enough electives to fufill the major. As a result we can observe the rush to mergers of social sciences departments in many third-tier public schools.

Sociology, anthropology, and political science departments are consolidating. At Cameron State University in Lawton, Oklahoma, the two philosophers on campus are now in the social science department (which includes the traditional social science disciplines), where they teach courses such as business ethics. To maintain viability, the department has majors' programs in occupational specializations such as a large major in social welfare, a vocational sequence designed to train counselors and low-level professionals in the criminal justice system, a thriving industry in the state. Lacking a social and a political theorist, these required courses are taught by a criminologist. With almost 500 majors, the eleven full-time members of the department each teach more than 120 students in four course loads a semester, in addition to academic and professional advisement of bachelor and master's students. Many courses are taught by adjuncts. Since the university has many business majors, a favorite of dozens of third-tier schools, the humanities and social science departments are crucial for fulfilling the shriveling "breadth" requirements.

Economic pressures as much as the ideological assaults on the liberal arts account for the sea change in the curriculum that is in process in public higher education. As I have noted, the students and their families feel more acutely the urgency of getting a leg up in the race for survival. The relative luxury of the liberal arts might be reserved for the few who are liberated from paid work during their college years. The consequence is that the human sciences are squeezed from the bottom as well as the top as students demand "relevance" in the curriculum and lose their thirst for reflection.

It may be safely declared that only in the larger cities, and there not uniformly, have faculty and students successfully defended the liberal arts. At CUNY a decade of determined faculty resistance has slowed, but not reversed the trend. As the new century dawned, the CUNY administration was preparing its version of distance-learning, one of the more blatant efforts to end the traditional reliance on classroom learning in favor of a model that focuses on the use of technology to produce more standard packages of predigested knowledge. In addition, distance-learning offers an answer to the fiscal crisis suffered by many public schools because it reduces the number of full-time faculty, transforms brick and mortar into cyberspace so that building and maintenance costs are reduced, and, through standardization, eliminates the mediation of a critical intellect to interpret transmitted knowledge. The last item does not primarily involve cost-saving, but rather the centralization of political and social control.

The bare fact is that neither the discourse nor the practices of critical learning are abroad in public higher education except as the rear-guard protests of a much exhausted faculty and a fragment of the largely demobilized student body. Blindsighted by the sixties' rebellions, many educators went along with student demands for ending requirements and ended up with the marketplace in which demand-driven criteria determine curricular choices. In other words, neoliberalism entered the academy through the back door of student protest. Yet for progressive educators the task remains: to demand a rigorous core of knowledges as a requisite of any postsecondary credential. This is today a radical act. To capitulate to the "market," which arguably wants something else because it is in a panic about an uncertain future—students and their parents really do not believe in the palaver of the "boom economy"—is to surrender the idea of higher education as a public good. Educators would be acknowledging that these institutions, largely paid for by working-class and middle-class people, should not promote critical thinking, should not explore the meaning of citizenship in the new neoliberal era, and should abhor the project of democratic appropriation of both Western and subaltern (marginal) traditions through attitudes of bold skepticism.

Perhaps it is too early to propose that public higher education be throughly decommodified and shorn of its corporate characteristics, that all tuition costs be paid by a tax system that must be reprogressivized. Perhaps the battle cry that at least in the first two years only science, philosophy, literature, and history (understood in the context of social theory) be taught and learned and that specializations be confined to the last two years, is so controversial, even among critics of current trends, that it remains too countercultural. Yet if higher education is to become a public good in the double meaning of the term—as a decommodified resource for the people and as an ethically legitimate institution that does not submit to the business imperative—then beyond access we would have to promote a national debate about what is to be taught, and what is to be learned if citizenship and critical thought are to remain, even at the level of intention, the heart of the higher learning.

Justifying Privilege

Pierre Bourdieu

Max Weber said that dominant groups always need a theoretical justification of the fact that they are privileged. Competence is nowadays at the heart of that which is accepted, naturally, by the dominant—it is in their interest—but also by the others. In the suffering of those excluded from work, in the wretchedness of the long-term unemployed, there is something more than there was in the past. The Anglo-American ideology, always somewhat sanctimonious, distinguished the "undeserving poor," who had brought it upon themselves, from the "deserving poor," who were judged worthy of charity. Alongside or in place of this ethical justification there is now an intellectual justification. The poor are not just immoral, alcoholic, and degenerate, they are stupid, they lack intelligence. A large part of social suffering stems from the poverty of people's relationship to the educational system, which not only shapes social destinies but also the image they have of their destiny (which undoubtedly helps to explain what is called the passivity of the dominated, the difficulty in mobilizing them, and so on). Plato had a view of the social world that resembles the world of our technocrats, with the philosophers, the guardians, and then the people. This philosophy is inscribed, in implicit form, in the educational system. It is very powerful, and very deeply internalized. Why have we moved from the committed intellectual to the "uncommitted" intellectual? Partly because intellectuals are holders of cultural capital and, even if they are the dominated among the dominant, they still belong among the dominant. That is one of the foundations of their ambivalence, of their lack of commitment in struggles. They obscurely share this ideology of competence. When they revolt, it is still because, as in Germany in 1933, they think they are not receiving their due in relation to their competence, guaranteed by their qualifications.

Athens, October 1966

(SOURCE: *Acts of Resistance*, The New Press)

PART FIVE

Health

18

Punishment or
Public Health:
Why the War on Drugs
Is a Failure

Jessie Corlito

"The American people want their government to get tough and stay on the offensive,"[1] said Ronald Reagan over fourteen years ago when describing American drug policy as a "war on drugs." The Reagan administration began its drug war by creating mandatory prison terms for drug users and expanding public funding for the criminal justice system. Although the Clinton administration does not use the term "war" to describe its approach to drug use, our national drug control strategy continues to expand the criminal justice system. The drug control budget for 1998 was $16 billion.[2] Approximately 70 percent of this amount is allocated for government bureaucracies and law enforcement rather than providing money for preventive health care and drug treatment.[3] Why do we continue to support a punitive policy against drug users rather than developing an effective public health strategy? Can we justify the incarceration of drug users as ethical public policy?

The criminal penalties against drug users are defended as reasonable because drug addicts are believed to be a danger to society. Incarcerating drug users is defended as ethical policy based on social utility because it deters drug use. When examining the applications actually made of our drug laws, we cannot defend them as ethical practices of retribution or social utility for the following reasons: (1) Although illegal drug users are from all racial and economic backgrounds, the criminal prosecution of drug users is almost exclusively enforced on African Americans and people of color who are from a lower economic background; (2) rather than stopping drug addiction, the incarceration of African American and

Latino drug users has created the largest prison population in American history that is addicted to drugs and infected with HIV; and (3) We continue to allocate enormous funding for prisons while ignoring the social resources needed for public health and economic development in communities that are continually deteriorating in American society. I will elaborate on each of these points and further explain why a public health strategy must replace our criminal justice policies on drug use.

The enforcement of our national drug control strategy is a racially and class-biased form of punishment. The National Institute for Drug Abuse reports that African Americans and white Americans use cocaine and marijuana at roughly the same rate, yet African Americans suffer five times the number of arrests compared with whites for using the same drugs.[4] According to a recent report from the National Justice Commission, police find more drugs in urban ghettos because that is where they look for them. The majority of people filling our prisons come from impoverished backgrounds and lack a formal education.[5] Police officers are not making drug raids on Wall Street or in middle-class, white, suburban neighborhoods. A recent study by the Sentencing Project reveals that 90 percent of those who are incarcerated in state prison for drug possession are African American or Latino.[6]

Instead of stopping drug use, our drug laws have created the largest prison population of people of color in U.S. history. The United States has over 1.5 million people behind bars, and 89 percent of these inmates are there for nonviolent offenses. Of these, nearly two out of three are convicted of a drug offense.[7] Increasing our prison population has not decreased drug use over the last fifteen years, but instead has increased a prison population that is addicted to drugs, infected with AIDS, and/or without adequate job skills for future employment.[8] AIDS is one of the most deadly consequences of our current drug war philosophy. The drug war has increased the spread of AIDS by its "getting tough" philosophy, which prevents free needle exchange or the sale of clean syringes without prescriptions in most states. The sharing of dirty needles among addicts is now the leading transmission route of HIV, and AIDS is now the number-one killer of African American men between the ages of twenty-five and forty-four. Drug-related AIDS is also rising among Latinos.[9] Finally, AIDS is skyrocketing in some state and federal prisons, causing a further shortage of supplies and medical care.[10]

When one examines the facts, it is clear that our current drug war is not an ethical practice of retribution or social utility. Rather than preventing social harm or improving understanding of drug use, lawmakers often promote social fears by portraying all drug users as dangerous criminals who deserve punishment. Certainly, some addicts may commit violent acts under the influence of drugs or alcohol. However, most drug users who are incarcerated are nonviolent offenders.[11] What is the ethical basis for incarcerating individuals who ingest potentially harmful substances when they have not harmed others by their actions?

An ethical drug policy should recognize that the use of potentially harmful substances may lead to addiction, but addiction is best understood as a public health concern, not a criminal justice issue. A clear example of this is the use and abuse of alcohol. In contrast to prior views of alcohol abuse as a moral weakness, alcoholism is now recognized as a disease process that has biological, psychological, and social aspects that require treatment.[12] Penalties are only imposed on alcohol users when they cause potential harm to others with such behavior as driving while intoxicated. An alcoholic cannot recover from the social isolation of prison solely through personal strength. He or she requires a biological intervention of detoxification, as well as assistance with the psychological and social factors that contribute to alcohol dependence. Many alcoholics have recovered successfully by means of medical intervention, mental health care, and increased social support through organizations such as Alcoholics Anonymous.[13]

Some Americans may accept alcoholism and drug use as health problems, but they may not support a notion of social responsibility for preventing addiction. Conservatives may ask, Why should our tax dollars fund health care that is needed because of bad personal habits? This question reduces addiction to bad choices made by individuals. Clearly, individual choice is an important influence in maintaining health. We should persuade individuals to use good judgment and avoid harmful substances; however, we cannot reduce the process of addiction merely to bad judgment. A more accurate understanding of drug addiction is given through the biopsychosocial model of health. Within my practice as a psychiatric nurse, I have found the biopsychosocial model successful because it addresses addiction as a multidimensional process that has biological, psychological, and social factors. For example, when examining the specific needs of low-income people of color who are addicted to drugs, we cannot simply tell individuals to "just say no" to drug use or incarcerate them. An addict cannot "just say no" if he or she has already become biologically dependent. Once a person becomes biologically dependent upon drugs, the only safe intervention is a medical process of detoxification. After the biological aspects of addiction have been treated, the psychological and social aspects of addiction must be addressed. A step to recovery among members of Narcotics Anonymous that is widely endorsed is accepting that addicts are powerless over addiction. What this means is that addiction is not conquered merely by personal strength. Recovery is a lifelong process that requires support from others to maintain abstinence from drugs and, sometimes, to make changes in every area of one's life. The biopsychosocial model of health also treats addiction as under the sway of a kind of soft determinism. Individual choices are shaped by biological and social limits. For example, chronic addiction can lead to severe illnesses, such as AIDS, cirrhosis, or hepatitis, that make recovery more difficult. The availability of family or other social support is also vital in the prevention and treatment of addiction because most addicts complain of overwhelming feelings of loneliness or powerlessness.

Making health care readily available to all addicts is vital to recovery, especially for people of color who have been targeted by the "war on drugs." We should replace our criminal justice policies with an innovative public health approach to drug use and addiction that reduces social harm. To meet this challenge, access to drug treatment and basic health care should be a "right" for all Americans, not merely a privilege for those with the best managed-care plans. In the 1990s, 20 million Americans were uninsured throughout any given year and 20 million more had too little health insurance to protect them from the financial burden of a major illness.[14] There is a clear conflict of interest between the policies of managed care that limit patient services for profit and an ethical distribution of social resources that are required for public health. Public mental health services are nonexistent in many communities, whereas most HMOs provide minimal coverage for inpatient drug treatment or psychotherapy.[15] Why have we allowed the profit-making of the insurance industry, rather than sound scientific and ethical principles, to dominate health care policy?

A universal health care plan that includes drug treatment and mental health services should be developed by a coalition of concerned scientists, physicians, nurses, educators, and other informed citizens. Not only should we fund a universal health plan with our tax dollars, we should make a basic legal requirement for the adequate distribution of public health resources that replaces our current

market-driven approach. Moral philosophy can be helpful in exploring our social obligations for providing access to resources for health. One model of social
development that would be useful in designing drug policy is described by
philosopher Martha Nussbaum and economist Amartya Sen as the "capabilities"
approach.[16] The capabilities approach does not reduce social development or
health to abstract economic terms. It is not merely the GNP of a nation or the income of a household that promotes health. Development is measured by evaluating how a society provides for human beings under universal categories of human capabilities.[17] The capabilities in these universal categories are ones for
those "activities ... performed by human beings that are so central that they seem
definitive of a life that is truly human."[18] Some capabilities that Nussbaum mentions are as follows: bodily health and integrity, emotions, practical reason, affiliation, and control over one's environment.[19] These categories are broadly construed, according to Nussbaum, so that we can allow for much individual
variation under universal categories of human experience.[20]

In applying Nussbaum's capabilities approach to addiction, it is not enough to
simply detox a person from drugs and alcohol without evaluating what social resources are needed to improve the person's capacity for physical, emotional, and
social well-being. Some specific questions a capabilities approach may lead us to
are the following: (1) Do American ghettos affected by the drug war require not
merely better clinics, but also new economic and educational opportunities? (2)
How can we rebuild communities and, specifically, what resources are needed to
increase the capacity for physical and emotional health? (3) How has racism influenced the war on drugs and our perception of drug users? and (4) What social
resources are needed to increase the capacity for affiliation in neighborhoods
that are isolated by the effects of poverty or in individuals whose families are
fragmented under the effects of the criminal justice system?

Nussbaum's capabilities approach, largely influenced by Aristotle's emphasis
on the importance of proper cultural values, education, and practices in shaping
our ability to be flourishing human beings, differs from market-driven notions of
development. Her approach also differs from traditional notions of distributive
justice, since she sees wealth, income, and possessions not as good simply in
themselves, but only as tools that we use to shape ourselves and the world
around us.[21] She argues that Aristotle's central question is not "How much do
they have?" but rather "What are they able to do and to be?" Government has
not done its job if it has not made each and every person in society capable of
functioning well—even if it has given them many things.[22]

Some philosophers may object to a public health project such as the one that I
am advocating on the grounds that it is just too expensive or that it would require a paternalistic intervention of socialism from the state. Postmodernists may
argue against any essentialist or universal claims regarding health because they
regard health as a social construct with the potential to oppress individuals who
differ from the desired norm. I think differences and individual rights should be

given careful consideration in shaping health policy, but I am not convinced that a capabilities approach to public health is incompatible with respecting individual rights and difference. A racially diverse coalition of activists should assist in identifying what is required to increase the capacity for public health in deteriorating American communities. It is clear that diversity and difference are not the emphases of our current "war on drugs," which is a class-biased and racially biased form of punishment for a potential health problem.

Increasing funding for a capacities approach to public health may also be critiqued as an outdated form of "big government" by many today. This is a short-sighted claim because making a legal commitment to public health promises to lead to a more effective approach to drug use than the current criminal justice approach. Rather than merely building more federal law enforcement bureaucracies and more prisons, we should create new jobs for recovering addicts who could participate in the rebuilding of their neighborhoods. Increasing employment opportunities through a public works program, run principally at the local level, that assists with the rebuilding of schools, housing, small business, and public transportation may be one method of improving American neighborhoods. American ghettos that lack safe and respected schools, adequate housing, public gathering places, and quality medical care are social environments where even the strongest individual may have extreme difficulty in flourishing. Emphasizing the importance of community building is an aspect of Nussbaum's capacity approach that is compatible with a social ecology that emphasizes the importance of sustainable communities for healthy human development. Insisting on improving the ecology of neighborhoods is also vital for increasing the capacity for human flourishing in communities affected by the drug war. This means insisting on clean water and air, access to a variety of fresh and safe foods, the preservation of land without toxic dumping or overcrowding, and efficient and environmentally responsible forms of transportation.

We cannot continue to justify our current drug policy as a deterrent to drug addiction or as a just form of punishment. Although personal choice is vital in maintaining health, our ability to interact with our natural environment, to work, and to build a sense of community and affiliation is necessary to maintain healthy development. To ensure that each person in our society has the capacity to become and stay healthy, we must expand our present notion of public health beyond the cost-containment practices of managed care and government cutbacks. Access to medical care and the ethical distribution of social and ecological resources will make thriving communities possible. Improved access to public health care and vital resources should be a basic human "right" for all, regardless of race or economic standing.

Notes

1. Donzinger, Steven, *Real War on Crime*, 115.
2. Office of National Drug Control Policy, *National Drug Control Strategy 1998*, 55.
3. Ibid, 56–58.

4. Donzinger, *Real War on Crime*, 115–116.
5. Ibid.
6. Mark Mauer and Huleg Tracy, *Report from the Sentencing Project*, October 1995.
7. Donzinger, *Real War on Crime*, 27-33.
8. American College of Physicians, "The Crisis in Correctional Health Care: The Impact of the National Drug Control Strategy on Correctional Health Services," in *The Annals of Internal Medicine* 117, 1992, 71–76.
9. Common Sense for Drug Policy and the Criminal Justice Policy Foundation, "The Spread of Drug Related Aids Among African Americans and Latinos," in *Health Emergency*, 1995, 1–13.
10. American College of Physicians, "The Crisis in Correctional Health Care: The Impact of the National Drug Control Strategy on Correctional Health Services," in the *Annals of Internal Medicine* 117, July 1992, 73–76.
11. Donzinger, *Real War on Crime*, 15.
12. Taylor, Shelley, *Health Psychology*, 12–21.
13. Ibid.
14. Wolfe, Barbara, "Reform of Health Care for the Nonelderly Poor," in Danziger and Sandefur, eds., *Confronting Poverty*, 255.
15. Boyle and Callahan, *What Price Mental Health?* 4.
16. Nussbaum and Sen, *The Quality of Life*, 30–51.
17. Nussbaum, Martha, "Women and Cultural Universal," in *Sex and Social Justice*, 40.
18. Ibid., 39.
19. Ibid.,41–43.
20. Ibid., 47–50.
21. Nussbaum, Martha, "Aristotelian Social Democracy," in *Liberalism and the Good*, 210.
22. Ibid.

Bibliography

American College of Physicians. July 1992. *Annals Of Internal Medicine*, vol. 117, no. 1.
Boyle, Philip, and Daniel Callahan. 1995. *What Price Mental Health?* Washington, D.C.: Georgetown University Press.
Common Sense for Drug Policy. October 1995. *Health Emergency*. Washington, D.C.: Dogwood Center.
Danziger, Sheldon, Gary Sandefur, and Daniel Weinberg. 1994. *Confronting Poverty*. Cambridge, Mass.: Harvard University Press.
Donzinger, Stephen. 1996. *The Real War on Crime*. Harper, N.Y.: The National Center on Institution Alternatives.
French, Peter. Winter 1996. *Journal of Social Philosophy*, vol. 27, no. 3. St. Petersburg, Fla.: University of South Florida.
Gordon, Diana. 1995. *The Return of the Dangerous Classes: Drug Prohibition Policy and Politics*. New York: W. W. Norton.
Kohut, Heinz. 1977. *The Restoration of the Self*. Madison, Conn.: International University Press.
Nussbaum, Martha. 1999. *Sex and Social Justice*. New York: Oxford University Press.
Nussbaum, Martha, and Amartya Sen. 1993. *The Quality of Life*. New York, Oxford: Clarendon Press
Mauer, Mark, and Tracy Huleg. 1995. *Report from the Sentencing Project of October*. Washington, D.C.
Office of National Drug Control Policy. 1988. *The National Drug Control Strategy 1988*. Washington, D.C.: U.S. Government Printing Office.
Taylor, Shelley. 1995. *Health Psychology*, 3d ed. New York, Los Angeles: McGraw-Hill, Inc.
Trebach, Arnold, and James Inciardi. 1993. *Legalize It? Debating American Drug Policy*. Washington, D.C.: American University Press.

19

A Case for Taking Health Care Out of the Market

Milton Fisk

In the United States, the public debate over national health insurance has been going on for half a century. As we enter the new millennium, the failure of corporate-managed care to control costs and the increase in the number of uninsured have given that debate new life. From the time of President Truman's late 1940s effort to get national health insurance,[1] Americans have periodically polled sizable majorities in favor of national health insurance. Such a system would take health care out of the market by establishing a single payer within a framework of public accountability. The U.S. health care system as a whole would become a public good. In many countries, like Canada, England, and Germany, a market in health insurance and for-profit health care are secondary features of the health care system, which thus functions as a public good.

My case for taking health care out of the market relies on what I take to be our general expectations regarding health in our society. Thus I give a central place to a social goal. With that goal in mind, it is not difficult to determine the kinds of health care institutions that need to be built. Giving a central place to social goals is not the starting point for a rights- or justice-based ethics, which has recently been the main form of ethics. But as I shall suggest toward the end, trying to establish what is just apart from social goals is a hopeless task.

Of course, our current expectations regarding health needn't have been those of earlier periods. So even if satisfying our expectations calls for a health system that is a public good, this needn't be the case for all prior and future expectations about health. Failing this, it is tempting to look for a universal prescription in regard to the kind of health care system people need by analyzing the nature of health care itself. This has led to attempts to show that health care is of itself unfit to be an object for sale.[2] But these attempts end up showing only that treating health care as a commodity is incompatible with the social goal we currently aim at in regard to health.

I shall work out from a social goal regarding health in talking about its implementation through certain institutions. Conversely, I shall work toward it in talking, more briefly, about conditions motivating its adoption as a goal people are willing to work for. At the level of implementation, there is need for an insurance system that, like all insurance systems, makes for collective provision. This insurance system won't do what it is supposed to do unless the health care system of which it is a part is a public good. At the level of motivation, there must be a measure of compassion and solidarity for a broad agreement to arise around working for a social goal. And without an advance toward equality this measure of compassion and solidarity will be absent.

Common Goods

A goal people have for a society is realized by the society's taking on a certain feature. We refer to such a feature when we speak simply of a society as being educated, democratic, healthy, or nondiscriminatory. In each case the feature referred to is a robust disposition on the part of the society to deliver certain individual goods.

So an educated society, under a variety of even unfavorable circumstances, routinely educates educable people. A society that only by some accident manages to have educated people in it will not be likely to reproduce an educated population in the next generation. It lacks the robust disposition needed to call it an educated society. When people want a certain kind of society they don't want just a widespread distribution of similar goods. They want a society structured to ensure such a distribution on a regular basis.

This kind of social feature is what has often been called a common good. It has two sides to it, an objective one and a subjective one. On the objective side a common good provides individual goods. It is the robust disposition I've already spoken about. It differs from a general good, which is something similar between disperse individuals but not a feature of the society common to them. The common society need not be that of only one country, but could be that of a region of countries or even of the whole international community. But in talking about health care, I'll be talking about the United States. After all, it not only has a market for most of its health care but also promotes the market in health care around the world through agencies such as the World Bank.[3]

On the subjective side a common good requires a broad agreement on it as a goal.[4] It is crucial to note several things about such an agreement. An agreement on a social goal—a goal that is a feature of the society—will be empty if it is either a forced or a selfish agreement.

If it is forced, people will sooner or later find the collective effort to realize it too burdensome. They will abandon that effort either through demoralization or the discovery of an alternative to it. If it is selfish, people will have adopted the goal only because of the personal benefit they will derive from its realization. But when they join the cooperative effort to realize the social goal only for personal benefit, they will sooner or later erode the cooperative effort through mistrust and manipulation and then exit from it in search of personal solutions.

Both democracy and solidarity are necessary conditions for the broad agreement that is the subjective aspect of a common good. Instead of being forced, the agreement must come as the result of a process of struggle, advocacy, and discussion of the sort that makes the core of democratic practice. This condition comes not from stipulating the superiority of democracy over other political practices but from noting the ineffectiveness of forced agreements for implementing social goals. Rather than being selfish, the agreement must represent a self-transcendence for those who enter it. What this means is that, instead of wanting to realize the goal solely for personal benefit, each will want to realize it for all. If an effort to get and then maintain a society of a certain kind is to be successful, solidarity has to extend across most of it. A market society, with its emphasis on getting ahead by individual effort, creates an obstacle to solidarity that can be overcome when enough people find—as they already have in health care—that the market often fails them. The existence of exploited classes and of oppressed peoples—blacks, Hispanics, women, gays—is also a great obstacle to realizing the solidarity needed for people to commit themselves to getting a common good. Struggles of these groups for recognition and equality have been necessary for getting as far as we have in committing ourselves to education, health care, and shelter for everyone in the United States.

A Healthy Society

There are a number of indications that today in the United States there is still a goal in the area of health that is a common good. People are outraged that so little has been done recently to reduce the percentage of the population that is uninsured. When HMOs close down operations for Medicare patients, people sense that profits have illegitimately been put before health. When managed care organizations deny patients procedures their doctors say they should have, solidarity with these patients becomes the response of the rest of us.

These and other reactions don't make sense apart from a widely shared view of the kind of society people want. They want a society that would be healthy in something like the following way. It would have a disposition to control threats to individual health. But there is a comparative element that enters in as well. One can take the actual situation as a baseline for determining how well threats to health are controlled. The society people want would control these threats in a way that represents a maximal feasible improvement over their control at this

baseline. Those reactions to today's U.S. health care system express discontent over the fact that we seem to be backing away from such an improvement. That this discontent exists shows a desire to reverse the trend and move toward a healthy society. Maximal feasible improvement today will very likely involve a shift from an emphasis on "heroic" medicine, with its expensive efforts to cope with serious malfunctions, toward a reduction of the incidence of such malfunctions. This will involve improving the environment, changing diets, education that enables individuals to control their conditions, preventing addictions, reducing stress produced by oppression and exploitation, and attacking occupational health hazards.

However vague this ideal is, it is specific enough to rouse practical opposition. In the name of the corporate interest, there are those who want carte blanche to pollute air and water and to subject employees to hazardous conditions. In the name of the free market, there are those who reject public solutions to the problem of the uninsured. In the name of the national interest, our leaders insist on wars that kill, cripple, and poison its own citizens, not to speak of the greater damage it does to others. This practical opposition to making the United States a healthy society creates rather than controls obstacles to individual health. It creates these obstacles not to serve other common goods, but to serve special interests in profit or power. Moreover, this opposition discourages agreement on a common good like a healthy society on the grounds that by calling for solidarity it runs counter to self-reliance. The existence of this opposition provides the reason behind an important qualification. I spoke only of a broad or widely shared agreement on common goods. And that's about the most we can expect. True universal agreement, dreamed of by some moralists,[5] is not feasible, either in regard to health or in the case of most other common goods.

Where will the constituency for a broad agreement on a matter like health be found? We need to look for an identifiable group. A random collection of people won't do. Its interests wouldn't be stable enough for the lengthy struggle to pursue and maintain a common good. So we need to look for a group that, because of its position in the society, is sensitized to a problem that calls for changing features of the society that contribute to that problem. It is the actual or potential health care underserved who make up the primary constituency for agreement on the healthy society. This gets us to the social basis for the opinion polls favoring universal health care. Those in this constituency will have become actually or potentially underserved since they are, by and large, those who have to or have had to work for a living.

I will then speak of a common good even where the society is divided. This calls for caution if we are to avoid getting into trouble for ignoring minorities. Such caution is actually built into the requirement that the process of coming to broad agreement needs to be democratic. So even a group that doesn't become part of the agreement is recognized as part of the process of trying to come to agreement. Its cooperation in not blocking implementation of a broad agreement is sought through efforts at building understanding of the seriousness of the problem and at avoiding needless infringements on interests in solving it. A group that can't agree will be guaranteed the benefits others will receive once the common good is realized. Still, such a group might find that none of this is enough. Instead it might decide to use its power to try to prevent a solution to the problem that pursuing a common good is supposed to address. In this case, the mutual recognition needed to continue wrestling with the issue is threatened, leading to the possibility of the society's fragmenting.

Where there is, as in the United States, a broad agreement on a healthy society as a goal, there needn't be a will to realize it. What we have learned so far is that, if the agreement can be implemented, it can't be forced and it can't be selfish. Still, in the United States the broad consensus has been unorganized, leaving individuals who are part of that consensus with a mere ideal without a will to action. As a result, their wanting to realize the goal for others is tempered by their not finding the conditions ripe for action. The solidarity involved is left at the level of a desire for the good of others without reaching that of a decision to pursue it.

Thus, later on we must discuss conditions that will motivate turning an agreement on a healthy society as a goal into a decision to realize it.

Public Goods

Once having identified a healthy society as a common good, we have to ask what institutions can realize it. These are the institutions that once fully functioning will promote the society's having the robust disposition that constitutes it as a healthy society. It is not evident from the start that these institutions should be public rather than private or mixed. And it is not evident that they should be ones whose services or products are to remain outside the market rather than to exist as commodities in it. In this discussion, the market is not restricted to the ideal market of economic theory; it can also be one in which the number of competitors is quite small and in which there is a certain amount of government regulation. For our purposes, the crucial thing about a market will be that in it firms are trying to increase their share of sales and to perform well enough to attract investors. What I shall try to show is that the institutions making up a health care system that promotes the realization of a healthy society will have to be a public good, and not such a market firm.

But first, what is a public good? It is an organization of human and material resources that advances the realization of a common good. To play this instrumental role, a public good must satisfy both the objective and the subjective requirements of a common good. It must not only move toward generating a feature of a society—like its being healthy—but also move toward it in a way that is compatible with its being agreed to in a democratic process and its being something people solidarize around. So a public good will have to be controlled in a publicly accountable way. Otherwise one can't ensure that what was agreed to in the democratic process is what is being advanced. In addition, the public good cannot make realizing the common good secondary to realizing a private goal, such as corporate profit or a feeling of racial superiority. Behind this requirement is a denial of the famous invisible-hand thesis according to which pursuing private goals will, by chance rather than design, realize common goods. We have seen that without each wanting a common good for all, the effort to realize it will fray into a search in different directions for private solutions. We know that troubled for-profit HMOs drop loss-making members in order to become profitable again. And we know that many doctors don't recommend for black and women patients the same thorough tests and aggressive treatment they recommend for comparable white and male patients. These are cases of putting private profits and prejudices ahead of the common good of a healthy society.

This gives us a general picture of public goods. But it doesn't pick out the specific types of institutions that would qualify as a public good in a given area like health care. Moreover, the sketchy arguments I've given for making any instrument for realizing a common good publicly accountable and not-for-profit are not enough. More needs to be said to make a convincing case that common goods have to be realized by public goods. But instead of making such a general case, I shall try to make the case for a healthy society as a specific instance of a common good. Doing this will also allow me to be more specific on the kinds of institutions a public good in health care demands.

In outline, my strategy will be as follows. At least in recent times when health care was conceived as having whole populations as its object rather than merely tiny strata of the well-off, insurance has been an integral part of health care systems.[6] So in looking for specific institutions that could be considered means to a healthy society, insurance should be considered among them. The rationale, to be discussed shortly, for including insurance among such institutions is a fairly general one I shall call the principle of collective provision. As a first step in my strategy, I shall show that any health care system in which this principle is satisfied will be a public good. The second step—a much easier one—will show that our agreement on a healthy society as a common good commits us to the principle of collective provision. Combining these two steps leads directly to the result that our agreement on a healthy society calls for a health care system that is a public good, and hence for taking health care out of the market.

It needs noting that the concept of public good adopted here is a more full-bodied one than that made familiar by postwar welfare economists. Their notion was that a public good is relatively inexhaustible and nonexcludable.[7] That is, apart from extraordinary demand such as would occur in an epidemic, in feeding uprooted populations, or in a drought, it is not exhausted by those deriving individual goods from it. And, apart from disputed political jurisdictions, no one person or group can claim its benefits solely for themselves to the exclusion of others. Now these characteristics of public goods in welfare economics follow from our conception. For the robust disposition to supply certain individual goods that a public good gives rise to makes for its being inexhaustible. And the solidarity on the basis of which this disposition is created makes it available to all and hence nonexcludable.

What's missing in the welfarist notion of a public good is reference to the existence of a social goal emerging from a democratic process and realized by a solidaristic struggle. This played into the delegitimation of public goods in the 1980s and 1990s. It allowed for the imposition of social goals that had then to be realized bureaucratically. A people serious about wanting a certain kind of society will insist on controlling the monitoring of the institutions set up to realize it. In addition, the decisions made in those institutions will need to involve the various groups working in them. Otherwise, the special goals of a dominant group among them will supplant the common good to be served by the institutions.

Collective Provision

Insurance is a response to problems that have no individual solution. Thus it is collective in nature. The problems addressed are for practical purposes unpredictable. Of course, one can say roughly how many people will be injured in car accidents in Utah in 2000. In that sense there is predictability. But one can't predict that one will be injured in an accident next year. It is this sort of individual unpredictability that insurance deals with. Associated with the unpredictable harms insurance deals with are the relatively large economic burdens those harms often entail. The treatment and care needed by individuals for recovery are provided through an expensive system, so the economic burdens of providing them will be great. Being large, they are unbearable by most individuals, though for some they may be bearable. One can't assume that one will be lucky enough to suffer only economically bearable harms when harms happen to come one's way.

People handle the existence of unpredictable harms that impose unbearable burdens through pooling funds to cover their risk. Individual responsibility for covering the expenses incurred by unpredictable harms directly gets canceled. In its place a collective responsibility—represented by the liability of the collective fund to indemnify—is created. We can speak of a principle of collective provision being at work in shifting responsibility away from the individual for the sake of avoiding unbearable burdens. What's left to the individual is only the responsibility for joining a plan for shared responsibility. One's ignoring such responsibility inevitably shifts the burden of one's losses to those contributing to a fund.

For my purposes the key idea here is the aim of making serious burdens bearable. This idea does not fit with having each person pay equally into the insurance fund. In fact, equal premiums would introduce results that are paradoxical in light of the principle. Paying equally would end up making the burden of relief for those least able to pay smaller and that for those most able to pay greater. Equal premiums would systematically reduce burdens unequally. Moreover, for the least able to pay, paying equally with the rest might introduce a burden they can't bear. Thus, paradoxically some people would be faced with an unbearable burden as a condition for their eligibility to avoid unbearable burdens. An income-indexed premium scheme such as Germany's or a progressive-tax scheme to support government health insurance such as Canada's would then be in keeping with a principle of collective provision.[8] An insurance market, in which premiums are not different because of different incomes, would not be in keeping with it.

Those who act in accord with a principle of collective provision will see it in their interest to cover prevention with their fund, thereby making prevention a part of collective provision. HMOs complain that the costs of new, high-tech procedures are making yearly double-digit premium increases necessary. One needs to ask, though, whether covering more preventive measures for their members wouldn't reduce the need for such expensive procedures. With the addition of preventive coverage to the principle of collective provision, it can be stated as follows. Individual responsibility not just for the possibly unbearable economic burdens brought on by unpredictable harms but also for the economic burdens of trying to prevent such harms is to be replaced by shared responsibility for setting up a common fund. The harms referred to are what have to be dealt with directly by treatment or prevention. The economic distributions from the fund are to cover charges for dealing with the harms. They are indirect in relation to the harms. It is assumed that these distributions are for high enough quality treatment and prevention so that these are generally effective. Thus collective provision is not only a matter of equitable distribution but also one of assuring quality.

Since this principle plays an important role here, something needs to be said about its justification. I prefer to see its justification as a matter of troubleshooting, rather than a basic structure of society.[9] The operative question becomes: What is needed to get rid of trouble that would otherwise become recurrent? Unpredictable harms entailing large burdens do crop up in some areas, and we look for feasible ways to indemnify against them. Insisting on individual responsibility will leave most of these burdens unmet. But collective provision of such a kind that only the better-off can afford it in a form that gives full coverage doesn't deal with the trouble. For those excluded from it will continue to demand inclusion under collective provision. The resulting bitterness and conflict is enough to indicate that without satisfying the principle of collective provision there will be recurrent trouble. People eventually discover that it is better to try an arrangement that promises not to keep facing them with the problems individual responsibility failed to address. This means applying the principle of collective provision.

Collective Provision and the Insurance Market

Why would an insurance market be in conflict with the principle of collective provision? The actors in a market pursue competitive success; they pursue goals that give them advantages in getting more business. In the insurance industry, more business means more premiums. With more premiums, the sum of the unspent parts of premiums tends to rise. In addition, with more premiums there is more to keep invested in financial instruments and real estate. Chasing big returns in these ways leads insurance companies to adopt policies that limit collective provision. These policies take various forms.

Suppose an insurer indexed premiums to income so that the less advantaged could come under collective provision. This would make this insurer vulnerable in competition with those who do not index. With a single rate for all classes, each of them is able to carry the more advantaged at lower premiums than the insurer with indexed premiums. The more advantaged will then take their business to those insurers who don't index premiums.

The consequence for the insurer who indexes would be a loss of the funds that make it possible to carry the less advantaged. So the indexing insurer would have to drop indexing or go out of business. The numerous people who cannot afford the premiums of the insurers who don't index end up without collective provision. To increase their business, these insurers would try to sell less expensive insurance to the less advantaged. But it would be insurance with sizable out-of-pocket expenses and with no coverage for important treatments.[10] It would not then satisfy the principle of collective provision, which calls for covering unbearable burdens, not for leaving them uncovered.

Once established, an insurance market will not be willing to give much room to government insurance programs, like Medicaid and Medicare in the United States. In particular, there will be opposition to extend these programs to cover all the uninsured. The reason is simply that if the gap is closed an area of expansion for the insurance market is closed. Suppose that Medicaid coverage is guaranteed by the government to everyone in families earning less than one-and-one-half times the actual poverty level.[11] This would provide coverage to around 45 million people, enough to get within striking range of universal health insurance. By closing the gap in this way, an expansion of the insurance market into a large segment of the preretired population would be foreclosed. Insurers would not be able to exploit this segment of the population, even with the sale of partial coverage plans.

Actually, insurers, including vertically integrated insurer-providers, hope for an expansion of the insurance market not just through limiting government health programs but also through ending them. Instead, they want the government to supply vouchers to the individual so he or she can buy private insurance. The poor and the elderly would then expand business for the private insurers enormously. The government would no longer have the role it has now in setting prices ceilings for the treatment of those in its programs. The poor and the elderly would use their vouchers for insurance that costs what the market will bear to have coverage for treatments whose prices are uncontrolled. The inflation already characteristic of the private insurance sector would carry over to the premiums bought with vouchers. The amount of health care that insurance bought with vouchers covers would diminish rapidly, leaving those relying on vouchers with fewer benefits and more out-of-pocket expenses than they had under government health programs. So the drawback of marketing government programs is simply that those who had depended on them would get even less coverage.[12] This would signal a further departure of the market in insurance from the principle of collective provision.

In all these ways it is clear that a market in insurance is incompatible with the principle of collective provision. Without a market in health insurance, the health care system, financed largely through insurance, will be a nonmarket system. Will this nonmarket system be a public good? Were it not a public good, it would have to fail one of the three features we have attributed to a public good. But it is clear that failing one of these would also lead to a failure of the principle of collective provision. For the principle of collective provision is about sharing the economic burden of dealing with and preventing illness. Part of sharing that burden will be to build a health care system that can deal with and prevent illness. Such a health care system will be a public good—there for the health needs of all, not subordinating those needs to profits, and running in a publicly accountable way.

This public good will be a nonmarket system even though providers—doctors, laboratory personnel, hospitals, and drug companies—may still charge for their services and products. How can this be? Those charges won't make commodities out of their services and products since what they are paid will not be determined by a market. Instead remuneration will be set by negotiations with an insurer having the distinctive trait of not being part of an insurance market. This may not be sufficient to keep what they get paid from being excessive.[13] But at least what they get won't be a market price. In principle, then, it is not necessary to have a national health service system to end the market in health care; a national health insurance system will do.

The Common Good and Collective Provision

The troubleshooting approach to justifying collective provision avoided reliance on anything more than the frustration of individuals denied collective provision. We can, though, find a positive basis for collective provision. Since we have already pointed out that there is agreement on a vague conception of a healthy society, this agreement is available to back up the principle of collective provision. To reach a healthy society calls for removing obstacles to health. Yet a failure to make collective provision would leave illnesses untreated and health hazards ignored by leaving individuals to cope with them on their own. The result would fall short of a healthy society.

When there is a failure to make collective provision, why can't any problems that result from this failure be avoided by a market in insurance? A market in insurance would put the common goal of a healthy society beyond reach. The reason it would do this is simply that common goods can't be realized by markets since markets have winners and losers. Among the losers are not just suppliers whose prices aren't competitive but also consumers who can't pay the market price. By pricing some consumers out of the health insurance market, one creates rather than reduces barriers to individual health, thereby falling short of advancing a healthy society. After all, markets are about winning through exclusion, whereas common goods are about organizing for inclusion. The winners exclude suppliers who can't compete and consumers who can't pay.

At what I called the level of implementation, we have now established two important connections. The first was that the principle of collective provision could not be satisfied in a health care system that failed to be a public good. The second connection was, as we just saw, that realizing a healthy society as a common good can't be done without satisfying the principle of collective provision.

At the level of implementation of a common good there is one more connection worth mentioning. It brings in an important notion of political morality, that of justice. We try to be fair in resolving conflicts by setting limits on what the different sides gain and lose. The norm for setting such limits comes from an overarching social goal that the sides could be expected to find agreement on. The kind of society people want helps, then, to settle disputes among them in a fair way. So if a healthy society is a shared goal, as I've claimed it is in the United States, then distributions of gains and losses made by a public good, which is instrumental to realizing that goal, are just. Moreover, a long-standing commitment to a healthy society will lead to a widely shared sense of what is just in health care. In making health care decisions, this sense of justice becomes instrumental for realizing the common good in health care.

Such a sense of justice may leave a lot of questions about justice unresolved. At any given time, the goal of a healthy society will not be backed up with full specifics in regard to what constitutes individual health. There will be disputed questions and new areas. As in other matters, justice in health care can be neither a complete nor a static norm. It may be clear that denying standard health care to people for either economic or political reasons is not just. But despite recent changes in outlook, we are still divided on whether it is just in all cases to maintain life by artificial means. Moreover, the meaning of being a healthy society could be altered by making techniques for enhancing human capacities accepted parts of the system of health care taken as a public good.[14]

Motivation

To agree on the kind of society we want is one thing; it is another to carry through to get it. There's lots of hard work involved in creating a health care system that is a public good, yet this work has to be done to realize the common good of a healthy society. So agreeing on a healthy society won't mean much without the motivation to have collective provision, a public good, and fair distributions. What, then, are some of the conditions for agreeing on a healthy society in a way that goes beyond desire to action?

The struggle for public goods is closely related to that for greater equality—greater equality in regard to class, race, gender, nationality, and sexual orientation. One can't have either public goods or greater equality without the other. Without public goods an important means of enhancing equality is ignored. For public goods guarantee a provision of goods and services that might otherwise not be accessible to some because of income inequality. Conversely, without advances toward equality a social cleft can develop that isolates the haves from the have-nots and the oppressors from the oppressed. They can be separated far enough so they no longer feel one another's vulnerability. The basis for their wanting things for one another is then eroded. So estranged, they are not likely to cooperate on projects to construct public goods. With this mutual dependence, it is no wonder that greater equality erodes the reign of the market.

The increase in income and wealth inequality in the United States in the 1990s coincided with a decrease in willingness on the part of the better-off to continue support of public goods. Not just Medicare and Medicaid, but also public schooling and Social Security pensions came under intense fire. As an alternative to public goods, powerful corporate interests were promoting systems of subsidized individual buying. With their own funds to manage, people's attention would be diverted from the issue of how everyone is being served. The better-off would of course supplement their subsidies to buy good education, good pensions, and good health care. The rest would be provided less adequately at a second or a third tier within the respective systems.

We cannot just wish away the reality and the culture of inequality that characterizes neoliberalism. But the financial crises of 1998 have shown that some things have to be changed. The fragility of the export model of development, which is based on domestic austerity, has been revealed. The changes needed won't, of course, come about without pressure from below for reducing inequality. If pressure occurs for higher wages and better benefits and is moderately successful, the greater equality thereby promoted would reduce resistance to implementing public goods.

The link between equality and public goods is, as just noted, a more unified society. This means, in particular, that people will be brought close enough together through equality so that compassion and an activist solidarity become possible. People who are in more or less equal positions can make the imaginative projection needed to recognize in each other their own vulnerability.[15] Each can then feel the anxiety the other has over being vulnerable and the pain the other has when the loss to which there is vulnerability actually occurs. As class and status differences become more pronounced, making that imaginative projection becomes more difficult. Those who are this different do not see one another as vulnerable in the same ways. With compassion reduced by inequality, one will have a weaker desire for others to have the benefits of solving common problems. Thus a weakening of compassion also weakens solidarity.[16] The desire for all to get what each wants can be weakened to the extent that there is no will to carry through on a common project. Solidarity as a desire becomes weak enough so that there is no activist solidarity. But without an activist solidarity, common goods won't be implemented. As a good from which all can benefit, however, a common good was seen to be one that self-interest was not sufficient to implement.

In the case of sickness and accident, the barrier raised by inequality to compassionate responses shows itself in a variety of stratagems. We often avoid having to witness the pain of those we see as unequal. When the pain is nonetheless unavoidably present, we make a studied refusal to be affected by it. Or we adopt the comforting myth that the harsh life of those not our equals keeps them from feeling much pain. Still, those separated by inequality may agree with one another that it would be well if there were a healthy society. But the lack of compassion in the society would undermine the possibility of the activist kind of solidarity that could implement such a common good through a health system that is a public good. So we need to recognize several conditions for getting the motivation to realize a healthy society. Among those vulnerable to or actually suffering from illness or accidents, there needs to be a relatively high degree of equality and as well of compassion and solidarity.

Notes

1. Monty M. Poen, *Harry S. Truman Versus the Medical Lobby* (Columbia, Mo.: University of Missouri Press, 1979).

2. Thus Robert Kuttner says, "Much of the recent history of health policy in the United States has been a hapless effort to bring 'market efficiency' and 'pro-competitive reform' to a sector that is inherently extra market." See his *Everything for Sale: The Virtues and Limits of Markets* (New York: Knopf, 1997), 111.

3. Consider, for example, a World Bank recommendation for Palestine's health system. It promotes dialogue between private insurers and the Government Health Insurance system for the purpose of establishing an effective private insurance market, including supplementary private insurance for those on GHI. See *West Bank and Gaza: Medium Term Development Strategy and Public Financing Priorities for the Health Sector*, vol. 1 (World Bank Report no. 17053-GZ, December 24, 1997), appendix 7a, 2, v.

4. A purely objective view of the common good was held by many in the Aristotelian tradition. See, for example, Thomas Aquinas, *Summa Contra Gentiles*, book 3, chap. 27. Others, however, thought there had to be a process of social bonding, rather than domination, before there could be the good of the political community. See the remarks on Henry of Ghent in Anthony Black, "The Individual and Society" in *The Cambridge History of Medieval Political Thought: c.350-c.1450*, ed. J. H. Burns (Cambridge: Cambridge University Press, 1988), 596–597.

5. The Kantian tradition of emphasizing universality is still upheld with great fervor, for example, by Jurgen Habermas, "Remarks on Discourse Ethics," in his *Justification and Application*, trans. C. P. Cronin (Cambridge, Mass.: Massachusetts Institute of Technology, 1993), chap. 2.

6. On this transition, see Paul Starr, *The Social Transformation of American Medicine* (New York: HarperCollins, 1982), 200–209.

7. For example, Paul A. Samuelson, "The Pure Theory of Public Expenditure," *Review of Economics and Statistics* 36, 4 (1954): 387–389.

8. On financing German and Canadian health insurance, see Joseph White, *Competing Solutions: American Health Care Proposals and International Experience* (Washington, D.C.: Brookings Institute, 1995), chap. 4.

9. An appeal to the nature of society in calling for a health care system that is a public good is made by Michael Walzer, *Spheres of Justice* (New York: Basic Books, 1983), chap. 3.

10. Some of these points are ably treated in a discussion of the market failures of private insurance by Robert G. Evans, *Strained Mercy: The Economics of Canadian Health Care* (Toronto: Butterworths, 1984), 37–45.

11. In the 1993–1994 Clinton health plan, those making up to 150 percent of poverty income guidelines could apply to their health alliances for subsidies, which would vary with income, to help pay their premiums. *Health Security Act: Bill to the 103rd Congress* (Washington, D.C.: U.S. Government Printing Office, October 1993).

12. On the proposed voucher system for Medicare, see Thomas Bodenheimer et al., *Rebuilding Medicare for the 21st Century* (Oakland Calif.: California Physicians Alliance, February 1999). Also Robert Dreyfuss, "Next Victim: Medicare," *Nation*, March 15, 1999, 16–22.

13. Negotiated remuneration to providers would be excessive if it included an allowance for profits that could either be used to enhance competitiveness of individual firms within the system or be taken out of the health care system by them in the form of dividends or investments.

14. On the issue of enhancement and health care, see Eric T. Juengst, "Can Enhancement be Distinguished from Prevention in Genetic Medicine?" *Journal of Medicine and Philosophy* 22, 4 (1997): 125–142.

15. On the importance of compassion in public reasoning, see Martha Nussbaum, "Compassion: The Basic Social Emotion," *Social Philosophy and Policy* 13, 1 (1996): 27–58.

16. Sandra Barkty has elaborated on the idea that compassion itself without solidarity will remain passive. See her "Sympathy and Solidarity: On a Tightrope with Scheler," in *Feminists Rethink the Self*, ed. D. Meyers (Boulder, Colo.: Westview, 1996), 177–196.

20

Mental Health: Public or Social Good?

Richard Lichtman

The Illusion of
the Private Self

One of the most pervasive myths of modern social theory is the view that contemporary capitalism is characterized by extreme individualism. So, in an essay
that explores the isomorphism between psychoanalytic concepts and the logic of
Anglo-American cultural values, Suzanne R. Kirschner maintains:

> These cultural beliefs and values are manifest both at the level of formal ideology and
> in (often unstated or implicit) roles of behavioral display and social interaction.
> Prominent among these desirable characteristics are *self-reliance* (self-sufficiency, self-
> confidence, and the avoidance of displays of dependency ...), [and] *self-direction* (the
> capacity to know what is in one's heart and mind ...).[1]

K. E. Read contrasts the individual in New Guinea with the inviolate individual of the West, maintaining that in the latter setting

> the moral duties of the person are greater than any of the duties which the individual
> possesses as a member of society. His moral responsibilities both to himself and oth-
> ers transcend the given social content, are conceived to be independent of the social
> ties that link him to his fellows.[2]

Or Philip Cushman:

> Many authors have described how the bounded, masterful self has slowly and un-
> evenly emerged in Western history. This is a self that has specific psychological
> boundaries, an internal locus of control, and a wish to manipulate the external world
> for its own personal ends.[3]

More and more in the twentieth century the focus has come to rest on the isolated, self-contained individual.[4]

Or consider Louis Dumont, for whom a most basic contrast exists between ancient hierarchical societies and modern egalitarian society whose individualistic
ideology prizes "the independent, autonomous ... and essentially nonsocial moral
being ... " [5] Or again, Benjamin Constant who maintained that the modern individual thinks of himself as free because he is "independent in his private life."[6]

Perhaps the most magisterial and influential statement remains that of Clifford
Geertz:

> The Western conception of the person as a bounded, unique, more or less integrated
> motivational and cognitive universe, a dynamic center of awareness, emotion, judg-
> ment, and action organized into a distinctive whole and set contrastively against other
> such wholes and against its social and natural background, is, however incorrigible it
> may seem to us, a rather peculiar idea within the context of the world's cultures.[7]

Habits of the Heart

But rather than cite the limitless number of such assertions it will be most useful
for our purposes to consider the contention that grounds *Habits of the Heart,* a
work that has come to play a central role in accounts of contemporary individualism, and that has the additional advantage of contributing some interesting discussion of the nature of contemporary therapy, the immediate subject of our inquiry.

Habits of the Heart is a study of American traditions and character, concerned
primarily with the nature of individualism. "It seems to us that it is individualism, and not equality, as Tocqueville thought, that has marched inexorably
through our history. We are concerned that this individualism may have grown
cancerous ... "[8] for one of the keys to understanding "the survival of free institutions is the relation between private and public life ... "[9] The modality of the
study involves interviews with persons who are primarily of the white middle
class. In focusing on private life "we decided to study love and marriage ... and
therapy, a newer, but increasingly important, way in which middle-class
Americans find meaning in the private sphere."[10]

The authors introduce their view of therapy in contemporary America in the
course of an interview with the therapist Margaret Oldham. Her understanding of her own practice as a therapist is grounded in a principle of tolerance

that respects the views of others and places individual fulfillment above social attachment.

> I just sort of accept the way the world is and don't think about it a whole lot. I tend to operate on the assumption that what I want to do and what I feel like is what I should do. What I think the universe wants from me is to take my values, whatever they might happen to be, and live up to them as much as I can.[11]

In keeping with the liberal tradition, Margaret Oldham believes strongly in individual responsibility and self-reliance and, as a consequence, the necessity of "being alone."

As the authors of *Habits of the Heart* understand our current situation, the therapist is, like the contemporary manager, a specialist in mobilizing resources for effective action, only here the resources are largely internal to the individual and the measure of effectiveness is the elusive criterion of personal satisfaction.... Although the culture of manager and therapist does not speak in the language of traditional moralities, it nonetheless proffers a normative order of life.... Its center is the *autonomous individual,* presumed able to choose the roles he will play and the commitments he will make, not on the basis of higher truths but according to the criterion of life effectiveness as the individual judges it (emphasis added).[12]

According to this "individualistic" view of therapy one advances one's own system of wants and desires. Of course, this arrangement implies that one knows what one wants, which incites the inclination to "try everything at least once."[13] The typical therapist of the individualistic school maintains that "It's not so hard for people to figure out what they want ... what makes them feel good."[14] How does one confirm the true autonomy of one's desires and guarantee the lack of influence by others? The sense of "being good" is the internalized judgments of others, which is most often opposed to one's own sense of "feeling good." It is one of the primary functions of the therapist to facilitate this distinction.

The predominant ethos of American individualism seems more than ever determined to press ahead with the task of letting go of all criteria other than *radical private validation* (emphasis added).[15]

Therapy, then, would seem to be an exercise in the establishment and maintenance of autonomy. The therapeutic practice eschews external validation and valorizes the worth of the individual—as given. The ... "ultimate purpose of the therapist's acceptance, the 'unconditional positive regard' of post-Freudian therapy, is to teach the therapeutic client to be independent of anyone else's standards."[16]

In a sense that the philosophers of the Enlightenment would have found a most corrupt perversion of their own conception of autonomy, the contemporary individual is expected to act independently of objective moral criteria. Human beings were, for Kant, the source of their own moral judgment in the sense that they followed the dictates of their reason. To be determined by any other natural influence was to be reduced to heteronomy. For contemporary individualism, however, "... the therapeutic attitude denies all forms of obligation and commitment in relations ... "[17] and reinforces traditional American individualism "... including the concept of utilitarian individuals maximizing their own interests."[18]

To sum up Bellah's first account of therapy as atomization we can do no better than cite a passage from *Mental Health in America* that Bellah himself notes with approval:

> Psychoanalysis (and psychiatry) is the only form of psychic healing that attempts to cure people by detaching them from society and relationships. All other forms— shamanism, faith healing, prayer—bring the community into the healing process, indeed use the interdependence of patient and others as the central mechanism in the healing process. Modern psychiatry isolates the troubled individual from the currents of emotional interdependence and deals with the trouble by distancing from it and manipulating it through intellectual/verbal discussion, interpretation, and analysis.[19]

Reality and Illusion

Thus far *Habits of the Heart* has been clear and straightforward: therapy functions within the orbit of American individualism to detach persons from context, relationship, and obligation, for the sake of maximizing their potential for personal self-gratification. However, a second current runs through the work and completely undermines this first position. On the very same page that had Bellah likening the therapist to the manager of internal resources, the context of the managerial metaphor is extended:

> The manager and the therapist largely define the outlines of twentieth-century American culture. The social basis of that culture is *the world of bureaucratic consumer capitalism* that dominates, or has penetrated, most older, local economic forms.[20] (emphasis added)

This assertion presents us with a quite different perspective from the earlier focus on individualism, for we are now informed that the therapist "takes the functional organization of industrial society for granted."[21] The entire therapeutic enterprise is seen in a new light, for although the previous individualistic interpretation took the function of therapeutic "cure" to be the facilitation of individual gratification in the face of imposing obstacles, the new view must redefine "cure" as overcoming "the lack of fit between the present organization of the self and the available *organization of work,* intimacy, and meaning ... "[22] (emphasis added). Emphasis is now directed to the lack of fit between the organization of the self and the larger and underlying structure of the capitalist mode of production.

We have been led by Bellah into a different orientation, an orientation that is the manifestation of a different mode of social existence. I will refer to the previous notion that therapy facilitates individualism as the ideological interpretation of therapeutic experience; it is a mode of false consciousness grounded in the mystification of individual experience in capitalist society, a perversion of consciousness that inverts cause and effect, figure and ground. For though on this ideological view therapy serves as the midwife to a "second birth" of ourselves, a separation from the society and family into which we were born, this new view, more fully grounded in reality, forces us to recognize that

> just where we think we are most free, we are most coerced by the dominant beliefs of our own culture. For it is a powerful *cultural fiction* that we not only can, but must, make up our deepest beliefs in the isolation of our private selves.[23]

Simply put, "individualism" is a mystification, or in another more fully developed tradition, individualism is an ideological inversion of the basic structure of capitalism, treating the individual as the cause rather than the consequence of social relations.

For the authors of *Habits of the Heart* American individualism is inseparable from the relinquishing of objective moral standards. Only private gratification serves to determine the decisions of private life. The self so constituted is seen as purely formal and merely empty, the semblance of a self that is in fact hollowed of all content. But, as Bellah asks, "... what guarantees the autonomy of so radically empty a self against invasion from outside?"[24] This question touches upon and simultaneously inverts an important issue: the nature of the self's "emptiness." For Bellah's approach here suggests that the self is first made empty by its own decision and then invaded "from the outside." The obvious truth, however, is that the self is made "empty" (a mystifying and finally unintelligible term) by the same forces that weaken its power of thoughtful opposition.

The account we are offered is particularly confused, for after referring to Locke's "tabula rasa," and Goffman's notion that "there is no self at all," Oldham is once again cited to the effect that "values are shaped by the way you are brought up." But the two claims cannot both be true: It cannot be the case that the self is both empty and shaped by its social environment. The authors continually vacillate between two notions of the self's privatized, empty relativism. On the one hand they view this tendency as the essence of extreme individualism, and on the other, they approach understanding that this particular mode of selfhood is the essential structure of contemporary capitalism.

It is the latter view that emerges in the assertion that the relevance of therapy is enhanced by the fit of the therapeutic attitude of self-realization and empathic communication to the increasingly interpersonal nature of the work we do.[25]

The claim of a fit between the therapeutic attitude and work comes closer to prevailing reality, though the authors, by hiding behind the ambivalence of the notion of "fit," avoid any awareness that the structure of socioeconomic relations produces therapeutic sensibility. "The very procedural structure of therapy, including its market exchange mode of fee for service ... ties it into the bureaucratic and economic structure of the larger society. Therapy's stress on *personal autonomy* presupposes *institutional conformity*"[26] (emphasis added).

We have finally arrived at the clearest confrontation of ideology and reality: "personal autonomy" in ideological opposition to "institutional conformity"; the illusion of individualism in stark and violent contradiction to the power of economic structure.

What we are required to realize through the analysis that *Habits of the Heart* itself provides, is that despite its claim that anomic individualism lies at the heart of contemporary therapy, the structure of present psychological diagnosis and "cure" is actually an ingredient in contemporary capitalism, particularly in the form of market exchange through which it facilitates conformity; the very manner in which therapy is consumed becomes the antidote to the "emptiness" that capitalism constructs. "Recognizing the uniqueness of each individual appears here as an expressive end in itself *and* as a method of putting people to more efficient use as human resources."[27] Once again we are presented with ideological facade and instrumental reality. Because *Habits of the Heart* is incapable of transcending the myopia of liberalism, it never questions the relationship between the individual as an "expressive end in itself," and the manipulation and exploitation of people that derives from the "efficient use of human resources." The foundations of contemporary therapy, communication, and sympathy cannot fully humanize the world of bureaucratic work, but they can make it more comfortable and cooperative. They can smooth out conflict between people and help them through the regulated channels they must negotiate to get the job done while looking out for themselves. "It *is* a jungle out there, and you *do* have to look out for number one," concedes the welfare supervisor, "but you can do it without hurting people and creating more jungle."[28]

This procedure is described as the "monitoring" of human responses, one's own and others, so that self-expression can be "subordinated to the organization's 'bottom line' goals."

Bellah has made it abundantly clear that the *form of individualism that marks contemporary capitalism functions precisely to advance the aims of the capitalist system.* This is not the individualism of the isolated person facing an external bureaucratic capitalist structure; it is the individual inherent in that very structure, constituted and defined by it. We can clarify the arrangement by simply referring to this new human being as the capitalist individual, and as the therapeutic modality so deeply entrenched in this personal life as the precise mode of management of the capitalist individual established within the underlying social mode of production. Atomism and relativism are not the reality we actually encounter; they are the ideological expressions of the mode of social control that drives relentlessly toward dominance and exploitation. They are the distorted conscious expression of the underlying mode of social structure that requires manifestation as their inverted truth. The matter was put clearly and succinctly by Marx 150 years ago:

> The more deeply we go back into history, the more does the individual, and hence also the producing individual, appear as dependent, as belonging to a greater whole: in a still quite natural way in the family and in the family expanded into the clan;

then later into various forms of communal society arising out of the antitheses and fusion of the clans. *Only in the eighteenth century, in "civil society," do the various forms of social connectedness confront the individual as a means towards his private purposes, as external necessity. But the epoch which produced this standpoint, that of the isolated individual, is also precisely that of the hitherto most developed social ... relations.*[29] (emphasis added)

Therapy as Common Good and Ill

If, as Bellah's argument actually provides, the function of therapy is to establish conformity to capitalist requirements while maintaining the illusion of individual freedom, we are able to simplify our analysis of therapy as a common good by clarifying the human benefits and costs of such an accommodation and mystification. The ostensible advantages of contemporary therapy are essentially twofold: the amelioration of private suffering and the development of insight into the deformities of personal life. Neither of these virtues is inconsequential. Nobody who has experienced the ravages of guilt, rejection, anxiety, depression, hopelessness, or immobility can feel anything but gratitude for a procedure that ameliorates these devastating experiences. Those who have been aided in their private lives, who have moved from a crippling sense of helplessness to the occasion of future possibility, will certainly reject the notion that therapy is a useless discipline, of no value to its participants. To emerge from the darkness of terror or compulsion into a light of normality is a secular conversion that is surely an improvement in personal life that therapy makes possible.

The same can certainly be said for those therapeutic encounters that illuminate one's life and offer some insight into the conditions of one's fall and present rise. To understand how we have been formed in the crucible of family life and continue to carry the seeds of that formation with us into our later "development" is certainly an awareness more valuable than much of the rest of our ordinary comprehension.

What then is the structural limitation of individual therapy, or to go further, the complicity of therapy in the system of capitalist domination? Bellah has already provided the necessary clue. Therapy is a mode of conformity to the prevailing system of corporate and state domination. Its fundamental mode of activity is to raise individuals from the realm of *abnormal pathology* to the circumstance of *normal pathology,* to that determination of individual and social existence that characterizes the nature of capitalist relations and capitalist personal being. Its primary function, both manifest and latent, is the substitution of individual priority for the commitments and sensibilities of collective social life.

If, as Bellah's analysis indicates, therapy effects cure by producing conformity to capitalism, what is the origin and nature of the ailments to which it ministers? In a strict positivist medical account, ailment and cure are logically independent of each other. There is nothing in the technique of setting a broken bone that itself produces the break in question. Nor does the development of diagnosis itself create the condition it is designed to understand. This is true whether the aliment is historically of long standing, like bodily wounds, or contemporary, like AIDS. In the positivist perspective, the same paradigm is used to comprehend therapeutic phenomenon. So narcissism would be viewed as an objective human frailty, like bodily impairment, and cures would occur according to the independent logic of medical or therapeutic discovery.

But are the "making" and "taking" of mental illness independent facts? Might it not be the case that the nature of cure and illness are dialectically related? Marx has maintained that production and consumption cannot be separated:

> Production is also immediately consumption.... The individual not only develops his abilities in production, but also expends them, uses them up in the act of production.... The act of production is therefore in all its elements also an act of consumption.... Consumption is also immediately production.... Production, then, is also immediately consumption, consumption is also immediately production.... But at the same time a mediating movement takes place between the two. Production mediates consumption; it creates the latter's material; without it consumption would lack an object. But consumption also mediates production, in that it alone creates for the products the subject for whom they are products.[30]

If we adopt an intrinsically social view of illness and cure along the lines that Marx has suggested in relation to production and consumption, we are moved to consider that both ailment and cure are simultaneously the result of an underlying system of social structures. We will then approach the claim that contemporary therapy facilitates conformity to capitalism by asking whether such conformity may not itself contribute to the ills that therapy is then enlisted to ameliorate. Bellah does not say much about the production of specific pathologies in America, but there are suggestive clues:

> Communication and sympathy cannot fully humanize the world of bureaucratic work, but they can make it more comfortable and cooperative.[31]
>
> The relevance of therapy is enhanced by the fit of the therapeutic attitude of self-realization and empathic communication to the increasingly impersonal nature of the work we do.[32]

The latter remark strikes me as quite peculiar. How can it be the case that therapy, defined as self-realization and empathic communication, fits what is simultaneously described as the "increasingly impersonal" nature of contemporary work? We can disregard Bellah's self-serving claim that therapy cannot *fully* humanize bureaucracy; in fact, it cannot humanize it at all. But what it may be able to accomplish to some degree is the obfuscation of the nature of work and the penalties that work exacts from the lives of laborers. For therapy can speak for the ideological claim of capitalist labor, the claim of self-fulfillment, social harmony, and reciprocal human recognition. What it is debarred from even seriously attempting is the actual recognition, let alone realization, of these aims. For the claim of self-realization through therapy is undermined by the nature of the capitalist system: its collective production and individual isolation; social interdependence and personal atomism; exploitation and alienation of social life; the alienation of human power; and the mystification of lived experience.

Common, Public and Social Goods in the System of Capitalism

Discussions of the terms "public goods," "common goods," or "social goods" often fail to offer a substantial account of the meaning of the term "good." The reasons are obvious: first, economics tends to eschew value judgments and therefore uses the notion of "good" to mean roughly the satisfaction of some want or need. This is the meaning of the term in the classical economics of Smith and Ricardo and the usage is followed by so radical an innovator as Marx, who employs the term "use value" with no moral connotation. Second, a full account of "the good" would amount to a treatise on ethics, a difficult undertaking, and one that will not be attempted here. I will hold to the point previously argued, that the individual and society are dialectically related, and that any notion of the good life must include the notion of a good society. And, for purposes of this chapter, I will further stipulate that any society that claims legitimacy must be intrinsically democratic. This last property entails several others; equality, reciprocal concern for the well-being of others, substantive knowledge of the basic laws and processes of social life, recognition of moral principles, and the desire to further this good life. I will return to this point later in this essay.

The public realm exists in several modalities and therefore the term "public" has several meanings; in other words, there are various ways in which "goods" may belong to the public realm. "Public goods" might well be defined in relation to the agency that initiates their introduction; "common goods" refer to a different dimension of the social situation, the right of universal participation in regard to the value in question. According to the traditional liberal framework, which includes the variation known as welfare economics:

A "good" may be common in the obvious sense that it is an actual or potential "good" for everyone in a given society; that is, that it satisfies some want of all the members of a given society. This is the ground of insisting upon its general availability. Since there are few "goods" which, when specified, will be embraced by every individual in a democratic society, the validity of the notion of "common good" depends on an analysis of the "potential" value of various goods under some set of ideal conditions. This position has received more careful attention in the conservative rather than the liberal tradition, which is reluctant to discuss "goods" that are not the objects of actual choice and desire.

The obvious and often cited examples of public goods are roads, bridges, lighthouses, and military defense, not in the sense that each member of the community owns a part of the whole, but that all may claim full participation in the whole. The basic argument in behalf of "goods" of this sort is that they are required for commerce or security but are not feasibly produced by regular market forces. They are not the sort of "goods" that are bought and sold in the marketplace because it is not profitable for market participants to engage in such exchange. Nevertheless, it is essential to realize that the historical introduction of public goods has most often been directed at expediting or correcting the activity of the marketplace. So, public goods are historically tied to capitalist society. If one maintains, as I think plausible, that public goods in a capitalist society fundamentally aid the operations of that society, then a significant measure of suspicion must arise in regard to their introduction and function.

Public "goods," not available through the market, require introduction through political decision. The determination may be made by a dictator, a totalitarian regime, a hereditary republic, or a collective democratic constituency. In each case the decision occurs beyond the procedures of the marketplace. It is this political fact about the introduction of public goods that leads to their defense among liberal supporters who are critical of the unregulated market. In a democracy public "goods" will often be introduced even though many individuals have no direct interest in them because a majority is sufficient for their support. In this regard, the struggle for their provision often leads a disadvantaged majority to curtail the power of the minority. This may be a progressive development, but in itself tells us nothing about the character of the "goods" themselves.

Public "goods" provide for want satisfactions that are unavailable through the market. The reverse side of this market failure is the situation of "externalities," what Kapp, in *The Social Cost of Private Enterprise*, defines as all "direct and indirect losses suffered by third persons or the general public as a result of private economic activities."[33] Regarding the political struggle to introduce legislation that circumvents the defects of the market, Kapp notes:

> The political history of the last 150 years can be fully understood only as a revolt of large masses of people (including business) against the shifting of a part of the social costs of production to third persons or to society. [34]

Externalities are "negative effects" of enterprise that are produced by one party and imposed on another. A standard example is the pollution caused by a factory, the effects of which burden those beyond the confines of the factory itself. In both the instances of public goods and externalities an attempt is made to remedy the defects of the market system, which remains the basic structure of the classical and neoclassical analysis.

The introduction of protective social legislation, restraining and inhibiting the actions of those responsible for detrimental externalities, has often improved the circumstances of large numbers of the population. However, it is vital to understand the *remedial* nature of these public goods; the remedy that is introduced through public goods may require the introduction of a procedure the market cannot provide, or it may necessitate compensation or penalty for some procedure that occurs in the course of market exchange. In classical economics and its variations the notion of "goods" and "ills" remain rooted in individual decisions that do not involve a moral assessment. Although it remains true that a political decision is required to supplement the competitive forces of the market, nothing is assumed about the particular "goods" that are implemented by this decision.

In particular, nothing can be inferred about the private or social nature of the "goods" themselves, and nothing can be inferred about the moral contribution of the public good in question. Military power may legitimately protect a threatened nation; it may just as well extend the imperialist ambitions of an expansive national policy. A competitive examination for college entry sponsored by a state agency may well advance the opportunities of some portion of the population, but it may also encourage competitiveness and a greater concern with one's own well-being at the expense of indifference to others. And the fact that a public agency dispenses medical services cannot tell us anything about the value of those services. In fact, a great expenditure on public health may only indicate that the society is producing ill health that it must then address through costly ameliorative measures.

I have chosen to use the terms "health" and "mental health" in an explicitly social and normative manner. It is essential to realize that terms like "public health" may refer to the institution that dispenses health services, to the procedure by which the decision is exercised, or to the nature of the good, "health" in this case, that is being distributed. "Health," as I shall use the term, is a social value of a different sort from a lighthouse; it is a requirement of any satisfactory life and is therefore a normative requirement of all human beings. It is, furthermore, an *intrinsic* value, as is not the case with a lighthouse that exists to facilitate some other activity deemed important. So, in this sense, it is a common and social value in that it is necessary for the well-being of all and depends on a particular social arrangement for its realization. It is logically conceivable that individuals living in isolation from each other could all require and satisfy the conditions of health without social support. However, because in fact this good is the good of human beings living in a society, health, although it most literally resides in individuals, can only be achieved through social institutions that cure disease and make the fuller healthful existence of individuals possible. It is therefore not only a common value in that all require it, but a social value insofar as it can only be realized through the institutions of an appropriate society.

Social values have a positive and a negative aspect. The positive provision lies in the assessment of valued experience or life that the good makes possible or embodies. Such is the case with parks, education, and health. The negative and more legal aspect of this consideration is the provision that no individual can be excluded from participation in the institutions of the social good: ideally, no one can be denied access to parks, education, or health. Of course, these are ideal concerns still commonly violated, for though there may be formal access corresponding to the legal prohibition on exclusion, it is obvious that there is no substantive equal right to participate or be protected against exclusion. This is a powerful indication of how rooted such social values are in the antisocial structures of an unequal society.

A value may also be social in the sense that it is relational, as are the values of "equality" and "reciprocal concern" referred to above. Love and justice are not individual goods: They can only exist through the particular structure of relations that bind one individual to another in accordance with specific normative requirements. Human concern advances my well-being through the same activity that enhances your own. These goods are of value to all members of an ideal society, but they cannot reside in the individuals themselves in isolation or, for that matter, as the sum of their private lives. It is clear that these values cannot be incorporated in a marketplace for procedural and substantive reasons: The market lacks any mechanism for registering values that cannot be located as the private possession of distinct individuals; and the market functions through competition although such values require reciprocal concern for the other's well-being.

Finally, there is transcendent, that is, organic value, both emergent and directive, that constitutes the placement of differentiated roles, functions, and determinate values that make up the entire social structure. This is usually what we mean by "culture." It is the normative structure of the society as a whole, that systematic organization of values that includes knowledge, love, justice, culture, beauty, play, erotic fulfillment, security, and self-determination, ordered for the sake of the maximum human realization of the members of the political community. This organic structure is the "meaning" of the life of the community, an ultimate good not reducible to the individual values whose order it structures, though it obviously cannot exist independent of their presence. It is the value of the ultimate distribution of values in the good life and can therefore be regarded as immanently transcendent. Its relation to its aspects is similar to the beauty of a work of art in that it is certainly not the sum of the various aspects that constitute it but clearly would not exist without their more specific determinations.

Considering, then, the features of public goods, it appears they can be graded in terms of their inherent sociability. Some public values, uniform weights and measures, for example, are useful as means to the private ends of commerce and trade. The latter may be deemed social in regard to the human contact they encourage, but their immediate purpose is the enhancement of the possibility of individual gain. The construction and maintenance of dikes represents an instance of mutual dependency since they can only be maintained by all and their failure would be experienced as a disaster by all. Finally, justice, as has been noted, is not a means to any further end though a just society may produce more general satisfaction than any other. In this instance, the quality of satisfaction, its distribution, is the relevant factor, not merely sheer quantity.

Capitalist Destruction
of the Social Good

Capitalism cannot serve the common social good; its entire structural directive is dependent upon increasing class exploitation, alienation, competition, fragmented labor, and ideological mystification. The "goods" that emerge from this social order are mediated through a system of market exchange now dominated by powerful transnational corporations systematically entwined in a net of state bureaucracies. It is not necessary to engage in a protracted comparison of capitalist "well-being" with that of the thousands of other societies that human beings have constructed to realize that capitalism has introduced the greatest assemblage of productive forces in world history and provided the expanding benefits of that technology for a small and shrinking portion of the world population. The values that capitalism makes possible are predominantly individualized forms of personal experience or relational forms that tend to be marked by exploitation, fragmentation, and social obfuscation.

In traditional therapy the criteria of "mental health" reflect current standards of "normal" functioning, personal identity, and interpersonal relationships. These are, of course, aspects of the present social system, which is de facto in effect, and which determines the definitions that become the standards of therapeutic work. In short, the capitalist system, like all other systems, judges the health of its members in accordance with the basic principles of its own, capitalist functioning.

Freud, for example, spoke of the necessity of work and love for healthy human existence, but I am unaware of any instance in which Freud actually considered the nature of work as a social-economic enterprise, an arrangement by which some set of human beings gains control over the labor power of others through the exercise of propertied domination. Again, although paranoia is regarded as a pathology marked by pervasive, illusory belief in the malevolence of others, there is no designation in the DSM for the incapacity of individuals to recognize the malevolence of the system that exploits their labor and turns it back upon themselves as alienated but "natural" domination. So, belief in malevolence that does not exist is a pathology; denial of malevolence that does exist, is not. Nor are structures of participation in one's own self-destruction seen in relation to patterns of masochism and self-abuse. In short, one form of illusion is seen as pathological and so described in official doctrine; the other is not seen at all and makes up the "normal" obfuscation of the ordinary life world.

So therapy is grounded in what I previously referred to as "normal pathology," a degradation of human existence codified as appropriate functioning. It is the average functioning, the normal "adjustment to reality" necessary to maintain the existence of the present capitalist system. When such views are articulated in their darkest form, as in the writings of the Frankfurt School, one is inclined to reject them as caricatures of contemporary life. Certainly there is more vital existence, play, friendship and love, compassion and hope than the pessimism of a total regime of commodity relations will permit. True. However, the reasons for this humane divergence are twofold: First, much of what is best in life occurs outside of the system of capitalist domination; and second, capitalism must always hold out the promise of happiness and fulfillment, and so, must permit some limited realization of these ends. Were it never to fulfill its promise, it would be reduced to a rule of violence incompatible with its need for participatory subordination.

Can therapy resist the prevailing forms of human exploitation? It cannot accomplish this end even if it were to choose to do so. Freud was quite frank about this issue:

> The function of education, therefore, is to inhibit, forbid and suppress, and it has at all times carried out this function to admiration.... [35]
>
> It has been said—and no doubt with justice—that every education is partisan; it aims at making the child adapt itself to whatever social system is the established one, without consideration of how valuable or how stable that system may be. If, it is argued, one is convinced of the shortcomings of our present-day arrangements, one cannot think it right to give them the added support of this psycho-analytical education of ours. We must place before it another and a higher aim, one which is emancipated from the social standards that are dominant today. I do not feel, however, that this argument is valid.... Psychoanalytic education will be assuming an unwarranted responsibility if it sets out to make its pupils into revolutionaries. It will have done its task if it sends them away *as healthy and efficient as possible.*[36] (emphasis added)

What, however, is the meaning of "efficiency" if not accommodation to the prevailing structure of capitalist logic? Of course Freud is only one voice in the analytic tradition, but I believe that on this point his position is authoritative. Certainly there have been revolutionary psychoanalysts such as Reich and Fanon, but the analytic establishment has consigned them to the exciting but unstable periphery. And though there are newer forms of therapy highly critical of the entire Freudian tradition, they rarely reflect critically on the necessity of radically transforming the present society of alienated dehumanization, whatever their claim to exploring interpersonal relations.

We have already been introduced to the "fit between the therapeutic attitude of self-realization and empathic communication and the increasingly interpersonal nature of the work we do." Bellah himself well noted that therapy's "stress on personal autonomy presupposes institutional conformity." The reason for this congruence is simply that the autonomy that is able to realize itself within pre-

sent circumstances is the autonomy of capitalist alienation. Autonomy is by its very nature relative to the structure of available possibilities that the self defines as necessary to its fulfillment. So, autonomy can always be had at the expense of contracting the choices among which the self determines its existence. To the extent that I surrender my claims to equality, cooperative self-determination, the end of exploitation, and the humanization of nature, to that extent I am permitted to act freely within the remaining circumscribed arena of passive consumption, acquiescence in the prevailing realm of "civilized" violence, and terror against those who protest.

The structures of the self through which autonomy can be formed and effectuated in this society are the needs and identities that, to a very large extent, are the modes of existence our political economy make possible and necessary. Therapy is an adjunct to the realization of these possibilities. To be autonomous in this sense is to be able to move without excessive hindrance within the current flow of events. It is decidedly not the autonomy to transcend this system, to struggle with hope for a location beyond the limits of capitalist exploitation, and to move with others toward a transcendence of contemporary capitalist logic.

To be truly autonomous is to be responsible, which requires that one is able to gauge the effects of reciprocal social action, which in turn implies that we understand the purpose and meaning of those actions, which itself necessitates the presence of a common code that derives from the collective action of those who are bound by its authority. Our social codes are alienated, exploitative, and mystified. We are more the subjects of these codes than their agents, and they remain generally opaque in their larger functions. Of course the possibility of such a restructuring remains; but the inertia of the system weighs heavily upon those who would confront it. Therapy as commonly practiced and understood leans on the support of this structure. Freud was honest and clear on this point.

Whether the consumer is faced with the fetishism of commodified exchange, a private fee for service arrangement transpiring between two insulated individuals abstracted from the direct life of the community, or the fetishism of the state apparatus, concerned with the potential disruptive influence of citizens unable to engage in the minimal activity required by the social economy, the general function of therapy is, as Bellah noted, conformity to prevailing power.

Beyond the specific fact that therapy is a commodified exchange, what is the significance of the general market structure of social life within which therapy operates? The dynamic of commodification establishes the need for separate and private persons to appropriate through individual consumption the external and apparently "natural" resources that are actually of their own making. The external system of commodification is vital because it represents the manifestation of the alienation of the labor that has produced it. What is appropriated in all forms, whether as competitive advantage and the display of power or the very formation of the self through the reflective instrumentalization of self-construction, is the system of abstract and reified norms that govern and direct the social world.

For Descartes, self-knowledge is an act of immediate intuition. For Hegel the certainty of one's own self-consciousness is dialectically related to one's awareness of the self-conscious recognition of one's self-consciousness by another self-consciousness. In the modern era this abstract mediation of self by other proceeds through the criteria of production, consumption, distribution, and exchange as embedded in the culture of personified commodification and represented, for example, by advertising. Here commodities come alive and play the "human" counterpart to their fetishized existence. The automobile exudes power, the tube of toothpaste assures confidence, the appropriate undergarments pulse with erotic desire, the affluent home embodies success. The fetishism of commodities presents objects as independent of the human activity that has created them; the personalization of commodities returns a "human meaning" to these entities, but the meaning is reconstituted through the false consciousness that promises personal fulfillment as the compensation for the loss of collective social control.

The cures offered for "mental illness" appear as objective and natural as the sufferings they promise to alleviate. And it is not merely the implicit goals of therapy that serve the larger society. It is obvious that therapy exists to relieve distress without challenging the parameters of current power. What is more revealing is the manner in which the formal structure of therapy replicates the formal structure of capitalist exchange. For writers like Philip Cushman, therapy involves the consumption of the soothing presence of the therapist, a consumption that serves to fill the emptiness of the self. Although there is certainly truth in this account, the therapeutic situation may also be viewed, particularly through a socially enhanced theory of object relations, as a vast and intricate construction of exchange. In this version of contemporary psychoanalytic theory, the self is understood as a system constructed out of the continual acts of projection and introjection; but these acts in fact merely parallel, on a psychic level, the larger processes of exchange that serve as the metabolism of the social world. The infant is understood to be constantly expelling aspects of itself into those others upon whom it vitally depends for its nurturance and its very existence. It makes its rage, terror, desire, oral aggression, and destructiveness part of the being of these others, and then, through the reciprocal process of ingestion, "takes in" again what it has thrown out of itself, usually with considerable distortion. Much of therapy deals with the location and amelioration of this system of reciprocal determination.

What is almost always overlooked in the theory of psychic exchange is that the "original" material is itself largely socially constructed. There are of course mental states and processes that must be attributed to the infant at birth; a tabula rasa view of our original condition is clearly impossible. But from the moment of its coming to its own being, the infant enters into a relation with the adult world that immediately begins to form the "original" material of its infant life. The entire rhythm of its feeding, holding, play, separation, recognition, darkness and light, cleaning, and touching vary culturally from the moment of its birth. Such "exchange" of mental states as are postulated within object relations theory (probably best understood as interpretations of the actions of others and interpretations of their interpretations of one's own actions rather than as mysterious processes of psychic transport) must always be grasped within the structure of power and meaning that adults exercise over the lives of their infants, a structure of power embedded in and following from the larger social world they inhabit.

Of course "therapy" recognizes that adults exercise power over infants and children, but it tends to believe that this disparity disappears as children grow to adulthood and come to their own maturity. What is critically overlooked, however, is the structure of social domination that is transferred to the child through the mediation of the family. Theories of "psychic exchange," crucial to object relation theory, systematically ignore the larger social realm of power. As the uneven and exploitative nature of class domination is masked by theories of "pure exchange," so a similar result often appears in studies of infant development. The fact that the infant grows eventually to substitute its own self-monitoring for external parental control is completely removed from consideration of the nature of that "self-monitoring" and the subordination of self that is established through its mediation.

In sociological theory the well-established position of exchange theory also serves to obscure the nature of social power. So, commenting on Homans's theory of social exchange and his assertion that under conditions of equilibrium, *"power differences tend to disappear* and neither party will change his behavior any further,"* Zeitlin comments insightfully:

> What this arbitrary and bizarre conception tends to do is to overlook entirely the perpetuation of power in persisting relationships—with the parties to the relation being not only unequal, but with one of them successfully dominating, subjecting, or coercing the others.[37]

In both cases, exchange is understood as an abstraction from the disparities of domination that root the individual in the social system.

Despite this purported constant traffic in psychic exchange, there is, as I previously noted, a prevailing and quite common view that the self is empty. The persuasiveness of this position derives from an analysis of need that holds that the self is perpetually dissatisfied and *devoid of* the commodities it feels it requires to fulfill its nature. The constant, restless striving for the next essential object of display or consumption (and it is interesting how much consumption would be curtailed without display) seems to vindicate the theory of the "empty self." But, in fact, the self is quite full and heavy with the ceaseless burden of instrumentalized self-reflection, continually assessing and reconstituting itself in accordance with calculations concerning the most efficient means to maximizing commodified gratification, and particularly, the one means that make all such possibilities viable—money.

For the circuit of desire more and more runs through the channels of commodification, which by their very nature, facilitate private interest at the expense of the common good. For a therapist to oppose this tendency would require a position antagonistic to the social parameters that establish the present boundaries of the self. At one point in *Strategy for Labor* Gorz asks:

> Does the man who eats red meat and white bread, moves with the help of a motor, and dresses in synthetic fibers, live better than the man who eats dark bread and white cheese, moves on a bicycle, and dresses in wool and cotton? The question is almost meaningless. It supposes that in a given society, the same individual has a choice between two different life styles. Practically speaking, this is not the case: only one way of life, more or less rigidly determined, is open to him, and this way of life is conditioned by the structure of production and its techniques. The latter determine the environment by which needs can be satisfied, and the manner of consuming or using these objects.[38]

This statement presents the deeper reason that Freud unconsciously manifested in eschewing the revolutionary patient and choosing instead the life of *health and efficiency.*

It must be recalled that the efficiency of capitalist society involves enormous waste and the simultaneous impoverishment of fundamental social needs; waste and scarcity in dialectical counterpoise. At one point in a discussion to which we will return, Stephen Mitchell presents the hypothetical case of

> a little girl who decides she will become a physician through a mixture of motives that we will divide into two groups. Group A includes genuine interest in the work- ings of nature in general and bodies in particular, sexual curiosity, a concern with helping others, and counterdependent defenses against getting sick herself. Group B includes a strong desire to please her parents' thwarted longings to be educated as professionals, identification with their social class aspirations.[39]

Mitchell notes that since the group A motives reflect "internal" concerns whereas the motives in group B are "external," the prior motives appear to be more authentic. However, the situation is more complex than first appears since the second motives may have become internalized while the originally in- terior motives

> could not emerge in an interpersonal vacuum or flower in a simply mirroring, facili- tating environment. They must have identificatory meanings embedded in the inter- actions with important others, complex reverberations and resonances within vari- ous relational configurations.[40]

This seems quite ordinary, unexceptionable contemporary therapeutic reflec- tion. However, note what is omitted: Nothing is said of the nature of the medical school she will attend nor of the system of health care through which her "con- cern with helping others" will be mediated. Recall Gorz's admonition regarding "the structure of production and its techniques [that] determine the environment by which needs can be satisfied, and the manner of consuming or using these ob- jects." And shall we ignore the prevailing understanding of nature, illness, and cure that obtains in her particular historical and cultural milieu? When Mitchell notes that even the more interior motives "could not emerge in an interpersonal vacuum.... They must have identificatory meanings embedded in interactions with important others, complex reverberations and resonance within various re- lational configurations," he does not appear to recognize the "relational configu- rations" of capitalism and the specific manner in which it privatizes the meaning of health. Nor does Mitchell note that internalization is a purely formal criterion of psychic development that is incapable of distinguishing between the appropri- ation of a humane or destructive political perspective.

The contradiction between profit motivated and humane medicine does not make up the agenda of contemporary therapy. Nor do any of the other capitalist structures that thwart the human need for education, communal affiliation, pro- tection of the natural environment, rational economic planning, and provision for livable space. Therapy cannot degenerate into a series of lectures on the political economy. However, although it is true that therapy is not a didactic enterprise, it is equally true that the present system of therapeutic practice merely assumes the contours of contemporary capitalism. The task is to find a new therapy that will, in Brechtian fashion, alienate alienation and turn a critical light on the social structures that have generated the private sufferings and then made them subject to private amelioration.

Nothing better illustrates the incapacity of contemporary therapy to grasp these considerations than the present use of the notion of "the true self." The search for the "true self" has been something of a perennial human concern, as the history of the great religions attest. However, although in previous epochs the self was understood in its connection to the universe, God, the spirits of one's ancestors, or the customs and practices of the community, with the beginning of the bourgeois period the self was sought more and more in separation from the world, in that interior realm to which individuals claimed ownership as they claimed any other private property they came to possess in the marketplace.

Winnicott's work, best known for its insistence on the primacy of the infant-mother dyad, nevertheless retains a commitment to the most extreme notion of isolated selfhood since Kant's conception of the noumenal self:

> principle governing human life could be formulated in the following words; only the true self can feel real, but the true *self must never be affected by external reality*, must never comply.[41] (emphasis added)

Of course, complying with the external world and being affected by it are two very different notions. The latter idea is absurd on its face and Winnicott surrounds this notion with more credible remarks concerning the infant's dependency upon its mother. But the notion of not complying is also quite absurd. Mitchell put the matter this way:

> Consider Winnicott's depiction of the earliest feeding experiences, which he established as the basis for the split between true and false selves. In pathological feeding, he suggests, the infant takes his cues from impingement from the outside. The baby's own impulses and needs are not met by the mother, and the baby learns to want what the mother gives, to become the mother's idea of what the baby is. Authentic feeding experience, on the other hand, derives from the baby's spontaneously arising gestures, which the mother meets and actualizes.[42]

This extraordinary summation of Winnicott's position informs us that infant feeding is pathological to the extent that the infant takes his cues from his mother and "learns to want what the mother gives," rather than from its own "spontaneously arising gestures." Of course, Mitchell has too much common sense not to protect himself by the use of the phrase *"derives from* the baby's spontaneously arising gestures."

Nevertheless, there are critical difficulties with Winnicott's conception: first, it completely neglects the diversity of feeding patterns in the great variety of world cultures. All of them channel, form, and organize the infants' "spontaneous" hunger through highly differentiated and quite specific ways of interpreting this given fact. For example, the infant may be fed before its hunger is consciously articulated, immediately upon its manifest urging, on a precise schedule of given hours, or any combination and melding of these alternatives and others we do not comprehend. There is no single way to respond to hunger, so either the infant is quite malleable in this regard, or almost all of the world's cultures engage in pathological feeding although only one, perhaps, recognizes the infant's spontaneous gesture.

Second, the infant's original response cannot be a "gesture" because gestures are acts that have been culturally interpreted and given cultural meaning.

Finally, Winnicott seems forced to the logic that the true self does not in fact change, since it does not permit itself to be affected by external reality. And in fact he endorses

> the theme not so much of society that changes as of human nature that does not change. Human nature does not change. This is an idea that could be challenged. Nevertheless, I shall assume its truth and build on this foundation. It is true that human nature evolved, just as human bodies and beings evolved.... But there is little evidence that human nature has altered in the course of hundred of thousands of years.[43]

Of course no evidence is offered for this contention and the fact that humans evolve but are not altered is simply left as the contradiction it appears to be.

The great appeal of Winnicott's distinction between true and false self, the primary reason for the widespread embrace of this concept among therapists and lay public alike, lies in the fact that it speaks to a real division within our being. There is undoubtedly a distinction between something "true" and something "false" in the way we experience our lives. But the division is not between a primary, given, unchanging humane nature and conformity to society. It is, rather, between our curtailed existence and the adumbration of a fuller being that speaks to us beyond the confines of this most limited world. The "true self" is the potentiality latent in a new social existence that we presently glimpse darkly but with deep longing and desire. It is not something already present in our nature at birth, but something we aspire to become in a yet uncreated communal existence. It is not the distinction between a true, spontaneous, primitive given and social conformity, but between primitive social existence and a genuinely human social life.

Winnicott's underlying assumptions seriously parallel what Macpherson has designated as "possessive individualism," a founding conception of liberal political thought:

The assumptions which comprise possessive individualism may be summarized in the following propositions:

> What makes a man human is freedom from dependence on the wills of others.
> Freedom from dependence on others means freedom from any relations with others except those relations which the individual enters voluntarily.
> The individual is essentially the proprietor of his own person and capacities, for which he owes nothing to society.[44]

It is striking to note the parallels between these two views: one the foundation of seventeenth-century political thought and the other a foundational assumption of a significant twentieth-century psychotherapist.

It may be noted in response that however atomistic or insular some of its assumptions, therapy certainly acts on behalf of those with psychological ailments. So, paradoxically, whether the true self is altered by external reality or not, the therapist attempts to transform the nature of that self as it enters into the therapeutic relationship. Whether the "true self" can be affected by external reality or not, Winnicott, it would seem, acted to increase the autonomy of his patients. So, despite the extreme contention of Winnicott's theory of the psychic homunculus, is it not the case that therapy cannot only minimize the suffering of patients but also, indirectly contribute to the social good?

Certainly therapy can ameliorate suffering. However, this is not equivalent of maintaining that it moves us beyond personal experience toward a common good. Reduction of pain is undoubtedly a good thing, but in itself, prima facie, it is an individual, private advantage. For therapy to transcend this individual realm its practitioners need to recognize and treat conditions that are common to the otherwise fragmented, alienated individual members of our society, or restructure the relations among them so that they more closely approach the ideal configuration of a good society. Therapy as generally practiced today is directed toward neither of these ends, for the reasons that I have advanced in this essay: therapy reinforces the basic assumptions of capitalist culture in regard to its definition of the self and its boundaries, the system of its needs, and the material relations it establishes among social members. Its gravitational pull is insular, "deeper" within the individual, personal relationship, or family.

This privatization, however, is not sufficient to establish the "social good." Another way of noting the point is to return to the claims made on behalf of therapy as providing personal insight. On the basis of our analysis of the formation of the capitalist self, we have become aware that the nature of such insight as therapy provides is limited at best and inverted, at worst. For in tracing our present malaise back to the conditions of our early childhood, therapy abstracts from those social structures that determine the functions of the family and its contribution to capitalist reproduction. For all its sophistication regarding the genesis and morphology of personal development, therapy is singularly ignorant of the larger social function of both the family and its own practice. In this crucial sense therapy shows itself to be as afflicted by bourgeois ideology as any other aspect of prevailing capitalist culture.

These considerations explain one of the major functional paradoxes of therapy; its capacity to ameliorate the conditions of individuals or of small groups while simultaneously strengthening the larger system of social control. It can certainly be argued that an improvement in the condition of the individual is likely to improve the condition of those close to the individual in question and so on, indefinitely. The often assumed inference is that the continual expansion of this process, one individual at a time improving the lives of others, will eventually lead to the total transformation of the larger society. This is precisely the nodal point of the fallacy in question. Each individual "improvement," based on a technique that reproduces the underlying political-economic structure, simultaneously reinforces social deterioration. The very most that can be claimed for therapy is that it can increase the happiness of one's private life. The least that need be said is that this "improvement" occurs at the expense of one's life as a member of society. For the shadows of public powerlessness and alienation fall back upon the individual and leave personal life divided between an intensified involvement in one's individual existence and a growing sense of the meaninglessness of personal "success." Therapeutic consumers experience small personal victories within the context of larger social despair; their private unhappiness may be diminished, but their sense of human existence is similarly curtailed.

Were the state to make therapy, as presently practiced, available to every individual in our society, such therapy would satisfy the definition of a "public good," but would fail utterly to promote the "social good." The discrepancy between these two notions is profound. "Public goods" are, in our situation, contrivances of liberal society designed to ignore the social structure of exploitative production for the sake of a redress of market ills or more equitable distribution of presently available advantages. Once again we need to follow Marx in insisting that the manner of production determines the value of distribution, exchange, and consumption. For every human being in our society to have access to "mental health" would still tell us nothing of the nature of the "health" to be promoted. In the case of mental health, the practice of therapy is inseparable from the ideology that grounds the therapy and is consequently unintelligible as a "pure" or "neutral" development. Therapy is not like setting a broken bone; the action of therapy is inseparable from the development of a conviction regarding human nature and its relation to society. If the conviction rests upon a belief that is distorted it may provide some sort of gratification, but it can only further the conditions that have contributed to the original difficulty.

Conclusion

Therapy, as a bourgeois "technique," is as much structured and constrained by the imperatives of capitalism as any other form of market technology. This is its basic limitation; however, this very restriction also suggests that freed from the narrow confines of its present political subservience, therapy can emerge as a truly emancipatory activity. Marx's terminology may seem archaic, but therapy evidences the same contradiction between productive forces and social relations that afflict the remainder of the capitalist enterprise. On the one hand, material techniques and accompanying liberal values introduce new possibilities for human fulfillment. However, the same historical processes that introduce these advances also curtail their fuller development, or even present regressions from previous standards of social life. Like machinery utilized by the capitalist, or such liberal values as equality, therapy as presently structured represents an ambivalent advance over previous practices.

The essence of the psychodynamic practice that grounds therapy provides us with the possibility of a new understanding of the nature of human development and its malformations. Psychotherapeutic theory and practice contributes to our comprehension of the manner in which the social world is appropriated by the conscious and unconscious subjectivity of human beings. We can begin to understand how this social appropriation is organized by the deeper dynamics of our being in the world, and through this insight we begin to understand some of the procedures by which individuals come to acquiesce in the structures of power that root them in subservience and apathy. We are capable of a more profound understanding of the nature of ideological mystification, for psychotherapy adumbrates the manner in which the interior of the self is afflicted by the same processes of alienation and reification that the Marxist tradition discovered in the political economy.[45]

A socially informed, progressive therapy needs to acknowledge simultaneously (1) the deeper economic and political structures that ground the lives of the individuals to whom it ministers and (2) the manner in which these lives are penetrated and misconceived through the formations of false consciousness. A mature therapy will have to recognize the relationships that obtain among the structures of social reality, the lived experience of those relations, and the forms of ideology that obfuscate the character of these experiences. A skeletal characterization might begin:

Socialist Reality	Experience	Ideological Distortion
Capitalist domination	alienation	"second nature"
Isolation	anxiety	autonomy
Competition	dread	initiative
Interdependence	conformity	participation
Alienation	meaninglessness	personal choice
Insularity	helplessness	intimacy
Exclusion	loneliness	privacy

An adequate theoretical system requires an analysis that integrates the structural and phenomenological considerations of social life. On the one hand, capitalist structures are not directly experienced. The imperative for constant capital expansion is not in itself directly perceptible; but the radical transformation of technology and dependent social institutions is a pervasive experience of modern life. On the other hand, lived experience is so permeated by pervasive forms of ideological mystification that the two are extremely difficult to separate. This is a propitious point for a reconstituted therapeutic approach, for the articulation of obscure aspects of experience is one of its specific sensibilities.

This promise remains unfulfilled, however, as the techniques of potential enlightenment remain themselves mystified. The instruments of potential revelation are themselves contaminated; human activity and theories of human activity are similarly obfuscated. The remedy in both cases requires as one of its preconditions an understanding of how both the maladies of individualism and the theories of its cure are rooted in individualist assumptions that are the product of a specific form of interdependent social existence. Can therapy itself produce such an understanding? The answer is as ambivalent as the question, for everything depends on the meaning of the phrase "produce an understanding."

There is every reason to believe that therapy cannot lead an otherwise reified social consciousness beyond its current apathy; there is also reason to believe, however, that therapy may be quite useful in furthering a process of change already in progress. It is not an accident that Reich and Fanon were deeply rooted in larger emancipatory movements. For the essence of the therapeutic process is the articulation of processes present *in* the psyche, but not yet *for* the psyche, not yet raised to the level of self-consciousness. The argument of this chapter has been that these processes are dialectically related to the larger social movements that surround the individual, since the individual both reflects and reproduces that pervasive social world. For these processes of production to become available to human beings, the therapeutic practice that "treats" them must itself recognize the social individual as its primary locus. But it cannot present this explanation as sheer didactics, as theoretical explanation that replaces lived comprehension.

The most progressive therapy, therapy that furthers a radical social process, may well need to recognize the social both in its theoretical structure and its practical location. The group is the final logical setting for a therapy that intends to incorporate the social world, as the process of reciprocal intersubjectivity in the group provides each individual with the condensed material of society. The group makes possible the awareness that my "pathologies" are not my own, that they do not belong to me as individual possessions. When I experience through others the conflicts, obfuscations, thwarted desires, and denials that I experience in myself, my collective or common nature is manifest as experience rather than abstract idea. It is no wonder that in the psychoanalytic establishment group therapy has always been held in less esteem than individualized "treatment."

We may regard the practical setting of therapy, individual or social, as the internal condition of social realization. In traditional therapy both the setting and the theory are distinctly individual and the process of social realization ideological and alienated. Traditional therapy isolates the individual as much as possible from the larger society and treats the subjective processes of individuals, though they are largely socially constructed, as primary, given, often innate mental constituents. A radical therapy using social categories and set in a more socialized group context may hope to provide an emancipatory social realization. Nevertheless, this process, though necessary, is not sufficient. It needs to occur in the course of a larger movement for democratic social change.

Such a development necessitates a significant transformation in capitalist society. Therapy cannot in itself conjure up a public good out of the fragmented and isolated elements of current society. Although the human needs that therapy articulates and manages are intrinsically "social," that is, created in society, present therapeutic practice views them ideologically, as "primitive," individual, psychic constituents. This is perhaps one reason why the enormous expansion of therapeutic activity in capitalist countries, particularly the United States, has not led to any proportional increase in personal well-being. Distress accumulates as the means of its cure expand. This is not to claim that therapy in itself is the cause of the malaise; however, the ideological distraction provided by therapy contributes to deeply misplaced expectations.

We have previously cited Marx to the effect that needs expand in proportion to the means of their satisfaction in the context of the prevailing mode of production. That mode of production and the means of consumer satisfaction are directed toward the expansion of private profit. Utility is not the end of capitalist production. It is notorious that the apparent diversity of commodities masks a depressing social uniformity whereas the codified pathologies of the DSM expand with similar profusion. The new, the novel, the unique mode of being continues to rest on a familiar ground of congealed power. Growing affluence masks an ever-expanding accumulation of waste that easily coexists with such profound unmet needs as those for education, housing, and health. This prevailing irrationality imposes itself on the consciousness of society; however, since there seems little opportunity for eradicating the difficulty, it is redefined as a normal or "natural" social fact.

Capitalism must fail to meet the more fundamental individual and social needs of its participants because it lacks any mechanism for satisfying such requirements, as our analyses of physical or mental health have made evident. Market calculation both ignores and corrupts such values as cannot be organized within an orbit of corporate profit: in the former case because values that are not provided with social recognition atrophy; in the latter, because values that the market commodifies are reduced to standards of quantifiable profit. Selling medications may well be profitable, but the conditions of sound health cannot be isolated, packaged, and marketed, as they depend on a radical transformation of social life that is not only beyond the capacity of the market, but which is anathema to its survival. Since such values cannot be obtained by private means and market mechanisms, they become an imperative of the political process and therefore public, social, common needs and goods. Socialist society can recognize and prioritize values that are beyond the logic of the marketplace; so socialism itself becomes a truly public and collective need.

It must be understood that there is a functional "rationality" involved in consumers' dependence on commodities and on a commodified aspect of themselves. Commodities are reasonable because they are available. As Gorz has noted, "The possession of an automobile becomes a basic necessity because the universe is organized in terms of private transportation."[46] So it is possible to buy an individual home in which to live but it is not possible to purchase a well-planned social life devoid of extreme disparities of wealth and poverty, alienated labor, imperialist foreign policy, and mass destruction of the environment. Those needs that can be satisfied by individual commodities appear more rational and "natural" because of the very fact that the prevailing system raises them to a level of priority; fundamental social needs are relegated to the category of fantasy since the means of their satisfaction are impossible to procure.

The need for "mental health" is ultimately the need for decent human existence; for recognition, support, creativity, empowerment, agency, and efficacy. It is true that in the best of therapeutic relationships these values may be adumbrated, and it is undoubtedly because of this fact that improvement occurs. But these occasions are isolated from the larger social world, unequal in authority, contracted as payment for service, and directed toward specific practicable ends. Individuals are required to purchase as private consumers what has been lost to them as members of a dehumanized society.

The capitalist trust appropriates or uses up air, light, space, water, and (by producing dirt and noise) cleanliness and silence gratuitously or at a preferential price; contractors, speculators, and merchants then resell all of these resources to the highest bidder.[47]

We might add well-being to the list of basic necessities, for it follows the same pattern of confiscation and repurchase. And the continued expansion of psychic maladies to which I have referred attests to nothing so much as the fact that the expansion of capital produces a growing reification of social life in which individuals believe more and more that their human satisfaction is to be achieved by the continual specification of particular "ailments" that can be cured by contracting specific specialists and dependent upon their particular technologies. The instrumental medicalization of the social world simply means that distress is separated from its social roots and redefined as the personal failure of the individual in whom it resides. The recipients of social ills are viewed by society and by the afflicted themselves not as the victims but as the hosts or even the perpetrators of their own suffering.

Such "pathologies" as narcissism are not the result of recent discoveries by an ever more acute therapeutic science. Narcissism is a condition of isolated, self-absorbed, privatized selfhood frantically struggling toward a reciprocal recognition that a more responsive society might make possible. One has to play one's own other in the absence of that actual presence. So, it is no contradiction that such self-directed concern exists in conjunction with mass consumption, mass culture, and mass domination. Freud noted, in one of his many trenchant social asides:

> The neurosis takes in our time, the place of the cloister, in which were accustomed to take refuge all those whom life had undeceived or who felt themselves too weak for life.[48]

When the collectivity disintegrates, the individual is left alone to deal with the "undeceived" nature of reality. No church will intercede on our behalf, for we are, in matters of faith, undeceived. And in this historical moment we lack the practical understanding that would empower us to transform this brutal reality. In our time mass production and consumption and their facilitating state organizations take the place of the cloister and hold out the promise that we can achieve by individual participation in these dehumanizing structures the values of a promised social world. It is not surprising that this society is saturated by apathy and sentimentality; the former because hope has been consumerized in fantasies of private makeovers;

> land of Just Add Hot Water and Serve
> from every B.V.D. -
> let freedom ring
> > —e. e. cummings

The latter because sentiment has fled the world, as Park noted: "Money is the cardinal device by which values have become rationalized and sentiments have been replaced by interests."[49]

But our longing remains. In those intimate areas of social life where human beings, against the tide of alienation, treat each other as transcending the structure of commodification, some semblance of humane culture presents itself. A therapy rooted in and responsive to such conditions may still redeem itself by seizing this moment and culturing its potentialities. The appropriate soil for the growth of such a therapy is any stirring of human spirit in which the present social arrangement is being contested. It might be argued that this is everywhere the case, but this is another argument for another time. What is clear enough is that therapy must transcend its present limits and align its praxis with a larger development of human life and its social condition. In so redefining itself it may fan the embers of such movements as exist and present a small model of the sort of responsive community that must appear in a new social arrangement.

Notes

1. Suzanne R. Kirschner, "The Assenting Echo: Anglo-American Values in Contemporary Psychoanalytic Developmental Psychology," *Social Research* 57, no. 4: 835–836.

2. K. E. Read, "Morality and the Concept of the Person Among the Gahuku-Gama," *Oceania* 25:280.

3. Philip Cushman, "Why the Self Is Empty," *American Psychologist* 45: 600.

4. Philip Cushman, *Constructing the Self: Constructing America* (New York: Addison Wesley, 1995), 77.

5. Cited in Alain Renault, *The Era of the Individual* (Princeton: Princeton University Press, 1997) 31.

6. Benjamin Constant, "The Liberty of the Ancients Compared with That of the Moderns," in *Benjamin Constant: Political Writings*. trans. Biancamaria Fontana (Cambridge: Cambridge University Press, 1958), 312.

7. Clifford Geertz, *Local Knowledge* (New York: Basic Books, 1983), 59.

8. Robert N. Bellah, Richard Madsen, William M. Sullivan, Ann Swidler, and Steven M. Tipton, *Habits of the Heart* (Berkeley: University of California Press, 1985), viii.

9. Ibid., viii.

10. Ibid., ix.

11. Ibid., 14.

12. Ibid., 47.

13. Ibid., 78.

14. Ibid., 78.

15. Ibid., 79.

16. Ibid., 99.

17. Ibid., 101.

18. Ibid., 104.

19. Ibid., 121.

20. Ibid., 47.

21. Ibid., 47.

22. Ibid., 47.

23. Ibid., 65.

24. Ibid., 80.

25. Ibid., 123.

26. Ibid., 124.

27. Ibid., 125.

28. Ibid., 125.

29. Karl Marx, *Grundrisse: Foundation of the Critique of Political Economy* (Baltimore: Penguin Books, 1973), 84.

30. Ibid., 90–91.

31. Bellah et. al., *Habits of the Heart*, 125.

32. Ibid., 123.

33. K. William Kapp, *The Social Costs of Private Enterprise* (New York: Schocken Books, 1975), 13.

34. Ibid., 16.

35. Sigmund Freud, *New Introductory Lectures on Psychoanalysis* (New York: W. W. Norton, 1933), 204.

36. Ibid., 206.

37. Irving M. Zeitlin, *Rethinking Sociology* (Englewood Cliffs, N.J.: Prentice Hall, 1973), 78.

38. Andre Gorz, *Strategy for Labor* (Boston: Beacon Press, 1964), 77.

39. Stephen A. Mitchell, *Hope and Dread in Psychoanalysis* (New York: Basic Books, 1993), 135.

40. Ibid.

41. D. W. Winnicott, *The Maturational Process and the Facilitating Environment* (New York: International Universities Press, 1965), 133.

42. Mitchell, *Hope and Dread in Psychoanalysis*, 132.

43. Winnicott, *Maturational Process*, 93.

44. C. B. Macpherson, *The Political Theory of Possessive Individualism* (London: Oxford University Press, 1962), 263.

45. See Richard Lichtman, *The Production of Desire* (New York: Free Press, 1982).

46. Gorz, *Strategy for Labor,* 88

47. Ibid., 90.

48. Sigmund Freud, "Origins of Psychoanalysis," in *General Selections from the Works of Sigmund Freud,* ed. John Rickman (New York: Doubleday Books, 1975), 31.

49. Robert E. Park, "The City: Suggestions for the Investigation of Human Behavior in the Urban Environment," in Robert Park, Ernest Burgess, and Roderick McKenzie, *The City,* (Chicago: 1925), 16–17.

About the Editors and Contributors

Anatole Anton is professor of philosophy and chair of the Philosophy Department at San Francisco State University. The focus of most of his research and writing is in the areas of political philosophy, philosophy of social science, Hegel, and Marx. He is general editor of the San Francisco State University Series in Philosophy.

Stanley Aronowitz is Distinguished Professor in sociology and director of the Center for Cultural Studies at the Graduate Center, City University of New York, where he has taught since 1983. He studies labor, social movements, science and technology, education, social theory, and culture. He is the author or editor of seventeen books, including *The Knowledge Factory, Dismantling the Corporate University and Creating True Higher Learning*. He received his Ph.D. from the Union Graduate School in 1975.

Jessie Corlito holds an M.A. in philosophy and public policy from American University. She is currently an Adjunct Professor of philosophy at Prince George's Community College in Largo, Maryland, and also practices as a psychiatric nurse.

Angela Y. Davis is professor of history of consciousness at the University of California, Santa Cruz. She has been engaged in organizing and research around prison issues for the last thirty years and is the author of a forthcoming collection of essays on the prison industrial compex.

John Exdell is associate professor of philosophy at Kansas State University. His specialty is social and political philosophy. He is currently doing research on the idea of personal desert as a norm of social justice, and the application of this theme to debates in the United States relating to welfare policy, race, and gender.

Zsuzsa Ferge was born in 1931 in Budapest, Hungary. She studied economics and sociology. She started to do research and teaching about social policy in Hungary in the seventies. She is a professor of sociology, has published extensively, and is a member of the European Academy and the Hungarian Academy of Sciences.

Ann Ferguson is professor of philosophy and director of women's studies at the University of Massachusetts at Amherst. She has written two books in feminist theory, one of which, *Sexual Democracy: Women, Oppression and Revolution*, 1991, Westview, will be out in 2d edition soon. She coedited a book on ethics and politics with Bat Ami Bar On, *Daring to Be Good*, 1998, Routledge. Currently she is doing solidarity work and research with the women's movements in Central America and Spain and with the welfare rights movement in the United States.

Milton Fisk is emeritus professor of philosophy at Indiana University at Bloomington. He has been active in efforts to get a single payer health insurance system and is currently active in Jobs with Justice. His book, *Toward a Healthy Society*, was published in 2000 by the University Press of Kansas.

Nancy Folbre is professor of economics at the University of Massachusetts, staff economist with the Center for Popular Economics, associate editor of the journal *Feminist Economics*, and cochair of the MacArthur Foundation, To Work on Research on the Family and the Economy.

Michael H. Goldhaber is the author of *Reinventing Technology*. He introduced the concept of attention economics and writes a column on this and related topics in *Telepolis*, a web magazine. He is a visiting scholar at the Institute for the Study of Social Change at UC Berkeley. Earlier in his life, he was a theoretical particle physicist.

Nancy Holmstrom is a professor of philosophy at Rutgers University in Newark. Her primary areas of research are Marxist theory and feminism. Her reader, *The Socialist Feminist Project*, will be published by *Monthly Review* in 2001.

Richard Lichtman has a background in philosophy and psychotherapy and has written widely on Marxism, social theory, psychoanalysis, and their interrelation. He is currently a professor at the Wright Institute in Berkeley, California.

Andrew Light is assistant professor of philosophy and environmental studies at the State University of New York, Binghamton, and resident fellow at the International Center for Advanced Studies at New York University. He is the author of over forty articles, reviews, and book chapters on environmental ethics, philosophy of technology, and philosophy of film, and has edited or coedited ten books (in print and forthcoming), including *Environmental Pragmatism* (1996); *Social Ecology After Bookchin* (1998); *Beneath the Surface: Critical Essays on Deep Ecology,* (2000); and *Technology and the Good Life?* (2000). He is currently finishing a book on pragmatism and the relationship between environmental ethics and environmental policymaking.

 Subcomandante Marcos. No one seems to know who Subcomandante Insurgente Marcos is. The Mexican government claims he is Rafael Guillen, but they're literalists. He says he's a Mexican like any other, born somewhere between the Atlantic and Pacific Oceans and between the northern and southern borders. He says he wears a ski mask because he is no longer who he was. So now he's a soldier in the army of the Zapatistas, and he lives in the jungles of Chiapas.

Robert W. McChesney is professor of communication and library science at the University of Illinois at Urbana–Champaign. He is the author of seven books, including *Rich Media, Poor Democracy: Communication Politics in Dubious Times* (University of Illinois Press, 1999).

Nel Noddings is Lee Jacks Professor of Child Education, Emeritus, Stanford University, and professor of philosophy and education at Teachers College, Columbia Universtity. Her most recent book is *Justice and Caring*, edited with Michael Katz and Kenneth Strike.

Kurt Nutting is a philosopher and attorney who currently teaches at San Francisco State University and other universities in the Bay Area.

Bill Resnick is a lawyer, writer, radio producer, and activist in Portland, Oregon. His forthcoming book, *The Long Revolutions Continue: Popular Democratic Struggle in the Age of Global/Mobile Capital,* contends that the big conservative story of U.S. life— "triumphant economy/troubled people"—is dead wrong, and that the great alleged social crisis is, like the economic "boom," rightist mythology. It demonstrates that the real social trajectory, in, for example, child rearing and sexuality, is best described as democratic recomposition, though to be sure muddled, troubled, and intertwined with the privatism and self-seeking generated by a polarizing worrying conservatizing economy.

Richard Rorty has been professor of philosophy at Princeton and professor of humanities at the University of Virginia. He is now professor of comparative literature at Stanford.

Jim Syfers received a Ph.D. in philosophy from the University of Iowa in 1963; he is currently a member of the Philosophy Department at San Francisco State University, and serves on the board of the Meiklejohn Civil Liberties Institute in Berkeley, California.

Iris Marion Young is professor of political science at the University of Chicago. Her books include *Justice and the Politics of Difference* (Princeton, 1990), and *Intersecting Voices: Dilemmas of Gender, Political Philosophy and Policy* (Princeton, 1997). In fall 2000 Oxford University Press will publish *Inclusion and Democracy*.

Index

Aaron, Henry, 205
ABC, 264, 349
Abington School District v. Schempp
Abnormality, 127–128, 129
Abnormal pathology, 415
Access
  to drug treatment, 388
  and higher education, 369, 370–371
  and universally accessible environment,
    128–129
Act for the Relief of the Poor, 192
Acts of Enclosure, 8
Addiction, 387–389
  capabilities approach to, 389
Administrative functions, 191–192
Administrative Procedures Act of 1946,
    152
Advertising
  and competition, 338–339
  and desire, 339
  and journalism, 351
  and preferences, 72
Advertising Age, 348–349
AFDC. *See* Aid to Families with
    Dependent Children
Affective community, 80
Affirmative action, 25
  and prison industry, 136–137
Affordable housing
  and metropolitan areas, reconstructing,
    260
Africa, 198
African Americans
  and drug control, 385–386
  and punishment industry, 133–138,
    142(n11), 142(n12)

African National Congress, 6–7
Aggression
  and caring capabilities, 106
Aid
  for human rights, 166(n21)
AIDS
  and drug control, 386
Aid to Dependent Children, 232
Aid to Families with Dependent Children
    (AFDC), 232, 249
Air pollution
  and Environmental Protection Agency,
    58–59
  See also Environmental quality;
    Pollution
Alberta, Canada
  and environmental quality, regulation
    of, 209–210
Alcoff, Linda, 119
Alcohol consumption
  as publicly provided good, 221–222
Alcoholics Anonymous, 387
Alcoholism, 387
Alcohol sales
  regulation, in Canada, 210, 221,
    225(n13)
American Dream, 255. *See also* New
    American Dream; New urbanism;
    Suburban dream
American Educational Research
    Association, 287
American Note (Dickens), 140
Americans with Disabilities Act, 128
Amish
  and public schools, 285
Amsterdam Declaration, 188

443

New progressives, 187
New public order
  and class struggle, 59–60
News Corporation (China), 361
New social democrats, 187
Newspapers
  and journalism, 349–351
Newsweek, 261
New Testament, 171–177
New urbanism, 255
  and commercialism, 263–265
  and subsidies, 265–266
  See also American Dream; Suburban
    dream
New York
  ballot access in, 311
  growth boundaries in, 267
  and prison industry, 136
New York city, 6
New Yorker, 261, 351
New York Times, 7, 267, 349, 354
New York Times Magazine, 349
Nicaragua, 30
NIEO. *See* New International Economic
    Order
Nike, 348
Nonanthropocentrism vs.
    Anthropocentrism
  and environmental quality, 211,
    224–225(n4)
Nondepletability, 9
Nonexcludability, 9
Nonrivalrous, 9
Nonrivalrous consumption, 10
Nonviolent offenders
  and drug control, 386
Normality, 127–128, 129
Normal pathology, 415, 421–422
Norquist, Ken, 298
Northern Land Office (Australia), 35
Nostalgic primitivism, 35–36
Novato, 267
Nozick, Robert, 11
Nussbaum, Martha, 102, 389

OECD. *See* Organization for Economic
    Cooperation and Development
Office of Management and Budget, 65

Ogilvie & Mather, 357
Oldham, Margaret, 410–411, 413
Olivas, Michael, 132–133
Oliver, April, 355, 356
Olson, Mancur, 70–71, 74
One-dimensional consciousness
  and power, 34
One-Dimensional Man (Marcuse), 34
One-dimensional society, 33–34
On Liberty (Mill), 294(n1)
*On the Penitentiary System in the United
    States and Its Application in France*
    (Tocqueville and Beaumont),
    139–140, 143(n30)
Open admissions
  and higher education, 371–372
Operation Wetback, 132
Opp, Karl-Dieter, 75
Oppressed
  preferences of the, 73
Oppression, 274(n4)
  and difference, politics of, 109
Oppressive functions, 200
Oregon, 266
  growth boundaries in, 267
Organic value, 420
Organization for Economic Cooperation
    and Development (OECD), 167(n56)
Organized labor, 65

Packwood, Robert, 119
Palestine
  health care in, 406(n3)
Parents
  and public education, control of,
    284–285
Park, Robert E., 436
Parks
  and metropolitan areas, reconstructing,
    258
Parochial schools. *See* Religious schools
Partiality
  and confrontation, 124–125
Patents, 13, 327
  and competition, 337–338
  and pharmaceutical companies, 27
Patriarchal religion
  and education, 280–283